Professional
Windows® Desktop
and Server Hardening

Professional
Windows® Desktop and Server Hardening

Roger A. Grimes

Wiley Publishing, Inc.

Professional Windows® Desktop and Server Hardening

Published by
Wiley Publishing, Inc.
10475 Crosspoint Boulevard
Indianapolis, IN 46256
www.wiley.com

Published simultaneously in Canada

ISBN-13: 978-0-7645-9990-3

10 9 8 7 6 5 4 3 2

1MA/RS/QU/QW/IN

Library of Congress Cataloging-in-Publication Data:

Grimes, Roger A.
  Professional Windows Desktop and Server Hardening / Roger Grimes.
    p. cm.
  Includes index.
  ISBN-13: 978-0-7645-9990-3 (paper/web site)

  1. Computer security. 2. Computer networks—Security measures. 3. Microsoft Windows (Computer file) I. Title.
  QA76.9.A25G775 2006
  005.8—dc22

                          2006003777

For general information on our other products and services please contact our Customer Care Department within the United States at (800) 762-2974, outside the United States at (317) 572-3993 or fax (317) 572-4002.

Wiley also publishes its books in a variety of electronic formats. Some content that appears in print may not be available in electronic books.

About the Author

Roger A. Grimes

Roger A. Grimes (CPA, CISSP, MCSE: Security, MVP, CEH, CHFI, TICSA) is a 20-year computer security consultant, writer, and teacher. He has written over a 150 national magazine articles on computer security, and this is his fifth book on Microsoft Windows security. He has consulted for many of the world's best-known enterprises (including McAfee, Microsoft, Verisign, and IBM), multiple universities, cities and school systems, plus every branch of the U.S. armed forces. He is currently a highly rated instructor teaching Windows and Linux security in Foundstone's Ultimate Hacking classes. He has presented at many of the industry's largest conferences, including MCP TechMentor, Windows Connections, and SANS. He was a contributing editor for *Windows IT Pro* magazine, and is the security columnist for *InfoWorld* magazine. He has written several advanced security courses, including for Microsoft. He is a three-year recipient of Microsoft's Most Valuable Professional (MVP) award, and was the creator and team leader of the successful www.hackiis6.com contest.

Acknowledgments

Twenty years ago, I thought I knew the world. Now, I know that I only barely grasp what would fit on the end of a technological fingernail. To that end, I want to thank the computer scientists and mailing lists that have had the most impact upon my learning.

I want to thank Microsoft and all the members of the par excellence MVPSec mailing list. You guys and gals are my doctorate education. I especially want to thank the following MVPs for their constant written responses to my endless questions: Susan Bradley, Chris Quirke (my tech reviewer), Joe Richards, Alun Jones, Obiwan, Bill Sanderson, Stephen J. Friedl (the Unix guru), Karl Levinson, Ron Chamberlin, and Harry L. Waldron.

Thanks to Microsoft for all the help and assistance in reviewing material and allowing me to read and experience the new stuff coming in Windows Vista, Internet Explorer 7.0, and IIS 7. Special thanks to Brett Hill, Microsoft's IIS Evangelist (and my friend for many years) for reviewing the chapter on IIS.

Thanks to Dshield, SANS, Bugtraq, and Securityfocus for the best practical public computer security mail lists on the planet. I especially want to thank Stephen Northcutt for his continued mentoring and guidance. I could not ask for a better employer, Foundstone, who pays me to teach and hack.

Thanks to Tim Nolan for reviewing my password chapter, making sure it was up to date and accurate. Thanks to Andrew Aronoff of Silent Runners.org for his script and excellent list of malware vectors. Thanks to Brian Livingston for feeding the world Windows facts for over a decade. Thanks to Ed Foster (the Gripeline) for fighting the hardest battles all the time. Thanks to Paul Ferguson, who invited me to disassemble my first computer virus back in 1987.

A big thanks to Carol Long who had the vision, and patience, to let me write the book I wanted to write. Thanks to Kenyon Brown, who suffered through my multiple drafts at all unexpected hours.

Lastly, thanks to my readers for frequently e-mailing me, asking me questions, and for frequently taking me to task over my various suggestions, forcing me to do more research. Our debates have made this a better book.

Credits

Executive Editor
Carol Long

Development Editor
Kenyon Brown

Technical Editor
Christopher Quirke

Production Editor
William A. Barton

Copy Editor
Luann Rouff

Editorial Manager
Mary Beth Wakefield

Production Manager
Tim Tate

Vice President and Executive Group Publisher
Richard Swadley

Vice President and Executive Publisher
Joseph B. Wikert

Project Coordinator
Michael Kruzil

Media Development Specialists
Angela Denny
Kit Malone
Travis Silvers

Graphics and Production Specialists
Carrie A. Foster
Denny Hager
Alicia B. South

Quality Control Technicians
John Greenough
Brian H. Walls

Proofreading and Indexing
Techbooks

Contents

Contents

Contents

Contents

Contents

Introduction

Welcome to *Professional Windows Desktop and Server Hardening*! This book contains practical Microsoft Windows security advice, much of which you will read nowhere else, that I've been dispensing for over 18 years. Can you believe that Microsoft Windows 1.0 was released over 20 years ago on November 20, 1985? While the operating system and some of my advice has changed over the last two decades, the security issues really haven't. Today's überviruses, worms, and trojans use substantially the same mechanisms they did back in the days of IBM's PC DOS. Sure, the languages change and the Internet made nearly every computer connected, but the attacking malware and malicious hackers are using the same tricks they always have.

Last week, I read how a new worm is encrypting user's data and asking for a $200 ransom to unlock it. Ho hum. The PC CYBORG AIDS trojan horse (`http://ciac.llnl.gov/ciac/bulletins/a-10.shtml`) did the same thing more successfully back in 1989. Lately, I hear some of my fellow security experts telling users how Windows-based rootkits are the scariest malware bug ever and how they will eventually lead to the death of antivirus software. I've heard the same warning about macro viruses in 1995, polymorphic viruses in 1993, and multi-partite boot viruses in 1992. Somehow, antivirus vendors learn how to detect the new critters and life moves on.

I've heard how today's new stealth worms, which proactively hide from detection software and prying investigators, are somehow new. What was the first stealth malware program? The Pakistani Brain diskette boot virus (`http://vil.nai.com/vil/content/v_221.htm`) in 1986. It was the first IBM-compatible PC virus, and it spread around the world without involving the Internet. If someone looked at an infected boot sector while the virus was in memory, it would return the moved original boot sector instead.

The media is always writing about how tomorrow's Internet worm will be worldwide and devastating. They neglect to remember that the real disasters are our loved ones in a hospital emergency room; everything else is just a nuisance. Or that the first worm that "took down the Internet" was the Robert T. Morris worm (`http://en.wikipedia.org/wiki/Morris_worm`) of 1988. The first malware program to affect the real world outside of the Internet was the ILoveYou worm (`http://www.cert.org/advisories/CA-2000-04.html`) in May 2000. Launched from the Philippines, it infected so many computers in one day that it caused my cell phone network to go offline for most of the first day (as it dealt with an overload from Internet-based e-mail messages heading to cell phones and pagers). The local telephone company's circuits were also overloaded for a few hours, but the icing on the cake was my morning paper being delivered at 5 P.M. that night. Not even Ronald Reagan's attempted assassination or the space shuttle disasters had done that.

The SQL Slammer worm (`http://www.cert.org/advisories/CA-2003-04.html`) of January 2003 has the notoriety of being the fastest recorded Internet malware to date. Within 10 minutes of its first exploited victim computer, it had infected nearly every Microsoft SQL server and Desktop Edition client it could reach on the Internet (`http://www.cs.berkeley.edu/~nweaver/sapphire`). Launched at 1 A.M. E.S.T., by the time network administrators around the world had wakened, not only was the attack over, it had been over for nearly a normal business work day. And no security expert I know thinks its speed record will stand much longer.

Even the future is old news. There is barely a security expert alive that hasn't warned about cell phone and PDA viruses becoming ever-present in the new millennium—and they are probably right. But the first successful cell phone virus that caused a countrywide problem was back in August 2000. A script worm (`http://wirelessreview.com/news/wireless_viruses_raise_flags`) infected Japan's DoCoMo i-mode cell phone network, prompting users to answer whether they would drink out of a girl-friend's coffee mug if she had a cold. If they answered yes the script then dialed the equivalent of our 911 system, eventually flooding Tokyo's emergency phone number with bogus calls. It was not only a cell phone malware attack, but also one that could potentially kill a person indirectly.

In my 18 years of dealing with malicious code, perhaps only the Nimda virus (`http://www.sarc.com/avcenter/venc/data/w32.nimda.a@mm.html`), with its six-plus angles of attack, and the 1992 Sara virus (`http://www.avp.ch/avpve/poly-gen/mte.stm`), the first polymorphic virus, really did something unique and unexpected. Everything else has been a small modification of someone else's idea or just a regurgitation of an old idea. It's perhaps more surprising to us "ole" computer security veterans that someone hasn't made something more malicious and that professional hacking is just now starting to be a daily economic force.

The biggest recent change in hacking is how many of the attacks are compelled by the profit motive. Until 2004, most viruses, worms, and hackers were done by hobbyists, motivated by peer recognition and personal goals. Now, more and more, both automated attacks and hackers are motivated by dollar signs. The media is full of stories of corporate espionage. Governments are reporting wide-scale, sophisticated attacks against their national infrastructure systems. Hackers are gathering hundreds to thousands of hacked machines into malicious bot networks that are sold to the highest bidder. Organized crime figures routinely steal hundreds of millions of dollars scammed from online purchasers. People's identities and their credit card information are being stolen by the hundreds of thousands on a daily basis. It is not hyperbole to say that professional hackers will challenge our world's data networks like no other category of crime has ever been able to accomplish. I would be surprised if stronger governmental regulation of the Internet and software did not occur in the next half decade.

What hasn't changed is the ways computers are attacked and how you can defend against those attacks. I cover the various attack methodologies in Chapter 1, "Windows Attacks." If you know what is attacking you, you can always design successful computer defenses. I already know how to stop viruses, worms, trojans, and malicious hackers. The hard part is implementing defense strategies in a consistent way so that all computers receive identical, consistent protection. Chapter 14, "Group Policy Explained," and Chapter 15, "Designing a Secure Active Directory Infrastructure," will take everything you learn in the chapters in between and make a security policy that is consistent and enforceable.

Why Another Book on Windows Security?

There must be over a dozen Microsoft Windows security books on the market, each purporting to be THE book on Windows security. Unfortunately, they all miss the mark for one reason or another. I even tried to convince my publisher to title this book "Everyone Else's Windows Security Book Sucks" but for sound, logical reasons they declined.

The other books contain a lot of useful information, but not a lot of useful advice. Most address the wrong problem . . . that of the dedicated, wily hacker, and hence, the advice they dispense leads the reader to a false sense of security. This book covers the real threat to Windows computers and offers practical guidance to protect those systems.

My advice is proven in businesses large and small over two decades. Knock on wood, not a single client following my advice consistently has ever suffered a single successful malware or dedicated hacker attack. It may happen one day, but as of the publishing of this book, my record remains intact. How do I do it? It's no secret. I have published over 150 magazine articles in the world's leading computer magazines (plus four other books on Windows security), and I speak several times a year at the largest industry conferences. But after each client consultation or public speaking engagement, somebody always asks where he or she can read about all my advice. Prior to this book, I had to recommend that they google me on an Internet search engine and look for all my separate articles and presentations. This book contains my entire library of advice in one place. This is my treatise, my opus.

A lot of the advice in this book is unheard of in most circles unless you've read my articles or attended my presentations. The rest of the world keeps following the same drab advice and wondering why they still end up infected or exploited. I've frequently shared my creative advice with Microsoft for possible inclusion in new end-user recommendation guides. I have done a fair amount of technical work for Microsoft, but with a few exceptions, most of my unique advice has been discounted.

And perhaps that is the strangest realization of all. In my perfect world, when I come up with some good advice and share it with Microsoft, I envision the security workers there testing my advice and then embracing its simplistic approaches. In the real world I do have a few advocates within the Redmond-based company, but more often I get complete rejections of my advice without any testing done to prove or disprove its efficiency. Microsoft is full of very smart people, perhaps the smartest collection of people I've ever come across in any company. But like many large organizations, they suffer from a groupthink mentality that I can only liken to the pre-9/11 thinking of our intelligence agencies. My good ideas are only but a small cry within a very large bureaucracy where a thousand other good ideas are contending to be heard.

That's not to say that some of my ideas haven't been adopted by Microsoft. Some have, but they aren't spotlighted like they need to be in order to make Windows users more secure. Other ideas in this book were invented by Microsoft and heavily promoted since day 1. For example, the single best way to protect your Windows computer against malicious compromise is using NTFS permissions. As Chapter 3, "NTFS Permissions 101," will reveal, sometimes the best advice is so commonplace it is ignored. If everyone followed the default security permissions' guidance that Microsoft has been promoting since Windows NT 3.1 in 1993, perhaps 70–90% of all viruses, worms, and trojans would have been defeated. This book will reemphasize great advice, old and new, and teach you the way Windows really works.

Other chapters, like Chapter 5, "Protecting High-Risk Files," and Chapter 6, "Protecting High-Risk Registry Entries," are a little off the mainstream, but worth their weight in gold. They are why I am well compensated to consult with companies valuing computer security. I've even heard how some of my advice would make a Windows system unsupportable—as if my advice would somehow permanently impair a computer system. I'll teach you how to take any advice I recommend and remove it with three clicks of the mouse. When you remove my "damaging" advice and the software problem you're still trying to solve still isn't resolved, critics will have to look for the real problem.

What I do have is a compendium of good, practical advice. Even better, the vast majority of the advice can be implemented with just the tools that Microsoft put in Windows for free. I promise you that if you follow any of my advice, your Windows network environment will be substantially less at risk for attack than before. In the process, I will simplify explanations of complex technologies and discuss how Windows really works. Your knowledge, computers, and networks will be significantly stronger. And automated malware and hackers will look elsewhere for easier targets.

Who Is This Book For?

This book is intended for Microsoft Windows network and security administrators with at least 1–2 years of experience. While a beginning administrator can easily implement any of the discussed techniques, it helps to have a firm foundation of Windows basic fundamentals and TCP/IP before reading any book of this nature. In most scenarios, I will explain all topics from A to Z, and assume all readers need a complete understanding. In my experience, people who claim to be an expert in a particular technology don't understand the basics as well as they thought. Heck, that's me some of the time, too.

What's in This Book?

This book is made up of 15 chapters covering four areas. Part I covers the basics and gives the reader a detailed understanding of the underlying technologies so they can implement the recommendations handed out in the rest of the book. Part II covers operating system security—securing it past the Microsoft defaults. Part III describes, step by step, how to harden commonly installed applications such as e-mail, Internet Explorer, and Internet Information Services. Part IV finishes the book by discussing how to best automate Windows security. Here's a chapter summary:

Part I

Part I, "The Basics in Depth," contains three chapters covering Windows threats, some basic defenses, and ends by discussing NTFS permissions probably better than you've ever heard them discussed before. Chapter 1, "Windows Attacks," starts off by correctly defining the real problem. You can't plan the appropriate defense-in-depth strategy without understanding the right enemy. This is where most textbooks and lecturers go wrong. Chapter 1 discusses viruses, worms, trojans, buffer overflows, hybrid attacks, and the dedicated manual hacker methodology. One of the most valuable parts of the book is a listing of every place malware can hide in a Windows system.

Although this book focuses on efficient unconventional defenses that most Windows administrators don't use, but should, Chapter 2, "Conventional and Unconventional Defenses," covers the normal recommendations of physical security, patch management, firewalls, and antivirus software. It offers specific best practice recommendations and warns you about the problem areas that concern network administrators the most.

Correctly set NTFS permissions are the number one way to fight malicious exploits, but most administrators don't have a clue about how to set them. Chapter 3, "NTFS Permissions 101," covers default NTFS permissions, dispels some widely held myths, and details how your Windows security permissions should be set. Don't skip Chapter 3, as many seasoned veterans will be tempted to do. You will learn many new things and its lessons are integral to the forthcoming chapters. One of the best parts of this chapter is a table summarizing the default NTFS permissions for Windows Server 2003 and XP Pro.

Part II

In Part II, "OS Hardening," Chapters 4 through 8 discuss practical ways to secure the Windows operating system beyond the Microsoft defaults. Understanding authentication and preventing password crackers is central to securing Microsoft Windows computers. Chapter 4, "Preventing Password Crackers," covers the various types of Windows authentication protocols, when they are used, and which should be implemented when. After learning how Windows password authentication works, this chapter teaches you how to prevent password crackers in five easy steps.

Microsoft's latest operating systems come with a fair amount of default security built in, but it isn't enough. Chapter 5, "Protecting High-Risk Files," covers high-risk files needing additional security and how to secure them. While a lot of this chapter was seen for years as avant-garde, more and more security guides are recommending the advice it contains.

Like Chapter 5, Chapter 6, "Protecting High-Risk Registry Entries," details how to protect the operating system by increasing security beyond the defaults recommended by Microsoft. Defending and securing your registry is one of the best ways to prevent automated malware attacks. A few simple registry permissions can significantly secure your Windows computer. Chapter 6 covers high-risk registry keys and how to secure them.

Chapter 7, "Tightening Services," discusses the specialized topic of Windows services. You will learn how services and service accounts differ from the other Windows security principals, how hackers exploit services, and how to strengthen Windows service security.

IP Security is a vender-neutral method for encrypting and authenticating network communications between two computers. Unfortunately, IPSec is complex to understand and almost as complex to use. Chapter 8, "Using IPSec," explains IPSec in the easiest terms available and helps you leverage IPSec as a part of your normal security policy.

Part III

Part III, "Application Security," discusses ways to harden Microsoft's most commonly attacked applications.

If you can't stop unauthorized application installation or execution, you ultimately cannot prevent maliciousness. Preventing unwanted applications from launching is one of the best ways to prevent viruses, worms, and trojans. Chapter 9, "Stopping Unauthorized Execution," discusses the various ways to stop unwanted software execution with a special focus on Software Restriction Policies.

Internet Explorer (IE) is perhaps the weakest link of Windows security and Microsoft has made it impossible to remove (even when you think you have). So, if you have to live with it, secure it. Chapter 10, "Securing Internet Explorer," covers how IE functions behind the scenes, its multitude of security settings, and the recommended configuration.

Most malware attacks arrive as file attachments or embedded Internet links. Chapter 11,"Protecting E-mail," covers essential e-mail security. It covers the biggest threats, how to defend against them, and recommends e-mail best practices.

Internet Information Services (IIS) has become a very stable and reliable product. IIS 6 has had only one or two vulnerabilities announced since its introduction (compare that to dozens on its nearest competitor, Apache). Read Chapter 12, "IIS Security," and learn the steps you can take to harden IIS 6 beyond the already very acceptable levels implemented by Microsoft. Many of the lessons were learned during the very successful www.hackiis6.com contest.

Microsoft's Encrypting File System (EFS) is an excellent way to provide seamless and secure file encryption. In fact, EFS is so secure that unprepared users often find their files encrypted permanently without a way to unlock them. Read Chapter 13, "Using Encrypting File System," to learn how EFS works and what you need to know and do before implementing EFS.

Part IV

Part IV, "Automating Security," includes two chapters that cover automating all the security settings covered in the previous chapters. It details hundreds of group policy settings and the best way to apply group policy objects.

Microsoft Windows comes with over two thousand different group policy settings. Chapter 14, "Group Policy Explained," covers them, discussing which ones should be implemented when, and finishing with how to create your own customized security and administrative templates.

Knowing how to secure a Windows computer isn't hard. It's consistent implementation that is difficult. Chapter 15, "Designing a Secure Active Directory Infrastructure," covers how to automate all the previously discussed steps. It covers when to use local computer policy, group policy, and administrative templates, and what should be set at each level.

The lessons taught here apply to all the current versions of Microsoft Windows, including 2000, XP, and Server 2003. Most of the information is centered on Windows XP and Server 2003. In most cases, the differences between the newest versions of Windows and its legacy versions (9x, ME, NT, etc.) are noted when appropriate. Most of the lessons taught in this book will work with the forthcoming Windows Vista client and the "Longhorn" server versions expected in 2006–2007. Any discussion of Vista and Longhorn should be understandably tempered by understanding that their features and security mechanisms will change prior to their final release. I've covered the features I think will be in the final product.

One last warning before we begin. The term *hacker* will often be used to describe malicious attackers even though the author and the publisher realize many hackers never participate in wrongdoing. However, through its overuse and misuse in the conventional media, the word hacker has been forever associated with malicious intent. For that reason, it is often used in this book without intentionally meaning to malign all the good hackers in the world. Now, join me on a journey of heightened awareness. By the conclusion of this book you will have gained the knowledge that dozens of the world's leading corporations use to secure their Microsoft Windows computers.

Conventions

To help you get the most from the text and keep track of what's happening, we've used a number of conventions throughout the book.

> **Boxes like this one hold important, not-to-be forgotten information that is directly relevant to the surrounding text.**

Tips, hints, tricks, and asides to the current discussion are offset and placed in italics like this.

As for styles in the text:

❑ We *highlight* new terms and important words when we introduce them.

❑ We present code in two different ways:

```
In code examples we highlight new and important code with a gray background.

The gray highlighting is not used for code that's less important in the present
context, or has been shown before.
```

Source Code

As you work through the examples in this book, you may choose either to type in all the code manually or to use the source code files that accompany the book. All of the source code used in this book is available for download at `http://www.wrox.com`. Once at the site, simply locate the book's title (either by using the Search box or by using one of the title lists) and click the Download Code link on the book's detail page to obtain all the source code for the book.

> *Because many books have similar titles, you may find it easiest to search by ISBN; this book's ISBN is 0-7645-9990-9 (changing to 978-0-7645-9990-3 as the new industry-wide 13-digit ISBN numbering system is phased in by January 2007).*

Once you download the code, just decompress it with your favorite compression tool. Alternately, you can go to the main Wrox code download page at `http://www.wrox.com/dynamic/books/download .aspx` to see the code available for this book and all other Wrox books.

Errata

We make every effort to ensure that there are no errors in the text or in the code. However, no one is perfect, and mistakes do occur. If you find an error in one of our books, such as a spelling mistake or faulty piece of code, we would be very grateful for your feedback. By sending in errata you may save another reader hours of frustration and at the same time you will be helping us provide even higher quality information.

To find the errata page for this book, go to `http://www.wrox.com` and locate the title using the Search box or one of the title lists. Then, on the book details page, click the Book Errata link. On this page you can view all errata that has been submitted for this book and posted by Wrox editors. A complete book list, including links to each book's errata, is also available at `www.wrox.com/misc-pages/booklist.shtml`.

If you don't spot "your" error on the Book Errata page, go to `www.wrox.com/contact/techsupport .shtml` and complete the form there to send us the error you have found. We'll check the information and, if appropriate, post a message to the book's errata page and fix the problem in subsequent editions of the book.

p2p.wrox.com

For author and peer discussion, join the P2P forums at `p2p.wrox.com`. The forums are a Web-based system for you to post messages relating to Wrox books and related technologies, and interact with other readers and technology users. The forums offer a subscription feature to e-mail you topics of interest of your choosing when new posts are made to the forums. Wrox authors, editors, other industry experts, and your fellow readers are present on these forums.

Introduction

At http://p2p.wrox.com you will find a number of different forums that will help you not only as you read this book, but also as you develop your own applications. To join the forums, just follow these steps:

1. Go to p2p.wrox.com and click the Register link.

2. Read the terms of use and click Agree.

3. Complete the required information to join as well as any optional information you wish to provide and click Submit.

4. You will receive an e-mail with information describing how to verify your account and complete the joining process.

You can read messages in the forums without joining P2P but in order to post your own messages, you must join.

Once you join, you can post new messages and respond to messages other users post. You can read messages at any time on the Web. If you would like to have new messages from a particular forum e-mailed to you, click the Subscribe to this Forum icon by the forum name in the forum listing.

For more information about how to use the Wrox P2P, be sure to read the P2P FAQs for answers to questions about how the forum software works as well as many common questions specific to P2P and Wrox books. To read the FAQs, click the FAQ link on any P2P page.

Part I
The Basics in Depth

Chapter 1: Windows Attacks

Chapter 2: Conventional and Unconventional Defenses

Chapter 3: NTFS Permissions 101

1

Windows Attacks

Sixth century B.C. Chinese war philosopher Sun Tzu is popularly credited with first publishing the "Know Thy Enemy" battle strategy. In order to set up a secure computer defense, you have to define the enemy correctly. This is where many computer security defense courses, books, and articles go wrong. They spend the majority of their time telling you how to defend against the dedicated, manual attacker while either ignoring or giving improbably brief coverage to the much more realistic threat of malicious mobile code and malware networks. And if they can't define the problem correctly, how can they tell you how to successfully defend your computing environment? This chapter summarizes the various types of attacks that malware (and the dedicated hacker) can use to compromise Windows-based computers, and discusses the vulnerable areas of Windows in detail. Table 1-1, "Where Malware Hides," at the end of the chapter, is the most exhaustive list available in any publication.

Attack Classes

When all the various types of possible attacks against *any* computer system are analyzed, four descriptive classes are noted: automated malware versus the dedicated, manual attacker and remote versus local execution (see Figure 1-1). This section discusses the four categories and then breaks down the methodologies that each employs.

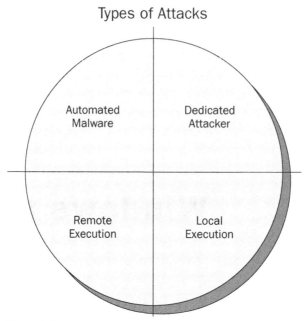

Figure 1-1

Automated Versus Dedicated Attacker

Automated malware is composed of any rogue code designed to exploit and replicate with a minimum of human intervention. The category includes worms, viruses, trojans, spyware, bots, and spam, or phishing attacks launched through any of the former types. Indeed, 99.9% of all computer attacks occur from automated malware! As simplistic as this statement seems, it appears that much of the world still doesn't get it. For reasons still unknown to me, most Windows security courses and defenses concentrate far too much time on the dedicated attacker threat, when automated malware is considerably more prevalent and dangerous. Part of me thinks it is because of the "mysterious intrigue" the evil hacker provokes. It is just human nature to be more concerned with an unpredictable and emotional warm-blooded threat than with the predictable automated attack of a coded program. Whatever the reason, too many books, classes, and people concentrate on the wrong threat.

This is not to say that classes concentrating on the very real threat of hacker's are a waste of time. No, the threat of hackers is a real threat, and the skills learned from those classes can be applied against automated malware. It's just that so many classes ignore the bigger threat of automated malware.

If this text appears overly defensive about the issue, it is because the idea of malware being the largest threat goes against conventional wisdom in many circles and has been the subject of a few heated debates among computer security experts. I've been asked many times to provide proof of my conclusions. My first response is "Go check your own firewall logs!" Any network or security administrator can tell you that their security and antivirus logs are full of daily attacks from automated threats. My web sites and honeypots receive hundreds of attempted exploits a day. Almost all are from automated malware scans. Today, the biggest threats to Windows computers are malicious e-mail attachments, Internet scanning worms, and botnets.

Today, the most popular e-mail worms exploit tens to hundreds of thousands of machines in a single day; and even those barely rate mentioning in the press anymore. It takes a 10-minute infector like the SQL.Slammer worm for the automated attack to become noteworthy. How many sites can a single hacker successfully exploit in a night without having to rely on automated malware? A handful, maybe. The sheer mechanics of automatic attacks alone suggests the veracity of my claim. Once an automated malware program is released, it can exploit millions of computers in a day. They keep on infecting and exploiting until the hole they use is closed or the technology moves on.

The first (known) IBM PC virus, Pakistani Brain, spread around the world with no problem, albeit it took months in the era before the Internet. It infected only 5 1/4-inch floppy diskettes.

The Brain virus remained one of the most popular viruses until the 3.5-inch floppy diskette and hard drives became more prevalent and the original PC floppy drive disappeared.

The Wild List (`www.wildlist.org`) reports each month on the most popular viruses still seen "in the wild." Its November 2005 list (`www.wildlist.org/WildList/200511.htm`) has several viruses from the 1990s, including a few from 1994 and 1995. Once released into the wild, an automated malware program can never be recalled. If a hacker stops hacking, whether through maturity or being incarcerated, the hacking stops immediately.

Statistics

If you don't believe me and your firewall logs, let's look at some verifiable statistics. According to the FBI's respected 2004 Computer Crime and Security Survey (available at `www.gocsi.com`), 78 percent of reporting businesses detected a computer virus on their network, making it the number one reported computer threat. Although I'm not sure how the survey defines computer virus in the results (for example, does it include worms and Trojans?), I'm fairly confident that many cases went unreported.

The 2004 ICSA Labs Tenth Annual Computer Virus Prevalence Survey (`www.cybertrust.com/intelligence/white_papers.html`) has numbers even more in line with most corporate administrators' experience. The survey reports an average of 392 automated malware encounters per 1,000 computers in the typical large corporation, with an average of 116 successful infections per site per month. Has anyone you've known received 116 manual hacker attacks in a given month? Average recovery cost from a virus outbreak in 2004 was $130,000 (with an average server downtime of 23 hours). Despite the fact that nearly all (99%) the companies surveyed had antivirus measures on at least 90% of their computers (84% claimed 100% coverage), only 12% of the respondents felt that the automated malware problem was the same or better than in the past. This means 88% of the survey takers perceive the problem being worse than ever!

Several computer security reporting agencies have reported that nearly 100% of active e-mail addresses have received spam, viruses, and fraudulent e-mails. MessageLabs, a leading e-mail security service provider (`www.messagelabs.com/emailthreats/intelligence/reports/monthlies/april05/default.asp#t7`) reports that 69% of all e-mail is spam, and 1 in 43 contains a virus. They also report (`www.messagelabs.com/emailthreats/intelligence/reports/monthlies/march05/default.asp`) that over 70% of all spam (including phish e-mails) is created and sent by automated bots that have compromised the computers of innocent users.

The Anti-Phishing Workgroup (`www.antiphishing.org`) reports in its February 2005 report (`www.antiphishing.org/APWG_Phishing_Activity_Report_Feb05.pdf`) that fraudulent "phishing" e-mails have been increasing at a rate of 26% per month since July 2004, with an estimated 75 to 150 million phishing e-mails sent `daily` (`www.antiphishing.org/APWG-FDICCommentaryLetter.doc`). The average conversion rate (i.e., the percentage of users revealing personal identification information to the phisher) ranges from about 2% to 15%. Even the lower end is not miniscule when you consider the overall volume. Spyware is an even more prevalent problem.

A Dell Computers survey (www1.us.dell.com/content/topics/global.aspx/corp/pressoffice/en/2004/2004_10_15_dc_000?c=us&l=en&s=corp) revealed that 90% of all computers in the United States have spyware installed, and most users aren't aware of its presence. Another report (http://around cny.com/technofile/texts/tec082904.html) claims that the average PC has 50 to 70 spyware infections, but PCs with 900 or more infections are not uncommon.

Connect a computer directly to the Internet and it will begin to receive probes within minutes to hours. Before the first 24 hours have passed, it will have received dozens to hundreds of attempted exploits. You can recognize automated attacks versus the manual methods by looking at the type of attacks and the timing. Automated attacks rarely port scan a particular host looking for a vulnerable port, or try to fingerprint any found services. They immediately launch their exploit against a particular host without even trying to figure out whether the host could ever be successfully compromised by its specific exploit. A common web site malware script program tries nearly 100 different attacks in five seconds. About half would only work against Microsoft's Internet Information Server (IIS), the other half would only be successful against the open-source Apache web server. The automated malware program tries all attacks regardless of the found host, and it needs only one to be successful. It then e-mails the originating hacker (who is using a free and hard to trace e-mail account) if it is fruitful. Another common Microsoft SQL Server malware program attempts dozens to hundreds of different passwords against found SQL connections, one right after another. I can tell the SQL malware program is automated because of the speed of the password guesses and the fact that it launch against any PC advertising the standard SQL ports, regardless of whether a SQL login prompt is offered.

Without a doubt, automated malware, not the dedicated lone hacker, is the biggest threat to computers. But in my many years of teaching Windows security, no class I've been hired to teach (outside my own) has focused on automated attack types. Most courses teach the classical hacker methodology (covered below) by teaching students how to be would-be attackers, and then teach how to defeat the hacker menace. Students love becoming ethical hackers. I love teaching them. But it really doesn't do much to make their systems more secure.

Some readers may ask if it makes a difference whether we are defending against a dedicated attacker or automated malware. Yes! First, it is very difficult to stop dedicated manual attackers. Usually, they are well trained, methodical, and patient. You would have to ensure perfect security on every computer you manage to keep them out. Hackers only need to find one hole, one unpatched machine, one gullible end user—and your network is theirs. Dedicated hackers can change their attack methodology based upon what they learn during the early course of the attack. If they start out attacking your web server or router and come across your even weaker SMTP server, they can change their attack on the fly. Automated malware can't do that. It does only what it was predefined to exploit. Small defense changes can completely defang an automated attack tool.

Simple things, like renaming the Administrator account or changing the default port number on a service, will defeat automated malware. A dedicated hacker can use *anonymous enumeration* (covered in the forthcoming chapters) to find a renamed Administrator account, and a hacker can easily port scan a particular host and then do connection probes to find out where you moved a particular service's listening port. Automated malware can do the same thing, but they are rarely investigative. For instance, I have one of my honeypot Microsoft SQL Servers listening on the default TCP/IP ports of 1433 and 1434. It receives nearly a hundred SQL brute-force password guessing attempts a day. Another honeypot running the same version of Microsoft SQL on a non-default port has been up for over two years with zero attacks. It has only received three probes at the redirected ports, none of which were SQL-based. So, forget the conventional wisdom — security by obscurity as a defense works, and works well for automated malware!

Anyone that says otherwise isn't fighting the right problem or practicing critical thinking. For example, if I move a service's default listening port to something other than its expected value, how could I be doing anything but strengthening security? I liken it to a house that is covered with entrance doors on all four externally facing walls. Only one is the right door that will allow entry into the house. If a thief shows up to check out the entry door (i.e., a port scan) to determine whether the door is unlocked (i.e., a vulnerability), by having multiple doors I've increased the thief's workload by a multiplication factor equal to the number of additional doors. Automated malware usually only looks for one door, and only in front where it expects to find it. A dedicated manual attacker can check all the doors until it find the right one. Automated malware can do the same thing, but I've yet to run into the worm or virus that ever looked for a non-default service port or checked for any admin account that wasn't named Administrator or root. Chapter 2 covers more unconventional thinking.

Remote Versus Local

Another big attack distinction that is significant to attackers and defenders alike is whether the attack can be accomplished remotely or must be executed locally by the end user. Remote attacks without any end user intervention are the most devious kind. The attacker runs a manual or automated program from a remote location and takes over the user's computer. *Buffer overflows* are the most common example of this type of attack. Most security experts worry about remote attacks much more than local attacks because they can, if coded right, exploit every vulnerable machine the rogue code can contact very quickly. SQL Slammer worm anyone?

Fortunately, most malware requires some input from the end user in order for the exploit to occur. As Microsoft's first law of the Ten Immutable Laws of Security (`www.microsoft.com/technet/archive/community/columns/security/essays/10imlaws.mspx`) states, if a bad guy can persuade you or a program on your system to run his program, it isn't your computer anymore.

The vast majority of malware requires that end users (or their computers) be tricked into executing the code locally. E-mail worms, which, according to the ICSA Survey mentioned above, make up 92% of all automated malware attacks, almost own this category. Most e-mail worms are transmitted in malicious e-mail attachments, although a smaller but growing category tricks the user into accessing the malware through a rogue Internet link. E-mail worms can also use malformed attachment formatting, embedded scripts, and other HTML auto-run vulnerabilities to accomplish their malicious deeds.

If we could get all end users to stop clicking on every file attachment or HTML link they get in e-mail, our current malware craze would be almost non-existent. But end users will always ignore the security advice you give them and there will always be at least one person on the network who will execute every file attachment no matter how often warned, so you need to keep reading this book.

Tricking the user into running the malware program can also be done by constructing a malicious web link and embedding it into an HTML e-mail. Most e-mail programs readily execute HTML content, so the malware program or commands can be auto-launched simply by a user opening an e-mail. As we will cover in Chapter 11, *Protecting E-mail*, the two best things you can do for e-mail users is to block malicious file attachments and disable HTML content.

One of my favorite examples of an embedded HTML link trick is when a malicious web link executes a program the user isn't even aware they have installed, like an instant messaging or telnet client. The link then uses the launched program to carry out further malicious instructions on the compromised system. Over the years, I've seen several malicious HTML links embedded in otherwise normal-looking e-mails that launched previously unused software to install worms and other malware programs.

Perhaps the user doesn't even use Instant Messaging (IM). No bother, the web link starts the program, downloads the malicious file, and then executes it. If the user doesn't regularly use IM, it is almost certain that the IM client hasn't been updated with the recent version and is vulnerable to the exploit. Another example, the Blaster worm, used the Trivial File Transfer (TFTP) program located on every Windows computer to download its main body. No regular users that I know have ever heard of the TFTP program, much less one that allows anonymous file transfers to their computer. That's why I always recommend removing unused software. The software you don't use can still be used to hurt you. We will cover how to stop unauthorized software execution in Chapter 8.

In a related category, if hackers can gain physical access to your computer, they can also execute malicious code locally. This is often the case in privilege escalation attacks, password cracking attacks, and data theft cases. Local attacks can be devastating, but remember that if hackers have local access to your computer, then they can do anything. They can steal the computer. They can douse it in lighter fluid and set it on fire. Fear of local attacks is usually concerned with preventing a trusted insider from gaining higher unauthorized access and privileges.

To summarize the previous information, all computer exploits can be divided into four categories: automated or manual, remote or local. Automated malware allows fast exploitation, but cannot be as creative as a dedicated attacker. Remote exploits are the most dangerous because they don't require end user interaction to execute. Most exploits require that the end users (or their computers) be tricked into executing harmful code locally on the system. With few exceptions, automated remote exploits, such as SQL Slammer or the MS-Blaster worms, have been involved in the fastest and most widespread malware outbreaks.

Lastly, it must be recognized that many, if not most, of today's exploits are a combination of multiple categories. Often a hacker will use automated malware to find computers susceptible to the initial exploit and allow the malware to compromise the computer. The malware then is predefined to contact the hacker (e.g., via a secret IM channel), whereby the attacker can pick and choose his targets at his leisure. Today, it is rare to hear of attacks accomplished solely by a hacker manually typing commands on a keyboard one at a time against a remote host, although they do exist.

Types of Attacks

There are many different types of attacks, including the dedicated manual hacker, automated malware, and blended attacks.

Dedicated Manual Attacker Methodology

The 1983 movie *War Games,* starring Matthew Broderick, kicked off the world's fascination with computer hacking. Several computer historians point to that single film as launching pad for youth hobbyist hacking. In the movie, Broderick's character, David Lightman, spends his free time *war dialing* (i.e., serially dialing multiple phone numbers one at a time until an active phone number is found, looking for unsecured modem connections. Along with co-star Ally Sheedy, he ends up infiltrating a military computer and unwittingly almost sets off World War III. It received three Oscar nominations and made stars of the two young protagonists.

Early on, computer hacking often involved war dialing for analog phone connections. That was before the Internet. Now, hackers scan the Internet looking for live Internet hosts and probe them for weaknesses. Here is the conventional methodology of the dedicated manual attacker:

1. Hacker uses a TCP/IP scanning program to find an active host on the Internet. In the early days, hackers manually and methodically pinged random IP addresses until they found a responding host. Eventually, the earlier phone war dialing programs were converted to look for active IP addresses. Note, this type of reconnaissance requires that the remote host has an IP address and responds to a *ping* (ICMP Echo Request). As firewalls and routers began to prevent ping responses in order to thwart hackers, hackers started scanning for open TCP or UDP connections instead.

2. After an active IP address is located, a TCP/IP port scan is done against the remote host. This should reveal any open TCP or UDP connections. If a port is not opened, a TCP connection probe is reset by the remote host or the source IP address is sent a *host unreachable* ICMP message (if a UDP port is involved). Firewalls (in *stealth mode*) will block all probes to closed ports from reaching the protected host, forcing the originating prober's computer to wait for a connection timeout.

3. Depending on the TCP/IP ports found, the hacker can learn what services are running on a particular host. For instance, if port 80 is found, the host is probably running a web server. If port 25 is found, it is probably a SMTP e-mail server. If ports 135, 137, 139, and 445 are found, the host is probably a Microsoft Windows computer (this is covered in more detail in Chapter 2).

4. Once the TCP/IP ports are identified, the hacker will begin to fingerprint the host and its services. The hacker can manually connect to each found open port or use an automated fingerprinting tool. Many times, simply connecting to a port will reveal the service and its version number. Popular fingerprinting tools, such as Nmap (`www.insecure.org/nmap`) or Xprobe2 (`http://xprobe.sourceforge.net`), can be used to identify the operating system. Identifying the operating system helps identify the associated applications. For instance, IIS 6 only runs on Windows Server 2003. IIS 5 runs on Windows 2000, IIS 5.1 only runs on Windows XP, and IIS 4 only runs on Windows NT 4.0.

5. Once a service and its version are identified, a hacker can begin to attempt exploits built for just that particular software version. For example, if the hacker found IIS 5.0, he could search the Internet for all the IIS 5.0 exploits available. Several web sites allow this type of research, including Secunia (`www.secunia.com`). Currently, Secunia shows 11 IIS 5 vulnerabilities (`http://www.secunia.com/product/39`). If the software is fully patched, then the hacker must exploit a misconfiguration or host application error. Apparently, these are not hard to find. According to a November 2004 Gartner Research report (`www.g2r.com/DisplayDocument?doc_cd=124806`), "two out of three `successful` attacks exploit misconfigurations rather than vulnerabilities or missing patches."

6. Finally, the attacker manually hacks his way into the remote computer.

What happens at this point depends on the hacker. If the hacker isn't logged in as an administrator, a privilege-escalation attack may be attempted. Most of the time, hackers spends their next few minutes making sure they can easily break back in when needed. They may set up a new backdoor program, create a new user account, or set up a new malicious listening program. Many times, hackers then close the hole that allowed them to break in. Surprising as it may be, sometimes the first sign that network administrators receive that they've been hacked is that their systems are fully patched. This was especially notable when many network administrators held off on applying Windows XP Professional's Service Pack 2 (SP2) because of incompatibility issues. They were surprised to find SP2 installed even after they had specifically configured Windows not to install it. It was their complaint to Microsoft about the service pack installing even when requested that it not be that led to the malicious hacker being discovered. I always think it is sad when the hacker does the patching before the administrator.

A fast-growing percentage of professional hackers will inspect the hacked PC to determine whether there is any valuable information to compromise. Often this means they look for credit card or financial information. The hacker may install other malware programs to do keystroke logging or remote control. Before professional hacking became popular, the hobbyist hacker would often use the newly exploited computer as a repository for illegally copied games and videos. Other hackers would set up remote control trojans and start to attack other computers on the Internet. Then, if the secondary hack gets discovered, the evidence trail stops at the intermediary hacked computer instead of at the hacker's true location.

When doing forensic analysis on a hacking crime, two things need to be looked for:

1. How did the hacker or malware initially break in?
2. What did the hacker or malware do after the initial compromise?

The first question will help you prevent future occurrences of the same hack; the latter will help you understand why a particular computer was hacked. Unless the hacker has an interest in a particular company, the found victim computer was probably randomly selected. I don't mean to imply that a dedicated hacker isn't ever trying to attack a particular company. Interesting entities such as NASA, popular web sites, and Fortune 1000 company web sites receive dedicated hacker traffic each day. But most companies aren't being especially targeted by the dedicated hacker, or if they are, it is only by raw luck of the draw. More often, hackers use automated, roving malware to find and exploit vulnerable hosts.

Types of Hackers

Hackers don't come in just one flavor. The vast majority of hackers are called *script kiddies*. These are individuals whose enthusiasm for hacking far outweighs their own hacking abilities. Rarely can they do dedicated manual hacking, keystroke by keystroke. More often they download hacking utilities, tools, and scripts that automate the entire process for them. They just plug in an IP address, and the tool does the rest of the work.

Don't Run with Knives

Here's a humorous story. In May 2005, I hosted an IIS hacking contest at www.hackiis6.com. It was hugely successfully, withstanding up to 250,000 hack attempts and probes per second during the contest. Few of the attacks were interesting. Most attacks came from automated attack tools used by script kiddies. What surprised me was how many of the attacks were meant for Apache web servers — the attacks would never be successful against Microsoft IIS servers. I never knew whether the hackers thought maybe I was kidding when I said it was an IIS server or if they just fired off the only web site hacking tool they could find. Even funnier was another strange story of sweet revenge. One of the popular security mailing lists where budding hackers like to lurk was discussing how to hack my contest site. A participant

---

uploaded a script that he said was sure to hack my web site. Even though the script was written in Shell script (a Unix/Linux scripting language), which is not my specialty, I was able to determine that the 13-line script did not attack my web site. Instead it sent the root password of the user who executed it to the script's creator. With a bare minimum of programming knowledge, they could have easily seen that it had nothing to do with my web site and was only grabbing their password and sending it to a remote person. Instead dozens of hacker wanna-bees executed the script. There were even days of e-mails from the script kiddies asking why the script didn't hack my IIS web site even though they were executing it over and over. A few claimed it worked. Too funny!

Although script kiddies aren't very knowledgeable, they probably accomplish most of the hacking that you hear about. They don't need to be experts; the knowledge is built into the tool they are using. They usually aren't very good at covering their tracks and can usually be caught with a minimum of forensic investigation.

Unfortunately, a smaller subset of hackers *are* knowledgeable attackers. They can use and modify a plethora of different hacking tools to accomplish their task at hand, following steps that somewhat mimic the manual dedicated hacker progression listed above. They can switch and modify tools from their defaults to be successful in their compromise pursuit. This type of hacker is persistent and patient. They are smart enough to cover their tracks and can avoid immediate detection. Hackers at this level may write their own malware, but the techniques they use are known. An even smaller subset of dedicated hackers are the master technicians — the überhackers. They develop their own tools and methods for breaking in. Their original malware uses new malware techniques or pushes existing envelopes. They are confident and don't often participate in security mailing lists. If they discover a new hacking hole, they keep it for themselves or sell it to commercial interests. This is the professional hacker and the one defense experts fear most. Although it is difficult to tell how many master hackers there are at any given time, the recent, significant increase in professional computer crime suggests they are on the rise.

Microsoft employee Robert Hensing has written a short guide (http://weblogs.asp.net/ robert_hensing/archive/2004/08/09/211383.aspx) *discussing the various hacker personas, as he calls them. Robert has spent years on the front lines at Microsoft fighting hackers and discovering new malware and hacking techniques. Although he also summarizes the various hacking skills over three levels, his discussions are more in depth.*

Keeping the dedicated manual hacker out of your computing environment is very difficult. You have to be perfect. Every computer attached to the Internet has to be perfectly configured, fully patched, and secured. The patient, dedicated hacker only has to find one hole. But even the dedicated hacker often resorts to using automated malware to speed up the process.

Automated Malware

The more popular attack method is using automated malware. Most automated attacks can be categorized by the three main parent types: virus, worm, and trojan.

Virus

Computer viruses are malicious programs that must rely on other host programs or code to spread. In most cases, the virus inserts itself into a legitimate host program (or boot sector) so that when the host is executed, so is the virus (see Figure 1-2). The smallest working PC-based virus is called Define (`http://vil.nai.com/vil/content/v_346.htm`). At only 30 bytes, it is the minimalist blueprint of every virus. It finds a host file, adds its own code to the host file (actually, it overwrites the original host file), and closes the file. When the infected host is run, the process repeats. The other 60,000 plus viruses are just more sophisticated versions of the same routine. Some infect boot sectors, others infect program files, and others infect data files (e.g., macro or script viruses). Some infect at the beginning of a file, others at the end, others in the middle, and still others don't infect the original host at all. A small subset of viruses, called *companion viruses* (aka *twins* or *spawners*), rely on operating system tricks to fool users into executing the malicious code first when trying to execute the legitimate host.

Some viruses print messages to the screen, make funny noises, draw graphics, and mess with print jobs. Others cause damage. They format hard drives, erase files, and corrupt data. A computer virus can do anything that is programmatically possible.

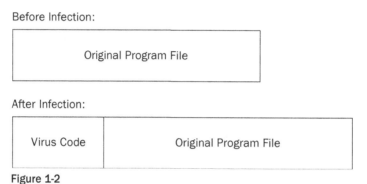

Figure 1-2

The first personal computer virus, the Apple-based Elk Cloner, was written by teenager Richard Skrenta (`www.skrenta.com/cloner`) in 1982. Early on, only a few viruses came out each year, mostly for the Apple and Amiga platforms. When the IBM PC started becoming the PC of choice, viruses migrated to the new platform. Although Trojan Horse programs (i.e., trojans) had been around longer than viruses, viruses quickly became the malware writer's program of choice. Before the end of the century, there would be over 60,000 different viruses.

Today, computer viruses aren't as prevalent on the Windows platform because Microsoft created a system file protection mechanism known as *Windows File Protection (WFP)*. Ostensibly only created to fight the programming problem known as "DLL hell," WFP will replace any modified, renamed, or deleted Windows system file with a legitimate copy. WFP had the net effect of decreasing the easy spread of computer viruses because when the virus infected a protected file, it was immediately removed.

Along the way, antivirus mechanisms got significantly better at preventing attacks. From 1995 to 2000, macro viruses enjoyed malicious success, but today, Microsoft-enabled programs have, for the most part, defeated the threat. A few years ago, viruses migrated to malicious script files (e.g., VBScript, JavaScript, and HTML applications), but even those threats have been mostly minimized.

Trojans

Trojan programs masquerade to the end user as one type of program (e.g., game, program, etc.), but usually have a hidden malicious agenda. A common trojan ploy is for trojan code to be added to a real, legitimate commercial program. This is often accomplished using a program known as a *linker*. The compromised legitimate program is offered free on the Internet. Users, looking for pirated software, download the program and install it. The program installs as it normally would and this is all the user sees, but the trojan installs "invisibly" behind the scenes.

The defining characteristic of a trojan is that it does not automatically spread or replicate (as does a worm or virus). In order to spread from computer to computer, it relies on different users downloading and executing it prior to being identified as malware.

Trojans are just starting to get the respect they deserve. Trojans often install keylogging programs, which record everything the user types in, including passwords, bank account numbers, and other confidential information. Once a trojan has successfully compromised a computer, the exploited computer can be redirected to do anything. If the trojan infects the PC and awaits further commands from the originating hacker, it is called a *zombie* or *command and control* trojan. For decades, trojans were designed to attack and exploit just the one computer they infected. They would infect the computer and then "dial home" to the hacker and announce their presence. The hacker then would manipulate the single exploited machine. In some cases, the trojan enables the hacker to do anything to the computer that he wants—sort of like a malicious PC Anywhere remote control program. These remote access trojans (or RATs), can record user keystrokes, manipulate files, steal passwords, capture screen shots, and even capture video and sound if the computer is equipped with a working video camera and microphone. The dangerous aspect of a RAT is that even after the malware is gone, the user usually has no idea what the hacker did or learned while the RAT was active. A RAT was the first type of malware program to be able to cause problems well past its removal. Now, multiply that unknown risk by 100,000 or so.

Today, hackers use trojans to compromise as many innocent machines as they can, creating huge networks of compromised machines under the control of a single hacker or group. These *botnets* can then be used do the bidding of the malicious attacker. The hacker may use the compromised machine to attack other targets. If the secondary target attempts to trace back the attack, it ends at the trojan-controlled machine, and not at the originating hacker's machine. Botnets can be comprised of tens of thousands to over 100,000 computers.

In a few months, Honeynet Project researchers (www.honeynet.org/papers/bots) tracked more than 100 different botnets, some containing over 50,000 compromised machines. Symantec tracked over 30,000 botnets over a six-month period (www.securityfocus.com/infocus/1838). According to Baylor University professor Randal Vaughn, the most popular trojans used to make botnets in 2005 are (in order of popularity) Korgobot, Spybot, Optix Pro, rBot, and other Spybot variants (e.g., AgoBot, PhatBot, SDbots, etc.)

Professional hackers will accumulate as many computers as they can in their botnet and then sell or rent the botnet to the highest bidder. One report (www.securityfocus.com/infocus/1838), says a botnet can be rented for *as little as* $100 per hour. Spammers and other professional hackers then use the botnets for their own reasons, including distributed denial of service (DDoS) attacks, spreading spam, hosting malicious web sites, spreading other malware, manipulating online games and polls, and participating in identity theft. Several other companies and researchers have estimated that hundreds of thousands of PCs unwittingly become involved in botnets each month. The company CipherTrust, which tracks zombie nets, estimates (www.ciphertrust.com/resources/statistics/zombie.php) that in May

2005, 172,000 new exploited PCs appeared each day. This figure is probably on the high side, but obviously a huge number of PCs are under the control of someone other than their owners. Most of the compromised machines are in the United States or China. Go USA??

Another emerging trojan type is the *rootkit*. A rootkit malware program spends extra effort to hide itself from casual observers and the dedicated forensic inspector. Rootkits use stealth-like mechanisms to hide any sign or symptom of their infection when inquiring eyes or processes query for their existence. Rootkits used to only be a concern for Linux/Unix administrators, but are now moving into the Windows world. There are several web sites dedicated to Windows rootkits, including `www.rootkit.com`. Many security experts are concerned because a properly coded rootkit can be very difficult to discover. In theory, since every PC can possibly be compromised with a rootkit, every forensic investigator needs to take a heavy-handed approach when dealing with an exploited PC, even if it's just suspected of being compromised by a normal virus, worm, or trojan. Although rootkits can be more problematic, the author feels that the antivirus and other security defense companies will rise to the challenge, and rootkits will pose no more harm than yesterday's DOS stealth viruses. For example, you can download Sysinternal's RootKitRevealer (`www.sysinternals .com/utilities/rootkitrevealer.html`) to search for hidden Windows rootkits.

Worms

As common as trojans are, computer worms are even more so. According to several resources, e-mail-based computer worms make up over three-fourths of all attempted attacks against a PC. A worm is a malicious program that does not need to infect a legitimate host program to replicate — it is self-replicating. E-mail worms usually arrive as e-mail attachments pretending to be something legitimate (in that way, they are like trojans). When clicked, they install themselves in such a way as to ensure that they execute when the computer is rebooted (see "Where Malware Hides," below). The worm uses its own coding to spread. Often the worm will look for the infected user's e-mail address book, retrieve potential e-mail addresses, and then send themselves to the new recipients. Early on, e-mail worms used the user's SMTP server to send themselves. Today, most contain their own SMTP sending engines.

Worms don't need e-mail servers to spread. They can spread using any service or program shared among PCs. Internet worms often scan large swathes of public IP addresses looking for computers to exploit. The SQL Slammer worm exploited servers and workstations running Microsoft's SQL software. The MS-Blaster worm exploited the Windows RPC service. Many worms target web servers. The truth is that a worm can target any listening port and service on a computer. These days, when vulnerability exploit details are released, someone is making a worm to exploit more PCs faster. Whereas we used to have a few weeks or months to patch our machines, automated worms have decreased the low-risk period to a few days or less.

When reviewing a malicious mobile code program, it helps to categorize its overall behavior as a worm, virus, or trojan. A worm can replicate on its own and probably hasn't directly infected other legitimate files. A virus has infected other host files, and those will need to be cleaned up or replaced. A trojan isn't as hard to remove, but what its controlling hacker did while the trojan was in control of the PC is usually unknown. Today, like most e-mail worms, many malware attacks borrow techniques from multiple parent classes. These hybrids, although not new, are becoming more and more common.

Remote

Remote attacks, which successfully compromise a computer without the end user being involved or making a mistake, concern security analysts the most. The idea that a remote attacker can connect to an innocent remote PC and compromise it is a compelling issue. Common remote attacks include denial-of-service, buffer overflows, misconfigurations, sniffing, and man-in-the middle attacks.

Denial of Service

Sometimes a computer doesn't have to be exploited or modified to be maligned. A *denial-of-service (DoS)* attack causes a listening port or service on a remote computer to become hung and unusable by legitimate users until it is restarted. Hackers have used botnets for years to bring some of the world's most popular web sites down, including eTrade, eBay, Microsoft, and popular gambling web sites. Denial-of-service attacks work by sending a listening service too much fake traffic or something it is not coded to expect, causing the program to crash or go into an endless loop. For example, an attacker using a large botnet can send millions of packets per second to a single web site, overwhelming it, and making it unavailable to legitimate users. Steve Gibson of Gibson Research Corporation has one of the best accounts of an extended DoS attack (`http://grc.com/dos/grcdos.htm`). His company was held hostage by a 13-year-old kid offended by a quote that was misattributed to Steve. It's a great story full of technical detail, if you have time to read it.

Other types of DoS attacks malform network packets to accomplish their task. For instance, a *LAND attack,* which recently reappeared to successfully compromise Windows XP and Server 2003 (`www.eweek .com/article2/0,1759,1773958,00.asp`) for a few months, sends packets with identical origination and destination IP addresses and port numbers to hosts. The destination host receives the packet and attempts to respond to the bogus origination host, but ends up in an endless loop responding to itself. The scary thing about DoS attacks is that the Internet's primary protocol (IP version 4) is pretty much useless to prevent them. Many web sites have been down for days while fighting DoS attacks, finding and shutting down remote connections from DoS bots one-by-one to filter out the illegitimate traffic from the legitimate.

Buffer Overflow

The most common type of remote exploit is accomplished using a *buffer overflow*. A buffer overflow attack sends more information to a receiving program than the receiving program is prepared to accept. The receiving program incorrectly accepts the overly large data sent its way and inadvertently places the rogue data (which is composed of malicious machine-language commands) into executable memory where it is subsequently executed as program code by the CPU.

A buffer overflow can simply result in a DoS attack or result in a complete system compromise. If the buffer overflow attack results in a complete system compromise, the attacker gets logged into the remote system in the security context in which the remote service was executing. Unfortunately, most Windows services run in the LocalSystem context, which gives the hacker absolute control of the PC. Buffer overflows always occur because the program and/or the programming language did not control the inputted size of the data being submitted (as they should).

Related to the buffer overflow attack are invalid data *injection* attacks, where applications are sent malformed data that then tricks the application into executing commands instead of the intended normal database actions. SQL injection attacks are the most popular of these attacks, but they occur with PHP, CGI, and dozens of other programs and languages. Injection attacks can only be fixed with program patch updates and better program coding that checks for these malware data types. Drastic changes are being made to Windows and to the supporting computer chips to prevent buffer overflows. Windows XP and Windows Server 2003 have undergone extreme code review cycles (several rounds of manual and automated review) to prevent buffer overflows. Still, patches fixing Windows buffer overflows occur at least every few months.

Misconfiguration Weaknesses

Contrary to popular belief, it isn't only unpatched software that gets exploited. Dedicated attackers (and penetration testers) often exploit machines through configuration errors induced by the computer administrator, programmer, or application program.

The author of this book regularly sees the following misconfigurations on remote computers:

❑   The Everyone group has Full Control permissions to all files and folders on a file server.

❑   The null session Anonymous user credential is given Full Control permissions to all files and folders on a domain controller.

❑   The IIS Anonymous user account is given Full Control permissions to all files and folders on an Internet-facing PC.

Computers and computer programs are complex, and complexity is the enemy of security. Most computer administrators are overworked and undertrained. Security is just one part of their job. Getting the computer up and getting the applications working for the end user is job number one. In their rush to satisfy multiple user requests, it is easy to see how administrators could misconfigure a computer. All it takes is answering yes to one unknown message box and Windows will do the rest. Misconfiguration errors can only be resolved by better training, configuration management, more secure software defaults, and configuration reviews.

Sniffing

Network protocol analyzer programs (i.e., *sniffers*) capture network packets crossing through their network interface card. By default, most network interface cards will drop network traffic not intended for them. A sniffer modifies the network interface card's network protocol stack so that the sniffer program can capture every packet that the card sees (called *promiscuous mode*). An attacker using a sniffer can capture anything that passes along the network in unencrypted form, including passwords and confidential information. Sniffing attacks were much more common in the early days of local area networks, where Ethernet hubs passed all information headed to and from any host on the hub to all other hubs. Ethernet switches replaced dumb hubs starting in around 1995. An Ethernet switch, by default, allows each connected PC to see only the traffic headed to and from it (plus broadcasts). This effectively killed the eavesdropping sniffer for about 15 years as a popular means of attack.

Today's proliferation of unprotected wireless local area networks (WLANs) has lead to a huge resurgence in wireless sniffing attacks. A remote attacker, listening in with a portable and small computing device, can listen in on any unprotected wireless network. Unfortunately, even the first popular wireless encryption protocol (Wired Equivalent Privacy) wasn't all that secure. Today, anyone can walk around and find dozens to hundreds of hackable wireless networks, which they can then exploit to capture confidential information, steal free bandwidth access, or inject malicious code.

A more sophisticated form of the sniffing attack is a man-in-the middle (MitM) attack. After establishing an eavesdropping session between two hosts, a MitM attacker can forge his identity to appear as the other host to each participating host. The MitM hacker can then capture information, or even more dangerous, manipulate the communication session to change the data sent between sender and receiver (without either innocent party being aware of the change). There have been some scary MitM attack demonstrations. The hacker program Cain & Able (www.oxid.it/cain.html) allows MitM attacks to be carried out with a few clicks of the mouse. Using the tool, an attacker puts the program into sniffing mode and captures the IP and MAC addresses of the machines it can listen to. Then, by simply clicking the mouse a few times, the Cain & Able user can initiate a MitM session. I've seen Cain & Able used to successfully intervene in SSL and RDP encrypted sessions. To prevent MitM attacks, the two hosts (or their programs) must use some sort of session authentication protection (e.g., IPSec, asymmetric cryptography, etc.).

Other Types of Attacks

Other types of attacks include physical, insider, obscurity, directory transversal, password cracking, social engineering, adware, spyware, spam, phishing, and pharming.

Physical

It's important in any computer security defense plan to consider physical security. If attackers have physical access to a computer, they can do anything to it. They can install hardware keyloggers, steal files, crack passwords, and just about anything else they want to do. They can steal the PC or set it on fire. Physical security is covered in Chapter 2.

Insider

Many surveys claim that trusted insiders account for 70-80% of all corporate computer crime. It makes sense that a trusted authorized employee, with intimate knowledge of a particular computer, has a strong chance of compromising that system, compared to the unknowledgeable outsider. But according to a May 2005 report prepared for the Secret Service (`www.secretservice.gov/ntac/its_report_050516.pdf`), insiders account for only 29% of all successful intrusions. Current, former, and contract employees were the most common insiders to commit a computer crime. In 62% of cases, a negative work-related event trigged the crime. In 82% of cases, the individual "acted in a concerning manner in the workplace prior to carrying out the crime." More than a third of them had already been arrested for other crimes. When hired, most had authorized, highly privileged access, but less than half did at the time of the crime. The majority of them used remote access to gain access to an unauthorized account, created a backdoor, and then launched a malicious attack. What does this say? A disgruntled employee or contractor is responsible for most insider attacks. Your security policy should take these statistics into account.

Obscurity

Many attacks work by fooling users or their programs into believing they are headed to a legitimate web site or network location, but instead redirect them to a malicious location. Obscurity attacks also used to fool computer security defenses. The simplest obscurity attack might be a user receiving an e-mail directing her to `www.microsoft.com.site.com/downloads` to download a proposed Microsoft patch. Those of us who understand URLs understand that the example URL would direct the user to a computer located on `site.com`, not `www.microsoft.com`. But most end users don't know the details of how URLs work and would probably be fooled. Typical obscurity attacks are even cleverer than the simple example. Usually the e-mail would be full of legitimate official links, and the `site.com` portion of the URL would be an IP address or a hexadecimal encoded (or decimal dot notation) location instead.

Obscurity attacks fool even the most secure of devices. Frequently, content and links that would normally not be allowed are passed through computer security defenses only to be converted into their legitimate locations on the computer endpoint. This is because many Internet standards require that inspection devices, computers, and browsers be able to take instructions and commands in many forms besides the normal ASCII form. This leads to inherent conversion problems of which the hackers take advantage. These types of attacks can be difficult in the short term to defeat, as hackers have been ingenious in creating ways to bypass the created defenses. For example, in 2005, there have been several obscurity attacks against many of the common Internet browsers. Browser developers responded by developing special tools that would alert the user when the presented URL did not match the web site to which they were being redirected. Enterprising hackers coded their malicious web pages to post "messages" that looked like the user's normal screen over the resulting warning messages. Very tricky indeed.

Directory Transversal

Directory transversal attacks are similar to obscurity attacks in that they attempt to use an obscure or encoded representation of a directory path in order to access a directory location or file to which they would normally not have access. For example, an older (now patched) attack, `http://hostdomain/../../../../../../../windows/system32/cmd.exe?/c+dir+c` will be converted to `c:\windows\system32\cmd.exe`. In unpatched versions of IIS 5, it would allow a remote attacker to have command-line shell access to the web server even though IIS is specifically coded to prevented anonymous access to that location. All of the popular web servers and web browsers, and many computer security devices, are susceptible to these types of attacks. The vendors close up one hole only to have another discovered a few months later. The defenses against these types of attacks will be covered in chapters 10 and 12.

Password cracking

If an attacker can gain physical access to a Windows computer in its default configuration, its password database is very susceptible to attack. Remotely, an attacker is usually forced to guess at user logon names and passwords to be successful. Unfortunately, most networks are full of many weak passwords that are easy to guess. Chapter 4 will cover password cracking thoroughly.

Social Engineering

Sometimes the easiest hack isn't a hack at all. The world's most controversial and popular culture hackers have all been masters of social engineering. Instead of using a malware program or trying to manually break into a system, they just ask for the necessary information. Most people's overly helpful nature leads to an unnatural trust that social engineering hackers exploit. Social engineering doesn't always require elaborate ruses. Frequently, company receptionists are called by external hackers claiming to work for the telephone company. They ask the helpful receptionist for an outside line to help troubleshoot a problem. The hacker then makes free long-distance calls at his leisure. Often, when I've been hired to do penetration testing, I'll walk up to the CEO's assistant and explain that I've been hired to do penetration testing, including password strength testing. I then ask for the CEO's password to test it. I've never not gotten the password. The only defense against social engineering is good computer security policies and employee training.

Adware, Spyware, Spam, Phishing, and Pharming

Spammers and mischievous advertisers are making the virus, worm, and trojan problem of the past two decades seem like child's play. Spam e-mail is more common on the Internet than legitimate e-mail. An unprotected, unpatched PC will often have dozens to hundreds of installed adware, spyware programs and tracking cookies after a few days of surfing the web. Some "free" software programs install hundreds of malicious programs that the user is unaware of as a cost of using the free program. Adware and pharming attempt to direct the user to a predefined location instead of where the user intended to go in order to sell a product. Adware usually does this by modifying the user's browser configuration or DNS client information (see "Where Malware Hides," below). Pharming (`http://en.wikipedia.org/wiki/Pharming`) tricks DNS servers or clients into having fraudulent information in order to misdirect end users. Pharming attackers are interested in either Adware-like activities or stealing the user's identity. Phishing attacks send malicious, but legitimate-looking, e-mails to users asking them to re-verify their credit card information. Phishing e-mails look quite realistic, even often reminding users not to be fooled by phony phishing e-mails at the same time as they scam the user.

Spyware attempts to capture a user's personal information in order to sell the information to dubious vendors or criminals.

All five types of attacks previously mentioned are on the rise, despite increased legislation and better computer defense tools. They install themselves in elaborate, multi-angled attacks, which make it difficult to remove. They have software installers that install other software installers that install dozens of programs, each from multiple, moving malicious web sites. Trying to track down who is spreading the spam, spyware, or phishing attack is one of the most difficult computer forensic challenges possible. It takes massive coordination of several networks and security administrators to capture a single bad guy.

> *Read the multi-part SANS Handler's Diary article, "Follow the Bouncing Malware"* (`http://isc`
> `.sans.org/diary.php?date=2004-07-23&isc=00ee9070d060393ec1a20ebfef2b48b7`),
> *to get a better understanding of how difficult the task can be.*

Malware Trends

There are three major trends in malware today. Attacks are becoming more:

❏ Professional, with criminal intent

❏ Blended

❏ Self-updating

This means the attacks are getting more sophisticated, more secretive, and more likely to cause financial harm. The single biggest change in malware during 2005 was the evolution of malware from a teenage hacker's hobby to a professional criminal enterprise. Almost all the malware released in 2005 attempts to steal personal or financial information. Symantec's Internet Security Threat Report VIII (`http://` `enterprisesecurity.symantec.com/content.cfm?articleid=1539`) reported that 74% of the most popular malware programs monitored in 2005 had the ability to steal information. This is a tremendous change from the past, when most malware programs were created for bragging rights or to upload pirated software. The use of malware programs to commit computer crime is so prevalent that a new malware classification, *crimeware*, has been coined to accurately state the intent.

Second, attacks are often are blended to include automated portions directed by a dedicated attacker. What starts out as a trojan ends up writing a worm that "drops" a virus. The virus downloads a spam bot, and the cycle continues. Lastly, many viruses and worms are pulled from one or more centralized (often illegally compromised) web sites. Once these malicious web sites are recognized, the owning ISP can be identified and they can shut down the web site.

Today, the malware searches for victim web sites to compromise. Then a worm from the first compromised web site starts to infect client machines. The subsequently infected client machines reconnect to the original *mothership* malware web site and download new malware. The new malware instructs the client to connect to another malicious web site, where it downloads a new malware program, and so on. Using this method, the malware mothership web site is always changing. By the time authorities shut down one malicious web site, a hundred more are compromised. And the code downloaded from each malware web site changes with each version, so the malware is self-updating. The originating hacker can drop off new malware programs with different infection and damage routines anytime they want to.

Even with all the attack types mentioned previously, we are just discussing the tip of the iceberg. There are literally hundreds of attack types and more than 100,000 different malware programs. Malware is as varied as real programs. Rogue programs are becoming more complex, and will follow technology wherever it goes. Today, malicious e-mail attachments and embedded links are the most popular malicious code types. In the future, wireless worms or rogue XML code will probably take center stage. It is doubtful that we will ever see a complete defeat of malware and a completely safe computing environment. There may be more than 100,000 programs, but they use the same few dozen compromise methods.

Where Malware Hides

With few exceptions (e.g., notably the SQL Slammer and Code Red worms), almost every malware program programmatically exploits Windows to ensure its continued survival. Table 1-1 contains the most extensive listing of where malware can hide in a Windows system of any publication. In summary, malware tries to use applications, files, folders, registry keys, and other mechanisms that are automatically executed when Windows (or another common program) starts. The forthcoming lessons in the remaining chapters are based upon defending Windows computers against these common malware exploitation techniques.

Table 1-1

Area	Name	Function	Notes
Application	Archive files	Malware can be hidden or launched from within archive file formats.	Archive file formats, such as PKZIP, Cab, Stuff-it, and Tar, manipulate/obscure the original file and can allow malicious files to bypass detection mechanisms. Malware files can be hidden in nested archive files, and won't be detected unless detection mechanisms use recursive scanning; even then the key is how "deep" the recursive scanning will try. Denial-of-service attacks and detection bypass have been successfully caused by overly large uncompressed file names, overly "deep" directory structures, etc. Exploded archive files have also be used to overwrite other legitimate files in directories the user did not intend.

Area	Name	Function	Notes
Application	Auto-run application files	Malware can launch from any auto-running file associated with a particular application.	Examples include MS-Office auto-run macros. Archive files can also have auto-run files executed after the archive is opened.
Application	Embedded or linked files	Many applications and their file formats allow other document types to be embedded/executed.	For instance, MS-Word files can have MS-Excel files embedded that are automatically executed when the Word file is opened.
Application	Microsoft Word	Embedded scripting can be used to manipulate remote file systems— to write over, copy, and delete files on the system which opened the MS-Word file.	It has been demonstrated that a maliciously crafted MS-Word file can secretly send a named document to a remote intruder.
Application	Cross-site scripting (XSS)	HMTL-based forms and e-mail allow malicious scripts to be embedded by a rogue hacker and executed on other computers that innocently view the HTML code.	Very common malware vector. Most HTML-based e-mail services have been the victim of one or more cross-site scripting attacks. Has also affected many web sites, blogs, and databases. Can only be defeated when the HTML-based service prevents the insertion of malicious scripting into input fields that are later displayed to other viewers.
Application	Outlook	Malware can manipulate Outlook to send other recipients malicious e-mails.	Can be done by malware becoming an add-in (e.g., Hotbar adware). Can be done by manipulating SMTP server settings or the HOST file and intercepting sent e-mail. Can be done by adding malicious script as an unauthorized e-mail signature (ex. JS.Fortnight worm). This exploit occurs more in Outlook Express than Outlook.
File	Alternate Data Streams	Malware can hide itself in the Alternate Data Streams (ADS) of a Windows file.	ADS example: regularfile.exe: malware.exe If executed, ADS process (i.e., malware .exe) will appear as regularfile.exe in Task Manager. No built-in Windows utility to show ADS files, but many companies, including www.sysinternals.com and Microsoft (Resource Kits), have tools to do so.

Table continued on following page

Area	Name	Function	Notes
File	Any executable	Viruses can modify any executable, script file, or macro file to run.	Works in DOS and any version of Windows. Microsoft system executables cannot be modified in Win ME and W2K and above because of Windows File Protection (System File Protection) in Win ME.
File	Autoexec.bat	Loads real-mode programs prior to Windows loading	Works with DOS, Win 3.x, and Win 9x. Replaced by Autoexec.nt in NT and later, and even then only gets called when a DOS session is started. Stored in root directory. Not commonly used by malware today. If used by malware, malware often inserted dozens of blank lines to the end of the file and pushed malicious commands below the normal viewing area of the file to fool inspectors. Win 9x looks for Autoexec when it starts, not necessarily Autoexec.bat; so an Autoexec.com or C:\Autoexec.exe could be run instead. Other variations relevant to Win 9x are C:*.DOS, C:*.WOS, C:*.W40, and C:*.APP files.
File	Autoexec.nt	File allows real-mode programs to be associated with specific 16-bit or 32-bit command shell sessions.	Works with NT family. Stored in %windir%\system32. Not common with malware.
File	AUTORUN.INF	Autorun file; runs commands or programs referenced by open= or shellexecute= after inserting (or choosing to Autoplay) media storage (i.e., CD-ROM discs).	Works with Win 9x and later, and can work with any type of media. By default, it doesn't work with most USB memory keys. Media that works with the Autorun.inf file can be modified using registry edits and third-party apps (such as TweakUI). Not widely exploited by malware, but the potential exists. By default, hard-drive volumes are enabled for Aurorun.inf processing.

Area	Name	Function	Notes
File	Batch or Command files	Will run listed programs or commands	Batch file viruses will search for these types of files to infect. Although not rare, most malware programs do not use this vector anymore. Windows fails to verify file content when opening a .BAT, .CMD, or .PIF file, so if a raw code .EXE is renamed as any of these, then it will still run as raw code. This is not the case with .LNK file, which is a threat only in that it is a shortcut that can be used to execute other files or load web sites.
File	Boot.ini	File used by NT OS family to determine which OS to load and where OS is located on disk	So far, not successfully manipulated by malware, but is sometimes the target of payload damage attacks.
File	Bootsect.dos	DOS boot sector on NT systems that dual boot with earlier versions of Windows or DOS	Could be infected by viruses in early versions of Windows and DOS. Pointed to by Boot.ini file in dual-boot scenarios in NT and later. In reality, any type of code can be referenced to run in the Boot.ini file (e.g., Recovery Console). Not widely exploited by malware.
File	Command.com	Default DOS shell in Windows 9x and earlier	Could be infected by viruses in early versions of Windows and DOS. Not possible in Win ME and W2K and later because of Windows File Protection.
File	Config.nt	File allows real-mode programs or drivers to be associated with specific 16-bit or 32-bit command shell sessions	Works with NT family. Stored in %windir%\system32. Not common with malware.
File	Config.sys	Loads real-mode programs or drivers prior to Windows load	Works with DOS, Win 3.x, and Win 9x. Replaced by Config.nt file in newer OSs. Stored in root directory. Not commonly used by malware today. If used by malware, malware often inserted dozens of blank lines to the end of the file and pushed malicious commands below the normal viewing area of the file to fool inspectors.

Table continued on following page

Area	Name	Function	Notes
File	Desktop.ini	Used to customize folder behavior. It is meant to allow users to customize folder appearance and behavior, but can be used to hide files and auto-launch programs when referred to folders are viewed.	Several worms (ex. WuKill, Rusty, Opposum, and Expobot) use Desktop.ini to launch their malicious executables when a related folder is viewed. Can be used to hide files and auto-launch programs. Desktop.ini is usually marked hidden. Folder.htt is used instead of desktop.ini when desktop is in "Web view". MSDN link: http://msdn.microsoft.com/library/default.asp?url=/library/en-us/shellcc/platform/Shell/programmersguide/shell_basics/shell_basics_extending/custom.asp
File	DOSSTART.BAT	Would load listed real-mode programs when starting a command prompt session or when booting to a command prompt session during Safe mode	Works with Windows 3.x and Win 9x family. Located in %Windir%. Superseded by registry key.
File	HOSTS	Used to place static DNS resolution entries	Works with Win 9x and later. Located in %windir%\System32\drivers\etc in NT and later. Malware or adware will often modify this file to redirect a user or program to a bogus location when the associated DNS entry is queried.
File	IERESET.INF	Used as the "initial" values when Internet Explorer is *reset*. Can be manipulated to place malicious entries.	Not used in the wild, yet. Proposed by Andrew Aronoff of SilentRunners.org. Default security is Read & Execute by normal users; requires Admin rights to modify.
File	LMHOSTS	Used to place static NetBIOS resolution entries	Works with Win 9x and later. Not commonly used by malware, but could be modified to do bogus NetBIOS name resolution redirection. Located in %windir%\System32\drivers\etc in NT and later.

Area	Name	Function	Notes
File	Msdos.sys, Io.sys	Default boot files in earlier versions of Windows and DOS	Could be infected by viruses in Windows 3.x and DOS. In Win 9x, Msdos.sys is used as an editable configuration file, not as a system file. In Win 9x, the original Msdos.sys and Io.sys files are renamed Io.dos and Msdos.dos. If you boot to DOS with Win 9x, the files are renamed Winboot.sys and Msdos.w40. Could end in other extensions, including .Wos and .App. In Win 9x, if Winboot.ini exists (it is normally deleted by the OS after a completed setup), then it can override the use of Msdos.sys. Not used in NT, 2000, and later, but may be present because of upgrades or dual booting situations. Not very dangerous these days. For Win 9x, also C:*.DOS and C:*.W40, which toggle these into active status via the F8 boot menu's "Previous MSDOS" option. If a C:\WINBOOT.SYS exists, it is automatically copied over C:\IO.SYS when a Win 9x boots; As far as I know, this hasn't been used by malware, much to everyone's relief. If a C:\WINBOOT.INI exists when a Win 9x boots, then it is processed instead of C:\MSDOS.SYS.
File	Normal.dot or any .dot file	Microsoft Word document template	Used by macro viruses. Not commonly manipulated anymore because default MS-Office security minimized success of macro viruses.
File	Ntldr	NT family OS boot code loader	So far, not successfully manipulated by malware, but is sometimes the target of payload damage attacks. Protected by Windows File Protection.

Table continued on following page

25

Area	Name	Function	Notes
File	OLE2 document trick	OLE2-formatted documents can be executed no matter what their file extension	Many applications, especially Microsoft applications, use the OLE2 file format, including Microsoft Office applications, MSHTA, SHS, and SHB files. Files with an OLE2 format will be run by the related application (as indicated by the OLE2 file's embedded OLE2 Root Entry CLSID value) regardless of the file name or extension. Thus, harmless.txt could really be a macro virus or hta malware script. The OLE2 file format is also known as Compound Document file format. OLE2 documents are essentially their own little file systems ("file system within a file"), resembling something like a FAT disk subsystem with its own root entries and subsections and files. The OLE2 trick is used in the wild by spammers, etc. The Root Entry CLSID can be found in OLE2 files following the string label R.o.o.t. .E.n.t.r.y.
File	Rasphone.pbk	Can be used to modify dial-up network settings, including which DNS servers (IpDnsAdress and IpDns2Address) the dial-up connection uses and to place unauthorized long-distance calls.	Located in %UserProfile%\ Application Data\Microsoft\ Network\Connections\Pbk folder. Don't forget to look in AllUsers profile. Trojans and malicious "Dialer" programs frequently manipulate this phonebook file, including Flush.D trojan and HotPleasure Dialer. Can be present with Windows 9x and above PCs. Key is not present (or a threat) unless you use Dial-up networking.
File	SYSTEM.INI [boot] scrnsaver=	If referenced by 16-bit Windows applications, will load the screensaver listed	Works with Windows 3.x and Win 9x family. Located in %Windir%. Screensaver files usually end with .SCR, .EXE, or .DLL extensions. Common malware vector in the Win 9x days. Replaced by registry entry in the NT family.

Area	Name	Function	Notes
File	SYSTEM.INI [boot] shell=	If referenced by 16-bit Windows applications, will load command shell listed (e.g. explorer.exe).	Works with Windows 3.x and later. Located in %Windir% . Only referenced by 16-bit Windows programs. Superseded by registry entries in NT and later.
File	WIN.INI [windows] load=, run=	If referenced by 16-bit Windows applications, will execute programs listed. Run= loads programs in maximized state, load= runs programs in minimized state	Works with Windows 3.x and later. Located in %Windir%. Only referenced by 16-bit Windows programs. Superseded by registry entries in NT and later.
File	Wininit.ini	Contains pending file operations (e.g., rename, copy, etc.) to be executed on the next reboot of Windows	Works with Win 9x and NT, but not in W2K or later. Located in %windir%. Replaced by registry key in later version of Windows. For more information, see `http://support.microsoft.com/kb/140570`.
File	Winsock.dll or Winsock2 service provider dlls	Used by Windows for network communications	Often used by trojans for their dirty work. Usually located in C:\%Windir%\System32 and protected by Windows File Protection in Win ME and W2K and later. Trojan versions may be located elsewhere (e.g., %Windir%\System or %Windir% folder). Trojan Winsock service providers can be added to Windows and can manipulate any network communications. Can be removed by Winsock service provider cleaners, such as Lsp-fix.
File	WINSTART.BAT	Would load listed real-mode programs prior to Windows loading or when user exited command prompt session.	Works with Windows 3.x and Win 9x family. Located in %Windir%. Superseded by registry key.

Table continued on following page

Area	Name	Function	Notes
Folder	%Windir%\ Favorites*.url %UserProfile%\ Favorites*.url %Windir%\ Favorites\Links\ *.url %UserProfile%\ Favorites\Links\ *.url	Lists Favorites in Internet Explorer	Often manipulated by adware, but has also been manipulated by malware
Folder	%Windir%\Start Menu\Programs\ Startup %Windir%\All Users\Start Menu\Programs\ Startup %USER PROFILE%\ Start Menu\ Programs\ Startup %ALLUSERS PROFILE%\ Start Menu\ Programs\ Startup	Default Startup folders; any program or command listed in one of these folders will be automatically executed when the user logs on	Works with Win 3.x and later, depending on default location for the particular version of Windows. Default is C:\Documents and Settings\ %userprofile%\Start Menu\Programs\ Startup in Windows 2000 and later. Default is C:\\%windir%\\%user profile%\Start Menu\Programs\ Startup in NT. Default is %windir%\Start Menu\ Programs\Startup in Win 9x family. Startup folder location determined by registry key. HKLM\Software\Microsoft\ Windows\CurrentVersion\Explorer\ User Shell Folders.
Folder	Recycler	Recycle Bin's temporary storage location for deleted files and folders	Often used by malware to store malicious code. Earlier versions of antivirus scanners would often skip the Recycle Bin storage area, and hence, escape detection.
Folder	System System32 %Windir%	Malware often writes itself to Windows system directories	Non-admins usually do not have permissions to write to System folders. In Win ME and W2K and later, because of Windows File Protection, legitimate system files cannot be overwritten, deleted, renamed, or modified, but new files can be written if the program has Write access. By default, most users have Read & Execute permissions to System folders.

Area	Name	Function	Notes
Folder	Tasks	Lists Task Scheduler Tasks	Works with Win 3.x and later. Located in %Windir%.
Folder	Temporary Internet Files	Malicious files are often stored/hidden in Internet Explorer's Temporary Internet Files (TIF) folder.	In 2000 and later, TIF is C:\Documents and Settings\<logonname>\Local Settings\Temporary Internet Files. Can be modified in Internet Explorer. If malware exploits System account (i.e., using a buffer overflow) and uses IE or Wininet APIs, the TIF location will be located under the Default User or Network Service profile directories (which are hidden by default). Some web browsers will have their own web caches that may hold the "as-arrived" form of malware dropped by web sites, as well as potentially exploitable application startup axes and/or settings locations.
Other	ActiveX Control	Installed ActiveX Control	If already installed, may be able to re-install other malware/spyware automatically even after removal. May need to set Kill Bit to defeat.
Other	Executable pathway	The PATH statement determines which paths OS should try if the file is not found in the default directory it was called from (i.e., Frog.exe vs. C:\Program Files\ Frog.exe)	Was a bigger problem in the latter days of DOS (.bat, .com, .exe). Some malware programs (ex. Spawner or twin viruses) rely on defects in the way Windows executes files when only the relative file name or path is given (ex. Frog.exe vs. C:\Program Files\Frog.exe). The PATH statement can be set by the DOS PATH command (located under Environment variables in NT family) or by the registry key. In Win 9x and earlier, autoexec.bat file could be modified to change the PATH statement. Can still be a problem today.

Table continued on following page

29

Area	Name	Function	Notes
			For example, some malware places itself in default application directories, which the application executes instead of the legitimate program executable. One trojan placed its malicious code in the user's My Documents folder. Because the malware was named after a legitimate MS-Word executable, MS-Word would always load it first instead of the legitimate version located under Program Files. More detail on path-spoofing: Set statements in Config.sys can define the PATH too, as can DOSStart.bat and DOS mode .pif for Win95 and Win98. Additional extensions may be set up as "executable" via file associations, and precedence override set by PathExt environment variable and registry setting in NT. Registry AppPaths, and possibly other locations where code overrides can be effected, may offer opportunities to spoof "companion" code into place. FaberToys (`www.faberbox.com`) is a free tool that includes program aliases as one of the integrations it lists. Any executable can be run as an associated "batch file" via a .PIF.
Other	Hidden files	Hidden (or system) files/folders will not appear to casual searches.	Dir *.* /ah /s will search and reveal all hidden files. Many legitimate files are marked as hidden or system. Mostly concerned with hidden executables, script, or batch files in root, %Windir, or System32. You can use Windows Explorer or Attrib.exe to unhide files.
Other	System Restore	XP/ME Restore feature may inadvertently restore malware located in older restore copies.	Most AV and malware remove software programs suggest turning off this feature prior to any active cleanup. Enabled by default, and usually a good thing to have running unless you need the storage or CPU resources. Can be enabled or disabled manually, by regedit, or by GPOs. Note that WinME's Wininit.exe has inherent SR functionality that will populate the SR subtree even when SR has been disabled.

Area	Name	Function	Notes
Other	Task Scheduler	Will run listed programs and commands	Sometimes used by malware to reload malware at a predetermined time interval or to gain initial access. Some scheduled tasks are run in the System context, allowing privilege escalation attacks.
Other	Trusted Publisher	Vendors listed here can execute programs without prompting for end user approval.	Be very cautious about which vendors are listed here, as it allows them to execute any program without approval from the end user.
Other	Unusual folder/ file names	Hackers and malware often use unusual names to hide malicious files and folders.	Some tricks fool Windows-GUI, some command prompt, some both. Be wary of soundalikes (svchosts.exe, win.exe, win32.exe, service.exe, users32.dll, etc.). Be wary of legitimate file names located in the wrong directory (e.g., svchost.exe located in %windir% instead of System32). Overly long file names that make the file name appear to be blank or push the file name or extension offscreen. Files with multiple extensions (e.g., malware.txt.ext). Files with incorrect extensions can still be executed at the command prompt. Files with nonstandard character sets (http://weblogs.asp.net/robert_hensing/archive/2005/01/10/350359.aspx). Isoglyph "puns," e.g., reversed-case EXPiORER.EXE, Unicode tricks. Files with incorrect extensions (i.e., a readme.txt that is really a .dll file or vice-versa). In Windows 2000 and NT, ADS code is shown in Task Manager with the parent file's name instead, and may spoof past firewall per-application monitoring. Various registry settings will cause code in an incorrectly extensioned file to be run as raw code, even when the Windows generic "open" would not have failed to exclude it.

Table continued on following page

Area	Name	Function	Notes
			Registry content that is "too long" will not be shown via Regedit.exe but will run anyway; LVNSearch (`http://isc.sans.org/LVNSearch.exe`) is a free tool that seeks such exploits. Files with invalid dates (i.e., before 1/1/1980 or well into the future). Windows Search GUI's date filter will not find files with dates before 1/1/1980.
Other	URL Monikers	URL Monikers can be added to Internet Explorer to load associated programs when a particular keyword is typed.	Internet Explore can be modified to allow keywords typed in the URL to launch associated programs. Also known as URL handlers. For more information, see `http://msdn.microsoft.com/library/default.asp?url=/workshop/networking/moniker/monikers.asp` Malicious coded web sites or HTML e-mails can launch and maliciously manipulate local programs using URL monikers. For example, AOL's Instant Messenger program, AIM, installs a URL handler called AIM://. It has been used to load buffer overflows known to be successful with particular programs. The associated program need only be installed, not even used, to be launched. `HKCR\<urlhandler>\shell\open\command` is the registry location for URL handlers.
Registry	`HKCR\<fileext>` NeverShowExt	Real file extensions can be hidden.	Although most users know that Windows allows registered file extensions to be hidden (the default), most users don't know about the "super hidden" extension attribute, which allows selected files (dozens of file types, including SHS, SHB, SHC, LNK, PIF, XNK, and several shortcut and CLSID files) to hide their extensions even if you told Windows not to hide file extensions.

Area	Name	Function	Notes
			The super hidden file attribute can be enabled by creating a NeverShowExt registry entry under HKCR\<fileext>. To disable, search for and delete any occurrence of the NeverShowExt key under HKCR. Note that Never-ShowExt also overrides Explorer's option to "Show file name extensions for registered file types."
Registry	HKCU\ Control Panel\ Desktop Scrnsave.exe=	Will load listed programs or commands when the screensaver is configured.	Not commonly used by malware. Used by Petch trojan (`http://securityresponse.symantec.com/avcenter/venc/data/w32.petch.b.html`). Screensaver is significant in that it is applied in Safe mode, even Safe Mode Command Prompt Only. This could allow malware to activate during long unattended scanning procedures, although this particular trick appears yet to be exploited by malware.
Registry	HKCU\ Software\ Microsoft\ Internet Explorer\Main\ Start Page HKCU\ Software\ Microsoft\ Internet Explorer\Main\ Search Page HKCU\ Software\ Microsoft\ Internet Explorer\Main\ Search Bar	Configures Internet Explorer's Startup page or search bars.	Commonly manipulated by adware and spyware
Registry	HKCU\ Software\ Microsoft\ Internet Explorer\ SearchURL	Redirects any URLs typed in Internet Explorer to the defined URL.	Commonly manipulated by adware and spyware

Table continued on following page

Area	Name	Function	Notes
Registry	HKCU or HKLM \ Software\ Internet Explorer\ Explorer Bars	Malicious adware\ spyware could create new menu bars in Internet Explorer.	Allows new entries to be made to standard menu bars. Available in IE 4.x and later. Commonly manipulated by adware and spyware. Menu bar will be a CLSID subkey listed under Explorer Bars. Used by Hotbar adware (`http://securityresponse.symantec.com/avcenter/venc/data/adware.hotbar.html`)
Registry	HKLM\ Software\ Classes\CLSID\ {CLSID}\ Implemented Categories\ {00021493-0000-0000-C000-000000000046}	...93 defines a vertical Explorer bar	Commonly manipulated by adware and spyware
	HKLM\ Software\ Classes\CLSID\ {CLSID}\ Implemented Categories\ {00021494-0000-0000-C000-000000000046}	...94 defines a horizontal Explorer bar	
Registry	HKCU\ or HKLM\ Software\ Internet Explorer\ Extensions	Adware/spyware can add buttons to IE that connect directly to malicious programs and scripts.	Available in IE 5.x and later. http://msdn.microsoft.com/library/default.asp?url=/workshop/browser/ext/overview/overview.asp Commonly manipulated by adware and spyware, including Adblock.
Registry	HKCU\ Software\ Microsoft\OLE	Used to register Windows OLE programs	Available with Win 3.x and later. Not a common malware vector. Used by Bropia trojan (`www.sarc.com/avcenter/venc/data/w32.bropia.j.html`).

Area	Name	Function	Notes
Registry	HKCU\ Software\ Microsoft\ Windows NT\ CurrentVersion\ Windows\load	Runs commands or programs after the user logs on	Works with all versions of Windows NT and later. Replaces Win 9x's Win.ini Load= functionality. Executes programs in minimized state.
Registry	HKCU\ Software\ Microsoft\ Windows NT\ CurrentVersion\ Windows\run	Runs commands or programs after the user logs on	Works with all versions of Windows NT and later. Replaces Win 9x's Win.ini Run= functionality. Executes programs in maximized state.
Registry	HKCU or HKLM\ Software\ Microsoft\ Windows NT\ CurrentVersion\ Winlogon\Shell HKCU or HKLM\ Software\ Microsoft\ Windows\ CurrentVersion\ Policies\System\ Shell	Runs commands or programs after the user logs on	Works with all versions of Windows NT and later. Replaces Win 9x's System.ini Shell= functionality. Should only have 'Explorer.exe' as a data value, if any value is displayed. Should not include a directory path. Some malware points to a bogus Explorer.exe (not located in %Windir%. Should not have additional programs before or after Explorer.exe unless a program is known to be legitimate.
Registry	HKLM\ Software\ Microsoft\ Windows NT\ CurrentVersion\ Winlogon\ System	Runs programs after the user logs on	Key is present by default, but assigned no value.
Registry	HKLM\ Software\ Microsoft\ Windows NT\ CurrentVersion\ Winlogon\ Taskman	Runs programs in Task Manager after the user logs on	Key not present by default

Table continued on following page

Area	Name	Function	Notes
Registry	HKCU or HKLM\ Software\ Microsoft\ Windows\ CurrentVersion\ Policies\ Explorer\Run	Runs programs after the user logs on, when the Windows default shell (explorer.exe) runs for the first time during every logon	Works with W2K and later. Not unusual to find legitimate programs, such as Microsoft's ctfmon.exe, listed here. Does not require reboot. Does not execute commands if explorer.exe is executed manually. W2K will run any subkey with any program listed under this key. Discovered by Andrew Aronoff of SilentRunners.org.
Registry	HKCU\ Software\ Microsoft\ Windows\ CurrentVersion\ Policies\System\ Shell	Runs programs or commands after the user logs on, but before the desktop is displayed	Works with W2K and later. Shell subkey may not exist by default. Does not require reboot after modification. If malware creates the Shell key, and does not launch the Windows shell too, the desktop will not be visible. You can still use Task Manager to run commands, including regedit.exe. A similar System key exists under HKLM\; but the Shell subkey does not get executed.
Registry	HKCU or HKLM\ Software\ Microsoft\ Windows\ CurrentVersion\ Run	Runs programs or commands after the user logs on	Works with all versions of Windows 9x and later. Not run in Safe mode unless the value is prefixed by an * (asterisk). Often contains many legitimate programs. *The most popular registry auto-run key for malware, by a huge percentage.* W2K will run any subkey with any program listed under this key. Discovered by Andrew Aronoff of SilentRunners.org. Non-admin users cannot modify HKLM version. Run key also appears in the HK_U\.Default registry profile area, but does not copy over to new profiles. Cannot be disabled by holding down the Shift or Alt keys as sometimes reported.

Area	Name	Function	Notes
Registry	HKCU or HKLM\ Software\ Microsoft\ Windows\ CurrentVersion\ RunOnce	Runs programs or commands after the user logs on for the first time only after the key is created.	Works with all versions of Windows 9x and later. HKLM\RunOnce runs entries *synchronously* (in undefined order)—there is a defined order and all other keys and processing must wait for this key to process and clear before they can load. All other Run keys run entries asynchronously, which means they can load on top of each other. HKCU version will run once for any user given the key. HKLM version will only run the value for users with admin permissions to key. Regular users will not run the value, although they can read it. RunOnce key also appears in the HK_U\.Default registry profile area, but does not copy over to new profiles. Non-admin users cannot modify HKLM version. Not run if in Safe mode in W2K and later unless the value name begins with an asterisk. If an exclamation point begins the key value, then the key will not be deleted until successful completion of the program or command. Holding down the Shift key does not prevent execution. W2K will run any subkey with any program listed under this key. Discovered by Andrew Aronoff of SilentRunners.org.
Registry	HKLM\ Software\ Microsoft\ Windows\ CurrentVersion\ RunOnce\Setup	Runs programs or commands after Setup's first-boot activities or can be launched by the Add/Remove wizard when the user logs on for the first time. (Can be stored as part of the Default Users profile.)	Works in all versions of Windows. Not run if in Safe mode. Holding down the Shift key does not prevent execution. If an exclamation point begins the key value, then the key will not be deleted until successful completion of the program or command.

Table continued on following page

37

Area	Name	Function	Notes
Registry	HKCU or HKLM \ Software\ Microsoft\ Windows\ CurrentVersion\ ShellService ObjectDelayLoad	Runs commands or programs after the user logs on, although typically points to the CLSID of the associated .DLL file. Links programs to explorer.exe process.	Legitimate programs often located here, including Microsoft's webcheck.exe and systray.exe. HKCU is more popular than HKLM. Data value is CLSID of associated program as registered in HKCR\. Download.Ject trojan, Spyware Eblaster (`http://securityresponse` `.symantec.com/avcenter/venc/` `data/spyware.eblaster.html`) and the Webber trojan (`www.sophos.com/` `virusinfo/analyses/trojwebbera` `.html`) use this key.
Registry	HKCU or HKLM\ Software\ Policies\ Microsoft\ Windows\ System\Scripts	Runs scripts on computer startup/shutdown or user logon/logoff	Works with Windows 2000 and later. Scripts may be passed down by group policies and located in different registry keys. Not a common location for malware.
Registry	HKLM\ Software\ Classes\ <filettype>\ shell\open\ command HKCR\ <filettype>\ shell\open\ command Examples: HKLM\Software\ Classes\batfile\ shell\open\ command HKLM\ Software\Classes\ comfile\shell\ open\command HKLM\Software\ Classes\exefile\ shell\open\ command HKLM\ Software\Classes\ htafile\shell\open\ command HKLM\ Software\Classes\ piffile\shell\open\ command	Can be modified to run additional commands or programs when a particular file type is executed	Works on Windows 9x and later. HKLM\Software\Classes\<filetype> and HKCR\<filetype> are aliases of each other. If you change the value in one, you change it in the other. Most common malware modifications listed, although any file type can be modified. Most common modification is made to the exefile type. For example, Value should always be: "%1" %* PrettyPark worm (`http://security` `response.symantec.com/avcenter/` `venc/data/prettypark.worm` `.html`) changed value to: FILES32 .VXD "%1" %* Whenever an exe file was executed, it would execute the malicious Files32 .vxd worm program, too. If the entire data value is deleted instead of the original value being replaced, it causes execution problems with exe files. In XP, in that HKCR is no longer a simple alias for HKLM\Software\ Classes, but an overlay of the per-user Classes over this. This allows per-account file associations to be effected, including that of the Administrator account. Exploits can be made at two levels: at the linkage between .ext and

Area	Name	Function	Notes
	HKLM\Software\ Classes\ ShellScrap\shell\ open\command		file type (e.g., directing .EXE away from its normal exefile association) or by altering the actions defined within the file type. Some file association contexts default to the action called "open," while others look to which action is named as "default". More elaborate file association intrusions can be crafted via CLSIDs; in addition, other shell extensions can be added that will kick in as part of the namespace (left pane in Explorer), or as "persistent handlers" when the contents of folders are listed (right pane in Explorer).
Registry	HKCU or HKLM\ Software\ Microsoft\ Active Setup\ Installed Components\ <program's name or CLSID> Loads programs on PC startup	Works with Windows 98 and later. Look for Stubpath= value.	Contains many/mostly legitimate programs. Common method used by malware; for example, Prorat trojan (`www .sophos.com/virusinfo/ analyses/trojproratd.html`). HKCU doesn't usually launch anything. The HKLM Version value is compared at launch to the Version value under HKCU. If the HKLM value is greater, the executable is launched and the HKCU Version value is updated. At next boot, the executable doesn't launch again unless the HKCU Version value is deleted or the HKLM value is incremented. (Thanks to Andrew Aronoff of SilentRunners.org) Difficult to discern what is legitimate vs. malicious in this key.
Registry	HKCU or HKLM\ Software\ Microsoft\ Command Processor\ Autorun	Runs program or command when: Cmd.exe is executed, Windows is started in Safe mode with Command Prompt, or when a batch file (.bat) or command (.cmd) is executed.	Works with NT and later. Replaces previous functionality of Dosstart.bat. Does not run when Command.com is executed. Can be disabled when running cmd .exe manually by typing in **cmd.exe /d**. Modification of this key does not require a reboot to be effective.

Table continued on following page

Area	Name	Function	Notes
Registry	HKLM\Software\Microsoft\Internet Explorer\Search HKLM\Software\Microsoft\Internet Explorer\UrlSearchHooks	Determines how Internet Explorer searches for unknown entries	Works with Internet Explorer 5.x and later. Both keys contain legitimate values, but often commandeered by spyware and adware. Search subkey contains references to `http://ie.search.msn.com` by default.
Registry	HKLM\Software\Microsoft\Internet Explorer\Styles	Lists Internet Explorer style sheets	Can be created or manipulated by adware/malware to display malicious web sites or pop-ups.
Registry	HKLM\Software\Microsoft\Internet Explorer\Toolbar	Loads new menu bars for Internet Explorer or modifies existing toolbars	Works with all versions of Internet Explorer 5.x and later. Commonly exploited by adware.
Registry	HKCU\Software\Internet Explorer\Toolbar\ShellBrowser HKCU\Software\Internet Explorer\Toolbar\WebBrowser	Malicious adware\spyware could create new menu bars in Internet Explorer.	Commonly manipulated by adware and spyware. Menu bar will be a CLSID subkey listed under Toolbars.
Registry	HKLM\Software\Microsoft\Windows NT\CurrentVersion\Windows\AppInit_DLLs	All the DLLs that are specified in this value are loaded by each Microsoft Windows-based application that is running in the current logon session using the User32.dll API library (which is used by most programs).	Works with Windows NT and later. Not usually populated by legitimate programs, but can be. Common method used by malware and adware; for example, CoolWeb Search Adware (`http://security response.symantec.com/avcenter/venc/data/adware.cwsmsconfd.b.html`).

Area	Name	Function	Notes
Registry	HKLM\ Software\ Microsoft\ Windows NT\ CurrentVersion\ Winlogon\ GinaDLL	Loads Windows logon user interface; loaded interface passes interactive user's logon credentials to Winlogon.exe	Works with Windows NT and later. Microsoft's default data value is Msgina.dll. Has been a target of trojan attacks, attempting to capture end user logon credentials. PC Anywhere program will modify the value to be Awgina.dll. The Novell logon client will modify as well.
Registry	HKLM\ Software\ Microsoft\ Windows NT\ CurrentVersion\ Winlogon\ Notify	Used to run a particular program when a predefined event (e.g., Screensaver stops or starts, user logs on or off) occurs.	Works with NT and later. Many legitimate programs are stored here. Not a common malware location, but is used. For example, Haxor backdoor trojan rootkit (`http://security response.symantec.com/ avcenter/venc/data/backdoor. haxdoor.b.html`).
Registry	HKLM\ Software\ Microsoft\ Windows NT\ CurrentVersion\ Winlogon\ Userinit	Specifies the programs that Winlogon runs when a user logs on	By default, Winlogon runs %Windir\ System32\Userinit.exe, which runs logon scripts, reestablishes network connections, and then starts Explorer .exe, the Windows user interface. Not a common malware startup location; has been exploited in the wild. For example, Petch trojan (`http:// securityresponse.symantec.com/ avcenter/venc/data/w32.petch.b. html`).
Registry	HKLM\ Software\ Microsoft\ Windows\ CurrentVersion\ Explorer\ Browser Helper Objects	Programs are loaded when Internet Explorer loads; programs loaded also known as Add-Ons.	Works with an OS that can run Internet Explorer 5.x and above. Commonly exploited key Several programs help list and/or modify BHOs, including IE XP SP2 and above. Note that disabling "third-party browser enhancements" in IE6's Tools, Options, Advanced will not suppress these intrusions into Outlook Express if the BHOs also defined themselves there as well.
Registry	HKLM\ Software\ Microsoft\ Windows\ CurrentVersion\ Explorer\ SharedTask Scheduler	Task scheduler programs that are launched when Windows starts	Works with W2K and later. Not a common malware location, but is used. For example, Bookmarker trojan (`http://securityresponse .symantec.com/avcenter/venc/ data/trojan.bookmarker.c.html`)

Table continued on following page

Area	Name	Function	Notes
Registry	HKLM\ Software\ Microsoft\ Windows\ Current Version\ Explorer\ Shell Folders HKLM\ Software\ Microsoft\ Windows\ CurrentVersion\ Explorer\User Shell Folders \Startup \Common Startup	Determines location of Startup folders (i.e., Startup programs) and other common folders (ex. My Documents, My Favorites) for All Users profile	Works with Windows 9x and later. Used by malware to change Startup folder behavior. Malware can place itself in the newly be executed when the user logs on, but if the user checks the normal Startup folders, the malicious program will not be listed. Malware modifying these keys will often then execute programs and commands found in default Startup folders so the user is not suspicious.
Registry	HKLM\ Software\ Microsoft\ Windows\ CurrentVersion\ Explorer\Shell ExecuteHooks	Contains the list of the COM objects, listed by GUID, that trap execute commands	Must contain the %Windir%\ System32\Shell32.dll API program. Other listed programs must be deemed suspicious.
Registry	HKLM\ Software\ Microsoft\ Windows\ CurrentVersion\ RunOnceEx	Runs programs or commands after the user logs on, in a controlled order. Runs listed value each time any user logs on until a user with admin permissions to the registry key logs on, then it deletes the value after running.	Works with all versions of Windows 9x and later. Not run in Safe mode unless the value is prefixed by an * (asterisk). Only runs values under subkeys (does not run values placed directly under key) Non-admin users cannot normally modify. For more information, see `http://support.microsoft.com/?kbid=232509&sd=RMVP`.
Registry	HKLM\ Software\ Microsoft\ Windows\ CurrentVersion\ RunServices	Runs service after boot up prior to the user logging on.	Works only in the Win 9x family. There is also a HKCU version of the same key, but it doesn't appear to be used or able to launch anything.

Area	Name	Function	Notes
Registry	HKLM\ Software\ Microsoft\ Windows\ CurrentVersion\ RunServicesOnce	Runs service once after boot up prior to the user logging on, and then deletes itself.	Works only in the Win 9x family. If the value is preceded by an exclamation point, deletion will not occur unless the command is successfully completed. There is also a HKCU version of the same key, but it doesn't appear to be used or able to launch anything.
Registry	HKLM\ Software\ Microsoft\ Windows\ CurrentVersion\ Shell Extensions\ Approved	Lists programs that will run with associated file types	Works with Windows 9x and later. Usually contains dozens of legitimate programs. Most programs listed will be located in %Windir%\System32 or C:\ Program Files. Difficult to tell what is and isn't malicious.
Registry	HKLM\ System\ CurrentControl Set\Control\ MPRServices	Can be used to launch programs during predefined events	Used by the Win 9x family. Similar to the HKLM\Software\ Microsoft\Windows NT\Current Version\Winlogon\Notify registry key used by NT and later systems. Used by Haxdoor.B backdoor trojan (`http://securityresponse.syma ntec.com/avcenter/venc/data/ backdoor.haxdoor.b.html`).
Registry	HKLM\ System\ CurrentControl Set\Control\ SafeBoot	Used by Windows to determine what programs, services, and drivers are loaded in a Safe mode boot	Although not common, can be manipulated by malware to either prevent Safe mode from being run (i.e., values are deleted) or to add malware program to a Safe mode boot sequence. Used by Petch trojan (`http:// securityresponse.symantec.com/ avcenter/venc/data/w32.petch.b .html`) to delete all Safe mode listings.
Registry	HKLM\ Software\ Microsoft\ Windows NT\ CurrentVersion\ Image File Execution Options	Allows another program (or debugger) to be executed instead when another program is started	Key lists all the programs that have been defined to have alternative programs start instead. Normal to have dozens of legitimate entries here. Used by a few malware programs, including the Zellome worm and StartPage.O trojan. Thanks to Andrew Aronoff of Silient-Runners.org for the hint.

Table continued on following page

Area	Name	Function	Notes
Registry	HKLM\System\ CurrentControl Set\Control\ Session Manager\ BootExecute	Programs or commands will be executed upon next reboot	Works with NT and later. Replaces some of the functionality of Wininit.ini of earlier Windows versions.
Registry	HKLM\System\ CurrentControl Set\Control\ Session Manager\ Environment\ Path	Determines what directories to check for commands or programs typed in without a specific PATH statement (i.e., Frog.exe vs. C:\ Program Files\Frog.exe)	Some malware programs rely on defects in the way Windows searches for and executes files when only the file name (ex. Frog.exe vs. C:\ Program Files\Frog.exe) is given. The PATH statement can be set by the DOS PATH command (located under Environmental variables in NT family) or by the registry key. Should contain by default: %SystemRoot%\system32;%SystemRoot%;%SystemRoot%\System32\Wbem; Can contain other legitimate non-default entries (ex. C:\Program Files\Network Associates;) Not commonly used by malware, but can still be a problem today. For example, some malware places itself in default application directories, which the application executes instead of the legitimate program executable. One trojan placed its malicious code in the user's My Documents folder. Because the malware was named after a legitimate MS-Word executable, MS-Word would always load it first instead of the legitimate version located under Program Files.
Registry	HKLM\System\ CurrentControl Set\Control\ Session Manager\ Environment\ PathExt	Determines what file extensions are tried if the program name is typed in without an extension (e.g., Frog vs. Frog.exe)	Some malware programs (ex. Spawner or twin viruses) rely on defects in the way Windows executes files when only the file name (ex. Frog.exe vs. C:\Program Files\ Frog.exe) is given. Not commonly used by malware today. Should be the following by default: .COM;.EXE;.BAT;.CMD;.VBS;.VBE;.JS; .JSE;.WSF;.WSH

Area	Name	Function	Notes
Registry	HKLM\System\ CurrentControl Set\Control\ Session Manager\ FileRename Operations	Contains pending file operations (e.g., rename, copy, etc.) to be executed on the next reboot of Windows	Works with NT and later. Replaced the older Wininit.ini file.
Registry	HKLM\System\ CurrentControl Set\Control\ Session Manager\ StartPage	Configures Internet Explorer's Startup page	Commonly manipulated by adware and spyware
Registry	HKLM\System\ CurrentControl Set\Enum\Root	Used to registry legacy Windows services	Not normally used by legitimate programs today. Not commonly used by malware. Used by Wallz worm (`http://secu-rityresponse.symantec.com/avce nter/venc/data/w32.wallz.html`).
Registry	HKLM\System\ CurrentControl Set\Services	Will load program as service (i.e., prior to user being logged in)	Works with NT and later. Common malware vector. Difficult to determine what is and isn't malicious using this key alone.
Registry	HKCR\ Protocols\Filters or HKLM\ Software\ Classes\ Protocols\Filters	Malware program can load itself when a MIME file attachment (ex. Text/xml) is executed	For example, can be used so malicious program is loaded each time a text file is viewed in IE instead of Notepad. Frequently used by spyware and adware. Programs listed by CLSID below keys. Used by StartPage.I trojan. Both keys are just aliases for each other. Thanks to Andrew Aronoff of Silent Runners.org for this hint.
Registry	HKLM\System\ CurrentControl Set\Control\ Class\{4D36E96B-E325-11CE-BFC1-08002BE10318}\ UpperFilters	Malware program can modify I/O from input devices	Used by some keylogging trojans (ex.InvisibleKey Spyware) to capture data from the keyboard driver. By default, several of the same keys will exist. Do not delete or manipulate this value, because it often contains legitimate information, without backing up registry first. Thanks to Andrew Aronoff of Silent Runners.org for this hint.

Table continued on following page

Area	Name	Function	Notes
Registry	HKLM\System\ CurrentControl Set\Services\ Winsock2\ Parameters\ NameSpace_ Catalog5\ Catalog_Entries HKLM\System\ CurrentControl Set\Services\ Winsock2\ Parameters\ Protocol_ Catalog9\ Catalog_Entries	Allows trojan or worm to install itself as a Layered Service Provider so that it can monitor network traffic	Used by many trojans, spyware, and adware programs. Many legitimate keys are located here. Can be difficult to find unautho rized programs. Commercial Guardian Monitor spyware program and Redfall trojan uses this method. Thanks to Andrew Aronoff of SilentRunners.org for this hint.
Registry	HKLM\Software\ Microsoft\Office\ Outlook\Addins	Malware can add itself as an Outlook Add-in and manipulate incoming or outgoing e-mail	May contain legitimate entries, such as anti-spam or antivirus software plug-ins. A common malicious example is Hot-bar adware.
Registry	HKCU\Identities\ <Identity>\ Software\ Microsoft\ Outlook Express\ <version>\ Signatures	Malware can add a malicious script to Outlook Express e-mail signatures that retrieves malware automatically when opened by the recipient.	Documented in Outlook Express, but may be able to be exploited in Out look and other e-mail clients as well. Used by the Kak and JS.Fortnight worms.
Registry	HKCU\ Software\ Microsoft\ Internet Explorer\ Desktop\ Components\<#> \Flags \Source \SubscribedURL	Can be hijacked by adwareto redirect IE to unauthorized locations and malware	Source and Subscribed values are set to About:Home by default. Hint provided by Andrew Aronoff of SilentRunners.org.
Registry	HKCU\ Software\ Microsoft\ Windows\ CurrentVersion\ Explorer\ ShellState	The registry value controls many aspects of the desktop environment.	Including whether Active Desktop is enabled, and whether file extensions are visible. Not very commonly manipulated by malware presently. Hint provided by Andrew Aronoff of SilentRunners.org.

Area	Name	Function	Notes
Registry	HKCU\ Software\ Microsoft\ Windows\ CurrentVersion\ Policies\Active Desktop	Controls Active Desktop settings	Active Desktop, if enabled, opens up more potential attack vectors. Note that selecting particular types of display media (e.g., a .JPG as wallpaper) will enable Active Desktop in some versions of Windows, whereas disabling Active Desktop while a .JPG is set as wallpaper will cause an "Are you sure?" prompt that many users will back out of in order to use their "nice" wallpaper. Not present by default on most systems. Not very commonly manipulated by malware presently. Hint provided by Andrew Aronoff of SilentRunners.org.
Registry	HKCU\ Software\ Microsoft\ Windows\ CurrentVersion\ Policies\Explorer	Controls Windows Explorer settings	Not very commonly manipulated by malware presently. Hint provided by Andrew Aronoff of SilentRunners.org.
Registry	HKCU\ Software\ Microsoft\ Windows\ CurrentVersion\ Policies\System	Allows control of desktop system and some administrative tools	Often used to disable Task Manager (DisableTaskMgr=0x1), Registry Editor (DisableRegistryTools = 0x1), and Control Panel (NoDispCPL= 0x1). Key not present by default on most systems. Commonly manipulated by malware. Examples include HackerWacker keystroke logger spyware, Ronoper worm, and Ting adware. Hint provided by Andrew Aronoff of SilentRunners.org.
Registry	HKLM\ Software\ Microsoft\ Windows\ CurrentVersion\ URL\Default Prefix	Adds any string value as a prefix for any URL typed in the browser, effectively redirecting all typed-in URLs to the unauthorized web site first	Commonly used by Adware. Examples include SmartSearch and WorldSearch adware, the JS.Fornight adware worm, and Popdis Trojan. Default values are supposed to be *http://*. Hint provided by Andrew Aronoff of SilentRunners.org.

Table continued on following page

Area	Name	Function	Notes
	HKLM\ Software\ Microsoft\ Windows\ CurrentVersion\ URL\Prefixes\ Search		
	HKLM\ Software\ Microsoft\ Windows\ CurrentVersion\ URL\Prefixes\ Search		
Registry	HKLM\System\ CurrentControl Set\Services\ Tcpip\ Parameters\ DataBasePath	Can be used to point to a new, unauthorized HOSTS file instead of the HOSTS file in the normal location (i.e., \%SystemRoot%\ Drivers\Etc)	Used by trojans (ex. Qhosts) and adware (ex. TMKSoft.XPlugin). Value is also added to ControlSet001 and ControlSet002 by some trojans (ex. Qhosts). Hint provided by Andrew Aronoff of SilentRunners.org.
Registry	HKLM\System\ CurrentControl Set\Services\ Tcpip\ Parameters\ NameServer	Can be used to point to a new, unauthorized DNS server	Used by a few malware programs, including Qhosts trojan.
Registry	HKLM\System\ CurrentControl Set\Services\ Tcpip\ Parameters\	Sets overall TCP/IP communications values, including DHCP, DNS, and TCP/IP stack. These values are used unless a specific value is set under the \Interfaces subkeys on a particular interface.	Many subvalues on this key could be changed to cause problems—for example, to set a new default gateway, to change normal DNS resolution order, etc. Many legitimate settings are present by default. Many values can be modified to strengthen a Windows computer against denial-of-service attacks.
Registry	HKLM\System\ CurrentControl Set\Services\ Tcpip\ Parameters\ Interfaces\ <interface CLSID>	Controls all TCP/IP communications, including DHCP, DNS, and TCP/IP stack.	Many subvalues on this key could be changed to cause problems—for example, to set a new default gateway, to change normal DNS resolution order, etc. Many legitimate settings are present by default.

Area	Name	Function	Notes
			Used by Qhosts and Flush.D trojans. Look at CurrentControlSet001 and 002, as some trojans modify those values to (ex. Qhosts).
Registry	HKLM\System\ CurrentContro lSet\Services\ VxD\MSTCP\ NameServer	Can be used to force a client to use an unauthorized DNS server	Key not present by default. Used by Qhosts and Flush.D trojans.

New exploits methods are added every month. Go to www.wrox.com to get an updated list.

If you felt this comprehensive list was overwhelming, you can find some comfort in the fact that almost all automated malware hides in the HKLM\Software\Microsoft\Windows\CurrentVersion\Run registry key. If you suspect a malware program, go there first, but Table 1-1 will help you locate malware when that particular registry key does not reveal the rogue program.

Summary

Most malicious attacks can be classified into four categories: Automated, Dedicated Attacker, Remote, or Local Execution. A key point of this book and the success of your network defense depend on you understanding that the most common threats come from automated malware, where security-by-obscurity has value as part of a computer defense plan. Automated malware includes viruses, worms, trojans, and hybrid, blended programs. Remote attacks include buffer overflows, denial-of-service, obscurity, and sniffing attacks. Other attack types, such as social engineering, spam, and insider attacks also deserve consideration. There are more than 100,000 different malware programs and they can hide in more than a hundred different places in Windows. Chapter 1 ended with a comprehensive listing of where malware can hide. The details it provides will lead to the defenses covered in the forthcoming chapters.

Now that we understand what threats we are up against, we can begin to concentrate on the defenses. Chapter 2, "Conventional and Unconventional Defenses," summarizes the overall steps of a successful computer security defense plan. Conventional defenses, such as patch management and antivirus protection, will be discussed along with unconventional but efficient defenses not covered elsewhere.

Conventional and Unconventional Defenses

In 2005, the Carnegie Mellon University CERT Coordination Center counted 5,990 new vulnerabilities (www.cert.org/stats) compared with 1,090 in 2000 and 171 in 1995. The Information Technology-Information Sharing and Analysis Center (www.it-isac.org) reported 52 new vulnerabilities and 16 new proof-of-concept (POC) exploits in the five days from June 20 through 24, 2005 (the week this chapter draft was first written). Despite a worldwide acceptance of the hacker and malware problem, the threat only continues to get worse. We need a better defense plan.

This chapter is divided into thirds, discussing overall guiding computer security defense principles and conventional and unconventional recommendations not covered elsewhere in this book. Most of the conventional recommendations are well known and should already be implemented in every network. On these issues, best practices will be discussed to maximize their efficiency. But as the statistics show, conventional defenses aren't enough. This chapter provides unique advice that can significantly improve your security strategy.

Overall Defense Strategy

One of the most welcome changes in the computer security field over the last decade is its maturing rise toward becoming a legitimate profession. Professions have guiding practices, certifications, and membership-based governing bodies. Certifications and governing bodies exist to help committed professionals follow ethical, best practices and to advance the profession as a whole. Every profession has a credo of accepted beliefs and practices that members should follow. These guidelines lead to a better overall work product, more educated practitioners, and the respect of other legal and financial bodies. Guiding principles help professionals make better, more consistent decisions when faced with unusual situations.

For example, accountants (my former profession) follow something called Generally Accepted Accounting Principles (GAAP). GAAP is a collection of official opinions and statements (`http://cpaclass.com/ gaap/gaap-us-01a.htm`) that accountants can consult when faced with an accounting situation. They are particularly helpful with unique financial circumstances that the normal accounting rules haven't covered. GAAP puts out guiding principles (such as "revenues must be matched to the expenses that created them") to help accountants make the right decision when tempted by others to present a more optimistic (i.e., fraudulent) outcome. In recent years, several CEOs and corporate accounting officers have been arrested for not following GAAP. With this in mind, I want to introduce this book's guiding security principles. They lie behind all the statements and recommendations stated elsewhere.

We Will Never Defeat Hackers and Malware

We will never defeat hackers and malware! This is perhaps a bitter pill to swallow, but it's true. Viruses, worms, and hackers have been around since before Microsoft was in existence and will be around long after it is nothing but a historical footnote. Many computer administrators mistakenly believe that once Microsoft goes away, hackers and malware will too. They are fools without an appropriate understanding of history. The first viruses weren't on Windows PCs. They weren't even on personal computers. They, and their ilk, appeared on mainframe computers that were popular at the beginning of the computer age. They moved to Apple computers when they became popular and moved to Microsoft Windows when it became the dominant platform. Malware and hackers exist on every platform.

As long as computers allow flexibility and users have human ingenuity, there will be hacking and exploits. The best we can do is to strengthen our computers and networks to a point where other targets are more attractive and more likely to be broken into. Don't adopt the attitude that somehow there will be less hackers in the future and users will be eventually be allowed to compute without the fear of maliciousness. If fact, we do a relatively poor job at preventing old attacks, much less addressing the new attacks. Attacks from years ago are still very popular and successful. In the future, there will probably be more ways to exploit a computer, not less. I know many security experts who have burnout because their job just keeps getting harder and harder — and not easier.

Whatever Is Popular Gets Hacked

Whatever software is popular at the moment invites hackers. Many people believe that Microsoft Windows gets hacked so much because it has poor security. This may have been true in the days of Windows 95, but it certainly isn't true today. Windows XP and Windows Server 2003 have some of the best security of any popular desktop operating system. It's just that it runs on over 95% of client desktops, and popularity breeds attacks. This explains why the open-source Apache web server program, with 70 percent of the web server market, has had dozens of successful exploits against IIS's handful in the same time period. Is IIS more secure than Apache? I'm not sure. It would take a long-term analysis by experienced security evaluators to reach that conclusion. What I do know is that Apache is the most popular server and it gets hacked more.

Some Microsoft haters suggest that end users move to other platforms, such as open-source alternatives Linux, Firefox, and OpenOffice. These are the same people who often recommend that users move from Microsoft Office document formats to some other file format such as PDF or RTF. What they don't realize is that both of those file formats have already been exploited, the Adobe PDF format several times (`http://secunia.com/search/?search=Adobe+Acrobat`).

And if the computing world up and moved in mass to a new platform or new program, hackers would just follow. Just ask Firefox Internet browser users for their experiences. The open-source Firefox browser was released as a "secure" alternative to Microsoft's Internet Explorer. It has picked up 27 vulnerabilities since its release in August 2004. As I write this chapter, 2 of the 27 are unpatched (http://secunia.com/product/4227), and this is with only a 10% market share (www.clickz .com/stats/sectors/traffic_patterns/article.php/3500691). Let Firefox surpass Internet Explorer in popularity and it is sure to gain the notice of even more hackers.

Some other examples: Apple Corporation's new Macintosh operating system, OS X, is gaining Apple slightly more market share. OS X has had 63 (http://secunia.com/product/96) vulnerabilities patched since its release. Cisco, the world's most popular Internet router company, releases patches nearly every month. Its new router operating system, IOS 12.x, has had 36 public vulnerabilities (http://secunia.com/product/182). RedHat Linux has over 99 (http://secunia.com/product/1343).

The truth is that any software can be hacked. There is no perfect code without bugs and potential exploits. What matters is how seriously the vendor takes security and how quickly they respond to security vulnerabilities. You may end up initially decreasing your overall security exposure by switching to a less hacked platform or piece of software, but then you pick up interoperability and training issues. And if your new platform becomes popular, you're back in the same place after all the pain and bloodletting. Instead, if the vendor is being responsive to security problems, then spend your effort on securing your current environment instead of looking for temporary false solutions. On a related note, if you want to know where hackers and malware will attack in the future, just look for the popular software.

There Is No Perfect Security Solution

There is no single solution that will be best for all users and environments. For instance, users often ask me to recommend the "best" antivirus program. That's like asking a car mechanic for his recommendation for best car. It depends on what you value most. The car mechanic might value a car noted for its low-cost reliability, while maybe the buyer wants a sports car or something low on gas mileage. It's the same way with computer security. There are many good solutions, none perfect, and what works best for one organization doesn't work great for another. That's why if any security expert claims to know what is best for your environment without learning about the environment first, you're talking to a marketing guy, not a security techie.

Most people don't even really want the best security. The best security is almost always unusable in most organizations. The popular saying is that if you want a secure computer, lock it up in a closet without a network card or keyboard. If you don't want to be attacked from the Internet, don't allow the computer to connect to it. Outside of those types of efforts, everything else is just a cost/benefit trade-off. Usually, the more secure you make a system, the less user-friendly it is. A good security solution weighs end-user and management acceptance against the potential problems the security defense is surely to cause. The best security defenses are highly accurate at both preventing maliciousness and not preventing legitimate computing. In this book, each defense technique is taught along with best practice recommendations, but ultimately each decision must be decided by the administrator.

Focus on the Right Problem of Automated Malware, Not Hackers

As Chapter 1 covered, more than 99% of the attacks and attempted exploits any computer system will endure are automated malware. There are different defenses with higher levels of success that can be implemented if you accept this understanding. You still need to fear the dedicated malicious hacker, just don't focus the majority of your efforts on the wrong problem. The solutions presented in this book address both but concentrate on automated malware.

If a User Can Be Tricked into Running a Malicious Program, It Is Game Over

If users only ran the legitimate, authorized programs they needed to do their job, the life of the computer administrator would be an easy one. Instead, users frequently run programs they shouldn't, visit web sites they shouldn't, and execute every file attachment. Ultimately, if you cannot prevent end users from executing unauthorized software, everything else is for naught. That's because a malicious program, if so programmed, can get around any computer security defense. Malware can bypass any firewall, bypass any antivirus scanner, and undo any computer security protection. There is no perfect defense against executed malware. The key then is to prevent end users from running unauthorized programs and code they should not be executing. Much of this book is dedicated to those types of protections, especially Chapter 9, "Stopping Unauthorized Execution."

Security-by-Obscurity Works!

Too many security experts claim that security-by obscurity doesn't work when it is obvious that it does. And although security-by-obscurity doesn't work as a complete defense by itself, I'll venture to say that it is one of the best ways to secure a computer! Anyone that disagrees with this statement, just move your web server from port 80 to some other random port and compare before and after attack statistics. This chapter covers the best security-by-obscurity tips.

Don't Let End Users Make Security Decisions

I'm not a big believer in end user education. It's highly overrated. With few exceptions, coordinated end-user education programs have never worked! Think about it. The most prolific automated threat is malicious e-mail attachments. As reported in Chapter 1, they are involved in nearly 92% of all successful attacks. The entire class of attacks could be defeated if people did not execute unexpected file attachments. Is there a computer user alive who has not heard the warning, several times, not to execute strange file attachments? And even if nearly everyone on your network follows this advice, it takes only one clueless end user to infect the whole network.

Most end users aren't very computer security aware, and even if they are, they are more likely to choose the wrong answer when faced with a particular security decision than the reader of this book. When end users get e-mail file attachments, Windows warns them that the file attachment could be malicious and cautions them against execution. The default decision is not to execute the attachment. End users need only press their Enter key or click the OK button and the system will do the right thing. Still, end users continue to go out of their way to make the wrong choice.

How many computer systems have you been on where the Microsoft Automatic Updates program has downloaded all the current patches and is just waiting for the end user to acknowledge and apply them but the user has clicked the "do it later" button? I frequently see patches behind for eight months or more. When I query the end user, he or she acknowledges being bugged by the update warning, but still they go unpatched.

End users really shouldn't be faced with security decisions. They aren't as knowledgeable as the typical IT professional and they often aren't going to make the right choice. We need to make the right choice for them and prevent malicious exploits from reaching their desktops in the first place. We need to push out patches and block malicious file attachments. We need to prevent the accidental execution of rogue code and block access to malicious HTML coding. Don't allow malicious code to get to the user's desktop in the first place.

Assume Firewalls and Antivirus Software Will Fail

Assume that traditional firewall and antivirus solutions will fail, because they will. As showed in Chapter 1, nearly every corporation reports universal antivirus software deployment, and yet they still report the problem as being as bad as ever. Firewalls can help, but malware is increasingly coming in and going out on allowed ports. Heck, I think any malware program that doesn't use port 80 for its malicious communications must be written by an idiot hacker. Port 80 is open on every firewall; why not use it?

Firewalls and antivirus solutions are needed, but they are not perfect defenses. Practically, I assume they will fail a few times a year. Computer security defenses should be designed following the "defense-in-depth" principle and assume that secondary and tertiary defenses will be needed to prevent what was missed by the first layers.

Protection Should Be Host-Based

In order for malware to exploit a PC, it must be executed on a PC, in its memory. Malware and hackers can arrive via any input mechanism (see Figure 2-1). If bits can be sent to a PC over a connection, the input conduit can be used maliciously. This includes wirelessly, via the keyboard, modem, network card, USB devices, CD-ROMs, and floppy discs. A frequent location to put computer defenses is on the network edge or e-mail gateway. These are great locations but only as an adjunct. The best place to put a computer defense is on the computer desktop.

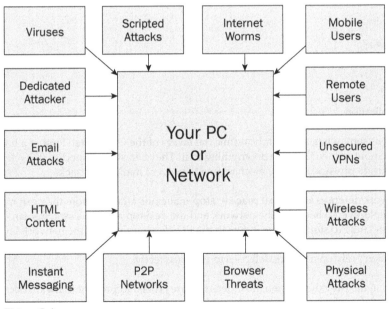

Figure 2-1

For instance, if you placed your antivirus software only on the e-mail gateway, you would miss nearly every other attack vector not occurring on port 25, including local execution and peer-to-peer programs. Sure, most of the attacks are currently coming via e-mail, but this trend isn't going to continue. Like the macro and boot viruses of yesteryear, malware will move on to other avenues once the current defenses prove consistently successful.

The August 2003 MS-Blaster RPC worm (`http://securityresponse.symantec.com/avcenter/venc/data/w32.blaster.worm.html`) proved that network edge protection isn't enough. When Blaster first came out, the conventional warning was that because most network Internet firewalls didn't allow port 135 traffic through it, the network and all its PCs were safe. Then remote laptop users and other infected mobile users (e.g., consultants, part-time workers, etc.) logged in a few days later with infected host computers. Once the Blaster worm was around the edge firewall, every unpatched PC host fell victim. The MS-Blaster worm proved that firewall protection must be moved down to the desktop.

If you deploy defenses on the desktop level, you will be able to catch the threat no matter where it originates. Having protection on *both* the desktop and the network is a great strategy, but if you have money only for one location, choose the desktop.

Practice Defense-in-Depth

With the latter point made, you should always practice defense-in-depth computer security when possible. No one computer security initiative works perfectly. Computer security will rarely be applied consistently across the environment. Somebody always misses something. Computers break, automation tools are never perfect, and it is a rare environment with nothing but the latest operating system tools and applications.

Defense-in-depth is the practice of placing security defenses at varying, often overlapping, logical locations within the enterprise. As Figure 2-2 shows, defense-in-depth includes the following locations:

❑ Physical

❑ Network

❑ Host

❑ Data

❑ Application

These locations somewhat, and rightly, mimic the layers of the OSI model. First, if a hacker has physical access to a computer, then they can do anything to it. They can steal it, modify it, hack it, or destroy it. You must provide physical security mechanisms to prevent malicious attack.

Second, network defenses are a great place to stop malicious attacks before they can reach the computers. For example, even when both the network and the desktop antivirus systems can catch a particular virus, it doesn't hurt to stop it before it gets to the PC. By stopping it at the network level, the PC's CPU resources don't have to be utilized to stop the viruses. Plus, network security devices allow centralized control. Just don't rely on network defenses to work perfectly.

As discussed in the previous section, host defenses are crucial to prevent malware because all malware must be executed on the host in order to be successful. Data defenses references how data can be used to compromise a computer. For example, a macro virus is made up of scripting languages and is stored in a document as data. SQL injection attacks use malformed data to extract confidential information from a database. Data has long been used to compromise computer systems, and application vendors and programmers need to write their programs to expect, and deal with, malformed data. Lastly, the applications themselves are frequently used to exploit a PC. Buffer overflows are the most frequent type of application attack, but you must include nearly every other type of malware program that accomplishes its work through end-user execution.

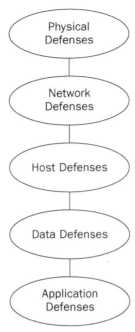

Figure 2-2

Defense-in-depth means including defenses at multiple layers to catch what others might have missed. Defense-in-depth also means overlapping different vendor products when possible and practical. There is no doubt that two products in the same defense class will always catch more malware than a single product from a single vendor. For example, consider using one vendor's product on your Internet gateway, another on your e-mail server, and still another on your computer desktop. The most successful e-mail security providers, such as MessageLabs (www.messagelabs.com) and Postini (www.postini.com), use multiple antivirus e-mail engines to catch more viruses. Many studies, (including this one on anti-spyware products at http://windowssecrets.com/comp/050127), proved that even when one product is vastly superior to others, using two products always increased detection rates. Of course, although multiple vendor products catch more malware and decrease overall risk, the strategy must be weighed against the added overhead and cost of managing multiple platforms.

Prevent Malware from Hiding Where It Likes to Hide

Most automated malware must hide itself in Windows in order to be executed when the computer is rebooted. Thus, a good security defense is to prevent malware from hiding where it normally likes to hide (see Table 1-1 in Chapter 1). In particular, Chapter 3, "NTFS Permissions 101," will describe how to prevent malware from hiding in the operating system; and Chapter 6, "Protecting High-Risk Registry Entries," will explain how to prevent malware from hiding in the registry.

Minimize Potential Attack Vectors, Decrease Attack Space

Every installed service, application, and running process on a PC is a potential attack vector. By decreasing the number of them, you will decrease the risk of successful exploitation. Chapter 5, "Protecting High-Risk Files," Chapter 7, "Tightening Services," and Chapter 8, "Using IPSec," discuss decreasing attack vectors.

Security Must Be Automated

Security is relatively easy. It's consistency that is hard. We know how to prevent viruses, worms, and trojans, but consistently applying the recommended security defenses all the time requires automation. If you don't automate security, it won't get done consistently. Chapters 14, "Group Policy Explained," and Chapter 15, "Designing a Secure Active Directory Infrastructure," discuss automation.

With these overall guiding principles in place, the practical defense steps can be discussed.

Conventional Defenses

Although this book is full of unique, unconventional tips, conventional wisdom is still needed. This section covers over a dozen common security recommendations, plus a few more less commonly known suggestions.

Don't Give Users Admin Access

In order for most malware to work, it must be executed locally by the end user. After execution, the malware typically works in the security context of the end user who executed it. This means whatever the user can do, the malware can do. Unfortunately, most administrators allow their end users to be logged in with administrator-level privileges. Most often the user is logged in with an account that is added to the local Administrators group. This is done so that normal end users can install software and configure their computers. In general, administrators have Full Control permissions to all local computer resources.

Non-administrative users (known as *Limited User Accounts* or *LUAs*) cannot do a host of normal administrative activities, including the following:

❑ Install or uninstall programs, including Internet Explorer programs

❑ Configure Windows system settings

❑ View or change security permissions

❑ Change network configuration settings (sometimes cannot view settings)

❑ Create new shares (but can map to existing shares)

❑ View the security log (but can view Application and System logs). They cannot clear any of the Event logs.

❑ View local computer policy settings

❑ Stop, start, load, or pause services

❑ Change most things in the System applet

❑ Add non-Plug-and-Play hardware or drivers

❑ Modify drivers in the Control Panel

❑ Add or change hardware profiles

❑ Change page file parameters

❏　　　Manipulate many taskbar programs

❏　　　Change system time or time zone

❏　　　Create new Performance logs, Counters, or Alerts

❏　　　Configure Remote Desktop/Assistance (but can request Remote Assistance if so enabled)

LUAs can usually manipulate anything to do with their desktop profile, including delete and add desktop icons, change desktop background and screensaver, and map and disconnect drive shares. They can execute existing programs, run commands, modify Internet Explorer security settings (strangely enough), change folder options, schedule tasks, add printers, and encrypt files.

Whereas administrative accounts have Full Control permissions to all local system resources, LUAs have only Read or Read & Execute permissions to most Windows system files and areas. They usually also have Write permissions to personal areas, such as their profile, home directories, My Document folder, and temporary file locations. We will cover this in more detail in Chapter 3. LUAs have mostly Read-only permissions to most registry keys, including the ones most popularly attacked by malware. They also have Write permissions to the Current User registry keys (covered in Chapter 6).

Computer administrators often give regular end users Administrator rights so they can install software and change Windows settings, when needed. To be fair, prior to the forthcoming Windows Vista (see the "Windows Vista" sidebar later in this chapter), Microsoft didn't give administrators an easy way to allow regular end users to install software without being an administrator, and in many cases all new user accounts are added to the Administrators group by default.

The net effect is that once malware is executed, it is running in the context of the local Administrator and can do nearly anything it wants to the system. Because of this risk, system administrators should not allow end users to be logged in with administrator-privileged accounts. If this rule were followed, it would defeat 70-90% of today's malware attacks. The truth is that there are many ways for malware to spread and do harm without needing administrator permissions, but most rogue programs are coded with the expectation that the user will be logged in as an administrator.

If your end user isn't an administrator, an account with administrative permissions will be needed to install software or reconfigure Windows system settings. This can be accomplished as follows:

❏　　　By having an administrator install all software and configure system settings

❏　　　Using the group policy software install feature to install program (covered in Chapter 14)

❏　　　Giving the user a second, more privileged account to install and configure with

With the latter option, users can be told of a second account that they should use when installing software and reconfiguring the system. You can rename the Administrator account something similar to the user's normal login account (such as Ray2, where Ray1 is used for normal operations) or call the account something like Software Installs. Although this technique would decrease the potential attack risk if utilized correctly, the propensity for the user to always be logged in as the elevated privileged account is high.

RunAs

Another option is to teach nonadmin users how to use the RunAs feature to invoke their higher privileged, admin account when needed. Microsoft created the RunAs feature in Windows 2000 and has increased its functionality in every version of Windows since. RunAs was developed so that even system administrators could stop being logged in full-time with administrative privileges. Microsoft realized that even administrators spend the majority of their time doing non-admin tasks, such as writing documents and picking up e-mail. Administrators are often responsible for accidentally running malware programs, and should therefore only be logged in as administrators when administrative permissions are needed.

The RunAs feature can be executed within the Windows GUI or at the command line. From within the GUI, you need only right-click any executable to get a RunAs option. Select *The following user* radio button (see Figure 2-3), and then fill in the name of the administrative account you want to use, preceded by the machine or domain name to which the account belongs, type in the password, and select Enter or click the OK button.

If the RunAs option does not appear when you right-click a file, try holding down the Right-shift key and then right-clicking the file. For reasons unknown to me, the Right-shift key makes the RunAs option appear when it doesn't without the right-shift key trick. Sometimes, the RunAs option will not appear with some executables, such as Format.com, either way.

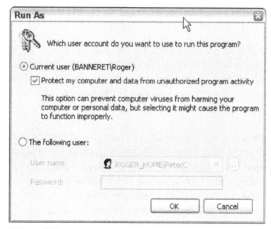

Figure 2-3

The Secondary Logon service must be running on the machine where RunAs is executed.

In Windows XP and later, RunAs uses the impersonated user's desktop profile (in Windows 2000 it used the Default Users' profile instead). At first, this might not seem like a big deal, but because drive mappings and other desktop settings are saved to a user's profile, there is a potential for the inputted command not to work.

Administrators can create desktop icons with the RunAs feature already selected by right-clicking on any desktop icon, choosing Properties, selecting the Shortcut tab, and then clicking the Advanced button. You will then be able to select the *Run with different credentials* option (see Figure 2-4). Then, when you click on the icon, you will be allowed to run the selected program with different credentials. Unfortunately, the new credential account will always need the password typed in, but security-wise this is desired.

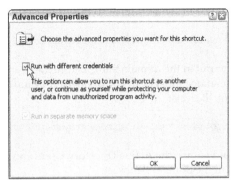

Figure 2-4

Command-line RunAs

If run at the command line, RunAs has even more features and flexibility. Running RunAs at the command prompt without any parameters results in the following output:

```
C:\>runas
RUNAS USAGE:

RUNAS [ [/noprofile | /profile] [/env] [/netonly] ]
        /user:<UserName> program

RUNAS [ [/noprofile | /profile] [/env] [/netonly] ]
        /smartcard [/user:<UserName>] program

   /noprofile      specifies that the user's profile should not be loaded.
                   This causes the application to load more quickly, but
                   can cause some applications to malfunction.
   /profile        specifies that the user's profile should be loaded.
                   This is the default.
   /env            to use current environment instead of user's.
   /netonly        use if the credentials specified are for remote
                   access only.
   /savecred       to use credentials previously saved by the user.
                   This option is not available on Windows XP Home Edition
                   and will be ignored.
   /smartcard      use if the credentials are to be supplied from a
                   smartcard.
   /user           <UserName> should be in form USER@DOMAIN or DOMAIN\USER
   program        command line for EXE.  See below for examples

Examples:
> runas /noprofile /user:mymachine\administrator cmd
> runas /profile /env /user:mydomain\admin "mmc %windir%\system32\dsa.msc"
> runas /env /user:user@domain.microsoft.com "notepad \"my file.txt\""

NOTE:  Enter user's password only when prompted.
NOTE:  USER@DOMAIN is not compatible with /netonly.
NOTE:  /profile is not compatible with /netonly.
```

In the simplest form, you can type in syntax similar to this example:

```
Runas /user:<domain>\<username> <pathname\programname>
```

It is important to remember to put in the domain name before the user name if you intend to use a domain account. The program name must be inside quotes if it includes long file names or spaces. An example command might look like this:

```
Runas /user:banneret\tgrimes "mmc g:\windows\system32\dsa.msc"
```

This example command would launch the Active Directory Users and Computers console in the context of the user account TGrimes in the domain Banneret.

The default RunAs command line allows the current user to use the impersonated user's profile and environment instead of his own. Running with the /noprofile switch can save time on most commands, but can cause problems. Try both ways. Starting with Windows XP (but not shown in the Windows XP command-line syntax listing) is a new feature called /savecred. Using the /savecred command, you can instruct Windows to save the impersonated user's logon name *and password* to be used next time when RunAs executes the same command. This feature requires the Stored User Name and Password functionality to be left enabled (it can be disabled with Group Policy, as covered in Chapter 14). You can use the command-line version of RunAs in desktop shortcuts to gain the additional functionality offered in the command-line version on the desktop GUI.

For an administrator to use RunAs routinely means learning how to execute many Windows GUI commands at the command line. For example, to change the system time or time zone, use RunAs with Timedate.cpl. Running Sysdm.cpl will launch the System applet. Or launch an administrative console using cmd.exe and then run the needed program or functionality.

RunAs Issues

Unfortunately, RunAs isn't perfect. Possibly most distressing is that it cannot run Windows Explorer, the utility often used by administrators to view and modify NTFS and Share permissions. A common solution dedicated administrators can implement is to use Remote Desktop and connect to the same desktop with administrative privileges. It's crude, but it works. Second, RunAs doesn't work with all installs. While RunAs can be used to run and install many programs, many install programs will not install. If you have problems, try running the Add/Remove Programs wizard using the Appwiz.cpl command. Lastly, it refuses to work with many programs for reasons unknown, and the failure often doesn't give you a good error message to troubleshoot. For instance, even when you start Internet Explorer (Iexplore.exe) using RunAs in an administrative context, Windows Update will not work. It will appear to be working and just fail.

Third-Party Privilege Escalation Apps

Consider using a third-party utility to accomplish elevated privileges, such as MakeMeAdmin (http://weblogs.asp.net/aaron_margosis/archive/2004/07/24/193721.aspx). When you run it, you get a command-line prompt running under your normal user account profile, but in a new logon session in which it is a member of the Administrators group. This command prompt and any programs started from it use your regular profile, authenticate as you on the network, but have full local administrative privileges. All other programs continue to run with your regular, unprivileged account. There is also a MakeMePU.cmd (PowerUser mode).

Extending LUA Protections

Often, the reverse behavior is wanted. Administrators who do need administrative credentials the majority of the time wish they could run some programs using an LUA account. For instance, many administrators realize the increased risk of using Internet Explorer and wish they could run just that program as a non-admin user. You can use RunAs to accomplish this or use another third-party application called RunAsAdmin (`https://sourceforge.net/projects/runasadmin`). RunAsAdmin allows you to utilize XP's and 2003's SAFER API (covered in Chapter 9) to run at a lower privileged logon token. It has a per-user startup interactive configuration option that enables the user to choose what restriction level to use on the fly. It was designed by a Microsoft MVP and can be trusted.

Keep Patches Updated

Many of today's popular attacks only work because administrators have not kept their Windows system patches up to date. Recently, a friend of mine who is a very knowledgeable and respected administrator for a Fortune 500 company called me to report an Internet worm outbreak in his organization. He said that over 1,500 computers were infected across multiple county offices and that his antivirus software was not detecting it. From his description of what the worm was doing (i.e., crashing the RPC service), I knew this meant that worm was attacking a vulnerability patched over a year ago. After I helped him repair his systems, we learned that the worm used three different vulnerabilities, but all were patched by Microsoft over a year ago. One of the vulnerabilities was over three years old. In my eyes, he was to blame for his company's downtime.

Sadly, I also understand the practical world. There are many companies who can't keep patches updated. For instance, another Fortune 500 company I work with has several hundred Windows NT 4.0 workstations and servers running in their production plants. They run a critical manufacturing program and the vendor refuses to warranty the software if it is patched beyond its installed Service Pack (SP) 2 level. The software has been paid for and does its job perfectly. To replace the functionality would cost tens of millions of dollars. The company weighed the potential risk of being down from a virus or worm against the replacement cost of the system. Security is always a formula of cost versus benefit measured in dollars.

Many other companies have overly small staffs already overburdened with current support duties. To do thorough regression testing on big patches is beyond their current staff's workload, especially if they aren't being hacked a lot currently. Many companies still haven't deployed Windows XP's Service Pack 2 even though it has been out since August 2004, and even though its application closes hundreds of attack holes. Again, I could complain about the lack of foresight, but this is the practical reality that many organizations face. And ultimately, this is how some organizations become extremely vulnerable to Internet attacks and worms.

Although there is no hard and fast rule, organizations should strive to deploy Windows system and other third-party application security patches within a reasonable window of time based upon the patch's criticality and the company's likely risk of exposure. Microsoft rates each patch it delivers with a severity rating of critical, important, moderate, or low (see `www.microsoft.com/technet/security/bulletin/rating.mspx` for more details). Before determining whether a particular patch applies, an organization should decide ahead of time how quickly it needs to deploy a patch based upon its severity rating. Table 2-1 shows an example of a patching deployment time line.

Table 2-1

If Patch Severity Rating Is . . .	Patch Should Be Deployed Across All Applicable Computers Within . . .
Critical	1 day–2 weeks (less than 1 week for high risk attacks)
Important	1–3 weeks
Moderate	3–8 weeks
Low	4 months

Patch Regression Testing

Of course, patches need testing prior to production deployment. The patch deployment team should create multiple test workstations that mimic the production environment. Ideally, there would be a test machine to match every configuration within the enterprise. When new patches come out, the team should deploy them to the test workstations and check for application compatibility. Microsoft is doing a better job of testing their patches before deploying, but at least once or twice a year a patch is released that causes widespread problems to a fair percentage of users.

After the patches have been deployed and tested on the nonproduction machines, they should be deployed in a limited fashion to selected production computers within the environment. The production machines testing should absolutely test all computer configurations and applications deployed across the enterprise. If the patch is determined to cause few or no problems, it should then be widely deployed across the enterprise using a patch management tool. The patch deployment team should have a patch rollback plan prior to deploying any patch in case something goes wrong. Consider reading Susan Bradley and Anne Stanton's excellent ebook, The Complete Patch Management Book (www.ecora .com/ecora/jump/pm99.asp) or Microsoft's patch management document (www.microsoft .com/technet/security/topics/patchmanagement.mspx).

Microsoft Patch Management Tools

Although there are many better third-party tools, Microsoft has many free and commercial patch management deployment tools, including System Management Server, Windows Update Service, Microsoft Update, Automatic Updates, and Microsoft Baseline Security Analyzer. I'll summarize each here:

❑   System Management Server (www.microsoft.com/smserver/default.asp)

System Management Server (SMS) is Microsoft's premier software deployment and desktop management tool. Although it can do far more than just deploy software patches, it is an excellent tool for doing just that. It has excellent fine-tuning controls, management flexibility, and excellent reporting. However, it is an expensive commercial tool and requires significant experience to operate.

❑   Windows Server Update Service (www.microsoft.com/windowsserversystem/update services/default.mspx)

Windows Server Update Service (WSUS) replaced the less functional Software Update Services (SUS) server product in June 2005. WSUS, like SUS, is Microsoft's best free tool for patch management. Although not as feature rich as other third-party products, WUS is a solid patch management competitor. You must install it on a Windows 2000 or 2003 server and have the appropriate client access licenses (CALs). It supports Windows 2000 and later clients. The clients must have the Automatic Updates service installed and configured to pull from the WSUS server. Then patch management administrators download and approve patches on the WUS server, which then deploys to the workstations.

❑ Microsoft Update (`http://update.microsoft.com/microsoftupdate/v6/default.aspx?ln=en-us`)

Microsoft Update replaces Microsoft's Windows Update web site. Whereas Windows Update could only check for and update the Windows operating system and a small subset of applications (i.e., Internet Explorer, Outlook, Outlook Express), Microsoft Update will check for and install patches to a wider range of applications (including Exchange, IIS, Microsoft Office, and SQL Server). Previously, with Windows Update, you had to visit additional web sites to patch all those applications. Microsoft promises to include additional applications at the Microsoft Update web site. Unfortunately, like Windows Update, Microsoft Update requires that the installer be logged on as an administrator, the process is manual, one machine at a time, and lacks any centralized control or reporting.

❑ Automatic Updates (`www.microsoft.com/downloads/details.aspx?FamilyID=799432fb-c196-4f01-8cce-4f9ea58d6177&DisplayLang=en`)

Automatic Updates is a client-side service first installed with Windows XP Pro Service Pack 1, but later installed in Windows 2000 Service Pack 2 and in Windows Server 2003. It can be installed manually by downloading from the link above. Automatic Updates connects to either Microsoft's Windows Update site or to a corporate WUS or SUS server. It can be instructed to check for new patches every day or once per week. Patches can be downloaded and installed automatically, or just downloaded or the end user notified. Automatic Updates installs patches using the LocalSystem context, and as such the end user does not need to be an administrator. If patches are downloaded directly from Microsoft's Windows Update web site, there is no centralized control or reporting.

❑ Microsoft Baseline Security Analyzer (`www.microsoft.com/technet/security/tools/mbsahome.mspx`)

Microsoft Baseline Security Analyzer (MBSA) cannot patch a Windows computer, but can be used to check for common security misconfigurations and missing critical patches. It can be run against Windows NT 4.0 and later machines (but it cannot be installed on Windows NT) and the person using it must have local administrator credentials on the machines being scanned. The File and Printer and Remote Registry services need to be running for MBSA to work remotely. It can be run against a single PC or against a network of machines. MBSA provides a nice XML-formatted report, but there is no easy way to get a single summary report for multiple machines.

Don't forget to patch your non-Microsoft applications. Some third-party applications, such as Sun's Java and Macromedia's Adobe Acrobat, seem to need patching as frequently as Windows. Also, don't forget to update and patch your hardware drivers, disk controller cards, and computer BIOSs. Keeping up on your patching is a significant way to prevent malicious attacks and exploitation.

Use a Host-Based Firewall

Every Windows PC should have a host-based firewall installed. Windows XP and Windows Server 2003 come with a Microsoft-built firewall called Windows Firewall (it was called Internet Connection Firewall in Windows XP pre-SP2 and Windows Server 2003 pre-SP1). Windows Firewall blocks all inbound connection attempts not initiated by an outbound connection or previously defined as an allowed inbound service. Because the Windows Firewall cannot block outbound connections, many security experts (including this author) have written about how poor it is. Now, however, after years of solely relying on it, I've come to appreciate it. I removed all my other firewalls, including my old favorite, ZoneAlarm (www.zonelabs.com/store/content/home.jsp), and my network perimeter firewall, SonicWall (www.sonicwall.com). Verdict? Even though my network is under constant attack and I travel constantly and attach to grossly infected networks, my machines have remained clean. Windows Firewall works! It's not the best host-based firewall, but it is free and it works.

Windows Firewall is a basic stateful firewall. It will block all inbound, unauthorized connections. If any connection prompts are displayed, they are concerning whether to allow an application to set up new inbound listener ports (called *exceptions*). Exceptions (see Figure 2-5) are the ports or applications that can accept inbound connections not initiated by an outbound connection. Windows Firewall has three main states: On (with exceptions allowed), On (with no exceptions allowed), and Off. Whether or not ICMP traffic should be allowed is also configurable. Disabling all ICMP traffic may prevent some legitimate programs from working. For instance, Active Directory uses ICMP probes to determine whether a slow link is detected for group policy purposes (www.microsoft.com/technet/prodtechnol/windowsserver2003/library/Operations/92c46246-7cb7-441e-92d6-2b6671c2980e.mspx).

Figure 2-5

Windows Firewall allows you to configure different firewall settings for different network connections. Thus, you can set one policy for laptop computers connected to your LAN and another for when they are away from the corporate network. In most cases, you would want the firewall policy to be more relaxed when connected to your LAN so that you can administrate the machine remotely but put its defenses up when away so that malicious code does not compromise it. In the corporate environment, you can use group policy to define particular groups of people that can access Windows Firewall-protected machines without being filtered by the firewall as long as they use IPSec. For more information on Windows Firewall group policy settings, read the document located at http://download.microsoft.com/download/6/8/a/68a81446-cd73-4a61-8665-8a67781ac4e8/wf_xpsp2.doc.

New Features of Windows Firewall

When Microsoft's Internet Connection Firewall was updated in XP SP2 and Windows Server SP1 to Windows Firewall, many new features were introduced, including the following:

Firewall enabled by default for all network connections

Firewall can be configured per connection or globally

Improved exception definitions (by IP address or subnet, by executable)

A default firewall policy is enabled during Windows startup, allowing only basic traffic, such as DHCP and DNS, to pass until the firewall is fully functionality (ICF did not protect during Windows startup). This default policy cannot be modified.

Can completely control using group policy

New Windows Firewall applet in Control Panel

PV6 support

IPSec support, and IPSec is Windows Firewall aware

IPSec traffic can be routed past the firewall without inspection, and can be done by Windows group (covered in Chapter 8)

Netsh support

> You can query the state of your firewall using the Netsh.exe command, as shown in the following commands:

```
Netsh firewall show state (will document the firewall's overall
settings)
Netsh firewall show logging (will tell you if logging is enabled
and how it is configured)
Netsh firewall show allowedprogram (will list program files
listed as Exceptions)
```

IAnother interesting feature is the capability to define specific groups of users or computers that can bypass the Windows Firewall inspection process. The specified user's computers must use IPSec to communicate with the intended host. The idea is that if the traffic is already protected and authenticated by IPSec, then the duplicative filtering abilities of the firewall aren't needed. This could be used to allow admin users to bypass the firewall or to allow use of remote management tools. Unfortunately, this sort of feature would also allow malware or a hacker to take advantage of the additional trust if they compromised a IPSec-connected computer.

On the downside, Windows Firewall has some significant weaknesses when compared to its competitors:

❑ It cannot block outbound connections (which means locally executed malware can connect to outbound to notify its originator, infect other computers, or update its own programming). The forthcoming Windows Vista firewall will block outbound connections.

❏ Logging is not turned on by default and even when turned on is very poor.

❏ It cannot send alerts to the user on unauthorized inbound connection attempts. Sometimes it is helpful to know when your machine is under attack

❏ It does not do application-layer inspection or identify specific attacks. Thus, if your machine were under a massive denial-of-service attack, Windows Firewall would only log each attempt separately, and is not able to aggregate the smaller attacks into one large, cohesive attack

A short Microsoft summary article on Windows Firewall can be found at http://support.microsoft.com/default.aspx?kbid=875357.

For those administrators looking for a better host firewall, consider the following products:

❏ ZoneAlarm (`www.zonelabs.com/store/content/home.jsp`)

❏ McAfee Personal Firewall Plus (`http://us.mcafee.com/root/package .asp?pkgid=101&WWW_URL=www.mcafee.com/myapps/firewall/ov_firewall.asp`)

❏ Norton Personal Firewall (`www.symantec.com/sabu/nis/npf`)

❏ Tiny Firewall (`www.tinysoftware.com/home/tiny2?la=EN`)

There are dozens of good host-based firewalls to choose from. My personal favorite is ZoneAlarm. It was recently purchased by CheckPoint (`www.checkpoint.com`). ZoneAlarm could be overly intrusive at times, but contained a feature unique to the host-based firewall world. Many host-based firewalls will block outbound attempts by executables not previously allowed. Unfortunately, most users aren't knowledgeable enough to know what should and shouldn't be allowed. Heck, most security people don't really know what they should allow. For example, should Microsoft Office and VMware be initiating outbound connections when they are installed? If you don't allow them, will you miss a security update or something else desirable? ZoneAlarm has a feature that consults a centralized database that makes the decision or tells the user what most people choose when faced with a similar decision about the same program. This feature is not included in the free product. After ZoneAlarm, I liked Tiny Firewall. It works well, has a small footprint, and has the least impact on legitimate communications. McAfee and Norton firewalls can also be installed in a wider suite of vendor offerings (i.e., antivirus, anti-spam, etc.).

No matter which host-based firewall you choose, you should install and use one. It is not enough to have only a firewall on the network's edge.

Use Antivirus Software

Most organizations are already using antivirus software, but there are some best practices to reinforce. Here are some antivirus recommendations:

❏ Administrators should make sure each end-user computer has a running, real-time scanning antivirus program with an updated signature database.

❏ An antivirus program should consistently rank high in terms of current and overall accuracy. Several web sites report on the accuracy of the most popular antivirus scanning products, including The Virus Bulletin 100 (`www.virusbtn.com/vb100/about/index.xml`).

❑   The antivirus product should have consistently accurate repairs when it removes malware.

❑   The signature update should be automated, either directly to the vendor (for laptops) or downloaded from a centralized corporate definition server.

❑   Antivirus software should be installed on e-mail servers (at least until malicious e-mail traffic subsides).

❑   If antivirus software is installed on a network edge gateway device, it should scan all ports allowed through the firewall and not just the default ports (usually 21, 25, 80, and 110).

❑   Antivirus software should cause minimal/acceptable slowdown on end-user computers.

❑   The antivirus vendor should have timely tech support and report on suspicious submitted files in a timely manner.

❑   The antivirus product should prevent regular end users from disabling the product.

❑   Antivirus software should allow all files or just selected file types to be scanned.

❑   Antivirus software should scan file headers to identify files and not just rely on the file extensions.

❑   With the proliferation of peer-to-peer (P2P) programs, any installed antivirus software should inspect P2P traffic.

❑   Antivirus software should recursively inspect all compressed file types.

Very few things in the computer security world are "rock-science," but antivirus scanning is. Today's scanners are a far cry from their early versions. They use incredibly efficient scanning techniques to look through tens of thousands of files per minute, they contain emulation environments to catch polymorphic and stealth works, they and contain accurate heuristic scanning engines. I rarely recommend a new, untested antivirus product to clients. I prefer to stick with the tried-and-true antivirus scanner vendors that have proven their accuracy and mettle over multiple years.

Use Anti-Spam Software

As reported in Chapter 1, spam is still a major problem. All e-mail should be protected by an anti-spam software program or device. Anti-spam defenses can be deployed at four locations:

❑   Desktop

❑   E-mail server

❑   Network gateway

❑   E-mail service provider

Interestingly, spam accuracy goes up the further you get away from the desktop. Desktop anti-spam products (currently) have the worst accuracy in detecting spam of any of its competitors. This is the exact opposite of the results I find in antivirus software. Anti-spam software deployed on e-mail servers is better, but still, in my opinion, unacceptable. If your anti-spam product isn't approaching 99% accuracy, then you need a better product.

Dozens of anti-spam products and appliances deployed on the network's edge have proven to be very accurate and efficient. Personally, I use an appliance called the Barracuda Spam Firewall (www.barracuda networks.com). Like many other of its competitors, it is highly accurate (99% or above), feature-rich, fast, and highly customizable. The only downside is that the spam e-mail must reach the device, and hence, your network, in order to be filtered. Several companies, such as MessageLabs and Postini, filter out spam before it reaches its destination networks. They are the most accurate anti-spam services available and are relatively low cost (per-seat pricing starts at $15 per year). These services tend to be less feature-rich and customizable compared to network gateway solutions, and you must route your e-mail (by repointing your mail MX record) to the provider. Even though they sign a confidentiality agreement, you will have to allow management to agree to third-party inspection of your e-mail. No matter which anti-spam solution you choose, you need to implement one. Spam is a leader in spreading malicious malware, spyware, and adware.

Use Anti-Spyware Software

Sadly, even though the major antivirus vendors are positioned to be the best spyware detectors, none of the major players seem to be taking the threat of spyware seriously. With antivirus programs running on the desktop inspecting all traffic headed to and from the PC, you would think the antivirus programs could add signatures for spyware and thoroughly protect the desktop. Maybe one day, but not now. You should select and use an accurate anti-spyware solution. There are dozens of free products on the market, including Lavasoft's Ad-Aware (`www.lavasoftusa.com`), one of my favorites, and Microsoft's own solution (`www.microsoft.com/athome/security/spyware/software/default.mspx`). Microsoft bought Giant Software's anti-spyware product. The Microsoft beta release has consistently tested among the most accurate products. Per Bill Gates, the individual version will remain free, but an enterprise-managed version will be commercially supported.

A big plus for Microsoft's product is that it is one of the few free products that blocks, as well as detects, spyware. Most free anti-spyware programs detect spyware after the fact, but do nothing to prevent new infections. Usually you have to buy the commercial versions in order to receive proactive protection.

There are dozens of anti-spyware product reviews — just be sure not to be fooled by the many bogus "spyware sites" that are really looking to add more spyware to your system. Here are two trusted legitimate spyware detector review sites:

- ❏   `www.pcmag.com/category2/0,1874,1639157,00.asp`
- ❏   `http://windowssecrets.com/comp/050127`

In a nutshell, no single anti-spyware product catches everything. And all products catch things that the others miss. Combining two anti-spyware products increases accuracy, but I can't seem to talk myself into using two different products even if it results in slightly better accuracy. Maybe it's because I'm already using/paying for a firewall, anti-spam, and antivirus software. Some antivirus vendors offer anti-spyware products as well, but I haven't found them to be very accurate in my testing. Anti-spam appliances, such as the Barracuda Spam Firewall, are also checking for spyware, but I haven't completed my testing to give an accuracy rating.

Physical Security

As discussed previously, if a hacker has physical access to your computer assets, there isn't much you can do to prevent malicious exploits, theft, or data destruction. All computers containing sensitive information should be protected by physical security measures. This includes building security, locks, doors, and passwords.

Boot-Up Passwords

Portable computers, such as PDAs, cell phones, and laptops should be protected with boot-up passwords. That way, if they are stolen, the thief will have a more difficult time accessing the computer. Most laptop thieves don't know how to disable the boot password and end up junking the stolen goods — better than some random criminal accessing your corporate or personal information. When PDAs and cell phones are boot password protected, it requires that the criminal wipe out all permanent memory in order to access the device. This, again, protects your data.

Boot Only from the Primary Hard Drive

All computers should be prevented from booting from any media except the primary hard drive. Many malicious hacks depend on the intruder being able to boot around Windows (using special tools or Linux boot discs), bypassing Microsoft's built-in security. By preventing booting from anything but the primary hard drive, you have significantly reduced your risk from a physical attack. On a related note, this will also prevent boot viruses from infecting the computer. If you need to boot on a floppy disk or CD-ROM disc for troubleshooting purposes, you can always modify the BIOS back to the appropriate setting.

Password-protect the BIOS

After configuring the computer's BIOS to only boot on the primary hard drive, password-protect the BIOS from unauthorized changes. This will prevent a physical attacker from switching the computer back to booting on malicious media. Sure, a knowledgeable attacker can open the computer case and disable the BIOS password option, but if the intruder has that much access and time, you've got other problems to worry about as well. The BIOS password should not be the same password that you use for your Windows administrators. The BIOS password is likely to *not* be changed on a regular basis, and because of remote troubleshooting, is more likely to be given out to a regular end user.

Harden the TCP/IP Stack

The TCP/IP stack is the network software that takes packet data handed to it by the network interface card software driver and passes it to the operating system for further processing. Microsoft Windows has its own TCP/IP stack drivers, although additional drivers can be added by installed programs (such as Ethereal or Winpcap) or by Layered Service Provider (LSP) programs.

The TCP/IP stack can be attacked by remote hackers, usually in the form of a denial-of-service attack. Microsoft hardened the default stack in XP Pro SP2 and Windows Server 2003 SP1. Microsoft has registry settings you can use to strengthen the Microsoft TCP/IP stack on previous Windows versions against attacks using massive volumes of malformed network packets. Table 2-2 shows Microsoft's recommended registry keys and values to protect against DoS attacks directed at the TCP/IP stack.

Table 2-2

Value Name	Value (REG_DWORD)
The values below are located beneath the registry key HKLM\SYSTEM\CurrentControlSet\Services	
SynAttackProtect	2
TcpMaxPortsExhausted	1

Table continued on following page

Value Name	Value (REG_DWORD)
The values below are located beneath the registry key HKLM\SYSTEM\CurrentControlSet\Services	
TcpMaxHalfOpen	500
TcpMaxHalfOpenRetried	400
TcpMaxConnectResponseRetransmissions	2
TcpMaxDataRetransmissions	2
EnablePMTUDiscovery	0
KeepAliveTime	300000 (5 minutes)
NoNameReleaseOnDemand	1
The values below are located beneath the registry key HKLM\System\CurrentControlSet\Services\AFD\Parameters	
EnableICMPRedirect	0
EnableDynamicBacklog	1
MinimumDynamicBacklog	20
MaximumDynamicBacklog	20000
DynamicBacklogGrowthDelta	10
The values below are located beneath the registry key HKLM\System\CurrentControlSet\Services\Tcpip\Parameter	
DisableIPSourceRouting	1
EnableFragmentChecking	1
EnableMulticastForwarding	0
IPEnableRouter	0
EnableDeadGWDetect	0
EnableAddrMaskReply	0

The values listed in Table 2-2 are not the default values, and if the various registry keys do not exist, they will need to be created. You can get more detailed information about each setting at http://support .microsoft.com/default.aspx?scid=kb;en-us;324270.

> *Not all of the recommended settings in Table 2-2 are implemented in XP Pro SP2 and Windows Server 2003 SP1, but the new TCP/IP stacks are sufficiently hardened so that in most cases, no modification is needed on these versions of Windows or later.*

Malware, as discussed in Table 1-1 in Chapter 1, can also hide as LSP software by manipulating Windows' normal Winsock functionality. By injecting itself as LSP software, the malware effectively becomes part of the TCP/IP stack. When network traffic is intercepted by the network card on the way in or is sent by the operating system or applications on the way out, it is passed along the LSP software programs. Each LSP program can inspect and manipulate the reviewed data streams. I've seen this trick used more by spyware than by viruses and trojans, but it can completely disconnect a system from a network. This risk is often greatest when such malware is imperfectly removed!

Once while I was manually removing a particularly difficult NewDotNet adware program (http://securityresponse.symantec.com/avcenter/venc/data/adware.ndotnet.html), the system I had cleaned could no longer connect to the network. After researching the program some more, I realized that it had injected itself as an LSP program and caused network problems when I removed it. I downloaded a program called LSPFix (www.cexx.org/lspfix.htm). It revealed the hiding adware and enabled me to remove it. Figure 2-6 shows a snapshot of a normal XP Pro SP2 system without malware installed.

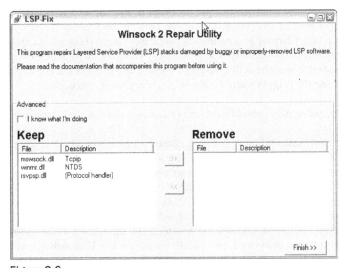

Figure 2-6

Several trojan and spyware programs, such as Riler (http://securityresponse.symantec.com/avcenter/venc/data/trojan.riler.html) and Daqa (http://secunia.com/virus_information/10835/win32.daqa.a), also use the LSP as a hiding place.

The LSP networking API has been strengthened in XP Pro SP2 and Windows Server 2003 SP1 to make it more resilient when nonstandard LSP programs are removed.

Unconventional Defenses

Here are some unconventional recommendations not covered in detail elsewhere in this book.

Rename Admin and Highly Privileged Accounts

Dedicated hackers and malicious software attempts to compromise the Administrator user account. You can make it harder to accomplish that by renaming the Administrator and other highly privileged accounts to names that don't suggest their function. Use a naming convention that is easy to remember and well known to your IT staff, but wouldn't be as obvious to a hacker. For example, if your user account names are first initial, last name, rename your Administrator account to BLovell. Rename the Guest account to RLovell. Rename other administrator accounts to SLovell, KLovell, and MLovell. One of my clients names his administrators after members of the rock group Kiss. Anything you and your staff can remember easily works. Be sure to change the name and description fields from their original defaults. The *Built-in account for administering the computer/domain* should not be left. Renaming the local Administrator and Guest accounts can be accomplished using group policy.

Now, create replacement bogus accounts. Create a new user account called Administrator (this must be done after the original is renamed). Give it the original Administrator's description. Create a long and complex password; it will never be used so there is no need to write it down or remember it. Then, using NTFS permissions or group policy, highly restrict this account. Make sure that it has Full Control-Deny permissions to all computer resources. Using group policy (Chapter 14), remove any normal special privileges and highly restrict any remaining rights. This can be accomplished more easily using a specially created group (see Chapter 3). The idea is that if by chance the hacker cracks the bogus account, then the access they receive is severely restricted. They would love to get Guest access rather than what this bogus Administrator account will give them. Repeat the process for your other highly privileged accounts, and rename the originals and create bogus placeholder accounts.

> *All highly privileged accounts should have long (15 characters or longer), complex passwords.*

Then enable Logon and Account Logon auditing. Nobody legitimate in your environment should be trying to use the bogus Administrator account. It's fake. If you see logon messages associated with the Administrator account, you know that a malicious hacker or program is trying to hack your computer systems. Starting with Windows XP Pro SP2 and Windows Server 2003 SP1, Microsoft added a Per-User auditing feature (www.windowsitpro.com/Article/ArticleID/46625/46625.html). Using it you can enable logon auditing for just the bogus accounts if you are worried about the noise generated from enabling the normal logon auditing feature. And Per-User auditing doesn't show up in the normal auditing configuration areas. If the hacker uses a tool to query your current audit policy, the Per-User settings will not show up.

Protect Other Highly Privileged Accounts

You need to take similar protections on any of your highly privileged accounts. Other highly privileged accounts include:

- ❑ Local or domain Administrators
- ❑ Directory Services Restore Mode account (i.e., local Administrator on a domain controller)
- ❑ Any account that is a member of the Administrators group
- ❑ Any account that is a member of the Domain Admins group
- ❑ Any account that is a member of the Enterprise Admins or Schema Admins groups
- ❑ Any account that is a member of the Power Users group
- ❑ Any account designated as a Data Recovery Agent (DRA) or Key Recovery Agent (KRA)
- ❑ Any account that is a member of the Account Operators or Server Operators groups
- ❑ Any account that is a member of the Group Policy Creator Owners group

- ❑ Accounts with delegated permissions
- ❑ Accounts with elevated Full Control permissions beyond the normal end user

Because these accounts are often normal user accounts, they usually don't have to be renamed. However, if any of them are named after their official role (e.g., DRA_Admin or ExchangeAdmin), you should rename them to something less notable. Consider instituting Logon and Account Logon auditing for any of these accounts.

SID EnumerationMany security experts argue that hackers can simply do SID enumeration to discover the true Administrator accounts. Every security resource in Windows is given a Security Identifier (SID) number. Built-in entities, such as the Administrator, the Guest, and the Everyone group, are given *well-known SIDs*, meaning they are the same across all Windows desktops. For instance, the Administrator always has a SID of 500. The Guest account's SID is 501. The Everyone group is a 1. The Domain Admins group is 512. Normal users and computers start at number 1000 and up, so the theory is that any hackers worth their salt will not trust the Administrator account name and will always enumerate the SID and discover the real accounts. The save to this potentially dangerous problem is that most hackers don't do SID enumeration, and certainly no automated malware ever has. Since 99% of your threats are automated, it means 99% of the "hackers" will not do SID enumeration. Even most malicious hackers don't do SID enumeration. They could, but they usually don't. They look for the Administrator account and if they find it, they don't look anymore.

SIDs will be covered in more detail in Chapter 3.

Added to this proclamation is the fact that anonymous SID enumeration (which is what most hackers would try initially anyway) doesn't work on XP Pro and above computers, unless they are domain controllers. By default, domain controllers must allow anonymous SID enumeration. It is the way they work. But Windows XP Pro, Windows Server 2003 stand-alone, workgroup, and domain member computers don't allow anonymous SID enumeration. In each case, the hacker would have to previously compromise the network with another legitimate account in order to do SID enumeration. Even then, most dedicated hackers find it easier to add their existing exploited account to the Administrators group than to directly attack the Administrator account. All in all, renaming the Administrator and other highly privileged accounts is a significant way to secure your Windows computers.

If you are interested in more details about designing and protecting Administrator accounts, be sure to download and read Microsoft's The Administrator Accounts Security Planning Guide (www.microsoft .com/technet/security/topics/serversecurity/administratoraccounts/default.mspx).

Run Services on Non-Default Ports!

When I found out that some of the world's largest banks got hit by the Slammer SQL worm, I was aghast. Not only did that mean that a financial institution's database servers were unpatched, and that they were placing mission-critical infrastructure on the untrusted Internet, they were also using default ports that take literally a registry entry to change. Lesson learned, whenever possible, install server software to non-default ports. For instance, I never run RDP or Terminal Services on TCP port 3389. I run PC Anywhere on any port but port 5132. I run my HTTPS servers on something other than 443. My FTP servers don't run on port 21 and I certainly don't run my SQL servers on ports 1433 or 1434.

If the service doesn't need to be on a default port, throw it somewhere else, preferably randomly high where port scanners won't readily find it or know what to do with it. For example, although RDP hasn't been exposed to a publicly announced exploit (since 2002), I run it where it can't be easily found. If an exploit does come out, it will usually be thrown in a worm and hit every possible victim in a few hours or days. I won't be found so easily.

I frequently change even public web servers to non-default ports. For example, I have a lot of health-care clients who exchange financial and patient data over the Internet using HTTPS. Besides using encrypted communications, I move the web server's default port to something random and high. Then all partici-pating parties are told to connect to the non-default port. It's as simple as sending the link in e-mail (ex: `https://www.example.com:38093`). We tell them to save it as a shortcut on their desktop. Legitimate users have no problem gaining access, and web worms are frustrated.

Install High-Risk Software (i.e., IIS) to Non-Default Folders

Along the same lines, whenever possible, install the OS and any software to non-default folders. Install Windows to C:\Windows or applications to C:\Program Files. Most Internet attacks are automated with predefined paths to access when the exploit is successful. Yes, there are ways for hackers and malware to check for the correct paths, but most don't. If you use IIS, change the default path to something other than C:\Inetpub. If you use IM software, install the software to a non-default folder and rename the default configuration file if you can. IM worms almost always only work if the default pathways are present.

Windows Vista

One of the biggest changes in the upcoming Windows client, Windows Vista, will be an extension of the Limited User Account (also called the Limited-Privileged User Account). Here are some of the features being discussed (remember that no feature is final until the product is released):

To begin with the quasi-admin group, the Power Users group is finally going away. Microsoft has been trying to kill this group and its members since Windows 2000.

Even if a user is logged in with administrative privileges, most programs will run in a non-admin context. For example, if the Administrator opens Internet Explorer, it will not be running in the Administrator's context. In order to do something administra-tive, Windows Vista will prompt the user for the admin credentials (again). This is a most welcome addition to the Windows OS, and it should stop a fair amount of tradi-tional malware from automatically installing.

Vista-compatible applications will contain a "manifest" file detailing who will need what permissions in order for the application to be installed and in order for it to run.

Another big feature is the ability of a LUA to install a program to a folder location named My Programs instead of to the shared Program Files or System32 directories.

Applications trying to write to protected areas of the file system and registry will be given "virtual" copies that they can manipulate, but that will not control the entire system.

An excellent blog discussion from a Microsoft employee can be found at `http://blogs.msdn.com/embedded/archive/2005/04/07/406412.aspx`.

Summary

This chapter contains over a dozen useful hints for minimizing the risk of malicious attack. It began by covering the computer security principles, which guide the specific recommendations. Guiding principles can be used to help the security administrator make the correct decision when specific guidance is not documented. Conventional defenses, such as not allowing the user to be logged in as an administrator, keeping patches up to date, using antivirus software, using anti-spam software, using anti-spyware software, hardening the TCP/IP stack, and providing physical security have always been necessary to any computer defense plan. Preventing boot up on anything other than the primary boot drive and password-protecting the BIOS configuration are not unique suggestions, but they bear repeating as they are not widely utilized.

Unconventional recommendations such as renaming highly privileged accounts, making bogus accounts, and installing services on non-default ports are great security-by-obscurity techniques. Often disdained by many security experts, these tips can significantly reduce the chance of a successful attack. Chapter 3 covers Windows NTFS permissions in more practical detail than you've ever read.

3

NTFS Permissions 101

I frequently ask students and clients to rank their NTFS permissions knowledge on a scale from 1 to 10, with 10 meaning they are an expert. Most administrators rank themselves as a 7 or 8. The truth is most are a 2 or a 3. I don't blame administrators for the lack of understanding of how NTFS permissions really work. Most are overworked and underpaid, and their teachers didn't teach it right in the first place. In the life of a busy administrator, the last thing they usually have is free time to explore the intricacies of Windows permissions. Yet, understanding how to correctly set NTFS permissions is among the top ways to prevent malicious exploits. This chapter discusses how Windows security really works, lists all the well-known SIDs, reveals all the built-in users and groups, discusses share and NTFS permissions in detail, summarizes the current permission settings in Windows, and finishes with recommendations. Chapters 5, "Protecting High-Risk Files," and 6, "Protecting High-Risk Registry Entries," build on the knowledge learned in this chapter. This is a big chapter, but it is worth its weight in gold. I wish it was the chapter I read when I was first learning about NTFS permissions and Windows security.

Common Misconceptions

Before we get started, here are some common misconceptions that will be corrected in this chapter:

- ❏ The Everyone group has Full Control to most Windows resources by default.
- ❏ Deny permissions always override Allow permissions.
- ❏ Effective permissions are determined by the intersection of NTFS and Share permissions.
- ❏ When both NTFS and Share permissions are involved, the effective permission granted is always the least permissive permission.
- ❏ Read permission only allows a user to view a resource.
- ❏ Read & Execute permission is necessary to execute a program.
- ❏ The Deny-Delete permission prevents deletion.

If any of these surprise you (and most people should see at least one surprise), when you are finished with this chapter, review this list again to see if your understanding has changed since the first time you read it.

How Windows Security Works

To understand how NTFS permissions control access to resources, you must understand the symphonic relationship of the various mechanisms involved with Windows security. When a security principal (i.e., user, group, computer, or service account) attempts to access a protected Windows resource (be it a file, folder, share, printer, or some other resource), it must prove to Windows that it has the necessary permissions to access the resource.

Access Control Phases

The process of a security principal (often called a *subject* in theory discussions) attempting to access a protected object is called *access control*. Regardless of the operating system, access control has four distinct phases:

❑ Identification

❑ Authentication

❑ Authorization

❑ Accounting/Auditing

Identification

Identification is the method a security principal uses to identify itself to an operating system. In Windows, this is done by the security principal submitting a unique name or value (in the case of smart cards or other security tokens). The submitted identity must be unique in the authentication database. In Windows, local security principal accounts are stored in a local database file called the Security Accounts Manager (SAM). Domain accounts are stored either in a SAM database on an NT domain controller or in the Active Directory database file (Ntds.dit) stored on Windows 2000 and later domain controllers. Each security principal in a Windows namespace must have a unique identity-unique friendly name, a unique GUID number, and a SID number (more on these numbers below). The key is that the security principal must be able to hand the authentication database a label or number that uniquely identifies it.

Creating identity labels takes more sophistication than just randomly making names. First, identity names should use a common naming convention. For users, it is often something like the user's first name initial followed by their last name. Many organizations use identity labels to represent the security principal's role or location (e.g., DallasAdmin, SouthVALegalPrintManager, etc.) As Chapter 2 shared, for security reasons, highly privileged identity names should not specifically identify the role the security principal fulfills in an enterprise. Lastly, identity labels should be documented and a centralized, secure process used for their issuance and removal.

Authentication

Once the security identity is handed over, the authentication database needs to prove that the submitting entity really "owns" the identity. To do that, the security principal must submit information that only the authentication database and it knows. Most often, this information is a password, but it could be a smart card, a security token, or biometric credentials. If the security principal successfully submits the expected confidential information proving ownership of its identity, the security principal is authenticated. We will cover the authentication process in detail in Chapter 4.

Authorization and Accounting

It's important to note that once the security principal's identity has been authenticated, the other access control mechanisms often can reliably take the identity's credentials without having to re-verify them. In practice, some authentication mechanisms do rely on the initial authentication and don't ever re-verify identity, and other access control schemes re-verify each access request. Thereafter, whenever the security principal wants to access an object, it submits its previously verified identity to the access control mechanism, along with its security credentials. The security credentials contain the permissions the security principal is given by the operating system. In Windows, the owner of the resource being accessed has previously assigned permissions to the appropriate security principals. In theory discussions of access control, this is known as the *discretionary access control* (or *DAC*) method.

The access control mechanism, called the *security reference monitor*, determines whether or not the security principal obtains access, and what type of access, to the requested object. If the security principal's request is successful, the request is authorized. Lastly, the request and its subsequent success or failure can be logged in a process called *accounting* or *auditing*. All Windows security principals must submit themselves to the process of access control, as shown in Figure 3-1.

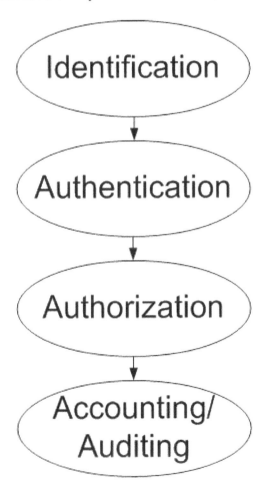

Identification:
This is who I am!

Authentication:
Prove it!

Authorization:
Can I access that object?

Accountability:
Here's who did what

Figure 3-1

The phases of access control listed previously are not unique to Windows. Most popular computer operating systems use a similar set of mechanisms. Now we can discuss each of the phases in more detail as it pertains to Windows.

GUIDs and SIDs

Although we humans track security principal accounts using their *common* or *friendly* name (e.g., Linda Smith), Windows tracks security principals using their permanently assigned *Globally Unique Identifier (GUID)* or *Security Identifier (SID)* numbers. Because of this, even when the security principal's name changes, the principal is still correctly tracked in Windows. If you rename a Windows security principal account, the new name will appear in most of the necessary dialog boxes and windows automatically.

GUIDs

Each Windows security principal and object has a unique 128-bit GUID number. GUIDs are assigned by the operating system to nearly every Windows object possible, including users, computers, groups, objects, programs, data elements, and programming components. Many programs referenced in the registry are identified by their GUID. Per Microsoft, the GUID should be unique to every Windows object in the universe. It is calculated using a formula involving the time, the date, network information, and a random routine that uses cycle frequencies from the computer's clock chip. An example GUID looks something like this:

```
e99e82d5-deed-11d2-b15c-00c04f5ce503
```

Once you are aware of GUIDs, if you weren't before, you will notice them everywhere. They are all over the registry, identify specific programs, identify ActiveX controls, and can be used as data in databases. However, trying to find a user object's GUID can be difficult. Oftentimes, the GUID will be revealed when using a troubleshooting tool, but in order to specifically list a particular object's GUID takes special utilities or coding. You can use the `Ldp.exe` program or `Adsiedit.msc` console located at `\Support\Tools\Support.cab` on the Windows XP or Windows Server 2003 installation CD-ROM discs to query GUIDs stored in Active Directory.

GUIDs exist in many operating systems, not just Windows.

Figure 3-2 shows a user account's GUID (and SID) using the Adsiedit console tool. Unfortunately, GUIDs are stored in hexadecimal string form in Active Directory and must be converted to a string-formatted GUID to be read correctly. The Microsoft Knowledge Base article located at `http://support.microsoft.com/default.aspx?scid=kb;en-us;325648` contains a VBS conversion script. Sometimes being able to convert a GUID to an object's name is helpful. For example, when searching in the registry for malware, you may come across an unfamiliar GUID. You can use Microsoft's Guid2obj tool (`www.microsoft.com/windows2000/techinfo/reskit/tools/existing/guid2obj-o.asp`) to do the conversion. Unfortunately, the Guid2obj tool works only on objects registered in Active Directory, not on objects registered locally.

For instance, on a user's workstation I found the following GUID being executed as an Explorer Shell (see Table 1-1 for more details):

```
{9EF34FF2-3396-4527-9D27-04C8C1C67806}
```

The Guid2obj tool could not convert the GUID to its common name. This meant the object wasn't registered in Active Directory. Then I used the Find feature in the Registry Editor tool (`Regedit.exe`) to search on the value. In a few seconds it found the value and its associated common name of Microsoft Antispyware in two registry locations, including registry key location `HK_LM\Software\Microsoft\Windows\CurrentVersion\Explorer\ShellExHooks`. This is an expected behavior of the software as it tries to intercept malware.

Program GUIDs are also known as Class IDs or CLSIDs. CLSIDs are frequently found in the registry and in HTML coding (e.g., CLSIDs identity the ActiveX control being executed).

Overall, finding and locating GUIDs can be hard work. Fortunately, an object's SID is usually more important to security administrators and easier to get than the GUID. GUIDs were discussed here so you would know that most objects have both a GUID and a SID and that they are different, and because GUIDs can be important when tracking down objects in the registry.

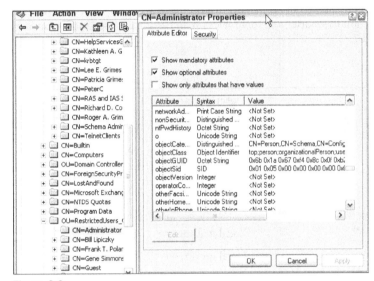

Figure 3-2

SIDs

All security principals have one or more SIDs but not all objects. For example, printer objects don't have SIDs. In Windows, only security principals (i.e., users, groups, computers, and service accounts) have SIDs, and they are assigned when the object is first created. SIDs are variable-length numbers with one or more dashes separating different numeric values. SIDs are guaranteed to be unique only in the domain, unlike GUIDs, which are guaranteed to be unique in the universe. It is the SID that most administrators and security processes are most interested in.

If you delete and re-create a security principal, even if it has the same name, it will have a different SID.

An example SID is

```
S-1-5-21-3333797343-2748683396-701768906-1111
```

All SIDs begin with S-1- and then are followed by a sequence of numbers separated by dashes. The next number following the 1- is called the *SID Top-Level Authority* value. It is usually a number between 0 and 5.

For local account SIDs, the number will be 2. For domain security principals, it will be a 5 (in Windows 2000 and later domains and workgroups). After this value, the SID will be composed of one or more 32-bit fields separated by dashes. The middle values usually indicate the domain in which the security principal is located. The domain portion will be identical for all objects in the same domain. The last value is called the *Relative Identifier (RID)*. The RID is generated at the time the object is created. Built-in security principals (e.g., Administrator, Everyone, Guests, etc.) have *well-known* RIDs that are identical for every similar security principal in every domain. Non-default security principals have RIDs starting with 1003, and the RID value is incremented for every security principal created. Most manually created security principals have RIDs beginning at 1100 and on up. A SID's format looks something like this:

```
S-1-X-X-X-X-RID
```

Because of the well-known SIDs and RIDs, it is possible to identify many security principals, no matter what they are named, based upon the SID or RID. Table 3-1 lists the well-known SIDs and RIDs. The values most important to security administrators are in bold. Each user and group is explained in more detail in Table 3-2.

Table 3-1

SID	Description
S-1-0	Null Authority
S-1-0-0	Nobody or Anonymous Null Session ID. Assigned when a security principal or its SID can't be identified or is non-existent.
S-1-1	World Authority
S-1-1-0	**Everyone** group
S-1-2	Local Authority
S-1-2-0	Local group
S-1-3	Creator Authority
S-1-3-0	**Creator Owner** group
S-1-3-1	Creator group.
S-1-3-2	Creator Owner Server, not used in Windows 2000 and later
S-1-3-3	Creator Group Server, not used in Windows 2000 and later
S-1-4	Non-unique Authority
S-1-5	NT Authority
S-1-5-1	Dialup group
S-1-5-2	Network group
S-1-5-3	Batch group
S-1-5-4	**Interactive** group
S-1-5-5-X-X	Logon session; X-X is a random unique number assigned to a particular logon session.

SID	Description
S-1-5-6	Service group
S-1-5-7	**Anonymous Logon** or **null session**
S-1-5-8	Proxy SID; not used in Windows 2000 and later
S-1-5-9	Enterprise Domain Controllers group
S-1-5-10	Self
S-1-5-11	**Authenticated Users** group
S-1-5-12	Restricted Code group
S-1-5-13	Terminal Server Users group
S-1-5-14	**Remote Interactive Logon group**
S-1-5-15	This Organization group
S-1-5-18	**LocalSystem** (or **System**) account
S-1-5-19	**LocalService**
S-1-5-20	**NetworkService**
S-1-5-21	Non-unique; SIDs are not unique
S-1-5-32	Built-in Domain
S-1-5-1000	Other Organization group
S-1-5-64-10	NTLM Authentication protocol
S-1-5-64-14	SChannel Authentication protocol
S-1-5-64-21	Digest Authentication protocol
S-1-5-x-x-x-500	**Local** or **Domain Administrator**
S-1-5-x-x-x-501	**Local** or **Domain Guest**
S-1-5-x-x-x-502	Krbtgt
S-1-5-x-x-x-512	**Domain Admins**
S-1-5-x-x-x-513	Domain Users group
S-1-5-x-x-x-514	Domain Guests group
S-1-5-x-x-x-515	Domain Computers group
S-1-5-x-x-x-516	**Domain Controllers group**
S-1-5-x-x-x-517	Cert Publishers group
S-1-5-x-x-x-518	**Schema Admins group**
S-1-5-x-x-x-519	**Enterprise Admins group**
S-1-5-x-x-x-520	**Group Policy Creator Owners group**

Table continued on following page

SID	Description
S-1-5-x-x-x-553	RAS and IAS Servers group
S-1-5-x-x-x-544	**Administrators group**
S-1-5-x-x-x-545	Users group
S-1-5-x-x-x-546	Guests group
S-1-5-x-x-x-547	**Power Users group**
S-1-5-x-x-x-548	**Account Operators group**
S-1-5-x-x-x-549	**Server Operators group**
S-1-5-x-x-x-550	Print Operators group
S-1-5-x-x-x-551	**Backup Operators group**
S-1-5-x-x-x-552	Replicator group
S-1-5-x-x-x-553	RAS Servers group
S-1-5-x-x-x-554	**Pre-Windows 2000 Compatibility Access group**
S-1-5-x-x-x-555	**Remote Desktop Users group**
S-1-5-x-x-x-556	Network Configuration Operators group
S-1-5-x-x-x-557	Incoming forest trust builders group
S-1-5-x-x-x-558	Performance monitor users group
S-1-5-x-x-x-559	Performance log users group
S-1-5-x-x-x-560	Windows Authorization Access group
S-1-5-x-x-x-561	Terminal Server License Servers group
S-1-5-x-x-x-562	Distributed COM Users group
S-1-6	Site Server Authority
S-1-7	Internet Site Authority
S-1-8	Exchange Authority
S-1-9	Resource Manager Authority

Where shown in Table 3-1, x-x-x represents the domain or workgroup SID.

Well-known SIDs were gathered from the author's own research and several published resources, including Microsoft documentation located at: `www.microsoft.com/resources/documentation/Windows/XP/all/reskit/en-us/Default.asp?url=/resources/documentation/Windows/XP/all/reskit/en-us/prnc_sid_cids.asp`, `http://msdn.microsoft.com/library/default.asp?url=/library/en-us/secauthz/security/well_known_sids.asp`, `http://support.microsoft.com/default.aspx?scid=kb;EN-US;Q243330`, and Jan De Clercq's Windows Server 2003 Security Infrastructures (Elsevier Digital Press, 2004).

Table 3-1 can be helpful when Windows displays the SID instead of the common name. For instance, I often see SID S-1-5-32-547 displayed when looking at NTFS permissions in the default security templates (covered in Chapter 14) on Windows Server 2003. Table 3-1 tells me this is the Power Users group, and the problem Windows Explorer is having is that Windows Server 2003 removes the Power Users group during a domain controller promotion.

The Power Users group is present in Windows Server 2003 non-domain controllers and in previous versions of Windows for backward compatibility, but it contains no members. Microsoft plans to remove the Power Users group in Windows Vista.

SID Viewing Tools

You can use several software utilities to view security principal SIDs, including the following:

- ❑ Whoami.exe
- ❑ Sid2user.exe and User2sid.exe
- ❑ Psgetsid.exe

There are a lot of Whoami program versions in the world, but the version that displays Windows SIDs is included in Windows XP Pro and Windows Server 2003 (the W2K3 version, which is more functional, can be copied and run on Windows XP Pro as well). If you type **Whoami** by itself, it returns only the currently logged in user's name preceded by their domain or workgroup name:

```
Example\ScottLovell
```

If you type **Whoami /user,** you'll get the current user's SID, looking something like this:

```
Q:\WINDOWS\system32>whoami /user

USER INFORMATION
----------------
User Name       SID
============= ===========================================
example\scottlovell S-1-5-21-3334797343-2748683396-701868904-1111
```

If you type **Whoami /user /groups,** you'll get a listing of the user and all the groups, and the related SIDs, to which the user belongs. For example:

```
USER INFORMATION
----------------
User Name       SID
============= ===========================================
example\mattlovell S-1-5-21-3334797343-2748683396-701868904-1114

GROUP INFORMATION
----------------
Group Name                      Type            SID             Attributes
================== ========================================================
Everyone                        Well-known group S-1-1-0
                   Mandatory group, Enabled by default, Enabled group
BUILTIN\Administrators          Alias           S-1-5-32-544
                   Mandatory group, Enabled by default, Enabled group, Group owner
BUILTIN\Users                   Alias           S-1-5-32-545
```

```
                         Mandatory group, Enabled by default, Enabled group
       NT AUTHORITY\INTERACTIVE            Well-known group S-1-5-4
                         Mandatory group, Enabled by default, Enabled group
       NT AUTHORITY\Authenticated Users    Well-known group S-1-5-11
                         Mandatory group, Enabled by default, Enabled group
       LOCAL                               Well-known group S-1-2-0
                         Mandatory group, Enabled by default, Enabled group
       EXAMPLE\Data              Group              S-1-5-21-3334797343-274868
       3396-701868904-1131 Mandatory group, Enabled by default, Enabled group
       EXAMPLE\Group Policy Creator Owners Group    S-1-5-21-3334797343-274868
       3396-701868904-520  Mandatory group, Enabled by default, Enabled group
       EXAMPLE\Domain Admins           Group        S-1-5-21-3334797343-274868
       3396-701868904-512  Mandatory group, Enabled by default, Enabled group
       EXAMPLE\Enterprise Admins       Group        S-1-5-21-3334797343-274868
       3396-701868904-519  Mandatory group, Enabled by default, Enabled group
```

The preceding examples are shown using the W2K3 version of Whoami. The XP version of Whoami uses the /all parameter to display the user's personal and group SIDs.

This is an excellent example of a user's SIDs. Pay special attention to the next few paragraphs because what they contain is essential to learning about Windows security. When a user logs on to a Windows computer, after the authentication is successful, the local machine or domain controller (if in a domain) queries for and gathers all the SIDs for the groups to which the user belongs. If the user is in a domain environment utilizing universal groups (i.e., groups available throughout the forest) the domain's *global catalog* is queried to return those groups as well. The domain controller queries itself for domain local and global groups (covered below).

The SIDs are collected together and become part of the security principal's *security token*. When the user wants to access an object, the Windows security reference monitor (SRM) asks for the user's security token, which is akin to asking the user what groups they belong to. In this example, the user belongs to the following groups: Everyone, Administrators, Users, Interactive, Authenticated Users, Local, Data, Group Policy Creator Owners, Domain Admins, and Enterprise Admins. This user has a lot of access. The user isn't the original Administrator account because his RID is 1114 and not 500. However, because he belongs to Administrators, Domain Admins, and Enterprise Admins groups, this user has almost as much access.

The original Administrator account is afforded a few other niceties that newly made administrators don't have. For example, on domain controllers, Windows will periodically (within a few hours) re-add the original Administrator back to any objects or resources to which their permissions were removed. Also, the original Administrator account cannot normally be locked out by Account lockouts (although you will learn how in Chapter 4).

This user will have every permission and privilege that is assigned to his listed groups, along with whatever is assigned to his individual user account. Note that the user belongs to many more groups than average administrators think they belong to. Besides the obvious groups manually assigned by an administrator, the user belongs to many built-in and action-oriented groups (covered below). It is the accumulation of permissions from all groups, assigned, built-in, and action-oriented, that gives the user his or her NTFS permissions. Often, when an administrator can't figure out why a particular user has different effective permissions than the administrator intended, look into each group the user belongs to, not just the obvious ones.

Viewing the current logged on user's SID is easy enough with Whoami, but it takes different tools to research a SID of a user who isn't the currently logged on user. Probably the most well-known SID query tools are Sid2user (which converts a given SID to the user, group, or computer account common name and User2SID (which converts a given security principal's common name to its SID). Programmer Evgenii B. Rudnyi wrote both utilities as companions to each other and they work well. For reasons unknown to me, he allows only the source code to be downloaded. To download it in compiled form to run in Windows, you can search any Internet search engine for Sid2user or download it from www.wrox.com.

You need to be an authenticated user in Windows XP or later to successfully run the utilities, and you need to run the utilities locally or have a NetBIOS connection already established to the computer. Prior to XP, you only needed to have a drive mapped by a null session user (no name, no password). This is still true of Windows 2000 and Windows Server 2003 domain controllers, a point hackers love to exploit. Here's an example of User2sid and Sid2user:

```
Q:\>user2sid TonyaLovell
S-1-5-21-3334797343-2748683396-701868904-1117
Number of subauthorities is 5
Domain is EXAMPLE
Length of SID in memory is 28 bytes
Type of SID is SidTypeUser

Q:\>sid2user 5 21 3334797343 2748683396 701868904 500
Name is BillLovell
Domain is EXAMPLE
Type of SID is SidTypeUser
```

Note that Sid2user has a slightly different SID format than you would expect. You must leave out the S-1- prefix and put spaces instead of dashes between the numeric values. The Sid2user outcome reveals a RID of 500, which means this user is the original Administrator account. This tactic, called *SID enumeration,* is often mentioned by security administrators as the primary reason for not renaming their highly privileged accounts. If the hacker has the appropriate access (an authenticated user on Windows XP and later or anonymous on a domain controller or Windows 2000 and earlier), he can use a SID enumeration tool and quickly find the highly privileged accounts. True, it's that easy. However, most hackers don't use SID enumeration, it isn't easy to do across the Internet (the hacker needs to map a drive or have access to the RPC or NetBIOS ports, which most firewalls block), and no automated malware I've ever seen does it. One day a hacker may build an automated tool that is incorporated into a worm or trojan to do SID enumeration (heck, Rudnyi's source code is widely posted on the Internet) but none do now. You can significantly increase your computer defenses by renaming your highly privileged accounts to something less notable.

You can also use Sysinternal's Psgetsid (www.sysinternals.com/Utilities/PsGetSid.html) utility. It works locally or remotely on Windows NT 4 and later. Although you still need NetBIOS access to the remote computer to run the utility remotely, you don't have to manually establish a drive mapping. Psgetsid will install itself as a service, using administrative credentials you must provide. It will return the user or computer's SID. I'm sure Microsoft probably has a few SID viewing tools in one of their Windows Resource Kits as well.

SIDHistory

Every security principal also has a field called *SIDHistory.* The SIDHistory field was originally created to allow smoother Windows upgrades and domain migrations. When a security principal is imported into another domain, its SIDs must change. Remember that most individual SIDs, as shown in Table 3-1, contain the security principal's domain in the SID. After a successful migration, the object's original SIDs can be moved to the SIDHistory field. During many security operations, the SIDHistory field can be checked, and the SIDHistory's SIDs used in security operations just as if the old SID were a current SID.

Hackers learned that they could programmatically add any SID they wanted to the SIDHistory field. There was never any authentication done or any validity checking mechanism enabled. Thus, the hackers could add highly privileged SIDs from the domain they were joining or becoming a part of through a Windows trust, and their new object would suddenly be elevated to the same status as the forged highly privileged account. Microsoft turned on *SID filtering*, in which the accepting domain filters out any SIDs in the SIDHistory field that claim to be part of the domain they are joining, in Windows Server 2000 Service Pack 2 and Windows Server 2003. It makes sense. Why would an object joining a domain already be a part of it? Unfortunately, the SIDs in the SIDHistory field also make up a part of a security principal's access token (covered below). You should make sure SIDHistory filtering is enabled in your environment, which it is by default.

Delegation and Impersonation

Two other poorly understood issues that impact Windows security are *delegation* and *impersonation*. Impersonation is another process acting on behalf of the user. In Windows, the security principal never accesses a resource or object directly. Instead, the program or process that the security principal used (e.g., Windows Explorer) impersonates the security principal (using the security principal's security token) to access the object. When a program or process impersonates a security principal, it means the process or program is operating in the security context of the end user. This is the way Windows works.

It can also lead to some strange security interactions. Over the years, Microsoft has had to deal with more than a few bugs because the impersonation process did not function correctly. In both examples that I can think of, it led to the end user having System-level access. In the first example, Microsoft Office 2003 had a bug whereby when the user went to open a file and got the normal File Open dialog box, it would enable the user to explore mapped drives and areas to which end users would not normally have access. The second example is still a problem currently (as this chapter is being written), whereby even when an end user has been purposefully prevented from modifying Internet Explorer's security settings (normally end users can modify IE's security settings, but this can be prevented using NTFS permissions, group policy, or the Internet Explorer Administration Kit [IEAK]), the user can access IE's security settings through the security settings feature of Microsoft Media Player. In both instances, the processes were impersonating the System account (as processes often do), instead of switching to impersonating the user.

Impersonation can be turned off and on per security principal account by setting the *Impersonate client after authentication* privilege in group policy or local computer policy. By default, service accounts and most Windows programs have this privilege. This privilege was introduced in Windows 2000 Service Pack 4 because of malicious use of impersonation. Occasionally, impersonation will need to be given to a program (e.g., a patch management program pushing out patches) if the service account it is using was not already allowed to impersonate.

Impersonation Levels

Actually, Windows 2000 and later has several impersonation levels, including the following:

❏ Anonymous

❏ Identify

❏ Impersonate

❏ Delegate

The levels reflect the authentication used between a security principal, a service, and the resource the service is accessing on behalf of the user. The first three impersonation levels allow a process to impersonate a user account for access to a local object; the last option deals with access to remote objects. We've already talked about the normal impersonation scenario in which the process impersonates the security principal using it. Anonymous impersonation means the process impersonates the anonymous user (i.e., the null session) and not the end user. The Identify level allows the process to access other local objects using the security principal's access control permissions, but it is not actually impersonating the security principal. In Identify mode, the service or process can identify the security principal to the SRM for the purpose of accessing the object, but the service or process does not "become" the security principal. The net effect is that the Identify level is more restrictive than the Impersonate level, and many access requests will fail. For that reason, most services and processes use the Impersonate level. Unfortunately, impersonation only works on local resources, not remote ones.

You can view impersonation on your system in real time using Sysinternal's TokenMon utility (`www.sysinternals.com/Utilities/Tokenmon.html`). It will reveal the processes using impersonation and what security principal accounts are being used (see Figure 3-3). If you use TokenMon, it will generate hundreds of entries in a few seconds. In this example, you can see the Microsoft Antispyware program (`gcasDtServ.exe`) impersonating the `Banneret\Roger` user account. You can also see that much of the impersonation is a process impersonating the System account. Every process in Windows manipulates objects in the security context of a security principal, although it is often the System account behind the scenes.

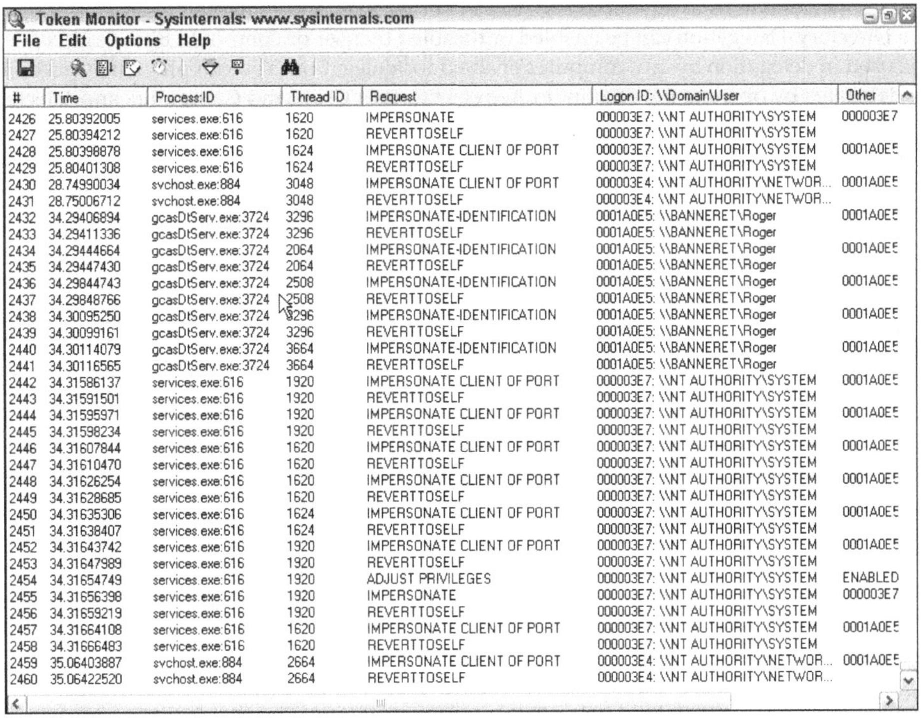

#	Time	Process:ID	Thread ID	Request	Logon ID: \\Domain\User	Other
2426	25.80392005	services.exe:616	1620	IMPERSONATE	000003E7: \\NT AUTHORITY\SYSTEM	000003E7
2427	25.80394212	services.exe:616	1620	REVERTTOSELF	000003E7: \\NT AUTHORITY\SYSTEM	
2428	25.80398878	services.exe:616	1624	IMPERSONATE CLIENT OF PORT	000003E7: \\NT AUTHORITY\SYSTEM	0001A0E5
2429	25.80401308	services.exe:616	1624	REVERTTOSELF	000003E7: \\NT AUTHORITY\SYSTEM	
2430	28.74990034	svchost.exe:884	3048	IMPERSONATE CLIENT OF PORT	000003E4: \\NT AUTHORITY\NETWOR...	0001A0E5
2431	28.75006712	svchost.exe:884	3048	REVERTTOSELF	000003E4: \\NT AUTHORITY\NETWOR...	
2432	34.29406894	gcasDtServ.exe:3724	3296	IMPERSONATE-IDENTIFICATION	0001A0E5: \\BANNERET\Roger	0001A0E5
2433	34.29411336	gcasDtServ.exe:3724	3296	REVERTTOSELF	0001A0E5: \\BANNERET\Roger	
2434	34.29444664	gcasDtServ.exe:3724	2064	IMPERSONATE-IDENTIFICATION	0001A0E5: \\BANNERET\Roger	0001A0E5
2435	34.29447430	gcasDtServ.exe:3724	2064	REVERTTOSELF	0001A0E5: \\BANNERET\Roger	
2436	34.29844743	gcasDtServ.exe:3724	2508	IMPERSONATE-IDENTIFICATION	0001A0E5: \\BANNERET\Roger	0001A0E5
2437	34.29848766	gcasDtServ.exe:3724	2508	REVERTTOSELF	0001A0E5: \\BANNERET\Roger	
2438	34.30095250	gcasDtServ.exe:3724	3296	IMPERSONATE-IDENTIFICATION	0001A0E5: \\BANNERET\Roger	0001A0E5
2439	34.30099161	gcasDtServ.exe:3724	3296	REVERTTOSELF	0001A0E5: \\BANNERET\Roger	
2440	34.30114079	gcasDtServ.exe:3724	3664	IMPERSONATE-IDENTIFICATION	0001A0E5: \\BANNERET\Roger	0001A0E5
2441	34.30116565	gcasDtServ.exe:3724	3664	REVERTTOSELF	0001A0E5: \\BANNERET\Roger	
2442	34.31586137	services.exe:616	1920	IMPERSONATE CLIENT OF PORT	000003E7: \\NT AUTHORITY\SYSTEM	0001A0E5
2443	34.31591501	services.exe:616	1920	REVERTTOSELF	000003E7: \\NT AUTHORITY\SYSTEM	
2444	34.31595971	services.exe:616	1920	IMPERSONATE CLIENT OF PORT	000003E7: \\NT AUTHORITY\SYSTEM	0001A0E5
2445	34.31598234	services.exe:616	1920	REVERTTOSELF	000003E7: \\NT AUTHORITY\SYSTEM	
2446	34.31607844	services.exe:616	1620	IMPERSONATE CLIENT OF PORT	000003E7: \\NT AUTHORITY\SYSTEM	0001A0E5
2447	34.31610470	services.exe:616	1620	REVERTTOSELF	000003E7: \\NT AUTHORITY\SYSTEM	
2448	34.31626254	services.exe:616	1620	IMPERSONATE CLIENT OF PORT	000003E7: \\NT AUTHORITY\SYSTEM	0001A0E5
2449	34.31628685	services.exe:616	1620	REVERTTOSELF	000003E7: \\NT AUTHORITY\SYSTEM	
2450	34.31635306	services.exe:616	1624	IMPERSONATE CLIENT OF PORT	000003E7: \\NT AUTHORITY\SYSTEM	0001A0E5
2451	34.31638407	services.exe:616	1624	REVERTTOSELF	000003E7: \\NT AUTHORITY\SYSTEM	
2452	34.31643742	services.exe:616	1920	IMPERSONATE CLIENT OF PORT	000003E7: \\NT AUTHORITY\SYSTEM	0001A0E5
2453	34.31647989	services.exe:616	1920	REVERTTOSELF	000003E7: \\NT AUTHORITY\SYSTEM	
2454	34.31654749	services.exe:616	1920	ADJUST PRIVILEGES	000003E7: \\NT AUTHORITY\SYSTEM	ENABLED
2455	34.31656398	services.exe:616	1920	IMPERSONATE	000003E7: \\NT AUTHORITY\SYSTEM	000003E7
2456	34.31659219	services.exe:616	1920	REVERTTOSELF	000003E7: \\NT AUTHORITY\SYSTEM	
2457	34.31664108	services.exe:616	1620	IMPERSONATE CLIENT OF PORT	000003E7: \\NT AUTHORITY\SYSTEM	0001A0E5
2458	34.31666483	services.exe:616	1620	REVERTTOSELF	000003E7: \\NT AUTHORITY\SYSTEM	
2459	35.06403887	svchost.exe:884	2664	IMPERSONATE CLIENT OF PORT	000003E4: \\NT AUTHORITY\NETWOR...	0001A0E5
2460	35.06422520	svchost.exe:884	2664	REVERTTOSELF	000003E4: \\NT AUTHORITY\NETWOR...	

Figure 3-3

A service trying to use impersonation to access a remote resource will end up sending the anonymous credentials (i.e., unauthenticated) for the logon attempt, which will cause many failures. *Delegation* is the process of a service impersonating the security principal to a remote server or resource. Delegation requires Active Directory and domain accounts, and only works on Windows 2000 and later computers located in the same forest. When delegation is enabled, a server or service can send the security principal's credentials to log on to the remote service. The remote service thinks the logon is coming directly from the security principal. Delegation is a good thing and is required in order for several services to work with remote clients (EFS, IIS's Integrated Windows Authentication, etc.).

For example, suppose you have a front-end web server connected to a back-end SQL database that requires the user to use his normal Windows user account to access the data. This is a very common scenario. Without delegation, the front-end web server would not be able to pass the user's logon credentials to the back-end database. In most of these cases, programmers were stuck with creating a single "master account" that was used to interface between the front-end web server and the back-end database (see Figure 3-4). This approach has several weaknesses, not the least of which is a single point of failure and a lack of individual accountability. With delegation, you can mark any Windows 2000 or later computer or service as *trusted for delegation*. When delegation is allowed, the in-the-middle front-end web server can impersonate the user and pass along their logon credentials to the back-end database (refer to Figure 3-4). Windows KB article#262291 (http://support.microsoft.com/kb/q262291) covers the various levels. Prior to Windows 2000, "identify" and impersonate were the only supported impersonation levels.

Any other impersonation level besides Delegate will prevent the impersonating service from sending your network credentials to any remote service or server, even those marked *trusted for delegation* in Active Directory. Delegation can be enabled or disabled by user or computer. By default, user accounts can be used in delegation by any computer enabled for delegation. You can prevent an account from being delegated by opening the account in Active Directory Users and Computers and selecting the Account tab (see Figure 3-5). There you can enable the *Account is sensitive and cannot be delegated* option.

Computers (usually servers) can be enabled or disabled for using delegation by opening the computer account in Active Directory Users and Computers and choosing the Delegation tab (see Figure 3-6). There you can disable the computer's capability to use delegation (i.e., the *Do not trust this computer for delegation* option), enable any service on the computer to use delegation (i.e., the *Trust this computer for delegation to any service (Kerberos only)* option) or specify which services and protocols can use delegation (i.e., the *Trust this computer for delegation to specified services only* option). The latter option, known as *constrained delegation,* is new in Windows Server 2003 and does not exist in Windows 2000 domains. It allows you to selectively choose which remote servers and services (as identified by their service account's *service principal name, or SPN)* can be sent delegated credentials. You can also use the three other authentication protocols (i.e., LM, NTLM, and NTLMv2) instead of Kerberos, if so desired. In Windows 2000, when a computer is trusted for delegation, it can impersonate a user to any other service on any other computer in the domain. Constrained delegation allows an administrator to significantly minimize a hacker's attack space on a server with delegation.

> *In order for an application to use an authentication protocol other than Kerberos in delegation, the application must specially be written to use the other protocols. Most applications, including Internet Explorer, only allow Kerberos delegation.*

Delegation is turned on by default for domain controllers but not member servers. Consider disabling delegation on highly privileged user and service accounts that do not require delegation. On Windows Server 2003 servers required to use delegation, enable constrained delegation.

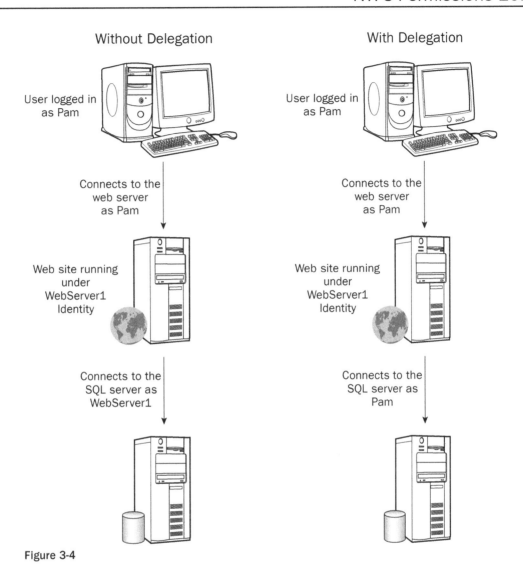

Figure 3-4

Figure 3-5

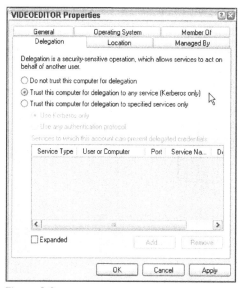

Figure 3-6

Groups

All Windows security principals are members of one or more groups. These groups can be built-in to Windows or manually added by administrators. Windows built-in groups can be added or modified by the operating system as the need arises. For example, promoting a member server to a domain controller causes all the local groups to be converted to domain groups, all the local user and group accounts to be deleted, and two new local user accounts to be created (Directory Services Restore mode Administrator and Guest). Installing new features and software to a computer often adds new groups. For example, adding Microsoft Exchange, DNS, DHCP, WINS, and Certificate Services adds new groups that are required for the software to function correctly.

> *If you haven't noticed already, Windows groups usually have a name that ends with an "s" in order to make it easier to immediately identify whether the security principal you are viewing is a user account or group. For instance, there is an Administrators group and an Administrator user account.*

Action-Based Groups

Some of the built-in Windows groups are very special in that membership changes based upon security principal actions and behaviors. For example, logging in to a computer using the local keyboard automatically makes the user a part of the Local group. Simply logging on and authenticating makes the user a member of the Everyone, Authenticated Users, Domain Users, This Organization, Interactive, and Users groups.

A security principal becomes a member of an action-based group simply because it or a process impersonating it did something. When the action is over, the security principal is moved out of the group. Other than stopping the action that places a security principal in a particular action-based group, there isn't any way to prevent a security principal from being in a particular group. It's in the group because of the action done. However, and this is important, you can still modify the permissions that an action-based group has to a particular resource. For example, an administrator can't stop a user account from being in the Everyone group. It was placed there simply by being created and logging on, but the permissions that the Everyone group gets to an object can be modified.

Here are the various action-based groups (see Table 3-3 for more detail on what each represents):

- ❏ Anonymous Logon
- ❏ Authenticated Users
- ❏ Batch
- ❏ Creator Owner
- ❏ Dialup
- ❏ Domain Computers
- ❏ Domain Controllers
- ❏ Domain Users
- ❏ Everyone
- ❏ Interactive
- ❏ Local
- ❏ Logon session X-X

❏ Network

❏ Other Organization

❏ Self

❏ This Organization

❏ Users

Administrators need to pay special attention to these action-oriented groups because they are often the cause for incorrect permissions being applied. Unless you are aware of all the action-based groups that might be appended to a security principal's security token, you might be stumped in a permissions problem.

Group Types and Scopes

There are two types of groups: security and distribution. *Security groups* are a traditional type of group most Windows administrators think about. You put security principal members inside of a group and apply security permissions to the group. All the members in the group inherit the permissions given to the group. *Distribution groups* are list groups. They can contain members but cannot have security permissions attached to them. The most common distribution group is the Global Address List (GAL) installed by Microsoft Exchange server. In Active Directory native-mode and higher, you can switch group types back and forth. However, if you switch a security group to a distribution group, it loses all its attached permissions permanently (unless re-applied by the administrator). There are no default distribution groups in Windows.

Groups have scopes that determine what types of members they can contain and what types of groups they can be members of. The Active Directory domain level has an impact on group scopes as well. A domain in mixed-mode can only have Local, Domain Local, and Global groups. A native-mode or higher domain mode level allows an additional security group called Universal.

> *In Active Directory mixed-mode, you can have a Universal distribution group.*

Local groups are managed using the Local Users and Groups console and are used to give permissions to local resources. Local group information is stored only on the local computer's SAM database, but each local group can contain members from the local computer, any domain, and any group within a reachable domain.

Domain Local groups are just like regular local groups, except they reside in domains and can be managed by the Active Directory Users and Computer console. Global groups exist in domains, and can contain any security principal in the current domain, or any group from any domain in the forest. For this reason, global groups are often thought of as domainwide groups. Universal groups were introduced with Active Directory in Windows 2000 and are considered a forestwide group. They can contain members from any domain in the forest and can contain any of the other types of groups. Universal groups and their memberships are stored on domain controllers hosting the *global catalog* function.

Groups can often be placed inside other groups, depending on the domain-mode, and this is called *group nesting*. In mixed mode, global groups can be members of other global groups, local groups, and domain local groups. In native mode and above, local, global, and universal groups can also be members of universal groups. The only group nesting not allowed in native and above mode is a universal group being a member of a local group (but a local group can be a member of a universal group). Table 3-2 summarizes this.

Table 3-2

Domain Mode/Feature Server 2003	Mixed Mode (default)	Windows 2000 Native and Windows
Security groups supported	Local, Domain Local, Global	Local, Domain Local, Global, Universal
Distribution groups supported	Local, Domain Local, Global, Universal	Local, Domain Local, Global, Universal
Group nesting allowed	Global into Global, Global into Local or Domain Local	All types of nesting allowed except a Global group cannot contain a Universal group

When a security principal logs on to their computer, the local computer, the domain controller, and the global catalog are all queried to provide a complete list of groups to which the user belongs in order to create the security token.

AGULP Method

With all these group scopes, you might wonder how to appropriately set NTFS permissions. Glad you asked. Since the introduction of Windows NT, Microsoft has been teaching and promoting a method called *AGLP*, or now with the introduction of Universal groups, *AGULP*. It is taught to every beginning Windows administrator. They learn it, test on it, and then forget it, which is sad, because it is the way security permissions should be set in Windows. Or let me be stronger: If you or your administrator is not setting security permissions this way, then you are doing it wrong. The AGULP method is the right way to set security permissions, the most efficient way to set permissions (is speeds up Active Directory replication and the SRM), and is probably the only way an organization can keep track of its permissions. The most secure organizations in the world use the AGULP method. Conversely, organizations not using it probably really don't understand what their permissions are, and hackers and penetration testers like organizations with a poor understanding of their security permissions.

The AGULP method says that whenever you are setting up security permissions to a resource (e.g., file, folder, share, printer, etc.), you should assign permissions like this:

1. Create a local (or domain local if you have a domain) group for that resource.

2. Assign the security permissions from the object to the local (or domain local) group.

3. Create a global group and add to it all the security principals desiring access to the resource as members.

4. Place the global group in the local (or domain local) group as a member.

Optionally, in a multi-domain environment, you can put the global groups into a universal group, and the universal group into the local (or domain local) group.

This is where the AGULP acronym comes from: security principal Accounts go into Global groups, which go into either Universal or (Domain) Local groups. The (Domain) Local group has all the Permissions to the local resource (see Figure 3-7).

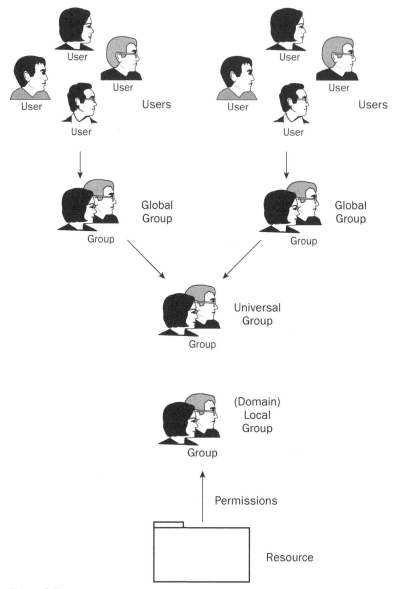

Figure 3-7

The efficiency of this design is that all the assigned permissions are always assigned to the (domain) local groups. When auditing a network, an administrator doesn't have to query every group type in the domain and figure out which group trumps the other group. Allowing security permissions to be set on each of the group scopes is a management nightmare. The mess is sure to lead to a security hole that a hacker can exploit. If the AGULP method is used, then an audit can query just the one set of groups and find out all the security permissions in a domain.

Some administrators will call the AGULP method crazy and cumbersome, worsened by the fact that you need a separate (domain) local, universal (if needed), and global group for each type of permission you need to give. For instance, if you want to give some users Full Control-Allow permissions and another set of users just Read and Write permissions, you'll need two sets of AGULP groups. In my experience, once administrators get used to the AGULP method, it takes an extra two minutes longer than most organizations' random permission assigning method. Some administrators say it takes too long to set up and is too confusing. I say, if you don't follow the AGULP method, you aren't setting up permission correctly and you are building in a security exploit disaster! Not using AGULP makes your security infrastructure too complex to manage, so you won't really be managing it. Is the AGULP method adding too much time to your security infrastructure or saving you time by letting you manage it effectively for the first time?

If you don't use the AGULP method now, stop all your other security projects, take a "stand down" week, and get your security house in order. Getting your NTFS permissions correctly defined and managed is one of the most significant security benefits you can make to any environment. While other organizations are spending money on advanced security products that often don't work, you can get more bang for the buck by refocusing on the basics.

Built-in Users and Groups

Like well-known SIDs and RIDs, Windows comes with dozens of built-in users and groups. Understanding what each does and what permissions and privileges each has is key to understanding Windows security. Table 3-3 lists all the built-in Windows users, and Table 3-4 lists all the built-in groups. Review all of them, but pay the most attention to (read the details about) the underlined users and groups.

Table 3-3

Account Name	Description
Administrator	Local or domain Administrator, depending on where found Local Administrator Has full access to all local resources and is a member of the local Administrators group, and cannot be removed Domain Administrator Domain administrator, usually has Full Control permissions to all domain resources. Can be renamed, but not deleted or disabled. Is a member of Administrators (cannot be removed), Domain Admins, Domain Users, and Group Policy Creator Owners groups by default. In the first domain in a new forest (i.e., the forest root domain), the Administrator is also a member of the Enterprise Admins and Schema Admins groups. This means the administrator of a forest root domain is significantly more powerful than other domain administrators in the same forest.

Table continued on following page

Account Name	Description
	In a domain, the Administrator account is created and its password set when you install Active Directory on the first domain controller.
	The first Administrator account in each domain is also a Data Recovery Agent (DRA) for EFS for that domain.
	Note: The local administrator account can be disabled in Windows XP and non-domain controller Windows Server 2003 servers.
	During a DCPromo, a server's local Administrator account is copied up to the domain and deleted in the local SAM.
Directory Services Restore Mode Administrator (named Administrator)	During a DCPromo, a server's local Administrator account is copied up to the domain and deleted in the local SAM. A new local Administrator account is created in the local SAM and is known as the Directory Services Restore Mode Administrator. It is named Administrator by default. Its password is set during the DCPromo. Account can only be used in Directory Services Restore mode.
	Account name and password is also used in Recovery Console operations
	This account is not replicated to other computers.
	Can change password using Netdom, Setpw.exe (in W2K, see KB article #239803), Ntdsutil (in W2K3), Dsrm, or Net Use.
Guest	Every computer has a local Guest account and every domain has a Guest account. Default account for guest logins. When used, will create a new local profile and remove the profile when the Guest user logs out.
	When used, does not need a password. Must be enabled for some legacy applications and functionality. If enabled, provides an avenue for malicious hackers to implement a privilege escalation attack.
	Disabled by default in Windows XP and later
	Local Guest account is a member of the Everyone and Guests groups, Domain Guest account is a member of Domain Guests and Domain User groups.
	Disabled by default. Can be renamed but not deleted.

Account Name	Description
HelpAssistant	Created when Remote Assistance is enabled and a remote assistance session is requested. Will be deleted if no remote assistance requests are pending. Has limited access to the desktop environment.
IUSR_<computername>	Not a default account, but added if Internet Information Server (IIS) is added. Used as the security principal account for all users connecting anonymously to an IIS web site. Member of the Domain Users and Guests groups by default, which can indirectly give more permissions than is necessary for the web site alone. In IIS, default anonymous account (IUSR_) can be changed to another security principal account.
IWAM_<computername>	Not a default account, but added if Internet Information Server (IIS) is added. This account is used for web sites running "out-of-process," which is used more often in previous versions of IIS. Member of the Domain Users and IIS_WPG groups.
Krbtgt	Kerberos-related account, appearing only on domain controllers. Disabled by default. Kerberos authentication is achieved by using tickets that are enciphered with a symmetric key that is derived from the password of the server or service to which access is requested. To request such a session ticket, a special ticket called *the Ticket Granting Ticket (TGT)* must be presented to the Kerberos service itself. The TGT is enciphered with a key derived from the password of the KRBTGT account, which is known only by the Kerberos service. Should not be deleted or modified.
Local Service	New security principal in XP, lesser-privilege account intended for use with service accounts. Account has same permissions given to the Users group. Accesses network services with anonymous credentials.
Network Service	New security principal in XP, lesser-privilege account intended for use with service accounts. Account has same permissions given to the Users group. Accesses network services with the same credentials given to its local machine account.
Support_<number>	Microsoft vendor support account. Disabled by default, it is part of the HelpServicesGroup group. It is intended as a default account for remote support through the Help and Support center.
System (also known as Local System)	Highest privilege account on the local computer — even more powerful than the administrator. Most of the operating system and kernel-mode applications run with the privileges of this security principal. Any Windows service running within the System context probably needs to stay that way, but each non-Windows service should be strictly evaluated before assigning it the Local System account. If a hacker gains control or buffer overflows a service running in the System context, they are all-powerful on the computer.

Table continued on following page

Account Name	Description
	Any process with the System SID is also made a member of the local Administrators group.
	When a system process accesses a network resource, it also picks up any SIDs belonging to the local computer account (e.g., Domain Computers and Authenticated Users)

Table 3-4

Group Name	Type	Description
Account Operators	Domain Local	Relatively powerful group that mimics a lower-privilege administrator
		Exists only on domain controllers
		No default members. Members can view and manage user, group, and computer accounts (except for objects in the Domain Controllers and Built-in containers). Can view, but not modify, high-privilege accounts. Cannot change group membership of highly privileged built-in groups. Can logon locally to domain controllers (which normal users cannot do).
Administrators	Domain Local or Local	Members have Full Control of local server(s)/domain controller(s) in the domain and any related security principal accounts
		The Administrator and System accounts are the only default members (you can't see the System account usually). This membership cannot be changed.
		Any object created by a member of this group is owned by the group, not the member.
		When a computer joins a domain, the Domain Admins group is added as a member of the local Administrators group. When a server becomes a domain controller, the Enterprise Admins group is also added. These memberships can be changed.

Group Name	Type	Description
Anonymous Logon (also known as the Anonymous session, null session, etc.)	Action-based	Security principals connecting anonymously (they access resources over a network connection by using a null user account name, domain, and password) are added as members to this group. Resources must specifically allow the Anonymous security identifier (SID) allowed in order for anonymous users or connections to access. Anonymous users are important to the operation of Windows, and if completely disallowed would cause service disruptions. In Windows Server 2003 and XP, the Everyone group does not contain this group as a member. In previous versions of Windows, anonymous users could access the same resources as the Everyone group, which caused potential security issues. Note: The Anonymous Logon security group is not related to the IIS anonymous user account.
Authenticated Users	Action-based	Includes all currently logged on users (interactive or network) who have authenticated with a logon name and password. Does not include the guest account, or in XP and later, the anonymous user account. The Authenticated Users group is a member of the Users group. The Authenticated Users group should be preferred over the Everyone group when assigning new permissions unless unauthenticated access is desired. Authenticated users from other trusted domains or forests are also placed in this group.
Backup Operators	Domain Local or Local	Members can back up and restore files regardless of other security permissions. They can also log on locally to domain controllers and shut down computers.

Table continued on following page

103

Group Name	Type	Description
		Has no default members
		Administrators also have the same restore and backup rights without belonging to this group.
		Tape backup service accounts should belong to this group instead of belonging to the Administrators group, if possible.
Batch		Includes all security principals logged on to the computer through a Windows batch queue facility (e.g., Task Scheduler). The security principal must have *Logon as batch job* privilege.
Cert Publishers	Domain Local	Members of this group are allowed to publish user and computer digital certificates to Active Directory. Usually contains computer accounts.
		Computers with Microsoft Certificate Services installed in Enterprise mode are automatically added to this account in their own domain, but may need to be added to other domains' or forests' Cert Publishers group if Certificate Services is to publish certificates to areas outside its home domain. No default members until Certificate Services is installed.
CERTSVC_DCOM_ACCESS	Domain Local	Installed with enterprise Microsoft Certificate Services. Default members are Domain Users and Domain Computers.
Creator	Action-based	This is a placeholder group that is replaced with the owner's primary group after the creation operation is complete.
Creator Owner	Action-based	This is a placeholder group that is replaced with the owner's account (not always the same as the creator's) after the creation operation is complete. This group is getting its own Access Control Entry (ACE) in NTFS DACLS permissions in Windows Vista (more on this below).
DHCP Administrators	Domain Local	Installed with Microsoft DHCP service, contains no default members. Members can configure DHCP using the GUI or the Netsh command, but cannot perform other administrative tasks on the server.

Group Name	Type	Description
DHCP Users	Domain Local	Installed with Microsoft DHCP service, members of this group have read-only access to the DHCP service. No default members.
Dialup	Action-based	Includes all security principals logged onto the computer by means of a dial-up connection
Distributed COM Users	Domain Local or Local	Members can execute DCOM applications on the local computer No default members
DNS Admins	Domain Local	Only available, by default, in domains or forests using Microsoft DNS. Members of this group have Full Control of all zones and zone records in the domains in which they contain members. No default members.
DnsUpdateProxy	Global	Members are allowed to perform DNS dynamic update on behalf of other clients. Normally only used if Microsoft DHCP servers are installed in a domain. By default, DHCP clients have their DNS records registered by DHCP, which then becomes the owner. If the DHCP server goes down, the client may have trouble updating its own DNS host records. By placing the DHCP computer accounts in this group, client host records are not secured and can be updated by other computers. Has no members by default.
Domain Admins	Global	Members are domain administrators, with Full Control to all domain resources. The Domain Admins group is the default owner of all domain objects created by any member of the group. The domain Administrator is a default member of this group. This group is a member of the local Administrators group on all domain computers.

Table continued on following page

Group Name	Type	Description
Domain Computers	Global	Group contains all computer accounts of computers joined to the domain, except domain controllers. Allows a computer to create a secure channel between itself and another computer for privileged communications (but communications are not encrypted by the channel itself).
Domain Controllers	Global	Group contains the computer accounts of domain controllers joined to the domain.
Domain Guests	Global	Any member it contains has Guest privileges. Contains only one member by default, the domain Guest account. A member of the Guests group.
Domain Users	Global	Group contains all user accounts created in the domain. Permissions given to this group are extended to all users in the same domain. Most new and built-in user accounts are part of this group, including Administrator, krbtgt, Support_#, and the IIS default user accounts. In Windows Server 2003, Everyone and anonymous are not part of this group.
Enterprise Admins	Universal in native mode domains, Global in mixed-mode domains	Members of this group have Full Control permissions to all resources in the forest. Can make forest changes, such as adding, deleting, and modifying domains, configuring sites, authorizing DHCP servers, and installing enterprise Certificate Authorities. By default, Administrator of first domain in the forest (i.e., forest root domain) is a member of this group. This group only exists in the forest root domain. By default, this group is a member of the Domain Admins group of all domains in the forest.
Enterprise Domain Controllers	Universal accounts in the forest	Includes all domain controller computer
Everyone	Action-based	This group includes all authenticated users and computers plus the members of the Guests group, (but *not* the anonymous null session by default in XP and 2003).

Group Name	Type	Description
Exchange Domain Servers	Global	Added with Microsoft Exchange, only Exchange domain servers need to be added.
Exchange Enterprise Servers	Domain Local	Added with Microsoft Exchange, only Exchange enterprise servers need to be added.
Group Policy Creator Owners	Global	Members can create and modify group policy objects. By default, Administrator of first domain in the forest (i.e., forest root domain) is the only member of this group. This group only exists in the forest root domain. Objects created by members of this group are owned by the member.
Guests	Domain Local or Local	Members have the same permissions and access as members of the Users group (although the Guest account is further restricted). Members of this group will have a temporary profile created during logon, deleted during logoff. Default members are Guest and IIS anonymous user accounts, IUSR_computername, and IWAM_computername (if IIS is installed). When a server becomes a domain controller, the Domain Guests group becomes a member of Guests local group.
HelpServicesGroup	Domain Local or Local	This group allows administrators to set rights common to all support applications. The Support_# user account and any Remote Assistance user will be added to this group.

Table continued on following page

Group Name	Type	Description
IIS_WPG	Domain Local	New group in IIS 6.0 used for worker processes. Members of this group usually serve as identities for specific namespaces and/or application pools. Application pool identities should belong to this group. The only default member is IWAM_<computername>, and this is only true if IIS is installed.
Incoming Forest Trust Builders	Domain Local	Members of this group can create one-way forest trusts to the forest root domain. No default members.
Interactive	Action-based	Includes all security principals logged on to the computer directly at the keyboard (i.e., local), using a Remote Desktop connection, or using a remote shell such as Telnet.
Local	Action-based	Includes all security principals logged on locally at the keyboard. Mutually exclusive from the Network group.
Logon session X-X	Action-based	X-X is a random unique number assigned to a particular logon session. Can be used to identify a particular logon session.
Network	Action-based	Members include anyone accessing the computer over a network connection (except Terminal Server users). Mutually exclusive of local, interactive, or dial-up groups.
Network Configuration Operators	Domain Local or Local	Members of this group can make changes to the network configuration settings (most often TCP/IP) and renew and release DHCP lease settings. No default members. Author had problems with this group during testing. It would not allow non-admin members to modify network settings correctly.
Other Organization	Action-based	Added to all users accessing a computer resource from another forest's domain across a forest selective trust. New in Windows Server 2003, mutually exclusive of the This Organization group.
Performance Log Users	Domain Local or Local	Members of this group can manage and create performance counters, alerts, and logs, without being members of the Administrators group. No default members.

Group Name	Type	Description
Performance Monitor Users	Domain Local or Local	Members of this group can view performance counters, alerts, and logs, without being members of the Administrators group. No default members.
Power Users	Local	Members of this group can install software, create security principal accounts, and modify and delete the accounts they have created. They can create local groups and then add or remove users from the local groups they have created. They can also add or remove users from the Power Users, Users, and Guests groups. Members can create shared resources and administer the shared resources they have created. They can start, but not stop, services.
		They cannot take ownership of files, back up or restore directories, load or unload device drivers, or manage security and auditing logs.
		No default members, unless the computer was upgraded from Windows NT 4.0, in which case it will contain the Interactive group.
		Does not exist on domain controllers and is being discontinued in Longhorn
Pre-Windows 2000	Domain Local	Members of this group have Read access to Compatible Access user and group objects in Active Directory.
		Exists only on Windows 2000 and later domain controllers
		By default, either the Authenticated Users or the Everyone group is a member, and is determined during a domain controller promotion (dcpromo.exe). If *Permissions compatible with pre-Windows 2000 servers* is selected, the Everyone group is added; otherwise, the Authenticated Users group is added. Essentially, the former selection can allow anonymous session connections (i.e., the null session) and read domain information. Provided for backward compatibility with legacy systems.

Table continued on following page

Group Name	Type	Description
		You may need to add users and computers to this group if they are running legacy systems.
		Domain Controllers and Exchange Enterprise Servers groups may be added as members by Active Directory.
Print Operators	Domain Local or Local	Members of this group can create, manage, and share printers, plus log on locally to domain controllers and load and unload device drivers. There are no default members.
RAS Servers	Domain Local or Local	Used for backward compatibility with NT 4.0 RAS servers
RAS and IAS Servers	Domain Local	Members of this group, usually server computer accounts, can read Account Restrictions, Remote Access Information, and Logon Information of user accounts. No default members. Pre-Windows 2000 RRAS and IAS server computer accounts should be added.
Remote Desktop Users	Domain Local or Local	Members of this group are granted the right to log on remotely.
		Does not exist in Windows 2000 or before
		No default members, and administrators do not have to belong.
		Equivalent to Terminal Server Users group on prior Windows versions
Remote Interactive Logon	Action-based	Includes all security principals logged on to the computer using a Remote Desktop session (Remote Assistance, Remote Desktop, Terminal Services, etc.). This group was added in Windows XP and later. Security principals in this group will automatically be members of the Interactive group, too.
Replicator	Domain Local or Local	Only used in NT 4.0 replication with File Replication Service. Usually should not be modified. Default member is domain user account used to log on to Replicator services on domain controllers.

Group Name	Type	Description
Restricted Code	Action-based	Used by any process executed in a restricted security context. Can be used by users using RunAs. When added to a user's security token, it significantly limits what a program running in that user's context can do to the local system (see below for more details). Longhorn will use this SID more.
Schema Admins	Universal in native mode domains, Global in mixed-mode domains	Members are potentially the most power ful account in the forest, even more power ful than Enterprise Administrators. Can modify Active Directory schema. By default, only Administrator of first domain in the forest (i.e., forest root domain) is a member of this group. This group only exists in the forest root domain.
Self	Action-based	A placeholder group during security operations. Can represent the security principal requesting the access or the security principal being impersonated by an object.
Server Operators	Domain Local	Relatively powerful group that mimics a lower-privilege administrator. Members of this group can log on interactively, access administrative shares, create, delete, and manage resources, manage services, backup and restore files, change system time, manage disks and volumes, format the hard disk, and shut down the computer Exist only on domain controllers No default members
Service	Local	Contains all logged on accounts with the *Logon as Service* privilege. All service accounts must have this SID in order for the service to be started by the security configuration manager (scm) utility, as all services are.
TelnetClients	Domain Local or Local	Allows non-administrative members to log on to Telnet Server services

Table continued on following page

Group Name	Type	Description
Terminal Server License Servers	Domain Local	Contains computer accounts of server(s) running Terminal Server License service
Terminal Server Users	Action-oriented	Includes all security principals logged on to the computer using a Terminal Services session In Terminal Services version 4.0 application compatibility mode (used for running Windows programs needing pre-Windows 2000 compatibility permissions).
This Organization		New to Windows Server 2003, identifies users who access resources locally within a trusting forest or across a trust that is not marked for selective authentication. New in Windows Server 2003, mutually exclusive of the Other Organization group.
Users	Domain Local or Local	Any user account created in the work group or domain becomes a member of this group. By default, Authenticated Users and the Interactive groups are members. Can perform common user tasks such as running previously installed applications and using local and network resources. Users can install applications only if the application supports per-user installation (which isn't common) and doesn't modify Windows system folders and registry locations. Initially the only member is the Authenticated Users group, but when a computer joins a domain, the Domain Users group is added to the local Users group on the computer.
Windows Authorization Access Group	Domain Local	Members can access the computed `token GroupsGlobalAndUniversal` attribute on User objects. This is necessary for some applications. Without this group, members would have to be added to the Pre-Windows 2000 Compatibility group. See Microsoft KB Article #331951 (`http://support.microsoft.com/default.asp x?scid=kb;en-us;331951`) for more details.

Group Name	Type	Description
		Only exists on Windows 2003 and later domain controllers
		Only default member is the Enterprise Domain Controllers group
WINS Users	Domain Local	Only added when the WINS service is installed for the first time. Members have read-only access to WINS service.
WSUS Administrators	Domain Local	Only added when Windows Software Update Services (WSUS or WUS) is added for the first time. Members can administrate WUS servers.

You can see the groups you belong to using Windows Server 2003's `Whoami.exe` or `Gpresult.exe`. I prefer Gpresult for several reasons. First, although it doesn't show you the SIDs, its overall output is significantly more informative. Second, it will show you what groups your computer belongs to. Most administrators never consider the groups their computer belongs to.

Everyone Group and the Anonymous SID

In Windows XP and Windows Server 2003, the Everyone group does not contain the Anonymous SID (as it did in Windows 2000 and NT). Practically, this means that only objects that have explicitly allowed anonymous access can be accessed by the anonymous (i.e., null session) user. This change makes Windows significantly harder to hack. In previous Windows versions, anyone connecting as an anonymous user could access any resource to which the Everyone group had access. Hackers loved this because administrators often assign the Everyone group a wide range of rights and object permissions.

Anonymous users, if allowed, still contain the Anonymous Logon SID and their network logon type SID (usually Network). This means an anonymous user still has access to objects that explicitly allow the Anonymous Logon and Network SID. The Network SID is an action-based group and doesn't generally have a lot of default access alone. It was created so programs and processes could determine whether the connecting security principal was Local or Network, and make different security decisions based on the findings.

In Windows Server 2003 domains, there is a group called the *Pre-Windows 2000 Compatibility Access* group. When creating a new domain, the administrator running `Dcpromo.exe` is prompted whether to include the Everyone and Anonymous Logon groups to the Pre-Windows 2000 Compatibility Access group. The default is to add the Authenticated Users and the domain controller to the group. If you need backward compatibility with pre-Windows 2000 machines, consider adding the Anonymous Logon group back into the Pre-Windows 2000 Compatibility Access group. You can also enable the group policy setting *Let Everyone permissions apply to anonymous users* to accomplish the same task. But do either with caution because doing so significantly weakens a Windows computer. As noted above, domain controllers are automatically added to the Pre-Windows 2000 Compatibility Access group, which means anonymous users can connect to most domain controllers. Even though this weakens the domain controller, anonymous connections must be allowed to a domain controller in order for it to do its normal duties. Allowing an anonymous connection is how security principals can connect in the first place to become authenticated users.

113

Restricted Code

This is a newly added well-known SID that when added to any user's security token significantly limits what access a program running in the user's security context can do to the local system. It is used by programs such as RunAs. For example, if a user chooses *Protect my computer and data from unauthorized program activity* when executing `RunAs.exe`, instead of running as another user, the Restricted group SID will be added to the user's security token. The Restricted token removes all current privileges the user might have except Bypass Traverse Checking, removes write access to the registry, removes privileged group memberships (i.e., Administrators, Power Users), and removes all access to the user's profile (e.g., cookies, Temporary Internet Files, etc.). This is done to prevent malicious unauthorized manipulation of the local system. This SID would be good to add to any Internet Explorer browsing sessions. Windows Vista will use this SID to do exactly just that. Even when logged in users have administrative privileges, when they execute normal programs, such as Internet Explorer or Outlook Express, those programs will run in the Restricted security context. See `http://blogs.msdn.com/aaron_margosis/archive/2004/09/10/227727.aspx` for more details.

Creator Owner

The Creator Owner group isn't a real group. It is a placeholder account. When a security principal with permissions to create an object does so, they become the object's creator owner. The Creator Owner group is used by Windows when the object creation is started and is replaced by the real user or group when the creation action is finished. The Creator Owner has Full Control permissions (subfolders and files only) to most folders. This means that if a security principal can create an object, file, or folder, it has Full Control to it. Creator Owners can fully manipulate the object, including changing permissions. Windows tracks Creator Owners for a variety of reasons, including security and disk quota management.

There are two small caveats to remember. First, oftentimes when a user is the Creator Owner of an object, the object is owned by a group instead. For instance, by default, when any member of the Administrator's group creates an object, it is owned by the Administrators group, not the specific administrator who created the object. You can change this behavior using group policy. Second, although a user may not have elevated permissions to a particular area or folder, the Creator Owner often does have access. If the security principal can create an object, it will end up with Full Control permissions to a place it otherwise didn't have elevated permissions. In most instances, the user will not be able to create the object in the first place, but I have seen some deviations to the normal treatment (an example is covered below). Just be aware of the Creator Owner's default permissions.

> *If the Creator Owner group displays in the Security Settings dialog box but doesn't appear to have any permissions, more than likely it has permissions to folders and files inside the current folder.*

The Creator Owner account will get its own DACLS access control entry (ACE) NTFS security permission in Windows Vista. This means that NTFS security permissions can be predefined on a folder or container and when an owner creates something, the new permissions can easily be predefined and viewed in Windows Explorer. The Creator Owner ACE will show up right next to the normal NTFS permissions, like Read & Execute.

The Creator Group is a related but different group from the Creator Owner. When rights are given to the Creator Group, when something is created by the user, permissions flow to the user's primary group, not to the user's individual accounts. This is the technique that allows any object created by an administrator to belong to the Administrator's group, instead of the individual administrator, thus preventing orphaned objects if the individual administrator is removed as a user account. Another related SID is Self. It acts as a placeholder so that permissions can be assigned to the parent of a newly created child object, before the parent is even defined.

Computer Accounts

Whenever a computer joins a domain, Active Directory creates a computer account (often called the *machine account*) for it. When the computer is turned on or reboots, the computer account logs on to the domain and goes through the same four access control phases listed at the beginning of this chapter. The computer account is named after your computer's name (it will have a $ at the end of the name in some utilities) and the password is set by the domain controller. The domain controller changes the password periodically, but you can force a password change using the Netdom.exe utility. There are two group policy settings that control computer account password changes, covered in Chapter 14.

> *Interestingly, if the computer and domain controller don't agree on the current password, then both will retry the authentication using the previous password.*

If the computer and domain controller ever lose password synchronization, an administrator will need to reset the computer account in Active Directory Users and Computers. Then when you reboot the problematic machine, it should re-sync with the domain controller.

When a computer logs on, it creates a *secure channel*, as Microsoft calls it, between the computer and the domain controller. This secure channel is then used to allow the other security principals (i.e., user, group, and service accounts) a more secure network communications link for their authentication traffic. Computer accounts are often involved in Active Directory events, and its membership can significantly impact the security of your network. For instance, most security settings in Active Directory are applied to computer accounts, not user accounts. Understanding what groups your computer belongs to is essential to understanding Windows security. I used Gpresult.exe to give me a listing of groups my computer belongs to:

```
The computer is a part of the following security groups:
------------------------------------------------------
      BUILTIN\Administrators
      Everyone
      BUILTIN\Users
      NT AUTHORITY\NETWORK
      NT AUTHORITY\Authenticated Users
      EXAMPLE_56978$
      Domain Computers
```

The results are common. In the typical domain environment, domain computers belong to the following groups:

❑   Everyone

❑   Users

❑   Network

❑   Authenticated Users

❑   Domain Computers

❑   Its own machine account (noted by the trailing $)

In this particular case, the computer was also a member of the Administrators group because the logged on user belonged to the Administrators group. Surprising to most students is the fact that domain computers belong to the Everyone, Users, and Authenticated Users groups as well. Besides the fact that if a hacker did compromise a machine account he would have a lot of access to a domain, the computer's "strange" group memberships allow most group policies (attached or inherited into an OU or container the computer is in) to apply to it by default. I suspect that if the group membership behavior wasn't as it is defined, many administrators would be wondering why their group policy objects were not applying. But since the Authenticated Users group has Apply Group Policy permissions, any computer-based group policy (appropriately placed) usually applies automatically to the computer hit by it.

Computer accounts are not created, or needed, until a computer joins a domain.

Domain controller computer accounts normally belong to the following groups:

- ❑ Administrators
- ❑ Everyone
- ❑ Pre-Windows 2000 Compatibility Access
- ❑ Windows Authorization Access Group
- ❑ Authenticated Users
- ❑ This Organization
- ❑ Computername$
- ❑ Domain Controllers
- ❑ Enterprise Domain Controllers (not always present)

You can see that the computer accounts (which most administrators don't even know exist) have a lot of security permissions and access. Thankfully, they are usually well protected and the passwords changed frequently and automatically by the domain controller.

Windows Trusts

In a multi-domain environment, Windows trusts also come into play. By default, all domains in a Windows 2000 and later forest have bidirectional, transitive trust to all other domains in the forest. In Windows 2003, in Windows 2003 forest functional level, you can also set up domain-to-domain trusts between forests. Other types of trusts and trust behaviors (e.g., nontransitive, external, etc.) are beyond the scope of this discussion, but two main questions need to be asked and answered:

1. What does a Windows trust really mean?

2. What permissions does a Windows trust give the trusted domain?

Remember that a trusted domain is the one being trusted by the resource domain. A trusted domain usually has the security principals wanting access to the trusting domain's resources.

On the first question, a Windows trust means that the trusting domain's SRM will trust the identity credentials and access token sent to it by the trusted domain. Effectively, the trusting domain is telling the trusted domain that it trusts the trusted domain controllers to do their identification and authentication phases so that when a security principal tries to access a resource in the trusting domain, the trusting domain's SRM will not redo the authentication. Conversely, if a Windows trust has not been set up between two domains, then the resource domain will ask the user domain security principal to authenticate again.

On the second question, people often hear that a Windows trust gives either no permissions or all permissions to the resources in the trusting domain. Here's the truth: The users in the trusted domain get the following group memberships in the trusting domain:

- ❑ Everyone
- ❑ Authenticated Users
- ❑ Users
- ❑ Interactive
- ❑ This Organization (unless from another forest using a selective trust)

Most obvious is that all users in the trusted domain immediately get access and permissions to whatever the Everyone and Authenticated Users group in the trusting domain has. In most domains, that's a lot of trust that just got transmitted. Be aware of this fact the next time you create a new Windows trust. Creating a new Windows trust is giving away a lot of trust!

Security Token

Now that you've got a better understanding of all the groups involved, we can focus our attention on the security token. As discussed before, after a security principal successfully logs on to a computer, the user and their group SIDs are collected for the security token (also known as an *access token* or *security access token*). The security token contains the following information:

- ❑ Security principal's account SID
- ❑ SIDs for groups to which the security principal belongs
- ❑ SIDs from the security principal's SIDHistory field
- ❑ A logon SID that identifies the current logon session (see Table 3-1)
- ❑ A list of the privileges held by either the user or the user's groups (covered in Chapter 14)
- ❑ An owner SID, which indicates what account or group becomes the owner of any object created by the security principal
- ❑ The SID for the primary group (used only in POSIX subsystems and indicated on the Users account information).
- ❑ A list of privileges given to the security principal and their status (i.e., enabled or disabled)
- ❑ The default NTFS permissions that the system uses when the user creates a securable object without specifying security permissions. The default permissions usually are the Creator Owner and System account having Full Control-Allow permissions.
- ❑ The source of the access token (i.e., Session Manager, LAN Manager, or Remote Procedure Call (RPC) server)

❑ Whether the token is a primary or impersonation token

❑ Current impersonation level (as discussed above)

❑ Session ID, indicating whether the access token is associated with a Terminal Services client session

❑ An optional list of restricting SIDs

❑ Other statistics

Every process working on behalf of the security principal (i.e., impersonation) has a copy of the security principal's access token. You can get a partial print out of a user's access token by using the `Whoami /all` command (the Windows Server 2003 version) on Windows XP and later. Here's example output:

```
[User]    = "EXAMPLE\ErinLovell" S-1-5-21-3334797343-2748683396-701868904-1112
[Group 1] = "EXAMPLE\Domain Users" S-1-5-21-3334797343-2748683396-701868906-513
[Group 2] = "Everyone" S-1-1-0
[Group 3] = "BUILTIN\Administrators" S-1-5-32-544
[Group 4] = "BUILTIN\Users" S-1-5-32-545
[Group 5] = "NT AUTHORITY\INTERACTIVE" S-1-5-4
[Group 6] = "NT AUTHORITY\Authenticated Users" S-1-5-11
[Group 7] = "LOCAL" S-1-2-0
[Group 8] = "EXAMPLE\Data" S-1-5-21-3334797343-2748683396-701868904-1131

(X) SeChangeNotifyPrivilege          = Bypass traverse checking
(O) SeSecurityPrivilege              = Manage auditing and security log
(O) SeBackupPrivilege              = Back up files and directories
(O) SeRestorePrivilege             = Restore files and directories
(O) SeSystemtimePrivilege            = Change the system time
(O) SeShutdownPrivilege            = Shut down the system
(O) SeRemoteShutdownPrivilege        = Force shutdown from a remote system
(O) SeTakeOwnershipPrivilege         = Take ownership of files or other objects
(O) SeDebugPrivilege           = Debug programs
(O) SeSystemEnvironmentPrivilege     = Modify firmware environment values
(O) SeSystemProfilePrivilege         = Profile system performance
(O) SeProfileSingleProcessPrivilege = Profile single process
(O) SeIncreaseBasePriorityPrivilege = Increase scheduling priority
(X) SeLoadDriverPrivilege            = Load and unload device drivers
(O) SeCreatePagefilePrivilege        = Create a pagefile
(O) SeIncreaseQuotaPrivilege         = Adjust memory quotas for a process
(X) SeUndockPrivilege            = Remove computer from docking station
(O) SeManageVolumePrivilege          = Perform volume maintenance tasks
(X) SeCreateGlobalPrivilege          = Create global objects
(X) SeImpersonatePrivilege           = Impersonate a client after authentication
```

Under the privileges section, an (X) means the privilege is granted, an (0) means the privilege is not granted. The Local Security Authority (LSA) program (`Lsass.exe`) is the component in charge of generating the security token. Whenever a service (or process or server) impersonates a user to access a resource, it hands the SRM the token. The SRM is a kernel mode component in charge of determining which security principals get to access to what objects and what permissions are given. Along with the security principal's access token is an *access mask*. The access mask is the access the process is requesting on behalf of the security principal, so although a security principal may have Full Control-Allow permissions to the object being accessed, the process may only be asking for Read permissions for the current request. The access mask changes as needed. The SRM takes the access token and access mask and compares them to the object's defined security permission settings (more on this shortly). Figure 3-8 shows a simplistic representation of the transaction. The SRM returns the allowed permissions or restrictions.

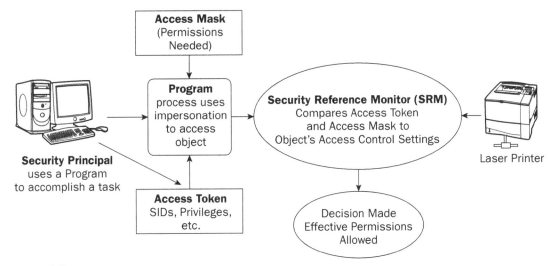

Figure 3-8

Share and NTFS Permissions

Microsoft Windows has both Share and NTFS permissions to secure access control to its protected objects. Each permission can be configured as Allow or Deny. Deny overrides Allow if set at the same level (see the "Inheritance" section below). Permissions can be set per file (except shares), per folder, per user, and per group.

Contrary to popular belief, Microsoft has some of the best security of any popular operating system on the market today. I challenge anyone to find a popular OS that has 28 different permission settings per file or folder. What Microsoft doesn't always have perfect are the default security settings. This section discusses Share and NTFS permission in detail.

Share Permissions

Share permissions apply only when a resource is contacted over a network connection (or even when accessed locally through Network Neighborhood or a NetBIOS connection). Share permissions are available whether the file system is FAT or NTFS but can only be set at the folder and printer level. If you want to share a file or group of files, you must place them in a folder and share them. If your file system does not use NTFS, the Share permissions are the only security permissions you have.

There are only three folder share permissions (see Figure 3-9):

❑   Full Control

❑   Change

❑   Read

When permissions are set at the folder level, they are inherited (covered below) by the objects contained in the folder and below by default, but objects permissions can be set to differ. And, of course, if there are underlying NTFS permissions, they apply as well.

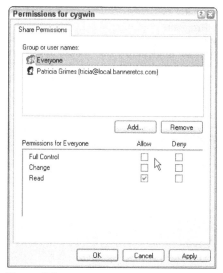

Figure 3-9

Most people think the Read permission only allows a security principal to view an object, when in fact a lot more can be accomplished. The Read permission allows a security principal to view, copy, and print (if applicable) the resource. If the share contains a program, the security principal can execute the program. The Read permission also allows the user to traverse a folder to get to another folder below it (more on traversing follows). The copy operation can be problematic securitywise.

If a user has Read access to an object, then that user can copy it to a new location and, in most cases, get Full Control to the new copy. This is because when an object is copied, a new, second copy ends up in the new destination. If the destination has Creator Owner permissions with Full Control (as is often the case), the security principal who copied the object is the Creator Owner of the new copy and gets Full Control. This is security as designed. The copier cannot copy the object, modify it, and then copy it back over the original object — the original object's integrity is protected. However, most administrators are surprised that Read access allows the reader to gain Full control of the copy, so be aware that everywhere users have Read access, they can make a copy of the object and do with it what they want.

> *Microsoft has a new digital rights management feature called Rights Management Services (www*
> *.microsoft.com/windowsserver2003/technologies/rightsmgmt/default.mspx) that can help prevent users*
> *from copying and printing objects, although it is not foolproof.*

The Change permission allows the related object (and any subfolders or files) to be added, viewed, copied, printed, modified, and deleted. No surprises here, although some administrators aren't always sure whether the Change permission allows the object to be deleted. It does. The Full Control permission allows a security principal to modify the share permissions (and any contained files or subfolders) as well, but the user must be a power user or administrator to access Share permissions in the first place, so usually this isn't a problem. This issue becomes more important when setting NTFS permissions (see below). Full Control share permissions also allow a user to Take Ownership if the underlying NTFS permissions allow it.

New Shares

Shares can be created by an administrator or power user by right-clicking any folder or printer object. The creator can then assign Share permissions and choose whether or not to limit the number of concurrent connections (Microsoft Windows workstation OSs are limited to 10 concurrent connections by default). *Home editions of Microsoft operating systems are often limited to a maximum of five concurrent connections.*

Regular end users cannot create shares. Sharing requires that the NetBIOS protocol and the File and Printing Sharing service be enabled.

The Everyone group is automatically given Read share permissions with new shares in Windows XP and later. In Windows 2000 and NT, the Everyone group was given Full Control share permissions, although in either case the underlying NTFS permissions control the effective rights given to a security principal. A commonly held mistaken belief is that all users get Full Control to all files and folders on a Windows PC. That was never true. As stated above, it was true for share permissions but never for NTFS permissions. The controlling NTFS permissions were whatever the administrator assigned them to be, or whatever the security principal inherited. If NTFS permissions are not set, then the most commonly inherited permission is Read & Execute. While this might be more permissions than an administrator might mean to give, it is a far cry from Full Control of all files and folders on the Windows PC.

A FAT-formatted volume would not have any offsetting NTFS permissions so the Full Control permissions of any shares would apply.

New Share Recommendations

Whenever creating new shares, administrators should remove the Everyone has Read permission and replace it with whatever is the least privileges necessary. Many resources recommend setting all shares with Everyone Full Control permissions, but this voids the least-privilege principle. You should strive to set the tightest permissions you can on both the share and NTFS permissions side.

Unfortunately, Microsoft has not made it easy to change the default share permissions on new shares to something other than Everyone Read. Microsoft did release a nonpublic regedit hack that allowed administrators to set new defaults for new shares, but the registry hack was wiped out accidentally by a hotfix and wasn't all that accurate anyway. It is hoped that Microsoft is renewing plans to allow administrators more granular control over new share permissions. Lastly, most non-admin users never need Full Control to a share. Consider giving Change permissions instead.

Hidden Shares

Since Windows 3.1x, Microsoft has allowed administrators to make *hidden shares*. By placing a $ (dollar sign) at the end of a share name when creating it, it becomes "invisible" to NetBIOS browsing. But if you know the name of the hidden share and the correct logon credentials, you can map a drive letter to the hidden share. Just be advised that several enumeration tools will reveal hidden shares. For the most part, hidden shares are just used to keep interested end users from discovering them too easily. By default, Windows makes a hidden drive share (called an *admin share*) for each active drive letter on a Windows system (i.e., C$, D$). Also, an administrator can create a *published share* in Active Directory that points to a NetBIOS share. They cannot be made hidden by placing the $ at the end of the name, and are not present in NetBIOS sharing lists. Active Directory published shares only show up in Active Directory object enumeration (e.g., Active Directory Users and Computers).

All drive shares, regular and hidden, should be password protected and require strong passwords. Many scanning worms look for drive shares and do password guessing against them. Weakly password-protected shares can result in compromised files. Conversely, password-guessing worms can sometimes cause inadvertent DoS attacks if account lockouts is enabled (see Chapter 4).

This section does not cover printer shares, which are at low risk for attack; nor does it cover other available file-sharing mechanisms such as FTP or Distributed File System (DFS).

NTFS Permissions

NTFS permissions are available to protect files, folders, registry keys, and other objects when the NTFS file system is installed. As long as NTFS is being used, NTFS permissions apply, whether the resource is being accessed locally or remotely. There are few legitimate reasons why NTFS can't be installed as the file system, with the notable exception of dual-booting machines with other operating systems that don't understand NTFS and troubleshooting issues that arise when NFTS used (i.e., a normal FAT boot disk can't be used to access NTFS-protected drives). NTFS must be installed to enable many Windows features, including the following:

❑ NTFS permissions — file and folder level

❑ Auditing

❑ Active Directory

❑ Disk quotas

❑ EFS encryption

❑ Compression

To modify NTFS permissions, simply right-click the object and choose *Properties ➪ Security*. There are seven different "summary" file and folder NTFS permissions (see Figure 3-10) created by a combination of 14 *special* permissions (see Figure 3-11).

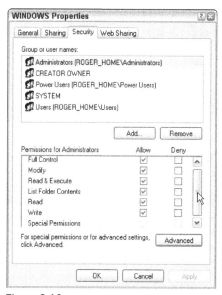

Figure 3-10

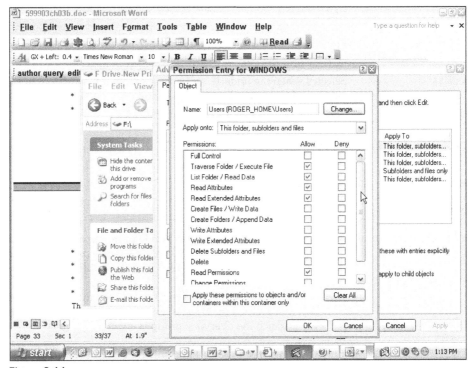

Figure 3-11

The seven summary file and folder permissions are described in Table 3-5.

Table 3-5

Permission	Effect
Read	View, copy, print, and rename files, folders, and objects. Cannot launch executable programs unless executing a script file that launches another executable with Read & Execute permissions.
	Can read object permissions, read object attributes and extended attributes (e.g., EFS, Archive bit, etc.). Lists files and subfolders in a folder.
Write	Read permissions, plus create and overwrite files and folders
List (Folders Only)	Allows viewing file names and subfolder names within the folder
Read and Execute	Read permissions, plus allows the execution of program files
Modify	Allows all permissions except the ability to Take Ownership and set permissions. Allows reading, deleting, changing, and overwriting of files and folders.

Table continued on following page

Permission	Effect
Full Control	Full control over this file or folder, including the ability to set permissions and Take Ownership
Special	Selected when the underlying 14 more granular permissions are selected or combined in ways that don't make up one of other six summary permissions. Also, includes the Synchronize permission.

Table 3-6 discusses what each special permission allows.

Table 3-6

Permission	Effect
Traverse Folder/Execute File	Traverse Folder allows moving through folders to reach other files or folders, even when the security principal has no permissions for the traversed folders. (Applies to folders only.)
	Traverse folder takes effect only when the security principal is not granted the **Bypass traverse checking** user privilege (which the Everyone group is given by default).
	For files: Execute File allows or denies running program files.
	Setting the Traverse Folder permission on a folder does not automatically set the Execute File permission on all files within that folder.
List Folder/Read Data	List Folder allows viewing file and subfolder names within the folder.
	List Folder only affects the contents of that folder and does not affect whether the folder you are setting the permission on will be listed.
	Read Data allows or denies viewing, copying, and printing files.
Read Attributes	Allows or denies a security principal the capability to see an object's attributes (e.g., Read-only, System, Hidden, etc.)
Read Extended Attributes	Allows or denies a security principal the capability to see an object's extended attributes (e.g., such as EFS, Compression, etc.)
Create Files/Write Data	Create Files allows or denies creating files within the folder. (Applies to folders only.)
	Write Data allows or denies making changes to the file and overwriting existing content. (Applies to files only.)

Permission	Effect
Create Folders/Append Data	Create Folders allows or denies creating folders within the folder. (Applies to folders only.) Append Data allows or denies making changes to the end of the file but not changing, deleting, or overwriting existing data. (Applies to files only.)
Write Attributes	Determines whether the security principal can write or modify standard attributes (e.g., Read-only, System, Hidden, etc.) of files and folders. Does not deal with writing files or folders, only their attributes.
Write Extended Attributes	Determines whether the security principal can write or modify extended attributes (e.g., EFS, Compression, etc.) of files and folders. Does not deal with writing files or folders, only their attributes.
Delete Subfolders and Files	Allows or denies deleting subfolders and files, even if the Delete permission has not been granted on the subfolder or file. See below for unexpected consequences of this permission.
Delete	Allows or denies deleting the file or folder. If you do not have Delete permission on a file or folder, you can still delete it if you have been granted Delete Subfolders and Files on the parent folder. See below for unexpected consequences of this permission.
Read Permissions	Allows or denies *reading permissions* of the file or folder, such as Full Control, Read, and Write. Does not involve reading the file itself.
Change Permissions	Allows or denies *modifying permissions* of the file or folder, such as Full Control, Read, and Write. Does not involve reading the file itself.
Take Ownership	Determines who can take ownership of a file or folder. Owners can always have Full Control, and their permission to the file or folder cannot be taken away permanently unless their ownership is taken away as well.
Synchronize	Not manipulated much by administrators. Deals with synchronization issues with multi-threaded, multiprocess programs and how multiple threads trying to access the same resource cooperate.

Windows Vista will also have the Creator Owner special permission, as discussed above.

Table 3-7 shows how the 14 underlying "special" permissions make up the seven summary permissions.

Table 3-7

Permission	Full Control	Modify	Read & Execute	List	Read	Write
Traverse Folder/ Execute File	X	X	X	X		
List Folder/Read Data	X	X	X	X	X	
Read Attributes	X	X	X	X	X	
Read Extended Attributes	X	X	X	X	X	
Create Files/Write Data	X	X				X
Create Folders/Append Data	X	X				X
Write Attributes	X	X				X
Write Extended Attributes	X	X				X
Delete Subfolders and Files	X					
Delete	X	X				
Read Permissions	X	X	X	X	X	X
Change Permissions	X					
Take Ownership	X					
Synchronize	X	X	X	X	X	X

Registry permissions are covered in Chapter 6.

Each possible access control permission that a protected resource can have is called a *Discretionary Access Control (DAC)* permission. There are also auditing permissions called *System Access Control (SAC)* permissions that are involved in object auditing, but this chapter doesn't cover them. A DAC is a specific permission descriptor, such as Read, Write, or Modify. When the DAC is related to a specific security principal (using the SID), it is considered an *Access Control Entry (ACE)* or permission. An example ACE is the Authenticated Users group having Read permissions to a particular folder. The collection of all the security principals and their permissions to a particular object is called the object's *Access Control List*, or *ACL* (pronounced "ack-kul"). If the ACL deals with only security ACLs, it can also be called a *Discretionary Access Control List*, or *DACL* (pronounced "dack-kul"). Most of the time when people are referring to an object's associated permissions, they call it ACL or DACL. When determining a security principal's access to an object, the principal's security access token is compared to the objects DACLs).

> *Starting with Windows Server 2003 SP1 (and in Vista), NTFS permissions (DACLs and SACLs) can be set programmatically on a per-socket basis. Essentially this means that permissions can be set on a per-connection basis. See http://blogs.msdn.com/michael_howard/archive/2005/10/23/484026.aspx for a quick discussion.*

Interesting Permission Interactions

Here are some other interesting permission interactions you may not have known.

Read Permissions vs. Read Attributes vs. Read Data

Must administrators get confused by all the Read labels in NTFS permissions. Read Permissions allows a security principal (or program impersonating them) to read the file or folder's NTFS permissions, and only the permissions. Without that permission, the object's permissions can't be read; the Security tab is grayed when viewing the object in Windows Explorer. Read Attributes and Read Extended Attributes refer to whether a security principal can read the NTFS attributes attached to a particular object. The attributes attached to an object change per object. File attributes are things such as Read-only settings, EFS, and files marked as System files. Read Data is the permission most people are referring to when they intend to let a security principal read the object's contents. The same thing applies to Write (i.e., Write Data, Write Attributes, Write Permissions) permissions. Don't be confused.

Read vs. Read & Execute

The Read permission alone will not allow a program to be executed unless the file to be executed is a script or data file associated with another program to which the security principal does have Read & Execute permissions. For example, if the user only has Read permissions to a folder, but the folder contains VBS script files, double-clicking on the script file will read it into memory and launch its associated program, Wscript.exe, to run the file. This rule holds true for IIS too. Script files do not need Read & Execute permissions, only Read.

What Full Control Really Means

If the user has every NTFS permission but Full Control, that user will lack only the Take Ownership and Change Permissions permissions. Unfortunately, this also means that any user with NTFS Full Control can change the permissions of the file or folder to which they have Full Control. Non-admin users are frequently given Full Control permissions to shares, files, their home directories, their My Document folders, etc. In most cases, you do not want users to be able to change their permissions on those folders. But they can, and they can even (temporarily) remove or deny permissions to administrators.

> *If administrators are ever prevented from accessing a resource because their permissions are removed, they can take ownership of the resource and reset permissions.*

You Can Write, But Not Read

You can be allowed to write to a file, once, without ever being able to read or view it. The write permission allows a user to overwrite a file, but modifying a file requires the user to have the Read permission as well.

What Is File Traverse?

File transversal allows a security principal to view or execute a file in a folder it would not otherwise have permissions to or see. The security principal or process must know the exact location to the folder and file to reach. By default, the Everyone group has the group policy setting that allows file and folder traversal by default. This privilege should not be modified unless you really, really know what you are doing. The File Traverse right is helpful when you want to allow users into a subfolder without seeing all the information in a parent folder. As Table 3-8 shows, the traversal permission is assigned to the Users group for `\Windows\Task` and `\Windows\Temp` folders. Because these are areas that can be common among several users, Windows attempts to keep non-admin users from seeing the others' content.

Users Can Delete When You Specifically Denied Delete

Sometimes an administrator will allow a user to Read and Write a file, but also selects Deny Delete so the user cannot delete the file. Surprisingly, the user can often still delete the file. What is going on? The file's parent folder has the Allow Delete Subfolders and Files permission. This permission allows users in the folder to delete contents. The Deny Delete permission is being overruled by the higher Allow Delete Subfolders and Files. To prevent users from being able to delete files, remove the Delete Subfolders and Files permission on the folder holding the file(s).

Deny Doesn't Always Override Allow Permissions

Another very important point is that although Deny permissions usually override Allow permissions (we saw an exception in the Delete vs. Delete Subfolders and Files permissions conflict), a permission set explicitly on an object will override an inherited deny. For example, I can place a user in a group that has Full Control-Deny permissions to the root directory and tell those permissions to apply to every file and subfolder. But if I go to a lower subfolder and explicitly give the user an Allow permission, the Allow will override the Deny. This is an important fact that will become the basis of a very useful defense in Chapter 5.

Changing Permissions

There are times when a file or folder's permissions may change because of some action. For instance, if you copy or move a file, it may change the file's permissions. When you copy a file, Windows always creates a duplicate new copy of the file in the destination area. The new copy will inherit the permissions of the new parent area by default. You can change them of course. If you move a file from one disk volume to another volume, the file will inherit the permissions of the new area. But if you move a file from one volume to another location on the same volume, the file will retain its original permissions. In class the saying is, "Move the Same Retains, Everything Else Inherits."

Also, normal Windows operations may overwrite the file and its original permissions. For example, when a hotfix overwrites an older file with a new version, it may reset the file's permissions to those of the parent folder. You learn how to use group policy and security templates to overcome this problem in Chapter 14. Another problem area is Windows File Protection (WFP). By default, when a protected Windows system file gets modified unexpectedly (e.g., `Notepad.exe` is deleted), WFP will note the deletion and replace the file. Unfortunately, the original file's permissions are lost and the new replacement file will inherit the permissions of the parent folder. You may come across other similar issues with Windows permissions.

Restoring from the Recycle Bin or System Restore retains the original permissions.

Inheritance

By default, all files, folders, and registry keys inherit their permissions from their parent container unless inheritance is turned off. Inheritance can be turned on by file, folder, or registry key, and can apply granularly to one or more security principals. Most administrators don't know that they can selectively turn on and off inheritance on a file-by-file basis, and make it apply on a per-user basis. That's because although inheritance is turned off or on holistically per file or folder, not every permission from above will automatically flow below (i.e., be inherited) between folders. As Figure 3-12 shows, the *Apply To* field determines whether a particular permission stays in the current container or flows below to subfolders and files. An administrator can set a permission (on a per-user basis) that either does or doesn't flow downward. In this example, the Everyone group has Read & Execute permissions, but the permissions do not flow down.

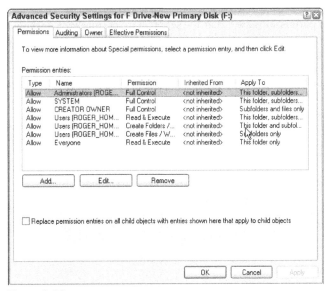

Figure 3-12

Effective Permissions

To refresh what you have learned so far: When a user tries to access a protected object, all the SIDs belonging to the user and the groups to which the user belong are collected together and placed into their security access token (along with other information). The user (or the process impersonating the user) hands the token to the Windows security reference monitor process, which compares the user's submitted SIDs to the object's DACLs. The DACL lists all the users and groups, and their allowed or denied permissions. The user's SID list (and access mask) is compared against the object's DACLs to determine what permission apply.

A user's effective permissions (i.e., their real permissions in practice) are calculated from a variety of factors. First, when trying to figure out a user's effective permissions, you must collect together the user's individual account and all the groups they belong to. A quick way to list most of the groups a user belongs to at a point in time is to run the Whoami /user /groups command at the command prompt while the user is logged in. This will reveal most of the groups, but potentially not all of the groups that the user is placed in at the moment of trying to access a file. For example, if you run that command at the user's workstation, it probably won't reveal that the user is placed in the action-based Network group on the remote server they are accessing. Of course, this factoid won't mean anything unless the Network group is assigned permissions to the particular resource the user is trying to access. Just remember that when troubleshooting permission problems, try to gather all the groups the user belongs to, obvious and not so obvious groups.

All the permissions assigned to all the user's SIDs are collected together. If there is a Deny permission set at the same level as an Allow permission, the Deny usually wins. If a Full Control-Deny wins, the user cannot usually access the object. By default, when NTFS and Share permissions are involved (i.e., the user is connecting to resource over a network share), the SRM must collect together all the Share and NTFS permissions. Up to this point, all permissions are collected together cumulatively, although the Share and NTFS permissions are kept separate.

The user's effective permissions are either the set of Share permissions or the set of NTFS permissions, whichever is less permissive (or most restrictive). This is another very important point. At the point of trying to determine the effective permissions, the outcome is the entire set of either the Share or the NTFS permissions, whichever gives less permissions. A large portion of administrators believe that the effective outcome is the least permissive permission, which is wrong. It is the least permissive *set of permissions* — either NTFS or Share. Let's use Figure 3-13 for our example.

Share Permissions	NTFS Permissions
Change Change Read	Modify Read
Read, Change	Read, Modify

Figure 3-13

In Figure 3-13, a user ends up with Read and Change Share permissions and Read and Modify NTFS permissions. As Figure 3-13 shows, initially the user had multiple Read permission occurrences because permissions cumulate from the various groups the user belongs to plus any permissions given to the individual user (not a good practice). All the Share and NTFS permissions are accumulated, but stored separately. Then the effective permissions are the most restrictive (least permissive) *set* of permissions. In this case, it is nearly identical. The effective permissions are Read *and* Change/Modify.

From having taught NTFS permissions for 17 years, I know that a large majority of Windows administrators think that the correct answer is the Read permission only — and that is wrong. They've been taught to take the least permissive permission (i.e., Read) at the end of the comparison instead of the least permissive *set* of permissions. But now you know, if you didn't already. This apparent conclusion is not as readily apparent as it seems, as I frequently see overly permissive permissions set on mission-critical resources. Make sure all the administrators on your staff know the correct answer and how it was derived.

Also, true effective permissions are determined by more than just NTFS and Share permissions. As discussed much in this chapter, the less apparent, action-based groups may be in place and adding their own permissions to the effective permission puzzle. Other Windows mechanisms, such as EFS, may come into play. For instance, if one of your end users has enabled EFS encryption on a file and you are not the Data Recovery Agent (covered in Chapter 13), then even if you have Full Control to the file, you won't be able to read it. Conversely, in order for an EFS user to open an EFS-protected file for viewing, that user must have Read and Write permissions on the file (because EFS decrypts the file upon viewing and rewrites it on-the-fly). This point is important to understand because effective permissions can be harder to figure than meets the eye.

Effective Permissions Tab

In Windows XP and later, Microsoft has included a new Effective Permissions tab (see Figure 3-14). Supposedly, anyone can access the new feature (right-click the object, select the Properties option, select the Security tab, click the Advanced button, and then select the Effective Permissions tab) and easily determine a particular user or group's effective permissions. In the past, all the individual and user account interactions would have to be figured out by the administrator. Now, with a few clicks of the mouse, the administrator can determine the effective permissions of a user or group.

Figure 3-14

Unfortunately, the Effective Permissions tab only works on NTFS permissions. It does consider the effects of Share permissions, action-based groups the user is not currently in, or other factors such as EFS. In this list of missing effects, not considering the impact of Share permissions is most inexcusable. The Effective Permissions tab is a needed but not overly accurate tool. Use it to get a general sense of what the effective permissions might be, but don't rely on it alone when determining critical permission settings. For that, rely on yourself and expertise.

Simple File Sharing

Windows XP has a setting called *Simple File Sharing* that, if enabled, effectively removes most NTFS permissions and sets them to something close to Share permissions. Even then, all connecting users either come in with full administrator rights or as Guest. Simple File Sharing is beyond the scope of this book other than to say you should never have your PC using it. Simple File Sharing causes many other issues, disables a ton of useful features, and effectively guts the security of Windows. It is meant for home users who need simply file sharing, but nearly everyone who knows about it wants Microsoft to remove it.

Current Permission Settings

To understand where you can harden the Windows operating system, you need to understand its current settings first. Table 3-8 lists the default security settings for Windows XP and Windows Server 2003 for the most interesting files and folders (permissions are inherited below unless noted).

Table 3-8

File or Folder	Default Permissions (beyond Administrators, System, and Creator Owners having Full Control)
%SystemDrive% (i.e., C:\ most often)	Users-Read & Execute, Create Folders-This folder and below Users-Create Files-Subfolders only Everyone-Read & Execute-This folder only
\Autoexec.bat \Config.sys	Users-Read & Execute Power Users-Modify
\Boot.ini \Ntbootdd.sys \Ntdetect.com \Ntldr	Power Users-Read & Execute Users have no permissions to these files
\Documents and Settings	Users, and Everyone-Read & Execute, Read, List Folder Contents Power Users-all permissions but Full Control
\Documents and Settings\Administrator	Administrator, Administrators, System-Full Control
\Documents and Settings\All Users	Users and Everyone- Read & Execute, Read, List Folder Contents Power Users-Modify, Read & Execute, List Folder Contents, Read, and Write
\Documents and Settings\Default User	Everyone- Read & Execute, Read, List Folder Contents (inherited) No Creator Owner permissions
\Documents and Settings\%UserName%	%Username%-Full Control No Creator Owner permissions
\Program Files \Program Files\Common Files	Power Users and Terminal Server User-Modify Users-Read & Execute, List Folder Contents
\Program Files\Windows Update	Power Users=Read & Execute, Write
\RECYCLER	Users-Read & Execute, List Folder Contents (inherited)
\System Volume Information	None for non-admin users
\Windows	Users-Read & Execute, List Folder Contents Power Users-Modify In W2K, the Everyone group has Read & Execute

File or Folder	Default Permissions (beyond Administrators, System, and Creator Owners having Full Control)
\Windows\System32	Users-Read & Execute, List Folder Contents Power Users-Modify
\Windows\System32\Drivers	Users and Power Users-Read & Execute, List Folder Contents
\Windows\System32\Netmon\Netmon.exe	Everyone, Users, and Power Users-Read & Execute
\Windows\System32\Spool\Printers	Users and Power Users-Traverse Folder/Execute File, Create Files, Read
\Windows\Tasks	Backup Operators-Traverse Folder\Execute Files, Read, Create Files In XP and later, non-admin users can't create tasks. In W2K, non-admin users can create tasks.
\Windows\Temp	Users-Traverse Folder\Execute Files, Create files and folders Power Users-Modify
\Windows\Regedit.exe	Users and Power Users-Read & Execute
\Windows\Repair	Users-Read & Execute Power Users-Modify
\Windows\Security	Power Users and Users-Read, Traverse Folder and Execute File
\Windows\System.ini	Users and Power Users-Read & Execute
\Windows\Prefetch	No access for non-admin users
\Windows\Help	Power Users-Modify Users-Read & Execute Terminal Server User-Read & Execute, Write
\Windows\System32\Config \Windows\System32\Catroot \Windows\System32\DHCP \Windows\System32\Drivers \Windows\System32\Logfiles	Users and Power Users-Read & Execute
\Windows\Application Compatibility Scripts	Interactive, Batch, Service-Read & Execute

The files under \Windows\System32 have two main permissions, as shown by Tables 3-9 and 3-10. It is interesting to note that the files in Table 3-10 cannot be directly accessed by Users and Power Users, but they can be by the Interactive group, which communicates the necessary Read & Execute permissions for non-Network users.

Table 3-9

\Windows\System32 Example Files with Permissions That Are: Users and Power Users-Read & Execute Administrators, System, and Creator Owners-Full Control
Acledit.dll, Adminpak.mis, Azman.dll, Browseui.dll, Clipsrv.exe, Dcpromo.exe, Diskmgmt.exe, Eventviewer.exe, Gpedit.exe, Kerberos.dll, Hal.dll, Kernel32.dll, Notepad.exe, Ntdll.dll, Ntds.dit,Ntoskrnl.exe, Progman.exe, Rasphone.exe, Rdpclip.exe, Regedt32.exe, Riched20.dll, Runonce.exe, Services.exe, Shell32.dll, Shscrpa.dll, Svchost.exe, Sysedit.exe, Systray.exe, Tlntsvr.exe, User32.dll, Userinit.dll, Win32k.sys, Winhlp.exe, Winlogon.exe, Winsock.dll, Winspool.exe, Wow32.dll, Wscript.exe, Wsoc32.dll

Any authenticated user can Read & Execute these files.

Table 3-10

\Windows\System32 Example Files with Permissions That Are: Interactive, Batch, Service-Read & Execute Administrators, System, and Creator Owners-Full Control
Append.exe, Arp.exe, At.exe, Bootcfg.exe, Calcs.exe, Chgusr.exe, Clip.exe, Cluster.exe, Cmd.exe (doesn't include Batch group), Command.exe, Comp.exe, Convert.exe, Debug.exe, Diskpart.exe, Diskperf.exe, Dsmove.exe, Edit.com, Edlin.exe, Eventtriggers.exe, Exe2bin.exe, Format.exe, Ftp.exe, Finger.exe, Gpresult.exe, Gpupdate.exe, Ntbackup.exe, Ntdsutil.exe, Openfiles.exe, Pathping.exe, Ping.exe, Powercfg.exe, Print.exe, Proxycfg.exe, Rasdial.exe, Rcp.exe, Recover.exe, Redir.exe, Reg.exe, Regsvr32.exe, Replace.exe, Reset.exe, Rexec.exe, Rsh.exe, Rsm.exe, Runas.exe, Sc.exe,Schtasks.exe, Share.exe, Taskkill.exe, Tasklist.exe, Telnet.exe, Tftp.exe, Tftpd.exe, Tskill.exe, Win.com, Wins.exe, Xcopy.exe

Because the Users group does not have access, but the Interactive group does, users connecting over the network (but not using RDP or Telnet), cannot Read & Execute these files remotely.

Interesting Points About Information in Tables 3-8 through 3-10

This section describes Tables 3-8 through 3-10.

%SystemDrive%

The permissions set in Tables 3-8 through 3-10 have the possibility of being inherited all the way down through the file system. The Everyone group is listed here has Read & Execute, *but only* to the folder. By default, the Everyone group has very few permissions to the rest of the file system (despite common misconceptions to the contrary). Creator Owner does have Full Control to any subfolders or files, and this permission is inherited below. Users can Read & Execute files and this permission is inherited below, but users cannot create files directly in the root directory.

Boot Files

Non-admin users do not have access to the boot files. While malware hasn't yet attacked these files, preventing non-admin access gives them additional security if your end users aren't logged in as administrators.

Program Files

By default, normal users only have Read & Execute permissions to the Program Files folder. This means they cannot modify existing programs or install new ones. In Windows NT 4.0, non-admin users could modify this directory and files. Often they had to because of the way applications, including Microsoft Office, were written. The `Compatws.inf` security template (covered in Chapter 14) gives Users Modify permissions if needed for legacy applications. One cautionary warning here: Terminal Server Users have Modify permissions by default. Terminal Server Users is a legacy group no longer needed in Terminal Server 2000 and 2003 versions, but it could still be present and used.

Windows and Windows\System32

As shown in Tables 3-8 and 3-9, by default, regular end users have Read & Execute permissions to all the files and folders in, and below, the Windows and Windows\System32 directories. These permissions are applied to dozens of files regular end users don't need access to. We will tighten those permissions in Chapter 5.

For reasons unknown to me at this time, the Everyone group is given access to the following files: `Calc.exe`, `Clipbrd.exe`, and `Write.exe`. Why did Microsoft single these out for special treatment? I don't know. It is more perplexing that `Write.exe` allows Everyone access, but `Notepad.exe` (even less likely to be used maliciously) doesn't. Just one of those Windows oddities.

System Volume

The System Volume Information (i.e., Sysvol) directory is used in Active Directory, but is installed even on stand-alone servers and Windows XP Pro. In XP, it is where System Restore stores its data. XP will spawn a new "System Volume Information" subtree on every new hard drive volume it sees, although not immediately — so it is usually possible to disable SR for that volume in time.

On non-domain controllers, it can contain miscellaneous items, such as log files. On a domain controller, it will contain group policy objects, File Replication Service (FRS) staging directories and files, user logon, logoff, startup, and shutdown scripts, file system junctions, and the Netlogon shared folder for pre-Windows 2000 computers. On Server 2003, Creator Owner, System, and Administrators have Full Control. In Windows XP, only the System account has access, so not even Administrators can access it.

Other Best Practice Recommendations

The following sections describe some other best practice recommendations.

Give Security to Groups, Not Users

It goes without saying that security permissions should be assigned to groups and not individual users. It can be tempting to assign a permission directly to a user when only one person needs the permission, but when you begin the practice of assigning permissions to individual accounts, you end up losing track of who has what permissions. Instead, follow the AGULP method for every permission assignment.

Don't Overuse Everyone Full Control

When setting up new security, avoid giving permissions to the Everyone group. Instead, make the group you give permissions to as selective as possible. At the very least, this means giving permissions to the Authenticated Users (or Users) group instead of the Everyone group unless you mean to allow guests to have access to your resources. Whenever you get ready to give Full Control to a non-admin user, ask yourself if they really need to change permissions and take ownership. If they don't, give Change or Modify instead. That's probably all they need most of the time anyway.

Set Security Using Special Permissions

Whenever possible, view and modify permissions using the more granular permissions. To access the more granular (i.e., special) permissions, choose the Advanced button on the regular Security permissions window (as shown in Figure 3-10) to reveal the special permissions (as shown in Figure 3-11). Although it may seem like more effort than is necessary at first, it is crucial that you follow this advice. First, by revealing the more granular permissions, you can better understand what the effective permissions are. Second, and more important, I've often seen the more granular permissions reveal something the summary permissions did not. For example, when securing an IIS web server, I kept choosing the Read summary permission. To my dismay, when I checked the underlying special permissions, the Read Data and the Traverse Folder/Execute File permissions were enabled, giving more access than was needed. I've seen similar "disagreements" over the past five years and when I call Microsoft they are unable to duplicate the issue, but I see it every few months. By setting permissions using the more granular settings, you can always be sure about what you are getting.

Summary

Whew, you made it! It is hoped that your understanding of Windows security and Windows permissions is significantly better than when you started the chapter. If you want, review the list of common misconceptions at the beginning of this chapter and make sure you understand why those statements are false. If you still don't understand one of them, review the related security or e-mail me (at roger@banneretcs.com). Chapter 3 ends the first portion of this book, *The Basics in Depth*. Here is a list of recommendations given in this chapter.

❑ Understand all the different built-in groups and users and when they should be used.

❑ Disable delegation on highly privileged users (and any computers) not needing delegation.

❑ On Windows Server 2003 servers required to use delegation, enable constrained delegation.

❑ Make sure the anonymous null session user is not part of the Everyone group (unless you have legacy support issues).

❑ Make sure SIDHistory filtering is enabled in your environment, which it usually is by default.

❑ Use the AGULP method to assign security permissions.

❑ Always assign permissions to groups and never to individual users.

❑ Use the special, more granular permissions when reviewing or setting NTFS permissions.

❑ Set Share and NTFS permissions as tightly as you can following the least-privilege principle.

❑ Use Share Change permissions instead of Full Control.

❑ Use NTFS Modify permissions instead of Full Control unless a user really needs Full Control.

❑ When assigning new permissions, give permissions to the Authenticated Users group instead of the Everyone group.

None of these security recommendations will protect your network if the hacker can crack your passwords. Chapter 4 will show you how to make your Windows passwords uncrackable.

Part II
OS Hardening

Preventing Password Crackers

Windows computers and networks can easily be made very resistant to password cracking attacks. Network administrators can implement a handful of automated security settings and prevent the success of every password cracking tool today. This chapter begins with a discussion of Windows password authentication, reveals how passwords are attacked, and explains how to prevent successful password attacks.

Windows Password Authentication

As Chapter 3 covered, there are four stages of access control: identification, authentication, authorization, and accounting/auditing. When logging into Windows, the security principal (user or computer) provides a unique logon name and password (ignoring other forms of authentication credentials for the purposes of this discussion). The password is a series of characters, numbers, or symbols that should only be known to the entity using the password and the authentication service. When the inputted password is confirmed by the authentication process, it confirms the identity of the security principal attached to a particular Windows session, and the security principal is considered authenticated.

How big can a Windows logon password be? Windows logon passwords can be quite big. A Windows 2000 and later logon password can be up to 127 characters long and contain 65,535 different characters. The character set includes every possible character and symbol that Windows supports. If people actually used all the possible symbols and made very long passwords, it would result in over 4.92×10^{611} possible unique passwords. That's basically the number 49 followed by 610 zeros. It's huge! If it were a crypt key, it would be 2,032 bits of encryption. The young kid in me wants to say something made up like *gazillion million billions*.

NT 4.0 passwords could only be made up of 142 different characters and the maximum password length was either 14 or 127 (many sources incorrectly say 128) depending on the tool used. If the password were set in User Manager or using the Net Use command, password length was restricted to 14, but the user could type in up to a 127-character password when changing in the normal password change GUI (i.e., Ctrl-Alt-Del). As discussed below, however, all NT 4.0 passwords were truncated to a maximum of 14 characters internally.

If Windows users actually used long and truly varying passwords, it would defeat every password guesser and cracker today and in the future. If the attacker had a million computers making a million guesses a second, it would take millions of years to find a correct password. There is not even enough hard drive space in the world, all combined, to store all the possible password combinations that result from 65,535 characters in passwords up to 127 characters long. Of course, most Windows users don't use very long and complex passwords.

Unicode Passwords

Many people think the only characters they can use in a password are the ones located on the keyboard, which totals 94 different symbols if you include both uppercase and lowercase letters. However, using either of the Alt keys along with a number from the numeric keypad (it does not work using the regular numbers above the letter keys) or other programmatic means will result in one of the 65,536 different Unicode symbols. And Unicode symbols can be used in Windows logon passwords.

Not all 65,536 Unicode characters can be created from the keyboard keys alone. Using the Alt key combinations results in a repeating pattern of a much smaller set of Unicode characters. In order to access all 65,536 Unicode characters, GUI-based and programmatic means must be used.

The Unicode character set is a way for operating systems to represent a wide variety of languages and symbols. Behind the scenes, underlying all the symbols and characters we see, is a numeric code. If the user or computer changes fonts, characters sets, or languages, the Unicode number will ensure that the new format representation is accurately reflected in its new form. For instance, a Unicode hexadecimal number 0101 (i.e., decimal 65) will result in a lowercase Latin letter *e*. Whenever the user or computer uses an e in Windows, behind the scenes it is stored as hexadecimal character 0101. If the computer or user changes the font, character set, or language, the e will be translated into whatever other representation it takes in the new format.

You can view many of the possible Unicode characters using the Character Map applet (click the Start button and choose All Programs ➪ Accessories ➪ System Tools ➪ Character Map. As Figure 4-1 shows, the Latin lowercase e is represented by hexadecimal code U+0065. To type in any Unicode symbol into a document or as a password, the user must hold down one of the Alt keys and then select the necessary decimal digits from the numeric keypad. If using the Character Map, the user might first need to convert between the hexadecimal number displayed in the Character Map and the decimal number needed to be typed in, although Character Map often displays the decimal equivalent in the bottom right corner of the dialog box. For a Latin lowercase e, the user would type in Alt-0101. Of course, for the lowercase letter e, the user would be better off typing in the e off the regular letter keys.

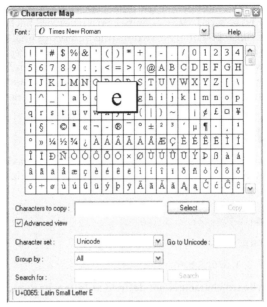

Figure 4-1

Passwords containing Unicode symbols are especially beneficial when the user uses a symbol that isn't already represented by one of the normal 94 keyboard characters that a password guesser or cracker would normally use. For example, the Unicode symbol ω (lowercase Greek letter Omega) can be typed in using Alt+911 (decimal 911was converted from hexadecimal number 038F using the Windows calculator). I've never seen a password cracker use this symbol in an attack. And because typing in an unusual Unicode character requires holding down the Alt key plus up to four other number keys, the idea is that it makes it more difficult for people shoulder surfing for passwords to easily view the password.

There are caveats if you choose to use a Unicode symbol in your password. First, not all systems and software support Unicode characters. Avoid using Unicode symbols on accounts that interface with older operating systems (e.g., MS-DOS, Windows 3.11, etc.), most web sites, and lots of other software that only expect the normal 94 keyboard characters. For instance, the Recovery Console feature in Windows 2000 and later does not allow Unicode symbols in the Administrator's password. Second, if you want to make the password more complex, don't use a Unicode symbol that is represented on the normal keyboard keys. That would just complicate the entering of the password with no increase in password complexity. Lastly, some Unicode characters are converted by Windows into normal alphabetic characters. For a complete list of Unicode characters to avoid, view the document located at `www.microsoft.com/technet/security/smallbusiness/prodtech/windowsxp/select_sec_passwords.mspx`.

The reality is that unless forced, most people use alphabetic characters only, and usually their password is a dictionary-based word (i.e., word, date, or name). So a password hacker doesn't have to cycle through a *gazillion million billion* potential passwords (the number of total possible password combinations if using all possible characters and combinations is known as the *key space*). Instead, the password key space used by a password guesser or cracker is at most a few hundred thousand words. In many cases, passwords can be guessed within a few hundred tries. A weak password will defeat strong security and allow any operating system to fall prey to a hacker. This fact is not lost on Microsoft.

Password Complexity

Starting with Windows XP Pro, increased password complexity is enabled by default. Windows password complexity requires that a user's password be a minimum of six characters long and contain characters from three of the five character types:

❑ **Uppercase letters:** A, B, C...Z

❑ **Lowercase letters:** a, b, c...z

❑ **Numerals:** 0, 1, 2, 3, 4, 5, 6, 7, 8, 9

❑ **Symbols (all keyboard characters not defined as letters or numerals):** ` ~ ! @ # $ % ^ & * ( ) _ + - = { } | [ ] \ : " ; ' < > ? , . /

❑ **Unicode characters**

The password cannot be the user's logon name or contain part of the user's name. It cannot be identical to one used before if tracked by Windows (i.e., Password history). These password complexity rules are enforced on local and domain logins. In a domain, the password policy rules are identical on all computers attached to the domain (although this might change in future versions of Windows). So, when password complexity is enabled or disabled, it is enabled or disabled across the domain and applies to all computers at once.

Windows NT has the ability to require complex domain passwords using an additional file called passfilt.dll (http://support.microsoft.com/default.aspx?scid=kb;en-us;Q161990). In Windows 2000 and later, password complexity can be enabled or disabled using a registry edit change, Local Security Policy, or a group policy object. The latter option is covered in more detail below and in Chapter 14. Local password complexity can be controlled by editing the Local Security Policy. To do so, click the Start button, select Run, type in **Gpedit.msc** and press Enter. This brings up the Local Computer Policy object. Then browse to Computer Configuration\Windows Settings\Security Settings\Account Policies\Password Policy (see Figure 4-2).

Password complexity is enforced when passwords are created, modified, or reset using the normal Windows tools. There are a few instances when password complexity does not apply:

❑ When typing in the Directory Services Restore Mode Administrator's password during a domain controller promotion

❑ Importing user accounts outside the normal GUIs

❑ When creating or modifying the password outside the normal GUI or using third-party tools

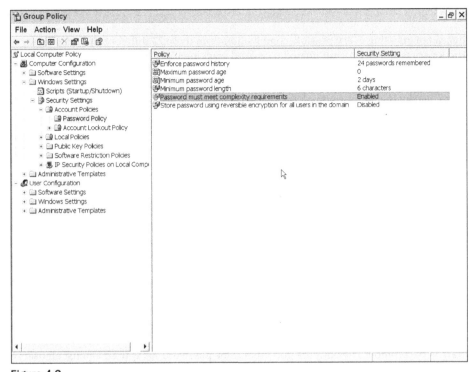

Figure 4-2

Are Complex Passwords Complex?

Even when password complexity is enabled, most user passwords aren't overly complex. Though they can theoretical use 65,535 different symbols, most users limit themselves to the basic alphanumeric character set of 62 characters:

abcdefghijklmnopqrstuvwxyzABCDEFGHIJKLMNOPQRSTUVWXYZ1234567890

And if strong password policies aren't enforced, most users pick passwords six characters long or less, and they choose an alphabetic character password that spells a word that could be found in the dictionary.

Many studies (for example, Microsoft's "The Great Password Debates: Pass Phrases vs. Passwords" at www.microsoft.com/technet/security/secnews/articles/itproviewpoint100504.mspx) have shown that even complex passwords can be guessed because most users employ predictable complex password patterns. Even when Windows password complexity is enforced, users select the basic alphanumeric list above, plus a few symbols. Many alphabetic characters aren't frequently used (e.g., q, x, and z). When users add a number to their password, they most often place it at the end and use the numbers 1 or 2. When special symbols (e.g., !@#$%^&*()?) are used in the password, the most commonly used symbols are !,@, $, and #. The @ symbol is most often used in place of the letter a, and $ is most often used at the end of passwords or in place of the letter s or the number 5. The ! and # symbols are most often used at the end of a password. And still the password contains a complete English dictionary word (on English-speaking user's computers, of course). Thus, a password cracker hoping to crack most Windows passwords need only use a modified character set (this is known as *hybrid dictionary attack*):

```
abcdefghijklmnopqrstuvwxyzABCDEFGHIJKLMNOPQRSTUVWXYZ1234567890!@#$%^&*()?<>
```

And instead of guessing every possible combination from these 75 different characters, they can start with dictionary words. Many automated password cracking tools come with a similar character set installed (covered more below) and crackers can pick and choose between varying character sets and load different dictionaries for the tool to use. Many password cracking tools allow hybrid password guessing whereby the various non-alphabetic symbols and numbers are tried in the common locations discussed above.

Using a Strong Password

A truly strong password has sufficient length (15 character minimum), contains one or more special characters (preferably not the common ones and not used in the common places), and does not contain a complete dictionary word. A user's password should not be easily guessable. For men, this means the password should not be something associated with their hobby or favorite sport. That CEOs use a lot of golf terminology in their passwords is not a big secret. For women, the most common passwords are derived from loved ones, often pictured in photos close to their computer. It's a sexist statement to make, but accurate, nonetheless. Tape backup service accounts often have the password "tape," "backup," or "tapebackup." Other common passwords include the word "password," "admin," "secret," "12345," or something like that.

Many common password lists are available on the Internet, sharing common passwords in use on most networks. The biggest list contains about 80 different passwords. The list is so small because many passwords are very common. The odds are good that if the password list is tried against all users on the network, one of them will strike. Popular computer worms (see http://securityresponse.symantec.com/avcenter/venc/data/w32.gaobot.alv.html for an example) often contain password-guessing routines. Their internal list contains maybe a few dozen passwords. How well do the worms' lists work? The worms successfully infect hundreds of thousands of machines.

Another common password problem is leaving the default password the system or device uses as assigned by its manufacturer. Although Windows doesn't use a default password, many software programs, other operating systems, and network devices do. Default password lists can be found all over the Internet. Example lists are located at www.phenoelit.de/dpl/dpl.html, www.cirt.net/cgi-bin/passwd.pl, and www.pentest.co.uk/documents/default-user.htm. Again, it is almost rare to find a network that hasn't left at least one default password intact.

To recap, a strong password is sufficiently long in length (we will talk more about this later), contains one or more non-alphabetic characters (preferably not in the usual places), is not a complete dictionary word, and is not readily guessable.

Windows Password Hashes

In most of today's operating system authentication systems, passwords are not stored in plaintext or transmitted across the network in plaintext. Plaintext passwords are too easy for a hacker to find and too easy for a network sniffer to capture. Instead, passwords are usually stored in an obscured form. Windows logon passwords are stored in either the security accounts management (SAM) database or the Active Directory database (Ntds.dit) in an encrypted hashed form.

A hash algorithm takes a given input and mathematically produces an output that is unique for the given input. A good hashing algorithm has several properties, including the following:

❏ The same input will always produce the same hashed output (called a *hash*).

❏ Different input should always result in a different hashed output.

❏ No two different inputs will ever result in the same hashed output. If two different inputs create an identical output, this is called a *collision,* and if these can be reliably produced non-trivially, it marks the hash algorithm as weak.

❏ It should be non-trivial to convert any given hash output to its original input.

Hashes are used in all sorts of cryptographic processes beyond storing passwords securely, including being used in authentication and verification routines. Figure 4-3 shows many common hash algorithms and their outcomes given the input string MARCELLA, using a hash calculator function of the hacking tool Cain & Able. MD5 and SHA-1 hash algorithms are used extensively in the computer world to identify specific files, although both have been found to have collision problems and will be replaced by more mature algorithms in the future.

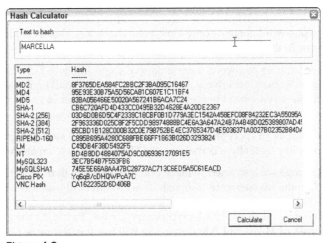

Figure 4-3

When Hashes Are Used

When a user types in a password for the first time, it is hashed and stored either locally in the SAM database or in a domain authentication database. No matter which authentication protocol you use (i.e., LM, NTLM, NTLMv2, or Kerberos) the stored password hashes use either LM or NT hash algorithms, or both. Every time a user logs on to Windows and types in his or her password, it is hashed, but Windows logon password hashes are rarely sent across the network.

LM or NT hashes

Windows logon passwords are hashed using one or two hash algorithms: LAN Manager (LM) and the Windows NTLAN Man (NT). The LM password hash has been used since the days of MS-DOS and Windows 3.11. LM password hashes are still stored by default in every authentication database, including Windows Server 2003 (by default). Windows NT introduced the NT password hash (also incorrectly called the NT hash by many resources). By default, Windows NT and later authentication databases will store both the LM and NT password hashes for any logon password for a user, computer, or service account.

Many sources call the NT password hash the NTLM password hash. This book will use the more common, and correct, NT form to further differentiate the NT hash from the NTLM authentication algorithm.

LAN Manager Hash

Invented by IBM and used by Microsoft, the LM hash is not a strong hash. In fact, it is so insecure and weak that most cryptographic experts refuse to call it a hash. Here's how the LM password hash is created:

1. Even though a password can be up to 127 characters long, the LM hash truncates all characters past the fourteenth position. If the password is less than 14 characters long (which is likely), the password is padded with easy to recognize null characters. This effectively negates the password strength to a maximum of 14 characters (but actually it gets worse).

2. All lowercase alphabetic characters are converted to uppercase. Thus, password guessers and crackers can eliminate all lowercase letters. The 94 keyboard character set is reduced to 68 characters. If the password contains only alphabetic characters, the hacker has only 26 characters to deal with — or 23 if you pull out the rarely used q, x, and z letters.

3. Next, the 14-character password representation is split into two 7-character halves. Each half is then treated on its own, effectively making each password half equivalent to a 7-character password. Therefore, even when the user types in a 128-character password, its effective security is about 7 characters if the password cracker can capture the hash.

4. Each half is used as an encryption key run through the DES symmetric cryptographic algorithm against a *secret* key (actually it is the constant "KGS!@#$%") to create two 64-bit outputs.

5. Both 64-bit strings are combined to make one 128-bit string that is stored as a 32-byte hexadecimal string (but the two separate 16-byte halves are still easily split into their separate origins).

Hence, the LM hash breaks all sorts of hash cryptographic rules, including the glaring problem that passwords, for example, of MARCELLA and marcella will result in the same LM hash. Any passwords whose first 7 characters are identical will result in the same LM hash. Thus, MARCELLA, MARCELL, marchella123456, and maRcellbD all result in the same LM hash: C49DB4F38D5492F5.

To be fair, passwords longer than 7 characters that share the same first 7 characters will result in a second LM hash component that may or may not be identical. But any password sharing the same first 14 characters will always have the same LM hash(es). Microsoft stores a null LM hash (i.e., a fake hash) for passwords longer than 14 characters or if LM password hashing is disabled. The null LM hash is

```
AAD3B435B51404EEAAD3B435B51404EE
```

which is the 16-bit null hash value AAD3B435B51404EE repeated twice. If you see the null hash repeated twice, it means that the password is longer than 14 characters or LM password hashing is disabled. If the password is shorter than 8 characters, only the second half of the LM hash will contain the null hash value — allowing password crackers to estimate password size as above or below 8 characters in size.

To be clear, if a password cracker can capture non-null LM password hashes, there is a high likelihood that they can convert the LM hashes to their originating passwords. An excellent summary of the LM hash algorithm can be found at www.harper.no/valery/PermaLink,guid,8cb9ada6-0f04-4ce0-a1b5-5b9a5f295df5.aspx.

NT Hash

Because the LM hash was so easy to break, Microsoft invented the NT hash. The NT hash overcomes many LM hashing problems. First, the NT hash is case sensitive, meaning it will not convert lowercase characters to uppercase. Second, long passwords are not truncated to the first 14 characters, and passwords are not padded with null characters. Lastly, NT hashing supports the full Unicode character set. Here's how a password is hashed with the NT hash algorithm:

1. The password is converted into a 16-bit Unicode string.

2. The Unicode string is hashed using the MD4 hash algorithm to make a 32-byte hexadecimal string.

NT hashing looks pretty simple, but the secrecy is in the fact that Microsoft used a more cryptographically sound hash algorithm (i.e., MD4) instead of making their own, and they no longer artificially truncate the original password.

NT password hashes have withstood the test of time and so far have not been found to be trivial to exploit. Password crackers have a hard time breaking NT hashes. LM hashes can often be compromised in seconds—the longest I've heard an LM hash crack taking is 1–2 days. NT password cracking, on the other hand, often takes days to months when the passwords are reasonably strong. In Figure 4-4, the Cain & Able program is being used to brute-force crack an NT password hash. As you can see in the figure, Cain & Able is predicting it might take 7.59×10^{10} years of cranking before it discovers the originating password. Note that this example shows the power of NT hashes used with long passwords.

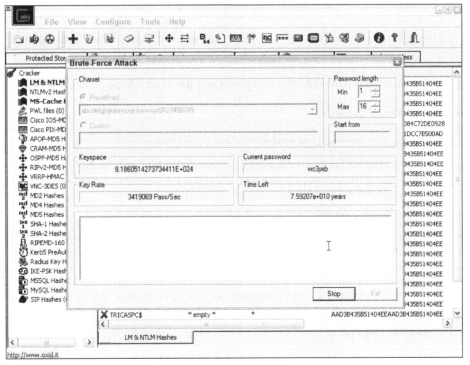

Figure 4-4

Windows Passwords Aren't Salted

A weakness with Windows password hashes is that they are not *salted*. Salted hashes are like regular hashes, except that a random value is added or mathematically applied to the password prior to any of the hashing functions. This ensures that no two identical passwords result in the same password hash. In the Unix/Linux world, passwords are often hashed one of 4,096 different *salt values* and the salt value is stored where it can be easily retrieved. Although retrieving the salt was intended to be easy, it still adds extra protection beyond that afforded to a Windows computer.

Microsoft's choice of not salting passwords has consequences. Extracting hashes (as shown below) can easily be accomplished. If an attacker notices several (non-null) accounts with the same password hash, if they crack the hash, the password is the same on all related accounts. Administrators often use the same password across all their highly privileged accounts. Non-salting makes password attacks easier.

Protecting Password Hashes Using Syskey

Instead of using salts, Windows relies on hash encryption. Starting with Windows 2000, all passwords stored in the local SAM database (but not Active Directory) are encrypted by default. Microsoft created a password hash encryption utility, Syskey in Windows NT 4.0 Service Pack 2, and mandated its use by default in Windows 2000. The SAM password database (located at `\%systemroot%\system32\config` (SECURITY and SAM files)) is encrypted by a master encryption key (64-bit or 128-bit depending on the version of Windows). Without Syskey, the master encryption key is stored in such a way that it is easily accessible to intruders if they boot around the operating system (e.g., using a Linux boot diskette).

With Syskey, the master key (also called the *local system key*) can be protected by the Syskey utility. It has three modes, which indicate where the master key is located:

❑ Local (default). The master key is stored locally in an obfuscated state on the local disk.

❑ The master key comes from the user typing in a password during bootup.

❑ The master key is removed from the system and stored on a floppy drive.

To use Syskey, follow these steps:

1. At a command prompt, type **Syskey**, and then press Enter.

2. In the Securing the Windows Account Database dialog box (see Figure 4-5), note that the *Encryption Enabled* option is already selected and is the only option available. When this option is selected, Windows will always encrypt the SAM database.

3. Click the Update button.

4. Click Password Startup if you want to require a password to start Windows. Use a complex password. The startup password must be at least 12 characters long and can be up to 128 characters long. Note: If you must remotely restart a computer that requires a password (if you use the Password Startup option), a person must be at the local console during the restart. Use this option only if a trusted security administrator will be available to type the startup password.

5. Click *System Generated Password* if you do not want to require a startup password. Select either of the following options:

    ❑ Click *Store Startup Key on Floppy Disk* to store the system startup password on a floppy disk. This requires that someone insert the floppy disk to start the operating system.

❏ Click *Store Startup Key Locally* to store the encryption key on the hard disk of the local computer. This is the default option. Click the OK button two times to complete the procedure.

6. Remove the SAM encryption key from the local hard disk by using the *Store Startup Key on Floppy Disk* option for optimum security. This provides the highest level of protection for the SAM database. Always create a backup floppy disk if you use the *Store Startup Key on Floppy Disk* option. You can restart the system remotely if someone is available to insert the floppy disk into the computer when it restarts.

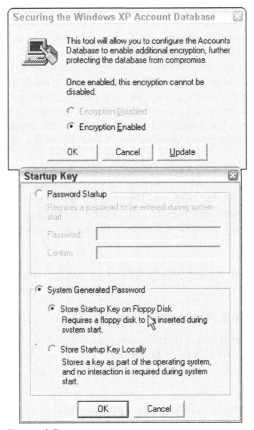

Figure 4-5

It is important to remember that Syskey was invented to prevent local intruders from readily accessing local SAM database hashes. There are some important caveats: First, once the computer is booted up, Syskey provides no protection. Second, Syskey is meant to prevent intruders from stealing passwords, but it does nothing to prevent a local intruder from resetting a password. Unfortunately, all passwords are stored in a known place in the SAM and it is trivial for a local intruder to completely blank or reset a particular user's password (including the Administrator's password). But if a local intruder has this type of local access, there are many other issues to be concerned with as well, and resetting local passwords is just one problem. Third and last, there have been hacking utilities developed that get around Syskey's protections, especially the default mode, but again just refer to the previous sentence. Administrators wanting strong local SAM protection should look into cryptographically sound external cryptographic hardware modules or BIOS hard drive encryption. A common feature on computers today is hard drive encryption built into the BIOS. Another simple protection is to prevent booting on any media other than the primary boot hard drive. Then attackers can't boot around the OS's protections and attack Syskey.

Windows Authentication

Sending password hashes across the network would open them up to network sniffing attacks. The attacker could sniff the network, extract the hashes, and then crack them to find the password. Actually, this is a legitimate form of password cracking, but Windows attempts to prevent this type of attack.

Most of today's popular operating systems don't send password hashes across the network. Instead they use a *challenge-response* mechanism. With challenge-response, when the client wants to log on, it sends a logon request to the local or domain authentication service (along with the local machine, workgroup, or domain name) and request to log on. The authentication service randomly creates a series of bytes (called the *challenge*) and sends it back to the client computer. The client takes the challenge and crypto-graphically manipulates the challenge according to an authentication protocol algorithm, using its password hash as one of the keys, and sends back the result (called the *response*). The logon authentication service runs the challenge through the same process the client used, and if the two results match, the client is authenticated.

The nice feature of challenge-response authentication is that neither the password nor the password hash is sent across the network, but both the client and the server must have the same stored password hash in order to create identical responses. In order for the client to send the correct response, it must have the correct password hash, and have directly inputted the correct password. It's a beautiful system when it works as intended.

> *Challenge-response mechanisms make it more difficult for password crackers to discover the plaintext passwords, but it only complicates the task — it is not impossible.*

Windows Authentication Protocols

Windows computers use one of four authentication protocols: LAN Manager (LM), NTLM version 1.0 (NTLM), NTLM version 2.0 (NTLMv2), or Kerberos.

LM Authentication

Like LM password hashes, the LM authentication protocol was created a long time ago and is considered easily exploitable. The LM authentication process flows like this:

1. The client makes an authentication request to the server.

2. The server generates a 16-byte random number, called a *challenge,* and sends it to the client (called a *Type 2 message*).

3. The LM hash of the password is created.

4. The 16-byte LM hash is null-padded to 21 bytes.

5. This value is split into three 7-byte thirds.

6. These values are used to create three DES keys (one from each 7-byte third).

7. Each of these keys is used to DES-encrypt the challenge from the Type 2 message sent by the authenticating server (resulting in three 8-byte ciphertext values).

8. These three ciphertext values are concatenated to form a 24-byte value. This is the LM response, which is sent to the server.

9. The server does the same calculation on its side, and then compares the response from the client. If the response matches the value calculated by the server, then the client is authenticated.

LM authentication remains a default authentication protocol for backward compatibility issues. LM is used to authenticate to early Microsoft LAN Manager (a pre-OS/2 network OS) servers, Windows 3.11, and Windows 9x systems. It is even used to authenticate Windows CE devices. Several cryptographers analyzed the LM authentication protocol and found it lacking.

NTLM

Microsoft created the NTLM authentication protocol with Windows NT. NTLM authentication works as follows:

1. The client makes an authentication request to the server.

2. The server generates a 16-byte random number, called a *challenge,* and sends it to the client (called a *Type 2 message*).

3. The client creates an NT hash of the password (as discussed previously, this is the MD4 digest of the Unicode mixed-case password).

4. The 16-byte NT hash is null-padded to 21 bytes.

5. This value is split into three 7-byte thirds.

6. These values are used to create three DES keys (one from each 7-byte third).

7. Each of these keys is used to DES-encrypt the challenge from the Type 2 message (resulting in three 8-byte ciphertext values).

8. These three ciphertext values are concatenated to form a 24-byte value. This is the NTLM response. The client sends the NTLM response to the server.

9. The server sends the following three items to the authentication server/service: username, the challenge sent to the client, the response received from client.

10. The authentication service retrieves the hash associated with the user, and then uses the hash to encrypt the challenge in a similar way.

11. If the result and the client's response match, authentication is successful and the DC responds to the server.

NTLMv2

Although NTLM authentication is significantly more secure than LM, another cryptographic review showed it to be trivial to exploit. Microsoft released version two of NTLM in Windows 2000 and back ported it to Windows NT in Service Pack 4. NTLMv2 fixed most of the noted weaknesses in NTLM. The NTLMv2 authentication process is as follows:

1. The client makes an authentication request to the server.

2. The server sends the client a Type 2 message challenge.

3. The client obtains the NT password hash.

4. The Unicode uppercase username is concatenated with the Unicode uppercase authentication target (domain or server name).

5. The HMAC-MD5 message authentication code algorithm (described in RFC 2104) is applied to this value using the 16-byte NT hash as the key. This results in a 16-byte value—the NTLMv2 hash.

6. A block of data known as the *blob* is constructed. The blob includes a timestamp, a client challenge, and other information from the Type 2 message.

7. The challenge from the Type 2 message is concatenated with the blob.

8. The HMAC-MD5 message authentication code algorithm is applied to this value using the 16-byte NTLMv2 hash (calculated in step 3) as the key. This results in a 16-byte output value.

9. This value is concatenated with the blob to form the NTLMv2 response. The client sends the NTLMv2 response to the server.

10. The server sends the following three items to authentication server/service: username, the challenge sent to the client, the response received from the client.

11. The authentication service retrieves the hash associated with the user, and then uses the hash to encrypt the challenge in a similar way.

12. If the result and the client's response match, authentication is successful and the client is successfully authenticated.

NTLMv2 has withstood the test of time and to date no exploits have been announced. NTLMv2 is harder to brute-force attack because it uses a 128-bit encryption key. Most attacks against NTLMv2 are only successful because of weak passwords (weak passwords will always do in strong authentication). For more information, check out `http://davenport.sourceforge.net/ntlm.html`, `www.security friday.com/Topics/ntlm_optimizedattacks.html`, and `http://msdn.microsoft.com/library/ default.asp?url=/library/en-us/security/Security/microsoft_ntlm.asp`.

Kerberos Basics

With Windows 2000, Microsoft created another authentication protocol. This time they picked a widely used open-source protocol created by MIT. *Kerberos* is only used in Windows 2000 and later domains involving domain logins. Local logins use one of the other three authentication protocols.

Writing about how Kerberos works could fill an entire chapter. The complexity, details, and nomenclature is astounding. Most students are introduced to Kerberos and all its complex terminology and end up not learning the basics of how Kerberos works, so instead of boring you with inane detail, this section describes it as basically as possible and leaves it up to you to decide whether you want to learn more about Kerberos.

The MIT version of Kerberos was developed with the authentication services being split among two or more Kerberos servers. In Windows, however, any Windows 2000 or later domain controller in a 2000 or later domain can act as the sole Kerberos server. Kerberos uses symmetric key encryption, and all participating computers' time must be within five minutes of the domain controller's time (by default). Here is a Kerberos summary:

1. The user authenticates itself to the domain controller as it normally would (Kerberos uses the NT password hash).

2. The Kerberos Authentication Service gives the client a token called a *Ticket Granting Ticket (TGT)*, which basically says the client is authenticated and can ask for session tokens. By default, the TGT is good for 10 hours. During this period, the client should not have to resubmit its logon credentials and be re-authenticated to any Kerberized server or service on the network. This minimizes the time authentication credentials spend on the network.

3. When the client needs to access a server process or service, it asks the Kerberos Ticket Granting Service (TGS) on the domain controller for a session ticket.

4. The Ticket Granting Service approves the request and gives the client a session ticket. The session ticket has been encrypted using the remote server's Kerberos token so that only the remote server can read it.

5. The client then hands the server it wishes to access the session ticket.

6. The server validates the session ticket and allows the client to access the process or service.

A slightly more detailed look is the Kerberos Authentication Service (AS) exchange:

1. The client's computer converts the entered password to the long term key.

2. The client computer creates a ticket request and then encrypts authentication credentials that include the current system time with the long term key. It sends this request to the Kerberos Distribution Center (KDC) service (i.e., the domain controller).

3. The KDC looks up the principal and its long term key from the Active Directory database. It uses the long term key to decrypt the authentication credentials, and compares the time against its local system clock. If the data can be decrypted and the time is within an acceptable window of difference, the identity is confirmed.

4. The KDC creates a session key for the client to use in future communications with the KDC. It also creates a user ticket specific to the KDC service that also contains the session key encrypted with the KDC's long term key. It encrypts a portion of the original time authentication credentials and the new session key with the client's long term key. It sends this encrypted data along with the ticket to the client's computer.

5. The client's computer decrypts the authentication credentials (i.e., TGT) to validate that the KDC actually has access to the long term key (i.e., mutual authentication), decrypts the session key, and stores it with the user's ticket in the credential cache.

6. After obtaining the TGT, the user will obtain a Kerberos session ticket for the computer on which the user is authenticating.

Kerberos Ticket Granting Service (TGS) exchange:

1. The client's computer creates a new ticket request for a resource, encrypts new authentication credentials (including a timestamp) with the KDC session key, and includes the user ticket. The data is sent to the KDC.

2. The KDC uses its own long term key to decrypt the user ticket and extract the session key. It then uses the session key to decrypt the authentication credentials. If the two match, it knows that the user was previously authenticated.

3. The KDC then processes the request for the new session ticket by looking up the resource server's long term key. It creates a new session key and encrypts it with the existing session key. It encrypts a portion of the original authentication credentials with the existing session key, and encrypts a service ticket with the resource server's long term key. This is all sent back to the client's computer.

4. The client's computer uses the existing session key to decrypt the authentication credentials, again assuring mutual authentication. It decrypts the new session key with the existing session key and stores it in the credential cache with the new service ticket.

Kerberos Client/Server exchange (the Application Exchange):

1. The client's computer retrieves the session key and service ticket for the resource server. It uses the session key to encrypt the authentication credentials and timestamp. The computer then includes an authentication request, the encrypted authentication credentials, and the resource server service ticket.

2. The resource server uses its long term key to decrypt the service ticket and retrieve the session key. It then uses the session key to decrypt the authentication credentials and compares the time to its own local time.

3. The resource server encrypts a portion of the original authentication credentials and encrypts it with the session key to prove its identity back to the client's computer (i.e., mutual authentication again).

Once authentication has completed, the server creates a local access token for the user that contains the SIDs of the user and any groups to which the user belongs, as covered in Chapter 3. You can use W2K Server Resource Kit utilities such as Klist and Krbtray (`www.microsoft.com/downloads/thankyou .aspx?familyId=9d467a69-57ff-4ae7-96ee-b18c4790cffd&displayLang=en`) to see the Kerberos tickets and keys in the credential cache. Microsoft has also released a Kerberos Network Monitor parser to help interpret network traffic captures of authentication traffic.

The benefits of Kerberos include the following:

❑ Mutual authentication — All participating parties authenticate to each other. Many authentication protocols are only one-way.

❑ Increased password protection because the initial authentication credentials are minimally retransmitted across the network

❑ Replay attack protection because of the timestamps

❑ Delegation of identity — This was covered in Chapter 3. Kerberos allows constrained delegation.

❑ Interoperability — Kerberos is an open standard (although Windows has its own Kerberos twists) and is supported by many operating systems, although interoperability can be a major challenge at times.

To date, Microsoft's version of Kerberos has withstood most attacks. MIT's Kerberos version is found to contain a vulnerability about twice a year. Microsoft's version has had only one report of a vulnerability and that is when the initial authentication takes place. If network sniffers can capture the initial authentication traffic, they can capture the NT hash and attempt to brute force it (covered more below). For more information on Kerberos, see the information at `http://support.microsoft.com/default .aspx?scid=kb;EN-US;217098` and `http://support.microsoft.com/kb/q266080`.

What Protocols When?

Windows 2000 and later can use all four authentication protocols. Windows 3.x and earlier can only do LM authentication. Fully patched Windows 9x and NT clients can do LM, NTLM, and NTLMv2 but cannot do Kerberos. Windows 9x clients need the Directory Services client to use NTLMv2, and NT needs Service Pack 4. Kerberos cannot be used as follows:

❏ With or to connect to Pre-Windows 2000 computers

❏ To connect domain computers to non-domain computers

❏ For authentication between non-domain computers

❏ When connecting to computers outside the forest trust

❏ On LANs where TCP/IP port 88 (UDP or TCP) is blocked between the client and the KDC

❏ For local logons

❏ With connections made with IP addresses only (there is a slightly complicated workaround)

❏ For Routing and Remote Access Services (RRAS) logons

❏ For Windows FTP and Telnet connections (without additional third-party software)

On Windows 2000, by default, Kerberos will be used to connect to any Windows 2000 and later domain controller or domain computer. If a Windows 2000 or later computer connects to an NT domain or a pre-Windows 2000 resource or local computer, it can be forced back to one of the other three modes.

Herein lies the problem. *Windows 2000 and later must use Kerberos and at least one of the other three protocols.* As discussed above, Kerberos and NTLMv2 are relatively secure protocols and should be the only authentication protocols used. Unfortunately, by default, Windows 2000 and later computers can use any of the four, and hackers can often force the older, insecure authentication protocols to be used.

There are many ways to trick a client computer into connecting to a rogue computer without the user's knowledge:

❏ The malicious hacker sets up a rogue web site and sends the user an e-mail with an embedded graphic link. If the user's e-mail doesn't prevent HTML content, when the user opens his or her e-mail, the embedded link can connect back to the attacker's rogue web server to download a small image. The rogue web server can be running IIS and request that the user's computer authenticate to the web server. The web server can tell the user's PC to use LM authentication. By default, when asked to authenticate, Internet Explorer, Outlook, or Outlook Express will authenticate with the user's currently logged on credentials. Today, most versions of Internet Explorer and the Microsoft e-mail clients will not send the user's currently logged in credentials to non-intranet sites without first asking, though early versions would. You can determine whether or not Windows tries to log into remote web sites with current credentials by modifying a setting in Internet Explorer (see Figure 4-6).

Many e-mail applications can selectively suppress the download and display of remote graphics, even if they display embedded graphics and other HTML message features.

❏ The user can be sent a malicious Microsoft Word document with an embedded link to a remote rogue web server. When the user opens or closes the document, a NetBIOS session is initiated to the remote web server. In Windows 2000 and later, the Web Client service will attempt to authenticate if requested by the remote server (see www.securityfriday.com/Topics/winxp3.html for more details).

❏ When a user clicks on Network Neighborhood, Windows will try to acquire a list of every available NetBIOS resource on the local LAN. A properly located intruder could trick the user's PC into authenticating to its malicious server.

❏   On a note related to the previous bullet point, by default Windows XP and later computers will seek out all NetBIOS resources on the local LAN whenever they are started. To prevent this behavior you must disable the *Automatically search for network folders and printers* option under Folder Options and Tools in Windows Explorer.

❏   Many hacker programs (see "SMB Attack Tools," below) can use the SMB protocol to force a Windows machine to incorrectly authenticate to the intruders machine.

Figure 4-6

SMB/NetBIOS

Server Message Block (SMB) is a communication protocol used for sharing files and other resources. Windows' implementation of SMB is called *NetBIOS*, but many operating systems, including Unix/Linux, use SMB (often using an open-source software program called Samba).

Windows NetBIOS works over ports 137, 138, 139, and 445 (Windows 2000 and later) and it is mostly used to map network drives, and to share folders and printers. In Windows 2000, Microsoft added NetBIOS over TCP/IP (NbT), because the original NetBIOS implementation was not easily routable.

Unless extremely hardened, every Windows system has its NetBIOS ports exposed to the network and will attempt to make connections (and accept connection attempts) to and from other NetBIOS computers on the network. Windows spends a lot of its time in the background sending and receiving NetBIOS traffic. It is in a large part how Windows works and how it populates the Network Neighborhood and Network browse lists. Many people are told that NetBIOS isn't needed anymore on today's Windows computers because of the increasing reliance on DNS resolution. This is hugely incorrect. A Windows computer without NetBIOS enabled doesn't communicate well with other Windows computers. Even Active Directory, which is closely tied to DNS, will not install without NetBIOS, and NetBIOS name resolution is still frequently used by Windows for many tasks.

Because NetBIOS is always available on any Windows computer and will activate with the slightest prodding, it is a favorite hacker target. Poorly secured Windows computers will accept, unbeknownst to the user, network drive mappings from other computers. And any Windows computer can easily be tricked into establishing network connections in the background.

Outbound NetBIOS connection attempts usually contain the currently logged in user's authentication credentials in obscured form. Windows authentication protocols (covered below) attempt to protect the authentication credentials from being converted to their plaintext original form by unauthorized intruders. Hackers have a variety of tools and techniques (many discussed in this chapter) to exploit NetBIOS mechanisms.

When any of these behind-the-scenes connections are made, the user's computer can be tricked into making an authentication request to the malicious server. The malicious server can then ask the client's PC to use the LM protocol, which the client's computer (by default) will happily do. The malicious computer can then capture the LM authentication process credentials and easily crack the password. We will discuss defenses against these sorts of attacks below.

Logon Process

During a normal Windows interactive logon, the `Winlogon.exe` process is responsible for managing the security-related user interactions to Windows, including the logon and logoff processes. `Winlogon.exe` calls the `Msgina.dll` (Graphical Identification and Authentication interface), which displays the standard logon box. `Msgina.dll` prompts the user for a logon name, password, and potentially more information, such as the domain name. The Winlogon process passes the inputted information securely to the Local Security Authority process (`Lsass.exe`), which determines whether the logon request must be authenticated locally or against a domain database and whether it requires LM, NTLM, NTLMv2, or Kerberos authentication (see Figure 4-7). Behind the scenes, Kerberos authentication is handled by something called the *Kerberos authentication package*, and the other types are handled by the MSV1_0 authentication package. You will sometimes see those names in the Windows event log, so it can't hurt to know what they are referring to.

One of the authentication protocols (LM, NTLM, NTLMv2, or Kerberos) is used to transmit the security principal's authentication credentials between the client computer and the server. A password hash is used during the authentication process. If the security principal is successfully authenticated, it is assigned a session ID, and the security access token is created (covered in Chapter 3). For most resource accesses from this point on, the user need only hand over the already authenticated identity and access token. The security reference monitor then determines whether the security principal is authorized to access the resource.

If the user supplies the wrong password, when the server being accessed is a domain controller, it contacts the domain's PDC emulator service. The PDC emulator service runs on a domain controller in each domain and is the ultimate storage place of security principal passwords. If a user changes their domain account password, the change is propagated from their computer to the PDC emulator. If the PDC emulator agrees with the server computer that the security principal has supplied a bad password, the server will then send a failed logon message back to the client and write an event to the Security log if so configured. A data field that tracks successive bad logon attempts is incremented by one. If the Account Lockouts (covered below) feature is turned on, and the maximum threshold figure is reached, the account may be locked out for the lockout duration period; although interestingly, in Windows Server 2003, if the security attempted to log on with a password identical to their last previous password (stored in the password history field), the bad logon attempt counter is not incremented.

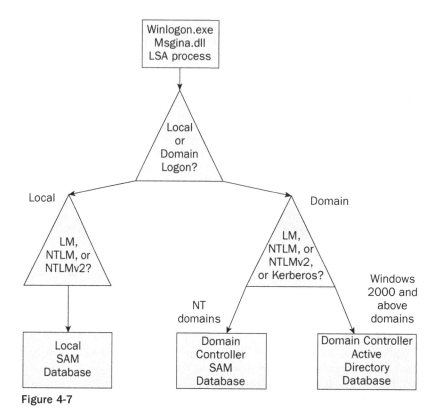

Figure 4-7

Passwords Attacks, Tools, and Techniques

Passwords can be attacked in one of five major ways: reset, guessed, captured, cracked, or socially engineered out of the user. This chapter covers the first four.

Password Resetting

At least once in their careers, most network administrators find themselves locked out of a computer because they don't have the correct Administrator password. Or the administrator is asked by human resources to break into a password-protected Microsoft Word file. Many administrators spend time trying to brute force the password or fiddling around with password crackers when what they really need is a *password resetter*.

Many of the programs claiming to be password crackers are really password resetters. They don't recover the current password, they just reset it to something the administrator creates or the tool just makes the current password be blank. In most programs and operating systems, and Windows is no exception, the location of the password(s) is known or easily found. It is much easier to locate a password and insert your own than it is to try to defeat the password's encryption.

Local Windows logons access accounts and passwords stored in the local SAM database. The SAM database is located on disk at `\%Windir%\System32\config` (SECURITY and SAM files and in the registry at the `HKLM\Security\SAM` subkey and duplicated to the `HKLM\SAM` subkey. The local SAM database (as compared to the Active Directory database) is most often attacked by password crackers and resetters. Because the local SAM is simply a file located on a hard drive, it is possible for attackers to steal the SAM database file, to extract password hashes from it, and to overwrite existing passwords with new passwords.

Domain passwords are stored in SAM database files on Windows NT domain controllers and in Active Directory database files on Windows 2000 and later domains. In Windows 2000 and later domains, all domain controllers in the same domain have a nearly identical copy of the Active Directory database. Active Directory passwords are stored in a file called `Ntds.dit` located in the `C:\Windows\NTDS` directory on a domain controller. Like the SAM database, passwords can easily be located in the Active Directory database when it is offline, although most password resetting and cracking tools only work with SAM databases.

Windows attempts to protect both SAM and Active Directory database passwords against unauthorized access. However, many hacking tools can successfully access these databases to extract the password hashes or to reset the current passwords. In most cases it requires local access, whereby the attacker boots around the Windows operating system and hence its protections, or it requires administrator-level privileges.

Theoretically, any boot diskette that allows you to boot up in its operating system and can read NTFS partitions can reset a Windows password. The attacker boots up on their boot image, mounts the NTFS partition as a read/writable volume, and then modifies the appropriate bytes in the SAM file. The hard part is determining the appropriate bytes for resetting or changing a password. And if you plan to set a new password, you need to be able to write in its LM or NT hashed form.

Nordahl Boot Diskette

Norwegian Peter Nordahl-Hagen gained underground popularity when he created an open-source floppy-sized Linux distro that contained a script automating Windows SAM database password resetting. You can download a bootable floppy diskette or CD disc image from `http://home.eunet.no/~pnordahl/ntpasswd`. Widely known as the *Nordahl boot disk*, its official name is the *Offline NT Password & Registry Editor*.

Once booted, a user must tell Peter's command-line script program which disk contains the Windows SAM file, the path to the SAM file if it is not in its default location, the SAM file name, and whether the password should be blank or changed to something else. In most cases, the user can simply take all the defaults and the password will be reset. Nordahl menus are similar to the following examples:

```
========================================================
. Step THREE: Password or registry edit
========================================================
chntpw version 0.99.2 040105, (c) Petter N Hagen

[.. some file info here ..]

* SAM policy limits:
Failed logins before lockout is: 3
Minimum password length      : 6
Password history count       : 20

<>========<> chntpw Main Interactive Menu <>========<>
```

```
Loaded hives: <sam> <system> <security>

1 - Edit user data and passwords
2 - Syskey status & change
3 - RecoveryConsole settings
  - - -
9 - Registry editor, now with full write support!
q - Quit (you will be asked if there is something to save)

What to do? [1] -> 1

===== chntpw Edit User Info & Passwords ====

RID: 01f4, Username: <Administrator>
RID: 01f5, Username: <Guest>, *disabled or locked*

Select: ! - quit, . - list users, 0x<RID> - User with RID (hex)
or simply enter the username to change: [Administrator]
```

Note that hexadecimal value 01F4 equates to decimal value 500, which indicates that the Administrator account is the true Administrator account. It hasn't been renamed. After selecting the Administrator account, the user will see the following menu text:

```
RID     : 0500 [01f4]
Username: Administrator
fullname:
comment : Built-in account for administering the computer/domain
homedir :

Account bits: 0x0210 =
[ ] Disabled        | [ ] Homedir req.   | [ ] Passwd not req. |
[ ] Temp. duplicate | [X] Normal account | [ ] NMS account     |
[ ] Domain trust ac | [ ] Wks trust act. | [ ] Srv trust act   |
[X] Pwd don't expir | [ ] Auto lockout   | [ ] (unknown 0x08)  |
[ ] (unknown 0x10)  | [ ] (unknown 0x20) | [ ] (unknown 0x40)  |

Failed login count: 0, while max tries is: 0
Total  login count: 3

* = blank the password (This may work better than setting a new password!)
Enter nothing to leave it unchanged
Please enter new password: *
```

After pressing Enter, the script will notify the user that the change has been made and re-confirm that the change should be written to disk. After rebooting the machine back to Windows, the new password should be in effect.

The Nordahl password reset diskette works very well and is frequently updated. There are some caveats, such as it may or may not work with dynamic disks and it doesn't always work. With that said, the price is right — it's free! There are many other Windows password resetting programs, free and commercial, including the following:

- ❏ Winternals Administrator's Pak (`www.winternals.com/products/repairandrecovery/index.asp?pid=ap`)

- ❏ NT Resetter (`www.mirider.com/ntaccess.html`). It is notable because not only will it reset a local Administrator password, but it can re-enable the account if it is disabled.

- ❏ Windows XP/2000/NT Key (`www.lostpassword.com/windows-xp-2000-nt.htm`). A commercial product that needs Windows install boot diskettes to work, but claims to reset domain administrator passwords and work with Windows Server 2003.

- ❏ EBCD-Emergency Boot CD (`http://ebcd.pcministry.com`)

- ❏ Austrumi (`http://sourceforge.net/projects/austrumi`). Another open-source bootable Linux image.

- ❏ O&O BlueCon XXL (`www.oo-software.com/en/products/oobluecon/index.html`). A commercial product that can reset local SAM passwords. Works with XP, 2000, and NT, but does not mention Windows Server 2003.

There is even an article detailing how to install a Linux-based password resetter on a USB flash drive or music player; see http://sl.mvps.org/docs/PasswordResetUSBDrive.htm.

Keep in mind that password resetting is often the solution to a missing or forgotten password problem, and hackers might be as happy resetting a password as they are cracking it.

Password Guessing

One of the most rudimentary ways to crack a password is to guess it. A password guesser could simply find an abandoned computer on the target network, press Ctrl+Alt+Del and begin guessing logon names and passwords. As discussed above, most networks have easily guessable passwords. Most penetration testers will tell you that they have never failed to get into a network by guessing at easy passwords, even when the target company requires complex passwords. The trick is finding input avenues that were overlooked by the administrator and looking for forgotten accounts. It is the rare enterprise that has all user accounts and passwords across the environment managed completely. There is almost always low-hanging fruit somewhere.

Most Windows password-guessing attacks use a remote connection to guess passwords, or they use the command-line Net Use drive mapping method. There are a few simple batch files you can find on the Internet to automate using the Net Use command for password guessing. Here's an example:

```
For /f "tokens=1,2*" %i in (Input.txt) do Net Use *:\\TargetIPAddress\Netlogon %j
/u:TargetIPAddress\%i^
2>>nul && echo Logonname %i Password %j >>Passwords.txt
```

Every password cracking tool is essentially a faster and more sophisticated version of the previous programming logic. In the Input.txt file, the attacker would have potential logon names followed by a space and then a potential password. Each line in the Input.txt file would have a separate logon name and password. If the intruder wanted to guess with multiple passwords using the same logon name, the login name would have to be repeated on multiple lines followed by the possible passwords. Here's an example:

```
Arcserve tape
Arcserve backup
Arcserver tapebackup
```

The resulting `Passwords.txt` file would contain only successful logon events. Unfortunately, manually guessing at the logon GUI or `Net Use` prompt can be slow — less than one per second even when automated by a batch file. Fortunately, there are tools that do faster password guessing. Several programs will answer a user name/password prompt with a predetermined list of user names and passwords. Brutus (`www.hoobie.net/brutus/brutus-download.html`) is one of the most popular.

Brutus

Brutus can do brute-force password guessing on a variety of mechanisms, including SMB, HTTP, POP3, FTP, Telnet, Cisco routers, NNTP, and SMTP. It can maintain up to 60 simultaneous connections. Brutus is a GUI tool, but it relies on two text files: `Users.txt` and `Words.txt`. `Users.txt` is an ASCII text file of the logon names you wish to try. `Words.txt` contains the passwords you wish to try for each logon name. Both files are meager with the default install, but you can download very large text files for both off the Internet. As Figure 4-8 shows, once Brutus is started, you simply choose which authentication method to attack (in this case, SMB) and type in a host name or IP address of the target computer. Brutus will do the rest.

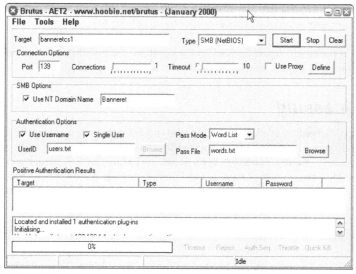

Figure 4-8

TSGrinder

TSGrinder (available at `www.hammerofgod.com/download.htm`) is a brute-force attack tool for Terminal Services and RDP connections. It works in conjunction with Microsoft's Roboclient (`ftp://ftp.microsoft.com/ResKit/win2000/roboclient.zip`) to mimic the keystrokes an intruder would manually take when trying to brute force a RDP connection. This means it connects to port 3389 and sends the normal RDP client connection request commands, and when prompted sends a logon name and password. It works great and you can see TSGrinder grinding away on the remote RDP connection in a nice GUI window. If the remote RDP service isn't running on default port 3389 (as I strongly recommend), you can run the accompanying ProbeTS (`www.hammerofgod.com/download/probets.zip`) or TSEnum (`www.hammerofgod.com/download/TSEnum.zip`) to find the moved ports.

A quick trick to defeat TSGrinder and other GUI brute-force attacks is to enable Windows logon banners (covered in Chapter 14). When a Windows logon banner is turned on, each time a GUI user tries to log on, they are first shown a banner warning dialog box that they must acknowledge to get to the normal user name and password logon prompt. Although it would be trivial to fix, I've yet to see a brute-force GUI attack tool that took the banner warning message box into account. Instead, they trip themselves up waiting for a logon prompt that isn't going to appear without an additional Enter.

SQL Brute Forcing

Microsoft SQL server is interesting in that it supports two types of logon authentication: normal Windows authentication and SQL authentication. There are tools to help locate active SQL servers (and MSDE clients), including SQLRecon (`www.sqlsecurity.com/DesktopDefault.aspx?tabid=26`) and the excellent GUI tool SQLPing2 (`www.sqlsecurity.com/DesktopDefault.aspx?tabid=26`).

Once you find active SQL servers, there are several tools that will automate attacks against Microsoft SQL servers, including command-line ForceSQL (`www.nii.co.in/resources/tools.html#fsql`), MSSqlPwd (`http://packetstormsecurity.org/Crackers/mssqlpwd.zip`), Sqlbf (`http://packetstormsecurity.org/Crackers/sqlbf.zip`), SQL Auditing Tool (`www.cqure.net/tools.jsp?id=6`), and Sqlbf-all (`http://packetstormsecurity.org/Crackers/sqlbf-all-src-1.0.1.zip`). The free tools located at `www.sqlsecurity.com` are among the best password auditing tools in existence.

There are brute-force guessing tools for nearly any application or service.

Password Capturing

Why spend time guessing the password when you can find or capture it? Social engineering is still a primary method for most professional hackers for gaining passwords. Even after all the warnings, help desks are still too eager to help "distraught" users reset their passwords. The problem seems worse the larger the company. Hackers, of course, look through garbage for passwords, and if physically onsite, shoulder surf or look for written passwords.

Keylogging Trojans

Password logging trojans are becoming ever more popular today. Many Internet worms, when installed, contain keystroke logging trojans. The trojans intercept the user's keystrokes as they type in passwords and store the collected information in a file. The hacker can then remotely pick up the file at a predetermined interval, or the trojan can e-mail, ftp, or use instant messaging to send the captured passwords.

An early password logging trojan was called FakeGina (`http://ntsecurity.nu/toolbox/fakegina`). In order to use, the hacker must modify the registry key `HKLM\Software\Microsoft\Windows NT\CurrentVersion\Winlogon` so that its original value of `Msgina.dll` (the legitimate Microsoft password GUI) is replaced with `Fakegina.dll`. When the user logs on using their normal Ctrl+Alt+Del sequence, their password is captured and written to a text file. FakeGina was startling when it was first released, but today there are many such trojans.

Why let all the hacker kids have all the fun? There are dozens of commercial products that brag about their ability to capture every keystroke. The keystrokes can be sent in real time or e-mailed at a later date. To find these types of products, just search the Internet for the keywords "divorce" and "spyware." Here are some links that lead to top-rated spyware products: `www.e-spy-software.com`, `www.netspysoftware.com`, and `www.win-spy.com/partnerlinks/Cheating%20Spouse%20Spy%20Software.htm`. You can't but shudder when you read some of the feature sets.

Hardware Keyloggers

Even more serious are the new hardware keystroke logging products (for example, see `www.keyghost .com`). Hardware keyloggers are small PS/2-looking devices that attach to the keyboard cable between the PC and the keyboard cable. Containing memory chips, they record thousands of keystrokes for up to months. Some hardware keyloggers will allow the installers to remotely download the data from a hidden file, although most require that the hardware logger be physically picked up to retrieve any captured information.

Hardware keyloggers have been involved in several large banking heists and have even been used to capture hackers. Hardware keyloggers are becoming a favorite evidence tool for the FBI and CIA. I've even heard several security vendors complaining about their customers using hardware loggers to capture the vendor's passwords while the vendor was onsite helping in an emergency.

The major distinction of all of the mechanisms in the password capturing category is that they capture the passwords in plaintext. No further computation is needed to find a usable password.

Password Cracking

Password cracking involves capturing the password credentials in a non-plaintext state and then using automation tools to attempt to find the original plaintext passwords. Usually, password cracking is done by capturing authentication traffic on the network or extracting password hashes from the password authentication database on the client or server.

Extracting Password Hashes

Extracting Windows password hashes can be done in one of two ways: offline or online. Offline attacks involve using bootable operating systems that support NTFS partitions to boot around Windows. But unlike the Peter Nordahl boot disk that simply resets passwords, these boot disks allow the user to extract the local SAM or Active Directory database and attack it offline. Once a SAM file has been extracted, there are several tools it can be imported into for analysis, including Cain & Able (`www.oxid.it`), John the Ripper (`www.openwall.com/john`), and LC5 (covered below). These types of attacks can be prevented simply by preventing booting on anything but the primary boot disk, and password protecting the BIOS to ensure that the boot order remains as you set it.

Pwdump

More common is an attacker accessing Windows while the password databases are online and in use. These methods usually require an administrator-level account connection. The most famous free attack tool in this class is called *Pwdump*. Invented by Todd Sabin, it has been taken over by several different programmer teams working independently of each other. Todd's last official version was Pwdump2 (`www.bindview.com/Services/RAZOR/Utilities/Windows/pwdump2_readme.cfm`). Pwdump2 can bypass Syskey protection and download password hashes from Active Directory. The original version could not extract password hashes from Active Directory. It was then upgraded to Pwdump3, which allowed remote extraction (you still need an Administrator-level account), and it would also extract Password History hashes. Pwdump4.02 (`http://pr.openwall.net/dl/pwdump/pwdump4.zip`) is the latest version and it fixes a few bugs found in Pwdump3. Be careful when downloading Pwdump. There are several trojan versions posing as legitimate copies.

Pwdump4.02 can extract password hashes from local or remote NT and later machines and dump the results to the screen (or text file). It accomplishes this by copying and executing a service called `Pwservice.exe` to the target machine and injecting a dll (`Lsaext.dll`) into the `Lsass.exe` process. It then enumerates the user accounts and intercepts the results from Lsass. The target machine must have an enabled Admin$ share, the Remote Registry service must be enabled, and the attacker must have administrator privileges. The output is displayed in l0phtcrack format, which is the industry standard for this sort of thing. Figure 4-9 shows an example Pwdump4.02 result.

Figure 4-9

Pwdump's output is formatted like this:

```
Account Name: SID: LM hash: NT hash: Password History1: Password History2:.
```

Figure 4-9 shows that the account called Administrator is the true Administrator because it has SID 500. The Krbtgt account exists only on domain controllers, so the queried computer must be a domain controller. ExampleW2K3$ is the domain controller's computer account. There are no Password History hashes revealing that either all the accounts are new or the passwords have not be changed since they were initially created. The Guest, krbtgt, and ExampleW2K3$ accounts have the null LM hash value in the LM hash field, but the other accounts don't. This means that these three accounts have passwords longer than 15 characters or they contain unusual Unicode characters. If LM hashing was disabled, all accounts would have the null LM password hash or at least the ones that had changed their passwords after it was enabled (but no account is showing a Password History hash).

A modified version of Pwdump3e, Pwdump6 is available at www.foofus.net/fizzgig/pwdump. However, it is largely untested, and it is unknown at this time how it compares to Pwdump4e's functionality (although it certain that Pwdump6 does not encrypt password hashes sent over the wire).

The Administrator, Elizabeth, and Amanda user accounts share identical LM and NT hashes. This means their passwords are identical. Crack one and you crack them all. Lastly, the Administrator, Amanda, Richard, and Elizabeth accounts all share the same first half of the LM hash field, but Richard has a different hash in the second half. This means Richard shares a common password root, at least the first 7 characters, with the other accounts, but it ends differently. You can learn a lot from a password hash dump. Once the hashes are extracted, they need to be imported into a password cracker.

Sniffing Authentication Traffic off the Network

Password hashes and authentication credentials can also be captured in network authentication traffic. The bare minimum requirement is that the sniffing machine must be able to physically capture the authentication traffic headed between the client and the server. If Ethernet switches are involved, the intruder may need to employ another adjunct tool called an *ARP spoofer*. ARP spoofing allows a third machine to initiate a MitM (Man-in-the-Middle) attack by fooling switch-connected computers into believing the attacker's PC is their intended legitimate target. ARP spoofers do this by flooding the switch and network with fraudulent Address Resolution Protocol (ARP) requests and replies. This falsely tells the involved computers that the IP address of their intended target is the intruder's IP address. It does this by spoofing layer 2 MAC addresses.

Hackers have developed many network sniffers to capture network authentication traffic.

SMB Attack Tools

As the earlier SMB/NetBIOS sidebar discussed, Windows SMB is a favorite hacker target. Dozens of hacker tools have been developed to exploit weaknesses in Windows' most frequently used protocol. Many tools either attempt brute-force password attacks against a particular computer's NetBIOS shares or trick the target computer into sending authentication traffic to a rogue server where it can be intercepted.

ScoopLM and BeatLM

One of the first Windows authentication–specific tools was ScoopLM (`www.securityfriday` `.com/tools/ScoopLM.html`). It captures LM, NTLM, and NTLMv2 authentication exchanges over SMB, NetBIOS, Active Directory, Telnet, HTTP (IIS), and DCOM traffic. Figure 4-10 shows ScoopLM in action. When started, the user first chooses which network interface is wanted for ScoopLM to listen on. Then the user clicks the Start button. ScoopLM will capture all the Windows authentication traffic (minus Kerberos) that it sees. When enough traffic has been captured, the user clicks Stop and saves the resulting data into an importable CSV file.

Then the user imports the CSV file into ScoopLM's companion product, BeatLM (`www.securityfriday` `.com/tools/BeatLM.html`). BeatLM conducts a brute-force attack against the authentication traffic but cannot decode NTLMv2 or Kerberos traffic. In my experience, BeatLM takes hours to days to successfully brute force passwords from authentication traffic, and if special Unicode characters are used it never breaks them.

Other SMB Attack Tools

The SMBRelay tool (`www.xfocus.net/articles/200305/smbrelay.html`) automates a MitM NetBIOS attack and then grabs NTLM authentication traffic and writes it to a text file for later brute-force analysis. SMBGrind (`http://packetstormsecurity.org/Crackers/NT/l0phtcrack/` `smbgrinder.zip`) is an optimized SMB authentication brute-force analysis tool. Attackers import SMB authentication traffic and SMBGrind works to reveal plaintext passwords.

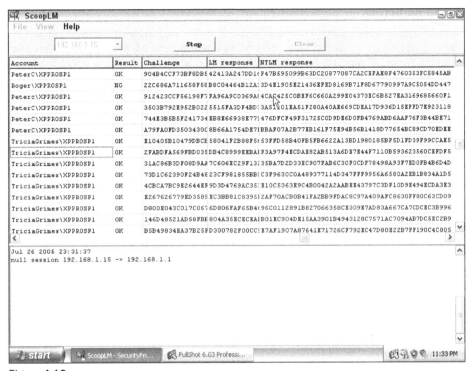

Figure 4-10

The SMB Auditing Tool (www.cqure.net/tools.jsp?id=1) is an extremely fast Linux/Windows SMB brute forcer for ports 139 and 445. It can attempt up to 1,200 SMB connections per second against a NetBIOS host. It scans for SMB servers and automatically enumerates the user accounts.

The SMB Downgrade Attacker (www.ntsecurity.nu/toolbox/downgrade) is a small utility that attempts to force clients using NTLM authentication to use the much more insecure LM protocol.

There are many other password-cracking programs capable of sniffing Windows authentication traffic and then brute forcing it. Both Cain & Able and LC5 are excellent GUI programs capable of capturing network traffic and then processing it. Cain & Able has the added benefit of being able to initiate an ARP spoof attack if needed. None of the previously mentioned tools can break NTLMv2 or Kerberos authentication traffic.

Share Password Attacks

When drive shares are created, they can be password protected. Windows 9x allowed the user to create a "share password" that was connected to the particular share, although most 9x users left it blank. Windows NT and later machines can manage shares using their normal Share and NTFS permissions and require local or domain authentication.

There are several password cracking utilities that attempt to crack Windows password-protected shares. Many computer worms and trojans do the same thing as part of their infection routine. One such utility is the Share Password Checker (www.securityfriday.com/tools/SPC.html). It acquires a list of shared folders available on the network, looks for blank passwords, and checks for old Windows share vulnerabilities.

Kerbsniff and Kerbcrack

The first published tools to attempt to crack Kerberos traffic are Kerbsniff and Kerbcrack (http://ntsecurity.nu/toolbox/kerbcrack). Like ScoopLM and BeatLM, Kerbsniff and Kerbcrack is a two-part program. Kerbsniff captures Kerberos authentication traffic and Kerbcrack then brute force cracks the resulting information. As shown in Figure 4-11, when Kerbsniff is started, it displays an asterisk for each Kerberos authentication packet captured.

Figure 4-11

The resulting text file with the Kerberos authentication information (see below) can then be fed into Kerbcrack to reveal the plaintext passwords.

```
KellyHiggins
LOCAL.BANNERETCS.COM
EDD657042B7CDB68060618FE9B0A29A9FE1387C98FF586946B3D98F762898D0E97926456C6A34857798
6900EDE3324A3AADC6862
#
LeeGrimes
BANNERET
DAF46AF38084F499472DF023303D04AE840CE65DBD5B5A1EF5606B36A91C10C3B493C7E1D680ED01587
CFE95B39FE5C3EF18CAF5
#
KathleenGrimes
BANNERET
F4DA6AF38084F499472DF023303D04AE840CE65DBD5B5A1EF5606B36A91C10C3B493C7E1D680ED01578
E9CF5B39FE5C3EF18CA5F
#
TriciaGrimes
LOCAL.BANNERETCS.COM
4D43FF7F3C35ACF31E817933B5968E7744A7BCF2156C23C4CFD34E45600C82D3503AD06C68020A4B3A9
36F4016D255E66199F5A6
```

Even though Kerbcrack can work through 1 million password guesses in less than 10 minutes on a Celeron 533 MHz computer, even slightly complex passwords seem to provide it a significant challenge. Once I knowingly captured a Kerberos authentication stream with the password of "password embedded" and left Kerbcrack running all day and night. When I came in the next morning, it still did not display the correct password. Kerbsniff and Kerbcrack work, but it will take optimization before it becomes a significant attack tool.

Guessing and Cracking Methods

Password crackers take an encrypted or obscured password representation and attempt to find its plaintext version. Because good cryptography is used to protect passwords, crackers most often resort to intense computations and permutations in their search for the correct password. Five main methods are used in automated password guessers and crackers: brute force, dictionary, hybrid, birthday, and rainbow tables.

Brute-Force Attacks

Brute-force password attack tools grind away at obscured passwords starting with the first symbol in their password list (often the lowercase letter a) and sequential increment symbols until they reach the very end of their symbol list. For example, a brute force cracking tool may try a, b, c...z, aa, ab, ac...az, and so on. It tries every possible combination without regard for what types of passwords are more common. Brute-force password attack tools are the most computationally expensive. They take a long time to work, but if configured correctly will eventually find any password. Every password cracking tool has a brute-force feature. Often the user selects a character set of all the possible characters or symbols it wants the tool to try and tells the password cracker the password size boundaries. Brutus was already mentioned above, but here are some other great password crackers.

Cain & Able

Cain & Able (www.oxid.it) is an excellent free password cracking tool. It has dozens of features and can crack dozens of different types of passwords and password hashes, including LM, NTLM, RDP, Cisco, VNC, MySQL, PWL, Kerberos, RIP, OSPF, SIP, and dozens of others. If you want a tool that nearly has it all in one place, Cain & Able is it. It has one of the best GUI interfaces of any password cracking tool and it's frequently updated. ARP poisoning and MitM attacks literally take a few clicks of the mouse. While Cain & Able isn't always the fastest password cracker, when you throw in its versatility and interface, it's a hard cracker to top.

Figure 4-4, earlier in the chapter, shows Cain & Able in the middle of a brute-force password attack against dozens of loaded LM and NTLM password hashes. The loaded character set consists of the 68 standard alphanumeric keyboard characters, but bigger character sets can easily be added. In this example, a maximum password length of 16 has been set. On most engagements, Cain & Able can find at least a few passwords within the first hour.

John the Ripper

Another open-source password cracker, John the Ripper (www.openwall.com/john), excels at speed. Available in both Windows and Unix/Linux versions, John (as hackers like to call it) works on the command line, saving every spare CPU cycle for computations, not a pretty GUI. It is widely supported by the open-source community, extensible, and supports a wide range of password hash attacks.

As a command-line tool, it intimidates many Windows administrators who would rather use a GUI. Many users are turned off by it and only see it as a brute-force guessing batch file on steroids. Don't be put off: John is the fastest free brute-force cracker in the business. It also has a companion Unix-only product, Distributed John (www.net-security.org/software.php?id=409), which works by distributing the password-cracking workload to two or more computers.

Figure 4-12 shows John the Ripper's overall syntax as well as the start of a successful password cracking attack. John has revealed two passwords, Brooks, belonging to two accounts, including one named Administrator. John cracked the first two passwords in under five seconds. You can stop and start John any time and it will begin where it left off. You can also ask John to calculate the estimated time to crack prior to beginning the analysis.

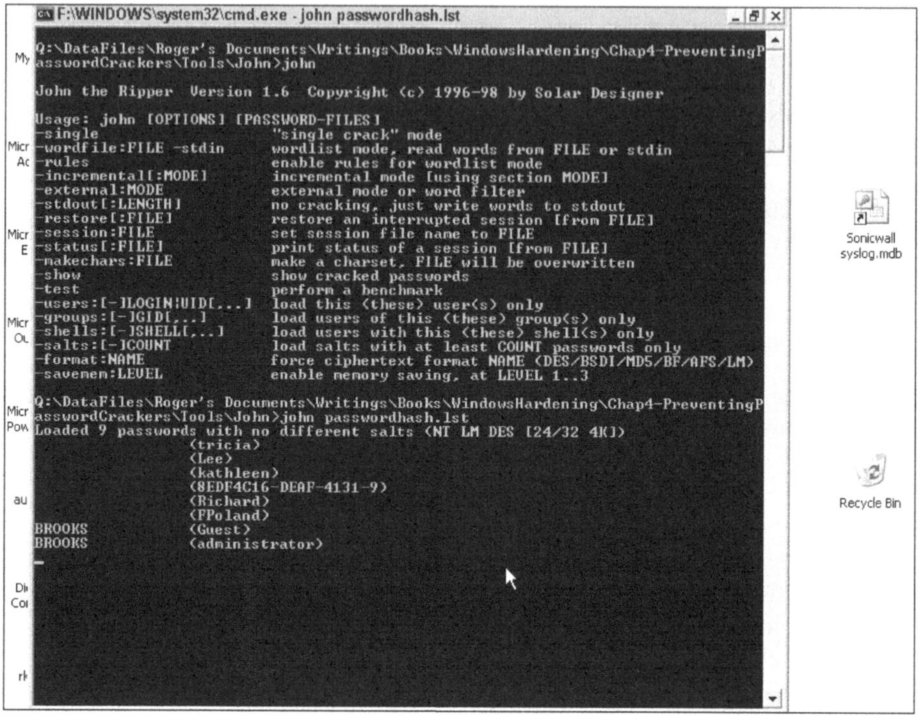

Figure 4-12

There are hundreds of free password crackers available on the Internet. Cain & Able and John the Ripper are at the top of the heap because of their feature sets, stability, and speed. The author of this book has used dozens of password crackers and each cracker has password types that it cracks faster than another tool. Overall, John the Ripper is pretty fast, but penetration testers often run multiple password-cracking tools at the same time. One quickly hits what another doesn't ever resolve. Using multiple tools, if you have the computational power available, ensures the fastest cracks overall.

Dictionary Attacks

Brute-force cracks grind away against the password keyspace without regard for which passwords are more likely to be used versus another. Good password crackers, such as Cain & Able, support dictionary attacks. With a dictionary attack tool, a dictionary (or word list) full of commonly used dictionary words is imported or linked to the attack tool. A good dictionary contains over 100,000 words. You can download huge password dictionary lists from all over the Internet. Some are GBs in size.

You can download specialized dictionaries that focus on foreign languages (e.g., Bulgarian, Yiddish, and Persian), Unicode characters, or themes. For example, one dictionary I've seen contains Star Trek terms and Klingon words. As strange as this sounds, if you know the network administrator is a trekkie, it's a good password dictionary to use. Other themes include common passwords, common phrases, dates, music, literature, names, religion, science, and sports. If you know your target user has a certain hobby or interest, attack them with it.

There are even dozens of programs designed to generate password dictionary lists. To find already generated lists, search the Internet using the terms "password dictionary" or "password word list." Two sites that will get you headed in the right direction are www.packetstormsecurity.org/Crackers/wordlists and www.geocities.com/SiliconValley/Port/5886/Dict.html??200523.

Hybrid Attacks

Hybrid attacks blend brute force and dictionary methods in an intelligent way. The hybrid method assumes that most users will still use as much of a dictionary word as possible even when forced to make the password complex. Hence, a hybrid attack will often do the following to a normal dictionary search:

- ❑ Substitute uppercase and lowercase letters throughout the dictionary word randomly
- ❑ Spell dictionary words backwards, with reverse spelling
- ❑ Add one or two numbers to the end of the dictionary word
- ❑ Add special symbols throughout the dictionary word, often substituting @ for a, and 5 for S, etc.

Cain & Able has the hybrid function built into its dictionary attack.

Birthday Attacks

Yet another methodology change often appears in password crackers: that of the *birthday attack*. Birthday attackers start by using one of the other methods (i.e., brute force, dictionary, or hybrid), but then randomly choose password attempts instead of sequentially cycling through from the beginning to the end of the potential password keyspace. The idea is that by randomly guessing, the password cracker is more likely to stumble upon the correct password than by using a sequential method.

The birthday attack gets its name from a mathematical theory that states that although the odds of any one person having a birthday on any particular day of the year is 1 in 365.25, when two random people compare birth dates, the odds of them sharing the same birthday are half of that. And as you add people into the mix, each additional person halves the odds. At the addition of the 18th person, the odds of two people having the same birthday (not including the year) approaches 50%. In demonstrations of this theory, the author frequently conducts the "birthday experiment" in his classes and lectures. Rarely has he had to reach the 18th student to find a birthday match. Many times, matches are made in the first few people.

Rainbow Tables

For a long time, password cracking theory involved optimizing the previous four methods and relying increasingly on more computing power to crack difficult passwords. Then someone stumbled upon the idea that has changed the current field of password cracking dramatically. Password cracking is difficult because password hashes, although known, are non-trivial to convert back to their original non-hashed password forms.

But what if all the possible hashing outcomes (millions and millions) were pre-computed and placed into a table? Basically, the password cracker takes a word list of all the possible password values and runs them through the hashing routine. Each result is stored along with the plaintext password that made the hash. When a hash is found, the password cracker need only look up the stored pre-computed password hash to find the original password. The first very popular implementation of this method was called *rainbow tables* and the name has stuck ever since.

The results were astounding. Good rainbow tables are GBs and GBs in size and contain billions of pre-computer password hashes. When a user plugs in a non-complex LM hash (which is what most networks are full of) the rainbow table program "breaks" the password in seconds. There are several online demonstration programs where you can plug in a password hash to see the outcome, including `http://lasecwww.epfl.ch/~oechslin/projects/ophcrack/index.php#Demo`. It has cracked thousands of passwords, most in under two seconds.

There are also optimized rainbow table programs that are pretty fast at cracking weak passwords. The Ophcrack (`http://ophcrack.sourceforge.net`) is probably one of the most popular. It comes with free 388MB and 720MB optimized rainbow tables for users to begin experimenting with. You can buy GB tables off the Internet and on eBay for prices ranging from $20 to $200.

You can even generate your own rainbow tables. Another popular rainbow table cracker is Rainbowcrack (`www.antsight.com/zsl/rainbowcrack`). Run by the Project Rainbow team, it enables users to generate their own rainbow tables. Demos have been shown using tables up to 36 GB in size. Thousands of people around the world are running clustered computers simply churning out larger and larger rainbow tables. In order to be faster and more accurate, the rainbow tables have to be larger and larger — to the point that available processing power, memory, and hard drive space is a consideration of every active rainbow cracker. The average PC starts to get bogged down when trying to create rainbow tables for passwords six characters or longer. A rainbow table with all the seven-character or less possible passwords would take several years to generate on the average PC. With that said, plenty of people have computed most LM password hashes to 14 places and are working on the NT hash keyspace.

The holy grail of Windows password hash cracking would be realized if a single database could hold every possible LM and NT hash and its plaintext equivalent (remember 4.92×10^{611} possible passwords). Currently it is computationally infeasible, because of computational and storage requirements, and probably will be impossible for the foreseeable future. But rainbow table makers realize that they don't need every possible password to be mostly successful, just the most likely passwords. Hence, they are falling back on the other four methods to choose the most likely candidates, and cryptographic scientists are coming up with optimization techniques.

Although rainbow tables can be frightening to network administrators, long, complex passwords beat them. Most rainbow tables can only break LM hashes, so if you disable them, your password hashes are relatively safe. If you make your passwords sufficiently long enough (say, 15 characters), and even slightly complex, few rainbow tables can break them.

LC5 and LCP

@Stake's commercial LC5 password-cracking program was considered the premier Windows password-cracking program for the professional enterprise. Its GUI interface, ease of use, and cracking and reporting capabilities made it a solid choice for password auditing, if you could afford it. Unfortunately, it was purchased by Symantec in 2004 and then discontinued in late 2005. If you are lucky enough to have a recent copy, it remains a top choice for cracking Windows passwords, at least until Windows password technology changes.

Currently, there are no other commercial programs for the enterprise on a par with LC5, although some company is sure to fill the void in the future. There is a relatively new program called LCP (`www.lcpsoft .com`), which appears to be a near clone of LC5, or a previous version (see Figure 4-13). It works almost identically to LC5, but contains a few bugs and is not nearly as trusted as LC5. The author of this book attempted to contact LCP's author via e-mail, but did not receive a reply. Because it has not been thoroughly reviewed for bugs and other potential issues, readers should be cautious when testing this program. For example, run it isolated in a virtual session until it becomes more trusted, or don't run it at all.

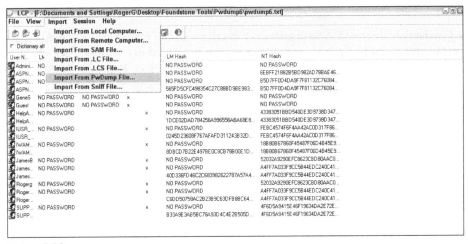

Figure 4-13

Password-Cracking Programs

There are literally hundreds of password cracking/recovery programs, one for nearly every program that uses passwords. Here is a partial list of the application programs with password-recovery programs available (this list isn't bulleted to save space): MS-Access, ACT, AIM, Apache, ArcServe, BIOS passwords, Cheyenne Innoculan, Cisco routers, CompuServe, EFS, MS-Excel, FTP, Hotmail, Intuit Quicken, IRC, Lotus, Lotus Notes/Domino, MySQL, MSN Messenger, Norton Antivirus, Novell Netware, MS-Office, OpenLDAP, Oracle, MS-Outlook, password-protected Outlook PST files, Palm PDA's, PDF, PGP secret keys, POP, PPP, PPTP, printers, RAR, RDP, Real Media server, routers, Shockwave, SSH, MS-SQL, Telnet, Terminal Services, VBA, web cams, brute force web site guesser, WEP, MS-Word, VNC, Wingate, WordPerfect, Yahoo news tickers, and Zip files.

One of my favorite sites to search for password crackers is `www2.packetstormsecurity.org`. Visit there and then search on any type of password cracker or resetter that you need. My general search returned over a 1,000 different programs, most of them free or open source. In my review, I found that perhaps only 50% would work on current and patched systems, but that is still a lot of hacker programs.

Other Types of Password Attacks

There are a lot of password mechanisms in Windows, which means a lot of passwords to be used and stored. A password cracker looks for passwords anywhere they can find them. Here are some common Windows password mechanisms and locations...

Cached Credentials

By default, Windows 2000 and later computers will locally cache the last 10 domain user credentials used to log on to a domain. Windows will allow up to 10 different user profiles to log on using cached credentials if the domain controller isn't available. The last 10 user profiles will be allowed to log on as many times as their want without interruption. Microsoft created cached credential storage in case the domain controller was down or too busy to respond. It is the cached credential feature that allows laptop users logged into their domain accounts to unplug from the network and continue to log onto their laptop, using their domain accounts (of course, any network resources will not be available).

Cached credentials are stored in the registry key HKLM\Security\Cache\NL$n, where n represents a number between 1 and 10. Cached logon passwords are not stored in clear text. They are encrypted using DES, RC4, and HMAC_MD5 cryptology algorithms, and the password hash is even salted with the user's username in Unicode form. These cached password hashes can be recovered and cracked using a program capable of cracking cached credential hashes. The domain Administrator account is almost always one that is present in the cache. This means a local admin can recover the domain admin's password. Recovering cached credentials is especially useful on shared or kiosk machines.

Cachedump (www.off-by-one.net/misc/cachedump-1.1.zip) is one such utility. It works by starting a new service on the fly and reading the Lsass.exe process' static encryption key from memory. The stolen key is then used to extract the cache credential values. In order for Cachedump to work, you must be logged on locally as an administrator and run the program from a local drive. Of course, there must be cached credentials to discover.

When successful, Cachedump returns the name and password hash of the cached credentials (see Figure 4-14). The extracted password hashes are not the same as the LM or NTLM password hashes, and they can only be converted to their plaintext password equivalents using a password-cracking tool that understands cached credential password hashes. John the Ripper (www.openwall.com/john), one of the best and most popular password hash crackers, can be modified to crank on cached credential password hashes (www.banquise.net/misc/patch-john.html). Also, although it is not readily apparent, two of the user accounts in Figure 4-14 share the same password, but you can see that all the password hashes are different. This is due to the salting, which, unfortunately, is not done with the normal LM and NTLM password hashes.

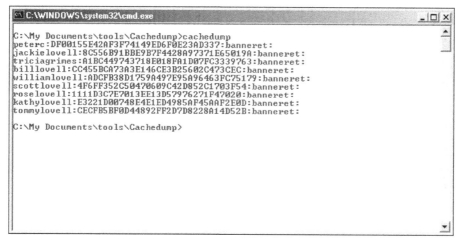

Figure 4-14

The cached logon feature can be disabled or limited using a GPO or registry entry. The number of cache logons allowed is set in the registry key HKLM\Software\Microsoft\Windows NT\CurrentVersion\ Winlogon\cachedlogonscount. In GPOs, you can find the similar setting at Computer Configuration\ Windows Settings\Security Settings\Local Policies\Security Options\Interactive logons: Number of previous logons to cache (in case domain controller is not available). The default value is 10. If set to 0, it disables cache logons all together. You should either disable cached logons or limit them to a smaller number of accounts — say, 1 to 3. Disabling cached logons completely might cause troubleshooting problems if the domain controller is down.

Computer Accounts

Don't forget that domain computer accounts also have logon names and passwords, although the passwords and password changes (every 30 days by default) are controlled by the domain controller. As shown in Chapter 3, computer accounts belong to many security groups by default, including the Everyone and Domain Computers group. There hasn't been a reported instance of a computer account and its password being used to compromise a network, but theoretically it could be done.

Service Accounts

Service accounts are normal logon accounts just like user accounts, but they have the *Log on as a service* user privilege. This allows the service account to log on and authenticate soon after Windows starts and prior to any user logging on. It also gives the service controller manager (Sc.exe) the ability to initiate each service account's logon and authentication. Each service account logs on using a logon credential as defined in its Log On tab in the Services console (Figure 4-15 shows an example).

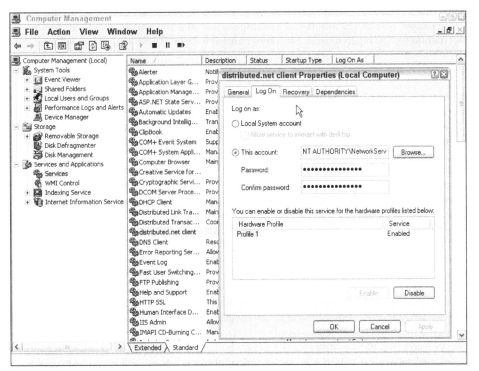

Figure 4-15

Most services use local SAM accounts, although some services may use domain-based accounts. Domain-based service accounts can use any authentication protocol to authenticate, including Kerberos. Most service accounts are installed when Windows is installed, and most use the highly privileged account Local System (although XP and later added LocalService and NetworkService service accounts and they are becoming more popular). Additional service accounts can be made manually, but most new service accounts are made when the administrator is installing software that requires a service account (such as tape backup software).

Service accounts are unique in that their logon names and passwords are not only stored in the local SAM or Active Directory database but also in local protected storage on the computer where the service resides. The local protected credential database is known as *LSA secrets*. The LSA stands for link state algorithm and the `Lsass.exe` process controls access to and from the LSA secrets. The LSA secrets storage area is located in the registry at `HKLM\Security`, but it normally isn't accessible to any user, even a local administrator—although if you can get in as Local System you can usually access it.

The LSA secrets storage area stores many things, including service account names and passwords, RAS credentials, dial-up networking account credentials, and FTP passwords. When you change a service account's password, you must change it in two places: the authentication database and the LSA secrets cache. Custom service account passwords (and many other passwords) are stored in plaintext in the LSA secrets cache storage area.

> *You cannot easily change the password of the default three service accounts (i.e., LocalSystem, LocalService, and NetworkService) and you should not manually change those passwords.*

Infamous whitehat hacker programmer Todd Sabin created the excellent Lsadump2 tool (`www.bindview .com/Services/razor/Utilities/Windows/lsadump2_readme.cfm`) for dumping the LSA secrets. Figure 4-16 shows Lsadump2 in action. Lsadump2 will dump the LSA secrets cache to screen although the information can be piped to a file for later analysis; for example:

```
Lsadump2 >lsasecrets.txt
```

In order to use Lsadump2, you must be logged in interactively on the machine you wish to examine and have the *Debug Programs* user privilege, which usually only administrators have. Lsadump must be executed from a local directory (it does not work over remote network drive shares). If successful, it dumps the LSA secrets in a somewhat raw format that can be a little difficult to decipher at first glance. Information is dumped a secret at time. The service account names and other names (e.g., RasCredentials) found are on the left (often followed by the SID). Service account names will often begin with _SC_. In Figure 4-16, the Fax Service service account name is _SC_Fax. Its password follows: B.r.a.g.3.3.f.r.o.g. You need to remove the separating periods to reveal the true password of Brag33frog. The service account's name will not be visible, so you have to go to the Services console and review the service's Log On tab to discover the service account's name.

If you need to be logged in as administrator in order to run this utility, you might wonder what benefit dumping the LSA secrets cache gives you. First, many, if not most, service accounts have full administrator privileges to the entire domain. This is certainly true of tape backup and antivirus service accounts. Plus, SQL server service accounts are also stored here. Thus, by simply being a local administrator (or regular user account with Debug Programs privileges), you can find out domainwide administrator accounts. And because changing passwords in service accounts requires two password changes for every service account, most administrators never change their passwords. What a juicy target: highly privileged, domainwide accounts with passwords that rarely change. It's a password cracker's dream.

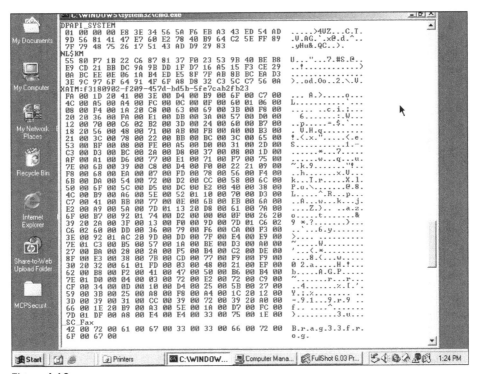

Figure 4-16

There are other password-cracking tools besides Lsadump2 that can dump the LSA secrets cache store, including Cain & Able. Lsadump2, and other tools like it, do not appear to work well on XP Pro Service Pack 2 or Windows Server 2003 Service Pack 1 and later machines. Microsoft must be addressing the weaknesses that allow these types of tools to work.

Credential Manager

Starting with Windows XP, Microsoft created a new password management mechanism called *Credential Manager*. It is used to store all sorts of other Windows password credentials (logon name and password), including those for drive shares, web sites, the RunAs/SaveCred feature, and .NET. Essentially any application that wants to use it can use it. The application need only use the Credential Manager API, and the Windows Credential Manager will securely store the passed credentials, and retrieve them when prompted.

Most users and administrators don't even know it exists, but if they have ever said yes to saving a password for automatic logging on, they have probably used it. To access the Credential Manager, a user needs to go to the User Accounts control panel applet and choose the Advanced tab, and then select the Manage Passwords button (see Figure 4-17). There the user can view, edit, and delete saved credentials. You can also use the third-party utility ClearCredCache (www.harper.no/valery/ct.ashx?id=deba 3b20-9d29-440f-b7bb5a61c50bd99d&url=http%3a%2f%2fwww.harper.no%2fvalery%2fcontent %2fbinary%2fClearCredCache.zip), written by a Microsoft MVP, to quickly clear all credentials.

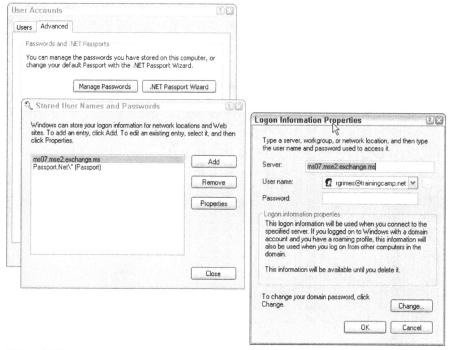

Figure 4-17

The protected credentials are stored in the user's profile (local or roaming) at `\Documents and Settings\%Username%\Local Settings\Application Data\Microsoft\Credentials\ %UsersSID\Credentials` or at `\Documents and Settings\%Username%\Application Data\Microsoft\Credentials\%UsersSID\Credentials`. These file locations aren't easily accessible to the normal end user.

Data Protection API

The Credential Manager credential database is protected by Microsoft's Data Protection API (DPAPI). DPAPI replaces Microsoft's earlier protection mechanism called Protected Storage. DPAPI protects other things besides the Credential Manager database, such as EFS private keys, S/MIME certificates, and other digital certificates. DPAPI uses a master key to protect valuable authentication credentials. The master key is at least 512 bits long, but in Windows Server 2003 domain controllers (at native domain mode or higher) it is 2,048 bits in length. By default, the master key is changed every 90 days.

Even though DPAPI is a secure, reliable technology, like the logon credential cache, the Credential Manager cache is exploitable by a logged on user with administrative permissions. You can use Cain & Able to view the saved credentials in clear text (see Figure 4-18) or use its stand-along utility, CredDump (`www.oxid.it/creddump.html`).

Because stored credentials are often common among varying resources (the logon name and password used in one location is often used in multiple places), finding a password here can lead to wider exploits.

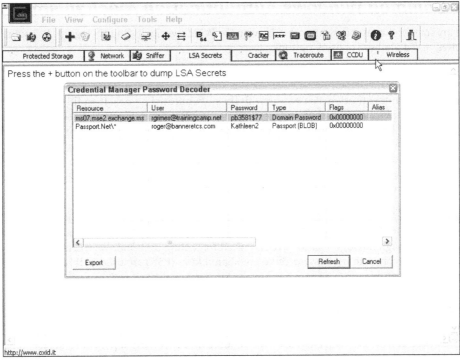

Figure 4-18

RDP Connection Objects

The Remote Desktop Protocol (RDP) is used to connect to several Microsoft Terminal Services technologies, including Terminal Services, Remote Desktop, and Remote Assistance. If an RDP connection is made frequently, Microsoft allows an RDP Connection object (click Start ⇨ All Programs ⇨ Accessories ⇨ Communications ⇨ Remote Desktop Connection) to be created so that in the future the user need only click on the icon to launch an RDP connection. RDP traffic is encrypted by default so that the remote logon password is never sent in clear text.

Although it is not the default, users can save their remote logon password with their connection object so that they do not need to enter the password to connect. If the password is saved, the Cain & Able program, using its RDP Decoder feature, will quickly reveal any saved passwords. It will reveal any RDP connection stored password in seconds, regardless of its complexity or length. An intruder would need local administrative access to use the RDP decoder, but the process is simplified greatly using Cain & Able. For this reason, you should not store passwords with your RDP connections.

Windows 9x and ME logon passwords are stored in PWL files using RC4 encryption. There are several password-cracking tools that will attempt to recover the passwords stored in PWL files, including Advanced Windows Password Recovery (www.tomdownload.com/utilities/security_encryption/advanced_windows_password_recovery.htm), Pwl Tools (http://lastbit.com/vitas/pwltool.asp), and Unix-based Windows 9x Password List reader (http://freshmeat.net/projects/pwl9x). If attackers can't recover user passwords from PWL files, they can delete the PWL file (essentially getting rid of the password protection) or create their own PWL files (just search on "PWL file creation" using any Internet search engine). PWL files are not used in Windows NT, 2000, XP, or later.

Other Common Windows Authentication Mechanisms

There are many other authentication mechanisms in Windows, including IIS logons, Password Reset Diskettes, and a plethora of other options.

IIS Logons

Windows logon authentication also occurs with IIS authenticated logons. If an IIS web site is not selected to require anonymous logon authentication, a connecting Windows client might send its current user credentials using LM, NTLM, NTLMv2, or Kerberos authentication. In Internet Explorer 6, the browser will only send anonymous credentials to non-intranet servers (see Figure 4-6 again), and will prompt the user before it sends non-anonymous credentials. On web sites (legitimate or not), the user's current credentials will be sent by default (older IE versions sent authenticated credentials by default to all IIS servers, even the ones requiring anonymous connections).

Other places that Windows users may be required to type in logon credentials is RRAS connections, locked screensavers, SQL databases, Outlook and Outlook e-mail connections, and SharePoint services. Passwords, although not logon passwords, are used for setting up Windows trusts, Cluster Services, and IAS client server connections. Passwordlike pre-shared keys (PSK) are used in IPSec, Radius, WEP, and 802.1x communications.

Password Reset Diskette

Stand-alone XP Pro systems can also store their local logon password on a diskette, called the *Password Reset Diskette*. It can be used when the user doesn't remember her current password to reset the password back to a previous password saved on the disk. When enabled (it's enabled in the Ctrl+Alt+Del dialog box), the user will be prompted for their Password Reset Diskette whenever they type in their password wrong. It's also a clue to a local intruder to look for the diskette when trying to do a local logon attack. To date, there are no publicly known crack attacks against the credentials stored on the diskette.

Password Authentication Mistakes

The media frequently reports on passwords sent in plaintext across the network, plaintext passwords visible in temporary files, or default blank passwords. Although Microsoft was famous for leaving plaintext passwords in temporary files, they have gotten significantly better over the years. Still, Dr. Watson memory dumps often contain plaintext passwords or password hashes.

In July 2005, SecuiTeam (`www.securiteam.com`) revealed that Dell-installed XP Pro computers have a hidden administrator account with a blank password (`www.securiteam.com/windowsntfocus/5KP091PGBO.html`). Many popular programs have been caught with password mistakes. For instance, although Microsoft Word allows a document to be password protected, at least two flaws have been found in Word's password protection scheme.

The first flaw is that Word uses RC4 symmetric encryption but does not randomly change what is called the *initialization vector (IV)* between document saves. This is a basic crypto flaw. It allows someone to save a protected identical document twice, and when the two documents are compared to each other using an XOR algorithm, the RC4 symmetric encryption key is rendered (`www.schneier.com/blog/archives/2005/01/microsoft_rc4_f.html`). The second issue is that any protected Word document can be opened in a text editor and the password simply blanked out (`www.tech-faq.com/word-password-recovery.shtml`). Microsoft is far from the only vendor to have problems with cryptographic routines, but it shows that even the largest companies with the best resources make mistakes. Creating new cryptographic routines takes extensive expertise, testing, and competent reviewers.

Let's not forget all the other places where passwords can be used and stored. Many web sites require logon names and passwords. Computers can require bootup or BIOS configuration passwords. PDAs and cell phones can have passwords. Routers and network devices have passwords. Many applications like Microsoft Office have passwords.

Island Hopping

The reason all these other passwords matter is that users often use the same or nearly identical passwords across multiple locations. The network administrator might institute the strong password protections possible in the world, but if the user uses the same password to manage their e-Bay account or to purchase online porno, the strength of the password is only as strong as every place it is stored. Hackers frequently setup bogus web sites asking users to establish login names and passwords. Then those credentials are used to break into the employee's work site, which they happily provided when applying to the online web site. When a hacker learns about a password in one location and uses it successfully to compromise a new location, it is called *island hopping*.

Create a password policy and encourage your users to use different passwords for personal use than they use at work. Consider requiring different passwords for the computer resources with the most value in your organization. Having separate passwords for different applications on the same network is counterintuitive to the single-sign-on push occurring in most organizations, but ease of use has to be measured against the subsequent risk from password island hopping.

Defending Against Password Attacks

With password hacking so prevalent, what's a network administrator to do? The typical Windows administrator can institute just the first five of the following steps and significantly decrease the password-cracking risk.

Disable LM Password Hashes

One of the single best things any network administrator can do is disable the storage of LM password hashes and force users to change their passwords after LM hash storage is disabled. This can be done several ways, including registry entry and GPO policy. To enable the disabling of LM password hash storage, in the GPO or local computer object, locate the option `Computer Configuration\Windows Settings\Security Settings\Local Policies\Security Options\Network Security:` *Do not store LAN Manager hash value on next password change* and enable.

You can also disable the storage of LM Manager hashes by requiring all passwords to be 15 characters or longer. Unfortunately, to date, Windows only allows the maximum size of the minimum password field to be set to 14 characters. This will change in future service packs and versions of Windows. Passwords longer than 14 characters will also confound password crackers and rainbow tables. The longer your password, the more difficult it will be to crack.

You can also disable LM hash storage by using certain Unicode characters. Table 4-1 shows the Unicode Alt character codes that cause the LM hash to be disabled.

Table 4-1

0128-0159	0306-0307	0312	0319-0320
0329-0331	0383	0385-0406	0408-0409
0411-0414	0418-0424	0426	0428-0429
0433-0437	0439-0447	0449-0450	0452-0460
0477	0480-0483	0494-0495	0497-0608
0610-0631	0633-0696	0699	0701-0707
0709	0711	0716	0718-0729
0731	0733-0767	0773-0775	0777
0779-0781	0783-0806	0808-0816	0819-0893
0895-0912	0914	0918-0919	0921-0927
0929-0930	0933	0935-0936	0938-0944
0947	0950-0955	0957-0959	0961-0962
0965	0967-1024		

Table from Microsoft's *Windows 2000 Security Hardening Guide* (www.microsoft.com/technet/security/prodtech/windows2000/win2khg/03osinstl.mspx).

As with any security advice, test thoroughly before implementing in a production environment. Many applications still rely on the LM hash, although most environments will not have any problems. Certainly continue using LM hashes if you have DOS, Windows 3.x, or other unpatched legacy systems in your environment. If you communicate with Unix/Linux clients using Samba, Samba may require LM hashes.

Require Long, Complex Passwords

Require long, complex passwords for all passwords in the enterprise. This means passwords that are at least 15 characters long, and contain at least one non-alphanumeric character. Consider requiring that highly privileged accounts, such as Administrator, have one non-keyboard character (although if the password is sufficiently long, no complexity is needed). If the password exceeds 15 characters, the likelihood of any password cracker finding it, even when no complex characters are involved, is remote.

Disable LM and NTLM Authentication

All Windows machines 2000 and later should use Kerberos and one other form of authentication. Disable LM and NTLM authentication options and force the computer to use secure NTLMv2 authentication when Kerberos can't be used. This can be done using a registry edit or group policy. In a GPO or local computer policy, find `Computer Configuration\Windows Settings\Security Settings\\ Local Policies\Security Options\Network Security: LAN Manager Authentication` `level` (see Figure 4-19). Choose the most restrictive setting possible—you'll need to test before implementing in your environment. If you can enable *Send NTLMv2 response only/refuse LM & NTLM*, you'll significantly reduce risk from network-sniffing password crackers.

Figure 4-19

Enable Account Lockouts

Enable Account Lockouts. Located in a GPO or local computer policy at `Computer Configuration\ Windows Settings\Security Settings\Local Policies\Account Lockout Policy`, it was created to prevent password-guessing attacks, manual or otherwise. When Account Lockouts is enabled, after a predetermined number of bad passwords are consecutively entered on a single security principal, the Windows Account Lockouts feature can disable the account for a predetermined amount of time or require an admin to re-enable it.

Microsoft is beginning to recommend that Account Lockouts not be enabled. Their reasoning is that if passwords are complex enough, then complexity alone will defeat guessers, and Account Lockouts is not needed. They are also worried about manipulative hackers or password-guessing worms using the Accounts Lockouts feature to cause a self-caused denial-of-service attack. I agree. But unfortunately, Microsoft has yet to provide us with tools that ensure that our passwords are really complex. As discussed at the beginning of this chapter, it is easy to make insecure passwords even when password complexity is enabled. The password *Password2* would meet complexity requirements and it isn't very complex.

Instead, I recommend enabling Account Lockouts, using the following settings:

❑ Set the *Account lockout threshold* to a certain number of acceptable bad password attempts—say, 3 to 5.

❑ Set the *Reset account lockout counter after* to 1 minute (the smallest it can be).

❑ Set Account lockout duration to 1 minute.

If someone types in a bad password too many times, they only have to wait a minute until it is reset. Having Account Lockouts enabled and set to anything defeats password guessers. Password guessers have to cycle through dozens to hundreds of passwords (it is hoped) to find the right one, sometimes thousands. By enabling Account Lockouts, you make the computational time too long. As far as a computer worm causing a denial-of-service attack is concerned, if I've got a computer worm guessing at passwords using all my users' logon names, I want regular users locked out until the computer worm is stopped anyway. And when the worm is gone, all user accounts enable in 60 seconds.

Usually you cannot lock out the Administrator account using Account Lockouts. This is a good thing. Who wants a hacker locking out the Administrator account? However, if you wish, you can enable Account Lockouts using Microsoft's Passprop utility (www.dynawell.com/reskit/microsoft/win2000/passprop.zip). I recommend not enabling this feature, as you should always have at least one account that cannot be locked out, to prevent a hacker from intentionally locking everyone out of the network.

Force Moderately Frequent Password Changes

Using group policy, set `Computer Configuration\Windows Settings\Security Settings\Local Policies\Password Policy\`*Maximum Password Age* to 90 days or less. Given enough time, any password guesser, cracker, or rainbow table would be able to defeat any password. The key is to change the password more frequently than the time needed by the attacker. Some high-security organizations force password changes at 30, 45, or 60 days. Any reasonable interval can be argued — just don't make it too short, forcing your users to write it down. Ninety days or less seems reasonable for most organizations.

Rename Highly Privileged Accounts

As discussed before, highly privileged accounts, such as Administrator, should be renamed to something inconspicuous. Be sure to remove the default descriptions. Then create bogus accounts with the original account's name and give them long and complex passwords. Turn on auditing (or Per-User Selective Auditing) to track password guess attempts against those bogus accounts. Yes, hackers can do SID enumeration, but most don't and automated password-guessing worms never do.

You can automate renaming the local Administrator and Guest accounts using group policy. You can change the names at `Computer Configuration\Windows Settings\Security Settings\Local Policies\Security Options\Accounts\`*Rename administrator account* and *Rename guest account*. This renames only the local accounts, not domain admin accounts.

Give Additional Protections to Highly Privileged Accounts

Highly privileged account passwords deserve more protection than most of the passwords on your network. Besides making admin passwords extra long and complex, consider these other recommendations:

- ❑ Change the password more frequently than normal passwords.

- ❑ Only use your most highly privileged accounts on trusted computers. You want to ensure that a hardware keyboard logger or trojan isn't intercepting the password.

- ❑ Use different passwords for your different administrative accounts. Your local administrator password should not be the same as your domain or enterprise admin password, and so on. Your Directory Services Restore Mode admin password should be different than all of the rest (and known by fewer admins).

- ❑ Separate domain admin and enterprise and schema admin roles (don't give both to same user account).

- ❑ Consider splitting up single passwords into two password halves, so that no single user has the entire password. This would force collusion to use the accounts, and fired employees would never have the passwords to attack the company with. If you use this option, the whole password should be written down and stored in two different, safe locations by an independent third party.

- ❑ Consider requiring smart cards or biometrics for admin logons.

- ❑ Don't forget to change passwords on the Directory Services Restore Mode admin account occasionally.

Microsoft has an excellent password guide for highly privileged accounts, called Microsoft Solutions for Security: The Administrator Accounts Security Planning Guide (www.microsoft.com/technet/security/ topics/serversecurity/administratoraccounts/default.mspx).

Enable Logon Screen Warning Messages

As discussed above, logon screen warning messages defeat many brute-force password-guessing programs. You can enable logon screen warnings in group policy at `Computer Configuration\Windows Settings\Security Settings\Local Policies\Security Options\Interactive logon\` *Message text for users attempting to logon* (and the related *Message title for users attempting to logon*).

Audit Passwords on a Regular Basis

Do it before the password hacker does. Using some of the tools in this chapter (e.g., Pwdump4 and John the Ripper or Cain & Able), scan for weak passwords on a regular basis. This will help you to ensure that users are using sufficiently long and complex passwords, identify areas of improvement, and document compliance.

Consider Using Random Password Generators

If passwords are long and complex enough, it defeats most password crackers. Consider using a random password generator to generate random-looking passwords if you are in a high-security environment. Unfortunately, unless the user runs this process, it defeats the purpose. If the administrator runs the random generation process and hands out the password, it immediately defeats the purpose of the password (uniquely known to prove identity). Also, users don't like inputting randomly generated passwords. You can find random password generators all over the Internet. An interesting site to visit is Funk's Password Amplification (`www.funk.com/radius/enterprise/pass_amp.asp`). It includes free software that takes a user's easy-to-guess password and attempts to make it more complex and harder to crack but not overly hard for the user to remember.

Don't Use a Password

Use two-factor or token-based authentication instead. Passwords alone will always be susceptible to compromise, if only from social engineering attacks, Two-factor authentication, smart card, USB token, biometric, asymmetric tokens, or other stronger authentication schemes should be considered where the value of the data warrants. These authentication methods invite their own sets of problems, but entities that replace passwords with stronger authentication methods where possible decrease their risk of successful attack.

Summary

Windows uses a variety of authentication mechanisms to protect passwords between the client and the server. Passwords can be stored in hashed form (LM or NTLM) to prevent easy interception, and four different authentication protocols are used to securely transport logon credentials. Passwords can be compromised through social engineering, guessing, brute force, or cracking. Five recommendations can significantly limit a network's exposure risk to password cracking:

- ❑ Disable LM password hash storage
- ❑ Require long, complex passwords
- ❑ Enable Account Lockouts
- ❑ Disable LM and NTLM authentication
- ❑ Force moderately frequent password changes

With a handful of changes, the threat of successful password cracking can be removed. Chapter 5 deals with protecting high-risk files from exploitation.

5

Protecting High-Risk Files

Microsoft Windows XP Pro and Windows Server 2003 copy over 8,000 files to the local hard disk when initially installed. There are dozens of files that are more likely to be used maliciously by attackers than legitimately by end users and administrators; and by default, regular end users have Read and Execute NTFS permissions to most files and folders (see Chapter 3 for details).

For example, Debug.exe is a legacy assembly program. It was commonly used by programmers in the early days of IBM and PC-DOS to create, view, and disassemble 8- and 16-bit executables (program files with .Com and .Exe extensions). Today, no legitimate programmers use it. For one, it is a very old program. It can only create legacy programs that Microsoft no longer wants to support. Two, its feature set and end-user friendliness are so poor that any programmers that might actually have cause to use it always use something else. However, malicious attackers can use it to create malware programs and overwrite legitimate files. In fact, in the last decade, it's probably fair to say that malware makers are the only ones still using Debug.exe. But even today, it is nearly impossible to remove it from Windows. Because of Windows File Protection, you can't delete, rename, or modify it. This chapter covers high-risk files such as Debug.exe, and details how to minimize their risk.

What Is a High-Risk File?

Ultimately, any file can be used maliciously. No matter how innocent and unremarkable a file format is, it can probably be malformed in some way by attackers to make it malicious. Even plaintext files can be used maliciously. In the days of DOS, an attacker could send a victim a pure ASCII text file that when read, formatted the user's hard drive. It worked because a driver file called Ansi.sys would convert embedded keyboard control characters into their action-based counterparts. The attacker would embed commands that would remap the user's keyboard so that the next key they pressed formatted their hard drive. These types of attacks were called *ANSI-bombs*.

Text files and text editors (such as Notepad and Wordpad) can be used maliciously to overwrite legitimate text files (e.g., `Autoexec.bat`, `Win.ini`, `Hosts`, etc.). Another text file trick, more common years ago but still possible today, is for attackers to create text files that when fed through `Debug.exe` will create malicious executables. Because antivirus programs and other types of security scanners will often flag malicious code being copied onto a new host, attackers can sneak the malicious file by as a "harmless" ASCII text file. With this trick, the text file contains the ASCII representations of machine-language commands. Figure 5-1 shows the Qaz trojan/worm (`http://securityresponse.symantec.com/avcenter/venc/data/w32.hllw.qaz.a.html` opened in Debug. The ASCII text file would look something like the two bottom middle columns of hexadecimal characters. When assembled with debug, it would be converted into machine language instructions, as shown at the middle top of Figure 5-1.

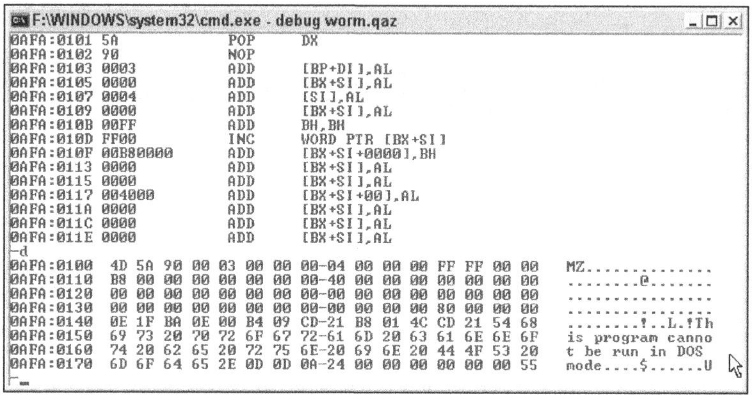

```
F:\WINDOWS\system32\cmd.exe - debug worm.qaz                        _ □ ×
0AFA:0101 5A               POP      DX
0AFA:0102 90               NOP
0AFA:0103 0003             ADD      [BP+DI],AL
0AFA:0105 0000             ADD      [BX+SI],AL
0AFA:0107 0004             ADD      [SI],AL
0AFA:0109 0000             ADD      [BX+SI],AL
0AFA:010B 00FF             ADD      BH,BH
0AFA:010D FF00             INC      WORD PTR [BX+SI]
0AFA:010F 00B80000         ADD      [BX+SI+0000],BH
0AFA:0113 0000             ADD      [BX+SI],AL
0AFA:0115 0000             ADD      [BX+SI],AL
0AFA:0117 004000           ADD      [BX+SI+00],AL
0AFA:011A 0000             ADD      [BX+SI],AL
0AFA:011C 0000             ADD      [BX+SI],AL
0AFA:011E 0000             ADD      [BX+SI],AL
-d
0AFA:0100  4D 5A 90 00 03 00 00 00-04 00 00 00 FF FF 00 00   MZ..............
0AFA:0110  B8 00 00 00 00 00 00 00-40 00 00 00 00 00 00 00   ........@.......
0AFA:0120  00 00 00 00 00 00 00 00-00 00 00 00 00 00 00 00   ................
0AFA:0130  00 00 00 00 00 00 00 00-00 00 00 00 80 00 00 00   ................
0AFA:0140  0E 1F BA 0E 00 B4 09 CD-21 B8 01 4C CD 21 54 68   ........!..L.!Th
0AFA:0150  69 73 20 70 72 6F 67 72-61 6D 20 63 61 6E 6E 6F   is program canno
0AFA:0160  74 20 62 65 20 72 75 6E-20 69 6E 20 44 4F 53 20   t be run in DOS
0AFA:0170  6D 6F 64 65 2E 0D 0D 0A-24 00 00 00 00 00 00 55   mode....$......U
-
```

Figure 5-1

Prior to assembling, a hacker could copy the ASCII source file from their machine to the victim's machine. Most antivirus scanners don't even attempt to scan text files. Even if they did, because the program is only ASCII text, the scanning program would only read the file as their literal character counterparts, as if it were reading a word processing document. Once past the scanners, the hacker would type in something like the following:

```
Debug <qaz.txt
```

The outputted program would be called `Qaz.com`. It could then be executed on the victim's machine, or a command could be added to one of the Windows startup files to execute the program when Windows restarts. The debug method works even when the user is a non-admin. This is because all users have Read and Execute access to the `Debug.exe` command.

Even pure data and graphic files can be used. Twenty years ago, security experts used to say that data couldn't infect a PC. That's before macro and script viruses came along and before malicious programmers learned to malform picture files into buffer overflow exploits. If every file type can be made malicious, a better question is what file types are considered high-risk files? That is, what file types have been used maliciously or will likely be used maliciously? High-risk files must meet some basic prerequisites before the actual flaws are even considered:

❏ The file type must be popular among a large class of users, ensuring that software that will be interpreting the file is commonly installed on a large percentage of computers.

❏ The file type is more likely to be used for malicious purposes by attackers than by authorized users for legitimate purposes.

❏ It must have a high incidence of malicious use, even if most of its use is legitimate.

Once those prerequisites are satisfied, the file type must contain a flaw or allow malicious use.

File Flaws

Files can be flawed by design or misused to cause unintended consequences.

Flawed By Design

Developers often create vulnerable file formats or allow the programs that run them to have insecure functionality.

Designed Without Security in Mind

For instance, when Microsoft's Windows Scripting Host first came out, any script file ending in .Hta, .Ws, or .Cs would automatically be executed by Wscript.exe or Cscript.exe when double-clicked or downloaded. Hta files could automatically launch in Internet Explorer and then have complete access to the system (under the user's logon credentials). When Windows Scripting Host first came out, there was no runtime message to warn the user, and scripts were allowed to modify system values and information without recourse. *Zero* security was built into Windows Scripting Host and there wasn't any for nearly a year. Hta and other scripting files became a hacker's dream. Visual Basic Script (.Vbs) files had similar treatment early on. Macro viruses became popular in the mid-1990s because of the same design flaw — no security risk evaluation was ever performed before the software was released.

Buffer Overflows

Another common problem is that the file format contains unexpected, exploitable holes that allow malicious use. For example, hackers are frequently malforming graphic file formats (e.g., PNG, GIF, JPG, ICO, etc.) so that the related rendering programs error out and initiate a buffer overflow. Open the wrong picture today and your computer is the hacker's. Often the program is as easy as typing the wrong file size in the header. For example, a hacker could create a graphic file with a file size of 1 or 0 written in the file's header. The program that interpreted the file would read the malformed file size, somehow calculate the file size to be a negative billion value, and result in a buffer overflow.

Embedded risks

Many file formats allow other embedded files and links to be embedded within the file. For instance, Microsoft Office files can contain links to other documents such that when the original document is opened, the linked document is downloaded and executed too. Many file types were originally fairly safe, but gained the capability to contain additional linked documents as their popularity grew (e.g., PDF, RTF, XLS, etc.). So whereas the original document type is still safe, the linked document can be used to accomplish the exploit. Many files, such as Program Information Files (.Pifs) and Scrap Shell (.Shs) files contain links to other documents by design. A security scanning tool, if it isn't programmed to look for and enumerate links, might miss the linked document. Hackers commonly exploit program GUI *skins* (i.e., GUI themes). The skins were made to allow users to create and easily transfer different program look-and-feels. Unfortunately, for end users, many skins are allowed to have embedded links, and the links can download or execute malicious code.

Misuse Flaws

Oftentimes, though, malicious hackers take files and programs and do unexpected things. For example, most OS platforms offer a variety of compression options for choosing a program archiver. In the Windows world, the most popular program archiver is the Zip file format (unarchiving is natively supported by Windows XP and later, and using Winzip and Pkzip on previous platforms). Its creators never intended the .Zip file format to be used maliciously, and probably didn't think about it being used maliciously. But today, attackers frequently use the .Zip file format to bypass security protections, including the following:

❏ Archiving malware programs inside of .Zip files so that programs that do not open archive files and scan contained files (called *recursive scanning*) will not detect the malware threats. Some viruses send themselves as password-protected .Zip files. The receiver is given the password to open the malicious archive, but the virus scanner skips scanning the file because it "can't see the password" and can't open the archive.

❏ Continually re-archiving the same file over and over again (called *nesting*) so if the scanning program does open scanned files, it might not de-archive the file enough to scan the original file contents

❏ Overwriting another legitimate file with a malicious version

❏ Using the file format to automatically run one of the contained programs when the file is opened

❏ Renaming other file types (i.e., MS-Word Documents) to .Zip file extensions so that when they are opened in Windows Explorer, the other document type executes instead

❏ Creating a subdirectory structure within the archive file format that, when opened, opens up dozens to millions of child directories. Some security scanners cannot or will not scan down past a certain number of subdirectories. Other attacks using this method have also created so many child subdirectories that the OS ends up out of usable space.

File Type Mismatches

Other flaws include header mismatches. A file may have a file extension claiming to be one type of program when it is in fact another type of program. In its "pretend state," it bypasses normal security mechanisms, but at some point in the execution path it is rendered in its intended malicious form. An example here is that any OLE2 file (i.e., most Microsoft Office documents) can be renamed to any extension (e.g., FISH.TXT), and when executed will run as the legitimate document type and attempt to open the normal MS-Office program.

The key is that the legitimate design of the program or file type unintentionally allows malicious behavior.

Configuration Import Files

Many programs allow configuration files to be created, and when the configuration file is clicked, it modifies the related system settings. For example, registry settings can be imported using .Reg files. A malicious hacker can e-mail a victim a .Reg file and if the registry edit file is clicked, it modifies the registry. .Ins files can be used to initiate unauthorized connections to Internet sites. .CER and .CTL files can be used to surreptitiously install an attacker as a trusted resource. Table 5-1 lists many common file types that will manipulate Windows or an installed setting simply by the user double-clicking on it.

Magic Names

Other files are more dangerous simply because of their file name. Windows has dozens of files that will be read and executed in a certain way just because of their name. For instance, a file called Autorun.inf located on a CD-ROM or DVD disk will be automatically executed when the removable media is first inserted. The Normal.dot file becomes the default Microsoft Word template simply because of its name. A file called Desktop.ini will take special precedence over any other file in a Windows folder when the folder is double-clicked.

Special thanks to Microsoft MVP Chris Quirke for this section.

High-Risk File and Program Examples

What is and isn't high-risk is different for different organizations. It is up to each system administrator to review the files and programs running on the computers under their control and determine what should and shouldn't be executing. While no administrator will come up with the same list, here are some starting points.

List of Potentially Malicious File Types

Table 5-1 shows many high-risk file types by extension and gives related details. You can use this list as a starting point to check off what is and isn't needed in your environment. This list can also be used in Chapter 11, "Protecting E-mail."

Table 5-1

File Extension	File Type	Malicious Use Details
.ade, .adp, .and	Microsoft Access project files	Can contain auto-executing macros
.ani	Windows Animated Cursor	Two exploits were announced by Flashsky Fangxing (flashsky@xfocus.org) on Dec. 23, 2004. First, a Windows Kernel DoS exploit: Windows XP SP2 not vulnerable, but most other Windows versions are (NT to 2003). Second, an Integer buffer overflow: most Windows versions are vulnerable (NT to 2003), caused by LoadImage API in USER32.Lib.

Table continued on following page

File Extension	File Type	Malicious Use Details
.arc	File Archive File format	Older, pre-Windows file archive file format. Still used occasionally by malware to bypass computer security defenses.
.arj	File Archive	Can be used by malware to bypass computer security defenses. Arj files can be created and unarchived using many popular programs, including Winzip. More detail on the .arj program can be found at `http://filext.com/detaillist.php?extdetail=ARJ`.
.asf, .lsf, .lsx	Streaming audio or video file	Can be exploited through buffer overflows, header malformation, or dangerous scriptable content
.atf	Symantec pcAnywhere autotransfer file	Can initiate a pcAnywhere file-transfer session
.bas	Visual Basic (VB) class module	Can contain malicious instructions
.bat	DOS batch file	Can contain malicious DOS command interpreter instructions. Also can contain executable .Exe code that will run even with the incorrect extension.
.bmp	Windows Bitmap graphics file	Integer buffer overflow, announced on Dec. 23, 2004. Most Windows versions were vulnerable (NT to 2003) until patched; caused by LoadImage API in USER32.Lib.
.cab	Microsoft cabinet archive file	Opens in Windows Explorer, IE, and can help install malicious files. Commonly used by Microsoft to install legitimate files, but could be used by malware to bypass computer security defenses. Unexpected CAB files arriving via e-mail or from untrusted web sites should not be opened.
.cbo, .cbl, .cbm	Microsoft Interactive Training file	User= field allows an exploitable buffer overflow (SEH pointer). Microsoft Interactive Training (Orun32.exe) must be present, although it is often present by default in OEM versions of Windows XP. First exploit of this file type announced on June 14, 2005 by iDEFENSE labs. Patched by MS05-31. HK_CR\MITrain.Document\shell\open\command is related to the Orun32.exe program.

File Extension	File Type	Malicious Use Details
.cer, .crt, .der	Security certificate	Can install a malicious certificate in IE to permit automatic downloading of malicious content
.chm	Windows Compiled Help File	Windows Help Files (.hlp) can be compiled for better performance and feature sets. Malformed Compiled Help Files have been involved in many announced exploits over the years, including Microsoft Security Bulletin MS05-031. Can be opened in Internet Explorer automatically without user intervention using Ms — its moniker.
.cmd	Command file	Contains batch-file-like DOS interpreter script commands. Can contain malicious instructions. Also can contain executable .Exe code that will run even with the incorrect extension.
.com	Program executable	Older, legacy DOS and 16-bit Windows executables. Still work under all Windows versions, except newer 64-bit Windows.
.cpl	Control Panel Applet	Executable program written to run in Control Panel context. Can be infected by viruses or used by malware programs to install themselves. Example includes a Win32.Beagle variant (`http://security response.symantec.com/avcenter/ venc/data/w32.beagle@mm!cpl.html`). If located so as to be part of Control Panel, listing the contents of Control Panel can run malware code even *before* any specific Control Panel item is "opened." This risk is fairly unpublicized and may not have been exploited as yet; it's known by-design functionality, however.
.css	Cascading Style Sheet	Used by IE and other browsers. Used by web developers to easily deliver a consistent look-and-feel style to a web site without having to recode the style on each web page. Has been exploited maliciously many times.
.ctl	Certificate Trust List	Could be used by a remote attacker to trick a victim into installing the attacker as a trusted publisher

Table continued on following page

File Extension	File Type	Malicious Use Details
.cur	Windows cursor graphic file	Integer buffer overflow, announced by flashsky fangxing (flashsky@xfocus.org) on Dec. 23, 2004; most Windows versions are vulnerable (NT to 2003); caused by Load-Image API in USER32.Lib.
.dbg	Debug file	Can contain malicious machine-language instructions that can be compiled by debug.exe into malware
.dll	Dynamic Linking Library	Most Dlls are legitimate program files containing pre-compiled library routines that other programs can call, or can contain complete programs. Have been involved in many viruses and worms. Because of Windows File Protection, most Windows system Dlls cannot be overwritten or modified by malware, but rogue Dlls can be installed. Dll code can also be run as a stand-along executable if run via RunDLL or similar generic .Dll "launching wrappers" that are legitimate parts of Windows. The advantage to malware is that these "wrapped" Dll processes are typically named in Task Manager by the parent wrapper name. Host-based firewalls and IDSs that monitor applications only see the parent wrapper name. That's why .Dll files in particular are commonly used by trojans.
.doc	Microsoft Office Word Document	Can contain malicious macros, scripts, objects, links, and executables. Very difficult to block because legitimate use is very common. By default, many malicious objects are blocked by default in recent versions of Microsoft Office.
.dot	Microsoft Office Document Template	Can be manipulated by malware to contain malicious objects that are then added to every new document that relies on the related template file. Very commonly manipulated by early Microsoft Office macro files, but not as commonly modified by malware today.
.dsm, .far, .it, .stm, .ult, .wma	Nullsoft WinAmp media file	Has been involved in malicious exploits

File Extension	File Type	Malicious Use Details
.dun	DUN export file	Can contain malicious dial-up connection information that initiates outward calls
.edt	Adobe Reader PDF ebook file	Involved in at least one announced exploit (www.idefense.com/application/poi/display?id=163) in 2004. If ebook functionality is not needed, it can be blocked without affecting overall Adobe Reader functionality.
.eml, .email	Outlook Express e-mail message	Used by Nimda and many other worms. Eml files are opened in Outlook Express even when some other e-mail application is the current default. Attachments can be hidden within the file and will be clickable, and any exploits affecting Outlook Express or the Internet Explorer rendering engine will be exposed.
.exe	Application file	Can be used to launch malicious executables
.fav	IE Favorites list	Can be used to list malicious web sites that the user then visits
.gif	Graphic file format	GIF stands for Graphics Interchange Format. Although normally just a picture or image data file, it has be malformed to cause improper application handling and buffer overflows. It has impacted several applications, including Microsoft Windows Messenger, which was patched to fix a GIF exploit (see Microsoft Security Bulletin MS05-022).
.gzip, .gz, .taz, .tgz	Gzip file format	Can be used by malware to bypass computer security defenses. Very common on Unix/Linux platforms, but can also be used in Windows. See .tar also.
.hlp	Microsoft Help File	Can be used in multiple exploits
.ht	Hyperterminal file	Can initiate dial-up connections to untrusted hosts
.hta	HTML application	Frequently used by worms and trojans
.htm, .html, .dhtml, .shtml	HTML file	Can initiate an IE session and be used to automatically download and execute rogue files. All the "active content" risks, e.g., scripting, apply here as well.

Table continued on following page

File Extension	File Type	Malicious Use Details
.htt	Explorer Stylesheet	Can be used/manipulated by adware/malware to display unwanted browser Windows and popups. Used by *the View As Web Page* display attribute as a way of integrating HTML content. .htt files have the potential to make any writable network share a point of malware entry from infected systems that can see that share.
.ico	Windows Icon graphic file	Integer buffer overflow announced on Dec. 23, 2004; most Windows versions were vulnerable (NT to 2003) until patched. Caused by LoadImage API in USER32.Lib.
.inf	Install configuration file/security template	A Setup Information installer configuration file, it can be used to maliciously manipulate existing programs or to install new malicious programs. As a security template, it could be used to downgrade existing security permissions.
.ini	Application configuration settings file	Can be used to maliciously change a program's default settings. Also, Desktop.ini can be used to auto-launch malicious programs. Desktop.ini and .htt files have the potential to make any writable network share a point of malware entry from infected systems that can see that share. It's a significant integration point, as it's tedious to find and check all Desktop.ini files for references that launch malware.
.ins, .isp	Internet communication settings	Can be used to initiate Internet connections to untrusted sources
.jar	Java archive file	Can launch Java attacks
.jav, .java	Java applet	Can launch Java attacks
.jpg, .jpe, .jpeg, .jfif	JPEG files	JPEG stands for Joint Photographic Experts Group. Although normally just a graphics file format, it has been malformed to cause buffer overflows in various applications.
.js, .jse	JavaScript (encoded) file	Can contain malicious code. JSE files are encoded JavaScript files that can easily be decoded and read by Windows and IE. These files are executed by Wscript.exe, Cscript.exe, or JScript.dll.

File Extension	File Type	Malicious Use Details
.lnk, .desklink	Shortcut link	Can be used to automate malicious actions
.lzh	Archive file format	Can be used by malware to bypass computer security defenses. Used on Windows platforms, especially by game developers or Japanese programmers, but is not common.
.mad, .maf, mda, .mas, .mag, .mam, .maq, .mar, .mat, .mav, .maw, .mdn, .mdt, .mdx	Access module shortcut	Can carry out macro manipulation that isn't controlled by Office security settings
.mdb, .mdbhtml	Access application or database	Can contain malicious macros
.mde	Access database with all	Can contain malicious macrosmodules compiled and source code removed
.mhtml, .mhtm	MIME HTML document	Can contain harmful commands
.mim	MIME file	Could become a target of future MIME exploits
.msg, .mmf	Microsoft Mail or Outlook Express item	Can carry a virus or worm
.msh	Microsoft Shell Command file	New file format in Windows Vista, used to replace previous shell language files (e.g., .bat, .cmd, etc.). Demonstration viruses have already been developed exploiting this file format (www.f-secure.com/v-descs/danom.shtml).
.msi, .msp	Microsoft Installer package	Can be used to install or modify software
.mst	Visual Basic test source file	Can be used maliciously
.nws	Outlook Express news message	Network newsgroup protocol. Can carry viruses, worms, and other malware.
.ocx	ActiveX control	Can be used to install malicious ActiveX programs
.oft	Outlook Template file	Outlook Template file that can contain malicious scripting or objects. Not commonly used by malware. E-mail worms and viruses can sometimes harvest legitimate e-mail addresses from OFT files.
.ovl	Program overlay file	Commonly used by legitimate programs. Can be used to install malware, or legitimate ones can be infected by viruses.

Table continued on following page

File Extension	File Type	Malicious Use Details
.pdc	Microsoft compiled script	Can contain dangerous code
.pdf	Adobe Reader Portable Document Format	Involved in several exploits over the years. Difficult to block because of widespread legitimate use. By design, Acrobat Reader can auto-run scripts (JavaScript) within Pdf files; this feature can be disabled in Adobe Reader 7.x or later versions.
.pif	Program information file	Can run malicious programs, and the file extension is always hidden throughout Windows by default. These files also define their own icons, as contained within the file, further assisting attempts to disguise them as "safe" file types, and potentially facilitating run-on-display "icon" exploits.
.pl	Perl script file	Can contain rogue code
.png	Portable Network Graphics file	PNG is an open-source graphics format with lossless compression (www.libpng .org/pub/png). Has been involved in several exploits, including multi-browser buffer overflows. Last PNG IE buffer overflow resolved by MS05-025.
.pol	Windows Policy file	Could be used to lower security settings on Windows 9x and later machines
.ppt, .ppa, .pot, .ppthtml, .pothtml	Microsoft Powerpoint presentation, add-in, or template file	Can contain scripted exploits
.prf	Outlook profile settings	Can override default or trusted settings
.pst	Outlook or Exchange personal store file	Can contain malicious attachments and be imported into Outlook or Outlook Express
.pwl	Windows 9x password file	Could be used to overwrite legitimate passwords
.py	Python script file	Can contain rogue code
.rar	WinRAR archived file	Used by malware to bypass detectors that normally open zip files but don't open RAR files. Used by Beagle worm among others. See http://schmidt.devlib.org/file-formats/rar-archive-file-format.html.

File Extension	File Type	Malicious Use Details
.rat	Internet Explorer content advisor ratings file	Part of Internet Explorer's content advisor rating feature. Can be installed to allow malicious web sites to be approved as secure. Also can be used on IIS web sites to pre-rate content to be delivered to visitors. If installed on IIS, could be used to execute malicious program instructions. Has been involved in a malicious buffer overflow announcement in the past.
.rdp	Remote Desktop Top connection shortcut	If an end user can be tricked into running a malicious RDP file, it could execute local commands, or map a drive (should provide warning in XP Pro and later) to remote malicious machine, giving the attacker access to local files. Currently not popularly exploited.
.reg, .key	Registry entry file	Can create or modify registry keys
.rtf	Rich Text Format file	Can script other attacks and contain embedded malicious links. This problem exists because MS Word will auto-run Word document macros within .RTF files, even though .RTF is supposed to be a "safe" file type for information interchange.
.scf	Windows Explorer command	Could be used maliciously in future attacks
.scp	DUN script	Can initiate rogue outbound connections
.scr	Windows screen saver file	Can contain worms or trojans. Essentially, a .Scr file is an .Exe file.
.shs, .shb	Shell scrap object	Can mask rogue programs by containing links to other programs. Shell scrap file objects can have hidden extensions even when Windows is told to display hidden file extensions.
.slk	Excel SLK data-import file	Can contain hidden malicious macros
.stl	Certificate Trust List (CTL)	Can induce a user to trust a rogue certificate
.swf, .spl	Shockwave Flash object	Can be exploited
.sys	Driver or configuration file	Used by many auto-run files, including config.sys. Can be used to install malicious programs. Legitimate .sys files can be infected by viruses.

Table continued on following page

File Extension	File Type	Malicious Use Details
.tar, .taz, .tgz, .tz	Archive file format	TAR stands for Tape Archive file format. Common Linux/Unix archive file format, but is used in Windows. Can be used by malware to bypass computer security defenses.
.url	Internet shortcut	Can connect user to malicious web site or launch a malicious action
.uu, .uue	Archive file format	UUecode file format is used to send program files and other objects through plaintext e-mail. Used to be common across most PC platforms in the early days of the Internet, but is not common today. Can be used by malware to bypass computer security defenses.
.vb, .vbe, .vbs	VBScript file	Can contain malicious code. VBE files are encoded VBScript files that can easily be decoded and read by Windows and IE. These files are executed by Wscript.exe, Cscript.exe, or VBScript.dll.
.vcf	vCard file format	Used in many e-mail clients, including Outlook and Outlook Express to communicate recipient addressing details. Has been involved in a few exploits.
.vxd, .386	Virtual device driver	Can trick a user into saving a trojan version of a legitimate device driver
.wbk	Word backup document	Can contain dangerous macros
.wiz	Wizard file	Used by Microsoft to launch end-user-friendly "wizards" that walk new users through common tasks. Could be used to automate a future social engineering attack but is not a common malware vector.
.ws, .cs, .wsf, .wsc, .sct	WSH file	Can execute malicious code
.xla, .xlb, .xlc, .xld, .xlk, .xll, .xlm, .xlt, .xlv	Excel file types	Can contain dangerous macros and code
.xls, .xlshtml, .xlthtml	Excel spreadsheet	Can contain dangerous macros and code
.xml, .xsl	XML file	Likely to be the next language of choice for malicious coders

File Extension	File Type	Malicious Use Details
.z	Gzip file format	Can be used by malware to bypass computer security defenses. Very common on Unix/Linux platforms, but can also be used in Windows.
.zip	Pkzip or Winzip archive file	Can be used maliciously several ways, including: 1) Can allow malware to bypass file integrity checkers and antivirus software that does not unzip (password-protected) zip files, 2) Can contain a zip file within a zip file (several levels of nesting possible) to bypass security programs that do not do recursive scanning, 3) Can be used to auto-launch programs when the file is unzipped, 4) Can be used to overwrite other legitimate files, 5) Can be used to create an overwhelming number of directories and subdirectories, causing quota problems, low disk space, and other operating system abnormalities. The latter problem has also been used to bypass security programs that do not handle long and "deep" directory names well.

Go to www.wrox.com to get an updated list of potential malicious files.

As exhaustive as this list may seem, many readers can probably add additional high-risk files. This list does not contain every file extension that could be used maliciously, just the most likely candidates. To find out all the file extensions registered with a particular Windows computer, open up Windows Explorer and choose Tools ⇨ Folder Options ⇨ File Types (see Figure 5-2). The average Windows installation contains hundreds of file associations. Each file association should be considered potentially exploitable and measured against the potential risk and benefit. With many file extensions (e.g., Remote Desktop Protocol), what can potentially be exploited is high, but the relative risk of exploitation is low because attackers aren't commonly using that method. The highest-risk files for your organization should be monitored, and the risk of attack minimized (see "Defenses," below).

A great web site to use for file extension research is The File Extension Source (http://filext.com).

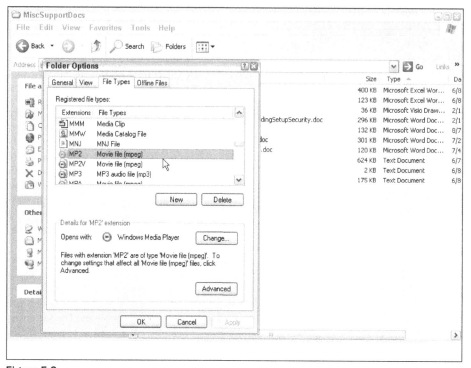

Figure 5-2

High-Risk Windows Files

Microsoft Windows installs with hundreds of executables and programs in the Windows and Windows\System32 directories. By default, all users have Read and Execute permissions. Again, what Windows system files are considered high risk depends on each administrator's environment. Table 5-2 lists the files the author considers high risk. All files are located in %Windir%\System32 unless notated. Even though all files listed in the table are considered high risk (i.e., more likely to be used maliciously than legitimately), not all risk is the same. Risk factor was determined by how often the file is used for exploitation and what the file can do.

Table 5-2

File Name	Description and Risk	Risk
Command.com	16-bit command-line shell. Can often be used much like Cmd.exe. Disable if not needed. Cannot be disabled by Software Restriction Policies (see below).	High

File Name	Description and Risk	Risk
Ftp.exe	File Transfer Protocol (FTP) client. Used by malware programs and attackers. Disable if not needed by end users.	High
Ntdvm.exe	Controls 16-bit DOS Virtual Machine environment. Disable to prevent 16-bit program execution.	High
Reg.exe	Allows manipulation of the registry.	High
Regedit.exe	Legacy registry editor. Non-admin users should not be able to manually view or manipulate the registry. Located in %Windir%.	High
Regedt32.exe	32-bit Registry editor. Non-admin end users do not need access.	High
Tftp.exe	Trivial file transfer protocol (TFTP) client. Used to initiate unauthenticated FTP sessions. Frequently used by malware programs and attackers.	High
Tlntsvr.exe	Telnet server. Disable if not used. Can be used by attackers to gain access.	High
Wscript.exe	Windows Scripting Host for running VBScript and JavaScript scripts outside of Internet Explorer. Disable if not used.	High
Clipsrv.exe	Clip book service. Allows *remote* access to the data stored in the local computer's clipboard. Disabled by default.	High-Medium
Cmd.exe	32-bit command-line shell. End users should not have access to DOS command-line shells unless access is needed or they run .BAT or .CMD files.	High-Medium
Cscript.exe	Command-line version of Windows Scripting Host. Not needed unless VBScript or JScript programs are run outside of Internet Explorer.	High-Medium
Mshta.exe	Allows HTML Applications (HTAs) to run outside of Internet Explorer. HTAs have been exploited several times. Disable if not needed.	High-Medium
Debug.exe	Legacy assembly program. Can easily be exploited. Rarely needed by legitimate users, administrators, or programmers.	Medium
Format.com	Used to format hard drives and floppy disks from the command line. Rarely needed anymore. Disable if not needed.	Medium

Table continued on following page

File Name	Description and Risk	Risk
Ntbackup.exe	Windows backup utility. Can be used to copy unauthorized information if the logged in user has backup privileges.	Medium
Ntdsutil.exe	Powerful Active Directory "swiss-army knife" utility tool. Not needed by non-administrators.	Medium
Regsvr32.exe	Allows users to register and unregister COM objects and .DLLs. Not needed by non-admin users.	Medium
Savedump.exe	Saves memory dump to a file. Not normally needed by end users.	Medium
Sc.exe	Used to view and modify services nformation. Not ineeded by non-admin users.	Medium
Schtasks.exe	Used to view, modify, and schedule tasks in Task Scheduler.	Medium
Secedit.exe	Used to view, apply, and compare security templates to a given PC.	Medium
Shutdown.exe	Used to shut down local or remote computers. Not normally needed by most end users.	Medium
Taskkill.exe	Allows user to kill running task. Not normally needed by end users. Occasionally used by malware.	Medium
Tscon.exe	Attaches user to a new Terminal Server (RDP) session. There have been some announced issues (including http://support.microsoft.com/default.aspx?scid=kb;en-us;302801).	Medium
Arp.exe	Address Resolution Protocol interface utility. Could be used to create false ARP entries and be involved with redirection attacks.	Medium/Low
At.exe	Legacy scheduling interface to Task Scheduler. Regular end users should not be able to schedule new tasks.	Medium/Low
Attrib.exe	Displays standard file attributes. Could be used to hide malicious files.	Medium/Low
Bootcfg.exe	Would allow a user to change many booting parameters.	Medium/Low
Edit.com	16-bit legacy command-line editor. Disable if not needed. Cannot be limited by Software Restriction Policies (see below).	Medium/Low
Rasdial.exe	Makes RAS connections. Disable if not needed.	Medium/Low

File Name	Description and Risk	Risk
Tsshutdn	Allows user to shut down local or remote Terminal Server (RDP). There have been some DoS vulnerabilities announced.	Medium/Low
Alg.exe	Service controlling Microsoft Internet Connection Sharing and Internet Connection Firewall/Windows Firewall. Non-admin users should be prevented from executing. Normally executes in the LocalService context.	Low
Append.exe	Legacy executable. Allows a user to extend the path statement variable to access files as if they were in the current directory when they are in fact in the appended path. This doesn't use the Path variable.	Low
Auditusr.exe	New API program interface to Per-User Selective Auditing feature introduced in XP Service Pack 2 and Server 2003 Service Pack 1. Use would display any Per-User auditing categories enabled.	Low
Cacls.exe	Allows users to view and manipulate NTFS permissions.	Low
Ddeshare.exe	Used to create DDE shares. Normally not needed by most end users.	Low
Dsadd.exe, Dsget.exe, Dsmove.exe, Dsrem, Dsquery	Active Directory command-line tools. Not normally needed by end users, although not popularly exploited at this time.	Low
Edlin.exe	Legacy command-line text editor. Not commonly used by anyone.	Low
Eventcreate.exe	Used to create custom events (http://support .microsoft.com/default.aspx?scid=kb;en-us;324145). Not needed by end users.	Low
Eventtriggers.exe	Used to define custom events that generate events. Not needed by end users.	Low
Exe2bin.exe	Can convert small .EXE files to .COM files. Not needed by end users.	Low
Finger.exe	Legacy application used to collect information from Finger identification services. Not needed by end users.	Low
Hh.exe	Windows Help. Only disable if concerned about Help file exploits or if a new, widespread Help file exploit has been announced that is not yet patched. Located in %Windir%.	Low

Table continued on following page

File Name	Description and Risk	Risk
Mmc.exe	Microsoft Management Console. Disable if not needed by end users.	Low
Msconfig.exe	System Configuration Utility used to display and modify some common Windows startup locations. Located in %Windir%\PCHealth\HelpCtr\Binaries. Like Regedit and Task Manager, this useful manual defense tool is often disabled by malware.	Low
Netdde.exe	Used to create DDE channels. Sometimes needed for applications that use DDE. Disable if not needed.	Low
Rcp.exe	TCP/IP Remote Copy Program. Not needed by regular end users.	Low
Recover.exe	Recovers lost file fragments. Can cause problems with data recovery. Disable unless needed.	Low
Regtrace.exe	Programming troubleshooting utility.	Low
Replace.exe	Allows files from source to replace files on destination. Not normally used by end users.	Low
Reset.exe	Resets Terminal Server (RDP) sessions. Not normally needed by end users.	Low
Rexec.exe	TCP/IP client command that runs commands on remote hosts running the REXECD service. Not normally needed by end users.	Low
Route.exe	Allows users to view and modify a Windows TCP/IP routing table. Could be used to set malicious routes.	Low
Rsh.exe	TCP/IP client utility that runs commands on remote hosts running the RSH service. Not normally needed by end users.	Low
Rsm.exe	Removable Storage Manager command-line interface, used for tape/storage media manipulation.	Low
Subst.exe	Legacy command, allows users to map a network drive path to a drive letter. Not normally used.	Low
Sysedit.exe	System Configuration Editor, legacy program used to view and modify legacy startup files.	Low
Telnet.exe	Telnet client. Disable if not used.	Low
Tskill.exe	Allows users to kill running Terminal Server (RDP) session. Not normally used by end users.	
Xcopy.exe	Allows files to be copied, including their attributes.	Low

Again, there are probably files that some readers can add or delete to the list. Files that are frequently used by the company (for example, `ftp.exe`) should not be listed as high-risk for that organization. Non-admin end users should be prevented from running the files listed in Table 5-2. Most of the files in the table are located at `%Windir%\System32`. Knowing a file's normal location is important because attackers will often create look-alike files with the same name, but in different locations.

Other Windows Files Needing Protection

Table 5-3 lists other common Windows files that need investigation. In most cases, regular end users need access to them, but administrators should audit their use and prevent modification if applicable.

Table 5-3

File Name	Default Location	Description
Hosts	%windir%\System32\Drivers\Etc in NT and above systems	Used for static DNS resolution
Lmhosts	%windir%\System32\Drivers\Etc in NT and above systems	Used for static NetBIOS resolution
Autoexec.bat, Autoexec.nt	Root directory for Autoexec.bat, %Windir%\System32 or %Windir%\ Repair for Autoexec.nt	In legacy systems, loads real-mode programs prior to Windows loading. Can be used to install malicious programs.
Autorun.inf	In the root directory on removable media (e.g., CD-ROM disks)	Can be used to automatically run commands or programs referenced by file. If concerned, you can disable Autorun using registry edit using the NoDriveTypeAutoRun registry value. The typical setting is 91 or 95 and should be changed to 9D (if you want CD disks to be autorun), BD (if both CD and hard drive autorun are to be suppressed), or FF (to suppress all devices). The settings are set per user.
Boot.ini	Root directory of system volume	File used by NT OS file to determine which OS image to load. A malicious Boot.ini entry can point to any file, anywhere, of any "DOS-visible" name, to be run as raw code on boot if that "OS" is selected. Not popularly exploited at this time.
Bootsect.dos	Root directory of boot volume	DOS boot sector on NT and later dual-boot machines. Can be maliciously modified. There's an equivalent Bootsect.dat for Recovery Console, if the Recovery Console is installed to HD.

Table continued on following page

File Name	Default Location	Description
Config.sys, config.nt	Root directory for config.sys, %Windir%\System32 or %Windir%\Repair for config.nt	In legacy systems, loads real-mode programs prior to Windows loading. Can be used to install malicious programs.
Desktop.ini	Can be located in any folder location	Used to modify desktop folder appearance, and can be used to launch new malicious code
Iereset.inf	%Windir%\Inf	Used as IE default values. Not used in the wild, yet. Proposed by Andrew Aronoff of SilentRunners.org.
Msdos.sys, Io.sys	Root directory	Only on legacy systems, contains DOS boot code
Dosstart.bat	%Windir%	If it exists, it should be examined or protected. Used by Win 9x for DOS programs set to run in DOS mode using the same configuration as Windows, which is the default mode for "Exit to DOS.pif" that is used for Shutdown, Restart in MS-DOS mode. If DOS mode .pif are set to "Specify a new..." then DOSStart.bat is ignored and the private startup files hidden in the .Pif are used instead.
Msdos.sys	Root directory	Legacy file. Can determine path to Windows and startup control in Win 9x environments. Was an OS boot file in MS-DOS.
Normal.dot	In \Documents and Settings\ %UserProfile%\Application Data\ Microsoft\Templates on non-legacy systems	Default template file for Microsoft Word. Commonly used by older macro viruses.
Ntldr	Root directory of system volume	NT and later boot code loader program. So far, not exploited but could be.
Rasphone.pbk	\Documents and Settings\ %UserProfile%\Application Data\Microsoft\Network\ Connections\Pbk	Could be used to modify dial-up network settings
Startup folders	\Documents and Settings\ %UserProfile%\Start Menu\ Programs\Startup	Any program, script, or executable files located in Startup folders will be automatically executed when the user logs in.

File Name	Default Location	Description
System.ini	%Windir%, if present	Legacy file. Could load malicious programs.
Win.ini	%Windir%, if present	Legacy file. Could load malicious programs.
Winboot.ini	Boot sector, if present	Legacy file. Can determine path to Windows and startup control in Win 9x environments.
Winboot.sys	Root directory, if present	Legacy file. Copied over C:\IO.SYS and then run by partition boot code at bootup.
Winstart.bat	%Windir%, if present	Legacy file. Could load malicious programs in Win 9x and earlier.
Wininit.ini	%Windir%, if present	"Run once" legacy file. Could load malicious programs.
*.Dos, *.W40, *.App, *.Wos	Root directory, if present	Legacy files for Win 9x, Startup settings and code files for "Previous version of MS-DOS" options on dual-boot systems.

The files listed in Tables 5-2 and 5-3 represent some of the most important Windows files, and the ones most likely to be involved with a malicious attack. Table 5-1 lists other types of files, including application files, that can be used in a rogue manner. Administrators should review the files in these tables to determine which of these should or shouldn't be running on their network.

Good web sites for looking up file names are Windows Process Library (www.liutilities.com/products/wintaskspro/processlibrary), I Am Not a Geek (www.iamnotageek.com/a/file_info.php), and Security Task Manager (www.neuber.com/taskmanager/process).

Malicious File Tricks

Malicious attackers have used a variety of rogue methods over the years to accomplish their activities. Here are some other tricks hackers have used to get their malware executed.

File Naming Tricks

Hackers have made an art out of renaming files for malicious purposes, and Microsoft is mostly to blame for this problem. By default, Windows will hide file extensions of known file types, although this behavior should be turned off (in Windows Explorer). Because this behavior is turned on by default, a malicious hacker can send a user a malicious executable called Readme.txt.exe and Windows will display just Readme.txt by default. Now, Windows contains several ways for the user to verify the extension:

❑   Hovering the mouse cursor over the file's path or full name

❑   Viewing file properties will reveal the file name

❑   The file's icon will be represented by the application associated with the file extension (in most cases).

Revealing File Extensions

You can tell Windows to display even registered file types by choosing the Tools menu option in Windows Explorer, then Folder Options, and the View tab (see Figure 5-3). Deselect the *Hide Extensions for Known File Types*. You should disable *Hide protected operating system files (Recommended)* to allow users to view Windows system files and profiles, and select *Show hidden files and folders*.

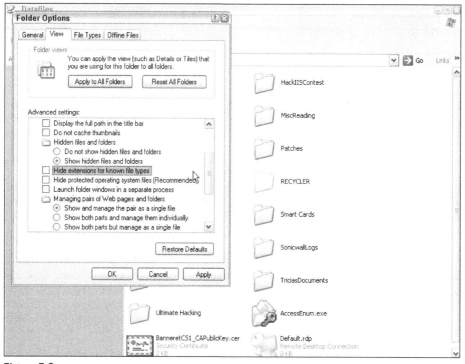

Figure 5-3

Super Hidden File Extensions

To make matters worse, even if you tell Windows not to hide well-known file extensions as discussed above, some register file extensions will still stay hidden (e.g., Scrap files). These file extensions are known as the "Super Hidden" file extensions. Each file association in the registry can be enabled or disabled regarding its Super Hidden status. Dozens of file extension associations have a registry value called NeverShowExt, including the high-risk files in Table 5-4.

Table 5-4

File Type/HR_CR Designation	File Extension
Internet Shortcuts	.Url
Desktop Shortcuts	.Lnk
Pif files	.Pif
ShellScrap file	.Shs
Explorer Command	.Scf

Super hidden file extensions allow hackers to name files like Readme.Txt.url that are really Internet browser links and will automatically download remote code, or Readme.Txt.shs, where the scrap file is really a shortcut pointing to an executable that is run instead. You should implement a registry edit or GPO to remove the NeverShowExt value for the file types listed in Table 5-4.

> *Be warned: If you reveal .Lnk and .Pif files, you will see the file extension revealed all over the desktop for many legitimate Windows files. Normally, this is not a problem, but it may surprise some users. The benefit gained by revealing the hidden extension overrides any temporary discomfort.*

Windows will always reveal or hide an extension depending on the existence of the AlwaysShowExt or NeverShowExt entry in the file type's registry subkey. The value of the entry doesn't matter, as long as the entry exists and is spelled correctly. When both values are present, the NeverShowExt value overrides the AlwaysShowExt value, which means it is hard to disable the NeverShowExt with a GPO (i.e., GPOs don't delete registry keys).

To delete existing registry keys, you can use an .Inf, scripts, or .Reg files. To manually remove the NeverShowExt value manually, use Regedit.exe and search for the NeverShowExt value. Delete it where found. The only issue to be aware of is that if you delete the NeverShowExt value, the file extensions related to those links will appear. For example, desktop shortcuts will end in an .Lnk extension. While this is a safe practice, you need to be aware of the results from the change, and warn end users if you deploy this suggestion widely. If you are pushing the change using a GPO, you'll need to deny Read permissions to the NeverShowExt registry key (if it exists).

Long File Names and Unprintable Characters

Hackers have also made file name roots containing something harmless-looking like Readme.txt that in reality was Readme.txt   .exe. The intervening spaces between the .txt portion of the file name and the real file extension (i.e., .exe) contained non-printable characters. Most screens that display the file name have an adjustable width for the file name column, and the default size would show Readme.txt. The true name would not be shown unless the user manually widened the column.

Sound-a-likes, Different Locations

When forensically investigating a computer for intrusion, always be on the lookout for sound-a-likes and files spelled right but in the wrong location. By default, WFP prevents Windows system files from being modified, deleted, or renamed. Instead, malware will install new rogue executables with official-sounding names in the normal system directories, or install a file with an identical name in a new location. Sound-a-like file names are ones like `Svchosts.exe` (instead of `Svchost.exe`) and `Regsrv32.exe` (instead of `Regsvr32.exe`). Or they load the malicious file, with a name identical to a normal system file, but from a non-default location. It can be hard to notice if you aren't familiar with file locations. For instance, is `Taskman.exe` loaded from `%Windir%` or `%Windir%\System32`? It's the former.

Rename Tricks

Any valid Windows system executable (at least `.Exes` and `.Coms` files) can be renamed to any file extension and still function identically on the command line (although not from the Windows Explorer GUI or Start, Run procedure). Thus `Format.com` can be renamed `Frog.gif` and still be executed. A new hacker trick is to upload their exploit tools to the victim's Internet Explorer Temporary Internet Files folder and name them after picture files. All users have access to the Temporary Internet File folder, and unless the user clears out the folder, the tools will probably stay undetected longer. Don't forget that any file format using the OLE2 file format (e.g., Microsoft Office documents) can be renamed without any file extension and it will still be executed by its appropriate related application if opened in the Windows GUI (doesn't work on the command line) or the application. Thus, an Excel spreadsheet named `Readme` will still be opened in Excel.

MIME Type Mismatch

When files are being downloaded in Internet Explorer and other multi-media-enabled applications, often Windows will look for the file's Multi-Purpose Internet Mail Extensions (or MIME) type. MIME was originally created so that SMTP mail servers and clients could exchange objects and media files beyond normal plaintext e-mail. Today, most web servers (and many other types of servers) send a file's MIME data type descriptor along with the file. The receiving application or operating system reads the MIME type descriptor and opens the file in the requested application.

Most MIME type descriptors are registered with the Internet Assigned Numbers Authority (`www.iana.org`), described in several RFCs, including RFC 1521 (`www.faqs.org/rfcs/rfc1521.html`). MIME type descriptors look something like this:

❑　Content-Type: text/plain

❑　type="application/x-shockwave-flash

The MIME type descriptor is read by the incoming application, which then looks up the application associated with each particular MIME type. In Windows, the MIME type application association is stored in the `HKCR` registry key under the appropriate application's file extension. In the first example, the `Notepad.exe` application is associated with the text/plain MIME type. In the latter, the Shockwave Flash application is associated with application/x-shockwave-flash.

Malicious exploits have been initiated by an intentionally malicious web server marking a file as one particular type of MIME file when the file's true contents were something else. The MIME type *mismatch* can cause application loading problems, DoS attacks, and even buffer overflows. MIME type mismatch issues have often been the reason why some security scanners failed to correctly catch malware problems.

Alternate Data Streams

Ever since Windows NT, Microsoft allows files and directories on an NTFS-formatted volume to have Alternate Data Streams (ADS). ADS was initially created to support Macintosh "resource forks" when Macintosh file support was added to NT. The idea is that one file or folder representation can have several other files associated with it. If copied or created with the appropriate ADS-aware tools, one copied file can contain all the support files its needs. When an ADS component is "attached" to a file, an extended attribute is attached to the file, and the ADS file is stored elsewhere on the disk. However, when the ADS file is needed, the file's extended attribute tells Windows that an ADS file is attached to the parent file and then where to look for the ADS file.

Although Microsoft uses ADS with some of its applications, ADS files never caught on big with other third-party legitimate programmers. Existing legitimate uses of ADS include the following:

- ❏   Handling "resource fork" material from Apple Macs (why ADS were invented)
- ❏   To store thumbnails
- ❏   By MS Office, to store document summary metadata
- ❏   By some antivirus (av) scanners, to hold integrity information

Hackers, however, occasionally use files with ADS to hide their malware or hacking tools. Because the ADS file is not stored directly with the file, even when the parent file (or directory) is modified to have an ADS stream, its file integrity does not change. This means that a hacker can basically store any number of programs or viruses attached to any file they like and MD5 hash checksum programs will not report different results. Although antivirus scanner programs can scan ADS files, they don't by default. It's an option that has to be turned on manually, and most administrators don't.

If you want to experiment with ADS files, try these steps:

1. Make a directory called C:\ADSTemp.

2. Copy Notepad.exe into C:\ADSTemp.

3. Copy Sol.exe (Solitaire) into C:\ADSTemp.

4. Do a directory (DIR) to get the file size and timestamps of Notepad.exe or run any hash integrity program you like.

5. Type **Sol.exe > Notepad.exe:Hidden.exe** and press Enter.

6. Now do another directory and checksum on the Notepad.exe file. Note that the information is the same, including size, date, and checksum. Figure 5-4 shows similar results.

7. Type in **Start c:\ADSTemp\Notepad.exe:Hidden.exe** and press Enter. The Solitaire program should have started.

8. Look in Task Manager (Ctl+Alt+Del) and see whether Notepad.exe is running as a process, and whether that reference indicates the difference between Notepad.exe and the ADS properly identified as Notepad.exe:Hidden.exe.

9. If you have a host-based firewall that does outbound blocking, repeat the preceding procedure, replacing Notepad.exe with an application that is allowed to pass through the firewall, and replacing Sol.exe with an application that will try to access the Internet but would normally be blocked from doing so by the firewall. Does the firewall pass or block the ADS?

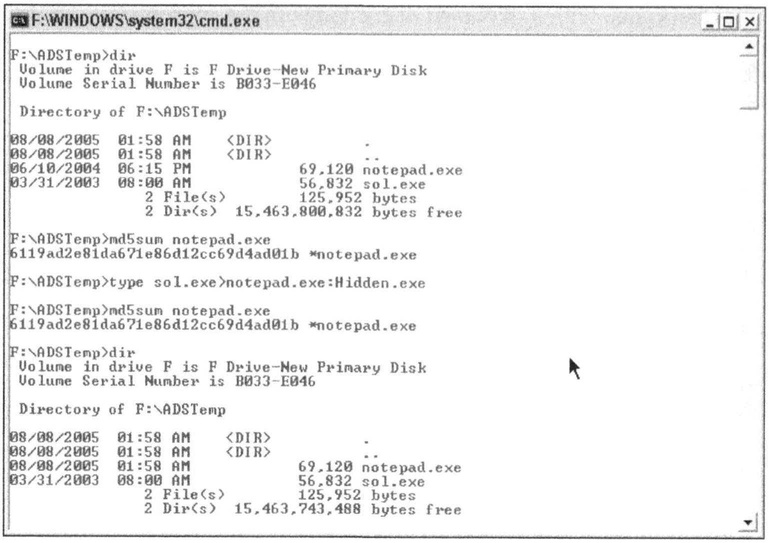

Figure 5-4

In this case, it was just two legitimate files, but it could have been a hacker tool just as easily. ADS file streams can be called using the `Start.exe` command and via browsers over HTTP. To find ADS files, you must download a Microsoft Resource Kit utility or use a third-party tool. My favorites are Foundstone's Sfind (`www.foundstone.com/?subnav=resources/navigation`) and Sysinternal's (`www.sysinternals.com/Utilities/Streams.html`).

Several risks associated with ADS have already being leveraged by malware:

❏   ADS aren't visible in Windows Explorer.

❏   Code running in an ADS is listed in Task Manager as the name of the parent file only in Windows 2000 and NT.

❏   Although antivirus programs can scan ADS files, they aren't checked for or scanned by default.

❏   As ADS have no directory entry, they can't be managed with NTFS permissions.

ADS files are an example of maliciousness from unintended consequences. When Microsoft created them, little thought was given to their potential abuses. The author of this book immediately saw the potential malicious use of ADS when NT 4.0 first appeared and reported it to a top AV vendor. They replied that they also knew about the potential problem, but that it wasn't a top priority since ADS files weren't being exploited. Years later when the first ADS viruses showed up, it wasn't surprising that several antivirus companies had solutions ready in a few days. It also taught me that many "zero-day" exploits are known by computer software defenders prior to their public release, but the defenses aren't released until after the public announcement to slow down the hacker vs. good guy war.

Dangerous Unused Applications

It is also important to remember that even when a file or application isn't used by the user, if it is installed, then it can be exploited. A common exploit method is for hackers to call a particular application via its URL moniker (this will be covered in more detail in Chapter 10, "Securing Internet Explorer"). A URL moniker is another file association type stored in HK_CR.

For example, the URL moniker Telnet:// will call the Windows telnet client to activate (see Figure 5-5). Suppose there were a known buffer overflow issue with the Microsoft Telnet.exe client program. A hacker could send a user an e-mail containing an embedded link that when clicked or automatically downloaded launched the client's Telnet program to contact the attacker's remote server, where a client-side buffer overflow was waiting. Similar tactics have been used against many programs.

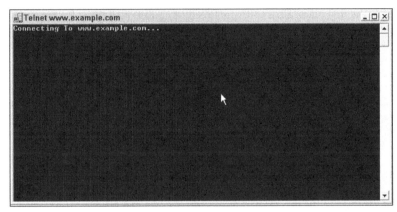

Figure 5-5

Another real-life example is the URL moniker aim://, which calls America Online's Instant Messaging (AIM) client. In the past, at least two exploits have been documented whereby a user is sent a simple URL link. Unknown to the user, the link contains the aim:// moniker; and with related commands fed to the user's browser, AIM is started and a file transfer initiated. The files transferred caused a buffer overflow in one instance, and allowed the unauthorized copying of files in the other.

Just an application being installed increases risk. Sometimes whether a user actually uses a particular program isn't a factor. In fact, when users don't use a program, they probably won't keep it patched and updated. How many times have you updated a program you never use?

Buffer Overflows

Lastly, any running program or service that can be overflowed gives an attacker a way to exploit a system. Buffer overflows (actually, there are over a dozen types of overflows besides a buffer overflow, but we'll just keep the discussion simple) either cause a DoS attack or allow complete compromise of the attacked system. When a program or service is overflowed, the attacker usually gets system access with the security context in which the program was running. In Windows, this is often the local system. You'll find out more about this in Chapter 7, "Tightening Services."

File Defenses

Now that we've discussed common high-risk files and programs, it's time to discuss how to minimize risk.

Uninstall, Remove, Delete, and Rename

The best way to minimize the threat of malicious exploit from high-risk files and programs is not to have them installed in the first place. Do a software inventory audit of all the software running on the systems under your control. Document software that is approved for use within the organization and remove everything else you can. Run uninstall programs, remove the programs manually if you have to, delete files and registry keys, or, as a last-ditch effort, rename the main executables.

> *If you rename a program file to stop it from being used, there is a risk of Windows tracking it. Once, when I renamed WScript.exe to WScript.ex! to disable stand-alone WSH script files, I found that related script files still ran. When I looked in the relevant parts of HKCR, I found that the "open" action command line was changed to WScript.ex!. I've also had hotfixes and service packs undo my renamed and deleted security protections.*

Unfortunately, that works only for non-WFP protected files.

Microsoft protects most of the executables in the %Windir% and %Windir%\System32 directories. Out of the more than 8,000 files installed with Windows, over one fourth is protected by WFP (called *System File Protection* in Windows ME). When a protected file is deleted, renamed, or moved, Windows will replace it with a legitimate copy (from the install media or %Windir%\System32\Dllcache). Although WFP can be disabled, it isn't easy or recommended. WFP provides nice (although not solid) protection against many file virus attacks.

Use NTFS Permissions

The single best way to prevent unauthorized program and file execution is to use NTFS permissions. For every high-risk file and unused application, prevent non-Admin users from being able to execute the file. By default, most Authenticated Users have Read & Execute access to all Windows system files. Make sure that administrators have Full Control to those files, but remove the Authenticated Users group from having Read & Execute permissions. Note that I didn't say deny permissions. Some readers may accidentally enable Read & Execute-Deny permissions to the Authorized Users or Everyone groups as a result of the recommendation. Unfortunately, administrators are also part of those groups so you don't want to be denying access. Instead, add Administrators and uncheck the Authenticated Users permissions. You may have to remove inheritance on some files and folders to change default permissions.

If you have ever wondered how to disable Outlook Express without disabling Outlook (Outlook requires Outlook Express files), use NTFS permissions. Find the Outlook Express executable (i.e., F:\Program Files\Outlook Express\Msimn.exe) and remove non-Administrators from being able to run it.

Remove Everyone Full Control Permissions

Consider replacing any permissions handed to the Everyone group with a more select group. At the very least you can usually replace the Everyone group with the Authenticated Users group and guarantee that anyone using a related protected resource at least had to provide valid authentication credentials.

One of the most fundamental computer security tenets is to assign security principals only the bare minimum permissions necessary to perform their duties — the principle of least privilege. For any protected resource to which non-Admin users have Full Control, consider changing to Modify permissions instead. Full Control is a lot of authority to give any non-Admin user. It gives them the capability to change permissions and to take ownership. Modify permissions is all most non-Admin users needed. Also remember that by default all Authenticated members of any trusted domain in the forest have the same permissions that your Authenticated Users and Everyone groups have. However, you can limit foreign domain users' access further by using NTFS permissions.

Create a Least Privilege Users Group

As administrators, we are continually asked to add new users who only need basic security permissions to a very limited subset of files and folders. Maybe it is an external consultant who needs access to the internal SQL database running on one server, or an external business partner who needs to log into your IIS server and pick up one file, or an onsite security consultant performing an audit. In any case, all administrators need to create user accounts that should only have access to exactly what they need and no more. Here's a solution.

Create a custom security group called `LeastPrivilegedUsersGrp`. Create a `LeastPrivilegedUsersOU` organization unit and place the `LeastPrivilegedUsersGrp` inside. Add any security principal that should have very limited access to both the OU and the group. Better yet, add membership to the LeastPrivilegedUsersGrp group using the Restricted Groups group policy feature (see Figure 5-6). You can find more about the Restricted Groups feature in Chapter 14, "Group Policy Explained."

Using a group policy object, severely restrict the User Rights and privileges of the members of the `LeastPrivilegedUsersGrp` to a common bare minimum. Create a `LeastPrivilegedUsersGPO` and attach it to the `LeastPrivilegedUsersOU,` and set it to be enforced (this will be explained in Chapter 14). Then, using the File Security feature of group policy, ensure that the members of the group have Full Control-Deny to all files and folders on every drive, starting with the root directory of each volume and working on down. Inheritance should do most of the work.

Then, wherever the members need access, go to those specific file and folder locations and grant specific access permissions. The specific permissions should override the inherited permissions set by the group policy. Using this method, you can create a group whose members have no rights to any file and folder in your network, except exactly where you want them to have access. No more having to wonder what files and folders these supposedly restricted users had before. Just drop the user into the OU, set their specific permissions needed, and let Active Directory do the rest. This is a great strategy for temporary workers, consultants, web site users, and web site pool identities.

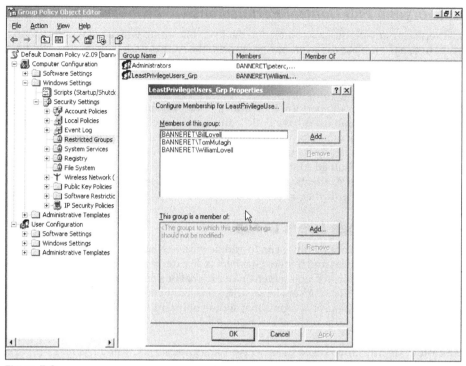

Figure 5-6

Use GPO Where Possible

Group Policy objects are a wonderful way to automatic almost any computer security setting, but they are especially helpful when setting file permissions. By default, when you delete or overwrite a file, it loses its set NTFS permissions. For example, if you delete a file protected by WFP, the permissions assigned to the replacement copy are inherited from the parent folder and do not necessarily match the permissions of the file deleted. The same thing can happen when Microsoft updates a file. The update overwrites the original and file permissions can sometimes be lost. Normally NTFS permissions are tied to the exact object they were set on. A new object, even if it has the same name, is a different object, so the original NTFS permissions are lost. Luckily this is not true when using a GPO.

By using group policy to set permissions, the NTFS permissions will be set on the file every time the GPO applies as long as the file's name and location do not change. The object the permission is being set on in the GPO must already exist on the machine where the GPO is being configured. However, you can make up any "fake" object as a placeholder, if you need to, to help with creating the policy. For high-risk files, use a GPO to ensure that the permissions are being applied and pushed out to all managed computers without having to worry about the files being updated or re-created and losing their permissions.

There are two security considerations. First, setting an object's permission via a GPO does not mean the logged in user cannot change the permission. When permissions are set via a GPO, the object's permissions are set, or reset, whenever the GPO re-applies. During the time interval between GPO applications, the file's permissions can be modified if the manipulator has the appropriate security permissions (i.e., Change Permissions). A GPO, by itself, only sets permissions. It does not prevent permissions from being changed otherwise if the manipulator has the necessary permissions.

Second, when a GPO is applied, it is not re-applied again for 16 hours by default (called the *maximum GPO refresh interval*) unless the GPO itself is new or changed. If the object being protected by the GPO is deleted or re-created (of course, the user or process doing this would have to have the appropriate permissions to do so), the predefined GPO permissions could take up to 16 hours to re-apply. You can manually force a GPO to re-apply immediately by typing in **Gpupdate.exe /force** at the affected workstation, or, more quickly, by telling the GPO to always re-apply during its periodic refresh interval (which by default is every 90 minutes with a random offset of 30 minutes). To turn on the latter feature, enable `Computer Configuration\Administrative Template\System\Group Policy\Security policy processing` and its child option of `Process even if Group Policy objects have not been changed`. You can download a security template with the default settings listed in this chapter from the Wrox web site.

Software Restriction Policies

Starting with Windows XP Pro, Microsoft introduced the concept of *Software Restriction Policies (SRP)*. SRP allows an administrator to specify what software is allowed to run on any managed computer. Software Restriction Policies require Windows XP Pro or later computers. Windows 2000 has a smaller subset of features similar to SRP but isn't nearly as versatile.

The SRP management console is accessed using Group Policy or Local Computer Policy. Choose `Computer Configuration\Windows Settings\Security Settings\Software Restriction Policies` to access SRP settings (see Figure 5-7). Group Policy, but not Local Computer Policy, allows administrators to configure SRP in the User Configuration area as well.

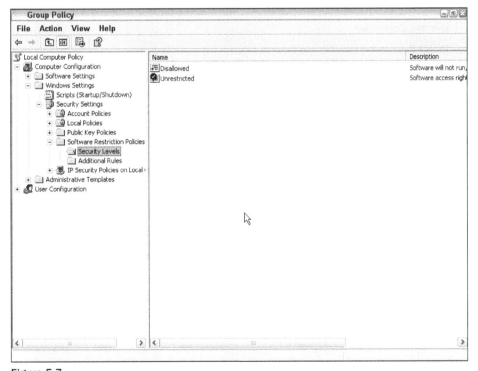

Figure 5-7

First, before administrators even begin configuring SRP, they need to establish what software should and shouldn't be allowed to run on a managed computer. This includes all user applications, utilities, Windows program files, etc. If the admin is going to restrict what files and programs are allowed to run, he or she must first get a list of what is to be allowed. Next, a major decision needs to be made. Is SRP going to deny all software by default, except that which is allowed, or allow all software to run by default, except that which is denied (the default when SRP is turned on)?

A good security policy is to deny by default all software except that which is explicitly allowed, much like a firewall should be configured. This method takes much longer to get working initially but pays back the biggest security dividend. If an administrator could stop unauthorized programs from running, it would stop nearly every computer security problem in the enterprise. Most of the recommendations in this book are because administrators are not willing to go this far in preventing unauthorized applications from running. This choice is called *Disallowed* in SRP. The other choice — that is, to allow all software to run except that which is explicitly denied — is called *Unrestricted*. Unrestricted is good at stopping specific nuisances, such as spyware, but it doesn't provide nearly as much security for the effort. You can also decide who SRP applies to — all users or all users except local Administrators.

Rule Exceptions

After that major decision is made, the administrator goes about setting *exceptions*. Exceptions are policy rules that either allow specific software (when using the Disallowed main setting), or deny specific software (when using the Unrestricted setting). There are four different types of exception rules:

❑   Certificate rules

❑   Hash rules

❑   Internet Zone rules

❑   Path rules

Certificate exception rules allow you to deny or allow software digitally signed by a specific digital certificate. For example, you can deny all VBScript files except those signed by an internal private digital certificate. It will stop VBS viruses and worms from running, but allow your own internal management scripts to run. Certificate rules require a code signing digital certificate to be trusted, and you must configure separately who can decide whether to trust a particular code signing certificate (any user or just Administrators). Certificate rules apply no matter where the file is or what it is named, as long as the file's integrity has been maintained and the certificate remains valid. Administrators can define whether certificate revocation checking is enabled on Certificate rules and how revocation is checked (Publisher, Timestamp, or both).

Hash rules allow you to input a valid MD5 or SHA1 file hash value (also known as a *digital fingerprint*). Like Certificate rules, they allow you to deny or allow a particular file or program no matter where the target resides or what the file is named. All that matters is that the related file meets its previously stored hash value (see Figure 5-8).

Most administrators using SRP use a lot of hash rules. The only problem is that software updates and patches frequently update the related executable referred to by the hash. This means the administrator is constantly adding and modifying hash rules every time a new file version comes out. With that said, the hash rule method is extremely accurate.

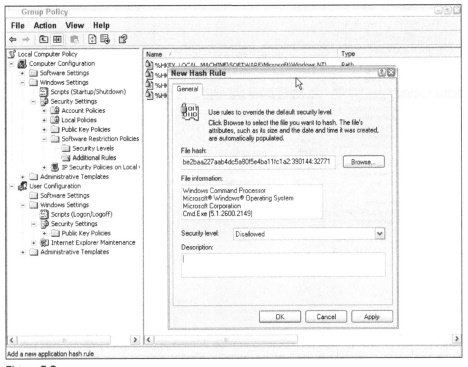

Figure 5-8

The Internet Zone rule is probably the least useful of the SRP rules. It will allow or deny all software installed and executed in a particular Internet Explorer Zone (more on zones in Chapter 10), but only if the file was installed with a Windows installer file (.Msi). Since most Internet-installed software programs do not install with an .Msi file, it practically makes the rule class useless.

Lastly, Path rules allow you to define exceptions using directory or registry paths. When SRP is enabled, Microsoft inserts four default Path rules ensuring that users don't lock themselves out of Windows the first time they enable the Disallow option. Path rules will accept the standard wildcard naming conventions (i.e., ? and *) in the path statements. SRP is fairly accurate at preventing the exact executable from executing, but can easily be bypassed by a semi-knowledgeable end user — for instance, if you right-click the protected executable and create a shortcut. That shortcut will run the executable without problem. If you rename the executable, it will run without problem. If you copy the executable elsewhere, it will run without problem.

There are some issues with SRP beyond figuring out what is and isn't allowed. It isn't perfect. For one, it only works with Windows XP Pro and later. Two, it cannot manage 16-bit executables (such as Command.com and Edit.com). If you wish to prevent 16-bit executables, use NFTS permissions on Ntdvm.exe. Three, it does not apply to all file types by default. The initial configuration (by file extension) is only 31 file types (see Figure 5-9). You can easily add more file extensions to SRP's file blocking mechanism, but it far less than the hundreds of file extensions defined in Windows by default. Lastly, there appears to be many ways to bypass each particular exception rule. Most users won't be able to guess how to hack around SRP, but it can be done. It is not a panacea. If you need absolute security, use NTFS permissions instead.

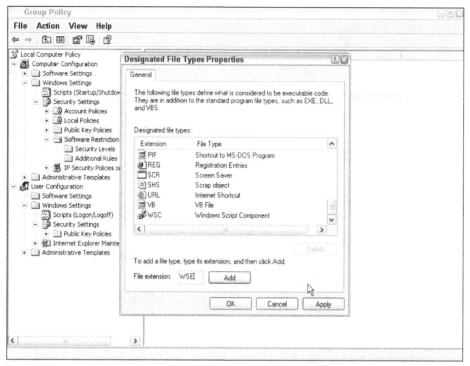

Figure 5-9

In at least one instance, SRP permissions are better than NTFS permissions. It is the problem of how to secure applications with NTFS permissions prior to them being installed. NTFS permissions cannot be set until the file or folder is already installed. SRP can be used with wildcards to allow or deny programs from the moment they were attempted to be first installed. You should use a combination of all the SRP and NTFS permissions to get the desired outcome.

Although SRP doesn't work on Windows 2000, group policy has SRP-like policies. Choose User Configuration\Administrative Templates\System. There are two similar settings called *Run only allowed Windows applications* and *Don't run specific Windows applications.* A few other options above and below will allow you to have some limited control over software execution.

There are many third-party tools that do the same thing as SRP, such as Desktop Standard's PolicyMaker (www.desktopstandard.com/PolicyMakerStandard.aspx) and NetIQ's Group Policy Administrator (www.netiq.com/products/gpa/default.asp). Go to www.microsoft.com/windowsserver2003/ technologies/management/grouppolicy/gptools.mspx for more Group Policy extension tools that can accomplish the same thing as SRP.

Enable Auditing

On high-risk files, consider enabling Object Access auditing. Turn on the audit categories you wish to monitor, and review event logs manually or with a tool looking for signs of intrusion. For example, enable auditing on the Hosts file. Set the default permissions on the Hosts file to be Read-only for non-admin users (or administrators, if you like). Enable Object Access auditing on the file and tell it to report any successes or failures for access requests beyond reading. If spyware tries to modify it, Windows will generate an event log entry. Consider doing this for any high-risk files that are especially critical.

Keep Patches Updated

Many file and program vulnerabilities are patched by the vendor. Keep your operating system and applications patched and updated.

Other Defenses

There are other defenses that can be taken to minimize the threat of unauthorized file and program execution, including the following:

❑ Blocking malicious files at the e-mail server and gateway devices. Any file-blocking device should allow file blocking by file extension or MIME types. Better devices actually inspect a file's header to determine its legitimacy (more on this in Chapter 11).

❑ Using NTFS permissions on high-risk registry keys and values can provide as much security as NTFS permission for files and folders. This will be covered in the next chapter, "Protecting High-Risk Registry Entries."

Summary

This chapter explained the concept of high-risk files and programs and how to minimize their risk. By default, Windows allows non-admin users Read & Execute permissions to most Windows system files. Administrators need to use NTFS permissions, Software Restriction Policies, Group Policy, Patch Management, and other techniques to prevent malicious misuse. As with any security advice, do not implement the recommendations in this chapter on production systems without adequate testing. Chapter 6 covers protecting high-risk registry entries.

Protecting High-Risk Registry Entries

Microsoft introduced the registration database (the *registry*) as a way for Windows to locate pertinent configuration information in one location. It exists in all versions of Windows, including 64-bit and Windows CE. Prior to the registry, most applications, and even Windows, installed their own configuration files (often ending with the .INI file extension). Ini files could be installed anywhere on the hard drive, and be structured however the developer liked.

Unfortunately, the use of separate configuration files led to end user confusion, lost configuration files, and operational problems.

The registration database offered a hierarchical database schema that developers and administrators could use to simplify registration and configuration information. Whether or not the registry met this goal is debatable. What isn't debatable is that malicious programmers learned to use the registry to compromise Windows machines with much success. Today, it is the rare malware program that doesn't manipulate the registry to do its misdeed. This chapter discusses the registry and its different sections in depth, lists the high-risk keys, and then describes defenses against malicious misuse.

Registry Introduction

Even though Microsoft heavily promoted the use of the registry instead of separate configuration databases, starting as early as Windows 3.x, many application developers, including Microsoft, continued to use their own configuration files along with the registry for many years after the registry was introduced. As Windows moved from the Windows 9x platform to the Windows NT family, existing .INI files were kept only for backward legacy compliance. The registry grew from a little-used database to a huge application configuration store refractory. Today, registry files over 100 MBs in size aren't uncommon (although 11 MBs is the limitation in Windows 98).

You can still view Windows default .INI files, System.ini, and Win.ini by running many commands, including Sysedit.exe and Msconfig.exe.

The registry solution solved one problem, a single location for system and program information, but introduced many more. Problems such as corruption, large size, single points of failure, and infrequent backups have made the registry a source of criticism since the beginning. Although officially Microsoft claims that end users and administrators should not directly edit the registry, almost every troubleshooting technician can mentally recall numerous keys easily because of their familiarity with its structure. Often, a registry edit is the only way to solve a Windows problem. And like many computer databases, once data is written to it, it never leaves, even if unneeded. The registration database is prone to corruption and its ever-growing size can delay Windows booting up a minute or more.

Microsoft intends to replace or supplement the registry with the Windows File System (WinFS) in upcoming releases of Windows XP, Vista, and Server 2003. WinFS will consist of XML-enabled style data values stored in a SQL-like database. WinFS was initially going to be released in Windows Vista, but it was pulled by Microsoft and will instead be included in Windows XP Release 2. Because current applications are developed to use the registry and not WinFS, if you're a Windows admin0 be prepared to troubleshoot both in the coming years.

Registry Structure

The hierarchical registry database is divided into five different major sections, called *hives* or *subtrees*. The five hives, as shown in Figure 6-1, are HKEY_CLASSES_ROOT, HKEY_CURRENT_USER, HKEY_LOCAL_MACHINE, HKEY_USERS, and HKEY_CURRENT_CONFIG. They are often abbreviated as HKCR, HKCU, HKLM, HKU, and HKCC by authors, including in this book. You can explore the registry (and view, search, modify, and delete information) using either of the common Registry editing tools, Regedit.exe or Regedt32.exe. There are also a plethora of third-party tools that show information or allow editing of the registry (e.g., HiJackThis, Autorun, etc.).

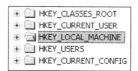

Figure 6-1

Under each hive are *keys*, *subkeys*, *values*, and *data* — making up thousands of separate database entries. Keys are the first level under the subtrees, followed by the lower subkeys, the subkey values, and the data of each value. There can be one or more values under each subkey. Each value can contain data, whether decimal, binary, ASCII string, or another representational data (covered below). In Figure 6-2, the hive is HKLM, the key is \Software, the subkey is \Microsoft\Windows\Current Version\Run, the value is dla, and the data is C:\Windows\System32\dla\tfswctrl.exe.

Hives can be completely independent storage areas or display values and keys of different hives. In NT and later, most hives are stored as physical files in %Windir%\System32\Config or the location indicated by HKLM\System\CurrentControlSet\Control\hivelist. The files in %Windir%\System32\Config are named Software, System, SAM, Security, Default, and UserDiff. Table 6-1 discusses each of the registry hive files. Unless otherwise noted, they can be found in %Windir%\System32\Config.

Figure 6-2

Table 6-1

Hive Name	Description
SAM	Contains information stored in the key HKLM\SAM regarding the Security Accounts Manager (SAM) database
Security	Contains the security information stored in the key HKLM\SECURITY
Software	Contains information stored in the key HKLM\SOFTWARE about the local computer's software configuration information
System	Contains information stored in the key HKLM\SYSTEM about the computer's system configuration
Default	Contains the default system information that is stored in the key KU\.DEFAULT
Ntuser.dat	Stored in the user's profile under \Documents and Settings\%UserProfile%, it represents the HKCU subtree.

As you can see, most of the files refer to the HKLM subtree. The registry files ending in the .Sav file extension are backup copies made just after the text-mode portion of the Windows install routine is finished. They are saved so that if the GUI mode portion of the install fails, the Setup program can restore the system to the end of the text-mode install and begin again. Forensic investigators can use their last modified file date to learn when the system was first installed. The files ending in .Log are transaction log files containing a record of the changes made to the registry.

Microsoft's Windows Vista will have registry virtualization for legacy (i.e., non-Vista) applications. It will redirect many HKLM registry changes to per-user locations. This will prevent many applications (and malware) installed by a single user from affecting all users on the same computer.

Registry Value Data Types

Most registry keys and subkeys eventually get down to the registry subkey values and the value's data. Data can be inputted several different ways (manually, scripting, GPOs, etc.) using a variety of different data types. The most popular data types are shown in Table 6-2.

Table 6-2

Data Type	Description
Reg_Binary	Hexadecimal characters type in two-digit, raw binary, hexadecimal form
Reg_Dword	Binary or hexadecimal characters type in as 4-byte ASCII characters. Related values are DWORD_LITTLE_ENDIAN (least significant byte is at the lowest address or in reverse) and REG_DWORD_BIG_ENDIAN (least significant byte is at the highest address or in normal forward order).
Reg_String or Reg_Sz	Fixed-length ASCII or Unicode character string
Reg_Expand_Sz	Variable-length ASCII or Unicode character string
Reg_Multi_Sz	Variable-length list or array of one or more ASCII or Unicode character strings

There are more data types than shown in Table 6-2. Not all versions of Windows have all data types. See http://support.microsoft.com/kb/256986/EN-US for more details.

HK_Local_Machine Subkeys

The HKLM subtree stores configuration information for hardware and software of the computer regardless of who is logged on. It contains five keys: Hardware, SAM, Security, Software, and System.

The Hardware key contains information about the physical hardware of the computer. The key HKLM\ HARDWARE is not stored as a file, because it is re-created each time the system starts. Any values created during the Windows session are discarded when Windows is shut down. Hardware information about local devices, interrupts, and hardware configuration is stored under this key. You can view a lot of this information by using the Device Manager applet under the Control Panel. Windows and other applications can access this key to interface with the hardware appropriately. Malware rarely manipulates this key.

The SAM key is the SAM database that stores authentication and security information about the different security principals (i.e., user, group, computers, etc.). It is usually protected from direct manipulation, even by the Administrator, but as discussed in Chapter 4, several password-cracking tools can access it and extract password hashes.

The Security key contains a plethora of security information related to the local machine. Default permissions don't allow even Administrators to view the subkeys and values, but you can change permissions (covered below) to allow more access. The Security key contains things such as the cached logon passwords and Lsasecrets. By default, Windows caches the passwords of up to 10 different user profiles to assist in faster logons. Those passwords are stored in the HKLM\Security\Cache subkey. The Lsasecrets, which include Service account passwords, are stored in HKLM\Security\Policy\Secrets. Different user security information is stored under HKLM\Security\Policy\Accounts, by account SID number. The \Security key stores a variety of other information related to the local machine. There are several attack tools (e.g., Creddump, Cachedump, as covered in Chapter 4) that attack this key, although most automated malware programs attack the next HKLM key.

HKLM\Software is the most popular Windows key by legitimate users and malware. \Software contains registration and configuration information for the operating system and application software installed on the local machine. It contains many of the registry auto-run keys (including the most popular auto-run key, HKLM\Software\Microsoft\Windows\CurrentVersion\Run). It contains subkeys for nearly every installed software program. Most of the subkeys and values of interest to malware are located at HKLM\Software\Microsoft\Windows\CurrentVersion and HKLM\Software\Microsoft\Windows NT\CurrentVersion. Table 1-1 in Chapter 1 listed the most popularly abused keys.

This is a good point to mention HKLM\Software\Policies. Most domain group policy settings under the Computer Configuration heading pushed down to the local machine by Active Directory are located here. Any policy setting configured here does not *tattoo* the registry—meaning if the group policy no longer applies, the pushed down settings are removed. Custom administrative templates can also push values to HKLM\Software\Microsoft\Windows\CurrentVersion\Policies, but this location creates *unmanaged* policies and they will tattoo the registry and remain in effect until the policy settings are deleted or modified (either manually or using group policy). On a related note, the HKCU\Software\Policies subkey holds the settings pushed down from the User Configuration portion of group policy (more on this in Chapter 14).

HKLM\System is second in malware popularity only to HKLM\Software. It contains operating system information that controls system startup behavior, device drive loading, service configuration and loading, and overall OS operations. An example is HKLM\System\CurrentControlSet\Control\Safeboot\Minimal. This subkey controls what services are loaded when the OS is booted in Safe mode. Many forensic investigators rely on Safe mode to remove any malware programs when searching for signs of infection and maliciousness. Many malware programs manipulate this key so that they are loaded and can thus manipulate or hamper forensic techniques even when the OS is in Safe mode. Several popular keys used by malware were shown in Table 1-1 of Chapter 1. If malware is attacking Windows, chances are greater than 95% that it will attack a subkey located under HKLM.

HK_Classes_Root

This subtree is used to list file associations, URI handlers (e.g., news://, aim:// in Internet Explorer), and COM file configuration information. HKCR is most commonly used to list the effective Windows file associations linking a particular file extension to one or more software programs which are supposedly designed to handle the particular file format. For example, clicking on a file ending in .Txt will normally result in Notepad being launched. Clicking a file ending in .VBS in Windows Explorer will result in Windows Scripting Host (Wscript.exe) being called, but clicking it in Internet Explorer will result in VBScript.dll being called to handle it. By default, Windows has hundreds of file associations.

File Associations in the Registry

HKCR lists the effective Windows file associations arising from the combination of HKLM\Software\Classes and HKCU\Software\Classes. Starting with Windows 2000, file associations can be viewed or modified in any of the following three registry locations:

❏ HKCR

❏ HKLM\Software\Classes

❏ HKCU\Software\Classes

Although file associations can be modified in any of the three locations, HKCR is only meant to be a registry area showing the effective associations. File associations set at the HKLM\Software\Classes location are in effect for all users of the computer unless specifically overridden by HKCU\Software\Classes. Associations in HKCU\Software\Classes take precedence for the currently logged on user. If a new value is written to HKCR and it does not exist in HKCU\Software\Classes, it is written to HKLM\Software\Classes and applies to all users on the computer. If the key or value already exists in HKLM\Software\Classes, the modification is written to HKCU\Software\Classes and only applies to the local logged on user. This is an important point to remember and one occasionally manipulated by malware. Forensic investigators, unaware of the other three file association location interactions, might be stymied by malware using the latter two keys instead of HKCR.

Under the registry key HKCR, applications are listed by either their file extension (e.g., Vbs), file type name (e.g., VBSFile), CLSID (e.g. {FDE424F3-AA10-471D-8A0A-6875C17B5914}), or handling module (e.g., Outlook.FileAttach). The HKCR subtree can be broken down into two main sections: upper-level file extensions and lower-level program modules and file associations.

The two different sections enable Windows to bind multiple file extensions into aggregate file types, and to simplify management of these. For example, one might have .Bmp, .Jpg, .Gif, .Tif, etc., all pointing to a file type called GraphicFiles, and define actions for these just once, under GraphicFiles. One could then define another file type called AlternateGraphicFiles and, by switching individual file extensions from one to the other, apply different sets of actions without having to destructively set these up for each file extension.

The upper level displays the file extensions associated with each registered program. Although most file extensions are three characters long, some file extensions are shorter and longer in length. The upper-level section is mostly a "pointer" to the related lower-level file associations. Together, both levels display a lot of information for each file type. The most important values include the following:

- ❏ File association
- ❏ File Extension
- ❏ Associated Program and Action
- ❏ CLSID (Class Identifier)
- ❏ Mime Type Identifier
- ❏ Default Icon
- ❏ File Extension Display
- ❏ File Handling (e.g., File Download Confirmation prompt)

Not all file associations have all these fields. At the top of HKCR (using Regedit.exe), you will see *. This subkey tells Windows how to treat all newly registered file types if not instructed by the installing program or user. Directly under the * subkey are hundreds of registered file extensions. Actually, not too much information is stored directly under the file extension subkey, but what is there is valuable and useful. For one, the Default value will list the associated registry key where more of the file association information is stored. For nearly every file association listed at the top of the HKCR key, there is another corresponding lower-level file association subkey holding more confirmation information. For example, the .Vbs file association has a Default value of VBSFile. VBSFile is a registry key located lower in HKCR and is where the majority of the information regarding the treatment of Visual Basic Script (.Vbs) files is stored. The top file association subkey will also list the CLSID of the associated program in the Persistant Handler value. The CLSID is a unique alphanumeric value given to each program or module. Windows and Internet Explorer often use the CLSID instead of the file extension to identify a file type handler.

The upper-level subkeys will also reveal MIME Type identifiers (discussed in Chapter 5). For example, the .Txt file association has the MIME Type identifier listed in the *Content Type* value, with data of text/plain. This means if a file is downloaded in Internet Explorer (or HTML-enabled e-mail) with a MIME Type identifier of text/plain, Windows will associate the file with the .Txt file association and the lower-level TxtFile subkey (as indicated by the *Default* value).

Heading down lower into the HRCR subtree will reveal more file association information. For instance, choosing the VBSFile file association (remember the .VBS file association's *Default* value said VBSFile), will display many key informational fields (see Figure 6-3). First, the *Default* value right under the VBSFile subkey describes the file type. In this example it is *VBScript Script File*. Although most administrators are familiar with the most common file extensions and their associated applications, there are dozens that are not well known. If you see *URL: <protocol handler>*, it tells you that the "file extension" is a URL moniker, not a file extension. For example, under the Telnet file association, the Default value has data indicating URL: telenet protocol. This means if **telnet://** is typed into Internet Explorer or on the command line, it will launch the Telnet program. All the registered URL monikers are a potential attack point because malware can get third-party programs to launch in Internet Explorer. This method has been used in several attacks in the past.

Another value is the FriendlyTypeName. This lists the .Dll file that will initially handle VBS files in Internet Explorer (i.e., Wshext.dll). Wshext.dll will eventually hand off VBS files to the VBSScript.dll program. The EditFlags decimal value of 0 (or 0x00000000 in hexadecimal) indicates that a file download confirmation dialog box will be displayed if the file is downloaded by Internet Explorer or other Windows programs and does not automatically execute. For potentially dangerous files, as listed in Table 5-1 in Chapter 5, this is a smart option to enable. If left disabled, a malicious web site or e-mail could automatically execute malicious code on the user's system without the user ever having a chance to deny the execution. A binary value of 01 in the third octet of the EditFlags value disables the download confirmation dialog box. The DefaultIcon subkey lists the executable from which the icon graphic is pulled when an associated file is displayed. In the VBSFile example, the icon is pulled from Wscript.exe. Malware has been known to manipulate this value in order to make a potentially harmful file appear harmless (e.g., .EXE file associated with the .TXT file icon) to trick the end user into executing it without the appropriate cautions.

Some file types point to themselves as the source of the icon, and this is a common point at which malware type spoofing occurs. When an icon is pulled out of the parent file, the file can display any icon it likes. This is why icons are an unsafe substitute for file name extensions as a determinant of file type.

The Shell\Open\Command subkey (see Figure 6-3) shows the program the file extension is associated with when executed outside of Internet Explorer. In this example, VBSFile is executed with the Wscript .exe program. The Shell\Open2\Command subkey displays another program, CScript.exe, which can be used to run VBS files at the command prompt. The Shell\Edit\Command subkey displays the program the file is opened in if opened for editing (versus executing). The \Shell\Print\Command subkey tells Windows how to print the file if told to print it (often using Notepad and the /P print command). Other subkeys instructing behavior you might see include New, Printto, and OpenAsReadOnly.

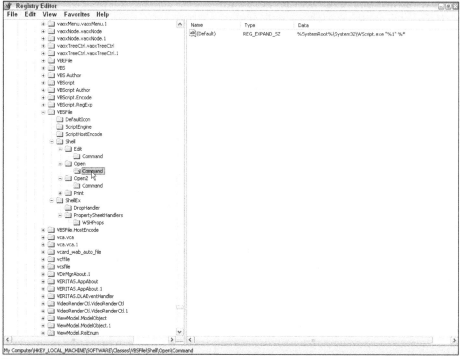

Figure 6-3

The `Shell\Open\Command` subkey has been manipulated by many malware programs. Worms and trojans have changed the default program to something more malicious. For example, the normal .Txt handler can be changed from `Notepad.exe` to `Wscript.exe`, for a malicious script file. A dangerous `VBScript` or `JSScript` file could then be sent to the end user as a .TXT file and it would execute using `WScript.exe` and be able to cause much more damage than if it were a plaintext file.

Trojans and worms have also manipulated the `Shell\Open\Command` value so that they were executed along with the normal file handler. For example, many e-mail trojans have manipulated the .Exe file association so that the malware program was executed along with any run .Exe executable. They do this by changing the .Exe file Default value from its normal setting of `"%1" %*` to `"malwareprogram.exe %1" %*`, where `malwareprogram.exe` is the malicious program's name. The following file associations are particularly popular with malware programmers using this trick:

❑ BAT

❑ COM

❑ EXE

❑ HTA

❑ PIF

But any file association is vulnerable. Other trojans have attacked .Chm, .Ini, .Reg, .Scr, and .Txt files.

The action named as the value of the key called `shell` is the default action that will happen if you double-click (or press Enter on) a file, and will be the action seen in bold if the file is right-clicked to access the context menu. But there are some shell contexts that will use whatever action is called "open" instead, whether this is set as the default action or not. This includes the "legacy" OpenWith programs list, and use of the Start command.

There are dozens of other possible registry fields related to the registry file associations, but these are the ones most interesting to malware authors and forensic investigators. Messing with file associations in the registry can be difficult and painstaking. Some forensic investigators prefer to use the Windows Explorer GUI to view and manipulate file associations, although GUI manipulation is very limited as compared to the registry interface.

File Associations in Windows Explorer

You can view the current file associations in Windows by choosing the Tools menu option from within Windows Explorer and then choosing Folder Options ⇨ File Types (see Figure 6-4). There are hundreds of registered file associations you can view, modify, and delete. Any changes made here (you need admin permissions) are written to the `HKLM\Software\Classes` subkeys and will override settings in the `HKCR` subtree. Currently, there is no way to view or modify file associations for the `HKCU\Software\Classes` subkey through the GUI — all changes must be made manually.

The Windows Explorer method only shows the direct file associations between file extensions and their related applications, but doesn't show handling modules or all OLE2 file types. By selecting a file extension and clicking the Change button in the File Types dialog box, you can view the associated application (see Figure 6-4) if you have admin rights. When clicking on a previously unregistered file association, Windows will prompt you to associate an application. If you are an administrator, you can select the *Always use the selected program file to open this kind of file* option (if the file has an extension) or let Windows use Web Services to search for the appropriate program (this almost never works).

If you select the Advanced button under the Folders Types dialog box, you get another set of features (see Figure 6-5). One, *Confirm open after download*, if selected will tell Windows and Internet Explorer to ask for the end user's permission before opening the selected file type in its associated program.

If the *Always show extension* option is enabled, it will force the file extension on the related file type to be displayed in Windows and related applications. By default, the related `AlwaysShowExt` registry setting is enabled on many existing file associations and all new and previously undefined file extensions (i.e., `HKCR\*` subkey). But as discussed before, many file associations have the `NeverShowExt` (i.e., Never show file extension) value enabled. Usually, if both the `AlwaysShowExt` and `NeverShowExt` values are present in the same file association subkey, the `NeverShowExt` wins.

> *The HKCR* subkey represents the default settings for all file types, and all file types will inherit actions and settings defined by it. File types that are not otherwise defined will inherit actions defined by "Unknown." For example, adding an action called BONG! to * shows up on all file types.*

It's important to note that any changes made in the Windows Explorer GUI usually affects the file association settings stored in `HKLM\Software\Classes`, not `HKCU\Software\Classes`, which is slightly different behavior than when directly modifying the registry.

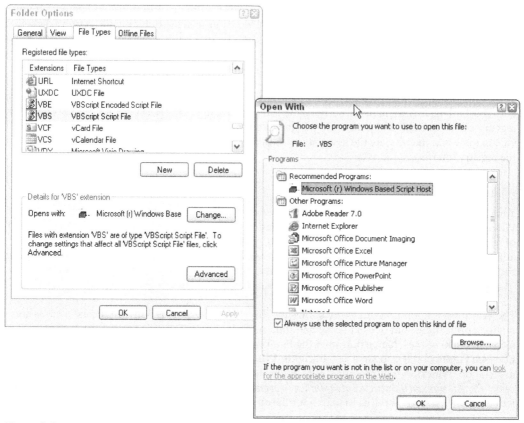

Figure 6-4

HK_Current_User

This lists the current configuration and profile information for the currently logged on user. Virtually any setting that affects the user's desktop experience can be found here, including background graphics, screen saver choices, folders, printer and drive mappings, whether or not the user can see hidden files, and hundreds of other settings. If similar values exist in both HKCU and under HKLM, the data in HKCU takes precedence. The HKCU location is not nearly as popular with malware but could lead to many of the same exploits accomplished using HKLM.

Spyware uses HKCU more often than any other type of malware. The consequences are that any anti-spyware scanner must be coded to scan multiple user profiles in order to remove all spyware.

HK_Users

HKU contains all the user profiles on the local computer. When a user logs on for the first time, their profile is created using the configuration information stored in the \Documents and Settings\Default User folder and the HKU\.Default key. Thereafter, when the user logs onto the machine using the same profile, their HKU\<profile> information is copied to HKCU for the user's session. The HKU\<profile> is tracked by security principal SID. Any changes made to the user's profile (in HKCU) are saved back to HKU\<profile>. Although malware could take advantage of the profile keys located in HKU, so far to date, they have not messed with it much.

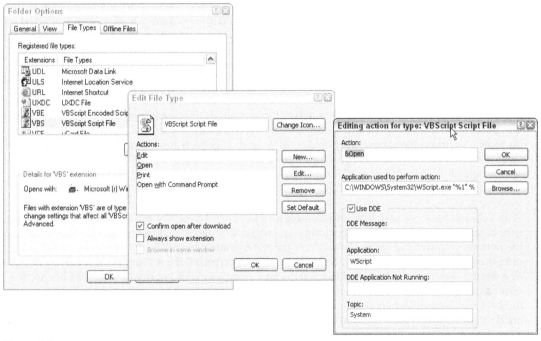

Figure 6-5

HK_Current Config

HKCC is an alias for `HKLM\System\CurrentControlSet\Hardware Profiles\Current` and data it contains can be changed in either location. Windows allows one or more hardware profiles to be created for a computer (under Control Panel ⇨ System applet ⇨ Profiles). If desired, varying hardware devices, drivers, and services can be turned on and off per profile. Profiles are most commonly used on laptops, going from docked to undocked states. It has not been frequently manipulated by malware.

All 64-bit versions of Windows store many HKLM\Software pre-64 bit registry keys (i.e., 32-bit) under a single location in the registry, HKLM\Software\WOW6432Node. 32-bit programs accessing HKLM\Software are seamlessly redirected to the new location.

Alternate Registry Storage Locations

Because the registry is so vital to Windows, backup copies are often created and stored. If these backup copies can be compromised by an intruder, they will significantly help the hacker with future attacks on the same computer. Registry file backups are made by Windows and many backup utilities. Although not current, backup copies of the registry files are made during the initial install and saved to `%Windir%\Repair`. These files can be used to replace a corrupted registry in an emergency recovery scenario. In Windows XP and Windows Vista, `Restore Points` will contain a copy of the registry files. `System State` backups made by the Backup Utility for Windows (formerly known as NT Backup) will contain a copy of the registry files, as will any backup job capable of backing up files in use.

Administrators can make individual backups of the registry using the Registry Editor's export feature or `Reg.exe` with the `/Save` parameter. Administrators should always make a backup of any affected registry key before they make modifications. One mistyped entry could cause Windows to have boot problems and STOP errors.

Registry Tools

The Microsoft registry editor tool comes in two forms: `Regedit.exe` and `Regedt32.exe`. `Regedit.exe` was the original tool delivered with Windows 3.x over a decade ago. `Regedt32.exe` was released with Windows NT. It contained new functionality, such as the capability to view and modify registry permissions and allows registry hives to be saved individually, but many users preferred `Regedit.exe`'s search capabilities. Starting with Windows XP, Microsoft's main registry tool was renamed back to `Regedit.exe`. If you type **Regedt32.exe,** it just runs the main `Regedit.exe` tool.

With `Regedit.exe`, you can save and load registry keys and hives. You can also modify the local registry database or connect to a remote computer's registry (the Remote Registry service must be active on the remote computer and the user must have the appropriate credentials). If the user connecting to the remote registry has administrative access, they can manipulate all the registry keys. If they are logged in as a regular user, they are restricted to what the particular user could normally see. If the connecting user has no authenticated access (i.e., connected as the anonymous null session), the user can only see the keys marked to allow anonymous viewing. The keys allowed to be viewed by the anonymous user are defined in group policy (or local computer policy) at `\Computer Configuration\Windows Settings\Security Settings\Local Policies\Security Options\Network access:` *Remotely accessible registry paths.* By default, the values in Windows XP Pro are as follows:

- ❑ System\CurrentControlSet\Control\ProductOptions
- ❑ System\CurrentControlSet\Control\Print\Printers
- ❑ System\CurrentControlSet\Control\Server Applications
- ❑ System\CurrentControlSet\Services\Eventlog
- ❑ Software\Microsoft\OLAP Server
- ❑ Software\Microsoft\Windows NT\CurrentVersion
- ❑ System\CurrentControlSet\Control\ContentIndex
- ❑ System\CurrentControlSet\Control\Terminal Server
- ❑ System\CurrentControlSet\Control\Terminal Server\UserConfig
- ❑ System\CurrentControlSet\Control\Terminal Server\DefaultUserConfiguration

You can add and delete keys from this list according to need, although no glaring holes are incurred by leaving it at the defaults.

Regedit Files and Scripting

Using `Regedit.exe`, you can view and modify registry permissions (see below), and search and find wanted registry keys and values. You can also manage the registry using `Regedit` files. `Regedit` files are text files, usually with .Reg file extensions, created to instruct Reg.exe in creating or modifying registry values. Regedit files have their own syntax, usually beginning with a command word determining which registry subtree to manipulate, followed by the registry entry to make.

For example, the following commands in a Regedit file would instruct Windows to open VBScript files in Notepad.exe instead of Wscript.exe. This can be done to prevent VBS viruses and worms (and legitimate VBScript script files) from activating properly.

```
REGEDIT4

HKEY_CLASSES_ROOT\VBSFile\shell\open\command]
@="notepad.exe \"%%1\""
```

Regedit files were a primary tool to programmatically manipulate the registry, but their use requires that the end user running the Regedit file be an administrator. You can find out more information about Regedit files at www.robvanderwoude.com/index.html or www.regedit.com.

Registry values can also be managed using Reg.exe, Group Policy, and scripts. Reg.exe is a default executable that allows registry hives and keys to be added, modified, or deleted manually. In Windows NT it was included in the Windows NT Resource Kit, but starting in Windows 2000 it was included in part of the default install. A good example web site demonstrating the Reg.exe command-line syntax can be found at www.robvanderwoude.com/index.html. Registry entries can also be manipulated via group policy, without the end user needing administrative access. Registry manipulation via group policy and local computer policy is discussed in detail in Chapter 14.

You can use any of several scripting languages, including VBScript, JSScript, and WMI, to manipulate registry entries. The following sample script demonstrates setting Notepad.exe as the default handler instead of using Wscript.exe for encoded VBScript files (.VBE extension):

```
Set WshShell = WScript.CreateObject("WScript.Shell")
WshShell.RegWrite "HKLM\Software\Classes\VBEFile\Shell\Open\Command\",
"C:\Windows\System32\Notepad.exe %1%", "REG_EXPAND_SZ"
```

For more information on using script files to manipulate registry keys and values see http://msdn .microsoft.com/library/default.asp?url=/library/en-us/script56/html/wsMthRegWrite .asp, www.winguides.com/scripting/library.php?id=6, or www.windowsitlibrary.com/ Content/314/2.html#5.

You can also use Microsoft's universal Logparser utility (http://www.microsoft.com/downloads/ details.aspx?FamilyID=890cd06b-abf8-4c25-91b2-f8d975cf8c07&displaylang=en) to view and record registry information. See http://www.logparser.com for more details.

Regmon

Sysinternals' free Regmon tool (www.sysinternals.com/Utilities/Regmon.html) is one of the most widely used registry troubleshooting utilities in the world. It comes in Windows 9x, NT, and 64-bit versions. When running, it displays and logs all registry requests. It can record all reads and writes, and their success or failure, to the registry and detail which process was involved. It is great for determining what access a particular program or user needs to which registry keys. Figure 6-6 shows Regmon in action. What surprises most people initially when querying for all registry requests is how frequently Windows is manipulating the registry even when nothing appears to be actively happening on the desktop. The example in Figure 6-6 collected thousands of registry reads and writes in just a few seconds. Most Regmon users end up filtering what registry events are collected in order to cut down on the "noise." Sysinternals' Filemon (www.sysinternals.com/Utilities/Filemon.html) utility is just as fantastic for troubleshooting file accesses.

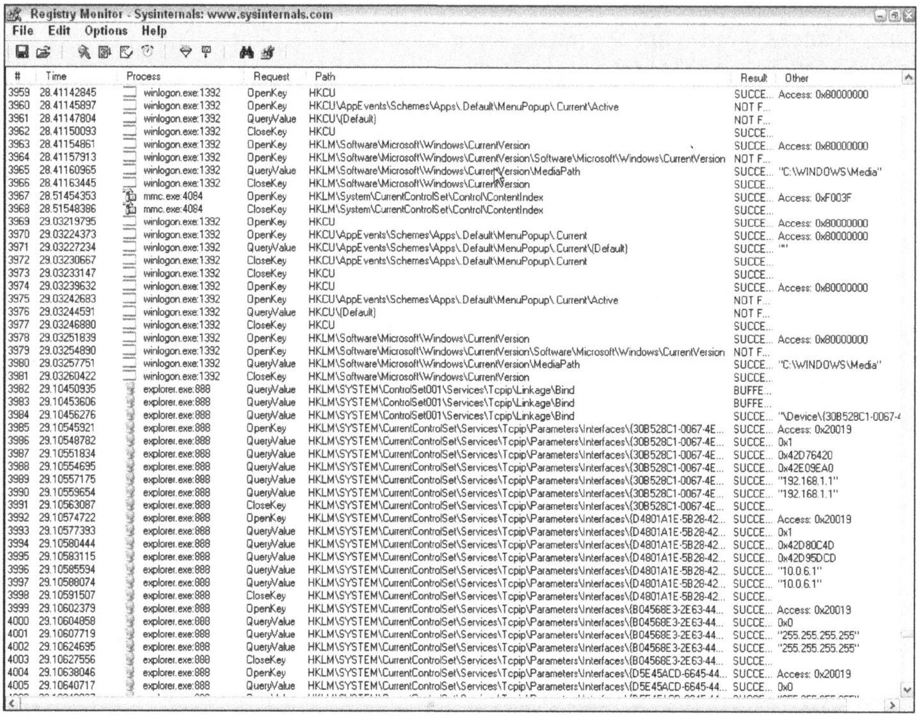

Figure 6-6

Another very useful tool is NifSoft's freeware Registry Scanner (www.nirsoft.net/utils/regscanner .html). It will return multiple keys back at once when searching for particular keys or data, so you can edit them all at once more quickly. It can also query registry entries based on last modification time and date.

In August 2005, it was found that overly large registry entries (those exceeding 256 characters in length) would not be read correctly by the default Microsoft Windows registry editor (i.e., Regedt32.exe). This could allow malware to make an overly large entry and escape easy scrutiny using Microsoft's tool. Many other third-party registry tools also suffered from the same problem, but most were fixed within a week or two of the announcement. Make sure your registry editor can see long registry entries.

Registry Permissions

Like files, the registry keys also have an extensive list of permissions, although they differ from their file and folder counterparts. To access registry key permissions, you can use `Regedit.exe` (or `Regedt32.exe` in Windows 2000 or NT) or the command-line `Subinacls.exe` tool. To view registry permissions in `Regedit.exe`, choose a registry key or value, then click on the Edit menu and choose Permissions. Like the NTFS permissions in Windows Explorer for a file or folder, the initial display shows only the higher-level permissions of Full Control, Read, and Special Permissions. Choose the Advanced button and then the Edit button on the Permissions tab to see the underlying 11 granular permissions (see Figure 6-7).

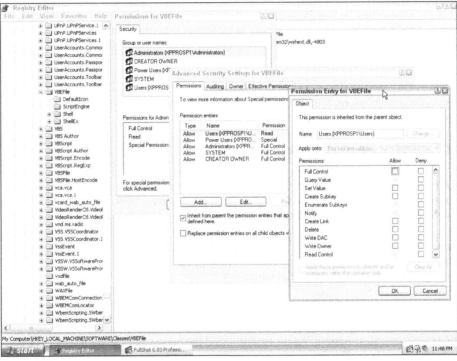

Figure 6-7

The 11 registry key permissions are as follows:

❏ Full Control — Allows full access to the registry key, including the ability to set permissions

❏ Query Value — Allows the value of the registry key to be read

❏ Set Value — Allows the value of the registry key to be written

❏ Create Subkey — Allows the creation of subkeys

❏ Enumerate Subkeys — Allows subkeys to be enumerated (found or listed)

❏ Notify — Required to request change notifications for a registry key or its subkeys

❏ Create Link — Used only by the operating system

❏ Delete — Allows a key to be deleted

❏ Write DACL — Allows key security permissions to be modified

❏ Write Owner — Allows the owner to be changed

❏ Read Control — Allows the auditing permission to be read

The Full Control permission contains all registry permissions. The Read permission is normally made up of special permissions Query Value, Enumerate subkeys, Notify, and Read Control. As with file and folder permissions, the Effective Permissions tab under the Advanced button will show you a security principal's effective permissions on a registry key. Normal inheritance rules apply: Permissions are inherited downward by default unless offset by a more granular permission.

You can also use Microsoft's Subinacls.exe (www.microsoft.com/downloads/details .aspx?FamilyID=e8ba3e56-d8fe-4a91-93cf-ed6985e3927b&DisplayLang=en) tool to display or modify registry permissions. It is useful in a script or when accessing Windows through a command shell window.

Default Registry Permissions

Windows XP and Server 2003 registry permissions are relatively secure by default. If the end user is not logged in as an administrator, then what they, or a program running in their security context, can manipulate is mostly in their own HKCU subtree. On most other subtrees, keys, and subkeys, non-admin users can only read the value. Table 6-3 shows the overall default registry permissions in Windows XP Pro.

Table 6-3

Registry Subtree	Default Permissions
HKCR	Administrators, Creator Owners, and System have Full Control, Users have Read access, and Power Users have Special access.
HKCU	System, Administrators, and the currently logged on user have Full Control. This is a subtree that malware could easily manipulate even when the end user is not logged in as an administrator.
HKLM	System and administrators have Full Control. Everyone group has Read access.
HKLM\Software	Administrators, Creator Owners, and System have Full Control. Users have Read access. Power Users and Terminal Service User group have Special permissions.
HKU	System and Administrators have Full Control and the Everyone group has Read access.
HKCC	Users and Power users have Read access. Administrators, System, and Creator Owners have Full Control.

On the subkeys below the main keys there are small deviations in the permissions, but for the majority of the registry keys and values, these parent permissions hold true through inheritance.

High-Risk Registry Entries

This section covers what constitutes a high-risk registry entry and describes specific concerns.

What Is a High-Risk Registry Entry?

A high-risk registry entry is any registry key or value highly likely to be misused by a malicious program or attacker. Some keys, such as HKLM\Software\Microsoft\Windows\CurrentVersion\Run are so often a target of malware that even their just as popular legitimate use cannot pull them off the high-risk list. High-risk registry entries fall into these main categories: File Associations, Auto-run areas, HKCU (because malware can write there even if a user is not an administrator), and Internet Explorer hijacking. Table 6-4 displays especially high-risk registry entries and the concerns associated with them.

Table 6-4

Registry Key	Description	Risk/Detail
HKCR\ HKLM\Software\Classes HKCU\Software\Classes	File Associations	Two main issues: 1. Rarely used file associations (such as scrap files, .SHS, .SHB, .SHC) are more likely to be used by malware than legitimate users and should be blocked. 2. Any file association with the NeverShowExt value can potentially allow malware to masquerade as another, more harmless, file type.
HKCU\Software\Microsoft\ Internet Explorer\Main\Start Page HKCU\Software\Microsoft\ Internet Explorer\Main\Search Page HKCU\Software\Microsoft\ Internet Explorer\Main\Search Bar	Configures Internet Explorers Startup page or search bars	Commonly manipulated by adware and spyware
HKCU\Software\Microsoft\ Internet Explorer\SearchURL	Redirects any URLs typed in Internet Explorer to defined URL	Commonly manipulated by adware and spyware

Table continued on following page

Registry Key	Description	Risk/Detail
HKCU or HKLM \Software\ Internet Explorer\Explorer Bars	Malicious adware\ spyware could create new menu bars in Internet Explorer.	Also allows new entries to be made to standard menu bars. Available in IE 4.x and later. Commonly manipulated by adware and spyware. Menu bar will be a CLSID subkey listed under Explorer Bars. Used by Hotbar adware (http://securityresponse. symantec.com/avcenter/venc/ data/adware.hotbar.html).
HKLM\Software\Classes\ CLSID\{CLSID}\Implemented Categories\{00021493-0000-0000-C000-000000000046}	...93 defines a vertical Explorer bar	Commonly manipulated by adware and spyware
HKLM\Software\Classes\ CLSID\{CLSID}\Implemented Categories\{00021494-0000-0000-C000-000000000046}	...94 defines a horizontal Explorer bar	
HKCU\ or HKLM\Software\ Internet Explorer\Extensions	Adware/spyware can add buttons to IE that connect directly to malicious programs and scripts.	Available in IE 5.x and later. http://msdn.microsoft.com/library/ default.asp?url=/workshop/ browser/ext/overview/overview.asp Commonly manipulated by adware and spyware, including Adblock.
HKCU or HKLM\Software\ Microsoft\Windows\Current Version\Run	Runs programs or commands after the user logs on	Works with all versions of Windows 9x and later. Not run in Safe mode unless the value is prefixed by an * (asterisk). Often contains many legitimate programs. *Most popular registry auto-run key for malware by a huge percentage.* W2K will run any subkey with any program listed under this key. Discovered by Andrew Aronoff of SilentRunners.org. Non-admin users cannot modify HKLM version. Run key also appears in the HK_U\.Default registry profile area, but does not copy over to new profiles. Cannot be disabled by holding down Shift or Alt keys as sometimes reported.

Registry Key	Description	Risk/Detail
HKCU or HKLM\Software\ Microsoft\Windows\Current Version\RunOnce	Runs programs or commands after user logs on for the first time only after the key is created.	Works with all versions of Windows 9x and later. HKLM\RunOnce runs entries *synchronously* (in an undefined order); there is a defined order and all other keys and processing must wait for this key to process and clear before they can load. All other Run keys run entries asynchronously, which means they can load on top of each other. HKCU version will run once for any user given the key. HKLM version will only run the value for users with admin permissions to the key. Regular users will not run the value, although they can read it. RunOnce key also appears in the HK_U\.Default registry profile area, but does not copy over to new profiles. Non-admin users cannot modify HKLM version. Not run if in Safe mode in W2K and later unless the value name begins with an asterisk. If an exclamation point begins the key value, then the key will not be deleted until successful completion of program or command. Holding down Shift key does not prevent execution. W2K will run any subkey with any program listed under this key. Discovered by Andrew Aronoff of SilentRunners.org.
HKLM\Software\Microsoft\ Internet Explorer\Search HKLM\Software\Microsoft\ Internet Explorer\UrlSearch Hooks	Determines how Internet Explorer searches for unknown entries	Works with Internet Explorer 5.x and later. Both keys contain legitimate values, but are often commandeered by spyware and adware. The Search subkey contains references to `http://ie.search.msn.com` by default.
HKCU\Software\Internet Explorer\Toolbar\ShellBrowser HKCU\Software\Internet Explorer\Toolbar\WebBrowser	Malicious adware\ spyware could create new menu bars in Internet Explorer.	Commonly manipulated by adware and spyware. The menu bar will be a CLSID subkey listed under Toolbars.
HKLM\Software\Microsoft\ Windows\CurrentVersion\ Explorer\Browser Helper Objects	Programs are loaded when Internet Explorer loads; programs loaded are also known as Add-Ins.	Works with an OS that can run Internet Explorer 5.x and later. Commonly exploited key. Several programs help list and/or modify BHOs, including IE XP SP2 and later.

Table continued on following page

Registry Key	Description	Risk/Detail
HKLM\Software\Microsoft\ Windows\CurrentVersion\ Explorer\Shell Folders HKLM\Software\Microsoft\ Windows\CurrentVersion\ Explorer\User Shell Folders \Startup\Common Startup	Determines the location of Startup folders (i.e., Startup programs) and other common folders (such as My Documents, My Favorites) for All Users profile.	Works with Windows 9x and later. Used by malware to change Startup folder behavior. Malware can place itself in the newly created Startup folder to be executed when the user logs on, but if the user checks normal Startup folders, the malicious program will not be listed. Malware modifying these keys will often then execute programs and commands found in default Startup folders, so the user is not suspicious.
HKLM\Software\Microsoft\ Windows\CurrentVersion\ URL\DefaultPrefix HKLM\Software\Microsoft\ Windows\CurrentVersion\ URL\Prefixes\Search HKLM\Software\Microsoft\ Windows\CurrentVersion\ URL\Prefixes\Search	Adds any string value as a prefix for any URL typed in the browser, effectively redirecting all typed in URLs to the unauthorized web site first.	Commonly used by Adware. Examples include SmartSearch and WorldSearch adware, JS.Fornight adware worm, and Popdis trojan. Default values are supposed to be `http://`. Hint provided by Andrew Aronoff of SilentRunners.org.
HKLM\System\Current ControlSet\Services\Tcpip\ Parameters\	Sets overall TCP/IP communications values, including DHCP, DNS, and TCP/IP stack. These values are used unless a specific value is set under the \Interfaces subkeys on a particular interface.	Many values should be modified to harden a Windows computer against denial-of-service attacks.

Table 1-1 in Chapter 1 displayed a more complete list of maliciously used registry entries. Table 6-4 lists just the popularly used registry keys or the ones most likely to lead to system compromise.

Defenses

The following defenses will help prevent malicious attacks against Windows computers.

Don't Let Non-Admin Users Be Logged On As Administrators

The number one way to prevent malicious attacks on the registry is to not give non-admin users Administrator-privileges. By default, as shown in Table 6-3, non-admin users usually only have Read-only access to most registry keys. If you have chosen to allow your regular end users to be logged on as administrators, consider manually hardening the high-risk registry locations listed in Tables 1-1 and 6-4 so that the user only has Read permissions (instead of Full Control).

Harden HKCU Registry Permissions

By default, even non-admin users have Read and Write permissions to the HKCU subtree. Consider giving users Read-only permissions to high-risk registry keys listed in Tables 1-1 and 6-4 for high-risk HKCU entries. Pay special attention to the HKCU\Software\Classes and HKCU\Software\Microsoft\Windows entries.

Block High-Risk File Associations

By default, Windows installs with hundreds of file associations (in HKCR, HKLM\Software\Classes, and HKCU\Software\Classes). Consider making a list of file extensions that should be allowed in your environment. Use Table 5-1 as your guide. Then, using registry permissions, block non-admin users access to high-risk file associations. For example, if your company does not normally use encoded VBScript files (file extension .VBE), block access to them. Take away the user's capability to read the file association key. Note that I didn't say give Read-Deny permissions to the Users group. Doing so, as some readers might have after having read the previous sentences, would result in Administrators (who are Users) from being able to access the key. Table 6-5 shows the especially high-risk file associations that should be blocked from casual use.

Table 6-5

File Extension	File Type	Malicious Use Details
.ani	Windows Animated Cursor	Two exploits were announced by Flashsky Fangxing (flashsky@xfocus.org) on Dec. 23, 2004. First, a Windows Kernel DoS exploit, Windows XP SP2 not vulnerable, but most other Windows versions (NT to 2003) are. Second, an Integer buffer overflow, most Windows versions are vulnerable (NT to 2003), caused by LoadImage API in USER32.Lib.
.asf, .lsf, .lsx	Streaming audio or video file	Can be exploited through buffer overflows, head malformation, or dangerous scriptable content
.bat	DOS batch file	Can contain malicious DOS command interpreter instructions
.chm	Windows Compiled Help File	Windows Help Files (.hlp) can be compiled for better performance and feature sets. Malformed Compiled Help Files have been involved in many announced exploits over the years, including Microsoft Security Bulletin MS05-031. Can be opened in Internet Explorer automatically without user intervention using Ms — its moniker.

Table continued on following page

File Extension	File Type	Malicious Use Details
.cmd	Command file	Contains batch-file-like DOS interpreter script commands. Can contain malicious instructions.
.com	Program executable	Older, some legacy DOS executables. Still work under all Windows versions, except newer 64-bit Windows.
.cur	Windows cursor graphic file	Integer buffer overflow, announced by Flashsky Fangxing (flashsky@xfocus.org) on Dec. 23, 2004, most Windows versions are vulnerable (NT to 2003), caused by LoadImage API in USER32.Lib.
.dbg	Debug file	Can contain malicious machine-language instructions that can be compiled by debug.exe into malware
.dsm, .far, .it, .stm, .ult, .wma	Nullsoft WinAmp media file	Has been involved in malicious exploits
.dun	DUN export file	Can contain malicious dial-up connection information that initiates outward calls
.eml, .email	Outlook Express e-mail message	Used by Nimda and many other worms
.hta	HTML application	Frequently used by worms and trojans
.pdc	Microsoft compiled script	Can contain dangerous code
.pif	Program information file	Can run malicious programs
.png	Portable Network Graphics file	PNG is an open-source graphics format with lossless compression (www.libpng.org/pub/png). Has been involved in several exploits, including multi-browser buffer overflows. Last PNG IE buffer overflow resolved by MS05-025.
.pol	Windows Policy File	Could be used to lower security settings on Windows 9x and later machines
.reg, .key	Registry entry file	Can create or modify registry keys
.scf	Windows Explorer command	Could be used maliciously in future attacks
.shs, .shb	Shell scrap object	Can mask rogue programs by containing links to other programs. Shell scrap file objects can have hidden extensions even when Windows is told to display hidden file extensions. This file type can itself run raw code.
.slk	Excel SLK data-import file	Can contain hidden malicious macros

File Extension	File Type	Malicious Use Details
.swf, .spl	Shockwave Flash object	Can be exploited
.vb, .vbe, .vbs	VBScript file	Can contain malicious code. VBE files are encoded VBScript files that can easily be decoded and read by Windows and IE. These files are executed by Wscript.exe, Cscript.exe, or VBScript.dll.
.vcf	vCard file format	Used in many e-mail clients, including Outlook and Outlook Express, to communicate recipient addressing details. Has been involved in a few exploits.
.ws, .cs, .wsf, .wsc, .sct	WSH file	Can execute malicious code

These file associations were chosen for the following reasons:

❑ They are frequently exploited by malware or attackers.

❑ They are infrequently used legitimately.

❑ Removal would cause few problems in most environments.

Modify your list based upon your environment's needs and expectations.

Block High-Risk URI Handlers

Don't forget to block non-admin access to dangerous URI handlers (e.g., `news://`, `aim://`, `telnet://`, `rlogin://`). URI handlers are the special keywords that can be added to the beginning of a URL to launch an external program. Not all URI handlers are dangerous. `Http://` and `Https://` are used legitimately most of the time, but malware has used a few other URI handlers in the past to exploit computers. Table 6-6 lists high-risk and other unused URI handlers that should be reviewed.

Table 6-6

URI Handler	Description
Aim	America Online Instant Messenger (AIM) program can be launched from an embedded HTML link. Has been used a few times in the past to conduct buffer overflows and steal files.
Callto	Will launch NetMeeting to call dial-up phone number. Has been used by malware to make expensive long-distance calls.
News, nntp, snews	Network News Transport (NNTP) protocol. Will launch Outlook Express (OE), even if OE is not used (and not patched). Has been used to spread malware. Involved in a Windows buffer over exploit as recently as June 2005.

Table continued on following page

URI Handler	Description
ftp	File transfer protocol (FTP). Will launch Internet Explorer (IE) in FTP-mode. Can be used to download malicious files. Can be used to exploit other ftp vulnerabilities, such as user name and password disclosures.
Gopher	Early Internet protocol. Can be used to launch IE, although Gopher has been disabled in IIS and IE for many years now by default. Not really a high risk, but it should be disabled because it is no longer used.
Ldap	Lightweight Directory Access (LDAP) protocol. Will launch OE by default. Not abused much by malware, but could be used to do e-mail address directory harvesting and to send malicious e-mails.
Ms-its	Allows compiled help files (.CHM) to be launched. Compiled help files have been used in nearly a half dozen different exploits over the years.
Rlogin	Remote logon is a Unix-style telnet utility (Rlogin.exe) included in several versions of Windows. Essentially a telnet utility. Not abused by malware, yet, but should be disabled because it is rarely used legitimately.
Telnet, Tn3270	Can be used to launch a remote telnet session. Not popularly exploited, but has been used in the past.

The URI handlers installed in Windows vary in each environment according to the version of Windows and what software has been installed. Administrators should query workstation registries to determine whether any other high-risk entries should be blocked. You can find URI handlers by searching for the data field, URL:, under HKCR.

Remove High-Risk NeverShowExt Values

Search for and delete the NeverShowExt values for high-risk file associations in HKCR, HKLM\Software\ Classes, and HKCU\Software\Classes. At the very least, remove this registry value for the following file types:

❏   SHS

❏   SHB

❏   SHC

❏   LNK

❏   PIF

❏   XNK

Block File Association Changes

By default, only Administrators (and Power Users) can create or change file associations. If end users are logged in as Administrators, you can still deny them the ability to change file associations through the Windows Explorer GUI (although they still could do it programmatically or using Regedit.exe). To enable the admin blocking feature, write a `Dword` value of `00000000` to the `NoFileAssociate` value (you may need to create) under `HKLM\Software\Microsoft\Windows\CurrentVersion\Policies\Explorer`.

Use Group Policy or Security Templates to Automate Registry Permission Changes

Lastly, use a group policy object, local computer policy, or security template to automate hardening registry permissions. Chapter 14 covers this advice in more detail.

Summary

This chapter covered high-risk registry entries. High-risk registry entries are registry keys and values more likely to be used my malicious attackers and malware than by legitimate users for legitimate reasons. Each registry key has 11 different registry permissions that can be set on each key. Windows XP Pro and later have pretty good registry security, but a few areas could use additional hardening. Chapter 7 discusses how to harden Windows services against malicious compromise.

7

Tightening Services

Attackers frequently attack services as a way to exploit a computer. Services, by their very definition, accept incoming connections and frequently accept network connections. If malicious attackers can exploit a service, they usually end up with the security permissions the service was running in — usually LocalSystem. This chapter discusses services and how they work in detail, including how to tighten services and secure them.

Why Tighten Services?

Services should be reviewed and tightened to present less attack surface, to lessen the risk of buffer overflows, to reduce the risk of denial-of-service (DoS) attacks, and to decrease overall management effort.

Less Attack Surface

Every service is a potential attack vector for the attacker. It can end up allowing unauthorized access, have unintended consequences, allow DoS attacks, and generally lead to full system compromise. As the number of services increases, so does the risk of compromise. As Table 7-1 shows, every newer version of Windows adds more services. Many service accounts associated with services have full access to the local system. Some have full admin access to the entire network. If an attacker cracks those accounts, it can mean complete system or network compromise.

Worse yet, many services cannot be disabled, even in a critical attack, without adversely affecting the legitimate processes of the operating system. Windows depends on many services to do its job. For example, during the Blaster worm attack, which attacked the Remote Procedure Call (RPC) service, turning off the RPC service would have effectively disabled Windows. It wasn't until Microsoft released a new patch in Service Pack 2 (many months later) that RPC was given additional protections to prevent Blasterlike attacks.

Reduce Buffer Overflow Risks

If a service is overrun, it results in DoS or complete system compromise. When a malicious programmer can reliably predict where in memory his code will land during a buffer overflow, he can crash the related service and gain whatever security context the service was running in. Most service accounts have full access to the local machine. Reducing the number of services overall and reducing the privileges given to the remaining services will reduce the risk of successful attack.

Reduce Risk of Denial-of-Service Attacks

Every service gives the hacker a potential DoS attack. Most services are network accessible and any that are can be overpowered. One type of DoS attack simply sends a very large number of requests and connection attempts in a short period of time, overwhelming Windows' ability to simultaneously respond to all requests. It sends Windows into 100% CPU utilization and makes it run out of available memory. Either way, Windows stops responding to new requests. Another type of DoS attack might stop or crash the Windows service and prevent legitimate use until it is restarted. Many services have had programming flaws that allowed DoS attacks to occur from as little as one malformed packet. The attacker could send one packet to each PC on a network and stop all computing or send one packet to an IIS server and bring the web site down.

Reduce Management Overhead

Reducing the number of services and minimizing the security risk of those that are needed reduces management overhead. Every active service must be maintained and applicable patches applied. Even services installed but inactive need to be patched. For instance, if a user has the ability to install and/or activate IIS on their computer, it needs to be patched regardless of whether it is actually used. Unfortunately, most Microsoft patch management tools do not look for inactive services. This means if the service is installed but not activated, many patch management tools (e.g., MSBA, Windows Update, Microsoft Update, WSUS, SUS, etc.) do not patch it. This ensures that if the user, or malicious intruder, can activate it, it is most certainly unpatched and exploitable. By tightening services, you can prevent unauthorized, and unpatched, services from executing. By analyzing needed services, removing unneeded services, and tightening remaining services, you can significantly reduce your risk of successful attack.

Services Introduction

Services are programs or processes that function to provide one or more services to the operating system and its security principals. In general, a service program usually has the following characteristics:

- ❑ It can start when the OS starts up.
- ❑ It does not require a user to be logged in to load.
- ❑ It often logs on with a security principal account that has full system access.
- ❑ It is controlled by the Service Control Manager (SCM) process.
- ❑ It creates and accepts local or network connections.

Although users or newly installed programs can install services, Windows installs with dozens of default services (although they are not all activated). As Table 7-1 shows, the number of installed and activated services increases with each new version of Microsoft Windows.

Table 7-1

OS	Total	Enabled by Default	Startup Type			Service Account		
			Automatic	Disabled	Manual	Local System	Local Service	Network Service
W2K	56	30	24	3	29	56	0	0
XP	79	41	35	4	40	65	10	4
W2K3	83	32	29	21	33	67	10	6
W2K3 DC	84	37	33	19	22	68	10	6

Table 7-1 reflects fully patched 32-bit domain member computers with default services installed, unless otherwise noted.

Table 7-1 reveals that the number of total services almost doubled between Windows 2000 and the newer operating systems.

These are just the default Windows services installed on a computer not running any special services or programs (the lone exception in Table 7-1 is the DNS Server service to provide DNS support for Active Directory domain controller services). Certainly, Windows Vista will have more available services than did any of the previous operating systems. Many Microsoft Windows applications install services, including IIS, SQL, Exchange, Certificate Services, SMS, SharePoint Services, ISA, BizTalk, and others. Each separate Windows application service can install up to 10 new services.

Original Equipment Manufacturer (OEM) computers, such as those from Dell, HP, IBM, and Compaq, install additional services. Sometimes the OEM vendor installs up to 20 new programs and 10 new services on each desktop and server computer they sell. In the past, OEM services have been just as likely to be exploited as Microsoft's default services. On top of this, many other installed software and hardware products install services. It is common to see one or more services installed to manage the network interface and video cards. Most often, the additional services aren't needed to use the component cards, but they add additional management interfaces. Software programs, such as tape backup software, antivirus programs, firewalls, Wincap, Microsoft SQL Server Desktop Edition, Seti@home, Distributed.Net, and thousands of other programs install new services. It is not unusual for a normal PC to be running more than 100 active services. Each of these services is taking up processor power and memory — and each is a potential attack vector for an attacker. Determining whether a service is legitimate or not is important to computer security.

Identifying Unknown Services

If you are unfamiliar with a service, you can search on its name by using any good Internet search engine (e.g., Google), by using Microsoft's Knowledge Base, or by searching in any of the Internet web sites that provide information on found programs and services (e.g., `www.theeldergeek.com/services_guide.htm`). When using a search engine, if the service name frequently appears on spyware or antivirus sites, it isn't a good sign. Although there are exceptions, any legitimate service should be well documented, and several links noting its legitimacy should be found. If no Internet information is provided and the service name is spelled correctly, disable the service and consider it suspicious until otherwise discovered.

All Microsoft services are well documented. Sysinternals' Autoruns program (`www.sysinternals.com/utilities/autoruns.html`) is also good for determining program legitimacy. As Figure 7-1 shows, Autoruns shows the service file name, location, size, and description. Autoruns can be configured to verify the code signatures of any service program and to hide verified Microsoft services by default. This enables an investigator to quickly reveal any unsigned services. Occasionally, Microsoft installs unsigned service applications, but not often. Any unsigned or non-Microsoft service should be investigated if its legitimacy is not known. Autoruns also includes an easy way to search Google for more information on the revealed service.

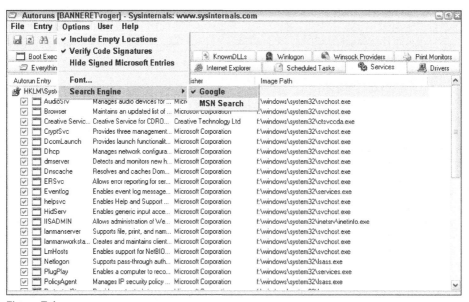

Figure 7-1

Service Details

Services and their details are normally accessed by running the Services console, `Services.msc`, or by right-clicking the My Computer icon, choosing the Manage option, and then choosing Services on the resulting Computer Management console. Using either method you can access local or remote computers. The console will open with the list of installed services (see Figure 7-2). You can choose between Standard and Extended views. The Extended view will display the service's description in the left pane when a service is highlighted. Both views have the description field and allow columns to be resized and sorted.

You can also run the command-line tool Sc.exe to display service information. It is included in some Windows versions by default or you can download it as part of the Windows Resource Kit utilities.

For analysis purposes, the Services console can be used to export a list of services and the information displayed in the main summary view. To export a list of services from the Services console, right-click the Services object in the top left pane, choose Export List, and choose the file name, type, and location of the exported file. The exported file can be easily opened in Microsoft Excel or Access for further analysis.

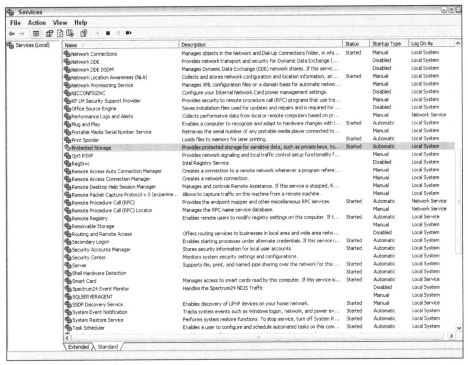

Figure 7-2

If the service is double-clicked on or opened, the Services console will reveal the following details (Windows 2000 and later): General, Logon, Recovery, and Dependencies.

General

As Figure 7-3 shows, the General tab displays many different useful fields regarding the service. The Service Name displays the service's *short name*. The short name is often how the service is referred to and is often required to use various service utilities. The Display Name is the service's name to be shown in the Services console (and other places). For example, the service with the short name of Browser has a display name of Computer Browser. Users often know it by its Display Name, but programmers and scripters know it by its short name. The Description field should hold some information about the service and why it is installed. Frequently, third-party, and occasionally Microsoft, services do not have a description. Services without descriptions should get extra scrutiny.

The path to the executable is an important field. Not only does it display the underlying executable that is executed with the service (and often the name displayed is not what would be commonly expected); it also shows the full path location (albeit with older 8.3 naming) to the executable and startup switches.

257

Attackers will often install rogue services with official-sounding Microsoft Windows names, but they have to install them in non-default locations (because they can't overwrite a legitimate file that is protected by Windows File Protection). The executable name here is usually what is presented in the Processes tab of the Task Manager.

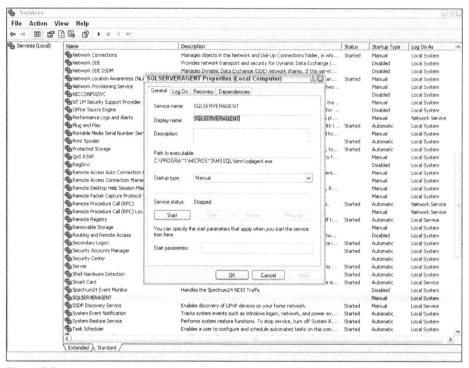

Figure 7-3

Multiple Services, One Name

The executable name is where it sometimes gets interesting. Although most service executables are named identically to the service's short name, others have no obvious relationship. Many services point to the same executable (e.g., Svchost.exe, Lsass.exe, Dllhost.exe, etc.). This is because the service's code is within the larger executable and is "called out." For example, all of the following services start using the Lsass.exe image: IPSec Services, Net Logon, NT LM Security Support Provider, Protected Storage, and Security Accounts Manager. At least two services start with the Dllhost.exe image: COM+ System Application and the MS Software Shadow Copy Provider. But the mack daddy image of them all is Svchost. %\Windir%\System32\Svchost.exe is responsible for nearly half of all default Windows services, including Alerter, Automatic Updates, Cryptographic Services, Computer Browser, DHCP Client, DNS Client, Messenger, Task Scheduler, Terminal Services, and Windows Firewall.

When an investigator looks at processes in Task Scheduler or using Netstat.exe -ano, instead of seeing the service's short name, they will see the executable name. If the investigator is not expecting it, they can be confused because several of the same file images are running at once, and many of the services may not appear to be running at all. When `Svchost.exe`, in particular, starts up, it queries the registry key (`HKLM\Software\Microsoft\WindowsNT\CurrentVersion\Svchost`) to find out which programs it should run and over how many separate instances of `Svchost`. The active processes running under each `Srvhost.exe` image can also be found by typing in **Tasklist /svc** at the command prompt. Its response might look something like this:

```
Image Name                   PID  Services
==========================  ====  =============================================
System Idle Process            0  N/A
System                         4  N/A
smss.exe                    1244  N/A
csrss.exe                   1364  N/A
winlogon.exe                1388  N/A
services.exe                1432  Eventlog, PlugPlay
lsass.exe                   1444  Netlogon, PolicyAgent, ProtectedStorage,
                                  SamSs
svchost.exe                 1628  DcomLaunch, TermService
svchost.exe                 1676  RpcSs
svchost.exe                 2016  AudioSrv, CryptSvc, Dhcp, ERSvc,
                                  EventSystem, helpsvc, lanmanserver,
                                  lanmanworkstation, Netman, Nla, Schedule,
                                  seclogon, SENS, SharedAccess,
                                  ShellHWDetection, srservice, Themes, TrkWks,
                                  winmgmt, wuauserv, WZCSVC
svchost.exe                  200  Dnscache
svchost.exe                  676  LmHosts, RemoteRegistry, SSDPSRV, WebClient
spoolsv.exe                 1268  Spooler
scardsvr.exe                1316  SCardSvr
alg.exe                      772  ALG
iexplore.exe                 568  N/A
tasklist.exe                2452  N/A
```

In this example, one `Svchost.exe` instance (with a PID of 2016) is running 14 different services, while other instances are running a single service. You can see what services are running under `Lsass.exe`, as well as the executable image behind each actively running service.

Startup Type

The Startup Type has three possible values: Automatic, Manual, and Disabled. Automatic means it starts when the system starts. A service with an Automatic Startup Type will run whenever the system starts, without having to wait for a user to log on. A service with a Manual Startup Type will not start automatically when the system starts, but can be started by other services or programs dependent on it, or manually by an administrator. Many services marked Manual start each time Windows starts, but just as many wait to be called by another program or process. For example, the Application Management service only starts when it is needed by Active Directory group policy objects trying to push down a software install. A service marked Disabled cannot be started by any program, process, or user until its Startup Type is changed. Table 7-2 shows the percentage of services with each Startup Type as compared to the percentage of services that start automatically when Windows starts (i.e., Manual or Automatic Startup Type).

Table 7-2

OS	Total	Started by Default	Startup Type		
			Automatic	Disabled	Manual
2000	56	54%	43%	5%	52%
XP	79	52%	44%	5%	51%
W2K3	83	39%	35%	25%	40%
W2K3 DC	84	44%	39%	23%	26%

You can see Microsoft's efforts to strengthen the operating system. Although the number of installed services has increased over time, the percentage activated by default has fallen and the percentage disabled by default has increased. This chapter builds on Microsoft's defaults.

Be aware that changing a service's Startup Type does not affect whether it is running or not at the current time.

Status can be Started, Stopped, or Paused. In XP Pro and later, by default only admins can change a service's status manually. There are many ways to stop and start a service, including using the Net Start or Net Stop syntax. For example:

```
Net Stop DHCP
```

This will stop the DHCP client. Note that the short name is used. Optionally, admins can pass the service command-line parameters to execute, although most of the time the switches are passed in the executable path field.

LogOn

The LogOn tab (see Figure 7-4) contains one of the most important fields of any service — the service account. All services log on using a service account (or service account principal). A service account is nearly identical to a normal user account. It can be local or domain-based but with a few differences. When a security principal account is registered as a service account, it gains the *Logon as a service user* right (in Local Computer Policy or a group policy object under Computer Configuration\Windows Settings\Security Settings\Local Policies\User Rights Assignment: *Log on as a service*). When this occurs, the service account logon will be managed by the Service Control Manager (SCM).

There is also a related service principal name (SPN) used for Kerberos delegation that this chapter will not be discussing. See http://pluralsight.com/wiki/default.aspx/Keith.GuideBook/WhatIsAService PrincipalNameSPN.html for more details.

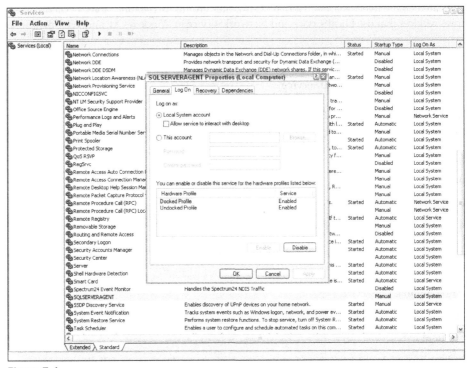

Figure 7-4

Default Service Accounts

You can enter any existing valid security principal account or use one of the three security principal accounts that exist in Windows by default: LocalSystem (known as System), LocalService, or NetworkService. The latter two accounts only exist in Windows XP and later, and were created to allow Windows services to be tightened. Prior to Windows XP, all services ran in the LocalSystem context. The LocalSystem context is the most powerful account in Windows. It has Full Control access to all objects; and even when an object's permissions are denied, it will be able to access the object with Full Control-Allow permissions.

To enable a service to use the LocalSystem account (sometimes displayed as NT AUTHORITY\System) as most services do, enable the *Local System account* option under the *Log on as* selection. Alternately, you can choose to enable *Allow service to interact with the desktop*, but this option is almost never enabled. If you allow a service to interact with the desktop, when the service displays information, it will be displayed on any currently logged in interactive user's desktop. A malicious user logged in interactively could take control of the service or attack it.

Although not used a lot yet (see Tables 7-3 and 7-4), LocalService and NetworkService can be used where LocalSystem access is not needed. When chosen, LocalService is displayed as NT AUTHORITY\ LocalService. The LocalService account has the same permissions as an Authenticated User on the local machine but connects to any remote computers using a null session (i.e., anonymous null session). NetworkService (i.e., NT AUTHORITY\NetworkService) accesses the local computer and network using the credentials of the local computer account. Typically, the local computer account belongs to the

Authenticated Users, Everyone, and Domain Computer groups by default. Tables 7-3 and 7-4 show common Windows services that use LocalService and NetworkService in Windows XP and Windows Server 2003.

Table 7-3

Services Logging On as LocalService
Alerter (disabled by default in XP and later)
Application Layer Gateway Service
Remote Registry
Smart Card
Smart Card Helper (only in Windows XP)
SSDP Discovery Service (only in Windows XP)
TCP/IP NetBIOS Helper
Telnet (LocalSystem in XP)
Uninterruptible Power Supply
Universal Plug and Play Device Host
WebClient
Windows Image Acquisition (not installed until an image device is installed)
Windows Time (LocalSystem in XP)
Windows User Mode Driver Framework (new in Windows Server 2003 SP1)
WinHTTP Web Proxy Auto-Discovery Service (only in Windows Server 2003)

Table 7-4

Services Logging On as NetworkService
ASP.NET State Service (not installed by default)
DHCP Client (LocalSystem in XP)
Distributed Transaction Coordinator
DNS Client
License Logging (in Windows Server 2003 only)
Performance Logs and Alerts
Remote Procedure Call (RPC) (made NetworkService in XP SP2 and Windows Server 2003 SP1)
Remote Procedure Call (RPC) Locator
Update Services (only in Windows Server 2003, not a default installed service)

The number of services listed in Tables 7-3 and 7-4 differ from the figures reported in 7-1 because Tables 7-3 and 7-4 include non-default services and cover both XP and Server 2003 operating systems.

Windows Vista will contain even more services running under the LocalService and NetworkService accounts.

When installing new services, consider using one of the newer, lesser privileged service accounts instead of using LocalSystem or an administrative-level user account.

Custom Service Accounts

Any user account can become a service account. It must have the *Log on as a service* user right and have access permissions to the objects it will manipulate. Simply enter (or browse to) the user account in the Services console Log On tab and type the password twice. Windows will automatically add the selected account as a service account, tell SCM to manage it, and store the password locally.

Service Account Passwords

Service accounts are also unique in that any entered passwords are stored both in the normal locations (SAM or Active Directory) and in the local system's LSA secrets cache (as covered in Chapter 4). (You should never change the passwords of the LocalSystem, LocalService, or NetworkService accounts. Windows maintains and changes them and ensures that they are sufficiently complex to prevent easy password hacking). As previously shown, it is possible for an admin user to extract those passwords in near plaintext using `Lsadump2.exe`, Cain & Able, and other programs. If you use a custom service account, make sure the password is long and complex and that it is changed more frequently than your normal user accounts. But also know that if a user has admin access to a computer with a customized service account, the logon name and password can be extracted even when the password is long and complex. This is not the case when the service account is one of the normal defaults (i.e., LocalSystem, LocalService, or NetworkService). The risk of having custom service account passwords cracked by an admin user must be weighed against the benefits of using a custom account in the first place.

You can also enable or disable any service on a per-service, per-hardware profile basis. Disable services when they are not needed in various profiles.

Recovery

As Figure 7-5 shows, the Recovery tab covers how Windows should treat an unnaturally stopped or nonresponding service. You can select how Windows should respond during the first, second, and subsequent failures. Windows response objects are *Take No Action*, *Restart the Service*, *Run a Program*, or *Restart the Server*. The default response is to Take No Action. The Recovery feature was made specifically to address overloaded, buggy, or maliciously attacked services. You can set how long failures are counted before the failure counter is reset to zero. Restart the Service allows a service to be recovered, at least temporarily, if being subjected to a massive DoS attack. You can set the number of minutes before restarting a service in order to allow another type of response or to send a message to connected users.

The default recovery action is often Take No Action or Restart the Computer for many services. For high-risk computers or services, consider instead setting the default action to Run a Program and send an alert to the first responders so they can troubleshoot or have early warning of a malicious attack. If you suspect that a service is going to be under attack, consider running a passive program to capture more detailed data, or another active response tool (such as an IPS or script). Figure 7-5 shows the command-line network packet capturing program, `Tethereal.exe`, being started on the third failure. If you decide to restart the computer, you can attempt to send a message to connected users.

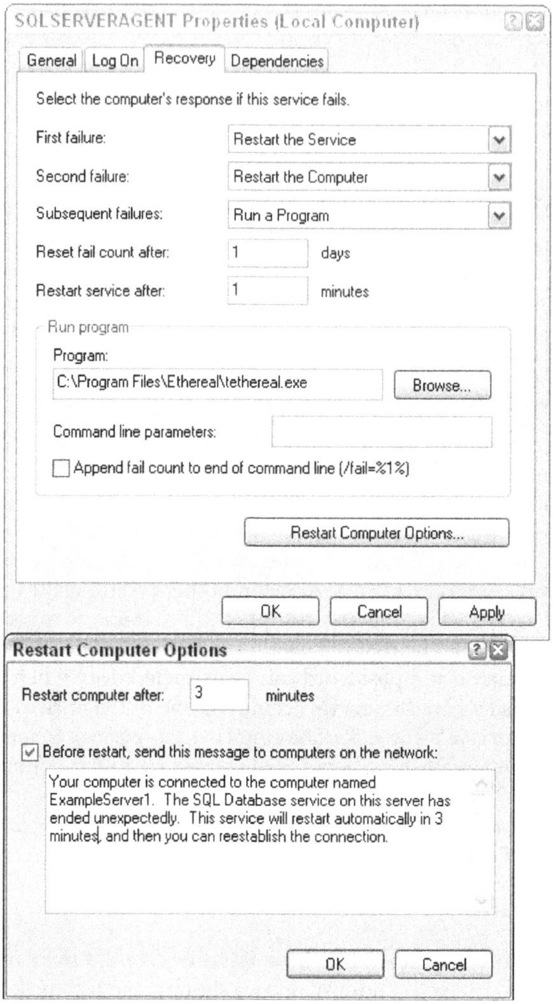

Figure 7-5

Dependencies

The Dependencies tab (see Figure 7-6) was added in Windows XP, but you can also see Windows 2000 dependencies if you open a Windows 2000 remote machine in an XP or later Services console. Dependencies show what services a particular depends on and what services depend on it. Prior to the Dependencies tab, a user would have to randomly shut off different services (or dig in the registry) to get warning messages to learn what services depended on what. Now one tab shows the needed information.

Figure 7-6

sc

Sc.exe is a helpful command-line tool to view, modify, and control services. Located in %Windir%\ System32, Sc.exe can work on local and remote services, return the results for one service, or extract information on all active services. It is often used to stop and start services, but it can do so much more than that. Here is an example of Sc.exe's output when typed alone to get the syntax:

```
C:\ >sc
DESCRIPTION:
        SC is a command line program used for communicating with the
        NT Service Controller and services.
USAGE:
        sc <server> [command] [service name] <option1> <option2>...

        The option <server> has the form "\\ServerName"
        Further help on commands can be obtained by typing: "sc [command]"
        Commands:
          query-----------Queries the status for a service, or
                          enumerates the status for types of services.
          queryex---------Queries the extended status for a service, or
```

```
                              enumerates the status for types of services.
           start-----------Starts a service.
           pause-----------Sends a PAUSE control request to a service.
           interrogate-----Sends an INTERROGATE control request to a service.
           continue--------Sends a CONTINUE control request to a service.
           stop------------Sends a STOP request to a service.
           config----------Changes the configuration of a service (persistant).
           description-----Changes the description of a service.
           failure---------Changes the actions taken by a service upon failure.
           qc--------------Queries the configuration information for a service.
           qdescription----Queries the description for a service.
           qfailure--------Queries the actions taken by a service upon failure.
           delete----------Deletes a service (from the registry).
           create----------Creates a service. (adds it to the registry).
           control---------Sends a control to a service.
           sdshow----------Displays a service's security descriptor.
           sdset-----------Sets a service's security descriptor.
           GetDisplayName--Gets the DisplayName for a service.
           GetKeyName------Gets the ServiceKeyName for a service.
           EnumDepend------Enumerates Service Dependencies.

       The following commands don't require a service name:
       sc <server> <command> <option>
           boot------------(ok | bad) Indicates whether the last boot should
                           be saved as the last-known-good boot configuration
           Lock------------Locks the Service Database
           QueryLock-------Queries the LockStatus for the SCManager Database
```

For example, I can type **SC \\10.1.1.20 queryex** to query all services. Here's a sample of that output from one service (although the command extracts similar data on all active services):

```
SERVICE_NAME: RpcSs
DISPLAY_NAME: Remote Procedure Call (RPC)
        TYPE               : 20  WIN32_SHARE_PROCESS
        STATE              : 4   RUNNING
                                 (NOT_STOPPABLE,NOT_PAUSABLE,IGNORES_SHUTDOWN)
        WIN32_EXIT_CODE    : 0   (0x0)
        SERVICE_EXIT_CODE  : 0   (0x0)
        CHECKPOINT         : 0x0
        WAIT_HINT          : 0x0
        PID                : 1676
        FLAGS              :
```

This indicates the state (i.e., Running), Service Name, Display Name, PID, whether or not a user or admin can stop or pause it, and other valuable information of interest to programs.

SC qc Rpcss can be typed to get information on the RPC service, resulting in output similar to this:

```
[SC] GetServiceConfig SUCCESS
SERVICE_NAME: rpcss
        TYPE               : 20  WIN32_SHARE_PROCESS
        START_TYPE         : 2   AUTO_START
        ERROR_CONTROL      : 1   NORMAL
```

```
BINARY_PATH_NAME    : C:\WINDOWS\system32\svchost -k rpcss
LOAD_ORDER_GROUP    : COM Infrastructure
TAG                 : 0
DISPLAY_NAME        : Remote Procedure Call (RPC)
DEPENDENCIES        :
SERVICE_START_NAME  : NT Authority\NetworkService
```

This time, it returns the Service Name, Display Name, Service Account, Dependencies, Startup Type, and Execution Path and command-line switches. SC is useful in a variety of situations.

RPC Services

Like Svchost.exe, RPC services need a bit more explaining. Many services are considered RPC services. An RPC service or program loads itself at a (usually) randomly selected TCP/IP port above 1023. The RPC Endpoint Mapper program running on port 135 gets requests from RPC programs, assigns an available port to the requesting service or program for the duration of the session, and records the assignment. When a remote computer wants to talk to an RPC service, it first contacts the RPC Endpoint Mapper on port 135, queries the mapper to find out where the service it is looking for is located, gets its answer, and then connects to the other service.

You can use a variety of tools to enumerate the RPC services as well, including SecurityFriday's RPCScan (www.securityfriday.com/tools/RpcScan.html), Bindview's RPCTools (www.bindview.com/Services/RAZOR/Utilities/Windows/rpctools1.0-readme.cfm), and Microsoft's RPCDump (www.microsoft.com/windows2000/techinfo/reskit/tools/existing/rpcdump-o.asp). Unfortunately, none of the tools work with XP Pro Service 2 or Windows Server 2003 Service Pack 1.

RPC Services are mentioned in this chapter to explain the appearance of many TCP and UDP ports just above 1023 on most Windows machines. Windows starts the RPC services, and the ports can be viewed using Netstat -an. For example, if you use Outlook to connect to Microsoft Exchange, they use RPC connections to communicate. Many administrators mistakenly believe that Outlook uses SMTP or POP3 protocols to talk to Exchange. Instead, whenever Exchange needs to talk to Outlook (e.g., maybe to report on a newly arrived message), Exchange contacts the Endpoint Mapper, obtains Outlook's RPC port, and then directly connects to Outlook.

Common Windows Services and Recommendations

Table 7-5 lists the default services found in Windows 2000 Pro, XP Pro, and a Server 2003 domain controller, the default Startup Type choice, and whether or not the service runs by default. Bolded recommendations are made under the Description field but are only intended to be general guidelines for environments with low to mid-level security requirements. Services must be enabled if your environment uses them. High-security environments can disable many of these services, as shown after the table. Test thoroughly before disabling any service in a production environment.

Table 7-5

Name	Description	W2K	XP	W2K3	Startup Type	Active by Default
Alerter	Notifies selected users and computers of administrative alerts. Some programs, such as antivirus consoles, use Alerter to send console messages. Must enable Messenger service to send an Alerter message across the network. A few low-risk vulnerabilities known. Should be **disabled** unless needed.	Y	Y	Y	Disabled	N
Application Experience LookupService	Installed with Service Pack 1, allows a specially coded application to ensure it is installed only on newer OSs. Only works locally, no network connections allowed. No risk in leaving **enabled**.	N	N	Y	Automatic	Y
Application Layer Gateway Service	Used by Microsoft and other vendors to interface and control Internet Connection Sharing (ICS) and Internet Connection Firewall (ICF). Keep **enabled** if you use ICS/ICF. No known vulnerabilities other than malware that sometimes turns off this service without the user's permission.	N	Y	Y	Manual	Y
Application Management	Only used with Active Directory software installation packages. Can be **disabled** if never used. No known vulnerabilities at this time.	Y	Y	Y	Manual	N
Automatic Updates	Needed for many Microsoft-based software patch management tools, including Automatic Updates service, SUS, and WSUS. No known vulnerabilities, it can be left **enabled** if used.	Y	Y	Y	Automatic	Y

Name	Description	W2K	XP	W2K3	Startup Type	Active by Default
Background Intelligent Transfer Service	Transfers IIS web site files in the background using idle network bandwidth. If the service is stopped, any services that use it may fail to transfer files if they do not have fail-safe mechanism features. IIS web sites such as Windows Update and MSN Explorer will be unable to automatically download programs and other information. Leave set to **manual**.	Y	Y	Y	Manual	May be Y
ClipBook	Not the same as the Clipboard app (Cut and Paste) most users are familiar with. Used by some programs as a universal, industrial-sized clipboard. Can be **disabled** or set to **manual** in most environments. No known vulnerabilities in years, but it is thought to be a potential future weak point. Requires the Network DDE service to be running.	Y	Y	Y	Disabled in XP and W2K3, Manual in W2K	N
COM+ Event System	Involved with distributing and running COM-based objects and programs. Unless you know that no COM- or DCOM-based applications are being used, it can be set to **manual** or **automatic**.	Y	Y	Y	Automatic in W2K3, Manual in XP and W2K	Y
COM+ System Application	Involved with distributing and running COM-based objects and programs. Unless you know that no COM- or DCOM-based applications are being used, it can be left at **manual**.	N	Y	Y	Manual	N
Computer Browser	Creates and maintains a list of computers on the local network and supplies this list to computers designated as browsers. Contrary to popular belief, NetBIOS is required on most Windows computers, and WINS is in a multi-network Exchange environment. Should be left **enabled** on all but high-security environments.	Y	Y	Y	Automatic	Y

Table continued on following page

269

Name	Description	W2K	XP	W2K3	Startup Type	Active by Default
Cryptographic Services	Heavily involved with providing the operating system and applications access to crypto-graphically protected files and resources. Should be **enabled** or **manual.**	N	Y	Y	Automatic	Y
DCOM Server Process Launcher	Provides launch functionality for Distributed COM services. **Don't disable** unless you are sure you don't have DCOM services in your network.	N	Y	Y	Automatic	Y
DHCP Client	Allows the computer to receive dynamic IP addresses and other DHCP information. Leave **enabled** if needed.	Y	Y	Y	Automatic	Y
DHCP Server	DHCP Server services. Keep **enabled**, unless not needed.	N	N	Y	Automatic	Y
Distributed File System	Creates and manages logical namespace storage volumes distributed across a network. Should be **enabled** on domain controllers in most environments, but can usually be disabled on member servers and clients. However, there are no known vulnerabilities, so it can be left in its default **enabled** state. Test this one first before disabling, even on member servers, if you have DFS enabled for client files.	N	N	Y	Automatic	Y
Distributed Link Tracking Client	Enables client programs to track linked files that are moved within an NTFS volume to another NTFS volume on the same computer, or to an NTFS volume on another computer. Can be left **enabled**.	Y	Y	Y	Manual in W2K3, Automatic in XP and W2K	Y in XP and W2K
Distributed Link Tracking Server	Enables the Distributed Link Tracking Client service within the same domain to provide more reliable and efficient maintenance of links within the domain. Can be left **disabled** unless needed.	N	N	Y	Disabled	N

Name	Description	W2K	XP	W2K3	Startup Type	Active by Default
Distributed Transaction Coordinator	MSDTC is responsible for coordinating transactions that are distributed across multiple computer systems or resource managers, such as databases, message queues, file systems, or other transaction-protected resources. Should be left **enabled** in network computers.	Y	Y	Y	Automatic in W2K3, Manual in XP and W2K	Y in W2K3
DNS Client	Resolves computer and service names to IP addresses. Used to locate Active Directory domain controllers and other services. Keep **enabled**.	Y	Y	Y	Automatic	Y
DNS Server	Enables DNS clients to resolve DNS names by answering DNS queries and dynamic DNS update requests. If this service is stopped, DNS updates will not occur. Keep enabled on servers providing DNS services to DNS clients.	N	N	Y	Automatic	Y
Error Reporting Service	Collects, stores, and sends unexpected application crash data to Microsoft. If this service is stopped, then Error Reporting will occur only for kernel faults and some types of user mode faults. Keep **enabled** unless you don't want users to have this service. No known vulnerabilities.	N	Y	Y	Automatic	Y
Event Log	Enables event log messages issued by Windows-based programs and components to be viewed in Event Viewer. This service cannot be stopped. Keep **enabled** in all environments.	Y	Y	Y	Automatic	Y
Fast User Switching Compatibility	Allows multiple users to log on to a single computer without first logging the other users off. When enabled, disables many features, including security features. Should be **disabled**.	N	Y	N	Manual	N

Table continued on following page

Name	Description	W2K	XP	W2K3	Startup Type	Active by Default
Fax Service	Allows the PC to send and receive faxes. **Disable** if not needed.	Y	N	N	Manual	N
File Replication Service	Used by file servers and domain controllers for domain communications and DFS. Should remain **enabled**.	N	N	Y	Automatic	Y
Help and Support	Enables the Help and Support Center to run on this computer. Although it can usually be left **enabled**, a few vulnerabilities have been found using it, so in a high-security environment consider disabling instead.	N	Y	Y	Automatic	Y
HTTP SSL	Allows IIS and other server apps to use HTTPS. Needed if HTTPS is used; otherwise, you can **disable**. No known vulnerabilities.	N	Y	Y	Manual	N
Human Interface Device Access	Allows "smart" keyboards, with predefined hot buttons, etc. Can also be used for some USB devices. Can be **disabled** if not needed. Could be used in an attack, but no known vulnerabilities.	N	Y	Y	Disabled	N
Indexing Service	Indexes contents and properties of files on local and remote computers. Has been involved in several vulnerabilities. **Disable** if not needed.	Y	Y	Y	Disabled in W2K3, Manual in XP and W2K	N
Internet Connection Sharing	Provides NAT and DNS services for computers connecting through ICS. Can be **disabled** if not needed. Could be used in an exploit, but so far no known vulnerabilities.	Y	N	N	Manual	N
Intersite Messaging	Used for intersite domain controller communications; otherwise, not needed and can be **disabled**. No known exploits.	N	N	Y	Disabled	N

Name	Description	W2K	XP	W2K3	Startup Type	Active by Default
IPSEC Services (called IPSEC Policy Agent in W2K)	Enables IPSec. Can be disabled if not needed, but IPSec is very helpful in many situations. Some low-risk vulnerabilities found when only using AH (and not ESP also) and with weak PSK. Can usually be left **enabled**.	Y	Y	Y	Automatic	Y
Kerberos Key Distribution Center	Needed on Active Directory domain controllers for Kerberos authentication, which is critical for Windows 2000 and later domains. Although a few low-risk exploits have been announced, including one Kerberos sniffing/brute-force attack, it should be left **enabled**.	N	N	Y	Automatic	Y
License Logging	Being phased out by Microsoft, this is used to track legacy licensing issues. Has been subjected to at least one exploit. Can be left **disabled**.	N	N	Y	Disabled	N
Logical Disk Manager	Used to manage logical disk activities and reports to different tools, such as Disk Manager. Can be set to **manual**, or disabled if not needed.	Y	Y	Y	Automatic	Y
Logical Disk Manager Administrative Service	Used to manage logical disk activities and reports to different tools, like Disk Manager. Can be set to **manual**, or disabled if not needed. The service only runs for configuration processes and then stops.	Y	Y	Y	Manual	Y
Messenger	Transmits net send and Alerter service messages between clients and servers. Has been involved in a few exploits and nuisance attacks (i.e., spam, phishing, fraud sales, etc.). Should be left **disabled** unless needed.	Y	Y	Y	Disabled	N

Table continued on following page

273

Name	Description	W2K	XP	W2K3	Startup Type	Active by Default
Microsoft Search	Creates full-text indexes on content and properties of structured and semi-structured data to allow fast linguistic searches on this data. No known vulnerabilities, it can be disabled or left **enabled** if needed.	N	N	Y	Automatic	Y
Microsoft/MS Software Shadow Copy Provider	Involved in Volume Shadow Copying used for file restoration and backups. **Disable** if not needed. No known vulnerabilities.	N	Y	Y	Manual	N
Net Logon	Maintains a secure channel between computers and domain controllers for authenticating users and services. Required for most computers — for logon, for registering SRV resource records in DNS, and for supporting NT 4.0 replication. Leave **enabled**.	Y	Y	Y	Automatic	Y
NetMeeting Remote Desktop Sharing	Allows a user to use NetMeeting to access a computer remotely. Can be **disabled** if not needed.	Y	Y	Y	Disabled in W2K3, Manual in XP and W2K	Y
Network Connections	Manages connections and objects in the Network and Dial-Up Connections. If disabled, users will not be able to view, browse, and modify network connections. Leave **enabled** at manual.	Y	Y	Y	Manual	Y
Network DDE	Needed for Dynamic Data Exchange (DDE)-enabled programs. Used by ClipBook service and sometimes by Microsoft Office applications. Can be **disabled** if not needed.	Y	Y	Y	Disabled in W2K3 and XP, Manual in W2K	N
Network DDE DSDM	Manages Dynamic Data Exchange (DDE) network shares, which are used by some programs. Used by ClipBook service and sometimes by Microsoft Office applications. Can be **disabled** if not needed.	Y	Y	Y	Disabled in W2K3 and XP, Manual in W2K	N

Name	Description	W2K	XP	W2K3	Startup Type	Active by Default
Network Location Awareness (NLA)	Notes when the computer's network location has been changed, and notifies interested applications. For example, if the PC uses DHCP, it will request a new lease when the network changes, such as when a laptop is plugged into a new location. Leave **enabled.** No known exploits, although theoretically there could be some attacks.	N	Y	Y	Manual	Y
Network Provisioning Service	Manages XML configuration files on a domain basis for automatic network provisioning. Can be **disabled** if not needed (most networks don't use it).	N	Y	Y	Manual	N
NT LM Security Support Provider	Provides security to remote procedure call (RPC) programs that use transports other than named pipes. Often needed, leave **enabled** at manual.	Y	Y	Y	Manual	Y in W2K3
Performance Logs and Alerts	Needed for Performance Log and Alerts monitoring. Can be **disabled** if not needed.	Y	Y	Y	Manual	N
Plug and Play	Used for Plug and Plug feature. Supposedly, stopping this service will result in system instability. Keep **enabled** even though it has been involved in more than one exploit. This should be able to be disabled, but it can't be without adverse legitimate effects.	Y	Y	Y	Automatic	Y
Portable Media Serial Number Service	For DRM, allows remote content providers to retrieve the unique serial number of any portable media player connected to the computer. If stopped, protected content will not download. **Disable** if not needed.	N	Y	Y	Manual	N

Table continued on following page

Name	Description	W2K	XP	W2K3	Startup Type	Active by Default
Print Spooler	Manages local and remote printer queues. Should be **enabled** if printing is needed, although it has been involved in at least one exploit.	Y	Y	Y	Automatic	Y
Protected Storage	Older Windows cryptographic method for protecting sensitive information, such as cryptographic keys, service passwords, etc. Being phased out, but still needed. Keep **enabled**. It h as not been exploited, but it can be used by malicious programs logged in as admin to access protected content.	Y	Y	Y	Automatic	Y
QoS RSVP	Provides control setup functionality for QoS-aware applications. Should be **disabled** unless needed.	Y	Y	N	Manual	N
Remote Access Auto Connection Manager	Per Microsoft, "Detects unsuccessful attempts to connect to a remote network or computer and provides alternative methods for connection. If this service is stopped, users will need to manually connect." Should be left **enabled** and manual unless remote connections are not needed.	Y	Y	Y	Manual	N
Remote Access Connection Manager	Manages dial-up and virtual private network (VPN) connections from the computer to remote locations. Should be **enabled** unless dial-up or VPN connections are not needed.	Y	Y	Y	Manual	Y in W2K
Remote Desktop Help Session Manager	Manages Remote Assistance. If this service is stopped, Remote Assistance will be unavailable. Can be **disabled** if not needed.	N	Y	Y	Manual	N

Name	Description	W2K	XP	W2K3	Startup Type	Active by Default
Remote Procedure Call (RPC)	The RPC Endpoint Mapper on TCP port 135 and COM Service Control Manager. If this service is stopped, programs using Remote Procedure Call (RPC) or COM services will not function properly. Leave **enabled**. Although it has been involved in several exploits, when disabled it creates many problems in Windows.	Y	Y	Y	Automatic	Y
Remote Procedure Call (RPC) Locator	Enables Remote Procedure Call (RPC) clients using RPCNs* APIs to locate RPC servers. RPCNs* APIs are not used internally in Windows, but can be used by other programs, such as Exchange. Leave **enabled** at manual unless you are sure you don't need them.	Y	Y	Y	Manual	N
Remote Registry	Enables remote users to modify registry settings and remotely administrate Windows machines. If stopped, will prevent many remote management applications from working. Leave **enabled** unless otherwise unneeded.	Y	Y	Y	Automatic	Y
Removable Storage	Manages and catalogs removable media devices and software. If this service is stopped, programs using removable storage, such as Backup, will operate more slowly. Leave **enabled** if needed.	Y	Y	Y	Manual in W2K3 and XP, Automatic in W2K	Y in W2K
Resultant Set of Policy Provider	Allows a remote user to verify effective group policy settings. No known vulnerabilities. Leave **enabled** at manual unless you don't want RSoP capabilities.	N	N	Y	Manual	N
Routing and Remote Access	Enables Routing and Remote Access (RRAS) services. Can be **disabled** unless needed.	Y	Y	Y	Disabled	N

Table continued on following page

Name	Description	W2K	XP	W2K3	Startup Type	Active by Default
Secondary Logon (called RunAs Service in W2K)	Allows programs and processes to be started using alternate user credentials. Leave **enabled** unless you intentionally want to disable the function.	Y	Y	Y	Automatic	Y
Security Accounts Manager	Interfaces with other programs to let them know the Security Accounts Management (SAM) database is ready to process requests. Leave **enabled**. If disabled, it can cause many problems.	Y	Y	Y	Automatic	Y
Security Center	Added in XP SP2, adds centralized Security Center console to manage Windows Firewall, antivirus software, and a multitude of security services and settings. Can be left **enabled**, but can be disabled if features and interface are not needed.	N	Y	N	Automatic	Y
Server	All file, print, and named-pipe sharing over the network for this computer. Usually leave **enabled**, but can be disabled if sharing is not needed.	Y	Y	Y	Automatic	Y
Shell Hardware Detection	Provides notifications for Auto Play hardware events, from CD-ROMs, USB memory devices, digital cameras, etc. Can **disable** to prevent "auto-play" attacks, but will also prevent "auto-display" events. If you disable, just remember the side effects.	N	Y	Y	Automatic	Y
Smart Card	Allows Smart Cards to be read by Windows without additional driver support. **Disable** unless used.	Y	Y	Y	Automatic in W2K3 and XP, Manual in W2K	Y in W2K3 and XP
Smart Card Helper	Needed for legacy Smart Card readers. **Disable** unless used.	Y	N	N	Manual	N

Name	Description	W2K	XP	W2K3	Startup Type	Active by Default
Special Administration Console Helper	Allows administrators to remotely access a command prompt using Emergency Management Services (EMS). Leave **enabled** unless not needed.	N	N	Y	Manual	N
SSDP Discovery Service	Enables discovery of UPnP devices on the local network. **Disable** unless needed.	N	Y	N	Manual	Y
System Event Notification	Monitors system events and notifies subscribers to COM+ Event System of these events. Leave **enabled** unless you know you don't have COM+Event-enabled applications. If disabled, it can cause problems with synchronizing applications and applications that pay attention to whether the computer is offline or online.	Y	Y	Y	Automatic	Y
System Restore Service	Performs and allows System Restore events. Leave **enabled** for backup purposes, but disable when cleaning up malware or to increase system performance.	N	Y	N	Automatic	Y
Task Scheduler	Enables the Task Scheduler application. Used by many applications for periodic jobs. Used maliciously in the past, it has been tightened by Microsoft. Leave **enabled** unless not needed.	Y	Y	Y	Automatic	Y
TCP/IP NetBIOS Helper Service	Provides NetBIOS over TCP/IP (NetBT) support allowing users to share files, print, and log on to the network. Leave **enabled** (disable only if NetBIOS is not needed, and NetBIOS is still needed often).	Y	Y	Y	Automatic	Y
Telephony	Provides Telephony API (TAPI) support for programs that control telephony devices and IP-based voice connections. **Disable** if not needed.	Y	Y	Y	Manual	N

Table continued on following page

Name	Description	W2K	XP	W2K3	Startup Type	Active by Default
Telnet	Telnet server. Allows remote telnet users to telnet in to command-line prompt. D**isable** unless used.	Y	Y	Y	Disabled in W2K3 and XP, Manual in W2K	N
Terminal Services	Allows users to connect inter-actively to a remote computer using many services using the RDP protocol, including Remote Desktop, Fast User Switching, Remote Assistance, and Terminal Server. RDP is commonly used, so leave **enabled** (can be disabled if not needed). A few exploits have been accomplished using RDP and Terminal Services.	N	Y	Y	Manual	Y
Terminal Services Session Directory	Only needed for Terminal Service clustering; otherwise, leave **disabled**.	N	N	Y	Disabled	N
Themes	Allows desktop themes to be activated. **Disable** if not needed.	N	Y	Y	Disabled in W2K3, Automatic in XP	N
Uninterruptible Power Supply	Manages an Uninterruptible Power Supply (UPS) connected to the local computer. Leave **enabled** unless not needed.	Y	Y	Y	Manual	N
Universal Plug and Play Device Host	Provides support to host Universal Plug and Play devices. Has been involved with exploits before. Can **disable** unless needed.	N	Y	N	Manual	N
Upload Manager	Per Microsoft, "Manages file transfers between clients and servers on the network. Driver data is anonymously uploaded from these transfers and thenused by Microsoft to help users find the drivers they need. The Driver Feed-back Server asks the client's per-mission to upload the computer's hardware profile andthen search the Internet for information about how to obtain the appropriate driver or get support. If this service stops, Microsoft willnot have access to the driver data."Leave enabled at **manual**.	N	N	Y	Manual	N

Name	Description	W2K	XP	W2K3	Startup Type	Active by Default
Utility Manager	Allows accessibility tools to be configured from one window. Can be **disabled** unless used.	Y	N	N	Manual	N
Virtual Disk Service	Provides software volume and hardware volume management service to VDS-enabled storage devices. **Disable** unless used.	N	N	Y	Manual	N
Volume Shadow Copy	Manages Volume Shadow Copies used for backup and user restoration purposes. If this service is stopped, shadow copies will be unavailable. Can be **disabled** unless used.	N	Y	Y	Manual	N
WebClient	Enables Windows-based programs to create, access, and modify Web DAV-based files. Normally, not needed, as its functions are covered in Microsoft Office and Internet Explorer. Has been involved in at least one exploit. **Disable** unless needed.	N	Y	Y	Disabled in W2K3, Automatic in XP	Y in XP
Windows Audio	Manages Windows audio devices. If this service is stopped, audio devices will stop working. **Enable** if needed.	N	Y	Y	Disabled in W2K3, Automatic in XP	Y in XP
Windows Firewall/Internet Connection Sharing (ICS)	Needed for Windows Firewall or Internet Connection Sharing. **Enable** if either of those two features are being used.	N	Y	Y	Automatic	Y
Windows Installer	Adds, modifies, and removes applications installed or uninstalled by the Windows Installer (*.msi) package. Also needed for group policy software installs. Can be left **enabled** at manual.	Y	Y	Y	Manual	N
Windows Management Instrumentation	Provides a common interface to WMI objects. Starting to be used heavily in Windows (e.g., RSoP) and other management software. Should be left **enabled**, although it could be used in an exploit.	Y	Y	Y	Automatic	N

Table continued on following page

Name	Description	W2K	XP	W2K3	Startup Type	Active by Default
Windows Management Instrumentation Driver Extensions	Used by WMI to monitor all driver and event trace providers that are configured to publish Windows Management Instrumentation (WMI) or event trace information. Should be left **enabled**.	Y	Y	Y	Manual	Y in W2K
Windows Time	Used for date and time synchronization on all clients and servers in the network. Required for Kerberos and other time-dependent services. Should be left **enabled**.	Y	Y	Y	Automatic	Y
WinHTTP Web Proxy Auto-Discovery Service	Per Microsoft, "Implements the Web Proxy Auto-Discovery (WPAD) protocol for Windows HTTP Services (WinHTTP). WPAD is a legacy protocol to enable an HTTP client to automatically discover a proxy configuration. If this service is stopped or disabled, the WPAD protocol will be executed within the HTTP client's process instead of an external service process; there would be no loss of functionality as a result." Can be **disabled** unless needed.	N	N	Y	Manual	N
Wireless (Zero) Configuration	Enables automatic configuration for IEEE wireless 802.11 adapters. If this service is stopped, automatic configuration will be unavailable. If enabled, Windows will often attempt to connect to any available wireless network (unless configured otherwise). Should be **disabled** unless needed.	Y	Y	Y	Automatic in W2K3 and XP, Manual in W2K	Y in W2K3 and XP
WMI Performance Adapter	Per Microsoft, "Provides performance library information from Windows Management Instrumentation (WMI) providers to clients on the network. This service only runs when Performance Data Helper is activated." Can be left **enabled** on manual.	N	Y	Y	Manual	N

Name	Description	W2K	XP	W2K3	Startup Type	Active by Default
Workstation	Creates and maintains client network SMB (file and printer) connections to remote servers. Both local file system requests and remote file or print network requests are routed through the Workstation service. This service determines where the resource is located and then routes the request to the local file system or the networking components. When the Workstation service is stopped, all requests are assumed to be local requests. If disabled, effectively disables file and printer sharing. Has been involved in several exploits, but is usually a necessary part of Windows. Leave **enabled** in all but high-risk environments.	Y	Y	Y	Automatic	Y

Note: Many of the services shown as not available in Windows 2000 Pro but available in Windows Server 2003 are available in Windows 2000 Server.

Nondefault Windows Services

Table 7-6 lists commonly installed Windows services that are not usually installed by default, gives recommendations for low-to-medium security environments, and lists the operating systems in which the service is available. Disable any unneeded services in Table 7-6.

Table 7-6

Name	Description	W2K	XP	W2K3
ASP.NET State Service	Provides support for out-of-process session states for IIS web sites running ASP.NET and using ASP.NET session states. There have been some ongoing concerns regarding ASP.NET. If enabled, opens port 42424.	N	Y	Y
Boot Information Negotiation Layer	Used in Remote Installation Services (RIS)	Y	Y	Y
Certificate Services	Installed with Certificate Services. Available in NT, 2000, and 2003 server products.	N	N	Y

Table continued on following page

Name	Description	W2K	XP	W2K3
Cluster Services	Installed with Cluster Services. Available in NT, 2000, and 2003 server products.	N	N	Y
File Service for Macintosh	Enables Macintosh computers to use NTFS shares. Available in NT, 2000, and 2003 server products.	N	N	Y
FTP Publishing Service	Installed as a component of IIS. Although FTP allows plaintext communications, no other known vulnerabilities have been found. Will probably invite a lot of hacker probes.	Y	Y	Y
Gateway Services for Netware	Allows access to file and print resources on Netware networks. Can be installed on NT, 2000, and 2003 server products.	N	N	Y
IIS Admin Service	Allows administration of IIS. If service is not running, you will not be able to run Web, FTP, NNTP, or SMTP sites, or configure IIS.	Y	Y	Y
IMAPI CD-Burning COM Service	Manages CD recording that uses IMAPI. No known vulnerabilities	N	Y	Y
Infrared Monitoring Service	Used for Infrared devices (often found on laptops and PDAs)	N	Y	Y
Internet Authentication Service (IAS)	Microsoft's version of the RADIUS authentication server. Can be installed in Windows Server 2000 or 2003.	N	N	Y
IP Version 6 Help (6to4) Service	Allows IPv6 traffic to be tunneled over IPv4	N	Y	Y
Machine Debug Manager Service	The Machine Debug Manager, Mdm.exe, is a program installed with the Microsoft Script Editor and other programs (i.e., Visual Studio) to provide support for program debugging. The Microsoft Script Editor is included with Microsoft Office 2000, or can be obtained from the Microsoft Windows Update website. It is needed only for programmer debugging purposes and can almost always be turned off.	N	Y	Y

Name	Description	W2K	XP	W2K3
Message Queuing Service Message Queuing Down Level Clients Service Message Queuing Triggers Service Microsoft Exchange Event Microsoft Exchange IMAP4 Microsoft Exchange Information Store Microsoft Exchange Management Microsoft Exchange MTA Stacks Microsoft Exchange POP3 Microsoft Exchange Routing Engine Microsoft Exchange Site Replication Service	Used for developing and implementing messaging applications. Commonly used with SQL applications.	N	N	Y
Microsoft Exchange System Attendant	Microsoft Exchange Server. Available on all Windows server products.	N	N	Y
MSSQL$UDDI Service	Used to find and identify new or available services in a web service application directory service. Most companies using web services aren't using the UDDI service yet, which can be likened to a whitepage directory lookup of web services. As web services mature and become plentiful, it is thought that Internet- and intranet-available UDDI services will be necessary.	N	N	Y

Table continued on following page

Name	Description	W2K	XP	W2K3
MSSQLServerAD Helper Service	Used by SQL services when SQL isn't running in the local system context	N	N	Y
.NET Framework Support Service	Provides .NET client run-time environment. Only needed when .NET programming exists in your environment.	Y	Y	Y
Print Server for Macintosh	Allows Macintosh computers to print to Windows printers. Installed on NT, 2000, and 2003 servers.	N	N	Y
Network News Transfer Protocol (NNTP)	Supports NNTP outside of Exchange on Windows 2000 and 2003 servers	N	N	Y
Office Source Engine	Installed with Microsoft Office 2003	N	Y	Y
Remote Storage Notification Remote Storage Server Services	Used only with Hierarchical Storage Management (HSM) secondary storage solutions	N	N	Y
SAP Agent Service	Used when connecting to Novell networks	N	N	Y
Simple TCP/IP Services	Provides Echo, Discard, Character Generator, Daytime, and Quote of the Day services	N	N	Y
Single Instance Storage Groveler Service	Used only by Remote Installation Services	N	N	Y
Simple Mail Transfer Protocol (SMTP)	Supports SMTP outside of Exchange	N	Y	Y
SNMP and SNMP Trap Services	Provides SNMP functionality. SNMP has been used in some attacks.	Y	Y	Y
SQLAgent$* Service	Needed for SQL server applications, such as tape backups	Y	Y	Y
TCP/IP Print Server Service	Allows Unix Line Printer Daemon emulation	N	N	Y
Trivial FTP Daemon Service	Unsecurable FTP server (no user name or password needed). RIS uses it, and all Windows 2000 and later clients have the TFTP client (Tftp.exe) installed by default.	N	N	Y

Name	Description	W2K	XP	W2K3
Web Element Manager	Used for web site remote administration	Y	Y	Y
Windows Image Acquisition (WIA)	Optional service added when digital image devices are added. Needed for scanners and cameras.	N	Y	Y
Windows Internet Naming Service (WINS)	Used for NetBIOS name to IP address conversion. Installed on Windows Server products.	N	N	Y
Windows Media Services	Used by Windows Media Services, a server version for distributing digital content	N	N	Y
Windows User Mode Driver Framework	Installed with Windows Media Player 10. If disabled, prevents synchronization between external player devices and WMP.	N	Y	Y
World Wide Publishing Service	Used for IIS	Y	Y	Y

Note: Many of the services shown as not available in Windows 2000 Pro but available in Windows Server 2003 are available in Windows 2000 Server.

Differences between Windows Platforms

Table 7-7 displays the service differences between a Windows 2003 stand-alone server and a Windows 2003 domain controller.

Table 7-7

Service Name	Windows Server 2003 Stand-Alone Server	Windows Server 2003 Domain Controller
Kerberos Key Distribution Center	Not Started, Disabled	Started, Automatic
Net Logon	Not Started, Disabled	Started, Automatic
Distributed Link Tracking Client	Started, Automatic	Not Started, Manual
Distributed Link Tracking Server	Not Started, Disabled	Not Started, Disabled (some Microsoft documents state this service is Started and Automatic on domain controllers)
DNS Server	Not installed	Started, Automatic (if DNS server is installed on domain controller)

Table continued on following page

Service Name	Windows Server 2003 Stand-Alone Server	Windows Server 2003 Domain Controller
File Replication Service	Not Started, Manual	Started, Automatic
Intersite Messaging Service	Not Started, Disabled	Started, Automatic
Remote Procedure Call (RPC) Locator	Not Started, Manual	Not Started, Manual (some Microsoft documents state this service is Started and Automatic on domain controllers)

Tables 7-5, 7-6, and 7-7 cover the most common Windows services. If a service is not needed, it should be disabled. Table 7-5 gave recommendations regarding the various services as they would apply in most low-to-medium security environments.

Securing Services

Tightening services means determining what services do and don't have to be running on a particular computer by determining its production role in the environment. High-security environments are easy to secure because you turn nearly every service off. Normal security environments are a bit tougher to secure because you must make security cost-benefit trade-offs.

High-Security Minimal Services

A high-security environment is one in which very little risk can be taken. An example is a public-facing web server or Internet bastion host supporting a security gateway or firewall. In these cases, every possible service that isn't needed can be disabled or removed.

The following services can be disabled on high-risk computers, if not needed: Application Layer Gateway Service, Application Management, ASP.NET State Service, Automatic Updates, Background Intelligent Transfer Service, Computer Browser, DHCP Client, Error Reporting, Help and Support, HTTP SSL, IPSec Services, Logical Disk Manager, Logical Disk Manager Administrative Service, Microsoft Software Shadow Copy Provider, Netlogon, Network Connections, Network Location Awareness, Performance Logs and Alerts, Portable Media Serial Number Service, Print Spooler, Remote Access Auto Connection Manager, Remote Access Connection Manager, Remote Desktop Help, Remote Registry, Removable Storage, Resultant Set of Policies, Smartcard, Special Administration Console Helper, Task Scheduler, Telephony, Terminal Services, Themes, Uninterruptible Power Supply, Upload Manager, Virtual Disk Service, Volume Shadow Copy, WMI Performance Adapter, and Workstation. If followed, a high-risk computing environment could potentially remove dozens of normally active or manually enabled services, significantly decreasing security risk in that environment.

Normal Security Environments

Which default services should be tightened in a normal security environment? Overall, Microsoft has done a good job in XP Pro and later. Most companies can leave the default settings and have a relatively good set of security on the default options. However, any service with LocalSystem access is potentially high risk, but turning them off often disables needed legitimate services. Sadly, some higher than normal risk services (e.g., RPC, Plug and Play, Server, Spooler, Workstation, etc.) are constantly exposed and constantly under attack. There isn't much we can do but keep patches up to date and try to prevent external malware from attacking internal computers.

Basic Recommendations

Table 7-5 describes which services could be disabled in most environments without large adverse effects. The main recommendation is to disable any service that is not being used for a legitimate production requirement. This always includes services such as Themes. Disable Wireless Zero Configuration if the computers do not use wireless. This advice even includes disabling legitimate services, which can have legitimate production value, if they are not used.

The basic recommendations made in Table 7-5 are tighter than you would find in most other guides. That's because most guides recommend keeping enabled services that you might not use but that don't currently have a demonstrated vulnerability against them. This book errs on the side of caution and assumes every service can be used in an exploit. If you don't need it, turn it off! Less attack surface equals less risk.

Make an enterprisewide list of what services are acceptable on your various servers and workstations. You should have different lists for different roles (i.e., file server, web server, etc.). Ensure that unnecessary services are disabled, or at least set to manual. If you are just beginning to harden your services, take baby steps. Turn off one service, or just a few, and reboot the computer a few times, running all your existing applications over a day or two to see whether any problems result. Carefully document any removed or disabled services by date. That way, if an application problem comes up in the future, you can use your disabled service list as a way to rule its involvement in or out.

Other Guides

Microsoft has excellent security guides for legacy, normal, and high-risk environments at `www.microsoft.com/technet/security/prodtech/windowsserver2003.mspx` and `http://go.microsoft.com/fwlink/?linkid=15160`. Many people used to go to the National Security Agency's (NSA) web site (`http://www.nsa.gov`) for Windows security advice. The NSA has approved Microsoft's default security templates, governing services recommendations, and the default templates for Windows XP Pro and Windows Server 2003.

The Center for Internet Security (`www.cisecurity.org`) has the best general-application Windows security guides available. Their CIS Benchmarking tools are available for Windows NT and later, Linux, FreeBSD, and Cisco routers (and more). What makes the tools great is that you can read the accompanying documentation to learn what is recommended and why, and then run a benchmarking tool to learn how your current environment differs. The CIS group has done an outstanding job!

Security Configuration Wizard

Windows Server 2003 Service Pack 1 came with the Security Configuration Wizard (`www.microsoft.com/windowsserver2003/technologies/security/configwiz/default.mspx`). It is an excellent tool for tightening Windows 2003 servers based upon the production role that they perform (i.e., file server, web server, Exchange server, etc.). The SCW conducts a series of interviewlike questions to ascertain what role(s) the server will be performing. It then leads the administrator through enabling or disabling various services (see Figure 7-7) based upon the roles chosen. SCW then makes a security template that can be applied (or rolled back) to the local server or any other computer that you wish. The resulting SCW file is an XML file that can be read or fed into other programs.

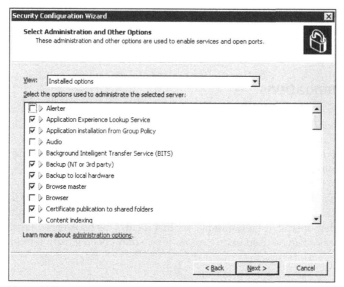

Figure 7-7

SCW is a great tool. Microsoft realized that most administrators don't have the time to become "services experts," so they automated the process as much as possible, although even the SCW tool doesn't automate the complete granularity of making a service-by-service decision. On hardened web servers and other high-security environments, I usually end up manually turning off more services than the SCW tool did. It's a great start though and one that I recommend on Windows Server 2003 SP1 and later computers. Future versions of Windows will continue to build on this excellent feature. For more information, see www.microsoft.com/windowsserver2003/technologies/security/configwiz/default.mspx.

How to Tighten Remaining Services

What about the services you can't uninstall or remove? Tightening services can be accomplished by disabling or removing unneeded services, using NTFS permissions to restrict the service, tightening the service account, and keeping patches up to date.

Disable or Remove Unneeded Services

If possible, uninstall or remove unneeded services. This is not always possible because Windows File Protection (WFP) will not allow you to remove, delete, or rename most default Windows services. Instead, mark the service with a Disabled Startup Type. Although a hacker or malware with admin access could potentially restart the service, disabling the service removes it from memory and prevents it from being used during an initial exploit. Remember that services marked Manual can often be started without much effort.

Use Permissions

Another excellent way to prevent unneeded services from launching is to use NTFS permissions. You can place Read-Deny or Read & Execute-Deny permissions on any service by researching its executable in the Services console or using Sc.exe. You can even use software restriction policies to prevent service image execution. This method will ensure that the service does not launch, although this hint is not easy to apply when one image file (e.g., Svchost.exe) is in charge of launching multiple services and you still need some of its services.

Instead, use the permissions available on each service in a GPO (see Figure 7-8). In every GPO you can define the Startup Type (i.e., Automatic, Disabled, or Manual) and push it down computers. This method is great when you need to turn off or enable a particular service across the enterprise in a short amount of time. GPOs also allow you to fine-tune permissions on the service object itself. You can give or take away various permissions that include deleting, starting, stopping, or pausing the service. I wish Microsoft allowed this inside of the Services console, but it doesn't.

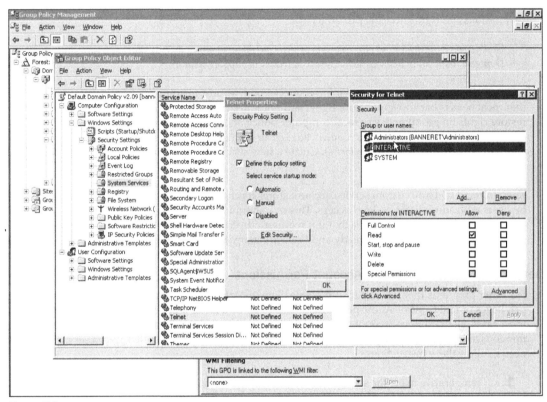

Figure 7-8

You can also view and set Service permissions using two command-line utilities. And you can use Sc.exe to display (Sc sdshow) and set Service permissions (Sc sdset). See www.microsoft .com/technet/prodtechnol/windowsserver2003/library/ServerHelp/0a658e97-51d5-4109- b461-a474c799964e.mspx for more details on Sc.exe. Unfortunately, setting permissions using Sc.exe requires knowledge and use of the hard-to-use Security Descriptor Definition Language (SDDL). See http://msdn.microsoft.com/library/default.asp?url=/library/en-us/secauthz/ security/ace_strings.asp for details on SDDL. The command-line utility Subinacl.exe (www.microsoft.com/downloads/details.aspx?FamilyID=E8BA3E56-D8FE-4A91-93CF-ED6985E

`3927B&displaylang=en`) can also set Service permissions, and without having to know SDDL strings and syntax. Although you may have to download `Subinacl.exe`, while `Sc.exe` is frequently installed by default, the former is significantly easier to use and can be used to set permissions on files, folders, and registry keys, too.

Create a Custom Service Account

When possible, create and use custom service accounts. Most services, when they install, automatically install using the LocalSystem account as their host service account. If the service doesn't need full LocalSystem access, don't allow it. Instead, create a new service account and give it a name that is similar to regular users and doesn't stand out (e.g., Richard Collier). Give the service account the *Logon as a service* right (or let the Services console do it). Then give the service account identity the least amount of permissions and rights necessary to do its job.

> *Don't change the default service accounts or their passwords for any default Windows-installed service. Doing so could cause instability and result in technical support issues.*

For example, most tape backup service accounts require an administrator-level account. In reality, all that most need is backup and restore rights and not Full Control-All permissions. The backup and restore rights (in group policy or local computer policy at `Computer Configuration\Windows Settings\Security Settings\Local Policies\User Rights Assignments\` *Back up files and directories and Restore files and directories*). Create a new service account and give it backup and restore rights instead of administrator.

Keep in mind that any custom service account stores its credentials locally, where they can be extracted by users with administrative-level access. This risk should be weighed against using a custom service account. But the practical reality is that if it requires admin access to exploit a custom service account, the intruder has admin access already and there are many things the intruder can do.

Determine Necessary Service Account Permissions

For other programs that you install, if it seems likely that the related service doesn't need administrator privileges or Full Control-Allow permissions to all files and folders, create a custom account instead. In most cases, all the service account needs is Modify access to its local files and folders, and Modify permissions to its related registry keys. To find out what permissions and access rights a service account needs, follow these instructions:

1. Temporarily make the service account a member of the Administrators group.

2. Configure the service to use the new custom service account.

3. Turn on Sysinternals' Filemon and Regmon utilities and filter for the service account's name and the services executable.

4. Turn on the service and let it do whatever it needs to do until you are satisfied it did all processes it was supposed to do (e.g., back up files).

5. Turn off Filemon and Regmon.

6. Analyze the results from the two monitoring utilities.

7. Apply the necessary permissions to the service account.

8. Remove the service account from the Administrators group.

9. Restart the service.

10. Monitor the computer and service for errors.

11. Check the event log for any errors.

Tighten the Service Account

Oftentimes you are stuck with using the default service accounts or allowing the service to use a highly privileged service account. Even though Microsoft attempted to tighten some services (see Table 7-3) by logging them on using the LocalService and NetworkService accounts, LocalSystem is used far too often. Nearly every service in Windows still logs on as LocalSystem. In most cases, these services need access only to the `Windows` and `Windows\System32` directories and maybe to a few other locations. Giving LocalSystem to most services seems overkill. Unfortunately, I do not recommend changing any default Windows service to another logon type. Doing so might have some unforeseen impact, cause hereto unforeseen issues, and make your Windows computers harder to support. Instead, concentrate your service account tightening efforts on non-default services, particularly third-party services.

Use Strong Service Account Passwords

Even though you should not change passwords on the three default service accounts, be sure to create long (at least 15 characters) and complex passwords on your service accounts and change passwords more frequently than you do on your nonservice accounts. Consider using a script to automate service account password changes. Here's a link to an excellent article and script by Redmond Magazine and Don Jones to automate the process: `http://redmondmag.com/features/article.asp?Editorial sID=398`.

Lock the Service Account to the Local Computer

Consider tying the service account to just the local machine. Many administrators make the mistake of making a service account a domain administrator, when all the service account needs is local administrator rights to the local machine. If the latter requirement is true, lock the service account to the local machine. You can do so in Active Directory Users and Computers or User Manager, by choosing the service account object, choosing the Account tab, and selecting the Logon to button. There you can specify one or more NetBIOS or DNS computer names the account is allowed to log on to (see Figure 7-9).

This technique will ensure that if the service account is compromised by an intruder, they cannot start an island-hopping spree from one computer to the next target.

Keep Patches Updated

When some service buffer overflows happen, the best you can do is to wait for a vendor patch or use another third-party tool (e.g., firewall, IPS, etc.) to prevent the malicious code from reaching your vulnerable service. In most cases, vendors, like Microsoft, are relatively quick to provide a patch update when a common service is exploited. Keeping up on your patches will decrease your overall security risk. Of course, these days hackers are building service-attacking worms out the patches that vendors release. In August 2005, Microsoft released more than a handful of patch updates. Malicious coders reverse-engineered the patches and had exploit worms live on the Internet in less than three days, so just as important as keeping up on your patches is realizing that the window for applying a patch once it has been released is decreasing significantly.

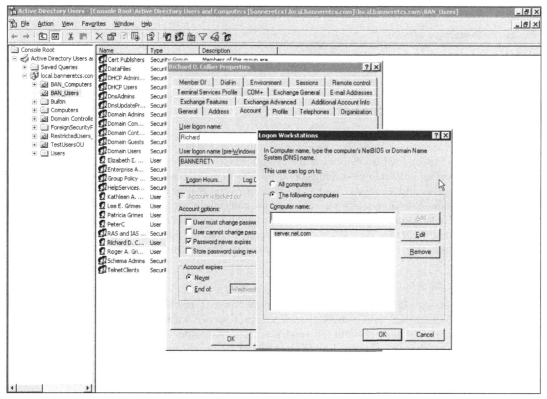

Figure 7-9

Summary

This chapter covered Windows services in detail. It began by discussion why services need to be tightened. Services often run in the context of highly privileged service accounts, such as LocalSystem. If attackers can buffer overflow a service, they usually end up with complete control of the machine. This chapter also discussed which services can be disabled and which must be left enabled on a service-by-service basis. Any unneeded service should be removed or disabled, and any remaining services should be tightened if possible. Chapter 8 covers the IP Security protocol.

Using IPSec

A chain is only as strong as its weakest link. Even when a network admin has implemented all the appropriate security controls on the computers under their control, if they have to share a network with someone else's insecure computers, there is risk of exploitation. If the other computers are compromised, malicious hackers can use them to spy on, sniff, and exploit the more secure computers. Worms infecting the less-protected computers can attack across the network and look for vulnerabilities. What is an admin to do?

If there is no legitimate business reason for the secure and insecure computers to communicate with each other, use IPSec to prevent unauthorized network connections. IPSec can be used to create VPN tunnels between two endpoints, be configured like a firewall, or require a valid digital certificate for two hosts to communicate. This chapter introduces IPSec, discusses Microsoft's implementation, describes how to create an implementation strategy and explains IPSec-specific attacks and defenses, and makes specific recommendations.

Introduction to IPSec

The *IP Security (IPSec)* protocol is a framework for authenticating and encrypting Internet Protocol (IP) traffic. Working at the third layer of the OSI model, IPSec is a series of multi-vendor open standards and protocols. It is proving to be one of the most common methods for securing endpoints and network traffic. IPSec can be used in the following ways:

❑   To create a virtual private network (VPN) from end to end

❑   To enforce network isolation

❑   As a host-based firewall, allowing and dropping filtered traffic

❑   To secure less secure protocols (such as RDP)

Although IPSec is optional for IPv4 traffic, it is mandatory for IPv6 traffic. Along with other popular open-source VPN solutions, like Secure Session Layer (SSL) and Transport Layer Security (TLS), IPSec will be a long-term security solution for network communications. Windows 2000 and later can natively participate in Windows IPSec.

> *Windows IPSec cannot be used to secure multicast or broadcast network traffic, but it can be used to block it.*

An Open Standard

IPSec became an open standard through the efforts of the Internet Engineering Task Force (IETF) Internet Protocol Security working group (`www.ietf.org/html.charters/OLD/ipseccharter .html`). Led by many companies and technologists, including Microsoft and Cisco, the IPSec working group's efforts resulted in dozens of *Request for Comments (RFCs)*. RFCs 2401 (`www.ietf.org/rfc/ rfc2401.txt`) to 2412 (`www.ietf.org/rfc/rfc2412.txt`) are considered the IPSec protocol standards. The IPSec standards cover how network packets should be secured, cryptographic key exchange, and the related protocol implementations. The IPSec working group officially disbanded in April 2005, although IPSec standards work still continues in several official sectors.

IPSec Basics

IPSec is an open standard involving numerous pieces, parts, and new terminology. In a nutshell, IPSec uses cryptographic hashes to establish packet and data integrity, and cryptographic ciphers to ensure confidentiality. Per RFC 2401, the security services offered include access control, connectionless integrity, data origin authentication, replay protection, data confidentiality, and limited traffic flow confidentiality. In order for two hosts to communicate using IPSec, they must be predefined to use common protocols, hashes, and cryptographic ciphers.

> *It is important to note that IPSec's data origin authentication is machine authentication, computer-to-computer. It cannot be used to authenticate a message (i.e., digital content) as belonging to or sent by a particular person.*

Working at Layer 3, the Network Layer, IPSec is independent of the upper-layer protocol traffic it is protecting. IPSec is implemented on network devices and on computers at the IP stack level. The participating upper-layer applications (and users) need not be aware of IPSec. Compare this to SSL or TLS, where the applications must be coded to implement, initiate, and understand the security protocol.

An IPSec connection is always between two participating end nodes (or endpoints). All IPSec traffic is only between one source endpoint and another participating, single destination endpoint. For example, if there are 200 client PCs connecting to a Windows server using IPSec, it means there are 200 separate IPSec VPN tunnels. Each connection can involve one or more *paths* (for example, multiple ports and application protocols) between the two endpoint hosts.

Tunnel versus Transport Mode

IPSec has two major mode types: *tunnel* and *transport*. Tunnel mode is used to create a VPN between two network devices (see Figure 8-1). The endpoints in this case are the two network gateway devices. They communicate with each other using IPSec. The PCs on either side of the networks are not using IPSec. Their traffic is sent clear-text across their local area networks and secured between the participating gateways. With tunnel mode, there are essentially two IP headers: an external one used by IPSec to route the packet from gateway to gateway and another internal IP header used to route the traffic to its ultimate intended destination once past the participating gateway.

Tunnel mode can be used to protect IP traffic over untrusted networks like the Internet. It can also be helpful when the participating computers cannot use IPSec natively (i.e., Windows NT or 9x). Tunnel mode protects the entire packet, including payload and packet header. Of course, in tunnel mode there is no guaranteed end-to-end security, only gateway-to-gateway security.

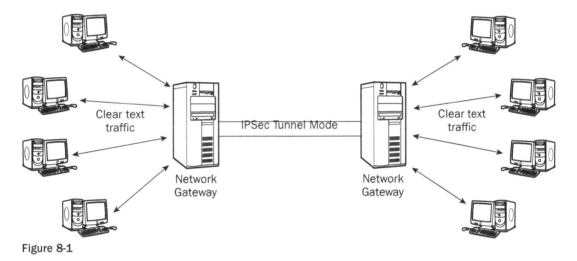

Figure 8-1

The limited data flow analysis feature of ESP is accomplished using tunnel mode because it obscures the ultimate source and destination of the data payload.

Transport mode is client-to-server security, typically between an endpoint PC and a server or VPN gateway device. Figure 8-2 shows examples of transport mode connections. With transport mode, protection is provided only to the upper-layer protocol or data, but not over the entire IP packet. A security gateway is only required to support tunnel mode, but computer hosts are required to support both tunnel and transport mode.

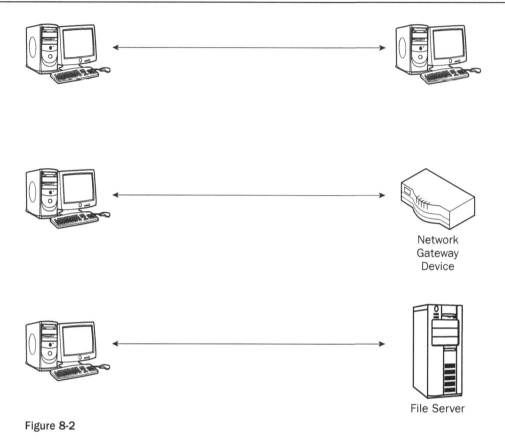

Figure 8-2

IPSec Security Protocols — AH versus ESP

IPSec can be used with two IPSec security protocols: Authentication Header (AH) and Encapsulating Security Payload (ESP).

Authentication Header

AH provides connectionless integrity, anti-replay (optional) services, and data origin authentication across an entire IP packet. It does not provide encryption. AH ensures that the packet came from where it says it came from, capable of stopping most man-in-the-middle attacks. Integrity is delivered using a cryptographic hash algorithm, usually 128-bit MD5 or 160-bit SHA-1. The IP packet hashes resulting from the applied hash algorithms are further protected by IPSec by applying a secret key only known by the IPSec endpoints. In most IPSec implementations, you can use either MD5 or SHA1 hash algorithms. Use SHA-1 when you can and MD-5 where you have to. Most IPSec implementations should support both, although Windows 2000 requires Service Pack 1 or later to support SHA-1.

Both MD5 and SHA-1 were found to have cryptographic weaknesses in 2005. Thus, in the future, it is expected that both will be replaced with better, cryptographically sound hash algorithms.

Encapsulating Security Payload

ESP provides payload data confidentiality (i.e., encryption) and limits traffic flow analysis but can also provide integrity services. Using ESP data confidentiality, the data payload is encrypted using a symmetric key algorithm, but the IP packet header is not protected. Like AH, ESP can also provide connectionless integrity, anti-replay services, and data origin authentication—but only on the payload data, not the entire packet.

ESP Encryption Ciphers—DES and 3DES

ESP provides encryption using symmetric key algorithms, such as Data Encryption Standard (DES), Triple DES (3DES), Advanced Encryption Standard (AES), and Blowfish (although Microsoft Windows only supports the first two currently). DES is a symmetric encryption algorithm chosen by the National Institute of Standards and Technology (www.nist.gov) as the government's official recommended symmetric cryptography algorithm in 1976. An updated NIST publication on DES can be found at http://csrc.nist.gov/publications/fips/fips46-3/fips46-3.pdf. DES' 64-bit encryption (actually 56 bits of effective encryption plus 8 parity bits) held up well over the years, but in the late 1990s, a few groups and contests "broke" DES in a few days' time. NIST recommended that *3DES* (called *triple DES*), with 192-bit encryption, be used in 1999, while in the middle of replacing DES and 3DES with a new standard.

In 2001, NIST announced the government's new official symmetric encryptions standard (http://csrc.nist.gov/publications/fips/fips197/fips-197.pdf), Advanced Encryption Standard (AES). Based on the Rijndael algorithm and starting at a 128-bit key size, AES is expected to be a default encryption choice for symmetric encryption (including in IPSec) for at least one to two decades. Microsoft's AES support is currently mixed, but getting better. Windows Server 2003 and Windows XP Pro SP1 support AES in several features, including wireless WPA and EFS. Unfortunately, AES is not currently available for Microsoft Windows IPSec.

Use 3DES when you can, and DES where you have to. Windows 2000 requires Service Pack 1 or later. IPSec implementations should support both symmetric protocols per the RFCs. You can also set ESP to <None> (also known as *ESP Null*), to turn off the encryption. If ESP is still enabled (i.e., integrity only), IPSec will only authenticate the data packet's origin and payload integrity.

AH or ESP?

IPSec must involve one or more protocols—AH or ESP, or both. If you intend to provide integrity and encryption across as much of the IP packet as you can, you want to use both. AH works using IP protocol number 51, and ESP works with 50. If firewalls are involved, these protocol numbers must be allowed through (for reference, the normal TCP protocol uses protocol number 6, and UDP uses protocol number 17).

When IPSec is enabled, each IP packet is analyzed to see if it needs IPSec protection or filtering. IP traffic is queried for its source and destination IP address, source and destination port numbers, protocol type (i.e., TCP vs. UDP), and other factors. The collection of identification values in IPSec is called a *security policy* or *rule*. There can be one or more IPSec rules per host. Rules are collected into the host's *security policy database*.

Security Associations

Each IPSec tunnel involves two or more *security associations (SAs)*. SAs are simplex (unidirectional) connections allowing two endpoints to be linked together. All traffic traveling in the same SA is given the same IPSec security treatment. SAs are identified using three pieces of information (called a *triple*): destination IP address, security protocol used (AH or ESP), and a *Security Parameters Index (SPI)*. The SPI is a unique 32-bit number relating two hosts with each other. The SPI is indicated in the IPSec packet and ensures that when multiple IPSec end nodes are communicating to one IPSec host the connections aren't confused.

The *Internet Security Association and Key Management Protocol (ISAKMP)* is a key-independent framework defining the procedures and packet formats to establish, negotiate, modify, and delete SAs. For normal two-way communications, two SAs — mirroring each other's information — are needed. A different SA must be used if AH and ESP are both involved. A host's security associations are contained in its *Security Association Database (SAD)*.

Key Management

Essential to IPSec is the issue of key management. What cryptographic keys to use and how they should be implemented and exchanged is controlled by a hybrid key management protocol called *Internet Key Exchange (IKE)*. IKE also uses the concept of SAs, but is not related to the SAs used in the endpoint IPSec tunnels discussed in the preceding section. IKE SAs are bidirectional.

IKE is composed of two other protocols: *Oakley* and *SKEME*, although it only uses each partially (hence the hybrid descriptor). Oakley is a key exchange protocol describing key secrecy, identity protection, and authentication. It uses the Diffie-Hellman protocol for public key exchange. Most of the IKE protocol is based upon the Oakley processes. SKEME allows flexible key exchange with anonymity and repudiability, along with easy and frequent key refreshment. IPSec key exchange normally takes place over UDP port 500. This port must be opened if a firewall is in between the two endpoints.

IKE Modes — Main, Aggressive, and Quick

IKE begins creating the SAs by negotiating which encryption and hashing protocols can be used, how long the keys can be used for, and whether or not *perfect forward secrecy* (covered below) is used. Multiple proposals can be sent in one offering. Once a proposal is accepted, the Diffie-Hellman protocol is used to exchange public keys and other information. The public keys are used to establish a secure tunnel, and further negotiation and communications can be protected.

Within IKE, there are two modes for establishing an SA. *Main mode* requires six packets back and forth between the two endpoints, but expends additional effort to ensure endpoint identity. *Aggressive mode* doesn't ensure endpoint identity, but is used to allow quicker associations. All IPSec hosts must have main mode implemented, but aggressive mode is optional. After the IKE SA is established, *quick mode* begins. Quick mode is similar to aggressive mode in that endpoint identification is not established (again, if main mode is used), although it is accomplished only after the encrypted IKE SA is initiated.

By default, Windows IPSec will keep quick mode SAs open for up to five minutes after no activity is noticed, but the default can be changed. Windows Server 2003 IPSec is both cluster-aware and network load balance (NLB)–aware, although it does not support instant failover. If a node is in a cluster, IPSec will detect its configuration and change the default quick mode configuration time to one minute, instead of five. This change is communicated to any connecting clients using IPSec; and it means that if the cluster node goes down, the clients will be reconnected to remaining cluster nodes after one minute.

In summary, main mode creates a bidirectional SA (known as ISAKMP or IKE SA), which creates a secure channel for quick mode SAs to then be established. Main mode then negotiates the security parameters to be used, exchanges the Diffie-Hellman keying information, and authenticates the identities of the IPSec peers. Quick mode then creates unidirectional IPSec SAs to secure the network traffic. During negotiation for the latter SAs, IPSec determines encryption and hashing algorithms, security modes (AH, ESP, or both), and whether it is tunnel or transport mode. IKE uses its own secret key with each IKE SA that is set up between each participating endpoint node. The IKE secret key, and the private channel it creates, is then used to securely pass the secret keys used with each SA, which is then used to secure the network communication's traffic.

NAT versus NAT-T

IPSec in ESP is compatible with Network Address Translation (NAT), but IPSec with AH is not. Because AH calculates integrity values based on the entire packet, when a NAT device modifies a protected IP packet (as NAT must do to convert between public and private IP addressing), it invalidates the AH integrity values.

To get around this problem, another IETF working group developed *NAT-Transversal (or NAT-T),* which is summarized in RFCs 3947 and 3948. It accomplishes this by encapsulating NAT in UDP traffic along with several other modifications and additions. NAT-T requires NAT-T-compatible endpoints. Windows XP SP2 and Windows Server 2003 natively support NAT-T, although strangely enough Microsoft often doesn't differentiate between NAT and NAT-T in their documentation and online help. In those versions, Microsoft's "NAT" is really NAT-T. You can also download a VPN client to support previous versions of Windows XP and the NT and 9x families (`www.microsoft.com/downloads/details.aspx?Family ID=6a1086dc-3bd0-4d65-9b82-20cbe650f974&DisplayLang=en`). NAT-T also requires UDP port 4500 to be open on any participating firewalls for IKE (NAT uses UDP port 500).

In March 2005, Microsoft became of aware of a potential security problem when Windows NAT-T clients connected to Windows servers behind NAT devices. The main issue is that IPSec can get confused if the remote private IP address behind the NAT device matches a valid local IP address on the local network. It could end up routing traffic to the local private address instead. Accordingly, Microsoft recommends that participating servers be assigned a public IP address instead and not use NAT/NAT-T. They changed XP SP2's default behavior to prevent connecting to a server behind a NAT device by default, although a registry change can be made to restore the older functionality. See `http://support .microsoft.com/default.aspx?scid=kb;en-us;885348` for more details.

Performance Issues

IPSec and its family of protocols provide integrity and encryption protective services on IP traffic. When implemented, IPSec's processing will slow down normal network communications and take up additional, although minimal, memory. How much slower and how much memory depends on the application, the number of SAs, and the vendor's implementation. In general, the slowest part of IPSec is the initial SA and key establishment, but every transmitted and received packet undergoes multiple cryptographic computations. In Windows, the initial establishment takes 1–4 seconds on most connections. After the initial establishment, the integrity and encryption features create ongoing cryptographic delays. How much total time IPSec adds to each transaction depends on the application, but in all cases it is measurable.

The author conducted an unscientific, one-time test, copying the same 340MB file dozens of times with and without IPSec between two relatively otherwise idle computers. Transmit times doubled in many instances with IPSec enabled, but the localized performance problems were just as noticeable. On both sides of the connection, with IPSec enabled, CPU utilization went above 75% (as compared to 10–20% without IPSec). LAN adapter network utilization dropped from 65-70% without IPSec enabled, to 20–40% with IPSec enabled.

Even IP packets not needing IPSec protection are slowed down a bit by the IPSec filter inspecting it to decide whether or not it should be included. In a normal LAN or remote access environment, the delays are usually acceptable (and to many users, unnoticeable), but in high-performance environments, software-only IPSec would probably be unacceptable. Environments needing high-volume IPSec transactions should consider using a VPN-accelerator hardware component or use external VPN devices. *IPSec offload adapters* are network cards with special hardware chips to take on the additional processing requirements of IPSec.

Now that you understand IPSec and some of its basic functionality, let's explore Microsoft's implementation in detail.

Windows IPSec

Microsoft first introduced IPSec in Windows 2000. When enabled, the driver file called `IPSec.sys` handles packet inspection and overall IPSec operations. Another file, `Oakley.dll`, is the IKE component. The *IPSEC Services* service also needs to be running, although it should be by default. IPSec policies can be created at the command prompt (using different tools and commands between Windows 2000, XP, and 2003) or using the *IP Security Policies* console. IPSec policies can be created and applied locally, or pushed down using a GPO. A computer can only have one active IPSec policy at one time, stored in `HKLM\Software\Policies\Microsoft\Windows\IPSec`.

> *Windows Vista will allow IPSec configuration using a new console called Windows Firewall with Advanced Security.*

IPSec Console

The most convenient way to configure IPSec is to use the IP Security Policies console. To use it, open the Microsoft Management Console (`Mmc.exe`) and choose File ⇨ Add/Remove Snap-in. Click the Add button, choose the IP Security Policy Management snap-in (see Figure 8-3) and click the Add button. Select the correct focus (usually the Local Computer) and then click Finish ⇨ Close ⇨ OK.

IPSec policies can also be created in GPOs and Local Computer Policies (under `Computer Configuration\Windows Settings\Security Settings\IP Security Policies`). This chapter will use the console in most of the examples.

IPSec at the Command Line

IPSec can also be controlled and configured at the command line. Windows 2000 uses the `Ipsecpol.exe` command (`www.microsoft.com/windows2000/techinfo/reskit/tools/existing/ipsecpol-o.asp`). Ipsecpol syntax can be a bit intimidating for the casual user. Some examples are provided at `http://support.microsoft.com/default.aspx?scid=kb;en-us;813878`. The following example syntax would block all outbound connections to any remote computer over UDP port 1434:

```
ipsecpol -w REG -p "Block UDP 1434 Filter" -r "Block Outbound UDP 1434 Rule" -f
0=*:1434:UDP -n BLOCK
```

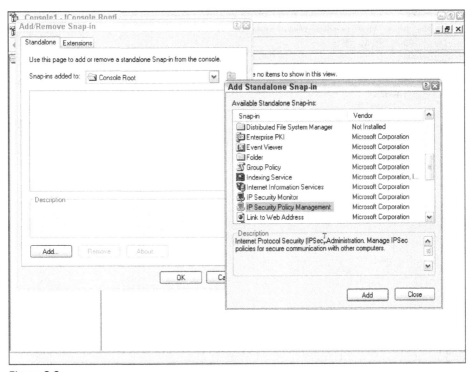

Figure 8-3

As cryptic as it may seem, Ipsecpol, and other configuration tools like it, allows IPSec policies to be generated quickly when using batch files and scripts. An admin requiring IPSec during a troubleshooting event could send a single batch file to a remote user that, when run, would completely configure and enable IPSec on the remote computer. Windows XP uses `Ipseccmd.exe` and Windows Server 2003 uses `Netsh ipsec`.

IPSec Monitor Tools

To use any of the IPSec monitoring tools you need at least a basic understanding of IPSec and its SAs. Windows 2000 computers can use the command-line tool `Ipsecmon.exe`. Windows XP computers can use the command-line tool *Ipseccmd.exe* with the `show all` syntax. Windows Server 2003 and later computers can use the `Netsh ipsec static show` or `Netsh ipsec dynamic show` commands. Better yet, Windows XP and later computers can use the *IP Security Monitor* snap-in GUI console. Any of these tools will show you whether or not an IPSec connection has been made and basic statistics (see Figure 8-4).

Detailed IPSec packet traffic can be recorded using many network packet sniffers, including Ethereal (`www.ethereal.com`) and Microsoft's own Network Monitor (Windows 2000 and later, and SMS versions). Figure 8-5 shows a small packet trace in Ethereal resulting from a ping test. You can see at the IP layer that the protocol number is hexadecimal 32 (which equates to decimal 50 or ESP). The SPI value for the SA is highlighted. Of course, if ESP encryption is enabled, you will not be able to see any payload data.

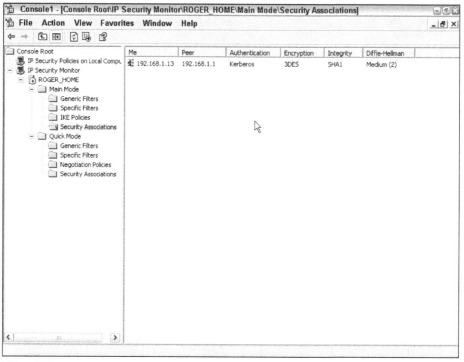

Figure 8-4

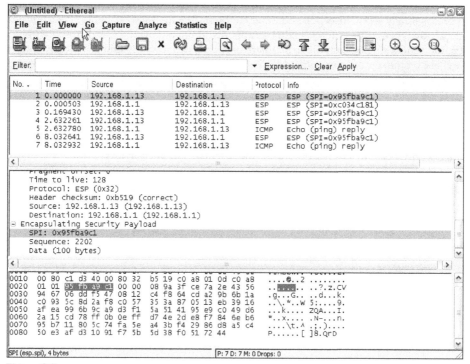

Figure 8-5

You can turn on rudimentary Oakley logging that can be enabled for the IPSec troubleshooting professional. When turned on, the `Oakley.log` file will be stored in `%Windir%\Debug`. I can be turned on in Windows XP by typing in **Ipseccmd set logike**, or in Windows Server 2003 by typing in **Netsh ipsec dynamic set config ikelogging 1**. Windows 2000 requires that a new registry key and value be made. It is `HKLM\System\CurrentControlSet\Services\PolicyAgent\Oakley\EnableLogging` and is set to 1. A new `Oakley.log` file is created each time IPSec is started. Previous versions will be saved as `Oakley.log.sav`.

You can also enable IPSec driver events to be logged to the Event log. To enable, set `HKLM\System\CurrentControlSet\Services\IPSEC\DiagnosticMode` to 1 and then restart the computer. IPSec driver events are written to the System log once every hour. You can also see IPSec policy changes in the Security log if you enable *Audit policy change*. IKE events can be recorded by enabling *Audit logon events*.

Default IPSec Policies

As Figure 8-6 shows, this will reveal three default IPSec policies in environments that have not modified the defaults. The three default polices are example policies that Microsoft created in order to help people create their own. Although they can be used, their settings are heavy-handed, meaning all traffic is treated a certain way. Custom IPSec policies are more flexible, and they are a good place to start learning.

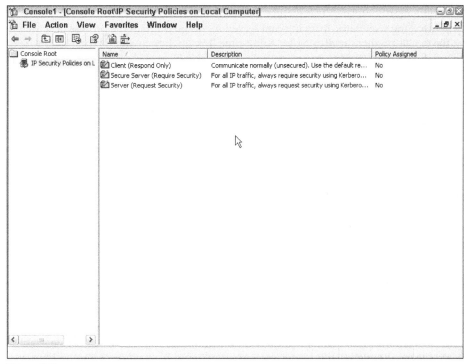

Figure 8-6

Table 8-1 describes the three default policies. All three policies use Kerberos to authenticate to computer peers, involve all IP traffic, and will use ESP encryption if allowed.

Table 8-1

Default IPSec Policy Name	Description
Client (Respond Only)	Will only enable IPSec security if requested to by another endpoint
Secure Server (Require Security)	Requires IPSec security on IP traffic, but allows ICMP traffic to pass without security
Server (Request Security)	Requests, but doesn't require, IPSec security on IP traffic, but allows ICMP traffic to pass without security

You can create as many IPSec polices as you like, but only one can be enabled (or *assigned*) per computer at any one time. You can assign a policy in the console by right-clicking the policy and choosing *Assign*. You can also delete, rename, and modify existing policies or create your own by clicking on a blank area in the console and choosing *Create IP Security Policy*.

Setting Up Windows IPSec

IPSec is a flexible framework. Unfortunately, that flexible framework and its myriad of terms can make IPSec configuration confusing. This section will lead you through the steps to create a very simple IPSec policy for securing web traffic to an internal server. As we go through the process of setting up an IPSec policy, the details might be confusing for a first-time IPSec policy creator. The basic IPSec setup process (see Figure 8-7) is as follows:

1. Only one IPSec policy can be enabled per computer.

2. Each IPSec policy can have multiple rules, each determining how to handle a particular type of traffic (as determined by the associated filter).

3. Each rule can only have one IP filter that defines a particular class of traffic (by IP address, protocol number, or port number).

Creating an IPSec Policy

The first step is to open the IP Security Policies console, right-click a blank area in the right-pane, choose *Create IP Security Policy,* and then click the Next button. When prompted, type in a name and description (see Figure 8-8) for your policy, and then click the Next button.

Next, you will be prompted about whether to *Activate the default response rule*. Enabled by default, the Default Response rule can be deactivated but not deleted. It can be used in any IPSec policy (as can most IPSec rules). The Default Response rule tells the affected computer to respond to any IPSec request by enabling ESP security if it matches the other endpoint request (or authentication if it matches the other endpoint request), and if not does not require security. In most cases, leaving the rule enabled will not causes problems, although in this case, I know we don't need it, so unselect the checkbox and click the Next button. Keep the Edit properties checkbox selected and click the Finish button.

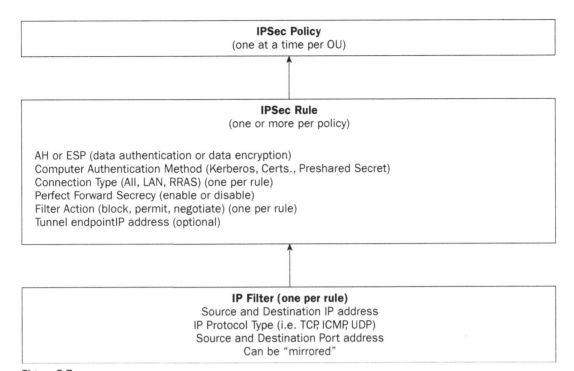

Figure 8-7

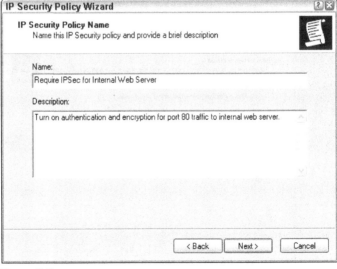

Figure 8-8

IPSec Rules

Now you can create or choose one or more IPSec rules. IPSec rules determine how to treat particular types of traffic (as defined by the IPSec filters). You can have one or more IPSec rules active in any single IPSec policy, but every IPSec rule is attached to only one IPSec filter. Click the Add button and then the Next button. The next dialog box will prompt the creator to input tunnel endpoints if necessary. Tunnel endpoints are only needed when the host on which the IPSec policy will be enabled will be a gateway endpoint participating in IPSec tunneling mode. If so, the creator would input the IP address of the other endpoint's network interface connecting the tunnel. We are setting up a transport mode policy, so just leave *This rule does not specify a tunnel endpoint* enabled and click the Next button.

Connection Type

When prompted to select the network connection type in the Network Connection dialog box, you can choose *All network connections, Local Area Network (LAN)*, or *Remote access*. Choose the appropriate option, although in this example, just accept the default of *All network connections* and click the Next button. Which option you choose is also dependent on whether you will be requiring just a particular type of traffic to be secured, or choosing to filter most traffic (and just to allow particular traffic). The latter case should always be *All network connections*, whereas the former might be more granular.

Authentication Method

As Figure 8-9 shows, the next decision is asked in the Authentication Method dialog box. In Windows IPSec, you can choose between three methods to authenticate the endpoints to each other:

❑ Kerberos authentication

❑ Certificate from a certification authority (CA)

❑ Pre-shared key

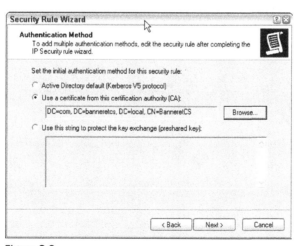

Figure 8-9

IPSec will not work unless the participating nodes can authenticate (i.e., machine authentication) to each other. You can choose up to three authentication methods and place them in order of precedence. If an end node can't do the first one listed, the others are offered up. The most secure method is the certificate, but it is also the most difficult to set up. First, each participating IPSec endpoint must have a machine certificate signed by a certification authority (CA) designated in the dialog box. Microsoft Certificate Services in Windows Server 2003 fills the bill, although its setup and configuration is beyond the scope of this book. For more information on setting up a CA using Microsoft Certificate Services, read *Microsoft's Windows Server 2003 PKI Certificate Security* (ISBN 0735620210). Although the certificate method is the hardest to deploy initially, it is the most secure method. It can be used on the LAN, across domains and forests, and remotely over the Internet.

The certificate selected in this step is the CA's certificate, not the endpoint's machine certificate.

The Kerberos authentication option is the easiest to deploy — just enable the selection and let Windows do the rest. In order for the Kerberos method to be used, the participating IPSec endpoint must have a valid computer account in the forest. If the Active Directory forest is a Windows Server 2003 forest, then Kerberos can be used across forests when a forest trust is established. The Kerberos method is the easiest to deploy, but it doesn't work well across the Internet or outside the trusted forest(s).

The pre-shared key (PSK) is also fairly easy to deploy. Just input an identical PSK (such as a password) on both sides of the IPSec connection and IPSec will do the rest. It works locally, across forests and domains, and over the Internet. Unfortunately, it is also the least secure method. Microsoft recommends only using it to test IPSec. I use PSK when initially setting up new IPSec connections to help rule out other authentication problems. After the PSK link is up, I move the IPSec connection to one of the other two methods.

If you use a PSK, be sure to enter a very long (longer than 15 characters) and complex PSK. Unlike most password treatments, the PSK will be displayed in plaintext in the IPSec policy window, so don't expect it to remain hidden. If you use PSKs, you should change them frequently. Unfortunately, much of the world uses short, non-complex PSKs that are never changed. This is an IPSec hacker's dream. As covered below, malicious hackers can capture traffic encrypted with the PSK and brute force it to learn the PSK. Once the PSK is discovered, it is trivial to exploit the rest of the IPSec protections. For this example policy, choose the weaker PSK method and type any short word as a PSK. I'm asking you to use the weakest method so you can see how it is displayed in the policy. Then click the Next button.

IPSec Filters

You can create as many IPSec filters as you like, and they are available for any IPSec policy, but you can only associate one IPSec filter per IPSec rule. Each IPSec filter can have one or more types of traffic (i.e., multiple protocols) associated with it. By default, Windows IPSec has two filters to choose from: *All ICMP traffic* and *All IP traffic* (Figure 8-10 shows the two defaults plus one custom filter). Let's create our own new rule to cover web traffic over TCP port 80. In the IP Filter List dialog box, click the Add button.

Type a filter name and description. Filter names are displayed in the IPSec Policy rules list in reverse alphabetical order. Their listed order does not affect the order in which they are applied if multiple rules exist, but you may want to consider the name carefully before entering one if you want a particular filter listing order. In this example, type **Web Port 80 Traffic Heading to Internal Web Site** and add an appropriate description. Click the Add button and then the Next button. The IP Traffic Source dialog box will then prompt you for the IP address for the traffic you plan to filter (see Figure 8-11).

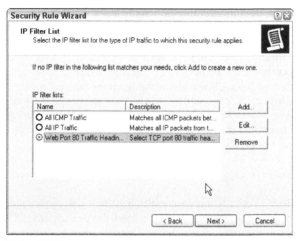

Figure 8-10

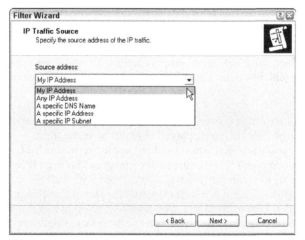

Figure 8-11

You can choose among the following options:

❑ My IP Address

❑ Any IP Address

❑ A specific DNS name (XP only)

❑ A specific IP Address

❑ A specific IP Subnet

❑ DNS Servers <dynamic>

❑ WINS Servers <dynamic>

❑ DHCP server <dynamic>

❑ Default Gateway <dynamic>

My IP Address is the first network card's first IP address if there are multiple network cards or multiple IP addresses. Windows 2000 has only the *Any IP Address*, *A specific IP Address*, and *A specific IP Subnet* options. Only XP has *A specific DNS name* (especially useful when an endpoint has a DHCP-assigned IP address that could change. Only Server 2003 and later have the latter four options. If they are chosen, IPSec will take the current values for those fields and update them if the related IP addresses change.

If the IPSec rule involves traffic headed from the current PC to another endpoint, choose the first option or specify the correct local IP address. If you want to filter traffic headed from another endpoint, choose its IP address or choose *Any IP Address*. For this example, choose *My IP Address*. When finished, click the Next button. You will then be prompted to fill in the *IP Traffic Destination* value in the next dialog box and click the Next button. For this example, choose *A specific IP Address* and fill in an IP address for a web server host you know that you can enable IIS and IPSec on for testing purposes.

IP Protocol Type

In the IP Protocol Type dialog box, you must indicate the IP protocol number for the involved IP transport layer protocol, or you can choose the *Any* option to allow the filter to inspect all transport layer protocols. In most cases, the value will be TCP, UDP, or ICMP, but there are many other values you can cycle through. Choose TCP for this example and then click the Next button.

IP Protocol Port

In the next dialog box, you must choose source and destination transport layer protocol numbers (e.g., 25 for SMTP, 53 for DNS, 80 for WWW, 443 for HTTPS, etc.). If most cases, if the current computer is connecting to another host, its source port number will be randomly generated as a number higher than 1023. In order to handle this, you must choose the *From any port* option. If the current PC is connecting to another computer's service with a well-known port, choose *To this port* and fill in the appropriate port number. In this example, type **80** (see Figure 8-12), click the Next button, and then click the Finish button.

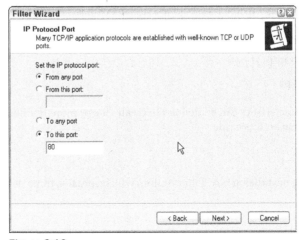

Figure 8-12

This will take you back to the IP Filter List dialog box. You can add more IP addresses and protocols to a single IPSec filter. In this example, add port 443. You should have a dialog box that resembles the one shown in Figure 8-13. Click the OK button and then select the new custom IP filter created (see Figure 8-10 again) and click the Next button. Filters can also be *mirrored*. Because an IPSec SA is a unidirectional entity, two-way communications (like most network traffic requires) needs an IPSec filter that mimics the original rule, only going in the reverse direction. In most cases (not all), enabling mirroring is necessary. Mirroring must often be disabled when setting up IPSec in tunnel mode.

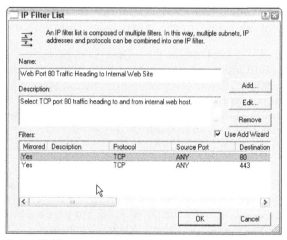

Figure 8-13

In summary, an IPSec IP filter allows network traffic to be intercepted according to the following characteristics:

❑   Source IP address

❑   Destination IP address

❑   Source address IP subnet mask (if a specific IP subnet is chosen)

❑   Destination address IP subnet mask (if a specific IP subnet is chosen)

❑   Source transport port

❑   Destination transport port

❑   IP protocol type

Each one of these characteristics can be defined to create one or more IP filters, which are then attached to a Filter Action within an IPSec rule.

Filter Action

Figure 8-14 shows the next dialog box, Filter Action, which contains three default options:

❑   Permit

❑   Request Security (Optional)

❑   Require Security

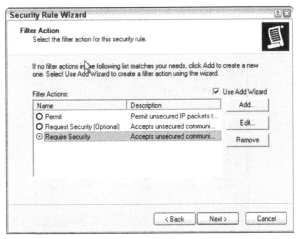

Figure 8-14

Permit allows the filtered traffic through without requiring IPSec security. Request Security will ask the other endpoint to enable IPSec encryption or authentication, but will still connect if the request is not met. Require Security requires that IPSec ESP encryption be enabled between the two endpoints for that traffic type before the filtered network traffic can be communicated.

You can accept and use one of the default three security methods or create your own and place them in order of precedence. The Request Security (Optional) option (see Figure 8-15) defines four security methods. The first method attempts to use the most secure encryption method currently available in Windows IPSec, 3DES. If the connecting endpoint cannot do 3DES, it will attempt to negotiate DES. Both of these methods have ESP integrity checking with SHA-1 enabled. If encryption can't be done, AH authentication is attempted, first using the stronger SHA-1, and lastly, MD5 if nothing else works. The Require Security method never attempts to use AH, only ESP encryption and integrity using various combinations of 3DES, DES, SHA-1, and MD5 (from strongest to weakest).

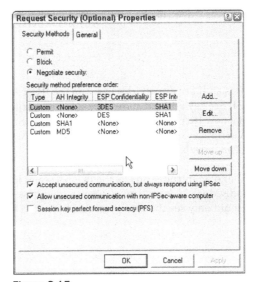

Figure 8-15

313

You can create your own security method and enable it in the Filter Action dialog box. Whatever security method you choose, the other connecting endpoints must support the same method in order for IPSec protection to be enabled. As Figure 8-16 shows, there are other options as well.

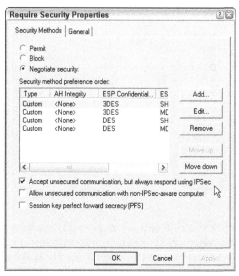

Figure 8-16

The *Accept unsecured communications, but always respond using IPSec* option tells an IPSec-enabled computer to allow unsecured requests, but to always reply using IPSec. While this would prevent a computer without IPSec from participating as an endpoint, it is a normal option to choose when the other endpoint uses the *Default Response* rule or *Client (Respond Only)*. The *Allow unsecured communications with non IPSec-aware computer* option is self-explanatory. Normally this option is only enabled when you want a computer that is IPSec-aware to always enable IPSec when contacted by IPSec-enabled computers but also still be able to initiate connections to computers not capable of IPSec. A good example of this is when you want to use IPSec inside your LAN, but not require it when it is connecting to Internet resources (which are probably not using IPSec). The *Session key perfect forward secrecy (PFS)* option requires more explanation.

Perfect Forward Secrecy

Perfect Forward Secrecy (PFS) is an IPSec option (discussed in the IPSec RFCs) that attempts to ensure that a compromise of any single IPSec key will not allow access to data protected by other keys. Master key PFS works by ensuring that a new IKA SA secret key is regenerated for each new session. Normally, without PFS, individual SA secret keys are generated from the IKE SA "master" secret key, which means there is a cryptographic link an intruder can follow.

If master key PFS is enabled and an intruder breaks the IKE SA secret key, it doesn't immediately give them help in cracking the individual SA keys. The attacker would have to attack each SA secret key individually, and even then it would only see the data protected by each SA secret key. One key compromise doesn't make it easier to compromise another. Without PFS, an attacker could use the information learned by breaking the IKE SA secret key to quickly compromise the SA private keys. Without PFS enabled, the master key is only regenerated when it has already been used to generate a predetermined maximum number of SA secret keys. Microsoft also allows PFS to be set on the SA private keys to further complicate cracking efforts.

Enabling PFS does provide stronger security, although in Windows it is disabled by default because it adds additional computational overhead and security often not needed in normal security environments. An environment with high-security requirements or expecting attacks against its IPSec infrastructure should enable PFS.

In summary, an IPSec rule can contain the following characteristics:

- ❑ Tunnel endpoint (if IPSec tunnel mode is desired)
- ❑ Connection Type (All, LAN, or remote)
- ❑ Authentication Method (Kerberos, Certificate, Pre-Shared Key)
- ❑ Filter List (covered above)
- ❑ Filter Action (Permit, Block, Negotiate Security, or custom)
- ❑ Other IPSec Rule Options

An IPSec policy can have one or more IPSec rules. When multiple rules are in effect, Windows automatically orders them operationally from most specific to least specific. This means that blocking or allowing specific endpoints will take precedence over larger ranges of affected computers. Some IP traffic is never considered or blocked in Windows IPSec.

IPSec Exemptions

By default, Windows makes certain exemptions (packet traffic types that cannot be blocked or controlled by IPSec) when IPSec is turned on. In Windows Server 2003, only IKE traffic, needed for IPSec establishment, is exempted from IPSec filtering. In Windows 2000 and XP, there are many more exemptions (see `http://support.microsoft.com/kb/253169`):

- ❑ Kerberos authentication
- ❑ IKE
- ❑ Multicast traffic
- ❑ Broadcast traffic
- ❑ RSVP traffic

You can also configure a registry key to control exemptions. `HKLM\System\CurrentControlSet\Services\IPSec\NoDefaultExempt` can be configured with a value from 0 to 3, as shown in Table 8-2.

Table 8-2

No Default Exempt Value	Description
0	Default in Windows 2000 and XP. Exempts Kerberos, IKE, Multicasts, Broadcasts, and RSVP.
1	Recommended exemption setting by Microsoft. Only exempts Multicast, Broadcast, and RSVP traffic. Requires SP1 or later in Windows 2000. Default setting in Windows 2000 SP4 and Windows XP SP2.
2	Only available in Windows Server 2003. Exempts only RSVP, Kerberos, and IKE.
3	Default in Windows Server 2003. Only IKE exempted. Not available in XP or 2000.

Caution: Although a setting of 3 might be desired for all participating IPSec nodes, requiring all broadcast traffic to have IPSec could cause a lot of problems (e.g., NetBIOS, ARP, etc.). For that reason, Microsoft's recommendation of putting the setting to 1 is a realistic trade-off setting. In the future, it would be nice for Microsoft to have a setting to only exempt IKE and broadcast traffic, or even better, let the end user define all exemptions. You can also set the NoDefaultExempt value on Windows Server 2003 using `Netsh ipsec dynamic set config ipsecexempt value` = *command. See http://support.microsoft.com/kb/811832/EN-US for more details on exemptions.*

For our current IPSec policy example, choose the *Require Security* option, and then click the Next and Finish buttons. If done correctly, the IPSec wizard will display the IPSec Rule as configured among multiple tabs (see Figure 8-17). This is the same view you would see if you disabled the *Create a IP Security Policy* wizard. As shown in Figure 8-17, for this example I added another two authentication protocols beyond the PSK method. I then placed the PSK method lowest down on the list since it has the most risk involved. Click the OK button to save the rule to the IPSec policy.

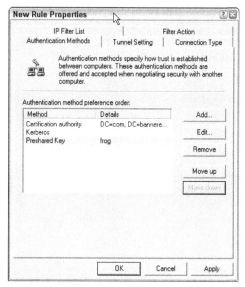

Figure 8-17

Once saved, you can edit the IPSec policy. You can add, delete, or edit rules/filters attached to the IPSec policy on the Rules tab. As discussed above, rule names are based upon IP filters and are displayed in reverse alphabetic order. The listed order has nothing to do with how they are applied. Rules/filters are applied from most specific to least specific (i.e., broad). On the IPSec policy General tab (see Figure 8-18) you can further define IPSec key characteristics, including whether the IKE SA uses *Master key perfect forward secrecy*.

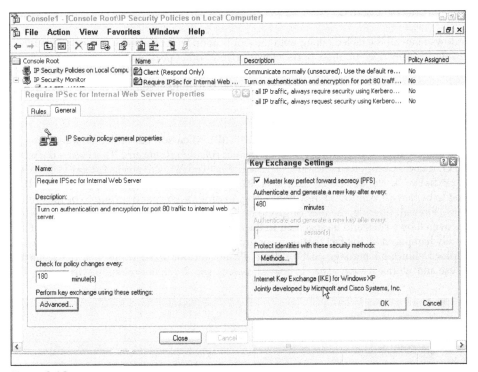

Figure 8-18

Once you are sure the IPSec policy meets the required criteria, you need to ensure that the other endpoint has a similar policy with mirrored rules and filters configured. You can manually create the mirrored policy, use one of the IPSec command-line tools and a script to create it, or, in the console, right-click the *IP Security Policies on Local Computer* option, and choose *All Tasks* and then *Export Policies*. The resulting file can then be imported on the other endpoint and the appropriate modifications made.

When both sides have the correct and aligned IPSec policies, you can assign them and test. If you are unsure about its functionality, use the IPSec Monitor console (or a tool) or a network sniffer to validate whether or not IPSec is working as intended. Additional configuration may be needed outside of IPSec in order to get it working. See Microsoft Knowledge Base article 816514 (`http://support.microsoft.com/default.aspx?scid=kb;en-us;816514`) for more step-by-step IPSec instructions.

Firewall Ports Needed

If a firewall is inline between the two participating IPSec endpoints, the following ports must be opened:

- ❏ UDP port 500 (for IKE traffic)
- ❏ UDP port 4500 (for NAT-T traffic only)
- ❏ IP Protocol 50 and 51

If Windows Firewall is enabled (along with the Application Layer Gateway service) when IPSec is enabled, it will automatically open up these ports. However, most other ports will need to be opened in IPSec for two hosts to communicate. For example, don't forget to allow DNS (TCP and UDP port 53) for clients needing DNS resolution. Most Windows hosts need NetBIOS naming resolution as well (ports 137 and 445).

Windows Firewall IPSec Bypass

In Windows XP Pro SP2 and Windows Server 2003 SP1, Microsoft has added an interesting Windows Firewall feature. If the GPO setting *WindowsFirewall: Allow Authenticated IPsec bypass* is enabled (located in a GPO or Local Computer Policy at `Computer Configuration\Administrative Templates\Network\Network Connections\Windows Firewall`), users and groups protected by IPSec can be allowed to bypass all Windows Firewall filtering. In order for a user or group to be allowed to bypass Windows Firewall filtering, the user or group must be communicating using IPSec secured traffic (i.e., traffic covered by a rule) and be specified in the GPO setting (see Figure 8-19). Unfortunately, the setting is severely hampered by the fact that users or groups can only be specified by a Microsoft Security Descriptor Definition Language (SDDL) string. Prolific author Mark Minasi has an excellent article on SDDL use and syntax at `www.minasi.com/showdoc.asp?docname=nws0502.htm`.

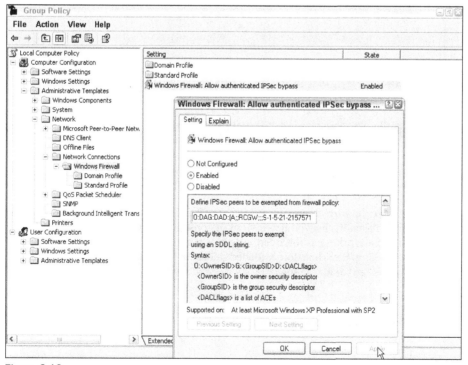

Figure 8-19

Windows Vista has a much-improved interface for IPSec and the Windows Firewall called the Windows Firewall with Advanced Security console.

Using IPSec Security

IPSec has incredible versatility. With appropriate setup planning, Windows IPSec can be used to protect any Windows 2000 and later computer, including workstations, domain controllers, web servers, and file servers. Successful IPSec takes a lot of setup planning. I'll use another example to illustrate the usefulness of IPSec.

Setup Planning

Here are some of the questions to consider:

❑ What role will the two IPSec endpoints assume in the network and with each other?

❑ Do you want to use IPSec to secure traffic between two endpoints or prevent all unauthorized traffic?

❑ Figure out what services are involved and what ports need to be secured.

❑ Using the IP rule and filter characteristics noted above, think about how your IPSec policy needs to be created.

❑ Will IPSec be used to authenticate, for encryption, or both?

❑ Do both endpoints recognize the same hashes and cipher algorithms?

❑ What authentication methods are possible?

When to Use IPSec

IPSec is an excellent solution for the following scenarios:

❑ Between two PC endpoints needing guaranteed traffic confidentiality and authentication

❑ Between two local area networks needing access to each other over the Internet

❑ As a requirement between critical computers and domain clients, ensuring that only managed domain computers and members can connect

❑ Along with Group Policy to allow only certain groups to access sensitive computers

❑ To allow only administrators to access management ports and consoles on remote computers

❑ Between laptop user at home and the corporate firewall (VPNs of this nature should terminate at a point that allows the perimeter firewall and other computer defenses to inspect and scan the traffic — to prevent the introduction of malware into the corporate network)

❑ To protect other insecure remote protocols — for example, to protect RDP traffic originating from insecure networks (currently, RDP traffic is vulnerable to man-in-the-middle attacks)

❑ To isolate a secure network from an insecure network (i.e., network or security domain isolation) when sharing common physical network media

❑ As a firewall to prevent unauthorized port connections

319

Example Scenario

Recently the author had an opportunity to manage a "Hack IIS 6" contest (located at www.hackiis6.com while the site was live) and security team. It involved a hardened IIS 6 honeypot server that the world was invited to attempt to hack. It was connected to a back-end SQL database and a side channel intrusion detection computer (see Figure 8-20).

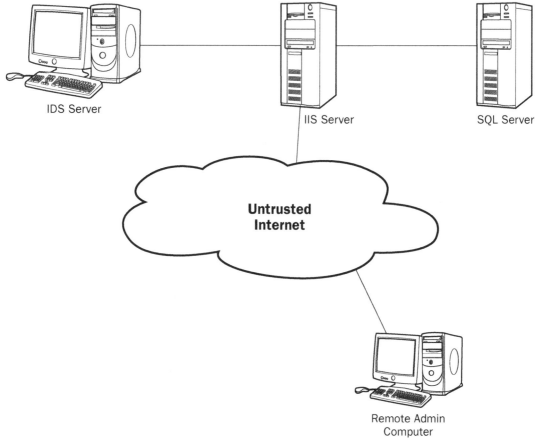

Untrusted Internet

IDS Server

IIS Server

SQL Server

Remote Admin Computer

Figure 8-20

It was remotely administered using Remote Desktop Protocol using TCP port 48064. The following IPSec rules were created:

❑ The web server was only supposed to allow untrusted attacks access to port 80. An IPSec rule was created that said to *Permit* traffic from any source IP to the web server's TCP port 80.

❑ All other ports to the web server *Required Security* using certificates. This effectively removed over 130,000 different UDP and TCP ports from attacker scrutiny.

❑ An IPSec rule was created to allow IPSec secured traffic (AH, and ESP integrity and authentication) from the remote management workstation's IP address from any port to the web server's RDP port, TCP 48064. It required a certificate to connect. Another similar IPSec policy was created to allow RDP over a non-default port to the SQL server to manage it.

❑　An IPSec rule was created to *Require Security* using certificates between the web server (any port) to the SQL server's TCP port 14034 (i.e., a non-default SQL port).

❑　Using IPSec on the SQL server, all other connections, other than from the web server to the SQL's server's non-default SQL server, were blocked (again using Required Security and certificates for all other ports). This allowed the SQL server to serve up just the one port that was needed between it and the web server. Another IPSec rule was created to allow the RDP remote administrator to connect to the SQL box, again using Required Security and certificates. All other combinations were blocked.

❑　An IPSec rule was created to Require Security between the web server and the IDS server to allow log collection from the web server using the FTP service. Initially, File and Printer sharing were enabled to allow the IDS server to pick up the IIS server's web server logs, but this was felt to be too much risk for the contest. Instead, FTP services were installed on the IIS server and secured with IPSec.

❑　The IDS server was locked down using IPSec. In order for the IDS server to capture all attack traffic headed to the web server, we could not block any ports completely. If we did, it would prevent the IDS server from sniffing network traffic. Instead we allowed all incoming traffic (so the IDS could sniff the traffic), but blocked all outgoing traffic (except to the one FTP port on the web server and one port on the RDP remote management machine). While not perfect security, it worked out pretty well.

❑　The RDP remote management machine could only connect to the hacking contest web server location using port 80, and the non-default RDP ports pointed to each participating server.

Using IPSec, we were able to block most of the 130,000 plus UDP and TCP ports each involved computer had and significantly tighten all the remaining ports (except for the web server's port 80). We had hackers attempting to hack night and day. For over three weeks the web site sustained over 150,000 attack packets per second. In the end, the web site wasn't hacked.

The contest didn't prove that IIS 6 wasn't hackable. Anything is hackable, and IIS 6 is bound to have holes. What it did prove was that by following simple hardening steps and implementing the correct tools, IIS 6 can be made fairly secure against most attacks. The hardened IIS 6 server and its well-researched applications probably had more to do with the web server going unhacked, but I'm certain the stringent IPSec policies contributed significantly to the project's success.

IPSec Attacks and Defenses

Although IPSec is used to secure network traffic and hosts, like any protocol it is susceptible to attacks itself. As shown above, IPSec traffic is easy to detect using a network protocol sniffer. An attacker finding an IPSec VPN might be motivated to try to break into the secure tunnel. This is because IPSec is often used to tunnel sensitive, and valuable, traffic past enterprise firewalls. Here are some common IPSec attacks.

Bypassing Firewall Defenses

IPSec VPNs are often terminated internally, past firewall and antivirus defenses. A compromised external host can be infected by a worm or virus, or exploited by a malicious hacker, who then uses the IPSec connection to compromise the more valuable target network. IPSec tunnels, and VPNs in general, frustrate firewalls and perimeter defense tools because they can make it impossible to inspect the payload for maliciousness.

These days, most of the popular Internet worms start out infecting offsite computers, laptops, and VPN computers. When the infected remote user connects into their parent's enterprise network, the VPN often lets the worm get past the perimeter defenses. If possible, terminate all external IPSec VPNs on a filtered segment which can apply normal defenses such as antivirus scanning and firewalling.

Trusted Man-in-the-Middle Attack

If attackers can learn the IPSec secret keys, they can perform a trusted man-in-the-middle (MitM) attack. To prevent these types of attacks, don't use PSK authentication except on hosts not connected to the production network. If you use PSK for limited testing of new IPSec tunnels, be sure to change it to Kerberos or certificate authentication before forgetting. There are even open-source tools, such as Ike-scan (`www.nta-monitor.com/ike-scan`) that can be used to brute-force and dictionary-attack PSK keys.

Denial-of-Service Attacks

Windows can minimize IPSec denial-of-service attacks, which attempt to overwhelm an endpoint using a large number of fraudulent SA connections. Per Microsoft, if Main mode is established, IKE will limit all current Main mode SAs to five per IP address/port pairs. If Main mode has not been established, IKE limits new Main mode SAs to 35 per IP address. If that limit is reached, IPSec will drop new connection attempts from the involved node until one of its current SAs has been dropped.

Other IPSec Links

Here are some other good IPSec links:

- ❑ www.microsoft.com/windowsserver2003/technologies/networking/ipsec/default.mspx

- ❑ www.ietf.org/ids.by.wg/ipsec.html

- ❑ www.unixwiz.net/temptips/iguide-ipsec.html

- ❑ www.cisco.com/en/US/tech/tk583/tk372/tsd_technology_support_protocol_home.html

- ❑ http://ipsec-tools.sourceforge.net

- ❑ http://secunia.com/search/?search=IPSec

- ❑ www.tcpipguide.com/free/t_IPSecurityIPSecProtocols.htm

Summary

This chapter covered using IPSec as a part of your defense-in-depth strategy. You can use IPSec to secure authorized traffic or to block unauthorized traffic. IPSec can be used to require security to ports that must be allowed to communicate, and to deny unauthorized access to all other ports. IPSec has two main modes: transport and tunnel, and two security protocols: AH and ESP. AH allows the packet integrity to be verified end-to-end, and ESP allows payload encryption and integrity. Both can be used at the same time to provide significant security to any IP network communications stream. Chapter 9 covers stopping unauthorized software execution.

Part III
Application Security

9

Stopping Unauthorized Execution

The holy grail of computer security is to prevent all unauthorized software, scripts, and instructions from running. Also known as a *software restriction policy*, the strategy is similar to the deny-by-default rule of firewalls, but on a desktop/application level. If appropriately configured and implemented, it would prevent all malware from executing locally and defeat most malicious exploits. Unfortunately, most of today's computing environments are exactly the opposite, or worse. By default, all software is allowed to run. And this is why we have the continuing magnitude of malware and hackers today.

Software restriction policies are known by many different terms, including white-listing, application control, and opt-in execution. Most end users are only vaguely familiar with the concept, using host-based firewalls, such as ZoneAlarm, that block unauthorized connections to the Internet. Conceptually, the goal is the same on all of these implementations—to prevent unauthorized software. This chapter discusses the overall issues behind preventing unauthorized software execution and then details the many ways a Windows administrator can accomplish it.

Deny-by-Default Software Execution

When a deny-by-default software execution policy is fully implemented, a managed computer will not be able to install or run any software or content (i.e., scripts, macros, ActiveX controls, etc.) not previously approved by the managing administrator. When developing a policy, it helps to understand the potential scope of the policy, the benefits, and the disadvantages.

Scope of Deny-by-Default Software Execution

Ultimately, a good security administrator wants to prevent any unapproved software program, script, macro, and set of instructions from being able to be installed and/or executed. Preventing normal software programs from being installed and executed is a large enough task, but today's interconnected Internet world requires much more. Here are the types of executions a global deny-by-default software policy would prevent if unauthorized:

- ❑ Installation and/or execution of normal software programs

- ❑ Downloading, installation, or execution of ActiveX controls and other executable content (e.g., Java applet) delivered through the browser

- ❑ Execution of scripts, macros, batch files, command files, and instructions

- ❑ Modification of existing programs

- ❑ Modification of existing data

- ❑ Manipulation of the operating system

- ❑ Initialization or inappropriate use of approved software

The first two bulleted points should be considered in any software restriction policy. The last point is particularly hard to enforce, but some restriction policies have varying amounts of success. For example, untrusted Java applets cannot manipulate local system resources. And Microsoft's ActiveX framework allows ActiveX controls to be initialized and manipulated only by their authorized parent routine, if so configured. Internet Explorer allows both of these content types to be configured on a per-security-domain basis. An ActiveX control might be allowed to run on any web located in the Trusted sites zone, but be denied execution in the Restricted sites zone. Internet Explorer zones will be covered in more detail in Chapter 10.

Benefits of Preventing Unauthorized Software Execution

Preventing untrusted software execution will prevent most malware programs, including viruses, worms, trojans, and spyware. Antivirus software vendors now report over 100,000 different malware programs. Nearly all would be prevented by implementing a strong software restriction policy. Besides preventing malware, an administrator preventing unauthorized execution can expect the following benefits:

- ❑ Higher performance
- ❑ Standardized computers
- ❑ Less staff support hours
- ❑ Less problems overall
- ❑ Less illegal licensing issues

Everyone knows that the more programs that are installed the slower the computer functions. Nearly every installed program installs one or more programs in one of Windows' auto-start areas. Fewer installed programs means faster computers, more free CPU cycles for existing programs, and more free hard drive space.

Every IT department support staff person knows that unapproved installed or misconfigured programs account for a large portion of their support calls. A standardized computer with standardized software applications lowers support costs and decreases the number of problems overall, for both the IT admin and the end user. Lastly, when unapproved software programs cannot be installed or executed, it results in less software piracy.

Disadvantages of Preventing Unauthorized Software Execution

If preventing unauthorized software execution has so many benefits why isn't deny-by-default software execution the rule today? Historically, the first issue involved with implementing a policy of this type was that it wasn't easy or inexpensive to do. Until the last few years, in order to implement a software restriction policy, IT had to purchase a third-party commercial program. Today, Windows XP and later computers support it.

The bigger issue is end user acceptance. End users don't like having their computing freedom curtailed. If the company provided them with a car, they would freely accept any terms the company might stipulate around the car, including when they can drive it, where they can drive it, and how they can drive. Put the same sort of restrictions on corporate computer end users for the first time and you're likely to see a lynch mob building for the IT team. When most network administrators are introduced to the concept of stopping all unauthorized software execution, they immediately think of the end user problems and hassles they would face if they implemented such a policy, and then discount it as unworkable. Instead, they prefer to fight security fires as they appear and have their staff deal with found security violations on a case-by-case basis. Having no configured software restriction policy may result in more overall work effort and vulnerabilities, but at least the users are not blaming IT for every program that doesn't work. And when a malware or hacker program does penetrate the less protected computers, the end users blame the hackers or the worm, not IT.

Implementing a software restriction policy requires a lot of up-front work and planning. Going from an environment where any program can be installed and executed to one in which freedom is restricted will absolutely cause a lot of problems — technical and otherwise. Many end users will lose their patience and regret their loss of freedom. It's inconvenient, if nothing else, to have to submit every new software program for IT approval.

Ultimately, it comes down to whether or not management finds great value in controlling which software runs on their owned assets versus the trade-off of employee freedom. Most corporations decide to accept the frequent infection of their computers by malicious software and hackers, but companies that need a higher-than-normal level of security will use a software restriction policy.

> *In my 19 years of experience, the corporate entities using a software restriction policy are among the most successful companies in preventing malware and hackers.*

It is important to understand that even if your environment cannot implement a total software restriction policy, lessons can be learned and subsequent steps taken to minimize malicious attack.

Developing a Software Restriction Policy

Implementing a software restriction policy involves several steps:

1. Get management's approval.

2. Decide on a default policy: deny-by-default or deny-specific software.

3. Decide which restriction methods to use.

4. Create a list of approved applications and publish to end users.

5. Publish and communicate the process of how applications get approved.

6. Review (and approve, if appropriate) new applications in a timely manner.

7. Communicate the software restriction policy to end users, including why it is needed.

8. Conduct a large testing phase to ensure rollout goes as planned.

9. Prepare IT support resources and staff accordingly for go-live.

10. Implement the software restriction policy.

11. Report successes and failures.

12. Adjust the software restriction policy as needed.

Besides appropriate planning and testing, the most important factor is to be responsive to end-user complaints and requests for new software installs. If you can minimize disruption and respond quickly to the resulting issues, a lot of end-user angst can be avoided.

A list of approved software must be created and communicated to management and end users. To create the list, begin by surveying computers for installed software. Ask the users what software is necessary to perform their job. Then create a list of approved software and ask management to approve it. Let management know that new software will need to be approved by end-user management and IT prior to its inclusion on the approved list. Record the default software folders and executables needed for each approved software program. Don't forget ancillary programs such as Adobe Acrobat Reader and Macromedia's Flash, which users might not think of but are probably installed and used on most systems.

Another key point to decide is whether the software restriction policy will prevent all unapproved software from running (i.e., deny-by-default policy) or whether you should just try to stop particular software from running. The latter policy is easier to implement initially, but doesn't have the security payback that the former stance does. With that said, some companies simply cannot implement the deny-by-default rule, even though it's better. End users would revolt and management won't approve it. Table 9-1 shows a list of executables that one company chose to block specifically instead of using a deny-by-default rule.

Table 9-1

Executable to Block	Software Program
Azureus*.exe	Azureus
Bitcomet.exe	BitComet
Bittornado*.exe	Bit Tornado
Blubstersetup.exe	Blubster
Bsinstall.exe	Bearshare
Bsliteinstall.exe	Bearshare
Cabos*.msi	Cabos

Executable to Block	Software Program
Dietk*.exe	Dietk
Edonkey.exe	EDonkey 2000
Grokster_installer.exe	Grokster
Imeshlight455re.exe	Imesh Client
Install_zultrax.exe	Zultrax
Kazaa_Setup.exe	Kazaa P2P File Sharing
Kutepp*.exe	KlRun
Limwirewin.exe	Limewire
Moodampinstaller.exe	Moodamp
Morpheous.exe	Morpheous
Mynap343.exe	MyNapster
P2psetup.exe	P2P Networking
Peanuts10.exe	Peanuts
Setupneonapster.exe	NeoNapster
Shareaza.exe	Sharea2a
Swappersetup.exe	Swapper
Winmx*.exe	Winmx
Xolox.exe	Xolox

Thanks to Chip Bendle for his personal block list.

The list contains many popular programs that are considered high risk or that install unwanted programs and spyware. Unfortunately, specific block lists (aka *black lists*) are difficult to maintain. The amount of unwanted software keeps increasing every day and a simple name change or update would allow the newer executable by. That's why, whenever possible, implement a deny-by-default (i.e., whitelist) strategy.

Methods to Prevent Unauthorized Execution

Several techniques can be used to prevent unauthorized execution.

Don't Let End Users Be Logged In As Admin

One of the single best things you can do to prevent unauthorized software installation is to prevent non-admin users from being logged in as administrators. Non-admin users cannot install most software, modify the HKLM registry key, or add programs to most Windows auto-start areas. Non-admin users normally cannot install programs from the Internet or modify existing program configuration information.

Unfortunately, this recommendation doesn't prevent normal users from running already installed software. Unless the user is restricted from running a program using permissions or some other method, Windows allows users to run most programs without administrative access.

Remove or Delete Software

If existing software isn't needed by any user, uninstall it, delete it, or rename it. As discussed earlier in this book, even when software isn't used, it can make a computer vulnerable. If possible, uninstall or delete the software or service. Using the program's official uninstall program is preferred, as it should remove associated files, folders, and registry entries. Unfortunately, many uninstall routines still leave unneeded files and registry entries even when they claim to be removing them. If the software being removed is high-risk, be sure to manually inspect the related files, folders, and registry keys, and delete if needed. Renaming the software executable or folder to something Windows or the end user doesn't expect can be useful when the software is difficult to remove. It's security-by-obscurity, but it can work in preventing easy execution.

Be aware that Windows will sometimes track name changes and update the pointers, icons, and shortcuts to the new name. Unfortunately, this method doesn't prevent re-installation. For example, if a network administrator removes America Online's Instant Messaging (AIM) client, there is little to prevent an end user from re-installing it if they have the appropriate admin permissions. Also, you cannot remove, delete, or rename Windows File Protection (WFP)–protected files. If you do any of the preceding, Windows just replaces them in a few seconds. Still, if you can successfully remove unneeded software, it is one of the best ways to strengthen the security of any computer system.

Use NTFS Permissions

You can use NTFS permissions to prevent the execution of existing installed software, and in some limited cases, prevent the installation of new software. NTFS permissions are the number one most secure way to prevent the unauthorized execution of existing software. If appropriately used, NTFS is hard to get around or trick.

Determine what software most normal users should be able to execute, and if the software cannot be removed completely (e.g., needed for admin purposes or other users on a shared computer), then use appropriately set NTFS permissions to secure it. In most cases, an administrator wants to take away a normal user's Read & Execute permission. As Figure 9-1 shows, a common decision would be to set permissions at the application's folder level and let the resulting permissions be inherited downward. In this case, Figure 9-1 shows the Everyone group's permissions being set to none (as if it had previously had permissions set). Administrators, System, and Service have the expected default Read & Execute permissions.

Remove any other groups that should not have permissions. There is no need to add the Everyone group (or any other group) and then remove the permissions if the group does not already have permissions. When Windows realizes that a listed security principal has no permissions set on a protected resource, it will remove it from the access control list completely.

Be careful. Do not set Read & Execute-Deny permissions for the Everyone or Authenticated Users group unless that is your true intent. Administrators and other privileged accounts belong to the larger groups as well and any permissions you set will also apply to the more privileged user accounts. Doing so could result in Read & Execute permissions unintentionally being taken away for the more specific groups. The key here is to remove Read & Execute permissions from groups that do not need access.

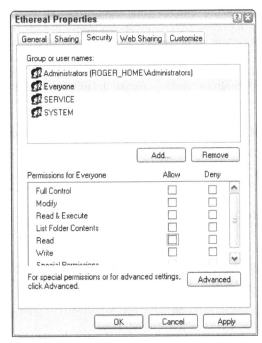

Figure 9-1

Preventing New Installs Using NTFS Permissions

The easiest way to prevent new installs using NTFS permissions is to not allow non-admin users to be logged in with admin credentials. Outside of that effort, another way to prevent new installs using NTFS permissions is to remove all permissions on the folders where the software is likely to be installed. Essentially, you want to take away the Read permissions from even the Administrators group, if end users are normally logged on with admin credentials. The true administrator can always take ownership and add back permissions if they are really needed.

For example, if you are tired of a particular software being installed (e.g., FreeRebates, a popular adware program), you can create its default directory ahead of time and remove all permissions. In this example, you could create a folder under C:\Program Files called FreeRebates, where the FreeRebates program would normally install itself. By creating the folder and removing all permissions, the FreeRebates install program will attempt to install itself but fail. This is because when it begins to create what it thinks is a new directory, the unseen directory will already exist and can't be created, and the install routine will fail. Simple error-checking code in the program's installation routine would prevent the failed installation, but most install routines do not contain the necessary programming. The same obscurity technique can be used to trick viruses and trojans. If a malware outbreak (that uses a particular file name) occurs and other defensive measures are not available, you can consider using this trick. For example, suppose a worm always creates a program called Mywife.gif in the C:\Windows\System32 directory. You can create a small text file with the same name and then assign it no or Full Control-Deny permissions. If the worm tries to exploit the modified system, it will not be able to create the expected file and will hopefully fail.

You can also try creating a directory with the same name as the file you wish to block. This often blocks malware that's smart enough to clear adverse attributes from a proactive blocking file but doesn't have the coding to deal with a directory with the same name. These methods are very crude and don't work all the time. The installing program or user might be able to install the software or malware using another folder or file name. But many malware programs install to a particular directory with predictable names, and end users almost always take the default install directory path when given a choice. It's a crude method, but it works in a pinch.

Preventing New Installs Using NTFS Registry Permissions

If an installed program relies on the registry to run, you can use registry permissions to prevent unwanted execution. As covered in Chapter 6, find the program's registry keys and remove Read permissions from the appropriate groups.

Use Service Permissions

If the program installs itself as a Windows server, you can use service permissions to prevent execution. As covered in Chapter 7, service permissions are most easily set using Group Policy Objects (GPOs) and the System Services leaf object. Alternately, you can set service permissions using the `Sc.exe` utility and its `Sdshow` (see Figure 9-2) and `Sdset` parameters along with the appropriate SDDL settings. With either method, you can control which security principals have the ability to stop, start, and read various system services. You can also disable services using the Windows hardware profiles feature (also covered in Chapter 7).

Figure 9-2

Don't Forget to Use Good NTFS Permission Setting Practices

Whenever using NTFS to set permissions, don't forget to follow best practices, including the following:

❑ Use the AGULP method to assign security permissions.

❑ Always assign permissions to groups but never to individual users.

❑ Use the Advanced Security Settings dialog box when setting NTFS permissions.

❑ Set Share and NTFS permissions as tightly as you can to meet the least-privilege principle.

❑ Using NTFS permissions is one of the best ways to prevent unauthorized execution of installed programs.

Unregister DLLs

There are times when it is important to temporarily disable COM objects or particular DLLs. Several Microsoft vulnerability warnings in 2005 (e.g., www.microsoft.com/technet/security/advisory/ 906267.mspx) recommended that specific files be "unregistered" as a workaround until patches could be developed, tested, and released.

By default, many programs, COM objects, and DLLs register themselves with Windows. They do this so they can easily be found and executed when appropriate in Windows. You can use the `Regsvr32.exe` or `/Unregister` command to unregister files.

For example, before the appropriate patch was released, Microsoft Bulletin 903144 (`www.microsoft .com/technet/security/advisory/903144.mspx`) advised concerned administrators to unregister the `Javaprxy.dll` COM object. It can be done using the following syntax:

```
Regsvr32.exe /u Javaprxy.dll
```

You must execute the command at the command prompt and in the current directory where the object is located (or otherwise provide the correct path). If done correctly, a message dialog box will pop up stating the success (see Figure 9-3).

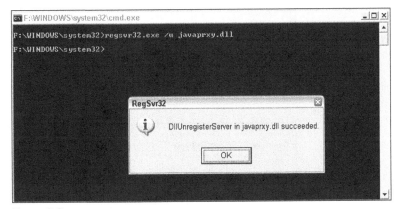

Figure 9-3

Any object unregistered using the `Regsvr32.exe` program can be registered by typing in the same syntax, but without the `/u` unregister parameter:

```
Regsvr32.exe Javaprxy.dll
```

Again, a successful message dialog box should appear. You can use the `/S` parameter (i.e., Silent mode) to prevent the popup dialog box from appearing. Most Dll and ActiveX controls (OCXs) files can be registered and unregistered using `Regsvr32.exe`. You must close and re-open any dependent applications if they are open when the `Regsver32.exe` command is executed in order for the new setting to be effective.

Larger applications often carry their own unregister commands. For example, the Windows scripting host HTML application host program, `Mshta.exe`, can be registered and unregistered using the `/register` and `/unregister` parameters:

```
Mshta.exe /register or Mshta.exe /unregister
```

Unregistering a program removes its file association in the registry. Figure 9-4 shows the .HTA file extension normally associated with `Mshta.exe`. Figure 9-5 shows the same screen after the `/unregister` switch has been executed. The HTA file extension is no longer listed.

Figure 9-4

Figure 9-5

Microsoft Visual Basic ActiveX controls can often be registered using the /regserver and /unregserver parameters (see http://support.microsoft.com/default.aspx?scid=kb;en-us;297279). Check each program's documentation for more information on the registration process.

Unregistering a program or Dll file is useful in instances when other alternative defenses are not available, but should not be used as a long-term defense. It's too easy for the unregistered program to be re-registered by a new software update or newly installed program. For long-term solutions, use NTFS or Software Restriction Policies (covered below).

Use the Kill Bit

Another technique similar to the registration solution is setting the kill bit. Administrators and users can set a kill bit flag in the registry to instruct Internet Explorer, Outlook, and other Windows programs to not load specific ActiveX controls. In order to set a control's kill bit, the control's CLSID must be known. To find an object's CLSID, you can:

❑ View the control's CLSID in Internet Explorer (not always accurate or possible).

❑ Contact the control's manufacturer.

❑ Use the Microsoft Resource Kit utility, Oleview.

❑ Query a database that lists various ActiveX controls and their CLSIDs.

❑ Search for it in the registry.

The Microsoft Resource Kit utility, Oleview (`www.microsoft.com/windows2000/techinfo/reskit/ tools/existing/oleview-o.asp`), is an excellent tool for hunting down unknown CSLIDs. You can see an example of it revealing Adobe Acrobat Reader's CLSID in Figure 9-6.

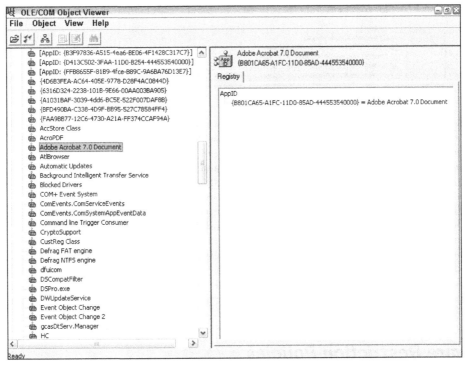

Figure 9-6

CastleCop's (`http://castlecops.com/ActiveX.html`) listing of ActiveX controls is one of the best on the Internet. Not only does it list control CLSIDs; it makes a determination about whether the control is legitimate or more likely to be considered unwanted by most users (i.e., spyware, adware, etc.).

Searching for a control's CLSID in the registry can be monotonous. Search for the Default string value for the `ProgID` key for each of the CLSID keys in `HKCR\CLSID`. Figure 9-7 shows an example searching for the Quick Time ActiveX control CLSID. In `Regedit.exe`, click on `HKCR\CLSID`. Choose the F3 key to search, type in **ProgID,** and then press Enter. Press F3 to repeat the search until you find the product name you are looking for. In this case, the QuickTime control's CLSID is `02BF25D5-8C17-4B23-BC80-D3488ABDDC6B`.

> *Nirsoft's RegScanner (www.nirsoft.net/utils/regscanner.html) is a good tool for registry scanning. It lists all matches of a single registry query in one list from which you can jump into edit. This is a lot better than finding and changing things one at a time via Regedit, when you realize you've done 37 such changes and the scrollbar suggests you have 75% of the registry still to go. It can also do queries based on modification date and time.*

Figure 9-7

After the control's CLSID is located, the following registry key must be located or created: `HKLM\Software\Microsoft\Internet Explorer\ActiveX Compatability\{CLSID}`. Locate the Compatibility Flag key. By default, it can be several values. Setting it to 400 will instruct Internet Explorer not to load the control. This is a good way for administrators to prevent known controls from running if they've had a problem with them previously. You can even proactively set the kill bit for ActiveX controls yet to be installed. The kill bit works only within Internet Explorer and other applications that rely on Internet Explorer to render graphics (e.g., Outlook), and thus some controls can bypass the settings. For example, I set the kill bit on Adobe's Acrobat ActiveX control. When I clicked on a PDF document in Internet Explorer, the control was not launched. However, I downloaded the same PDF document to my hard drive and clicked on it in Internet Explorer. Explorer automatically loaded Windows Explorer to handle the local file, which then loaded Acrobat and displayed the PDF document. This just re-enforces one of ActiveX's criticisms about security being handled by the browser. We will cover other methods to secure ActiveX controls in Chapter 10.

Software Restriction Policies

Starting with Windows XP Pro, Microsoft introduced the concept of *software restriction policies (SRPs).* SRP enables an administrator to specify what software is allowed to run on any managed computer. Software restriction policies (known as *SAFER* within Microsoft) require Windows XP Pro or later computers. Windows 2000 has a smaller subset of features similar to SRP but isn't nearly as versatile.

The SRP management console is accessed using group policy or Local Security Policy. Chose `Computer Configuration\Windows Settings\Security Settings\Software Restriction Policies` to access SRP settings (see Figure 9-8). Group policy, but not Local Computer Policy, allows administrators to configure SRP in the User Configuration area as well.

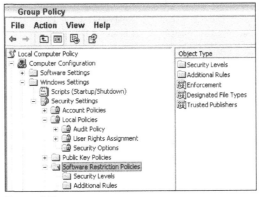

Figure 9-8

Overall SRP Decisions

First, before administrators even begin configuring SRP, a major decision needs to be made. Is SRP going to deny all software by default except that which is allowed, or allow all software to run by default, except that which is denied (the default when SRP is turned on)? Once the overall rule is set, *exceptions* to the major rule are defined. Hence, if you decide to implement the deny-by-default rule as the major rule, every program you want to run is then defined as an exception to the default rule.

The deny-by-default rule is called *Disallowed* in SRP. The other option, to allow all software to run except that which is explicitly denied, is called *Unrestricted*. This major SRP setting, called *Security Levels*, is made under the *Security Settings* leaf object (see Figure 9-9).

If you choose Disallowed, Microsoft has already created four exception rules (see Figure 9-10) that prevent first-time users from locking themselves out of their systems. The exceptions allow all executes in the root directory, the Windows directory, the System32 directory, and the Program Files folder to run, by default. These rules can be removed when you are familiar with SRP, but do so with caution.

You can also decide whether SRP applies to all Windows files or all Windows files except Dll files (see Figure 9-11). The default is all files except Dll files. This is because Dll files are often shared between multiple programs and throughout Windows. Most of the time, administrators mean to block normal executables. If an administrator chooses the Disallow default rule and also blocks Dll files, they could possibly cause problems with desired Windows programs. The *All software files* setting should be chosen with caution. You can also decide to whom SRP applies — all users or all users except local administrators. This allows a local Administrator to log in and run any executable they want for emergencies and troubleshooting but will prove useless if all users are logged in as local administrators.

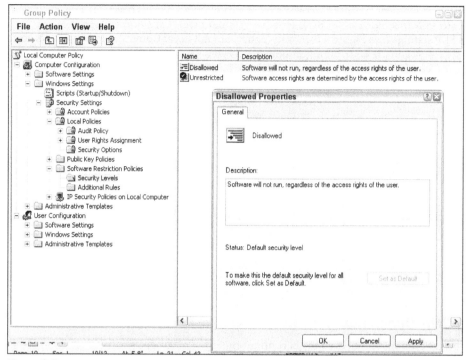

Figure 9-9

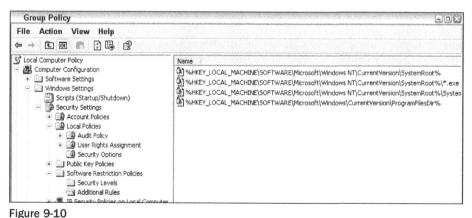

Figure 9-10

SRP can initially control only 31 different file types, including many of the highest-risk files. Default file extensions include ADE, ADP, BAS, BAT, CHM, CMD, COM, CPL, CRT, EXE, HLP, HTA, INF, INS, ISP, LNK, MDB, MDE, MSC, MSI, MSP, MST, OCX, PCD, PIF, REG, SCR, SHS, URL, VB, and WSC. You can easily add more file extensions (see Figure 9-12), but they will be far fewer than the hundreds of file extensions allowed to run in Windows by default. Use the file extension list presented in Table 5-1 as your guide.

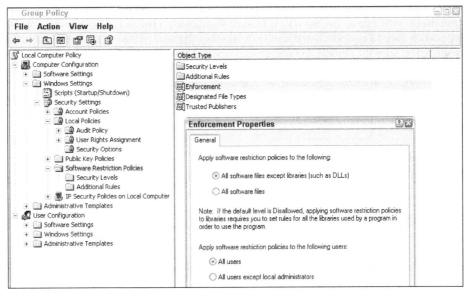

Figure 9-11

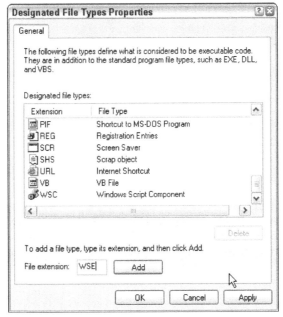

Figure 9-12

SRP allows an administrator to determine what level user (see Figure 9-13) can install a software vendor's publisher certificate as trusted (i.e., a Trusted Publisher). A trusted publisher can potentially install any application they like remotely without ever warning the user or asking for permission. Trusted publishers should be set with caution. In most cases, only local or Enterprise administrators should be installing trusted publishers, although this is not the default. You can also choose whether to require revocation checking on certificates using the publisher's name or the certificate's timestamp. In practice, revocation checking doesn't work as well as it should. You can enable it unless you have problems, but don't trust it to be accurate.

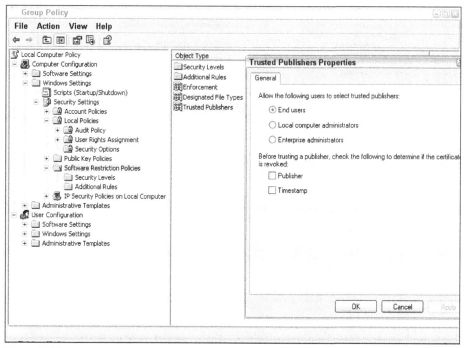

Figure 9-13

Exception Rules

After that major decision is made, the administrator goes about setting *exceptions*. Exceptions are policy rules that either allow specific software (when using the Disallowed main setting), or deny specific software (when using the Unrestricted setting). There are four different types of exception rules:

❏ Certificate rules

❏ Hash rules

❏ Internet Zone rules

❏ Path rules

Certificate exception rules allow you to deny or allow software digitally signed by a specific digital certificate (see Figure 9-14). For example, you can deny all VBScript files except those signed by an internal private company development digital certificate. It will stop VBS viruses and worms from running, but allow your own internal management scripts to run. Certificate rules require a code signing digital certificate to be trusted, and you must configure separately who can decide whether to trust a particular code signing certificate (see Figure 9-13 above). Certificate rules apply no matter where the file is or what it is named, as long as the file's integrity has been maintained and the certificate remains valid.

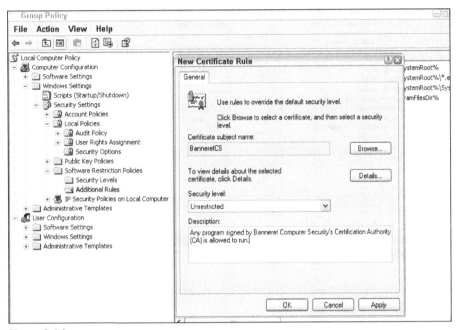

Figure 9-14

Hash rules allow you to input a valid MD5 or SHA1 file hash value (also known as a *digital fingerprint*). Like Certificate rules, it allows you to deny or allow a particular file or program no matter where the target resides or what the file is named. All that matters is that the related file meets its previously stored hash value (see Figure 9-15).

Most administrators implementing SRP use a lot of hash rules. The only problem is that software updates and patches frequently update the related executable referred to by the hash. This means the administrator is constantly adding and modifying hash rules every time a new file version comes out. With that said, the hash rule method is extremely accurate.

The Internet Zone rule (see Figure 9-16) is probably the least useful of the SRP rules. It will allow or deny all software installed and executed in a particular Internet Explorer Zone (more on zones in Chapter 10), but only if the file was installed with a Windows installer file (.MSI). Since most Internet-installed software programs do not install with an .MSI file, it practically makes the rule class almost useless. The Internet rule being established in Figure 9-16 would prevent any MSI programs from being installed from web sites lying within the Restricted sites zone.

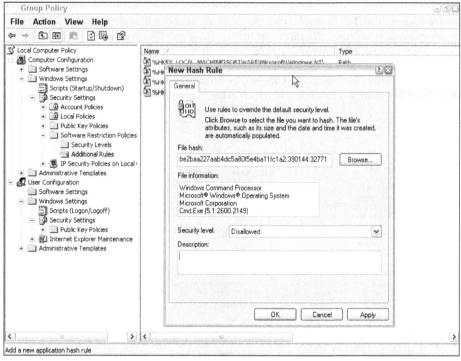

Figure 9-15

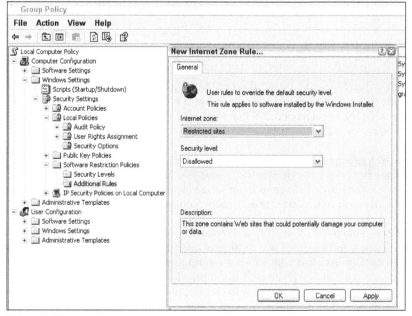

Figure 9-16

Lastly, Path rules allow you to define exceptions using directory (see Figure 9-17) or registry paths. Path rules will accept the standard wildcard naming conventions (i.e., ? and *) in the path statements. SRP is fairly accurate at preventing the exact executable from executing, but it can easily be bypassed by a semi-knowledgeable end user — for instance, by right-clicking the protected executable and creating a shortcut. That shortcut will run the executable without problem. If you rename the executable, it will run without problem. If you copy the executable elsewhere, it will run without problem.

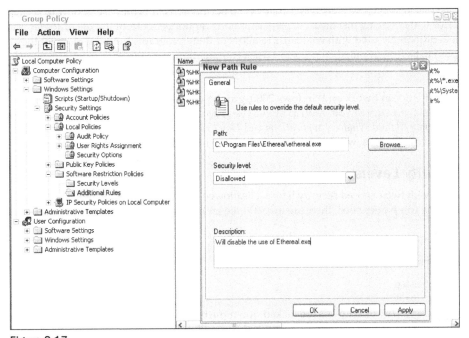

Figure 9-17

Setting up a deny-by-default SRP takes some planning and work. None of the rule exceptions by themselves work perfectly, but all four types used together can roughly enforce which software is and isn't allowed to run on a Windows XP and later computer. Figure 9-18 shows the type of message a user will get if the program is restricted by SRP.

Figure 9-18

There are some issues with SRP beyond figuring out what is and isn't allowed. It isn't perfect. For one, it works only with Windows XP Pro and later. Two, it cannot manage 16-bit executables (such as Command.com and Edit.com). If you wish to prevent 16-bit executables, use NFTS permissions on Ntdvm.exe. Three, it does not apply to all file types by default. Lastly, there appears to be many ways to bypass each particular exception rule. Most users won't be able to guess how to hack around SRP, but it can be done. It is not a panacea. If you need absolute security, use NTFS permissions instead.

In at least one instance, SRPs are better than NTFS permissions. It is the case of how to secure applications prior to them being installed. NTFS permissions cannot be set until the file or folder is already installed. SRP can be used with wildcards to allow or deny programs from the moment they were attempted to be first installed. You should use a combination of all the SRP and NTFS permissions to get the desired outcome.

Although SRP doesn't work on Windows 2000, group policy had SRP-like policies. In Group Policy, choose User Configuration\Administrative Templates\System. There are two similar settings called *Run only allowed Windows applications* and *Don't run specific Windows applications*. A few other options above and below will allow you to have some limited control over software execution.

More Security Levels

SRP comes with two exposed security levels: Disallowed and Unrestricted. While these two levels may be all that many companies need, there are in fact three more security levels that can be implemented in SRP:

❑   Basic User (also known as Normal User)

❑   Constrained (also known as Restricted)

❑   Untrusted

Constrained and Untrusted users are locked down further than normal users. For one, they cannot read the HKCU registry key or their own user profiles. Normally, all users have Full Control permissions to both these places. In Chapters 5 and 6, I recommended setting their permissions to Read-only to prevent malicious misuse. However, the Constrained and Untrusted security levels go even further, preventing even the reading of those keys. Unfortunately, the side effects of this treatment are unpredictable, varied, and hard to troubleshoot. I recommend that the Constrained and Untrusted levels be ignored until better utilized by Windows (as I'm sure it will).

The Basic User security level is a lot more useful than the other two and really should be a default setting in SRP. To expose the Basic User security level, you have to add a registry entry. Create a new Dword value called Levels under HKLM\Software\Policies\Microsoft\Windows\Safer\CodeIdentifiers. Set the value of Levels to hexadecimal 0x00020000 (see Figure 9-19).

This will reveal the Basic User security level when you go back into SRP (see Figure 9-20).

Now you can set the default SRP rule to be Basic User. Basic users run programs with permissions of non-admin Authenticated Users. An even better strategy is to set the overall SRP rule to Disallowed or Unrestricted as suggested before. But now use exception rules to force particular applications (e.g., Internet Explorer, Outlook, etc.) to run in the Basic User security context. Just define exception rules as you normally would, but instead choose Basic User instead of one of the other two options (see Figure 9-21).

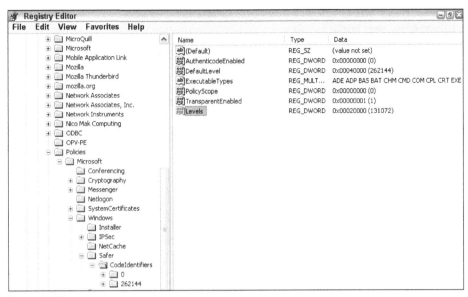

Figure 9-19

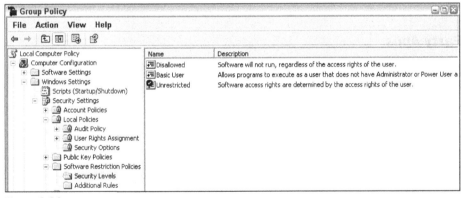

Figure 9-20

This is much like Windows Vista's new feature of running non-admin programs as lower-privileged users even when the current user is logged in as an administrator. You can use SRP to bring this feature to your Windows XP Pro and later computers. Microsoft security architect and book author Michael Howard has an excellent series of articles on the three additional security levels and SAFER programming at http://blogs.msdn.com/michael_howard/archive/2005/01/17/354708.aspx.

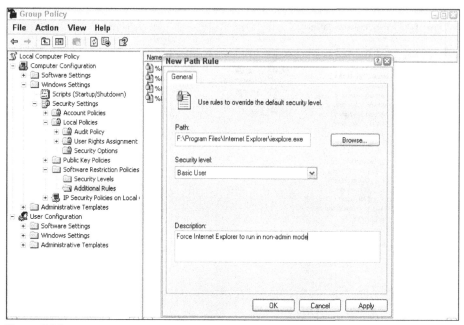

Figure 9-21

Third-Party Apps

Many third-party tools do the same thing as SRP, such as Novell's ZENworks (www.novell.com/products/zenworks), Desktop Standard's PolicyMaker (www.desktopstandard.com/Policy MakerStandard.aspx), and NetIQ's Group Policy Administrator (www.netiq.com/products/gpa/default.asp). Go to www.microsoft.com/windowsserver2003/technologies/management/grouppolicy/gptools.mspx for more Group Policy extension tools that can accomplish the same thing as SRP.

Summary

Chapter 9 covered the various ways to prevent unauthorized software execution, which is the number one way to defeat malware and malicious hackers. It recommends a deny-by-default rule and covers the various methods and techniques for locking down application software, including using NTFS permissions, unregistering programs, setting kill bits, and using software restriction policies. Chapter 10 will cover Internet Explorer security in depth.

10

Securing Internet Explorer

Internet Explorer (IE) is Microsoft's most attacked and vulnerable software. Much of the reason has to do with the fact that it is the most popular browser by a large majority and a very complex piece of software with a lot of functionality. Surely Microsoft is to blame for not making it more secure early on, but it is getting more secure and resilient over time. If you don't believe me, read *"IE Security Statistics,"* later in the chapter. This chapter discusses how Internet Explorer works, summarizes the different types of attacks against it, and covers security defenses.

Internet Explorer

First released in July 1995 (`www.microsoft.com/windows/WinHistoryIE.mspx`), Internet Explorer (IE) was Microsoft's first Internet browser. At the time, the Netscape browser had the majority of the market share, but by 1999 IE had captured first place. Since then, IE has remained the dominant browser, perhaps in a large part due to Windows' desktop dominance. Since 2001, IE has had 60-80% of the browser market share (try `www.w3schools.com/browsers/browsers_stats.asp` or `www.safalra.com/website/browsermarket`), depending on whose figures you read. IE works mainly on Windows platforms, but there is a Mac-based version as well (`www.microsoft.com/mac/products/internetexplorer/internetexplorer.aspx?pid=internetexplorer`). The most popular version is IE 6.x, followed by IE 5.x. Microsoft released IE 7 for XP SP2 and Windows Vista, partially in response to Firefox and partially to combat the increasing threat of phishing attacks. IE 7 is significantly more secure than previous IE versions, but unfortunately, requires Windows XP and later to run.

IE Features

IE is the most functional browser on the market today. It strives to comply with any popularly supported standard. It supports HTML, XML, DHTML, JavaScript, VBScript, FTP (both passive and active modes), URL monikers, multimedia, file downloading, cascading style sheets (CSS), program interfacing, custom interfaces, browser extensions, history listing, favorite links, content filtering, pop-up blocker, source-code viewing, offline web page viewing, digital certificates, script debugging, install on demand, user authentication, iframes, persistent user data, plug-ins (called add-ons in IE), Java applets, ActiveX controls, SSL, TLS, Auto Complete, resizable graphics, multiple security zones, privacy features, and a cookie manager.

New IE 7 Features

IE 7 is a major upgrade over previous versions, although the look-and-feel remain the same, with a few major changes, such as tabbed browsing and the anti-phishing filter. IE 7 added the following features (assuming they are left in the final release candidate):

❑ **Improved User Interface:**

  ❑ Cleaner interface, less icons, less clutter.

  ❑ Tabbed browsing. Mozilla introduced tabbed browsing, whereby multiple web sites are shown on one web page view, each on a different tab. The feature allows more efficient web surfing, and Microsoft adopted it too.

  ❑ Quick tabs feature, to enable users to view and manage multiple tabs with a thumbnail representation of all tabs in a single window.

  ❑ Improved search engine integration with five default search providers (i.e., MSN, Google, Yahoo, Ask Jeeves, AOL Search). End users can easily add more. Search engine companies can customize the end-user experience.

  ❑ Improved search result support. Search results are presented to the user in a better way. Result of work from the OpenSearch 1.1 (`http://opensearch.a9.com`) collaboration. Search results can be displayed as HTML or RSS.

❑ **Improved Security:**

  ❑ Significantly improved anti-spoofing features. Fixes many errors in past versions whereby a malicious web link or site could hide its true location.

  ❑ Anti-phishing filter. If enabled (IE asks before it enables it), will send any link you are connecting to Microsoft in real time to determine whether it has previously been reported as a fraudulent web site. If the web site has been flagged as a known phishing site, the end user will be warned (see Figure 10-1). Even when the web site has not been previously flagged but still contains known phishing or spoofing tricks, IE will warn the user and ask if they want to proceed. Users can also submit sites for verification testing.

  ❑ Protected mode (only available in Windows Vista), in which IE will prevent any code or software downloaded from the Internet from being written outside the Temporary Internet File (TIF) location. Should prevent many malware and hacker attacks.

  ❑ New security setting called *Medium-High* to be used for the Internet zone default security setting. This is more secure than the Internet zone's old setting of Medium.

  ❑ Trusted sites zone security will be move from Low to Medium security.

  ❑ Local Intranet security zone will be disabled for non-domain computers.

  ❑ SSLv.3.0 and TLS 1.0 will be used for HTTPS connections, instead of SSL v.2.0.

- ❏ Capability to use IE 7 in "No Add-ons" mode to quickly turn off any add-ons to decrease potential vulnerabilities

- ❏ ActiveX Opt-in: ActiveX controls will not be allowed to run in IE by default. In previous versions, most ActiveX controls could run in IE even though most are intended only to run in Windows (outside IE). IE 7 sets a new default behavior, but the list is user definable.

- ❏ Improved digital certificate handling and end user presentation and involvement

- ❏ Stronger enforcement of cross-domain security

- ❏ Better URL parsing to prevent spoofing, obscurity, and phishing attacks

- ❏ If run on Windows Vista, IE will run in User Account Control mode, whereby IE runs with Restricted Code privileges (see Chapter 3) even when the user who started it is an admin.

- ❏ Stronger content filtering (new Parental Controls will require Windows Vista)

❏ **New Features:**

- ❏ Support for International Domain Name (IDN)

- ❏ Really Simple Syndication (RSS) support. RSS is essentially a new way for web sites to do pseudo-NNTP. Previously, it required another client; now RSS support is built right in. Every web site will be examined for an RSS "feed," and if it contains one, a button on the toolbar lights up.

- ❏ A Page Zoom feature to allow users to magnify any part of a web page

- ❏ Improved PNG graphics support, including for transparent PNG files, whereby they become somewhat transparent so an underlying media presentation can be seen

❏ **Improved Printing:**

- ❏ Shrink-to-fit web page printing, finally, so all printed web pages fit on the printed page. No more cut off right margins.

- ❏ If the last printing page of a multiple-page document from a web site (called an *orphan*) covers only a minimal portion of the page, IE will resize the document to make it fit on the previous page. Of course, you can control this feature.

❏ **Miscellaneous Additions:**

- ❏ Improved CSS support

- ❏ Stronger compliance with HTML and other browser standards

- ❏ Improved XML support (native now, no longer needs a separate ActiveX control)

- ❏ A web developer toolbar for web application developers (will also be an add-on feature for IE 6)

- ❏ Improved group policy support for new and existing features

- ❏ And, of course, IE 7 contains multiple bug fixes.

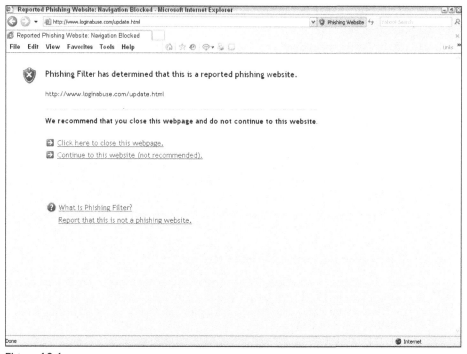

Figure 10-1

IE Competitors

There are other popular Internet browsers, such as open-source Firefox (www.mozilla.org/products/firefox), Mozilla (www.mozilla.org/products/mozilla1.x) , Linux-based Konqueror (www.konqueror.org), Opera (http://www.opera.com), Mac-based Safari (www.apple.com/support/downloads/safari.html), and text-based Lynx (http://lynx.isc.org).

Firefox has garnered a lot of attention lately and made the biggest gain into IE's dominant market share. According to a few resources, Firefox may have as much as 18% market share, especially in non-USA markets. Released in August 2004, Firefox was seen as a "safer" browser choice. Unfortunately, as covered in Table 10-1, it has suffered even more vulnerabilities than IE since its release. Because Firefox is constantly being exploited, its popularity has waned in recent months.

Netscape (http://browser.netscape.com/ns8) has become open source, but it will probably never be a serious challenge to IE and the other competitors. The Mozilla browser runs on Windows, Linux, and Mac OS X, but is coming in a distant third after Firefox. The Opera browser comes in commercial and adware-sponsored versions and is a sophisticated browser choice. Although it currently has slightly more than 1% market share, it should continue to be a viable browser choice for Linux and Windows users. Lynx is an interesting browser in that it is all text-based, and theoretically very difficult to exploit. Of course, it doesn't support many browser standards and features, and because of this doesn't have much market share, although security researchers often use it when linking to a suspected malware site. Several cell-phone vendors, such as Nokia (www.nokia.com) and NTT DoCoMo (www.nttdocomo.com), offer web-based browsers that are popular enough to a small, but measurable market share. Analysts expect cell-phone-based browsers to have some of the biggest market share increases over the next decade.

IE Security Statistics

To be a Microsoft proponent is to constantly hear about IE's security vulnerabilities from every open-source zealot. It has a lot. As of February 2006, version 6.x has had at least 91 announced security vulnerabilities since its release. But it is getting better. Table 10-1 shows some vulnerability statistics for IE 6.x and Firefox (FF) 1.x through December 2005.

Table 10-1

Year/Product	Total Number of Announced Vulnerabilities	Severity Rating- Extremely Critical	Vulnerabilities That Allowed Complete System Compromise
2003-IE 6.x	24	17%	14
2004-IE 6.x	34	15%	12
2005-IE 6.x	17	12%	7
2005-FF 1.x	22	4%	9

Figures and statistics taken from www.secunia.com.

Table 10-1 shows a few interesting facts. First, IE 6.x's number of vulnerabilities and vulnerability criticality rating has been decreasing over the years. In fact, the open-source Firefox browser had 30% more vulnerabilities than IE in 2005, and nearly half the Firefox vulnerabilities allowed complete system compromise. Symantec's Internet Security Report, Volume VIII (`http://enterprisesecurity .symantec.com/content.cfm?articleid=1539`) supports this finding.

Does this mean that IE is more secure than Firefox? No, not for sure. For one, new products being examined in the marketplace, like Firefox is, are expected to have more vulnerabilities than when the product matures. The only offsetting fact is that Firefox has a very small market share as compared to IE, and if its market share increases, so will the number of eyes looking to exploit it, and so will the number of discovered vulnerabilities. Second, the total number of exploits is only one measure of how secure a product is — it says nothing about how secure the product really is. And because of its popularity, an IE flaw is a higher risk than a flaw found in less frequently used Firefox. Still, seeing the data, I don't see Firefox as a more secure browser alternative.

The hard truth is that there are few safe browser alternatives. Lynx, a text-only browser, is probably as close as typical users will come to a relatively safe browser. It can display HTML and text files, and handle some cookies, but cannot display pictures or execute downloaded content. And it cannot reliably display most web sites. For this reason, it does not, and will not, have wide acceptance in the world.

Don't think browsers are difficult to secure? Lynx is a text-only browser, and it had two critical vulnerabilities in 2005 (`http://secunia.com/product/5883`). Regular, graphical-based browsers, capable of rendering complex web sites (as is IE and most of its competitors) are highly exposed (nearly every computer has one) and most contain multiple vulnerabilities — found and unfound. The two important factors are that a vendor establishes an acceptable level of functionality versus security and that when vulnerabilities are found, they are quickly patched by the vendor. On the latter point, Microsoft could improve.

Secunia.com currently (as of February 2006) shows that out of the 75 IE vulnerabilities, 28% of them are unpatched by Microsoft. Although few of them are ranked as high or extreme criticality, many are ranked as moderate issues (albeit most are non-severe). Several were announced as vulnerabilities in 2003 and 2004. The vast majority lead to either spoofing, security bypass, or information disclosure. To compare, Firefox only left 7% of their vulnerabilities unpatched, none highly critical. Mozilla is at 15% and Opera is 8%. To be fair, Microsoft has fixed many of the unpatched vulnerabilities in IE 7 (still in beta as of this writing), but with IE 6.x running on most of the world's desktops, Microsoft could respond quicker to patching IE issues.

How IE Works

When a user starts Internet Explorer using the normal `Iexplore.exe` executable, a lot happens under the hood. Hundreds of registry and file reads are done. Nearly 100 Dll files are loaded, including the following:

❑ `Ieframe.dll` is one of the main IE Dlls.

❑ `Shdocvw.dll` is the Web Browser Control, which is a main part of the browser. You can build your own browser program using this Dll.

❑ `Mshtml.dll` renders HTML coding, and is used by most Windows programs that display HTML, including Outlook and Outlook Express.

❑ `Msrating.dll` is involved with the Content Advisor feature, even if you don't use it.

❑ `Urlmon.dll` parses loaded URLs and includes lookups for URL monikers. It is the module that decides in which Internet Explorer security zone a particular URL or content will be placed.

❑ `Crypt32.dll` handles the Crypto API, which is needed for Digital Certificates, SSL, TLS, S/MIME, etc.

What Dlls are loaded depends on what IE is doing and rendering. For example, surfing to a site with VBScript coding will load `Vbscript.dll`. Surfing to a web site with JavaScript controls will invoke `Javascript.dll`.

Here is some of the startup process that occurs when a user first opens IE:

1. The user profile is queried to ensure that the correct IE settings are implemented.

2. GPO use is checked for and application of the GPO IE settings is verified.

3. The History file is loaded.

4. Cookie files and the index (`Index.dat`) are loaded.

5. Add-ins, such as Adobe Acrobat Reader, are loaded.

6. TCP/IP settings are verified.

7. MIME types (covered below) are loaded.

8. IE security zone settings are loaded.

9. Digital certificates and trusts are loaded.

10. Languages are verified and loaded.

11. Programs that are interfaced with IE to provide support, such as Notepad or Microsoft Word, are verified.

12. Internet Explorer is loaded.

When IE is up and running, it waits for a URL to be typed or loaded and for content to be retrieved or sent. Any loaded URL is parsed by `Urlmon.dll` and `Url.dll`, among several other support files. HTML content is rendered by `Mshtml.dll`. These Dlls can be called to work in any Windows Internet-enabled program. For instance, if an HTML-enabled e-mail is received by Outlook, it uses the previously listed Dlls to help with the displaying of the web content.

If content besides HTML is received, IE will load other helper files, `Javascript.dll`, `Vbscript.dll`, or an add-on such as Adobe Acrobat Reader or Macromedia Flash controls. What gets loaded depends on the content. Much of the content is determined by the MIME type descriptor (discussed in previous chapters). For instance, if the MIME TYPE instruction `TYPE="application/x-shockwave-flash` is found, then IE will load the Flash ActiveX control (`Flash.ocx`) to display the related Flash file. IE can also be instructed to download and run other executables and programs, download files, use SSL or TLS protection, run Java applets, run other scripts, and attempt user logons.

Uniform Resource Locators

The Universal Resource Locator (URL) is the standard naming convention used to locate and retrieve HTTP and other browser content. A URL includes information about the protocol it is using (i.e., the URL moniker), a colon, two forward slashes, and the content's fully qualified location, usually using DNS naming.

> *You may also see URLs referenced as Uniform Resource Identifiers (URI). URLs are actually a subset of URI, but both can be used when talking about browser content locations.*

The first part of the URL, the URL moniker, indicates the protocol type. Although it is usually http, it can be many other choices, including aim, telnet, ftp, news, and file (for local file manipulation). The next part of the URL indicates the server's name, which is usually www, but can be almost any name. The server's fully qualified domain location follows. Any typed-in DNS domain name is converted to its resultant IP address, although the URL can contain an IP address (i.e., `http://208.215.179.178`) instead of a DNS Name. After the domain name, URLs usually contain a folder or document name to retrieve. If the retrieved content contains URL references to other objects, they are downloaded as well. For example:

```
http://www.wrox.com/WileyCDA
```

In the preceding example, `Http` is the protocol, www is the server name, `wrox.com` is the DNS domain name where the server is located, and `WileyCDA` is the content location or virtual directory.

```
ftp://ftp.microsoft.com
```

In the preceding example, `ftp` is the protocol, `ftp` is the server name, and the server is located in the DNS domain `Microsoft.com`.

In the next example, the protocol is `http`, the server is www, the domain name is `ietf.org`, the content location on the server is `rfc`, and the document is `rfc3986.txt`:

```
http://www.ietf.org/rfc/rfc3986.txt
```

Normally, when a particular file or document is not specified in the URL, the browser or server will offer up default file names, such as `Index.htm` or `Default.htm`.

Internet Explorer Attacks

Let me count the ways. There are dozens of ways to attack a computer using its browsing client. Attack types include URL spoofing, buffer overflow, cross-site scripting, zone manipulation, file execution, directory transversal, malicious content, MIME type mismatch, cookie manipulation, browser interface manipulation, and plug-in exploits. The different types of attacks can result in a complete system compromise, system reboot, denial-of-service, privilege escalation, information disclosure, session hijacking, and defeat of security controls. Here's a summary of the different types of attacks.

URL Spoofing

This has been one of the most popular types of attacks of the past few years because of professional phishers. Phishers send fraudulent e-mails with spoofed URL links. Usually the message appears as though it were coming from some entity the user may have business with (e.g., eBay, a banking site, an ISP, etc.), and it urges the user to follow the enclosed links and reveal confidential information. Usually phishing e-mails are looking for credit card information. Users click on the provided links, thinking they are headed to a particular web site, but are instead headed to the phisher's fraudulent web site (mocked up to look like the official web site).

Figure 10-2 shows a phishing e-mail I received. It claims to be welcoming me to the Bank of America company as a VISA card user, but I do not have a Bank of America VISA card. None of the links point to the legitimate Bank of America web site (www.bankofamerica.com). One of the most telling signs of this phishing e-mail is the sender's e-mail address, BankofAmerica@get.mynewcard.com. The Mynewcard.com domain is not registered to Bank of America.

Figure 10-2

Most phishing e-mails are not as obvious as this one. Most contain links that do point to the legitimate web site. Maybe only one or two of the twenty links in the e-mail point to the fraudulent site, but it is the main link the phisher points the user to. Most phishing e-mail contains a statement that warns about fraudulent e-mail, or a message indicating that the current message was scanned and found to be free of viruses.

URL Obscurity

The phishers often obscure the true URL using a variety of methods. One of the most common methods is to encode the URL using something other than plaintext characters. The majority of URLs contain nothing but plaintext characters, but the formal RFCs on URL formatting allow URLs to be "encoded" many other ways besides plaintext characters. Originally, the idea to allow encoding was to allow the many different types of computer systems to share the same Internet. However, almost all legitimate sites on the Internet use plaintext characters (and maybe percent encoding — e.g., %20 for a space, etc.). The only people using the many obscure encoding techniques are malicious hackers. Table 10-2 shows some of the various ways that the www.wrox.com URL can be encoded.

Table 10-2

Encoding Example(s)	Type of Encoding/Description
http://www.wrox.com	Normal plain ASCII text DNS domain name
http://208.215.179.178	IP address (decimal-dotted). Uses normal IPv4 address instead.
http://3503797170	IP address in base 10 (double word or DWORD decimal)
http:// 0320.0327.0263.0262	IP address in base 8 (octal)
http://www%2Ewrox%2Ecom http://%77%77%77%2E%77%72%6F%78%2E%63%6F%6D	Percent hexadecimal (base 16) encoding
http://www.wrox.com/anythingIwant/.%2e	Percent encoding reverse — several *control characters* will "backspace" over the previous portion of the URL
http://0xD0D7B3B2	
http:// 0xD0.0xD7.0xB3.0xB2	Hexadecimal notation

Note 1: Not all of these examples work in Internet Explorer, and some depend on the version of IE. Most of the malformed examples have been disabled in IE 6 XP SP2 and IE 7.x.

Note 2: You can use the URL Calculator (www.searchlores.org/zipped/urlcalc.zip) to see some of the encoded outcomes of your favorite URLs.

The following reference is a good site for hexadecimal URL conversions: www.w3schools.com/tags/ref_urlencode.asp. A good paper on URL encoding can be found at www.technicalinfo.net/papers/URLEmbeddedAttacks.html.

There are several other ways of encoding, and of course all the methods can be mixed together to fool the nonsecurity-aware user. In order to defeat these types of encoding tricks, the browser must "normalize" the link first to its plaintext ASCII equivalent using great care, and then evaluate it. Sometimes a mixture of malicious encoding and other spoofing tricks works when complex encoding won't (see Table 10-3).

Table 10-3

Encoding Example(s)	Type of Encoding/Description
http://www.wrox.com/ www.microsoft.com.downloads .patches/.%2e	Percent encoding reverse — several *control characters* will "backspace" over the previous portion of the URL
http://208.215.179.178/ www.microsoft.com.downloads .patches/.%2e	Mixture of IPv4 address and the previous example
http://%77%77%77%2E%77%72% 6F%78%2E%63%6F%6D/ www.microsoft.com.downloads .patches	The end user only sees the Microsoft download reference
http://www.microsoft.com @downloads.example.com http://www.microsoft.com @%77%77%77%2E%77%72%6F% 78%2E%63%6F%6D	The @ sign in the middle of a URL is usually indicative of a login name and password being passed to the web site, but in this case it is just a hacker trick. The hacker's website will ignore the fake login, but the end user sees www.microsoft.com.
http://www.eBay.com.badsite.com	In this case, the user sees www.ebay.com and thinks the link is legitimate, but www.eBay.com is the server name at badsite.com.
http://www.BankofAmericaUSA.com	
http://support.micosoft.com/ downloads.patches	
http://wwwebay.badsite.com	Sound-alike web sites fool many users.

There really are an unlimited number of ways to fool unsuspecting end users. Phishers even write scripts that pop up dialog boxes, message boxes, or other windows that hover over the true URL, so that even though the browser is displaying the true web site URL, the end user sees the fake URL.

Phishers have even used legitimate web sites to redirect victims to the malicious web sites. Several legitimate web sites have functions that can be manipulated to redirect browsers to outside web sites. The format is something like the following:

```
www.goodsite.com/scripts/goodscript.asp?www.badsite.com/login
```

The legitimate good site contains a script or feature that allows the legitimate web site to quickly redirect the user to the bad site. Here's a real redirection example received by the author:

```
http://www.medicallab.com.tw/%20/https::/www.paypal.com/cgi-bin/webscr/update.html
```

Malware, especially spyware, will spoof the user outside of IE. Several malware programs have re-written the user's DNS HOSTS file so that legitimately specified URLs point to redirected sites. Other rogue programs poison the DNS server's cache (often completely unknown to the user) so that the legitimately typed address ends up redirecting the user to the malicious site. Spyware and adware programs often manipulate the browser's proxy settings so that all transactions pass through a malicious proxy server to and from the legitimate web sites.

To fix these types of attacks, the browser needs complex anti-spoofing mechanisms. Internet Explorer 7.x contains significant upgrades to its anti-spoofing and anti-phishing mechanisms. Good reading on the different mechanisms can be found at www.technicalinfo.net/papers/Phishing4.html. Microsoft has a good anti-spoofing article at http://support.microsoft.com/?id=833786.

Buffer Overflow

When a malicious hacker or program overflows a service or process, they normally get the permissions and credentials that the program was running in. Internet Explorer sustains several buffer overflows a year, although they are always quickly patched. Such was the case with the Web Browser ActiveX control (www.kb.cert.org/vuls/id/842160) in 2004 and the JPEG image buffer overflow (http://secunia.com/advisories/12528) in 2005. Unfortunately, too many users run IE using admin credentials. Windows Vista and its Protected Mode will run IE as a restricted user by default, decreasing the risk of IE buffer overflow. Luckily, Internet Explorer has not suffered a buffer overflow that was remotely exploitable that also allowed privilege escalation. IE 7 should make this less likely.

Cross-Site Scripting

Cross-site scripting (XSS) is a situation in which scripting in one IE window or frame (i.e., the malicious window) is able to interact with another window, web site, or frame in an unauthorized manner. In most cases, the malicious web site is attempting to steal confidential information intended for the legitimate site. A simple example would be when a user is tricked into visiting a malicious web site. The user either leaves the malicious site open or closes it, and then opens a legitimate web site. Maybe the legitimate web site is a banking web site asking the user to log on. The malicious web site might be able to launch a XSS attack whereby the logon prompt is spoofed and the information collected is sent to the malicious web site. The malicious web site can then send the stolen information to the legitimate web site where the user is none the wiser. The malicious web site could even spoof the SSL session. The user would see the 'lock" icon (i.e., SSL status) at the bottom of IE and think the web page is secure. However, the session they could be seeing as encrypted and authenticated would be between IE and the malicious web site, something they would not discover unless they clicked on the SSL icon and looked at the digital certificate.

Cross-site scripting attacks are very common. According to www.secunia.com, they accounted for 10% of IE vulnerabilities over the last three years. Microsoft has worked hard in IE 6.x and even more so in IE 7.x to prevent cross-site scripting attacks. One of the things they have done in IE 7.x is to make SSL/TLS session details more visible. A user clicking on the SSL icon can view the digital certificate and details (see Figure 10-3). An excellent discussion on cross-site scripting can be found at www.cgisecurity .com/articles/xss-faq.shtml.

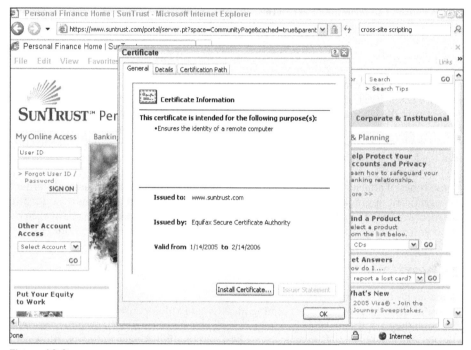

Figure 10-3

Zone Manipulation

Internet Explorer has five different security zones:

❏   Internet

❏   Local intranet

❏   Trusted sites

❏   Restricted sites

❏   Local Computer

Internet security zones allow users to granularly define specific permissions for different Internet or intranet resources. Mature IE users wish for more zones or the ability to make customized zones, but most other browsers do not have this type of feature at all. Internet Explorer allows users (or administrators) to define ahead of time particular security permissions and privileges for various web sites. Of course, if a malicious user or program can make their content "jump" between a zone of fewer privileges to one of more permissions without the end user's consent, many security vulnerabilities can take place. This indeed has been a long ongoing weakness and problem with IE and its security zones.

Local Computer Zone

The first four zones are readily accessible in IE (see Figure 10-4) by choosing Tools ➪ Internet Options, and then selecting the Security tab. The last zone is not easily user definable and represents content residing on the local computer. The Local Computer zone (also known as the My Computer zone) was one of the most privileged zones in Internet Explorer. All content residing in the Local Computer zone executes with the permissions of the logged in user and was not otherwise restricted until Windows XP SP2 and Windows Server 2003 SP1. In all of the latest Windows versions, the Local Computer zone is locked down with additional restrictions to prevent malware execution.

The Local Computer zone lockdown establishes the following new default behaviors:

❑ ActiveX controls may not run.

❑ Java applets may not run.

❑ Users may be prompted before they can run a script.

❑ Users may be prompted before they can open a data source belonging to a domain other than the original server.

Figure 10-4

The Local Computer zone cannot be manipulated in IE by the end user, but it can be configured using registry edits and programmatically. This is bad for the end user and administrator but good for malware.

The zones can be manipulated in the registry at `HKLM\SOFTWARE\Microsoft\Windows\CurrentVersion\Internet Settings\Zones`. Each zone is represented by the numbers 0 to 4, going from least to most restrictive. 0 is the My Computer zone, 1 is the Intranet sites zone, 2 is the Trusted sites zone, 3 is the Internet zone, and 4 is the Restricted sites zone. If you are interested in manipulating zones using the registry, read Microsoft KB article #182569 (`http://support.microsoft.com/?id=182569`). Editing zones via the registry allows a higher level of granularity than you can obtain through IE (i.e., defining of acceptable TCP/IP port numbers and protocols for each zone), but for most users IE zone settings are best configured in IE.

IE 6 SP2 for XP and IE 6 for W2K3 SP1 introduced increased protections on the Local Computer zone intended to prevent malicious code from exploiting the higher privileges of its local location.

Internet Site Zone

The Internet site is the default zone for all content not previously defined as residing in one of the other zones. Most of the time when you are surfing on the Internet using IE, the content being downloaded will reside in the Internet zone. The permissions and privileges in the Internet zone are moderately restricted (called *Medium* security) compared to the other zones. The security level is appropriate for most Internet sites but is too lax when unpatched vulnerabilities are prevalent. Many Internet attacks can be stymied when scripting and ActiveX controls are disabled, which the Internet zone allows by default. If a widespread vulnerability is present, users can benefit greatly by customizing the security (covered below) to disable scripting and other non-HTML content. Unfortunately, disabling the additional types of content all the time will cause errors on many web sites. Many security experts wish the most popular web sites used less special features and non-HTML content so that the Internet zone could be locked down more to prevent many malicious attacks without causing problems with legitimate content and web sites. Most users could benefit by customizing the Internet security zone to an acceptable level of usability and security.

The Internet site zone's default security level was moved to Medium-High in IE 7.

Local Intranet Zone

The Local intranet zone is a zone with high default privileges. The default security level is *Medium-low*. The intent is that users (or administrators) place internal trusted web sites in the Local intranet zone, and any sites in this zone will have elevated privileges. By default, all web sites residing on the local LAN (and other defined private IP subnets) will be placed in the Local intranet zone without the user having to specifically add the web site. External web sites can be added as well (see Figure 10-5), although users should remember that sites in this zone have elevated privileges.

Figure 10-5

As Figure 10-5 shows, along with the default selections, there are several options under the Local Intranet zone. The first is *Include all local (intranet) sites not listed in other zones*. This means that any server sites on the local network not listed in the Trusted sites or Restricted sites zone will automatically be included here. If you disable this option, sites on the local network will not automatically be included in the Local intranet zone. The *Include all sites that bypass the proxy server* option assumes that IE uses a non-transparent proxy to access the non-local site. By enabling the option, IE will add any sites that are excluded from having to be filtered through the proxy server. The reasoning is that only trusted sites would be excluded from being handled by the proxy server; and because they are trusted, they should be included by default in the Local intranet zone.

The *Include all network paths (UNCs)* option instructs Windows to include any NetBIOS shares in the Local intranet zone. This setting means that any security choices made on the Local intranet zone might impact regular Windows drive mappings. The Advanced button allows sites to be added manually. By default, the sites added to this location must be protected by using the HTTPS protocol to ensure site location authenticity, but this option is often deselected.

The Local Intranet zone will be disabled by default in IE 7 for non-domain computers.

Trusted Sites

Sites placed in the Trusted sites zone have minimal restrictions and a *Low* security level. Most actions and content will be allowed to execute without user intervention. Even the highest-risk actions only require the user to acknowledge before they proceed. Unlike the Local intranet zone, the Trusted sites zone has no included web sites by default. New sites can be required to be protected by HTTPS, the default, or just unsecured HTTP.

The Trusted sites zone's default security level was moved to Medium in IE 7.

Restricted Sites

The Restricted sites zone, as its name implies, restricts most non-HMTL content and activity by default. The security level is *High*. The only activity allowed without user intervention is pop-up ad blocking and font downloading. By default, no sites are within this zone. The Restricted sites zone has no HTTPS requirement option. Most users won't have any entries here, because if the web site is high risk, they should not go there. With that said, if a user plans on visiting a high-risk web site, they should put the web site's domain name here, although don't expect IE's High security level setting to prevent all attacks. Malicious web sites often have unknown "zero-day" attacks or use social engineering methods to trick the user into executing malicious code.

You can also create your own IE security zones programmatically or using registry edits, although these zones are not easy to configure and cannot be accessed using the IE GUI. For more information, see http://blogs.msdn.com/ie/archive/2005/01/26/361228.aspx. I hope that Microsoft creates an easy way for an unlimited number of new zones to be easily created and configured in the future. Why they have not done this already is a mystery. This chapter will cover each IE security setting and the default settings in each of default IE security zones in detail.

File Execution

Many IE attacks are successful at getting malicious content downloaded to the user's system and then executed. To do this, a malicious web site must instantiate one or more file downloads, and be able to trick the user into executing it or exploit a browser vulnerability. IE will not execute most potentially malicious content without the consent of the user, so malicious web sites will often attempt to download bad content to the user's local hard drive with the first command and then execute it with a second. If the malware is successful with both commands, the content, now considered part of IE's Local Computer zone, will be able to execute any future instructions in the context of the logged-in user. These attacks are known as *cross-zone* attacks, since the code originated from the Internet zone and was able to be placed in the more trusted Local Computer zone.

To prevent a web site or malware from easily accomplishing this process, IE downloads all content to a randomly created (and randomly named) file and subdirectories under the Temporary Internet Files (TIF) folder. Because the content is downloaded into unpredictable names and locations, malicious web sites cannot easily find and execute the content. At least, that is how the cross-zone defense is supposed to work.

Over the years, many malware programs have been able to find exploits in IE that allowed it to predict or determine where the malicious content would be downloaded and the temporary name given. IE 6, after many successful attacks, has been significantly strengthened against cross-zone attacks. XP Pro SP2 IE 6.x stopped most of the known cross-zone attacks and IE 7 is further strengthened. IE7 treats all downloaded code as belonging to the Internet zone even when it is stored or called from the local hard drive. Still, given the complexity of trying to keep the different zones separate, it would be unlikely that this class of attack would remain unexploited in the coming years.

> One of the key aspects of file execution attacks is that IE usually downloads the content to the TIF area for evaluation even when the content is not going to be executed. It would be better if the content were evaluated and then downloaded, but it often appears the other way around, and this leads to many exploits that would otherwise not happen. For that to work, IE would have to restrict itself to behavior promised by the file name extension. As this is not the case, the first part of the file would have to be pulled down to sniff the header data for MZ marker, etc. IE may also initiate the downloading of material before the Save As dialog box is dismissed for performance reasons (this is welcomed by most users paying by the minute for dial-up service).

Directory Traversal

One of the most frequent types of attacks, although growing less successful over time, is the directory traversal exploit. In this type of attack, much like the URL spoofing attack class, a malicious link or web site attempts to access content that should be protected against remote interaction. If the attack is successful, a malformed URL can allow a remote attack or program to access content that the normal security permissions should prevent. Directory traversal attacks usually do this by using a combination of one or more \ . . \ sequences. In Windows, a single period (i.e., .) in a directory listing means the current directory. Two periods (i.e., . .) means the parent directory. Legitimate users often use . . \ or \ . . \ to jump among various subdirectories under a common parent (e.g., cd . . \test to jump from c:\parent\ example to c:\parent\test). Malicious URLs will contain one or more of these sequences in order to confuse the HTML parser and access resources they otherwise could not.

Here's an example from a Windows Server 2003 IE traversal vulnerability (http://secunia.com/ advisories/9989):

```
<a href="shell:cache\..\..\Local Settings\examplefile.html">
```

Malicious directory traversals can only be stopped by a rewrite of the HTML parser or a third-party intrusion detection tool. Thankfully, after many example exploits, directory traversal attacks are becoming less successful.

Malicious Content

It goes without saying that the content the user downloads can simply be malicious from the start. If the user can be socially engineered into running a piece of malicious code, it can often bypass any warning system or defense mechanism. Users are almost always warned about potential maliciousness before they run it, but most users are willing to take the risk that the program they are running is what it claims to be and will almost always run the program (or click on the file attachment). To paraphrase another security expert whose name I can't remember, "Users will bypass any warning, click on any file, ignore any security teaching to download a screensaver with pigs flying out of someone's butt!" That is indeed the problem. Most users will ignore all the good advice that we have given them, and when a security decision is left up to them, they will often make the wrong decision. That's why all software, including IE, needs to be better about not allowing truly malicious software to reach the end user.

MIME Type Mismatch

As covered before, MIME Types is the way different types of content are identified in a browser (and other applications). The web site indicates the MIME Type in the "TYPE=" or the "Content-Type=" field of the web page hosting the content to be downloaded. IE used to take the web site's word that the MIME type indicated matched the file format. This led to several vulnerabilities. For example, IE would download a file indicating it was a "skin" overlay for a multimedia player, but after downloading the "skin" turned out to be a malicious JavaScript, and executed as such.

Now, IE looks at the MIME Type indicated by the web page, checks the HKCR\MIME\Database\ Content Type registry key, and locates the correct file extension. If IE thinks there is a problem between the indicated file type and the true file type, it will then read the first 200 bytes of the file (called *MIME sniffing*) and see if it can determine the true file format type. If it can determine the file format type from the MIME sniff, it will then run the correct related program. If IE cannot determine the file type at this point, it relies on the file extension used by the file and executes only the program associated with that file extension. IE will reject files it has determined are invalid or corrupted. IE 6.x, Windows XP SP2, and IE 7.x all have enhanced MIME typing abilities, although MIME Type mismatches are still found every now and then — enough to be on the lookout for them. Any browser that only uses file extensions to identify a file type is very prone to MIME Type mismatches. If you want more information on IE's MIME typing abilities, see http://msdn.microsoft.com/library/default.asp?url=/workshop/ networking/moniker/overview/mime_handling.asp

Cookie Manipulation

Cookies are text files placed on a user's computer in order to keep track of the session state of a particular web site from click to click. Without cookies (or other session state mechanisms), web sites would not be able to keep track of which user sent what click and request. A user trying to buy jeans would have to enter their information (i.e., jean size, jean brand, color, type, credit card number, name, address, etc.) all on one screen, or else the web site would lose track.

Instead, a cookie placed by a web site usually contains information identifying a particular user. Every time a web page is requested, the delivering web site can read the cookie, get the identifying information, and then use a backend database to keep track of which user is doing what. It's the way that Amazon always says hello to you and recommends books that might hold your interest every time you log in.

Early on, web vendors put the user's identifying information in plaintext, in the cookie. For example, banks would put the user's bank account number and PIN number in the cookie. Other e-commerce companies would put the user's account information and credit card information in the cookie, and use the cookie request to retrieve the confidential information.

Unfortunately, two main problems arose. One, if a malicious web site can retrieve another web site's cookie (as is often the case), the malicious site can then "become" the user on the legitimate web site. Two, if what was stored in the cookie was the user's plaintext account number and that account number could be predicted, a malicious user could spoof their own cookie and become another user.

For example, the malicious user could join a popular e-commerce site and see if the cookie contained a predictable account number. For example, if the malicious user joins multiple times under different names and reads their own cookie, they might see that every time they join, their account number is incremented by 1. Then, by modifying their cookie and incrementing or decrementing the cookie account number value, they can spoof and become another user. The web site is none the wiser; it's simply reading a cookie value. Unfortunately, this type of issue is still common. One of the world's largest online banks was just recently found to have predictable, plaintext user account numbers stored in their cookies. IE 6.x and later has very strong cookie handling, but ultimately it is up to web site programmers to ensure that their cookies can't be spoofed.

> *Some browser versions also allow scripts to be stored and executed from cookies, which can allow malicious execution on the local computer.*

Browser Interface Manipulation

As recounted in Table 1-1 in Chapter 1, spyware and adware has taken browser interface manipulation to a whole new level. There are dozens of ways IE can be modified, with or without the user's permission, to control the behavior of IE. Spyware often changes the way searchers are done, in order to direct users to locations other than where they would want to knowingly go. Menu bars are modified, added, or deleted; start or home pages can be modified; URLs are redirected; buttons, toolbars, and menu bars added; virtually the entire IE interface can be customized — for good or evil.

Plug-In Exploits

It's not just IE that is exploitable, but any program it loads. Browser plug-ins, also known as *Browser Helper Objects (BHOs)* or *add-ons,* add additional opportunities for the bad guys to break in. Nearly every popular add-on has had one or more exploits, including Macromedia's Flash, Sun's Java Virtual Machine, Microsoft Windows Messenger, and Winamp. The popular PDF viewer, Adobe Acrobat Reader, has had six vulnerabilities in the last two years alone. Without a doubt, every additional add-on software product added to IE increases the risk of a successful exploitation. IE 7.x has the ability to load with a quick "no-add-ons" feature to decrease vulnerabilities. IE 6.x with Windows XP SP2 and later has the ability to manage (choose Tools ⇨ Manage Add-ons) or delete add-on packages (see Figure 10-6).

Secunia.com is an excellent web site to search on previous and existing IE vulnerabilities. It displays vulnerabilities by IE version, date of discovery, criticality, details, and whether or not a patch is available.

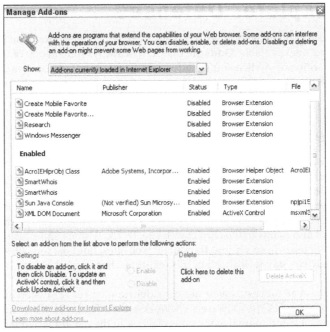

Figure 10-6

Browser Tests

At any given time there are between 6 to 20 unpatched IE vulnerabilities, although most of them aren't critical. If you are concerned about whether your version of IE is completely patched and what vulnerabilities it is still susceptible to, go to a browser test web site and let them check your browser for you. Most of them are safe. Here are a few browser test web sites:

❏   `http://bcheck.scanit.be/bcheck` (the best browser test site)

❏   `www.jasons-toolbox.com/BrowserSecurity`

❏   `www.anonymizer.com` (click on the Privacy Test, the only test that is a real concern is the Clipboard test)

When the author tested IE 7 beta 1 at the first browser test web site listed in the preceding list, it ran 24 checks. IE 7 passed all checks without a problem. The site maintains statistics and it claims that 32% of the browsers tested contained critical vulnerabilities. It also claims that IE had at least one unpatched, remotely exploitable vulnerability for 98% of 2004.

Internet Explorer Defenses

IE is a complex piece of popular software. Hackers are never going to stop attacking it, and it is unlikely to suddenly become unexploitable. Odds are that IE will always remain one of the most exposed and attacked pieces of software in Microsoft's platform. Still, running IE doesn't mean getting a guaranteed successful attack. Following are the many defenses you can take to prevent IE exploitation, going from most useful to least.

Don't Browse Untrusted Web Sites

The number one way to prevent malicious exploitation is to not visit unknown and untrusted web sites. Don't click on "weird" links sent to you in e-mail. Look out for strange-looking phishing URLS, like those listed in Tables 10-2 and 10-3. Too many encoded characters or sound-alike names and URLs should set off warning bells. Any company asking for your financial information unexpectedly is probably a fraud. Verify your SSL links by scrutinizing the accompanying digital certificate. Make sure all the information is valid and points to the correct web site. IE 7.x, with its anti-phishing filter, is making great strides in preventing users from visiting fraudulent web sites. But fake web sites can be made in seconds and more than likely can stay well ahead of IE's real-time checking behavior.

If you just have to visit an untrusted web site, consider running the IE session in a virtual environment such as Microsoft's Virtual PC or VMware's VMWorkstation. That way, if anything ugly happens, you can reset the session and minimize the potential risk to the real underlying OS. Microsoft has already released the Shared Computer Toolkit for Windows XP (`www.microsoft.com/windowsxp/sharedaccess/overview.mspx`), which, among other features, prevents permanent changes (i.e., made by malware) from being saved in between reboots. Also, consider using a less functional alternate browser or one that has been set to run no active content at all (e.g., Lynx) when visiting untrusted web sites.

Many people run less-functional browsers all the time with the hope that it will prevent malicious exploitation. While it may minimize the risk, at the expense of functionality, IE's coding cannot be removed from Windows. Even when you run an alternate browser, it is very possible for a malicious program to call IE's coding (e.g., via e-mail or an embedded link in Microsoft Office, etc.). Even if IE isn't your main browser, be sure to install all patches and updates. Not doing so, even if you don't use it, will increase exposure risk.

Don't Let Non-Admin Users Be Logged in as Administrators

Most IE malware will fail to work if the logged in user is not logged in as administrator. Several exploit types, such as buffer overflows, can still happen, but the vast majority of popular malware (i.e., spyware, adware, etc.) will fail to work if the user is not an administrator. Windows Vista's Protected Mode will run IE in a restricted user mode (with even fewer rights than a normal user) by default. The Microsoft Shared Computer Toolkit for Windows XP previously mentioned can also force IE to run in a restricted user's mode. You can also use Software Restriction Policies and the Basic User security identity (as shown in Chapter 9) to run any IE version on XP Pro and later in a restricted user mode.

Use IE 6 XP SP2 or IE 7

Microsoft's latest browsers are their most secure built to date. All Windows workstations should be running the latest version of IE possible. Fully patched versions of Windows 98 and later (including Windows NT 4.0) can run IE 6.x SP1. Windows XP Pro SP2 and later can run IE 6.x SP2 or IE 7.x. There is no excuse for running an earlier browser version unless you are running Windows 95, Windows 3.x, or Windows NT 3.x. Many resources suggest using a non-Microsoft browser, but as Table 10-1 showed, you lose functionality and end up having to patch the other browsers just as much as they become popular.

Keep IE Patches Updated

Once you are running IE 6.x or 7.x, keep on top of the patches. Patch any critical vulnerabilities as soon as you can after testing. These days, many IE exploits are getting released within three days of patch announcement. In the past you could afford to wait a few weeks. No longer. Immediate testing and deployment of critical patches should be a priority of any organization.

Customize Default Internet Explorer Security Zones

The default settings in IE's five security zones are often set at the right usability/security level for most users. However, administrators and users concerned with security are usually extremely, and rightly, paranoid about malware. Understanding each of the security settings in IE, and setting them to an acceptable level, can make surfing the Internet more enjoyable and secure. There are two major sets of security settings: those that can be set in each security zone and those available under the Advanced tab (both are available under Tools ➪ Internet Options). The Advanced options apply to all security zones.

Many of the setting options are Enable, Disable, or Prompt. Enable means the corresponding action described will occur without needing approval from the user. Disable means the action will be declined without user interaction. Prompt means the user will be prompted to approve or reject the action.

Let's start with the zone settings first. I'll discuss each feature, describe the potential vulnerability, give the default settings in each zone, and finish with my default recommendations for the Internet zone. A table will summarize the defaults and recommendations after the larger discussions.

The security settings discussed here are the ones available in IE 7 beta 1. Not all settings are available in all IE versions. The settings new in IE 7 will be noted.

.NET Framework-reliant components – Run components not signed with Authenticode

The .NET Framework is Microsoft's new client-server programming environment (loosely comparable to Java's virtual machine environment). Although .NET is not a dominant form of programming across the Windows platform at the time of this writing, it is expected to become dominant over the next few years. Code is signed to prove authorship. Authenticode is Microsoft's digital signing mechanism for authenticating code, scripts, and ActiveX controls. Any software publisher (i.e., vendor) can purchase an Authenticode digital certificate for code signing.

Running an unsigned component means that you cannot automatically authenticate who created and initially distributed the component (i.e., it is untrusted). Microsoft allows unsigned components to run automatically in all zones but the Restricted zone. I believe Microsoft was too lax on this setting. It should be set to disabled in Internet and Restricted sites zones.

This option and the next may not be available unless you have also installed the .NET Framework client software.

.NET Framework-reliant components – Run components signed with Authenticode

Signed code is rarely a problem. Signed code can contain bugs and viruses (hopefully, both unknown to the signer at the time the code was signed), but it is rarely malicious. If you trusted signed code to be non-malicious, you can accept it to run automatically. There have been some instances where spyware and adware companies used signed code to distribute their largely unwanted software. Microsoft enables this in all zones but the Restricted zone. Because of the spyware and adware issues, I suggest this setting be set to Prompt in the Internet zone.

ActiveX controls and plug-ins – Automatic prompting for ActiveX controls

ActiveX controls can be virtually any content, executable, or script delivered over a network through IE. Java applets are even delivered as ActiveX controls, in most cases. Windows uses dozens to hundreds of ActiveX controls. Most aren't needed in IE and one of the big changes in IE 7.x is to not allow any ActiveX control to run in IE by default, except those expressly authorized by the user or admin. This is the opposite behavior for IE 6.x and earlier.

This particular setting determines whether or not the user will be prompted (see Figure 10-7) by a pop-up dialog box to install an ActiveX control or plug-in. If disabled, the web site will attempt to download and execute the content, but IE will not prompt the user with a dialog box. Instead (when IE 6.x XP SP2 or later is installed), the user will be warned on the yellow information bar about an ActiveX control needing to be installed. The information bar warning is less obvious than a pop-up dialog box in the middle of the browser window.

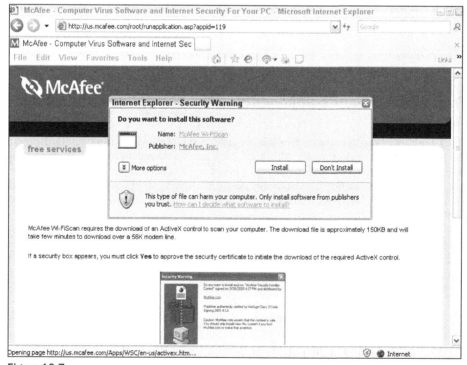

Figure 10-7

Microsoft enables this option in the Local Intranet and Trusted sites zones and disables it in the rest. Configuring this setting is up to the user, although I always like to be prompted in an obvious manner for any ActiveX controls that are trying to be installed. Otherwise, a web site feature may fail and it might not be readily apparent what is wrong.

ActiveX controls and plug-ins – Binary and script behaviors

Binary behaviors (`http://msdn.microsoft.com/workshop/browser/behaviors/howto/creating.asp`) were introduced in IE 5.5 and allow binary programs to be linked to and control HTML content. A binary behavior is a compiled object that can interact directly with the underlying OS. Its code cannot be read or examined using normal view source commands. They can be used to do many malicious things from a web page. Prior to Windows XP SP2 and Windows Server 2003 SP1 (where this setting first arrived), there was no way to prevent a binary behavior in any IE security zone, including sites residing in the Restricted sites zone. Now, by default, binary behaviors are disabled in the Restricted sites zone but allowed in the rest. I think binary behaviors are too powerful to allow from any Internet site. Accordingly, this option should be set to Disabled (or administrator approved).

ActiveX controls and plug-ins – Download signed ActiveX controls

Signed ActiveX controls usually present little risk unless signed by a spyware or adware vendor. Microsoft prompts the user to approve these on Internet sites and Local Intranet sites zones, enables them on Trusted sites, and disables them for web sites residing in the Restricted sites zone. These defaults are acceptable.

ActiveX controls and plug-ins – Download unsigned ActiveX controls

Unsigned ActiveX controls are highly risky and should be disabled usually or prompted if you expect to come in contact with needed unsigned controls. Microsoft disables them in all zones except Trusted sites, where the option is set to Prompt. The default settings are good.

ActiveX controls and plug-ins – Initialize and script ActiveX controls not marked as safe

Once an ActiveX control or plug-in (plug-ins are usually ActiveX controls) is downloaded (the options being decided in the two previous paragraphs), there is still the matter of whether to execute them. Vendors can mark their ActiveX controls as *Safe for Initialization* and *Safe for Scripting*. The first option determines whether the control can be initialized (i.e., started and executed). The second option determines whether it can be directed by scripting, which means it could have different outcomes based upon the script. If both options are selected, any web page can invoke them.

The idea is if the vendor determines the control is safe (i.e., can't be used in a harmful way), why not let other web pages and programmers re-use the control? Unfortunately, there is no official guidance or testing tool that a vendor can run to find out if their "safe" control is really safe. In over a dozen different exploits over the years, a control marked safe for scripting was used to do something malicious. In this particular option, IE is asking whether or not to allow web pages to initialize and script controls that are not marked safe. Considering that controls marked safe for scripting are potentially dangerous, ones that were tested and not found to be safe by their vendors definitely should not be allowed to run. Microsoft disables them in all zones, excepted Trusted sites, where the option is set to Prompt. The default settings are good.

ActiveX controls and plug-ins – Run ActiveX controls and plug-ins

This setting has a huge impact on IE. It determines whether IE can run ActiveX controls and plug-ins at all, regardless of their safety, and regardless of whether they are signed or unsigned. Disabling this feature defeats many, if not most, exploits that have attacked IE over the years. Unfortunately, it is such an all-or-nothing proposition that disabling it causes problems with most complex (i.e., popular) web sites.

Microsoft enables this option by default in all zones but the Restricted sites zone, where it is disabled. This is an acceptable default. However, if you are worried about a widespread, malicious IE vulnerability that can be stopped by disabling this option, consider disabling this option until a patch or other alternative defense can be applied. Alternately, IE can be instructed only to allow administrator-approved controls to run. In order to use this option, you must use group policy, an administrative template, a security template, or the IE Administrator's Kit — and know the control's CLSID.

ActiveX controls and plug-ins – Script ActiveX controls marked safe for scripting

This setting covers whether controls previously marked "safe" can be scripted (i.e., one-half of the marked safe for scripting and initialization dilemma). This is one of the toughest calls because it has been involved in many vulnerabilities, but to disable it is to cause problems with many legitimate web sites. Microsoft enables it by default in all zones but the Restricted sites zone, where it is disabled. This is an acceptable default. However, if you are worried about a widespread, malicious IE vulnerability that can be stopped by disabling this option, consider disabling this option until a patch or other alternative defense can be applied. Microsoft left this as Enabled in the High template used in Restricted Zones until comparatively recently, perhaps as late as (but not including) Windows XP. Always check this in older versions of Windows, especially after re-installing the OS or IE.

Downloads – Automatic prompting for file downloads

This setting determines whether the user will be prompted by a pop-up dialog box for normal file downloads. In most cases, the answer should be yes. It is always nice to know when a web site is trying to download content. If this option is disabled and the next option is enabled, then the user will download and potentially execute files without acknowledgment. That particular situation would be harder to defend. This option should be enabled on all zones. Interestingly, when this setting is disabled, most file downloads still prompt the user before proceeding. Internet Explorer contains the following hard-coded list of file types (by file extension) for which the warning dialog box cannot be disabled:

```
ASP, BAS, BAT, CHM (IE5 only), CMD, COM, EXE, LNK, INF, REG, ISP, PCD, MST, PIF,
SCR, HLP, HTA (IE5 only), JS, JSE, URL, VBS, VBE, WS, and WSH.
```

Downloads – File download

Disabling this option prevents all file downloads. If the previous option is enabled, it is usually safe to enable this option. Microsoft enables this option in all zones but the Restricted sites zone, where it is disabled. The defaults are acceptable.

Downloads – Font download

This option determines whether IE HTML fonts, normally needed for the correct presentation of a web page, can be downloaded automatically. It is enabled in all zones by default except the Restricted sites zone, where it is set to Prompt. The default settings are good.

Miscellaneous – Access data sources across domains

This setting determines whether a web page can retrieve data from another server located in a different domain. If set to disabled, it will only allow data to be retrieved from the same server the originating web page is being served from or from another server in the same domain. A few exploits have been accomplished when this setting is enabled. Most web sites access data on servers in the same domain. If this feature is not needed, keep it disabled. Microsoft disables it in most zones, including the Internet zone, but enables it in the Trusted sites zone and prompts in the Local Intranet zone. The default settings are acceptable in most cases.

Miscellaneous – Allow META REFRESH

A Meta-Refresh is an HTML command that instructs a browser to refresh the current web page after a periodic interval. It can also be used to redirect a user, without their permission, to another web page. It has been used maliciously many times, but as long as other critical vulnerabilities are patched, there is little risk. Legitimate use of Meta-Refreshes is common. Microsoft enables this option in all zones but the Restricted sites zone. The default option is normally okay.

Miscellaneous – Allow scripting of Internet Explorer Web browser control

This is a new option in IE 6.x XP SP2, although the control is not. The Webbrowser control is a stand-alone ActiveX control that can be used by programmers to add a mini-HTML browser to their application. After a few vulnerabilities were found by enabling this option by default, Microsoft disables it in the Internet and Restricted sites zones. The default option is acceptable.

Miscellaneous – Allow script-initiated windows without size or position constraints

New in IE 6.x XP SP2, this option determines whether or not a web site can open a new IE window anywhere and of any size. Unscrupulous web advertisers often did this to make it difficult for the user to close the pop-up advertising window. It is disabled by default in the Internet and Restricted sites zones. This is an acceptable default choice.

Miscellaneous – Allow Web pages to use restricted protocols for active content

This is a new option in IE 6.x XP SP2 and later. You can define, in the zone registry settings, which protocols and port numbers are allowed in a particular zone. Using this setting you can define whether or not web sites in this zone can use protocols and port numbers not explicitly defined in the registry. Microsoft has this new option set to Prompt in most zones, and disabled in the Restricted sites zone. The default options are acceptable.

Miscellaneous – Display mixed content

This option determines whether or not you will be prompted when a web page tries to display content from an HTTP and HTTPS communications streams at the same time. If it is set to Prompt, you may receive the following "Security Information" message on the web pages that contain both secure (https) and nonsecure (http) content:

```
This page contains both secure and nonsecure items.

Do you want to display the nonsecure items?
```

This is a very common occurrence on HTTPS web sites, although to be truly secure they should never mix content types. All but the security paranoid disable this feature, even though Microsoft's default on all zones is Prompt. The default is acceptable unless you are particularly worried about spoofed HTTPS web sites.

This option has been enhanced in IE 7. Users will no longer see the mixed-content dialog box prompt shown above. IE7 will only render the secure content by default, and offers the user the opportunity to unblock the nonsecure content using the new Information Bar. This is an excellent change because in previous versions of IE, the user was asked the question without really knowing the difference between the secure and nonsecure content. Now users will see the secure content first, separated from the nonsecure content. Besides preventing some types of malicious attacks, it will prevent a lot of web site advertising.

Miscellaneous – Don't prompt for client certificate selection when no certificates or only one certificate exists

This setting was introduced in IE 5.5 SP1. When this option is set to Enable, IE does not prompt the user with a "Client Authentication" message when it connects to a web site that has no certificate or only one certificate. When Disabled, IE will display the following "Client Authentication" message even if the web site does not have a certificate or has only one certificate:

```
Identification

The Web site you want to view requests identification. Select the certificate to
use when connecting.
```

Microsoft enables it in the Local Intranet and Trusted sites zones and disables it elsewhere. This is an acceptable setting.

Miscellaneous – Drag and drop or copy and paste files

This determines whether files and folders can be dragged and dropped between client and server, or whether files and folders can be copied and pasted between client and server. Strangely, if disabled in the Internet zone, it will not allow the described options between mapped drives on your computer if the NetBIOS shares were mapped using IP addresses instead of names. Dragging and dropping files is also helpful for FTP and WebDAV operations. Microsoft enables this setting in all zones except Restricted sites, where it is set to Prompt. There is little misuse possible, so the defaults are acceptable.

Miscellaneous – Installation of desktop items

This setting determines whether or not a web site can install shortcuts and content to the user's desktop. It should be disabled or set to Prompt in most zones. Microsoft enables it only in the Trusted sites zone, disables it in the Restricted sites zone, and sets it to Prompt in the other two zones. The defaults are acceptable.

Miscellaneous – Launching programs and files in an IFRAME

This determines whether programs and files can be executed in an inline floating IE frame (i.e., IFRAME). Several vulnerabilities have used this feature over the years. It should be set to Prompt or Disabled. Microsoft enables it only in the Trusted sites zone, disables it in the Restricted sites zone, and sets it to Prompt in the other two zones. The defaults are acceptable.

Miscellaneous – Launching programs and unsafe files

This determines whether or not the hard-coded file types listed above can be launched or their associated programs executed. This is Enabled on the Local Intranet and Trusted Intranet sites zones, disabled on the Restricted sites zone, and set to Prompt on the Internet zone. The default is acceptable.

Miscellaneous – Navigate sub-frames across different domains

This setting determines whether it is possible to open a child subframe that references a server located in a different domain than its parent. A malicious web site could mimic a legitimate web site by inserting a window as a frame within the legitimate web site's window. This feature was used in a few exploits years ago, but now is not considered overly dangerous. Microsoft enables this feature by default in all zones but the Restricted sites zone. I prefer to set the option to Prompt in the Internet zone.

Miscellaneous – Open files based on content, not file extension

New in IE 6.x XP SP2, this option determines whether IE will read the first 200 bytes of a file's header to determine whether the file matches the MIME Type the web site claims it to be. If the content never tries to execute using a MIME type other than the one it was downloaded with, IE does not check the file header. But if there is a disagreement, IE will read the file header in an attempt to determine the correct MIME Type. It has rightly been enabled in all zones except for the Restricted sites zone. I would enable it there as well.

Miscellaneous – Software channel permissions

This setting specifies the computer's level of access for web-based software distribution channels. The possible values are: High safety, Low safety, and Medium safety.

- ❑ High safety — This setting prevents users from being notified about software updates by e-mail, prevents software packages from being automatically downloaded to users' computers, and prevents software packages from being automatically installed on users' computers.

- ❑ Medium safety — Notifies users about software updates by e-mail, and allows software packages to be automatically downloaded to (but not installed on) users' computers. The software packages must be validly signed; users are not prompted about the download.

- ❑ Low safety — This setting notifies users about software updates by e-mail, allows software packages to be automatically downloaded to users' computers, and allows software packages to be automatically installed on users' computers.

The Internet zone and Local Intranet zones are set to Medium safety. The Trusted sites zone is set to Low safety. The Restricted sites zone is set to High safety. The selections are reasonable.

Thanks to www.websecurealert.com for the detailed information on channel permissions displayed above. However, be aware that some of the free software at this location contains adware.

Miscellaneous – Submit nonencrypted form data

This option determines whether HTML pages in the zone can submit unencrypted forms to, or accept unencrypted forms from, servers in the zone. Forms sent using SSL are always allowed. This option is usually enabled so that unencrypted data can be submitted without a warning. The defaults are good.

Miscellaneous – Use Phishing Filter

New in IE 7.x, enabling this filter tells IE to send each new domain URL to Microsoft's anti-phishing servers for inspection before allowing the page to be displayed. If a site has been defined as fraudulent, the user will be warned. It slows down web surfing, but increases security significantly. It should be enabled on Internet and Restricted sites zone, and these are the Microsoft defaults.

Miscellaneous – Use Pop-up Blocker

A new setting in IE 6.x XP SP2, this determines whether the built-in pop-up blocker is turned on. Like the previous setting, it should be enabled for Internet and Restricted sites zones. This is the Microsoft default as well.

Miscellaneous – Userdata persistence

This setting determines whether a web site can save data about the user or the current session on the user's hard drive, much like a cookie would be able to do. This feature is used by many legitimate web sites, and although it can possibly be used maliciously, it's best to leave it turned on. Microsoft leaves it turned on by default for all zones except the Restricted sizes zone, and this is acceptable.

Miscellaneous – Web sites in less privileged web content zone can navigate into this zone

This is a new setting that prevents less privileged content from initiating new connections into higher-privileged zones. This was created to defeat a new type of malicious attack. Microsoft has this option enabled in most zones but disabled in the Restricted sites zone. I believe it should be disabled by default in the Internet zone.

Scripting – Active scripting

Another important setting. This determines whether scripting is allowed in IE. If turned off, it will disable JavaScript and VBScript engines. Although many IE exploits rely on scripting to work, so do most web sites. Leave enabled unless you are trying to defend against a widespread attack that cannot be stopped using alternative defenses. Microsoft enables this setting on all zones except the Restricted sites zone, and this is acceptable.

Scripting – Allow paste operations via script

This determines whether a web page script (see the Privacy Test at `www.anonymizer.com`) can copy information off the user's clipboard. It is interesting to see a web page "retrieve" information residing on the clipboard, especially if it contains a now plaintext password or information we forgot about. Microsoft enables this option in all zones except the Restricted sites zone. I believe it should be disabled across most zones.

Scripting – Allow status bar updates via script

This new option determines whether web sites can update the status bar using a script. Some malicious web sites use scripts to fraudulently modify IE's status bar, such as indicating whether SSL is enabled or not. This setting should be disabled for Internet sites, and is by Microsoft.

Scripting – Scripting of Java applets

This determines whether Java applets can be scripted. Although dozens of Java exploits have been discovered over the years, only one has ever been widespread. The overall risk is low. You can enable the scripting of Java applets on all zones except the Restricted sites zone, which is the Microsoft default.

User Authentication

Lastly, this option determines how IE will respond to a request for the browser to authenticate the user. In previous versions of IE, IE would always respond to authentication requests by trying to log in with the current user's name and password. Unfortunately, it is possible for malicious web sites to force unprotected Windows computers to use older, weaker authentication protocols (i.e., LAN Manager), which are easy to crack.

A common ploy was for a spammer to send the victim a spam e-mail that contained a one-pixel graphic (called a *web spider* or *beacon*) that needed to be downloaded from the spammer's malicious web server to display in the e-mail. Previous versions of Outlook and Outlook Express would attempt to download the graphic automatically to display in the e-mail. The hostile web site would request user authentication to download the web spider, and tell the victim's computer that it only understands the LM authentication protocol. Thus, all the victim does is open an e-mail and their computer sends back their logon name and password in an easily hackable format.

Now IE will only send the user's current logon name and password if the site is listed in the user's Local Intranet sites zone. Otherwise, IE will try to logon anonymously or prompt the user for their logon name and password. IE's default settings are acceptable.

Table 10-4 shows the default settings for each Internet security zone and their recommended settings. Asterisks appear next to the recommendations that deviate from Microsoft's defaults.

Table 10-4

Security Zone Setting	Default Internet Zone Setting	Default Local Intranet Zone Setting	Default Trusted Sites Zone Setting	Default Restricted Sites Zone Setting	Recommended Internet Zone Setting
.NET Framework-reliant components – Run components not signed with Authenticode	E	E	E	D	*D
.NET Framework-reliant components – Run components signed with Authenticode	E	E	E	D	*P
ActiveX controls and plug-ins – Automatic prompting for ActiveX controls	D	E	E	D	*E
ActiveX controls and plug-ins – Binary and script behaviors	E	E	E	D	*D
ActiveX controls and plug-ins – Download signed ActiveX controls	P	P	E	D	P
ActiveX controls and plug-ins – Download unsigned ActiveX controls	D	D	P	D	D

Table continued on following page

Security Zone Setting	Default Internet Zone Setting	Default Local Intranet Zone Setting	Default Trusted Sites Zone Setting	Default Restricted Sites Zone Setting	Recommended Internet Zone Setting
ActiveX controls and plug-ins – Initialize and script ActiveX controls not marked as safe	D	D	P	D	D
ActiveX controls and plug-ins – Run ActiveX controls and plug-ins	E	E	E	D	E
ActiveX controls and plug-ins – Script ActiveX controls marked safe for scripting	E	E	E	D	E
Downloads – Automatic prompting for file downloads	D	E	E	D	*E
Downloads – File download	E	E	E	D	E
Downloads – Font download	E	E	E	P	E
Miscellaneous – Access data sources across domains	D	P	E	D	D
Miscellaneous – Allow META REFRESH	E	E	E	D	E
Miscellaneous – Allow scripting of Internet Explorer Webbrowser control	D	E	E	D	D
Miscellaneous – Allow script-initiated windows without size or position constraints	D	E	E	D	D
Miscellaneous – Allow Web pages to use restricted protocols for active content	P	P	P	D	P
Miscellaneous – Display mixed content	P	P	P	P	P
Miscellaneous – Don't prompt for client certificate selection when no certificates or only one certificate exists	D	E	E	D	D
Miscellaneous – Drag and drop or copy and paste files	E	E	E	P	E
Miscellaneous – Installation of desktop items	P	P	E	D	P

Security Zone Setting	Default Internet Zone Setting	Default Local Intranet Zone Setting	Default Trusted Sites Zone Setting	Default Restricted Sites Zone Setting	Recommended Internet Zone Setting
Miscellaneous – Launching programs and files in an IFRAME	P	P	E	D	P
Miscellaneous – Launching programs and unsafe files	P	E	E	D	P
Miscellaneous – Navigate subframes across different domains	E	E	E	D	*P
Miscellaneous – Open files based on content, not file extension	E	E	E	D	E
Miscellaneous – Software channel permissions	Medium safety	Medium safety	Low safety	High safety	Medium safety
Miscellaneous – Submit non-encrypted form data	E	E	E	P	E
Miscellaneous – Use Phishing Filter	E	D	D	E	E
Miscellaneous – Use Pop-up Blocker	E	D	D	E	E
Miscellaneous – Userdata persistence	E	E	E	D	E
Miscellaneous – Web sites in less-privileged web content zone can navigate into this zone	E	E	P	D	*D
Scripting – Active scripting	E	E	E	D	E
Scripting – Allow paste operations via script	E	E	E	D	*D
Scripting – Allow status bar updates via script	D	E	E	D	D
Scripting – Scripting of Java applets	E	E	E	D	E
User Authentication	Automatic logon only in Intranet zone	Automatic logon only in Intranet zone	Automatic logon with current username and password	Prompt for user name and password	Automatic logon only in Intranet zone

E=Enabled, D=Disabled, P=Prompt User for decision

Advanced Settings

Advanced settings apply consistently across all IE security zones. Some of the settings complement or override the options available in the separate security zones. In general, settings chosen here supersede the individual settings in the security zones (but not always). For that reason, a user or administrator must be aware not to set configuration options in conflict with one another. These issues are noted when applicable.

There are over 60 different advanced settings in IE 7.x. This section of the chapter will cover only the settings that can purposely affect IE's overall security.

Browsing – Always send URLs as UTF-8

UTF-8 encoding allows a user to use URLs that include non-ASCII and foreign language characters, regardless of the language of the user's' operating system and browser language. Without UTF-8 encoding, a web server must be based on the same language code page as that of the user's in order to correctly render URLs containing non-ASCII or foreign characters. Disabling this would prevent some URL obscurity spoofing attacks, such as double-byte encoding, but it would cause problems with many legitimate web sites. Microsoft has it enabled by default, and it should probably stay that way.

Browsing – Automatically check for Internet Explorer Updates

This option, which is enabled by default, tells IE to run Windows Update periodically to check for new Microsoft patches. This is a great feature to leave enabled. Disable it if patching is handled by a centralized management software program (e.g., SUS, WSUS, SMS, etc.) or if the logged in user is never logged in as a local administrator. Windows Update initiated patches require that the end user be logged in as a local administrator to install.

Browsing – Disable Script Debugging (Internet Explorer or Other)

These two separate options tell IE whether or not to check for script errors. If enabled (the default), it disables this ability. This is usually only useful for programmers. If enabled, IE will warn the user when script errors are located. Malicious web sites often have code bugs, so disabling this feature would show an interested programmer the coded mistake automatically if they were so inclined. The delineation between IE script debugging and other foreign debuggers is new to the latest versions of IE.

Browsing – Display a notification about every script error

If enabled, IE will display a notification message about every error it encounters in a script. It is disabled by default and this is usually an acceptable choice. Like the last option, there is little to gain by enabling this feature unless the user is a programmer and looking for security coding issues.

Browsing – Display enhanced security configuration dialog

If you have Enhanced Security Configuration enabled and a previously untrusted web site tries to use scripting or ActiveX Controls, a dialog box will appear to notify you. You can add the web site to the Trusted sites zone directly from this dialog box. If the Enhanced Security Configuration feature is disabled, it will have no effect on the browsing experience. It is enabled by default. It causes more problems than it solves, so disable. Read *"IE Enhanced Security Configuration,"* later in this chapter, for more information on this setting.

Browsing – Enable Install on Demand (Internet Explorer or Other)

This feature specifies whether to automatically download and install web components that can be installed by Internet Explorer Active Setup by using the component's cabinet information file (CIF) for setup instructions. Often, a web page needs to download new components to the browser in order to display the page properly or to perform a particular task. For example, a new language character set may need to be installed in order for IE to display a new language, or a media player may be needed to support multimedia content. If the component is not already installed, the Install on Demand feature can install the new components automatically. If the option is disabled, the user will be prompted to approve the new install prior to it actually installing. The Microsoft default is Enabled. Set to Disable in order to be notified of and approve new installed components.

Browsing – Enable third-party browser extensions

Enabled by default, this feature allows non-Microsoft signed browser add-ons (i.e., Browser Helper Objects). Turning if off can cause many problems with legitimate web sites, but also increases security, as all add-ons increase security risks. It can be disabled if a spyware problem involving BHO is suspected.

Note that this option has no effect on BHOs that modify Outlook Express directly.

Browsing – Use inline AutoComplete

Disabled by default, this determines whether IE's AutoComplete feature (which automatically tries to fill in requested information, such as a user's name and address) automatically fills in known information when a web site form requests it. It can be used maliciously by a remote web site or locally by an unauthorized user. Keep disabled unless needed.

Java (or Java-Sun) – Use JRE x.x for <applet>

This setting only appears when a Java Virtual Machine (JVM) environment is installed. There is some additional risk from running Java, but if you keep Java patched, you can leave this option enabled. It is often needed for legitimate web sites. If you use Java, be sure to keep up on the latest Java JVM and patches.

Security – Allow active content from CDs to run on My Computer

This new IE setting determines whether browser content can run in the Local Computer zone when launched from local CDs. If disabled, active content runs in the Internet zone. Leave disabled unless needed.

Security – Allow active content to run in files on My Computer

This new IE setting determines whether browser content can run in the Local Computer zone when launched locally. If disabled, all active content runs in the Internet zone. It has often been the cause of many exploits. Leave disabled unless needed.

Security – Allow software to run or install even if the signature is invalid

This option is disabled by default and should be left that way. If enabled, it allows unsigned and untrusted software to run.

379

Security – Check for publisher's certificate revocation

This checks to see if the publisher's (i.e., software vendor who signed the program) digital certificate has been revoked by the Certificate Authority (CA). You would never want to run a program whose publisher's certificate was revoked. This could mean that the publisher's private key was stolen and has been fraudulently used to sign a malicious executable. Unfortunately, when this setting is enabled, users will often get a message saying the certificate revocation could not be verified. Then it is up to the user whether to run the signed code or not. If the user is on a legitimate web site, it is normally okay to do so. It is enabled by default and should be left enabled.

Security – Check for server certificate revocation

If enabled, which it isn't by default, this will determine whether a server's SSL or TLS digital certificate is revoked, during the initial handshake connection. I recommend this feature be enabled, although when enabled it is not uncommon for many legitimate web sites' revocation to "fail" for one reason or another. Usually it is because the revocation link (called the *certificate revocation link distribution point*) is unreachable at the moment or not defined correctly. If the web site is legitimate and the digital certificate is legitimate, you can usually choose to ignore the certificate revocation message. Usually, the additional warning messages, if they occur, encourage users to further verify the SSL connection status, and anything that makes the end user more involved in verifying digital certificates without always accepting them by default is a good thing.

Security – Check for signatures on downloaded programs

This option is enabled by default and should remain that way. It ensures that any downloaded programs have verified digital signatures. Otherwise, it displays a warning about what is invalid about the digital certificate (or the digital signature may be missing all together). An invalid or missing digital signature means the software is at a higher risk for maliciousness (although most downloadable software on the Internet is not signed). Figure 10-8 shows the details of a digital signature as they were reviewed during an ActiveX control's download.

Security – Do not save encrypted pages to disk

Disabled by default, this option ensures that pages encrypted by SSL/TLS are also stored encrypted on the local disk. This option can be left disabled in most organizations unless the security risk of a local intrusion is higher than average. Normally, in order for an intruder to search and find downloaded Internet content belonging to another user, they must have admin rights to search the user's profile. If the intruder has local admin rights, this is just one of the many attacks that they can launch. Still, enabling this security option causes only slightly higher disk and CPU utilization. Most administrators only turn it on for computers with shared access.

Security – Empty Temporary Internet Files folder when browser is closed

Like the preceding option, this feature is disabled by default and only needs to be enabled if local admin attack risk is higher than normal. If turned on, the TIF area will be deleted every time IE is closed. This option does have a moderate to substantial performance penalty during the erasing actions. Most administrators only turn it on for computers with shared access.

Windows Vista will do more digital signature and certificate revocation checking, even outside of IE.

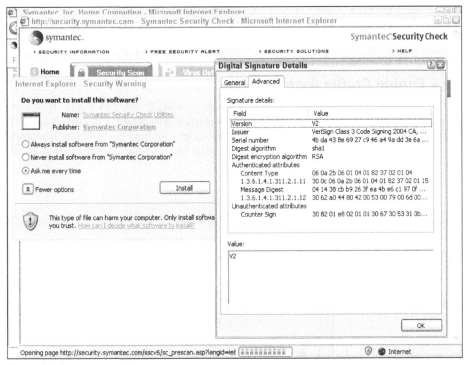

Figure 10-8

Security – Enable Integrated Windows Authentication

This setting works in conjunction with the security zone setting *User Authentication*, which defines whether authentication would happen automatically or not, and to which zones. This setting determines whether Windows logon authentication can be used, if prompted.

There are four types of Windows logon authentication protocols: LM, NTLM, NTLMv2, and Kerberos. If this feature is enabled, which it is not by default in IE 7.x, users can log on using Windows authentication to web sites that support integrated Windows authentication (such as IIS). The integrated logon will present the user's currently logged on name and password for authentication if requested. If the related zone setting is set to automatic, the authentication will occur without the end user having even been aware of the exchange. If the automatic authentication has not been approved, the user will be prompted for logon credentials.

By default, all newer versions of IE will connect to all web servers using anonymous authentication first. If the web server requires Windows logon authentication, in most cases users will be prompted for a logon name and password unless they are connecting to an intranet site. When enabled, the automatic use or prompting of integrated login can be controlled by an IE security zone. Even if this feature is turned on, Windows logon authentication methods normally only work on the local network (or forest), and over VPNs; and are not normally allowed over the Internet (without much planning, configuration, and management).

Although there is little risk to most environments by enabling this feature, you can leave it disabled unless needed. Remember to turn it on if needed (i.e., for SharePoint Services, IIS, etc.). If allowed to non-intranet sites, disable the use of LM and NTLM authentication protocols (covered in Chapters 4 and 14) to prevent malicious remote web sites from requesting insecure versions of user logon credentials.

Security – Enable Profile Assistant

Enabled by default, this option allows users to manage their My Profile (see Figure 10-9) settings in IE (from the Tools menu, select Internet Options, and then the Content tab). If disabled, the option will be grayed out, preventing the user from entering or managing contained information. If enabled, the user can enter in personal profile information that can be used by the AutoComplete feature to automatically fill in web site information.

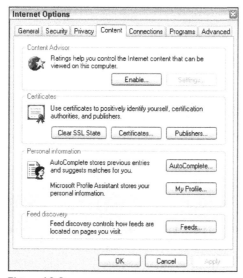

Figure 10-9

There have been a few spyware and adware attacks, including one used a zero-day JavaScript exploit, that have been successful at getting access to the information contained here. In most cases they "steal" the user's e-mail address to send spam. Some security-minded users will fill in the profile section with fake information to fool spyware and adware. You can choose whether to leave it enabled or disable depending on your risks and user population education.

Security – Phishing Filter Settings

New with IE 7.x, this option enables or disables IE's new anti-phishing filter option. I can think of no reason to disable it, other than the one- or two-second delay it incurs sometimes on new web site connections.

Occasionally, the phishing filter will not check on the web site and report whether the web site is a known phishing site until many seconds after the web page is loaded. It might appear as if a web page is not a suspected phishing site, and then 2–10 seconds later, the web site is accurately marked as a known phishing site. This may be a result of the performance trade-off that allows the web site to load at the same time the filter check is made, meaning there is the slight chance that a user could use the malicious web page for a few seconds prior to the warning.

There are three Phishing Filter options:

- ❏ Check Websites Automatically
- ❏ Do Not Check Websites Automatically
- ❏ Turn off Phishing Filter

If you turn the filter off completely, the *Check This Website* option (see Figure 10-10), which can be done manually on a per-site basis, is disabled. Choose the *Do Not Check Websites Automatically* option (from the Phish Filtering options in the preceding list) if you want to allow per-site manual checking. I frequently use the *Report This Website* option to report phishing and fraudulent web sites to Microsoft to benefit other users. After reporting the suspected web site, it goes through a review process before being made available as a confirmed phishing site to other users.

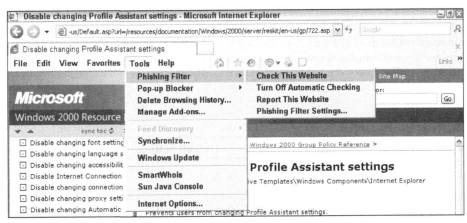

Figure 10-10

The anti-phishing filter can also be enabled or disabled using IE zone security settings. If the phishing filter is turned off in Advanced settings, it overrides setting(s) in the separate security zones. The current behavior (I hope it is fixed before general release) is that it could appear as if the phishing filter were turned on in a particular security zone, when in fact it is disabled across all zones.

Security – Use SSL 2.0, SSL 3.0, TLS 1.0

This option determines what version of SSL is allowed or if Transport Layer Security (TLS) is enabled. The last two options are enabled by default in IE 7.x. In prior IE versions, TLS wasn't enabled by default. TLS is the next version of SSL (i.e., there will be no SSL 4.0 standard). It works more securely at a lower layer of the OSI model and has many improved security features. SSL 2.0 should be disabled. A few web sites are still using it, but the overall percentage is not overwhelming. All the good commercial sites have long supported SSL 3.0 and later.

Security – Warn about invalid site certificates

This option is enabled by default and warns the user when a web server's digital certificate is invalid (if SSL/TLS are enabled in the previous setting). Legitimate sites with invalid certificates abound, unfortunately, usually because of expired useful life dates or because the current web site doesn't make the certificate's web site address. Still, warning users that a digital certificate is invalid raises awareness and may alert them to a spoofing or man-in-the-middle attack.

Security – *Warn if changing between secure and not secure mode*

This setting determines whether or not IE will notify the user that they are being directed between SSL/TLS and non-SSL/TLS sites. The default option of Enabled is acceptable.

Security – *Warn if forms submittal is being redirected*

Like the separate identical security zone setting, this option determines whether the user will be notified that the data they are submitting to a web site is being redirected to another web site. Although this can occur on legitimate web sites, the default option of Enabled should be left turned on to warn users of spoofing or man-in-the-middle attacks. There is a similar (but different) zone setting that determines whether the user can submit forms data unencrypted or not.

Table 10-5 summarizes IE 7.x's default settings, lists the default setting as set by Microsoft, and makes a recommendation for most users who surf the untrusted Internet. Differences between Microsoft's defaults and the recommended settings begin with an asterisk (*). Like security zone settings, advanced settings are a trade-off between functionality and security. Most users can implement the settings recommended in Table 10-5 for an acceptable level of security.

Table 10-5

Advanced Setting	Default Setting	Recommended Setting
Browsing – Always send URLs as UTF-8	E	E
Browsing – Automatically check for Internet Explorer Updates	E	E
Browsing – Disable Script Debugging (Internet Explorer or Other)	E	E
Browsing – Display a notification about every script error	D	D
Browsing – Display enhanced security configuration dialog	E	*D
Browsing – Enable Install on Demand (Internet Explorer or Other)	E	*D
Browsing – Enable third-party browser extensions	E	E
Browsing – Use inline AutoComplete	D	D
Java (or Java-Sun – Use JRE x.x for \<applet\>	E (if Java installed)	E
Security – Allow active content from CDs to run on My Computer	D	D
Security – Allow active content to run in files on My Computer	D	D

Advanced Setting	Default Setting	Recommended Setting
Security – Allow software to run or install even if the signature is invalid	D	D
Security – Check for publisher's certificate revocation	E	E
Security – Check for server certificate revocation	D	*E
Security – Check for signatures on downloaded programs	E	E
Security – Do not save encrypted pages to disk	D	D
Security – Empty Temporary Internet Files folder when browser is closed	D	D
Security – Enable Integrated Windows Authentication	D	D
Security – Enable Profile Assistant	E	E
Security – Phishing Filter Settings	Do Not Check Websites Automatically	*Check Websites Automatically
Security – Use SSL 2.0, SSL 3.0, TLS 1.0	E	E
Security – Warn about invalid site certificates	E	E
Security – Warn if changing between secure and not secure mode	E	E
Security – Warn if forms submittal is being redirected	E	E

E=Selected and enabled, D=Unselected, disabled Group Policy settings

There are literally more than 100 group policy settings to handle how IE looks, acts, and is secured. Group Policy settings will be covered in Chapter 14, "Group Policy Explained."

IE Enhanced Security Configuration

By default in Windows Server 2003, Microsoft has enabled the IE Enhanced Security Configuration security template and feature. It can be enabled in Windows XP Pro, but is not turned on by default. The Enhanced Security Configuration feature significantly tightens down the Internet zone. Essentially, it prevents all non-HTML functionality (i.e., JavaScript, add-ons, etc.). The feature moves the Internet security zone's default security level from Medium to High and moves the Intranet zone from Low to Medium (i.e., more secure), among other changes. When enabled, it will display a dialog warning to the user whenever they visit a site not already placed in the Trusted sites or Local intranet zones.

When warned, the user will be shown a dialog box (see Figure 10-11) and allowed to add the site they wish to visit to the more liberal Trusted sites zone. If the site is added, the site will no longer produce a warning. If the site is not added to the Trusted sites zone, it remains in the tightened Internet zone and most functionality beyond plain-HTML text is disabled.

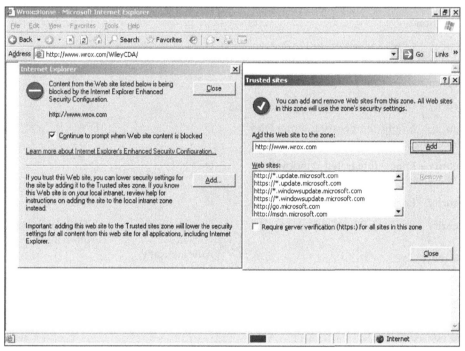

Figure 10-11

I do not like the IE Enhanced Security Configuration feature and recommend that it be disabled. This is because when it does appear, the user is allowed to conveniently add the desired web site to the Trusted sites zone. It was Microsoft's intention that on servers and other computers where this feature is enabled, IE users never visit web sites that should not be explicitly trusted. But real life is a different reality. Windows administrators frequently visit sites that they shouldn't be trusting from the server. Maybe it is to download a needed driver or piece of software, to conduct a search engine request, or to simply read a general news site (e.g., www.msnbc.com) while waiting for some administrative service to finish. What ends up happening is that all kinds of web sites that should never be marked as trusted end up in the Trusted sites zone. This is the exact opposite of what should be happening.

While the Trusted sites zone is modified to be more secure (i.e., Medium security level instead of Low, as is the case in IE 7 as well), it is all too easy for an administrator or group policy to accidentally reset the Internet zones back to their default security levels. I wish that Microsoft would instead change the Enhanced Security Configuration feature to allow newly visited web sites to be added to the normal (pre-Enhanced Security Configuration) Internet zone or make up a new zone. That way, most web sites that need to be visited can be added to the relatively secure new zone, instead of ending up in the modified Trusted sites zone. You can remove (or add) the IE Enhanced Security Configuration feature using the Add/Remove Windows Components feature available under Control Panel's Add/Remove Programs applet (see Figure 10-12).

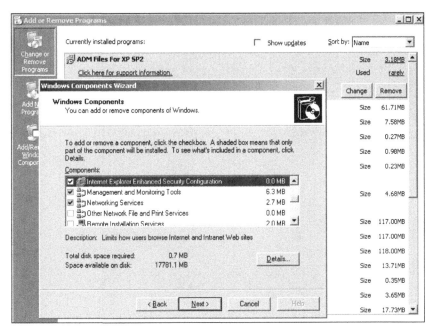

Figure 10-12

Remember that any setting made to the Internet zone or security level affects all programs that rely on IE's security (e.g., Outlook, Windows Media Player, etc.)

Third-Party Tools

Even though Microsoft is doing a better job at securing IE, historically there are usually many unpatched vulnerabilities at any given time. Correctly configuring IE security zones settings can offset a lot of those risks, but not all. There are many third-party products that purport to make IE more secure by default. Most either function as host-based intrusion prevention systems, such as Pivx's (www.pivx.com) preEmpt product (which the author highly recommends), or run IE in a virtual environment, such as Greenborder (www.greenborder.com), which allows all IE settings to be undone with a click of the button. Don't forget Microsoft's own Shared Computer Toolkit discussed above. Overall, I have more confidence in a product that prevents malware from being successful in the first place versus just cleaning up the resulting mess.

Summary

Chapter 10 covered the issue of securing Microsoft's most vulnerable and attacked piece of software, Internet Explorer. It described many of the common types of attacks made against Internet browsers, including URL spoofing, buffer overflows, cross-site scripting, zone manipulation, file execution, directory traversal, malicious content, MIME Type mismatch, cookie manipulation, browser interface manipulation, and plug-in exploits. This chapter covered the many ways administrators can make Internet browsing more secure, including individual recommendations for all of Internet Explorer's security settings. Tables 10-4 and 10-5 explain each setting and make a recommendation for most users' Internet zone. Chapter 11 covers how to secure e-mail from malware, spyware, and spam.

Protecting E-mail

Most e-mail is bogus or malicious. For several years now, spam has accounted for over 60% of all e-mail. That means more bogus e-mail is being sent than legitimate messages. And the percentage only increased even more after the United States CAN-SPAM Act was enacted on January 1, 2004. Most worm outbreaks in the last five years were delivered inside the corporate firewall via e-mail. E-mail value-added service provider MessageLabs (`www.messagelabs.com`) shows that on average, viruses and worms appeared in one of every 30 e-mails sent on the Internet in 2004 and 2005. During a popular worm outbreak, that figure routinely averaged one out of five e-mails for weeks at a time.

Malicious phishing e-mails remain a huge problem. Users are sent bogus e-mails posing as legitimate entities to trick users into revealing financial information. The Anti-Phishing Working Group (`www.antiphishing.org`) reported over 5,000 distinct phishing web sites in August 2005, largely driven by e-mail directed traffic. This is despite the fact that most companies routinely scan for malware at Internet and e-mail server access points, deploy antivirus software to the desktop, and run anti-spam software. Clearly, e-mail is a popular hacker target and needs to be a top priority in any computer defense plan. This chapter discusses the most common e-mail threats and how to protect against them.

E-mail Threats

Most e-mail threats fall into a handful of categories: malicious file attachments, devious embedded links, cross-site scripting, spam, and phishing. Each of these threats will be discussed below after you learn why e-mail is such a popular malicious attack mechanism.

Main E-mail Problems

Behind each of these categories are two main problems: lack of authentication and HTML-enabled e-mail. Like most security vulnerabilities, the real underlying issue is the lack of authentication — unauthenticated senders, untrustworthy content, and trojan file attachments. Malware and malicious coders know that the most frequently used application in the world is e-mail, and almost all of it is unauthenticated. Its ubiquitous use also ensures that a higher than normal percentage of users will be untrained in computer security and gullible to social engineering attacks. Unfortunately, most e-mail users almost universally open every e-mail and file attachment sent their way.

Ultimately, the safety of e-mail will only be improved by better authentication, from the first character typed in by the authenticated sender to the reception of the authenticated message by the receiver. There are a few e-mail protection standards and protocols that do this; unfortunately, none are widely used or accepted.

Most e-mail clients support HTML-enabled e-mail messages, meaning that everything that can be sent maliciously to an Internet browser can also be sent in e-mail. With many e-mail clients, including Microsoft Outlook and Outlook Express (OE), HTML e-mail content is rendered using the parsing engine and capabilities of Internet Explorer. Without HTML-enabled e-mail, it would be hard to trick many users into visiting untrusted sites. With e-mail, a massively productive worm, trojan, virus, or bot can send a link that claims to point to a legitimate resource but which really points to a site that the user would not normally trust. For instance, in Figure 11-1, the e-mail claims to be from eBay but really is from a malicious phishing site (as the underlying link reveals).

The dangerous combination of a ubiquitous application accepting unauthenticated content from around the world off the Internet is an attractive target for malware writers and hackers.

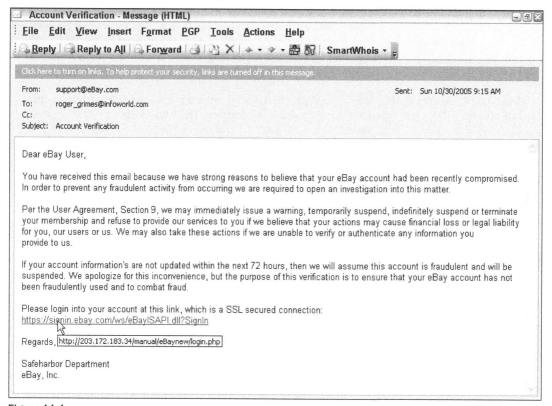

Figure 11-1

Malicious File Attachments

Malicious code runs in waves. Two decades ago, boot viruses ruled the landscape. Executable file viruses took over until 1995, when macro viruses became popular for four or five years. Although not the first e-mail worm (not even the first Internet e-mail worm), the success of the Melissa macro virus (`www.cert.org/advisories/CA-1999-04.html`) of March 1999 launched the next decade and a half of malicious attacks—Internet worms. Computer viruses started having less success because of Windows file protection features (Windows File Protection/System File Protection). Worms, which contain their own malicious program files and don't modify or overwrite other executables, were matched with e-mail to become a voracious combination.

The typical e-worm arrives as a malicious file attachment or embedded link along with message text engineered to fool the unsuspecting user into opening the attached file. Cybertrust's 2004 ICSA Labs Virus Prevalence Survey (`www.cybertrust.com/pr_events/2005/20050405.shtml`) shows that 92% of all malware infections arrive via an e-mail attachment. The accompanying message text comes in many forms:

- ❑   It may claim to be from an acquaintance of the recipient (i.e., sender address spoofing).

- ❑   The attached file executable name may be spoofed to appear as a non-executable (e.g., picture file, text file, etc.), as covered in previous chapters.

- ❑   The message may claim to contain something humorous or pornographic.

- ❑   It may pose as official communications from a trusted source (i.e., Internet service provider, bank, etc.).

- ❑   It may purport to be an antivirus program or software patch.

- ❑   It may be as vague as possible.

The key is enticing the unwary user (or system) into opening the attached file and running the malware. The malware can be a worm, virus, trojan, or bot. Figure 11-2 shows two bogus e-mails with malicious file attachments. The top example shows a social engineering trick whereby the e-mail claims to be from the user's e-mail administrator. It asks the user to run the attached program to check for a suspected trojan proxy server. Of course, if run, the attachment will install a new trojan proxy server. I noticed the maliciousness of this e-mail right away because in my company's domain (i.e., banneretcs.com), I'm the e-mail administrator and I didn't send myself the message. Still, it's a cause of concern that these automated e-mail attacks are smart enough to be DNS domain–specific. I can imagine that many users receiving a similar e-mail from their Internet service provider would be fooled.

The latter example in Figure 11-2 is courtesy of the Beagle.AV worm (`http://securityresponse.symantec.com/avcenter/venc/data/w32.beagle.av@mm.html`). This variant of Beagle looks for and disables over 30 different antivirus programs. It contacts a remote mothership server and updates itself. It then harvests new e-mail addresses by looking in over 30 different file types on the local computer, including e-mail address books, web pages, and databases. It contains its own SMTP engine and will send itself out to every e-mail address it can find. This Beagle variant arrived with a `.CPL` file attachment, which is the file extension for a Microsoft Windows Control Panel applet. Since it's almost unheard of, for a legitimate reason, to send a Control Panel applet via e-mail, this file type should have been blocked at the e-mail gateway.

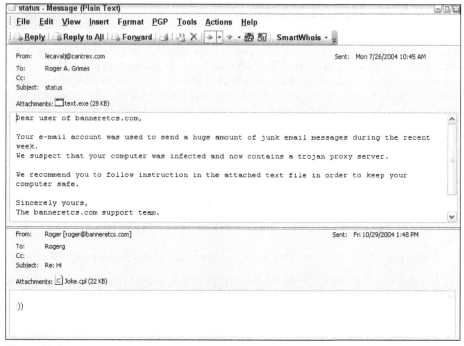

Figure 11-2

Even though we know that e-mail worms and trojans are the most popular method of malicious attack, and even though most organizations have implemented several layers of e-mail defense, the problem is still getting worse. MessageLabs' August 2005 report (`www.messagelabs.com/publishedcontent/ publish/threat_watch_dotcom_en/intelligence_reports/august_2005/DA_123226.chp.html`) reveals that the number of e-mail-based trojan programs has increased dramatically throughout 2005 in comparison with 2004. The peak number of trojans stopped in any one month in 2004 was 234, while in 2005 the highest number stopped in a month was 151,559.

Devious Embedded Links

While malicious file attachments are still responsible for the largest portion of automated malware attacks, hackers are changing their methods as network administrators get better at blocking suspicious attachments. Starting in 2005, a larger and larger percentage of malicious e-mails are arriving in inboxes with rogue embedded HTML links. The links either trick the end user into visiting a malicious web site (often another innocent victim web site that has been compromised by the same hacker or worm) and downloading the malicious file or automatically execute using an HTML vulnerability.

A currently unpatched Outlook exploit (`http://secunia.com/advisories/12041`) allows a malicious link with the HTML OBJECT tag descriptor to exploit e-mail when Microsoft Word is used as the e-mail editor and the e-mail is forwarded to another user. Outlook prevents the attack during the user's normal downloading and reading sessions but circumvents the default security checks when the mail is forwarded to another user.

January 2006 started off with one of the most devastating Microsoft Windows attacks, known as the WMF exploit (`www.microsoft.com/technet/security/advisory/912840.mspx`). It was the first widespread zero-day exploit successful against all fully patched versions of Windows. Worms and hackers exploited it using a malicious URL link that arrived in e-mail or via IM. If the user clicked on the link, it automatically loaded a malformed WMF file, which then buffer-overflowed the Windows graphics rendering engine and allowed complete control of the computer. Until Microsoft provided a patch, there were no guaranteed defenses.

Nearly every popular Internet browser suffers from exploits that allow remote execution of malicious code, privilege escalation, and security bypasses. Internet Explorer, as covered in the last chapter, certainly has its share of remotely exploitable vulnerabilities each year, but so does its closest competitors. Unfortunately, Internet Explorer is the most popular browser and a huge hacker target. According to Secunia (`www.secunia.com`), IE suffered 12 vulnerabilities in 2005 (as of October). A full 100% of the IE vulnerabilities were remotely exploitable, and half of those remain unpatched. Nearly half allowed system access or bypassed security. Many programs, such as Outlook and OE, are susceptible to the same exploits because they rely on IE for rendering HTML content. Whether through a file attachment or a malicious embedded web link, if an end user can be tricked into executing an untrusted executable, there is no perfect defense that can prevent all malware from successfully compromising the PC.

Cross-Site Scripting

Cross-site scripting (XSS) attacks are as possible in e-mail as they are in Internet browsers. As covered in Chapter 10, XSS attacks occur when an attacker is allowed to insert actionable HTML content into a web site or e-mail (or other HTML-enabled content) in such a way that it is unknowingly executed by the recipient. For example, when an attacker replies to a victim's online auction offering via an e-mail, the attacker's e-mail can contain code that steals the recipient's auction logon name and password when the e-mail is opened. eBay was hit by a JavaScript-enabled XSS worm called Ebayla in April 1999.

Cross-site scripting attacks remain one of the most popular attacks occurring today. When an XSS attack is executed, it normally executes in the context of the logged in end user. Those privileges are usually enough to carry out all sorts of maliciousness.

Spam

The spam problem is so bad that it no longer needs defining. Even though some of the majority producers of spam are being brought to justice and being put out of business, albeit slowly, it still compromises the majority of e-mail on the Internet today. The real questions are why do spammers do what they do and how?

Why Spammers Do What They Do

Spammers are motivated by easy money. The money is made either by selling products (legitimate or bogus), scamming money, or by selling validated e-mail addresses to other spammers. Spamming started out primarily as a cheap way to advertise, with spammers sending out millions of e-mails a day. According to The Spamhaus Project, the top 200 spammers (`www.spamhaus.org/rokso/index.lasso`) send out 80% of the spam. Each top spammer sends out tens of millions of e-mails a day.

Although this is no official accounting, most educated guesses put the spammer's conversion rate (i.e., the number of purchases made by spam readers) at somewhere around 3.6 sales per 1 million spams sent (i.e., 0.000036). Initially, that incredibly low conversion rate might seem unprofitable, but if the spammer makes a 100% markup (as they have claimed in many interviews) on a product with a sales price averaging $80 (this is the average sales price for products advertised by spam), then their daily revenue is $1,440 per 10 million spams. If they send 50 million spams a day, that is a daily revenue value of $7,200. Conservative estimates suggest that a spammer's operating expenses cost one-fourth of their revenue, leading to a potential profit of $1.5 million a year. Much of this money is made offshore, so taxes are little to non-existent.

Lest you think I'm overstating the money to be made, two convicted spammers successfully prosecuted in 2005 had to turn their assets gained from spam over to AOL and Microsoft. The turned-over assets included gold bullion, multi-million-dollar houses, Hummers, Porsches, and rare art. As another spammer (a former long haul trucker) said to attest to his wealth, "I know what it feels like to want, and I'll never have to know that feeling again."

In "Nigerian" scams, the spammer sends an e-mail claiming to be a close relative of somebody who recently died or was murdered. They ask for assistance in converting millions of dollars, and tell the recipient that they will receive 25% of the proceeds for assisting in laundering the money. Eventually, the scammers ask the recipient for financial or banking information so they can transfer the money, but instead (of course) steal the recipient's money. Because what the recipients are doing in the first place is illegal, they are hesitant to report the loss. Conversion rates have been reported to be as high as 2–3%, with victims losing tens of thousands of dollars. At one point, Nigerian scams were the second largest industry in Nigeria, but of course many scammer countries are competing now. Closely related to the Nigerian scams are foreign lottery winning notices. They claim the recipient has won some sort of lottery worth millions and ask for financial information (or money) to verify the recipient's identity.

Another major source of revenue for the spammer is selling verified, legitimate e-mail addresses. Although anyone can buy a CD containing over 2 million supposedly verified e-mail addresses, the CDs are often full of more bad addresses than good ones. Many spammers send e-mails selling no product, only hoping to confirm that the e-mail address it was sent to is valid and active. Spammers do this by inserting an HTML link in the e-mail that "dials" home when the e-mail is opened. The e-mail link often points to a one-pixel, transparent graphic (called a *web beacon*) that no normal user would notice. By opening the e-mail, most e-mail clients will automatically download any graphics referenced by the embedded links. The web beacon is uniquely named for each e-mail sent. When the graphic is downloaded, the e-mail address is positively identified as valid and active. The spammer then sells the validated address to hundreds of other spammers, and the whole cycle starts again.

Spammers are also spreading malware specifically coded to assist in criminal activities: mostly identity and credit card theft. The spammers can often make faster profit by creating large bot nets that can then be rented or sold to the highest bidding criminal enterprise. Symantec's September 2005 Internet Security Threat Report (`http://enterprisesecurity.symantec.com/content.cfm?articleid=1539`) said that 74% of the top 50 malware programs detected in 2005 had the ability to steal confidential information.

How Spammers Do What They Do

Spammers purchase or rent a series of computers and load them with bulk e-mailing programs. Search the Internet using the terms "bulk e-mailer" and you'll be astounded by what you find. Hundreds of programs are custom built for the spammer. Although not all bulk e-mailers are specifically made to help spammers, some of the features, such as purposefully misspelling the subject many different ways in order to bypass spam detectors, can only be of benefit to the spammer, not to the legitimate bulk e-mailer. For $125, the spammer can find a program that will drive the whole operation from beginning to end. It will create the e-mails, randomizing the sender's name, subject, and text enough to circumvent many anti-spam products.

Besides the computers and software that actually send the e-mail, the spammer needs a lot of Internet bandwidth. Although you would think that all ISPs would try to stop spamming, many ISPs cater to bulk e-mailers. They promise that the bandwidth given will be high-speed with high availability. These ISPs promise to help the spammer keep sending messages, and to fight any and all attempts to block their client's attempts to send unsolicited mail. These types of ISPs call their guaranteed spam-friendly protection *bullet-proofing*. Spam is big business for many companies beyond the originating spammer.

Everyone involved in the spam industry skirts the illegitimacy of spamming by claiming that all their e-mail lists contain legally obtained e-mail addresses from people who want such e-mails. They all claim that they would never knowingly send spam to someone who didn't want it. But when spammers and their infrastructure partners claim to be able to send to 200 million supposedly opt-in e-mail addresses a day, or 15 million web sites a day, just waiting for unsolicited advertising, they know they are lying.

A spammer's only real hurdle, besides the law, is how to collect enough legitimate e-mail addresses to make a profit. As mentioned above, they often buy validated e-mail addresses from other spammers and bulk e-mailers, but that's expensive. Instead, most spammers *harvest* e-mail addresses from the Internet using automated programs. The address harvesting programs will crawl the web looking for web pages with valid e-mail addresses, or use the information already collected in the most popular search engines. Why crawl the web when Google has done it already? Google, widely abused by spammers and hackers alike, contains logic that attempts to stop harvesting abuse, but there are other ways for the spammers to collect valid e-mail addresses, including the following:

- ❑ Mail server directory harvesting
- ❑ Harvesting public newsgroups and mail lists
- ❑ Address book harvesting (i.e., like most e-mail worms and bot do)
- ❑ Searching chat channels
- ❑ Query Ident and Finger servers (Unix services that can be used to identify individual users)
- ❑ Querying web browsers
- ❑ Utilize unpatched HTML exploits
- ❑ Hacking into mail and other Internet-facing servers
- ❑ Man-in-the-middle attacks
- ❑ Guessing

With mail server directory harvesting, a program connects to an Internet-reachable e-mail server and queries it for valid versus invalid names. Many SMTP servers support commands that are supposed to allow a remote e-mail server to check for the existence of a valid e-mail address before sending the data. Spam bots will check as many possible combinations of e-mail addresses as they can before being disconnected. If the participating victim e-mail server allows it, a spammer can guess all the valid e-mail addresses managed by the e-mail server.

No matter what the collection method, the spammers either collect the e-mail addresses themselves or purchase them from another source. The addresses are then fed into a bulk e-mail computer and launched onto the Internet. To get past the blocking defenses accorded by real-time black lists (see below), which allow e-mail servers to block e-mail from reported unsolicited bulk e-mailers, spammers must constantly change their sending e-mail address and e-mail domain name. However, using a false e-mail address is against many anti-spam laws (including the U.S. CAN SPAM Act). Thus, the average spammer is constantly on the run from the authorities, using offshore ISPs, and trying to cover their tracks to avoid being caught. Their evading techniques are often just as illegal, so when they eventually get caught, the list of violated laws adds up. Not surprising, many spammers are convicted felons for other nefarious business violations.

Phishing

Phishing is the malicious act of sending a bogus e-mail to a user that falsely purports to be from a legitimate service. The Anti-Phishing Working Group defines phishing as ". . . attacks [that] use both social engineering and technical subterfuge to steal consumers' personal identity data and financial account credentials." Most phishing attacks pose as the user's bank, online auction center, or ISP.

Most of the time, the phishing attack is not successful because the receiver of the e-mail is not affiliated with the bank or service the phishing e-mail claims to be from. But more and more often, phishers are making sure their victims belong to the *hijacked* brand name before they send the rogue e-mail. This is known as *spearfishing*, because the target is so narrow. Figure 11-3 shows a common phishing e-mail.

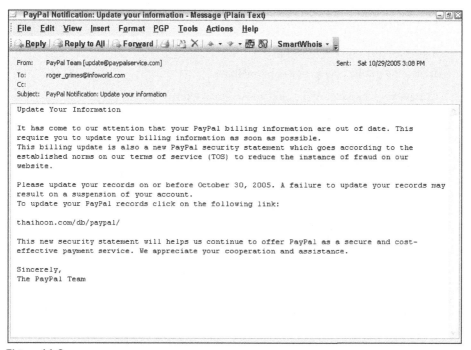

Figure 11-3

The recipient is being asked to update their PayPal account records, which most surely will include credit card information. The enclosed link, `thaihoon.com/db/paypal`, is not a PayPal-affiliated site. In this case, `www.thaihoon.com` is a Thailand-based web hosting service that allows users to put up free web sites. These types of sites are often used by the phishers, along with other exploited legitimate web servers, to avoid easy detection if the authorities get involved.

Conventional phishing attacks, where the user is sent an e-mail requesting confidential information, were on a slight decrease near the end of 2005. The newer phishing angle is to use another method to install a trojan to steal the confidential information without the user having to put the information into a bogus web site. According to both Symantec and the Anti-Phishing Working Group, the number of malware programs and phishing web sites hosting confidential information stealing trojans are both on the rise.

Related to phishing, *pharming* is a technique used to maliciously redirect a client's DNS request to a malicious server. Often what happens is that a vulnerable ISP DNS server is compromised, and rogue IP address data is installed. When the user or their e-mail client uses a URL, the connection request is routed to a malicious server coded to look like the real thing. For instance, a spearphishing e-mail arrives from a phisher claiming to be from the user's bank. The recipient independently verifies that the URL in the e-mail points to the bank's legitimate web site. When the receiver clicks on the e-mail's URL link, a *poisoned* DNS answer is sent to the client, redirecting them to a bogus site that is made to look like the user's real banking web site. The bogus web site may even redirect all requests to the legitimate web site so that the user can see their normal account information. Unbeknownst to the victim, their every keystroke, logon name, and password is being recorded.

Unauthorized Reading of E-mail

Although not an issue largely reported at this time, most e-mail sent through the Internet is plaintext. It can be read by anyone intercepting it along the way. The average number of intermediate routers between the source and destination e-mail servers on the Internet is 12 to 22. That's a lot of places for man-in-the-middle and interception attacks to take place. People routinely send confidential and sensitive information through e-mail that they would otherwise hope that unintended parties did not read.

There have been many cases of e-mail administrators reading otherwise confidential e-mails of company employees and management, executives snooping on other executives, and entire e-mail domains hijacked by hackers. Several very large companies and ISPs have had their e-mail DNS records hijacked by unauthorized parties. The redirected e-mail is then captured on a rogue server, where it can be read at will. Panix, one of New York's largest ISPs, had their domain hijacked for several days in 2005 (`www.panix.net/hijack-faq.html`). When Panix called to get their domain restored to the legitimate IP addresses, their DNS domain registrar did not answer their phone for several days. It turned out the DNS registrar, which allowed the hijacking to happen because of poor security, was located in Australia and the only person on call was not answering the phone. DNS domain hijacking has happened to eBay, Google, and thousands of other businesses. Authenticated and encrypted e-mail protocols would solve the problem.

E-mail is a catch-all depository for all sorts of maliciousness — malicious file attachments, devious embedded links, cross-site scripting, spam, phishing, DNS poisoning, and unauthorized reading. Fortunately, most of these problems can be minimized by implementing the following best-practice recommendations.

Securing E-mail

Securing e-mail takes a concerted effort of many defenses, including blocking malicious file attachments, disabling HTML content, securely configuring the e-mail client, blocking unauthorized e-mail clients, authenticating HTML links, antivirus scanning, blocking spam, anti-phishing protections, enabling e-mail authentication and encryption protocols, and securing DNS. Although these defenses can be applied to any e-mail program, Outlook and Outlook Express will be used to demonstrate the various techniques in this section.

Block Malicious File Attachments

Currently, the single best thing an e-mail administrator can do to stop the current wave of e-mail malware is to block any file type that is highly likely to be used maliciously. For example, is there any valid reason for executable files or Control Panel applets to be sent via e-mail in most organizations, as shown in Figure 11-2? In most cases, no, so block them by default. The high-risk file types covered in Chapter 5 apply here as well.

Administrators may even want to consider allowing only one file extension in and denying all others. End users can be instructed that anyone sending them a file via e-mail must rename the file to some otherwise unknown extension. For example, if your company is called Banneret Computer Security, maybe the file extension can be .BCS. All users wishing to do legitimate business with the company can be told ahead of time what the only valid extension is. This will stop any other file attachment, most of which are malicious.

Unfortunately, many file attachment blocking mechanisms don't allow a deny-by-default rule. Instead, they only allow "block by file extension" rules to be set. If that is the case, follow the recommendations in Chapter 5 and block those file types by default, essentially creating a crude deny-by-default rule.

Where e-mail file attachments can be blocked depends on the environment. Common locations include the following (going from external to internal):

- ❑ E-mail value-added service provider
- ❑ Internet router/gateway
- ❑ E-mail relay servers
- ❑ E-mail antivirus devices
- ❑ E-mail servers
- ❑ Client software

There are many good questions to ask when deciding which device or software should be used to block file extensions, including the following:

- ❑ How are file types blocked — by file extension or some other more intelligent method?
- ❑ Can new extensions be added?
- ❑ Can a deny-by-default rule be configured?
- ❑ Can file attachment blocking rules be applied to some users and not to others?

❏ What mail protocols can be examined — SMTP only, IMAP, POP, RPC, HTTP?

❏ Are intended recipients notified of blocked e-mail?

Most file-blocking mechanisms block by simply examining the file extension. While this may work most of the time, it ultimately is very inaccurate. A better mechanism would be for the file's header to be examined (and maybe more of the file's content beyond that) to accurately determine the file's true type. Make sure any e-mail file attachment blocker can handle multiple file extensions on the same file (e.g., Readme.txt.shs) and MIME-type mismatches.

Is it possible for some users, but not others, to be affected by the file blocking rules? If users complain that they don't want any files blocked because it gets in the way of legitimate work, it may be possible to let users who understand the risks of file attachments have more freedom (sort of like giving an e-mail driver's license to those users that are not likely to execute malicious code). Meanwhile, users who cannot be trusted to make the appropriate decision can be assisted by the file attachment blocking mechanism.

Many file attachment blocking mechanisms only work on SMTP and POP3, and maybe FTP and HTTP. The IMAP e-mail server and client protocol is becoming more popular for managing users' mail. Remote Outlook to Exchange connections may use RPC or RPC over HTTP connections. Can the file blocking mechanism monitor and block files on those protocols as well? Figure 11-4 shows the file blocking functionality provided by an anti-spam appliance.

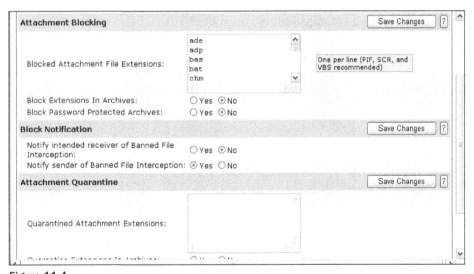

Figure 11-4

Microsoft Exchange and Outlook File Blocking

Microsoft Exchange server allows high-risk file attachments to be blocked by default. By default, Microsoft blocks the following file extensions: ade, adp, bas, bat, chm, cmd, com, cpl, crt, exe, hlp, hta, inf, ins, isp, js, jse, lnk, mda, mdb, mde, mdt, mdw, mdz, msc, msi, msp, mst, ops, pcd, pif, prf, reg, scf, scr, sct, shb, shs, url, vb, vbe, vbs, wsc, wsf, and wsh. These are known as Level 1 files. Any defined Level 2 files, for which there are no default entries, force the user to save the file attachment separately. The user cannot simply click the file attachment to launch. This seemingly simple step of forcing the end user to do a few additional mouse-clicks will prevent many e-mail attacks.

Both Level 1 and Level 2 file extension lists can be customized by the administrator or user (if allowed by the administrator). New file extensions can be added via the registry or in Exchange. In Exchange, an Offline template called *Outlook Security* must be downloaded from the Microsoft Exchange Resource Kit Tools, installed, and configured. Although it's a bit cumbersome at first, the template allows file blocking to be instituted on a per-organizational unit level and allows Level 1 and 2 file extensions to be easily modified. In order for Microsoft Exchange's method to work, the client must use Outlook and store messages in either an Exchange Mailbox (MDB), an Offline folder file (OST), or a Personal Folder (PST). Starting with Microsoft Exchange 2003, Outlook for Web Access (OWA) clients can also be managed.

Every version of Outlook and OE since 1998 has some version of file blocking, although Outlook 98 and 2000 required service packs to be applied. Outlook 2003 blocks the same Level 1 files as Microsoft Exchange does, plus adds the following: `app`, `csh`, `fxp`, `ksh`, `prg`, and `xsl`. Expect more and more file extensions to be added in each new Exchange and Outlook version. Outlook Express file attachment blocking functionality can be controlled using group policy administrative templates. Select `User Configuration\Administrative Templates\Windows Components\Internet Explorer\ Configure Outlook Express` (see Figure 11-5).

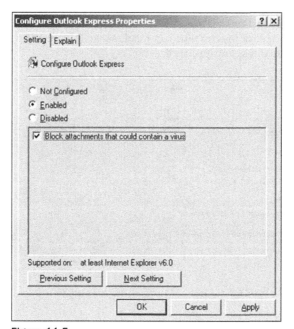

Figure 11-5

Hopefully, one day Microsoft will add a deny-by-default and an allow-by-exception rule to e-mail file attachments. Also consider using the other file and registry blocking techniques covered in Chapters 5 and 6. NTFS permissions can be a strong defense against high-risk malicious files. Unfortunately, you cannot block every file extension that is high-risk in e-mail using NTFS when the file type is used frequently outside of e-mail. For example, you cannot use NTFS or registry permissions to prevent the execution of .EXE or .CPL files because those types are routinely used outside of e-mail. In these cases, you are better off blocking the file attachments sent in e-mail versus applying file and registry security permissions. Ultimately, e-mail administrators want to stop users from blindly running every e-mail attachment. Stop most file extension types by default and educate trusted users about how to receive any file type if this functionality is desired.

Disable HTML Content

As e-mail attacks move from malicious file attachments to embedded URL links, it is important to limit the ability of users and their systems to easily and automatically connect to Internet content via e-mail. Most e-mail clients support the parsing and displaying of Internet content, and disabling this functionality causes many legitimate e-mails to display very poorly. However, as discussed above, most of the e-mails on the Internet today are malicious. The percentage of rogue e-mails versus legitimate e-mails is even higher when considering just e-mails containing embedded links. And because e-mail worms often prey on patched and unpatched HTML vulnerabilities, links do not always require that the user click on the link to activate.

Administrators should disable the displaying of HTML content by default. HTML content can be disabled in Outlook 98 and later and in Outlook Express 4 and later. The latest Microsoft Outlook and Outlook Express clients can be configured to display all e-mails in plaintext by default (see Figure 11-6). In Outlook 2003, the user can simply right-click any HTML-enabled e-mail that has been converted to plaintext back to its HTML-enabled representation. The idea is to prevent the automatic displaying of HTML-content — another deny-by-default rule.

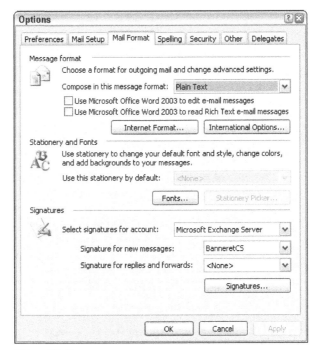

Figure 11-6

Outlook 2003 goes one better. Even when HTML content is enabled, it will prevent the downloading of remote graphic files off the Internet (see Figure 11-7). This effectively prevents spam web beacons from verifying the existence of an active e-mail address. Figure 11-8 shows the handful of settings Outlook 2003 has regarding its ability to download HTML content in e-mail. All of these options can be accessed by selecting Tools ➪ Options ➪ Security.

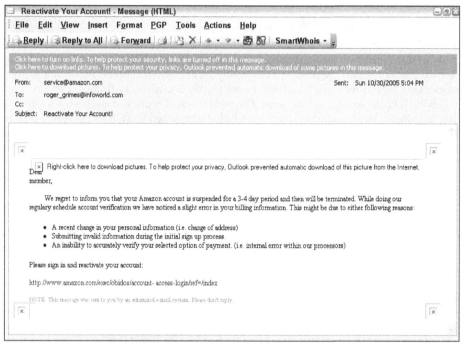

Figure 11-7

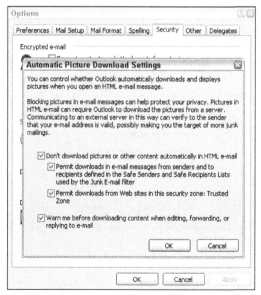

Figure 11-8

Configuring Outlook 2000 takes a registry edit. Under the key `HKCU\Software\Microsoft\Office\` `10.0\Outlook\Options\Mail`, create a new key: `DWord: ReadAsPlain`. Add `ReadAsPlain` as the value name and `1` as the value. In OE 6, choose Tools ➪ Options, and select *Read all messages as plain text*. Previous versions of Outlook and Outlook Express may be able to use the *NoHTML* add-on program (`www.ntbugtraq.com/NoHTML.asp`) that is widely available on Internet. It turns HTML e-mail into plaintext.

If the administrator doesn't mind more effort, they can create an e-mail security policy that doesn't force the user to choose between everything enabled or only plaintext content. Using Internet Explorer's security zones (covered in the last chapter), you can selectively allow or block different types of HTML content if plaintext e-mail is not possible. For instance, you can customize one of the default security zones (and select it under the e-mail Security dialog box) to disable scripting and ActiveX controls, while allowing the normal HTML formatting to come through. Many other e-mail programs allow this type of customization directly within the e-mail client.

Many e-mail administrators are concerned about the end user frustration they will create if they disable the displaying of HTML content by default. It's essential that administrators convince management and end users of the benefits of this tactic. The coming decade will be full of malicious attacks that launch using embedded URL links. Not only will users be protected from current threats, but many future threats as well. And displaying HTML-enabled e-mail is often as simple as one mouse-click or copying the link to an Internet browser. The cost/benefit measurement is easy to justify.

If the e-mail client used is HTML-based, this recommendation is considerably harder to implement. Still, attempt to configure any HTML-based e-mail client as securely as you can. Configure the browser involved to the minimum set of privileges that will allow the authorized HTML e-mail client to function correctly. Ensure that HTML e-mails are scanned for malicious code. If users are allowed to download files from their HTML e-mail, make sure the files are scanned before execution or launch.

Securely Configure E-mail Client

It almost goes without saying that e-mail clients should be configured to be as secure as possible. They should not allow the execution of malicious file attachments or devious embedded URL links by default. Most e-mail clients can be configured with varying levels of security. Outlook 2003 and current versions of Outlook Express, like most current e-mail clients, come with relatively secure settings by default. Most content is opened in the Restricted sites Internet Explorer zone (previous versions opened content in the less secure Internet zone). This will prevent nearly any content besides pure HTML code from being launched. Figure 11-9 shows the zone settings. As Outlook will warn you, if you modify the zone settings associated with any zone shown in this Options window, it will modify the settings in Internet Explorer as well.

As suggested in the previous section, make sure the e-mail client converts all HTML-enabled e-mails into their plaintext counterparts by default. Outlook allows HTML content in e-mail by default. This option should be disabled under Tools ➪ Options ➪ Preferences ➪ E-mail Options (see Figure 11-10). Don't confuse this plaintext setting option with the formatting option controlling outgoing e-mail. The latter option isn't nearly as important as the former.

Figure 11-9

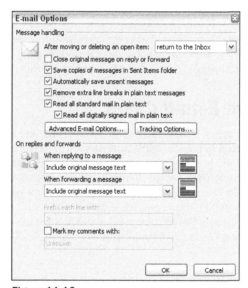

Figure 11-10

Turn Off Reading/AutoPreview Pane

Consider turning off the AutoPreview and Reading pane features (see Figure 11-11). By default, many e-mail clients, including Outlook, will display a portion of a message when the message summary is highlighted. This feature is supposed to allow users to quickly browse through all of their unread mail to determine what is and isn't a priority. Unfortunately, many e-mail clients will auto-execute HTML-content in the AutoPreview and Reading panes. In Outlook 2000, Outlook 2002, and Outlook Express 6, the AutoPreview and Reading panes are placed in the Restricted security zone, which should prevent scripts and active content from executing. Previous versions will execute any HTML content, including scripts, ActiveX controls, and plug-in content.

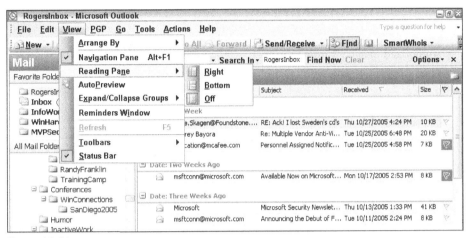

Figure 11-11

Consider Blocking Unauthorized E-mail

Even if an administrator secures the official e-mail client, if end users use additional e-mail clients and services beyond the corporate authorized clients, it increases security risk. If Outlook is the primary e-mail client and Microsoft Exchange server is the primary e-mail server, then the SMTP protocol is not used between client and server. Instead, Outlook utilizes a randomly chosen RPC port and Exchange sends and receives client e-mail on it. If the Outlook/Exchange combination is the only officially supported e-mail client in an organization, then the client's PC should never use the SMTP protocol port, TCP port 25. Firewalls should only allow port 25 traffic to and from the authorized SMTP servers. If SMTP traffic is noticed on firewalls between workstations and the Internet, it is highly likely that an SMTP worm is active.

Similarly, if corporate e-mail users are allowed to use unauthorized HTML e-mail, P2P, or instant messaging services, the risk of a security exploit increases. If clients are allowed to continue to use unauthorized e-mail clients or e-mail, every effort should be made to either eliminate them or secure them.

Authenticating E-mail Links

If HTML-enabled e-mail is allowed, the e-mail client or the related browser involved should be configured to prevent URL link spoofing. For instance, Internet Explorer 7 comes with several anti-spoofing mechanisms, but so, too, do many other browsers. Figure 11-1, at the beginning of this chapter, shows Outlook 2003/IE 7 revealing a spoofed link in a phishing e-mail. There are also browser add-ons that can be installed if your browser does not have special anti-spoofing mechanisms already included.

Antivirus Scanning

With tons of malware arriving via e-mail, an antivirus product that scans incoming e-mail is a must, and most antivirus clients directly support e-mail scanning. Antivirus products can be implemented at the following locations:

❑ Value-added e-mail service provider

❑ Internet router/gateway

❑ Authorized mail forwarding server

❑ Message content scanning server/appliance

❑ E-mail server

❑ E-mail client

Most corporations implement an antivirus scanning engine at centralized location (e.g., a gateway) and on the local client. This is a great cost/benefit decision. Scanning at the centralized location allows most of the e-mail malware to be caught prior to entering the local network or entering the client's PC. Scanning again on the local client will hopefully catch any malware arriving outside the normal e-mail service and provide addition protection from outgoing threats.

There are several different methods that antivirus vendors can use to scan your Exchange server:

❑ File-level

❑ MAPI-based scanners

❑ VAPI-, AVAPI-, VSAPI-based scanners

❑ ESE-based scanners

File-level scanners individually scan each physical file and aren't aware of Exchange-specific structures. These types of scanners can be very slow and problematic, and lock up Exchange server and its log files. If you must use a file-level scanner on your Exchange server, it should not scan the following folders and files:

❑ \Exchsrvr\MDBDATA, \SRS (all versions)

❑ \DSAData (only in Exchange 5.5)

❑ File extensions .edb, stm., and .log on an Exchange server

File-level scanners do not provide help with outgoing e-mail worms with their own SMTP engines and will not protect end-user workstations from e-mail worm attacks initiated from other vectors (macro viruses, embedded links, etc.).

Mail Application Programming Interface (MAPI)-based antivirus scanners were the first generation of scanning methods built for Exchange. They use the MAPI interface to log in to mailboxes and scan individual messages, not files. MAPI and newer Exchange-based scanners can usually scan messages whether they are using SMTP, POP, IMAP, or OWA. Unfortunately, MAPI-based scanners suffered a few problems. Under heavy workloads, they cannot guarantee that all messages are scanned before the user opens them. MAPI-based scanners cannot scan outbound messages, and under heavy workloads are extremely slow.

Microsoft remedied the problems of MAPI-based scanners by creating APIs just for Exchange-based antivirus scanners. Virus API (VAPI), Antivirus API (AVAPI), and Virus Scan (VSAPI) were created for a new generation of mail scanners. VAPI 1.0 was released in Exchange 5.5 SP3. While these types of scanners could scan Exchange servers without causing corruption or performance problems, file attachments were only scanned on access, and they could not tell you what viruses were removed. VAPI 2.0 released in Exchange 2000. It was not backwardly compatible but allowed proactive message scanning, with virus removal details and counters. VAPI 2.5 was released for Exchange 2000. It contained new features, bug fixes, and performance enhancements.

ESE (Extensible Storage Engine)–based scanners, such as Sybari's Antigen, turned out to be very fast and reliable. For years Microsoft refused to officially support ESE-based scanners, although they gave an unofficial tacit approval. Microsoft must have eventually really liked Sybari's approach, because in 2005 they purchased Sybari Antigen and will use it in their own upcoming anti-malware products.

Just remember that although server-based scanning methods work well, there are still ways e-mail-based malware can circumvent server-only scanners. The most obvious way is that it often takes antivirus vendors up to a complete day to include new detection signatures when a new malware outbreak is released. If an e-mail client bypasses Exchange server (picking up external POP, IMAP, and HTML-based e-mail), then e-mail malware could still end up in the Outlook/OE client and be executed. And malware can still end up transmitted to clients using any other method (P2P, IM, etc.). For these reasons, a client-side scanner should also be implemented.

Block Spam

Anti-spam solutions are based on a set of common technologies but are implemented in different ways and at different points in the spam trail. This section will cover the various methods used to identify and stop spam and then describe the most appropriate place to locate an anti-spam device or service. The various technologies used to catch spam are as follows:

- ❏ Address lookups
- ❏ Challenge-response
- ❏ Rate controls
- ❏ Real-time blacklists (RBLs) and whitelists
- ❏ Message analysis
- ❏ Human analysis

Address Lookups

One of the most common anti-spam methods is to read the incoming e-mail message's header, pull out origin information, and then use one of many types of address lookups to prevent message origination spoofing. Address lookup methods include the following:

- ❏ DNS lookups
- ❏ Reverse DNS lookups
- ❏ HELO lookups
- ❏ Sender confirmation
- ❏ Sender domain verification

A very simplified address lookup decision tree looks similar to this:

1. The e-mail says it came from this address.
2. Is the address valid?
3. If not, reject the e-mail.

A receiving e-mail server, officially called a Mail Transfer Agent, or MTA, can use a DNS lookup query to resolve the mail server identified in the incoming message's origination field to the IP address currently sending the message. Conversely, an anti-spam mechanism can first record the incoming IP address and compare it to the DNS name of the sending e-mail server identified in the message.

The HELO lookup method relies on the fact that incoming SMTP servers send a HELO command to initiate a send mail connection with another e-mail server and put their e-mail server name in the HELO command. The receiving MTA can use a DNS lookup to verify the e-mail server stated in the HELO connection. Sender confirmation happens when an MTA can verify that the sender's domain exists or that the sender's e-mail address is a valid e-mail address with the other server.

Unfortunately, these early types of address lookups suffered from their own simplicity. For instance, if the spammer simply uses valid domain or e-mail addresses, then the address lookups will return a high rate of false-negatives. This is further compounded by the problem that many legitimate MTAs do not have valid or accurate DNS lookup records, creating an offsetting high rate of false-positives. Lastly, spammers can subscribe to a "No-IP" service that will register a temporary domain address with the spammer's temporarily assigned IP address. These first-generation address lookup techniques have led to the latest anti-spoofing experiments and emerging standards.

Sender ID and Other Identity Authentication Schemes

There are several competing anti-spam proposals that attempt to defeat spam using spoofed origination domains by confirming the validity of either the incoming e-mail's SMTP reverse-path (i.e., where the e-mail claims it's from on an SMTP protocol level) or from the domain indicated in the sender's MAIL FROM field. When implemented, the receiving SMTP server can query the sender's DNS server to determine whether the sender's origination address is from the domain it says it is from and whether the message arrived from an e-mail server authorized to send e-mail in the originating domain.

At least four different proposals are trying to become the one and only standard. One of the first serious attempts was the Sender Policy Framework (SPF). SPF-aware servers read an incoming message's origination IP address and compare it to e-mail servers authorized to transmit e-mail for the origination domain. The idea is that if the spammer spoofed the domain, the registered SPF records on the origination domain's DNS server will not match the detected IP addresses. And if a client on a valid origination domain becomes infected with a worm that has its own SMTP engine, the client will not be authorized to send e-mail from the originating domain.

SPF-aware domains must identify valid MTA agents by adding SPF-specific records to their DNS servers and using SPF-aware server software. SPF uses the SMTP reverse-path (also known as return-path) on the message's SMTP connection, and cannot prevent a forgery in the MAIL FROM field. SPF, and other standards based on it, isn't really capable of stopping spam per se on their own, but its widespread use will prevent spammers from sending messages with spoofed domains. This means it will be easier to detect, track, and block spammers.

Microsoft proposed its own solution, based on SPF, now called *Sender ID Framework (SIDF)*. Although Microsoft hopes its standard will become widely accepted, and the license to use it is free, because it is a patented, proprietary protocol, several entities refuse to accept the standard. Many groups hope that whatever standard is developed and widely used is open source or public domain. Sender Policy Framework (SPF), DomainKeys (invented by a Yahoo! employee), Cisco's Identified Internet Mail, and the Trusted E-mail Open Standard (proposed by the ePrivacy Group) are competing alternatives.

The DomainKeys and Identified Internet Mail standards have merged into one solution called the DomainKeys Identified Mail (DKIM) specification, which hopes to become an IETF standard. This specification also protects the entire e-mail's authentication from sender to receiver. SIDF and SPF can only prevent domain spoofing, but cannot guarantee the validity of the message or even the sender's name. DKIM uses asymmetric cryptographic keys to create a digital signature on each message.

In August 2004, dozens of large vendors (e.g., Microsoft, Cisco, eBay, Earthlink, Symantec, Postini, etc.) asked the FCC to approve both standards. They want the IP-based, anti-domain-spoofing solutions to be recommended first, followed by the more difficult, and still emerging, digital signature standards. As of this writing, the FCC has not made an official recommendation. Microsoft and many others are supporting the Sender ID solution. Yahoo is supporting the DKIM solution, and many other entities have proposed their support for the pre-Microsoft SPF solution (now called *SPF Classic*).

A spam bot that infects a PC to generate spam and utilizes the PC's e-mail client to send the spam will not be detected by any of the proposed solutions, although a password-protected digital signature tool will probably make it harder. Indeed, these solutions were created only to address the problem of spammers using spoofed e-mail addresses and domains. Some experts claim that these emerging standards will cure nothing. There is some evidence of this, as most of the early adopters have been spammers. Spammers are rushing to change their spam to meet the new validation requirements of the solutions. The spammers are using dynamically created domains and registering their own SPF records. In essence, they are using the anti-spam tool to generate more spam.

Rate Controls

When spammers do something, they do it big. They don't send 50 messages, they send 5 million. They don't send a single message to 50 people; they send 5 messages to 50 million. By limiting the rate at which something in an SMTP e-mail can occur, it is hoped that many spammer attempts will be rejected. Here are some common rate controls:

- ❏ Connections per client
- ❏ E-mails per client
- ❏ Number of recipients per e-mail
- ❏ Distribution analysis

❏   Connections per client

❏   E-mails per client

❏   Number of recipients per e-mail

The first three rate controls are usually set on MTAs, something like *Reject any message with more than 100 recipients*. Rate controls have a high false-positive rate, but they can be fine-tuned and legitimate sources needing higher rates can be whitelisted.

Distribution Analysis

Distribution analysis is the process of watching one location send out thousands to millions of e-mails around the world to many different domains. Normally this can only be done on an anti-spam service value-added network that is able to review thousands to millions of e-mails very quickly. Because they get millions of e-mails a day for thousands of domains, they can see one sender sending out thousands of e-mails at once, and block all e-mails from the sender before they ever get to the recipient. Overall, distribution analysis has a pretty good false-positive and false-negative rate, but occasionally false-positives will result from legitimate broadcast e-mails from legitimate services (i.e., alumni newsletters, yahoo news flash bulletins, etc.). Vendors learn to whitelist those domains.

Real-Time Blacklists (RBLs)

Many third-party databases keep track of reported and known spamming domains, services, and (innocent) vulnerable open relays. RBLs are also known as *real-time blackholes* or *DNS black lists*. An MTA can link to RBLs, download the most current list, and then reject e-mails from entities on the list. There are several types of RBLs:

❏   **Relay Spam Servers (RSSs)** — A list of open mail relay servers.

❏   **Dial-up List (DUL)** — A list of dynamically assigned IP addresses from which an MTA can reject direct SMTP connections. Dynamic IP addresses are usually given to home-based client computers, which should be sending all their e-mail to their local ISP's SMTP servers. Hence, if e-mail is being sent directly from a home-based computer, it is probably from a spam bot.

❏   **Exploits Block List (XBL)** — A list of IP addresses with exploited computers (open proxies, spam worms, etc.) that are sending spam.

❏   **Personal Black and White Lists** — Most anti-spam products allow users to add their own blacklists and whitelists.

There are a handful of *popular* RBLs, including the following:

❏   `www.spamhaus.org`

❏   `www.mail-abuse.org`

❏   `www.ordb.org`

But there are hundreds of RBLs. For a larger list of RBLs, see `www.dnsbl.info`. Most anti-spam services and devices allow administrators to pick and choose between one or more RBL lists and to add their own personal lists (see Figure 11-12).

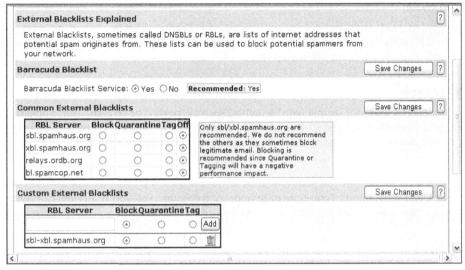

Figure 11-12

RBLs are not without their problems. Some have been shut down by heavy DDoS attacks by spam worms, after which their owners decided to take down the site (which they had been posting for free), rather than spend more of their money to fight the attack. But the biggest RBL problem is that of *true positives*. Innocent companies with an open relay can be placed on an RBL with one confirmed report. Being added to an RBL list can take 1–3 seconds, and being added on one list guarantees placement on dozens more automatically. Rarely is the infringing victim company ever directly notified by the RBL site of its placement on the RBL list. Normally the first indication that a company has that it has been placed on the RBL list is an e-mail being kicked back from a business partner days after being placed on the RBL. Once alerted to the open proxy, it only takes 15 minutes to fix, but it takes days to get off all the RBL lists so that a company can send and receive e-mail normally again.

Message Analysis

Up until now, most anti-spam methods have been directed at IP- and domain-level defenses. Anti-spam mechanisms also analyze message traits to determine whether a message is spamlike or not. Message analysis includes the following:

- ❏ Header analysis
- ❏ Keyword analysis
- ❏ URL analysis
- ❏ Image analysis
- ❏ Filtering
- ❏ Bayesian filtering/learning
- ❏ Fingerprinting
- ❏ Human-filtered lists
- ❏ Message analysis

Header Analysis

It's essential that anti-spam technology analyze message headers. This is where spammers often reveal their tricks. It is often used in combination with name address lookups. Header information that disagrees with displayed content will reveal spam.

Keyword analysis

Keyword analysis looks for simple word searches, such as *porno* or "weight loss" appearing in the same e-mail with other popular spam tricks, such as "Click here" links. It is not very accurate when done simply but becomes more accurate as patterns become unique to spammers.

URL analysis

Spammer URLs often point to one-time or temporary web sites. Anti-spam services can compare these against a database (sort of a URL RBL) of known spammer web site URLs.

Image analysis

Intelligent engines typically look for porno image characteristics such as too much skin color in the entire image, and shape recognition technology, along with key words in the image. It may scan pictures looking for words with OCR technology or look for web beacons. Spammers are now sending text messages as image files in order to defeat keyword filters, so image analysis is becoming more and more important.

Filtering

Filtering is a more complex set of searches than simple keyword searches. For example, if an e-mail contains x, y, and z, and has links in it, then it is spam. Filters must be hard-coded and defined before they can recognize spam. They can be updated for fine-tuning to become more accurate, but Bayesian filtering is better.

Bayesian Filtering

Bayesian filters look at the entire message, looking for predefined keywords, like a filter, but they rank keywords and techniques known to be used often by spammers and infrequently by legitimate users and sites. With regular filtering, every distinguishing feature marked as potentially spamlike has an equal rating. Bayesian filtering recognizes that the phrase "Buy Viagra" should have a higher ranking than the word "teen." Both are frequently used in spam, but the former is almost always spam and the latter is often used legitimately. Words like "frog" and "Einstein" will never rank as high as "Nigeria," "viagra," and "stimulant." And e-mails with the word "teen," an FF0000 HTML tag (for bright red), and containing web beacons should be very highly weighted as spam.

When a Bayesian filter analyzes a message, the findings are ranked statistically and assigned a value, usually between 1 and 10. A 1 would be a message that is almost certainly not spam and a value of 10 would indicate something almost certainly spam. Bayesian filters can be adjusted to be more accurate: to error on the side of false-negatives (see Figure 11-13). In this instance, as with several other anti-spam services and devices, the administrator can choose the values that will determine whether the message is marked as spam and detected, suspected as spam and quarantined, or passed as legitimate.

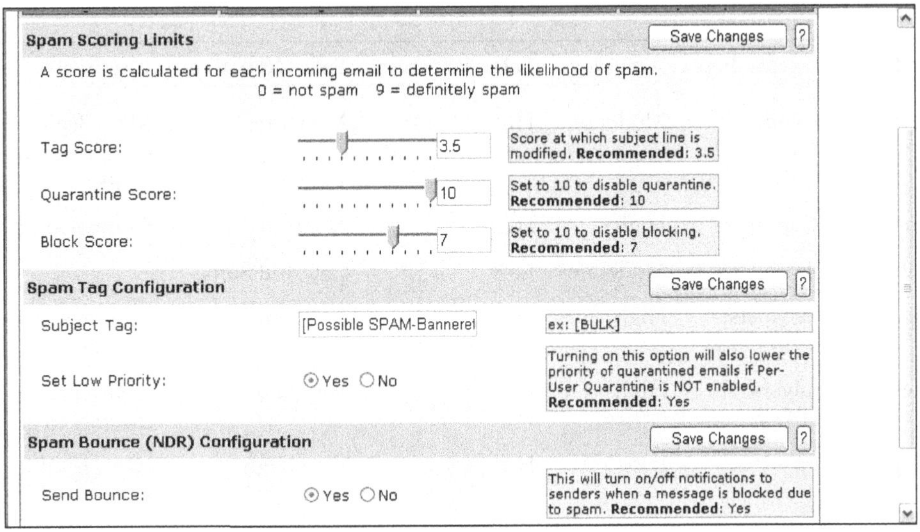

Figure 11-13

Bayesian filtering can "learn" what is and isn't spam when the administrator marks it as such. It fine-tunes the filter for each environment and can be used to re-fine-tune at any time. Bayesian filters must be trained over hundreds of spam and legitimate messages, and include message header evaluation. If an anti-spam filter can't learn, it isn't Bayesian, it's just plain filtering. Bayesian filtering can be very accurate — over 99.5% accurate, with 0.03% false positives.

Spammers fight Bayesian filtering by intentionally misspelling words, such as viiagra, v1gra, viaggra. Bayesian filtering fights back by installing the misspelled words into its filter lists. Spammers are using HTML tricks (e.g., columns, etc.) to bypass Bayesian filters — it's a war of sorts. But as filtering becomes better and spammers are forced to misspell their ads more and more, they become less effective.

Fingerprinting

Fingerprinting occurs when an anti-spam vendor captures a spam message and runs a CRC checksum against the included contents. New incoming messages can be compared against the stored CRC checksum, and if the results are the same, then a spam match has been identified. It's a nice adjunct technique that some anti-spam vendors add to their products to stop very popular spams with static content. Unfortunately, with so much spam generated on a daily basis, and each spam message made to appear unique, fingerprinting isn't overly reliable.

Human Analysis

Sometimes no matter how great the tool is, you can't beat a human for recognizing spam. Many solutions augment their technologies with a human team that delineates the hard-to-decide spam. The human decisions are passed along to the products as additional blacklists entries, keyword blocking, message analysis, and Bayesian filtering. Services and devices using human analysis are very accurate, of course, but slower than automated techniques.

Table 11-1 summarizes the benefits and disadvantages of the different anti-spam technologies.

Table 11-1

Anti-Spam Technology	Accuracy	False-Positives	False-Negatives	Comments
Address Lookups	Moderate	High	Moderate	Many legitimate companies are not configured right.
Challenge Response	High	High	None	Cumbersome
Rate Controls	Moderate	Low	Low, but Some	
Real-Time Blacklists	High	Low to Moderate	Low, but Some	Can cause more harm than good
Message Analysis	High	Low	Very Low	Bayesian filtering is the way to go
Fingerprinting	Low	High	Very High	Not a reliable option when used alone
Human Analysis	High	Low	Very Low	Slow, but adds to overall accuracy

Anti-Spam Device Location

The anti-spam device's location often has a big impact on its efficiency. Listed below are the most common locations for anti-spam devices and software:

❑ Hosted services

❑ Gateway

❑ Server

❑ Client

Hosted Services

Value-added e-mail providers are an excellent option to stop spam. Another company's MTA intercepts e-mail intended for your company (and maybe from your company) and filters out the spam. You have to point your DNS MX record to the vendor, but this option tends to be among the most accurate solutions in the field. They usually have all the anti-spam technologies running at once. These types of services are usually priced on an annual subscription per-seat basis, with costs running between $15 and $70 per seat/year. The benefits are as follows:

❑ "Lease it and forget it"!

❑ High accuracy

❑ The problem is stopped before volume hits your network.

❑ High customer satisfaction rate

❑ They usually offer multiple services, such as anti-porn and antivirus as either a default service or an add-on.

❑ Not server- or client-specific

❑ Can be managed anywhere you can get to a web browser

❑ Updated frequently

Disadvantages include the following:

❑ You're not truly managing your own e-mail (i.e., they can read it).

❑ It doesn't work with encryption.

❑ Tech support is a phone call away (in another country).

❑ They tend to be less customizable than other solutions.

❑ You may have problems sending out normal levels of bulk e-mail to clients and not having it marked as spam.

❑ Some services try to stop outgoing bulk e-mail as a default and it takes special arrangements to get legitimate customer e-mail through without a rate control blocking the e-mail.

The two most popular vendors in this category are Postini and MessageLabs. Both are great choices. Other enterprise class services include FrontBridge Technologies and Mi8. Smaller vendors include AlienCamel, ChooseYourMail, CleanMessage, and Spam Interceptor.

Gateway

The anti-spam solution can be placed on an Internet gateway chokepoint and can be either software or hardware. Software can be placed on another network perimeter device (i.e., firewall, e-mail antivirus server, etc.) or on a dedicated server. Hardware appliances are typically the client's software running on a Linux box.

Gateway Appliances

Gateway appliances are usually placed in front of your MTA. They offer the following benefits:

❑ Tend to be very accurate.

❑ Tend to be very fast.

❑ Not all are e-mail server or client-specific.

❑ You control your e-mail.

Disadvantages include the following:

❑ Requires that MX and/or reverse DNS records be changed to the intercepting gateway

❑ Spam volume is still making it to your network.

❑ Technical support can be spotty.

❑ Documentation can be weak.

Anti-spam appliance leaders include Barracuda Networks' Spam Firewall, MailFrontier, and Tumbleweed E-mail Firewall. Other appliance vendors include McAfee SpamKiller, Mirapoint Message Director, Dymeta Trimail Inbox, and Concentrico Keep/S. Prices start at about $1,200.

Gateway Software

Gateway anti-spam software can be installed on an already existing network perimeter device or on a dedicated server. If installed on an existing network device, the software must be compatible with the network device. Benefits include the following:

❑ Dedicated server products are usually e-mail server independent.

❑ Usually feature-rich and highly customizable

❑ Usually have other e-mail security features built in

❑ You control your e-mail (no privacy issues).

❑ Many choices (or is that a disadvantage?)

Disadvantages include:

❑ It isn't as accurate as the preceding solutions.

❑ Spam volume is still hitting the network (but not the server).

❑ May be a Unix-only product.

Popular vendors include Aladdin's eSafe, Symantec's Antivirus for SMTP Gateways, Sunbelt's iHateSpam, Spamassassin (open-source Unix), Brightmail Anti-Spam, and Trendmicro Spam Prevention Solution.

Server Software

Anti-spam server software is installed directly on the e-mail server. Benefits include the following:

❑ Can be highly integrated with Microsoft Exchange/Outlook

❑ Often from very familiar vendors

❑ Easy install

❑ Larger vendors offer stronger, consistent support

Disadvantages include:

❑ Spam volume is hitting the server.

❑ Not as accurate as previous solutions

❑ If the anti-spam feature isn't the main feature (i.e., product was originally antivirus only), the anti-spam feature set can be lacking.

❑ Anti-spam technology isn't updated as often.

Client-based Solutions

Client-based anti-spam solutions are installed on each end-user machine. Benefits include:

❑ Can be highly integrated with Outlook and several popular e-mail clients

❑ Can easily be managed by end users individually

❑ Often integrated with antivirus and anti-pop-up ads

Disadvantages include:

❑ Spam volume is hitting the network, server, and client.

❑ Lowest accuracy rating of all anti-spam tools in both false-negatives and false-positives

❑ A lots of terrible tools, even spam generators that pose as client products. Evaluate from new vendors at your own risk!!

❑ Harder to centrally manage

Popular vendors include Microsoft Outlook 2003 (some anti-spam features), Norton AntiSpam 2004, Clearswift MIMEsweeper, SpamCatcher, Cloudmark SpamNet, Sunbelt's iHateSpam, and McAfee Spam ·Killer.

Table 11-2 summarizes the benefits and disadvantages of each solution location.

Table 11-2

Anti-Spam Technology	Accuracy	Features/Customization	Comments
Host Services	Best	Moderate	A great choice if you can afford it and don't mind sending e-mail elsewhere
Gateway-Appliance	High	Moderate to High	Fast performance, low cost
Gateway-Software	Moderate to High	High	Feature rich, best reports
Server-based	Moderate	High	Often already bundled along with AV software
Client Side	Low	Moderate	Poor accuracy makes it hard to recommend

Administrators should pick an accurate anti-spam solution that works for their environment. If your solution is not 99% effective or better, get another solution.

Authenticate It

There are several ways to authenticate and encrypt e-mail. The most popular solutions are as follows:

❏ S/MIME

❏ PKI

❏ Digital IDs

❏ PGP

There are several new anti-spam initiatives, which authenticate the e-mail's originating domain or mail server, including Sender ID (`http://searchexchange.techtarget.com/sDefinition/0,290660,sid43_gci1005711,00.html`). Most of these early-generation solutions do not authenticate or encrypt e-mail back to the sender, which may prevent some types of phishing, but won't do much to stop spam using legitimate origination locations. Your environment should begin to implement an e-mail standard that will encrypt and authenticate critical e-mails.

Secure DNS

Pharming attacks rely on exploiting vulnerable DNS servers. Often the servers do not even have to be your own servers. In most environments, the company's internal DNS servers forward to an ISP's external DNS servers. Since you have no control over your ISP's DNS security, consider pointing your internal DNS servers to the root Internet DNS server for forward lookups. This will prevent DNS poisoning attacks on upstream DNS servers from poisoning your internal DNS servers. Also, use an updated DNS server. The latest BIND DNS services are immune to most DNS poisoning attacks, as well as any Microsoft DNS service after Windows 2000 SP2. Lastly, make sure your domain's name is secured with the registrar to prevent domain hijacking.

End-User Training

As covered in the introduction of this book, I do not put my trust in end-user education. If all end users could be educated, they would no longer be clicking on malicious e-mail attachments, clicking on devious URLs, or falling prey to phishing attacks. Still, end-user education does have value if you can teach them the risks of unauthenticated e-mail and about all the slimeballs out there trying to steal their money and infect their machines.

Summary

Chapter 11 summarized the various e-mail attacks that any organization or home user can face. It provided a multitude of defense steps that anyone can take to minimize the threat of e-mail-based malware, including blocking high-risk file attachments, disabling HTML content, authenticating URL links, running antivirus software, blocking spam, blocking unmanaged e-mail connections, securing DNS, and supplementing the defenses with end-user education.

This chapter and Chapter 10 covered client-side Internet risks. Chapter 12 will detail how to secure Microsoft's Internet Information Service, whether running on a server or a workstation.

12

IIS Security

What's hacked more, Internet Information Services (IIS) or open-source Apache server? It might surprise you to learn that Apache 2.0 has suffered at least 27 separate vulnerabilities since March 2003, the month IIS 6 was released to production; and IIS 6 has suffered only 3 vulnerabilities. As of February 2006, IIS 6 has not required a single critical patch. Much of that gap in vulnerabilities between IIS and Apache is probably explained by the fact that IIS runs on only 19% of the world's public-facing web sites, while Apache runs on 79%. Like Windows, anything popular will invite more hackers.

However, IIS 6 is the web server software used at some of the world's most popular web sites, including eBay, Hotmail, MSNBC, and Microsoft. Hackers are constantly assaulting these web sites hoping to exploit them and take them down, yet they stand relatively untouched. A majority of the Fortune 1000 companies run IIS, and IIS virtually owns the intranet space. IIS's default programming language, ASP.NET, has suffered a handful of vulnerabilities since its release. Open-source PHP seems to get a new vulnerability every week. Spam bots live for unpatched PHP servers.

The Code Red worm is the attack that many administrators and open-source advocates use to demonstrate how weak IIS is, and Code Red is still one of the most popular attempted attacks on the Internet. It was released in July 2001. The patch that prevented it from working was released by Microsoft two months prior. IIS hasn't suffered a major publicly exploited vulnerability since then. Isn't it time we stopped thinking of IIS as weak and easily hackable?

Of course, any software, especially web servers, can be hacked. The key is to make your web servers sufficiently secured against easy attack. Out of the box, IIS 6 is secure. You literally have to go out of your way to make it not secure. But sometimes that is easier said than done when installing a complex web site with multiple custom applications. One small mistake can open a huge hacker hole. This chapter covers how to secure IIS. It begins with IIS 6 basics, summarizes the security steps, and then describes each recommendation in detail.

This chapter will focus on specifics of IIS version 6. The details of IIS version 7s, which is in early beta as this chapter goes to press, will be discussed where known to deviate from IIS 6, but are subject to change.

IIS Basics

IIS is an application providing many network services, including World Wide Web (WWW) publishing, File Transfer Protocol (FTP), Network News Transfer Protocol (NNTP), Web Authoring Distributing and Versioning (WebDAV), Simple Mail Transfer Protocol (SMTP) virtual service, a web services platform, and many other applications and functionality. It natively supports many languages and protocols, including HTTP, HTTPS, HTML, VBScript, JScript, ASP, and ASP.NET protocols and languages. Its default functionality can be extended using Web Service Extensions (see below), which allows additional executables (e.g., ISAPI filters, CGI scripting, etc.) to be added to IIS.

IIS was originally only installed on Microsoft's file server products, but starting with Windows 2000, it was also available for workstation clients. Windows 2000 runs IIS version 5.0, and XP runs version 5.1. Starting with Windows Server 2003, IIS is available to be installed, but is not installed or activated by default. When installed and activated, IIS 6 installs with a bare minimum of services.

IIS is not available on XP Home Edition.

Table 12-1 shows the popular IIS versions and their default operating systems.

Table 12-1

IIS Version	Default OS
4.0	Windows NT 4.0 Server (NT 4.0 Workstation ran the Personal Web Server application)
5.0	Windows 2000 Server or Workstation
5.1	Windows XP Professional
6.0	Windows Server 2003 and XP Pro 64-bit version
7.0	Windows Vista/Longhorn*

*As of this publication, Microsoft has no plans to allow IIS 7.0 to run on previous platforms.

Windows Server 2003 introduced Web Server Edition, which is Windows Server 2003 without a lot of the enterprise features needed in a domain. The Web Server Edition of IIS 6 can support any number of remote users, but requires client access licenses for any users authenticating to a Windows authentication database or SQL server. Additional restrictions include the following:

❑ Cannot run Certificate Services

❑ Only a single RRAS VPN connection is allowed

❑ Cannot be a domain controller, but can be a domain member and participate in domain authentication

❑ No Volume Shadow Copying

❑ Cannot do the following: clustering, Terminal Server Application server mode, Internet Authentication Service (IAS), network bridging, Internet Connection Sharing (ICS), Internet Connection Firewall, removable storage management, RIS, Fax Services, Windows Media Services, or Services for Macintosh.

All Windows Server 2003 versions support Network Load Balancing (NLB).

Starting with Windows Server 2003, IIS is not installed by default on any Windows product. It must be installed by selecting Add/Remove Programs ⇨ Windows Components ⇨ Application Server. Under Application Server there are over two dozen components and subcomponents to choose from (see Figure 12-1). When installed, IIS 6 is installed in a locked-down state. Only static web pages can be delivered. All active scripting is disabled by default.

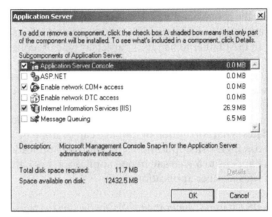

Figure 12-1

IIS can support multiple web and FTP sites at once (except workstation versions, which can only have one active web site at a time), each with varying degrees of functionality. IIS application files are located in a folder called `%windir%\system32\inetsrv`. The default IIS 6 install only supports static content, and installs only one web site, the *Default Web Site*. Files for the default web site are stored in `\Inetpub\wwwroot` by default and contain only a single static web page, indicating that the web site is under construction.

By default, three related services are installed: World Wide Web Publishing, IIS Admin Service, and HTTP SSL. All three run in the Local System context and will be started automatically, although the HTTP SSL service is set to manual and called by the World Wide Web Publishing service. When IIS is active, the web server will listen only on port 80 until otherwise configured. IIS runs using a multitude of files and processes. The main IIS process of `Inetinfo.exe`, running in the Local System context, is always present, but several other processes assist. It's important to note that in IIS 6 and later, no user code runs in these highly privileged processes.

Http.sys

When IIS 6 is installed and active, the `Http.sys` kernel mode driver installs as an HTTP protocol stack listener and intercepts and caches incoming HTTP requests. It also provides caching, logging, quality of service, and bandwidth throttling for the web server. Every active web site registers itself with the HTTP protocol stack. The `Http.sys` driver is the only default IIS 6 component to run in kernel mode, directly interacting with the operating system. Microsoft tested the security of `Http.sys`, making sure it was not susceptible to buffer overflows and other common security mistakes. All web site code and processes run in user mode, meaning that an exploited web site cannot normally modify the operating system.

IIS 7.0 will include four default protocol listeners: `Http.sys`, `Net.tcp`, `Net.pipe`, and `Net.msmq`. The `Http.sys` driver will include built-in support for HTTPS, SSL, and TLS, instead of requiring a separate service (i.e., HTTP SSL). The three other new protocol listeners will support Microsoft's new Windows Communication Foundation web services.

Worker Processes, Application Pools, and Identities

`Http.sys` forwards client requests to the associated web site's *worker process*. The worker process is user-mode-based code that does the actual handling, delivery, and response for the incoming HTTP request for a particular web site. For example, a worker process may retrieve additional HTTP content and send it to the requesting client, call an ISAPI filter to handle a particular type of request, or run a scripting engine.

Each web site runs in an *application pool*, which is a named worker process and logical memory allocation where one or more web sites or applications reside. When IIS 6 is installed, only a single application pool, called the *DefaultAppPool*, is created. Additional application pools can easily be created, and each web site and directory can belong to one or more application pools. Placing different web sites in different application pools isolates what corruption or damage can be done by one site to another. A web server administrator can run high-risk applications in their own application pool, separate from the web site. If a malicious action happens to a web site in one application pool, the vulnerability does not immediately compromise web sites in other application pools.

> *When referring to how IIS 6.0 works, application pools are the same as worker processes.*

In IIS 6's default worker process isolation mode, there is a separate worker process for each application pool. Each runs in the `W3wp.exe` process (see Figure 12-2). In previous IIS versions (or an IIS 6 web site running in IIS 5 isolation mode), `Dllhost.exe` is the default single instance worker process for all web sites. Applications and web sites running in *Low Application Protection* mode (e.g., ASP) use the `Inetinfo.exe` worker process. This means that in previous versions of IIS, a single compromise could allow easy access to all web sites on the server.

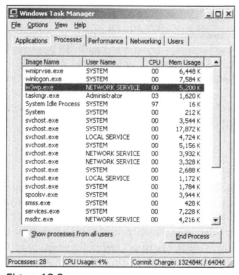

Figure 12-2

The W3wp.exe process will not launch until a web site on the web server is first accessed.

Each worker process and associated application pool run in the security context of an application pool *identity* (see Figure 12-3). The identity is a user or service account used to run the worker process and application pool (i.e., the security context in which the worker process and application pool runs). The default application pool identity is Network Service.

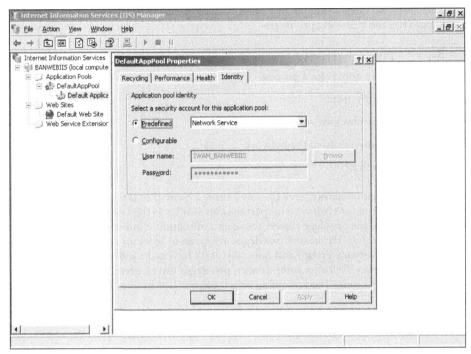

Figure 12-3

Introduced in XP Pro, the Network Service account has permissions similar to the Authenticated Users group, but accesses network resources using the web server's computer account. The Network Service account has the following privileges:

❏   Replace a process-level token

❏   Adjust memory quotas for a process

❏   Generate security audits

❏   Bypass traverse checking

❏   Access this computer from the network

❏   Logon as a batch job

❏   Logon as a service

❏   Impersonate a client after authentication

If you create a custom identity account (see below) with permissions similar to the Network Service account, make sure the custom account has the privileges listed above as a minimum requirement.

If a web site doesn't need access to other network resources (i.e., besides the normal remote requesting clients), the web site administrator can change the worker process identity to Local Service. The Local Service account, also introduced in XP Pro, has permissions similar to the Authenticated Users group, but accesses any network resources using an anonymous null session. In XP Pro and later, network resources cannot be accessed using the null session account, except to domain controllers. The Local Service account has the following privileges:

❏ Replace a process-level token

❏ Adjust memory quotas for a process

❏ Generate security audits

❏ Bypass traverse checking

❏ Access this computer from the network

❏ Logon as a batch job

The Local Service account does not have the *Impersonate a client after authentication* privilege. If you create a custom identity account (see below) with permissions similar to the Local Service account, make sure the custom account has the privileges listed above as a minimum requirement. *Bypass traverse checking* and *Access this computer from the network* privileges are given to any user or service account by default (by belonging to the Everyone group) and normally don't have to be individually assigned. *Logon as a batch job* and *Impersonate a client after authentication* privileges can be given by adding the custom account to the IIS_WPG built-in group. The remaining privileges must be individually given to any custom identity account.

IIS_WPG Group

The IIS Worker Process Group, IIS_WPG, was new in IIS 6.0. The default application pool identity, Network Service, belongs to this group by default (along with the IWAM, Local System, and Local Service accounts). Any custom application pool identity account *must* belong to this group as well. By default, IIS_WPG and its members have Read permissions to the default web server directory, \Inetpub\wwwroot.

The IIS_WPG group also has permissions to various other IIS directories, including IIS Temporary Compressed Files folder (if compression is turned on), %windir%\System32\Inetsrv\ASP (for ASP), and the %windir%\system32\Microsoft.NET\Framework\v1.14322\Temporary ASP.NET Files folder (if ASP.NET is installed).

Although you can modify the membership of the IIS_WPG group, you should be careful about changing the default permissions given to the group. First, if you accidentally remove a necessary permission, all of your web sites can stop working until you figure out what you did. With that said, you can remove the IIS_WPG group's right to high-risk files, folders, and registry keys (as detailed in Chapters 5 and 6). Be sure you don't deny write access to IIS_WPG to the default locations if you are running ASP.NET, as these permissions are required for .Net to write content to the server used for background processing. ASP.NET performs these operations as the process identity for the worker process, rather than the logged on user.

Creating a Custom Worker Process Identity

Application pool identities should have the bare minimum NTFS permissions and system privileges necessary to support the related web site. If the default three service accounts don't allow a least privilege security context to be used, a custom worker process identity account can be created and used. Here are the steps:

1. Create an identity account as you normally would in Local Users and Groups or the Active Directory Users and Computers console.

2. Make the account a member of the IIS_WPG group.

3. Assign the necessary additional explicit privileges to the new identity account: Replace a process-level token, adjust memory quotas for a process, and generate security audits. Identities wishing to access remote network resources need the *Logon as a service* privilege as well.

4. Assign the necessary NTFS permissions (e.g., Read, Write, etc.) of the necessary web site content and folders to the new identity account.

5. Test the web site from a client machine and look in the log for any IIS-related issues.

6. If the web site has problems from the custom identity, assign the application pool the normal Network Service identity and use Sysinternal's Filemon utility to troubleshoot what file permissions are needed in order for the web site to display successfully.

Web sites running on domain controllers using the Network Service account identity may need additional permissions set on the Network Service account and IIS_WPG group, because those permissions are taken away by the action of making a server computer a domain controller. See `http://support.microsoft.com/default.aspx?scid=kb;en-us;842493` for further information.

IUSR and IWAM

When a user connects to an IIS web site, the files are accessed in the context of an impersonated user. Whatever permissions and privileges the impersonated user has, so too does the connecting web site user. This is an extremely important point to remember when configuring IIS security. IIS allows authenticated and anonymous connections. Authenticated connections must use a valid SAM or Active Directory security principal account.

When IIS is installed, two default user accounts are created: `IUSR_<computername>` and `IWAM_<computername>`. The IUSR account is used by IIS for web sites supporting anonymous connections. Connecting users can access any web resource that the IUSR account is allowed to access. The IUSR account belongs to the Guests group, and has Read & Execute NTFS permissions to the Default Web Site's folder (i.e., `\Inetpub\wwwroot`) by default. Starting in IIS 6, the anonymous account has explicit Deny-Write and Deny-Delete permissions to the same folder to prevent anonymous users from uploading or modifying web content.

To recap, IIS 6.0 runs using a combination of one or more worker processes (`W3wp.exe` or `Inetinfo.exe`), the `Http.sys` protocol listener, applications pools, identities, and the web site's content. Figure 12-4 shows a theoretical example of IIS running three web sites within two application pools. Users accessing a particular web site run files in the context of an impersonated user, either by specifically authenticating or by indirectly using the IIS web site's anonymous user account (not to be confused with the completely unrelated anonymous null session built-in account).

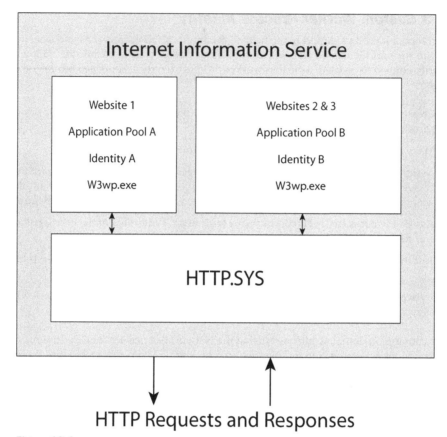

Figure 12-4

The IWAM account is used for out-of-process (e.g., COM+ application) connections and can usually be disabled in IIS 6. In previous versions of IIS, an application could run inside the web site (i.e., in-process) or external to the web site (i.e., out-of-process). When running out-of-process, IIS uses the process Dllhost.exe. You will see this process starting in IIS 6 when out-of-process communications (i.e., IIS 5 mode) is needed.

User names and passwords for these two accounts are stored in both the IIS *metabase* (see below) and the appropriate SAM or Active Directory database. Normally, IIS synchronizes the names and passwords of these accounts between IIS and the appropriate account database when IIS is first installed, but it needs to be manually maintained in both locations if the IIS default account names or passwords are changed. The initial passwords of these accounts are long and complex. When setting passwords manually, make sure the passwords are long and complex (i.e., 15 characters or longer).

You can view and set the IUSR account password manually in IIS using the IIS Admin console or using the Adsutil.vbs script located in \Inetpub\Adminscripts. See http://support.microsoft.com/default.aspx?scid=kb;en-us;297989 for details on how to view or set passwords using Adsutil.vbs. The IWAM account password cannot be changed in the IIS Admin console. It can be changed programmatically or by editing IIS's metabase.

In IIS 7, the IUSR account will be a built-in account with a well-known SID. This will enable permissions assigned to it to be easily copied to other web sites.

IIS Administration

IIS can be administrated locally or remotely. In IIS versions 4 to 6, IIS is locally managed using the IIS Admin MMC console (see Figure 12-5). To use the tool in IIS 6 or previous versions, the user must be a local Administrator on the web server. The IIS Admin tool allows nearly every facet of IIS and its web sites to be configured, including authentication, IIS permissions, SSL, application pools, and what web extensions are allowed.

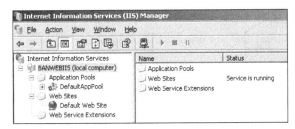

Figure 12-5

Remote administration can be accomplished using an internal IIS admin web site or an external remote admin tool, such as Remote Desktop. Although not installed by default, administrators can install a remote management web site called the *Administration* web site. To install, the administrator should select the *Remote Administration (HTML)* option under IIS components while installing IIS. It can be added after the initial install. This creates the new Admin web site, which runs on a randomly chosen TCP port (for example, 8098). To use the remote admin tool, simply surf to the normal supported web address, but begin the web site URL with `https://` and end the URL with : and the random TCP port number. For example:

```
https://www.example.com:8098
```

The default admin port is protected by SSL. If you forget to put the `https:` in the URL, an error message will be returned. There is another non-SSL admin port that is created as a listener, too, but it simply reports that you must connect on the HTTPS port. When you connect successfully, you must provide administrator-level credentials, and you may have to add the admin site to the Trusted sites security zone of your browser. Once authenticated, the Admin web site has nearly a full range of functionality, as compared with the MMC console tool. Figure 12-6 shows one of the management screens located in the remote management web site.

Metabase

IIS configuration information is stored to a file called the *metabase*, which only the local Administrator and system account have access to by default. The metabase is stored in a plaintext XML file called `Metabase.xml` located under `\System32\Inetsrv`. It can be edited manually, created and modified in the IIS Admin GUI, or modified programmatically. It can also be extended to add new schema objects in IIS. The schema structure is stored in `MBSchema.dll`. You can also back up and restore the metabase using several different tools, and IIS frequently makes its own backups and stores them in the `\System32\inetsrv\History` folder. The metabase can be imported and copied to other IIS servers.

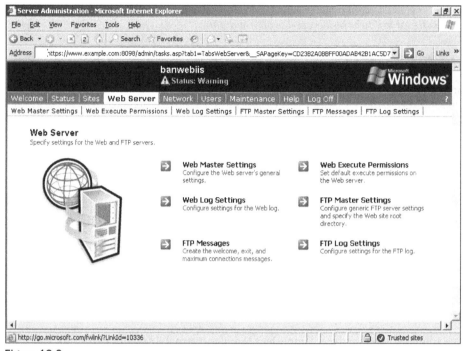

Figure 12-6

IIS 7 uses a new administrative tool called the *Web Manager*. Non-admin users can be delegated the capability to manage one or more web sites without having to be an administrator. Web Manager is a non-MMC console, completely redesigned for IIS 7. It separates the various aspects of web server administration into different categories (e.g., IIS, ASP.NET, Web Server Management, Server Components, Security, Performance, Health, etc.). The author has seen a beta copy of this tool and found it to be an improved interface over the IIS Admin console, once the administrator gets used to the new interface. In IIS 7, configuration settings are stored in two new XML files. The `Application.Host.config` file stores IIS server settings and each web site has its own `Web.config` file for site-specific settings.

IIS administrators can also use Remote Desktop or another other third-party remote control tool (e.g., pcAnywhere, VNC, etc.). Remote Desktop uses Terminal Services and Remote Desktop Protocol (RDP) over TCP port 3389 to provide a fairly reliable and encrypted communications session. Many administrators use IPSec tied to specific client and server addresses in conjunction with RDP to ensure authentication and encryption. Any of the remote admin tools allow complete control of the web server, and not just IIS, of course. Whatever remote admin tool is used, the administrator should take great pains to ensure that the admin port and connection are secure.

IIS Authentication

When a client machine connects to an IIS server, it will always connect as either the default anonymous user (i.e., `IUSR_<computername>`) or with an authenticated user account stored in Active Directory or the local SAM. IIS allows six different kinds of default authentication:

- ❏ Anonymous
- ❏ Integrated Windows Authentication
- ❏ Digest Authentication
- ❏ Basic Authentication
- ❏ Passport Authentication
- ❏ SSL Client-Side Mapping

Authentication methods can be configured in the IIS Admin tool by choosing the Directory Security tab and the Edit button under the Authentication and access control section (see Figure 12-7). One or more authentication methods can be selected per web site, per folder, or per file. For example, an administrator can allow anonymous connections to most of their web site content but require authenticated access to a particular folder or file. If anonymous and authenticated methods are allowed at the same time, most browsers will try the anonymous connection first.

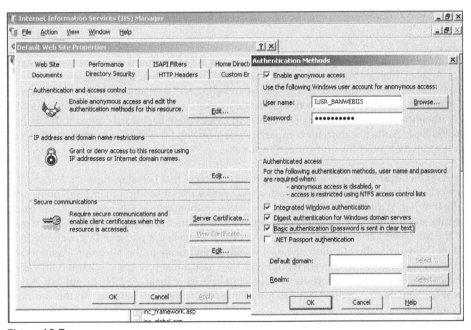

Figure 12-7

Anonymous authentication is the default impersonated user for most web sites. The IUSR_ <computername> account is a member of the Users and Authenticated Users groups. This membership gives the IUSR account Read and Execute permissions to most default Windows files. Luckily, these overly broad security permissions are offset by the less broad permissions of IIS. Any web site only requiring Anonymous authentication will not prompt the user for logon credentials.

Integrated Windows Authentication (IWA) allows a client to connect using one of the normal Windows logon authentication methods (i.e., LM, NTLM, NTLMv2, or Kerberos). This authentication method requires that the client and IIS server reside in the same domain, and for that reason IWA does not normally work over the Internet. NTLM and NTLMv2 can get past a firewall, but are generally stopped by proxies because NTLM is connection-based, and proxies do not necessarily keep connections established.

It is intended for internal intranet sites, where users should not be bothered by being asked to re-authenticate when they connect to the intranet server. Any web site in the user's Intranet sites zone using IWA will not prompt the user for logon credentials unless the logon credentials are valid. The default option of whether to always be prompted or not is set under each security zone's settings in Internet Explorer (covered in the last chapter). The remaining authentication methods will always prompt the user for logon credentials and pass them to the web server.

Digest Authentication allows remote clients to use Active Directory user accounts to authenticate if the web server is a member of an Active Directory domain. The server must use Windows 2000 and IIS 5 or later and the client must be IE 5.0 or later. The user's account must also have the *Store passwords using reversible encryption* option selected. If enabled, clients can authenticate using their normal user account, and the authentication transaction does not transmit the users in plaintext (unlike Basic Authentication). If Digest Authentication is used on a Windows Server 2003 web server running in a Windows 2003 domain, Digest Authentication can become Advanced Digest Authentication (using more secure MD5 hashes).

Basic Authentication is an older but widely supported HTTP standard allowing users to log on using a SAM or Active Directory account. Users are prompted to input their logon name and password, and the browser encodes the information using base 64 encoding and transmits it to the server. Although base 64 encoding is not plaintext, it is near enough, and extremely easy to decode back to its plaintext original. Basic Authentication should not be used except in cases where backward compatibility is needed. You can enable Basic Authentication for compatibility reasons and use SSL (or another protective tunnel-like IPSec) to strongly protect the authentication stream.

Passport Authentication is a proprietary Microsoft protocol that is losing support. Microsoft created it so that users could authenticate to participating web sites without sending their login name and password over the Internet. With Microsoft Passport, and other authentication schemes like it, the user establishes an identity and password at a centralized identity management location. In this case, it would be with one of the Microsoft Passport servers. Whenever the user visited a participating web site that supported Microsoft Password authentication, the user would authenticate to the Microsoft Passport site securely. Then the Microsoft Passport servers would give the client a token or cookie that would validate their authentication to the original web site. It is also possible to write an ASP.NET application that uses local Passport credentials so you don't have to use Microsoft's Internet databases, but this has not been widely adopted.

The user's identity and financial information (e.g., credit card information) would reside once at the centralized Microsoft Passport site, and not have to be stored on every web site from which the user wished to purchase goods. Unfortunately, the Microsoft Passport mechanism suffered from early security weaknesses and a lack of trust and use by end users. Microsoft is starting to discontinue its Microsoft Passport service for third parties, although Passport credentials are still used, and often required, for many Microsoft web sites and services.

SSL Client-Side Mapping is another potential default IIS authentication method. If SSL is enabled on a web site, the web site can also require that the client provide an authenticated SSL certificate as well. The client's SSL certificate can be stored in Active Directory (i.e., mapped), so that when the web site requests it, it can be retrieved from the user's Active Directory user object and handed to the server for validation.

This is a very secure form of authentication but requires heavy initial and ongoing administrative use of a PKI infrastructure.

The certificate can also be installed in the IIS metabase for backward compatibility with IIS 4.

IIS 7 has a new logon feature that can be installed on a web page by including the Login.aspx code. It presents the user with a logon name and password prompt screen that will then pass the credentials on — to IIS using one of the previously mentioned authentication types, to a SQL server database, or to any installed security provider.

You can do this with ASP.NET applications today. "Forms authentication" is available and in use by many web sites. However, in IIS 6, it only works for ASP.NET content. In IS 7, it will work for all content.

In IIS 6 and previous versions, each of the authentication methods came as one default package. If IIS was installed, then each of these methods could be used. Only the anonymous user was enabled by default on the Default Web Site, but any authentication method could be turned on with a simple mouse click. In IIS 7, each individual authentication method can be enabled or disabled on a per-module basis. For example, if the web site doesn't use Basic Authentication, the administrator can remove the Basic Authentication module, and the code will not be available in IIS for use or exploitation.

Table 12-2 summarizes the basics of each IIS authentication method.

Table 12-2

Method	Security Level	How Passwords Are Sent	Crosses Proxy Servers and Firewalls	Client Requirements
Anonymous Authentication	None	N/A	Yes	Any browser
Basic Authentication	Low	Base 64 encoded clear text	Yes, but sending passwords across a proxy server or firewall in clear text is a security risk because base-64-encoded clear text is not encrypted.	Most browsers
Digest Authentication	Medium	Hashed	Yes	Internet Explorer 5 or later
Integrated Windows Authentication	High	Hashed when LM or NTLM is used; Kerberos ticket when Kerberos is used.	No, unless used over a PPTP connection	Internet Explorer 2.0 or later for NTLM; Windows 2000 or later with Internet Explorer 5 or later for Kerberos

Table continued on following page

Table 12-2 (continued)

Method	Security Level	How Passwords Are Sent	Crosses Proxy Servers and Firewalls	Client Requirements
Certificate Authentication	High	N/A	Yes, using an SSL connection	Internet Explorer and Netscape
Passport Authentication	High	Encrypted	Yes, using an SSL connection	Internet Explorer or Netscape

Table 12-3 discusses the various advantages and disadvantages of the authentication protocols requiring logon credentials.

Table 12-3

Authentication Method	Advantages	Disadvantages
Digest	Supports authentication through firewalls and proxies. Encrypts user credentials. Requires Active Directory running on Microsoft Windows 2000 Server or later. Provides medium security.	Requires IE 5.0 or later. Requires that user password be stored unencrypted in Active Directory. Cannot be used to authenticate local accounts. Requires the associated application pool identity to be configured as Local System.
Basic Authentication	Doesn't require IE or Active Directory. Supports authentication through firewalls and proxies. Can be used to authenticate local accounts. Stores hash of the user credentials in Active Directory.	Plaintext transmission of credentials. Low security. Consider using adjunct security tunnel, such as SSL or IPSec, if Basic Authentication is desired.
Integrated Windows	Encrypts user credentials. Provides high security. Requires IE 2.0 or later (5.0 and later for NTLMv2 and Kerberos authentication).	Requires Microsoft clients. Will not work across a proxy server. May use low-level encryption for LM depending on the specifics.
Client Certificates	For server authentication (certificates stored on the server), your organization obtains certificates from a trusted certification authority. For client authentication, map certificates to user accounts stored in Active Directory running on Windows 2000 Server or later. Provides high security.	For client authentication (certificates stored on the clients), your organization has, or is willing to deploy, a public key infrastructure (PKI). For client authentication, you have a method of securely distributing the certificates to the clients.

Authentication Method	Advantages	Disadvantages
Passport	Supports authentication through firewalls and proxies. Encrypts user credentials. Requires IE 4.0 or later and Netscape Navigator 4.0 or later.	Requires Active Directory when account mapping is used. Requires your organization to license the .NET Passport authentication service, which is being discontinued.

Also, web administrators can implement third-party authentication schemes, whereby the user is prompted for logon credentials and the web site validates the attempt without involving the normal IIS authentication mechanisms. This is often done by using a front-end logon page that is back-ended to a SQL server, which functions as an authentication database. If this method is used, administrators must code their own logon method as securely as they can (no easy feat).

It's also important to remember that most of the IIS logon authentication methods are more concerned about transmitting authentication credentials between the remote client and the server and are not as concerned with integrity and confidentiality issues. To ensure those latter points, use an adjunction protection tunnel such as SSL or IPSec.

Permissions

Two types of permissions apply to IIS: IIS and NTFS. And IIS has two types of permissions: IIS permissions and Execution permissions. Share permissions do not affect IIS, although they could be used to access IIS files over NetBIOS connections (if allowed).

IIS Permissions

IIS has its own permissions that apply to each web site, virtual directory, folder, and file. These permissions are normally set under the Home Directory tab in IIS Admin (see Figure 12-8) after first selecting the web object focus (i.e., web site, virtual directory, folder, or file).

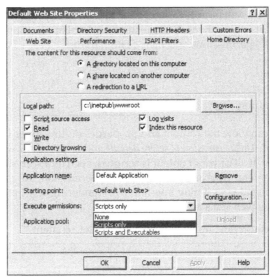

Figure 12-8

433

The IIS permissions are:

❑ Script source access

❑ Read

❑ Write

❑ Directory browsing

Script source access allows the client to read the web page's source code. This is normally okay, but might be disallowed if revealing the web page's source code or scripts can inadvertently reveal sensitive information (such as passwords). The connecting client must have Read or Write permissions in order for this permission to work.

Read permissions allow a client to download a web page, view or download files, navigate folders, or run scripts. Read is the default permission for all web sites, pages, files, and folders. If you disable this permission, the web page will not be displayed, although scripts and other executables will still be active and able to render. Write allows the connecting user to upload and modify content. This permission should not be given unless writing and modifying content (via HTTP PUT verb or WebDAV) is allowed. In some cases, Write permissions may not be required when using a program specifically designed for this purpose, such as FrontPage Server Extensions.

The Directory browsing permission is a unique one. If selected, clients will not download and display HTML content as they normally would. Instead, when the default document requested is not available, the directory is shown along with a listing of its contained files and folders (much like an FTP virtual directory might be displayed). Normal web sites normally do not have this permission enabled. However, enabling directory browsing is a convenient way to allow users to view, upload, and download files. You can also disable this permission, but allow Write, to create a "blind drop."

Administrators looking for an alternative to secure FTP should consider using directory browsing instead. Secure FTP clients and servers that talk to one another without issues are hard to find. Instead, enable directory browsing on an HTTPS web site containing the needed files and folders. Every user's browser will be able to connect and the content and authentication credentials will be authenticated and encrypted by default. Users will be able to right-click and Save As any file, and they can drag and drop uploaded files (or save directly to the web site using their local application if WebDAV is also enabled). Table 12-4 summarizes IIS permissions and their customary use.

Table 12-4

Permission	Description
Read	Users can view the content and properties of directories or files, and execute script content. *This permission is set by default* and required for web sites that have static content. If *all* of your content is scripted, such as a web site that only uses ASP content, you can remove the Read permission, but this is not generally recommended as it may interfere with rendering static content that may be mixed with the web site's application.
Write	Users can create, upload, modify, and delete content.

Permission	Description
Script Source Access	Users can access source files and scripts. If the Read permission is set, then users can read source or script files; if the Write permission is set, then users can modify source or script files. You must have either the Read or Write permissions set to enable. Set this permission when using WebDAV. If enabled, make sure that you require authentication for this site and that your file permissions are set correctly.
Directory browsing	Users can view file lists and collections, and download files. Enable Write permissions, too, to allow file uploading.

Execute Permissions

Execute permissions can be set on each web site, folder, and virtual folder (but not file). Execute permissions determine whether or not scripts or executable content can be executed, and define whether or not the script source code can be viewed. The Execute permissions can be seen at the bottom of Figure 12-8. Table 12-5 explains the permissions.

Table 12-5

Execute Permission	Description
None	Enable if you only want clients to access static content, such as HTML and picture files. Will not run scripts or programs.
Scripts only	Default setting. Enable to allow clients to run scripts, such as ASP, ASP.NET, and PHP (not installed by default).
Scripts and Executables	Enable to run both scripts and executable programs on the server

NTFS Permissions

NTFS permission play a huge role in IIS. Ultimately, if the connecting client "breaks out" of IIS, the NTFS permissions assigned to the web pool identity and impersonated user account are the security mechanism of last resort. All of this assumes you install IIS and the web site content on a NTFS partition. And you should never install IIS on anything but an NTFS partition!

NTFS permissions need to be set on two major categories of files: IIS server application files and web site content. IIS's application files are located in a folder called %windir%\system32\inetsrv. By default, only the System and Administrators security principals have Full Control to the folder and its contents. Users (and sometimes the Everyone group) normally only have Read & Execute permissions.

Because the IUSR anonymous account is a member of the Users group, it means anonymous connections would have Read & Execute permissions to this folder (and many others on the server) if the IIS engine were to allow remote users to put in URLs that could access these directories. IIS stops them, luckily, after years of early exploits. However, if a hacker learns how to break out of the site locations authorized by IIS, they could potentially have Read & Execute permissions all over the web server. I'm not sure why Microsoft places the IIS anonymous user in the Users and Guests groups, but I hope they have a good reason. Of course, the lack of IIS 6 exploits reinforces the fact that the offsetting defenses must be working.

Web server content files are installed to \Inetpub\wwwroot by default. Default permissions are as follows:

- ❑ System and Administrator have Full Control

- ❑ Users group has Read & Execute

- ❑ IIS_WPG group has Read

- ❑ The IUSR_<computername> anonymous user has Delete-Deny, Delete-Create, and Write-Deny permissions. Coupled with the permissions it gains from being part of the Users group, this account essentially has Read & Execute permissions but nothing else.

When creating any web site, the NTFS permissions assigned should be the bare minimum needed by the connecting user, impersonated account, and web application pool identity to reflect the web site accurately and thoroughly. Although this might seem confusing at first, the effective permission security of any IIS web site is determined by the union of the following:

- ❑ The NTFS permissions given to the application pool identity account

- ❑ The NTFS permissions given to the user account the client uses to authenticate to the web server (e.g., anonymous or an authenticated user account)

- ❑ The IIS permissions set on the web site, virtual directory, folder, or file

- ❑ The IIS execute permissions set on the web site, virtual directory, or folder

IIS 7 will introduce role-based security and delegation. It will define various common web server roles and NTFS permissions that can be given to each role. Then user accounts are added to each role, inheriting the appropriate permissions.

Understanding the effective outcome of these permissions on each folder and file in each IIS web site is essential to being a knowledgeable IIS administrator. Read-only web sites should be restricted by Read-only NTFS permissions. If executable program files are not needed, the Execute permissions should not be set to Scripts and Executables. Permissions are at the core of IIS security, but which features and functionality that IIS is running also plays a huge part.

Web Service Extensions

Microsoft intended IIS to be extensible by default. For example, an ISAPI filter (usually a Dll or program file) can be launched to handle specific types of content, or a PHP scripting engine can be added to handle PHP scripts.

When IIS 6 is installed, all web service extensions are disabled (called *prohibited*). Many built-in web service extensions can be installed and enabled if their functionality is desired. These will be covered below. Web service extensions should only be installed after thoughtful consideration. Each additional web service extension is a potential place for a vulnerability. Now that we have some of the basics covered, let's discuss how to take those same principles to harden IIS against malicious attack.

Step Summary

IIS is secure by default out of the box, but web servers are a combination of components (i.e., network environment, hardware, software, OS, and applications). Making sure that IIS and its running applications are secure means checking and verifying a lot of components beyond IIS. Here are the summarized steps that need to be performed to strongly harden an IIS server:

1. Configure network/perimeter security.
2. Ensure physical security.
3. Install updated hardware drivers.
4. Install the operating system.
5. Configure the host firewall.
6. Configure Remote Admin.
7. Install IIS.
8. Install patches.
9. Harden the operating system.
10. Configure and tighten IIS.
11. Secure web site(s).
12. Configure logging.
13. Clean and test.
14. Install and tighten applications.
15. Conduct penetration tests.
16. Deploy.
17. Monitor log files.

Now we'll cover each of those steps in detail.

Securing IIS

Use the following details to securely configure IIS. Most of the steps assume that the IIS server will be external-facing to the Internet, and need higher than normal security. Internal web servers may be fine with lesser settings.

Configure Network/Perimeter Security

Before hardening IIS can even begin, an administrator must make sure the network is safe and secure. The network should be free of rogue software, malicious mobile code, and malicious network sniffers. Any perimeter firewalls or routers should only allow the bare minimum of TCP/IP ports to or from the server. In most cases, that means just allowing TCP port 80 and maybe 443 (for HTTPS) from the Internet to the server. If the web server serves up only normal WWW traffic, the perimeter filters should not allow any other port, except maybe the remote management port, to have access to the server.

No port traffic should be allowed from the web server to the Internet, by default, unless it is a part of the web server's function. Temporary exceptions may be made for port 80 traffic (for browsing the web to get patch updates) and port 53 (for DNS queries). However, many web sites have these ports open from the web server to the Internet all the time, which is allowing too much access. If a hacker is successful in placing and executing a rogue program, and egress ports are allowed through the filter, the hacker may be able to send a command shell back from the server to his remote location over the open ports.

Ensure Physical Security

The web server computer should be in a physically secure location. Unauthorized users should not have physical access to the computer. Consider buying a computer that allows physical access to be controlled by a physical mechanism (e.g., lock or Smart card). Computers should have a locking case that prevents easy theft of the hard drive.

Unless otherwise contraindicated, IIS should always be installed on a dedicated computer. Any IIS server invites increased hacking attempts and puts any computer it is installed on at higher risk of successful exploitation. And any other application may make IIS vulnerable to a side-channel attack.

Prevent booting from anything but the primary boot drive. This will prevent local attacks that attempt to circumvent regular Windows security mechanisms (as covered in Chapter 4). It will also prevent boot viruses and other types of malware. Disable any unused USB, serial, and printer ports. Then password-protect the BIOS so that the configuration can be maintained. Use a BIOS password that is long and complex, but one that is not the same as your normal admin passwords.

Install Updated Hardware Drivers

Often forgotten, don't forget to check for and install updated hardware drivers for your computer's BIOS, motherboard, interface cards, video card, and hard drive controller cards. It is the rare computer that arrives with all the drivers updated. It would be a shame for a web server to be exploited because the server's hard drive controller card had a bug.

Install the Operating System

To prevent directory traversal attacks, IIS should be installed on a system with two separate, clean hard drives, each formatted with NTFS. IIS 6 has not been the victim of a directory traversal attack, but in the event that a hacker develops a successful one, having the IIS server software and content installed on one hard drive and the Windows operating system installed on another will prevent future traversal attacks.

Install the Windows operating system as you normally would. Most web servers should be installed as stand-alone servers, unless the web server will be participating in domain authentications (i.e., Integrated Windows Authentication, etc.). Unless you are dealing with an extranet server, most public-facing web servers don't need Active Directory. If Active Directory is accessible through the web server (because it is either a domain member or a domain controller), a successful hacker will be able to gather much more information.

*IIS should never be installed on a domain controller. If it is, the IUSR account is a member of Domain
Users, which by default is a member of Users on all domain computers.*

You want to install the OS with the minimal settings, applications, and services loaded. If possible, load
the OS with a static IP address. Dynamic IP addressing might give the hacker a way to exploit the server.
Optimally, the web server would not be connected to the network until after all patches were installed.

Configure the Host Firewall

As soon as the OS is installed, install a host-based firewall on the operating system. You want to protect
the web server from remote exploitation. Use Microsoft's Internet Connection Firewall or Windows
Firewall if you do not have another better host firewall. Both of these host firewalls do a fine job at protecting Windows by preventing all inbound connections not initiated by an outbound connection.

Keep the firewall enabled with no port exceptions until OS and IIS patching has occurred. When the server
is ready for operations, enable the firewall for only the port exceptions needed to run the web server. Often
these exceptions would be ports 80, 443 (if HTTPS is needed), and a remote management port.

Configure Remote Administration

Decide what your remote administration method will be. Don't use one if all administration will be
local. Remote Desktop is an excellent choice for remote administration, but it is susceptible to man-in-
the-middle and replay attacks. If you want to use RDP, though, make the following changes:

❑   Remote Desktop is often disabled by default. Enable it, and add to the Remote Users group any
    remote user you want to use Remote Desktop who is not already a member of the Administrators
    group. Remote Desktop can be enabled or disabled under the Remote tab in the System applet in
    the Control Panel.

❑   On the server, change the default RDP port from TCP 3389 to something else random and high.
    It is changed using a regedit at `HKEY_LOCAL_MACHINE\System\CurrentControlSet\`
    `Control\Terminal Server\WinStations\RDP-Tcp`. Change the value to decimal (versus
    hexadecimal). On the client side, the RDP client must include the port number at the end of the
    connection string to connect to a non-default port, for example: `www.example.com:33089`. See
    `http://support.microsoft.com/?id=187623` for more details.

❑   Specifically deny access to IIS anonymous user and anonymous null session. This can be done
    by adding the user accounts to the *Deny logon through Terminal Services* privilege in Group Policy
    or Local Computer Policy at `\Computer Configuration\Windows Settings\Security`
    `Settings\Local Policies\User Rights Assignment`.

❑   Enable *High level* encryption under `\Computer Configuration\Administrative Templates\`
    `Windows Components\Terminal Services\Encryption and Security\`*Set client connection*
    encryption level. In the same area, enable *Delete temporary folders on exit* and *Use temporary folders per*
    session, disable *Active Desktop*, set *Permission capability* to *Full Security*, and restrict each user to one
    session.

❑   Force users to close a session after being disconnected. These options are available in the
    Terminal Services Configuration console (see Figure 12-9) or in an Active Directory domain,
    under the user's Sessions tab in their User Account properties.

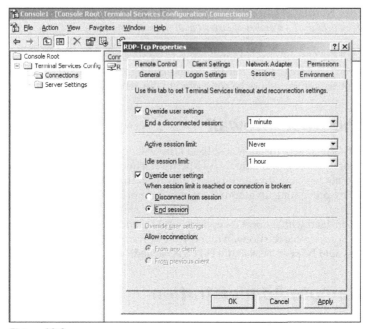

Figure 12-9

❑ Enable *Do not allow an initial program to be launched. Always show desktop* in the Terminal Services Configuration console. In the console, disabled all mappings except *Clipboard* under *Client Settings*.

❑ Last, and most important, protect RDP admin sessions using an adjunct protection tunnel, such as IPSec or SSL. The current implementation of RDP contains known weaknesses that, although not popularly abused at this time, are serious enough to require an offsetting protection. You can enable SSL for RDP on W2K SP2 and later. It is hoped that in the future, Microsoft will improve RDP so additional protections are not needed. For more information on remotely administering IIS, see http://support.microsoft.com/default.aspx?scid=kb; en-us;324282.

Install IIS In Minimal Configuration

Using Add/Remove Programs under Control Panel, install IIS with the default options. After hardening the OS and installing patches, we will install any additional IIS functionality needed.

Install Patches

Install all OS and application patches, making sure to install service packs before other patches. This may be complicated by the fact that the server may not be connected to the network, or a filtering device may be blocking access to Windows Update from the server (as previously recommended). Install as many patches as you can without connecting to the network. In most cases this means downloading OS and IIS patches from another already patched computer and then installing them manually on the server. If you must open port 80 to run Windows Update and download the patches from Microsoft, open only ports 80 and 53 outbound. Run Windows Update, install the patches, and then disconnect. Run the patching routine until no more patches are missing.

Administrators may want to consider enabling the Automatic Updates (AU) service. If so, AU should download the patches, but never automatically install. Consider installing and using the Microsoft Baseline Security Analyzer (MBSA) to check for any missing patches. If not connected to the Internet, you can download MBSA and the latest `Mssecure.xml` file from another patched machine and manually install and test. Delete any temporary folders used by the patches and reboot the server as required.

Harden the Operating System

Now is the time to harden the underlying OS. Basically, you want to disable or remove any service or feature that is not needed to support the web server, its applications, or its administration. This section will detail how to harden a stand-alone web server needing a bare minimum of services. Web servers with complex requirements (e.g., down-level client compatibility, domain membership, etc.) will not be able implement all the suggestions.

If you have Windows Server 2003 SP1, run the Security Configuration Wizard (SCW) and install the server in the role of a web server. The SCW (see Figure 12-10) can usually be launched right from the Start button. When prompted to choose a server role, choose only the *Web Server* role. Deselect all other roles, including File Server and Middle-tier Application Server (COM+/DTC), unless needed. Then use the SCW to turn off all services not needed, or manually configure.

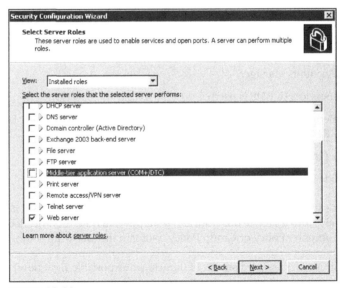

Figure 12-10

A stand-alone web server facing the Internet and not needing domain authentication only needs the following services enabled:

❏   Application Layer Gateway Service (if ICF or Windows Firewall is used)

❏   Automatic Updates (if used)

❏   Background Intelligent Transfer Service (if used)

❏   COM+ Event Service (if COM objects are used on the server; when in doubt, leave enabled)

❏   Computer Browser (only if needed to NetBIOS browse or connect to other computers' drives or printers)

❏   Cryptographic Services

❏   DCOM Server Process Launcher (if Distributed COM objects are used)

❏   DHCP Client (if used)

❏   DNS Client (if used)

❏   Event Log

❏   HTTP SSL (needed even if HTTPS is not needed)

❏   IIS Admin Service

❏   IPSec Services (if IPSec is enabled)

❏   Net Logon (if authenticated remote domain logons are used)

❏   Network Connections

❏   Plug and Play

❏   Protected Storage

❏   Remote Procedure Call (RPC)

❏   Security Accounts Manager

❏   Terminal Services (if RDP is used)

❏   Web Element Manager (installed with W2K3 Web edition, if the server is managed remotely using the Remote Admin web site)

❏   Windows Firewall/Internet Connection Sharing (if used)

❏   World Wide Publishing Service (of course)

Every other service should be disabled unless explicitly needed. See Chapter 7 if you need further guidance. When in doubt, turn a service off. Uninstall or remove all other non-needed applications and services. Use Local Computer Policy or Group Policy to obtain the following settings:

❏   Set the minimum password size to 14 (largest value possible right now).

❏   Give 15-character passwords to all custom application pool identity accounts.

❏   Enable password complexity.

❏   Enable Account Lockouts (3–5 bad passwords in 1 minute, locked out for 1 minute).

❏   Rename the admin account.

❑ Rename the Administrator and Guest accounts.

❑ Remove the Everyone group from *Access this computer from the network* user right.

❑ Under User Rights Assignment, remove Power Users and Backup Operators as members of the *Access this computer from the network* user right (unless you do remote backup of the web server).

❑ Change Unsigned Driver behavior from *Warn* to *Don't Allow*.

❑ Enable Message Text for Interactive Logon (just to defeat any brute-force logon tools).

❑ Disable *Logon caching*.

❑ Enable the *Do not allow the anonymous access of SAM accounts and shares* option (although this may disable some remote management tools).

❑ Enable the *Do not allow the storage of credentials or Passports for network authentication* option.

❑ Enable the *Do not store Lan Man hash value on next password change* option.

❑ Change the LM Authentication Level to NTLMv2; refuse LM and NTLM (unless you need down-level clients to authenticate using Integrated Windows authentication).

❑ Enable the *Clear virtual memory page file* option (although this will cause long shutdown and bootup times, so measure against availability concerns).

❑ Remove Posix as an optional Windows subsystem.

❑ Restrict CD-ROM and floppy drive use to local logged-on users only.

❑ Deny *Log On Locally* right to IIS anonymous users.

❑ Enable the *Interactive Logon: Do not display user info* option.

❑ Remove DFS$ and COMCFG from file shares that allow anonymous logon.

❑ Disable Active Desktop.

❑ Disable File and Printer Sharing in the Network Configuration dialog box.

If the web server is not Windows Server 2003 SP1 or XP Pro SP2 or later, harden the TCP/IP stack with the registry edits recommended at `http://msdn.microsoft.com/library/default.asp?url=/library/en-us/secmod/html/secmod109.asp`. This will prevent many network-level attacks and make the web server more resistant to denial-of-service attacks.

Reboot the system and troubleshoot any resulting error messages.

Configure and Tighten IIS

Now that the OS is hardened, let's turn out attention to IIS. Here are web server–specific changes to make (as compared to web site changes):

Installing Additional IIS Features

Now is the time to choose which IIS features to install. If features beyond static content are needed, rerun the Add/Remove Programs applet and install the needed IIS components. Table 12-6 discusses the various IIS components and subcomponents and makes recommendations.

Table 12-6

Subcomponent	Default Setting	Recommended Setting	Comment
Application Server Console	Enabled	Enable if required	Provides an MMC snap-in that includes administration for all of the Web Application Server (WAS) components. On a dedicated web server, this component is not required because only IIS Manager is used.
ASP.NET	Disabled	Enable if required	Provides support for ASP.NET applications. Enable this component when you need to run ASP.NET applications on the web server.
Enable network COM+ access	Enabled	Enable if required	Allows the web server to host COM+ components for distributed applications. Disable this component unless it is required by your applications.
Enable network DTC access	Disabled	Enable if required	Allows the web server to host applications that participate in network transactions through Distributed Transaction Coordinator (DTC). Disable this component unless it is required by your applications.
Internet Information Services (IIS)	Enabled (see below for subcomponents)	Enabled	Provides basic web and FTP services. This component is required on a dedicated web server. Note: If this component is not enabled, then all of its subcomponents are not enabled.
Message Queuing	Disabled (see below for subcomponents)	Enable if required	Provides guaranteed messaging, security, and transactional support for applications that communicate through messaging services provided by Message Queuing (also known as MSMQ). This component is required when your web sites and applications use Message Queuing. Note: If this component is not enabled, then all subcomponents are not enabled.

Subcomponent	Default Setting	Recommended Setting	Comment
Subcomponents of Internet Information Services (IIS)			
Background Intelligent Transfer Service (BITS) server extension	Disabled	Enable if required	BITS is a background file transfer mechanism used by applications such as Windows Updates and Automatic Updates. Enable this component when you have software that depends on it, such as Windows Updates or Automatic Updates to automatically apply service packs, hot fixes, or install other software on the web server.
Common Files	Enabled	Enabled	These files are required by IIS and must always be enabled.
File Transfer Protocol (FTP) Service	Disabled	Enable if required	Allows the web server to provide FTP services. Because the FTP credentials are always sent in plaintext, it is recommended you connect to FTP servers through a secured connection, such as those provided by IPSec or a VPN tunnel.
FrontPage 2002 Server Extensions	Disabled	Disabled	Provides FrontPage support for administering and publishing web sites. Disable when no web sites are using FrontPage Server Extensions. FrontPage extensions have been used in early hacking attacks.
Internet Information Services Manager	Enabled	Enabled	Administrative interface for IIS. Disable when you do not want to administer the web server locally.
Internet Printing	Disabled	Disabled	Provides web-based printer management and allows printers to be shared using HTTP. This component is not required on a dedicated web server.
NNTP Service	Disabled	Disabled	Distributes, queries, retrieves, and posts Usenet news articles on the Internet. This component is not required on a dedicated web server.

Table continued on following page

445

Table 12-6 (continued)

Subcomponent	Default Setting	Recommended Setting	Comment
SMTP Service	Enabled	Enable if required	Supports the transfer of electronic mail. This component is not required on a dedicated web server unless it is used to send e-mail from a web site. Required for servers running Exchange Server 2003. Users familiar with ASP.NET may consider using ASP.NET for SMTP delivery instead.
World Wide Web Service	Enabled	Enabled	Provides Internet services, such as static and dynamic content, to clients. This component is required. Note: If this component is not enabled, then all subcomponents are not enabled.
Subcomponents of Message Queuing			
Active Directory Integration	Disabled	Enable if required	Provides integration with Active Directory whenever the web server belongs to a domain
Common	Disabled	Enable if required	Required by Message Queuing
Downlevel Client Support	Disabled	Enable if required	Provides access to Active Directory and site recognition for clients that are not Active Directory–aware
MSMQ HTTP Support	Disabled	Enable if required	Provides the sending and receiving of messages over the HTTP transport
Routing Support	Disabled	Enable if required	Provides store-and-forward messaging as well as efficient routing services for Message Queuing
Triggers	Disabled	Enable if required	Provides support to associate the arrival of incoming messages at a queue with functionality in a COM component or stand-alone program. This component is required when your web sites and applications use Message Queuing and Message Queuing triggers.

Subcomponent	Default Setting	Recommended Setting	Comment
Subcomponents of World Wide Web Service			
Active Server Pages	Disabled	Enable if required	Provides support for Active Server Pages (ASP). Disable this component when none of the web sites or applications on the web server use ASP. You can disable this component in Add or Remove Windows Components, which is accessible from Add or Remove Programs in Control Panel, or in the Web Service Extensions node in IIS Manager.
Internet Data Connector	Disabled	Enable if required	Provides support for dynamic content provided through files with .idc extensions. A very old method, it can usually be disabled. Consider using ASP, ASP.NET, or a similar scripting language with equivalent functionality instead. Disable this component when no web sites or applications on the web server include files with .idc extensions. You can disable this component in Add or Remove Windows Components, which is accessible from Add or Remove Programs in Control Panel, or in the Web Service Extensions node in IIS Manager.
Remote Administration (HTML)	Disabled	Enable if required	Provides an HTML interface for administering IIS. Use IIS Manager instead to provide easier administration and to reduce the attack surface of the web server. This component is not required on a dedicated web server. Use an adjunct protection tunnel as well.

Table continued on following page

Table 12-6 (continued)

Subcomponent	Default Setting	Recommended Setting	Comment
Remote Desktop Web Connection	Disabled	Enable if required	Includes Microsoft ActiveX controls and sample pages for hosting Terminal Services client connections. Use IIS Manager instead to provide easier administration and to reduce the attack surface of the web server. This component is not required on a dedicated web server. Consider using RDP with an adjunct protection tunnel instead.
Server-Side Includes	Disabled	Enable if required	Provides support for .shtm, .shtml, and .stm files. Disable this component when no web sites or applications on the web server include files with these extensions.
WebDAV Publishing	Disabled	Enable if required	Web Distributed Authoring and Versioning (WebDAV) extends the HTTP/1.1 protocol to allow clients to publish, lock, and manage resources on the web. Disable this component on a dedicated web server. You can disable this component in Add/ Remove Windows Components or in the Web Service Extensions node in IIS Manager
World Wide Web Service	Enabled	Enabled	Provides Internet services, such as static and dynamic content, to clients. This component is required on a dedicated web server.

Choose to install only the options necessary to make your web server meet its operational requirements. Every additional feature is a potential attack point.

Enabling Web Service Extensions

In IIS 6, all web service extensions are disabled by default. Choose which extensions to enable, if any. There are six default options and you can add your own. Table 12-7 discusses the six default web service extensions.

Table 12-7

Web Service Extension	Description
Active Server Pages	Enable this extension when one or more of the web sites and applications contains ASP content.
ASP.NET	Enable this extension when one or more of the web sites and applications contains ASP.NET content.
FrontPage Server Extensions 2002	Enable this extension when one or more of the web sites use FrontPage Server Extensions.
Internet Data Connector	Enable this extension when one or more of the web sites and applications use the Internet Data Connector (IDC) to display database information (content includes .idc and .idx files).
Server-Side Includes	Enable this extension when one or more of the web sites use server-side include (SSI) directives to instruct the web server to insert various types of content into a web page.
WebDAV	Enable this extension when you want to support WebDAV on the web server.

Minimize the number of web service extensions to the bare minimum needed to meet the functional requirements of the web site.

IIS 7 Modules

In IIS 6, much of the core IIS functionality is built into a few monolithic Dll files. For instance, all the authentication methods, static rendering, and request processing are built into one Dll file. All the code for each authentication method is in memory whether the administrator ever uses it or not. IIS 7 has divided key functionality into dozens of task-specific Dll modules. These modules can be loaded and unload globally or per web site or per application. For example, if none of your web sites will ever use SSL client certificate mapping, you can unload the `Authmap.dll`. Table 12-8 shows some of the security modules that can be loaded or unloaded (details could change by IIS 7's release date).

Table 12-8

Module Name	Description	Module Dll
AnonymousAuthModule	Performs Anonymous Authentication when no other authentication method succeeds	Inetsrv\Authanon.dll
BasicAuthModule	Performs Basic Authentication	Inetsrv\Authbas.dll
CertificateMappingAuthenticationModule	Performs Certificate Mapping Authentication using Active Directory	Inetsrv\Authcert.dll

Table continued on following page

Table 12-8 (continued)

Module Name	Description	Module Dll
DigestAuthModule	Performs Digest Authentication	Inetsrv\Authmd5.dll
IISCertificateMappingAuthenticationModule	Performs Certificate Mapping Authentication using IIS certificate configuration	Inetsrv\Authmap.dll
RequestFilteringModule	Performs URLScan tasks such as configuring allowed verbs and file extensions, setting limits, and scanning for bad character sequences	Inetsrv\Modrqflt.dll
UrlAuthorizationModule	Performs URL authorization	Inetsrv\Urlauthz.dll
WindowsAuthModule	Performs NTLM integrated authentication	Inetsrv\Authsspi.dll

Taken from www.microsoft.com/technet/prodtechnol/windowsserver2003/library/iis7/TechRef/67f99d86-04ab-4140-8718-e873cc1e4b80.mspx

Strengthen NTFS Permissions

On dedicated web servers, remove NTFS permissions that are granted to the Everyone group on the root folder of disk volumes supporting web server content. Remove any compilers, development environments, or sample files.

If not needed, disable the IWAM and default IIS anonymous accounts in the User Manager tool. Create a new IIS anonymous account. This is an optional step but allows for better control over what access the IIS anonymous user has to the web server. Create an Anonymous Web Users group and add the new IIS anonymous user account to the group. Using Windows Explorer, set Full Control permission to Deny on the \%windir% and %windir%\System32 folders for the Anonymous Web Users group. Then add Everyone Deny permissions to the Windows\Temporary Compressed Files, unless web compression is needed. Deleted all files in the iisadmpwd folder.

Install URLScan 2.5

Download and install Microsoft's free URLScan version 2.5 tool (www.microsoft.com/downloads/details.aspx?familyid=23d18937-dd7e-4613-9928-7f94ef1c902a&displaylang=en). Much of URLScan's original functionality is already enabled in IIS 6, but the new version (versions newer than 2.0) has increased, must-have functionality not present in the included version.

URLScan will load itself as an ISAPI filter program, which must be enabled in Web Service Extensions. When enabled, it will inspect incoming commands looking for signs of maliciousness. You can and should further customize the information URLScan blocks. Look for the URLScan.ini file (see Figure 12-11) and make the following non-default changes:

❑ Set UseAllowExtensions to 1. This will enable URLScan to deny-by-default any extension not specifically allowed. Then, under the AllowedExtensions section, type in only the file extensions needed on the web server. Only content files being downloaded or uploaded need to be added. Be sure to add a period (.) to AllowedExtensions to cover files that don't end in an extension.

❑ Set MaxURL to 70 or some other number that indicates the maximum size of the URL string that your server will accept. You want to prevent overly long URLs, possibly containing buffer overflow or directory traversal attacks, from being uploaded.

❑ Set MaxAllowContent Length to 100000 or something acceptable that indicates the maximum size of any single content component. Again, the idea is to prevent unauthorized uploading or downloading.

❑ Set AllowVerbs to GET and HEAD, plus any other HTTP verbs that should be sent to the server. For instance, if the PUT command (which can place or write content to the web server) should never be used, it should not appear on the AllowVerbs list.

❑ Lastly, change the default URLScan log directory to a central log location to ease pick-up.

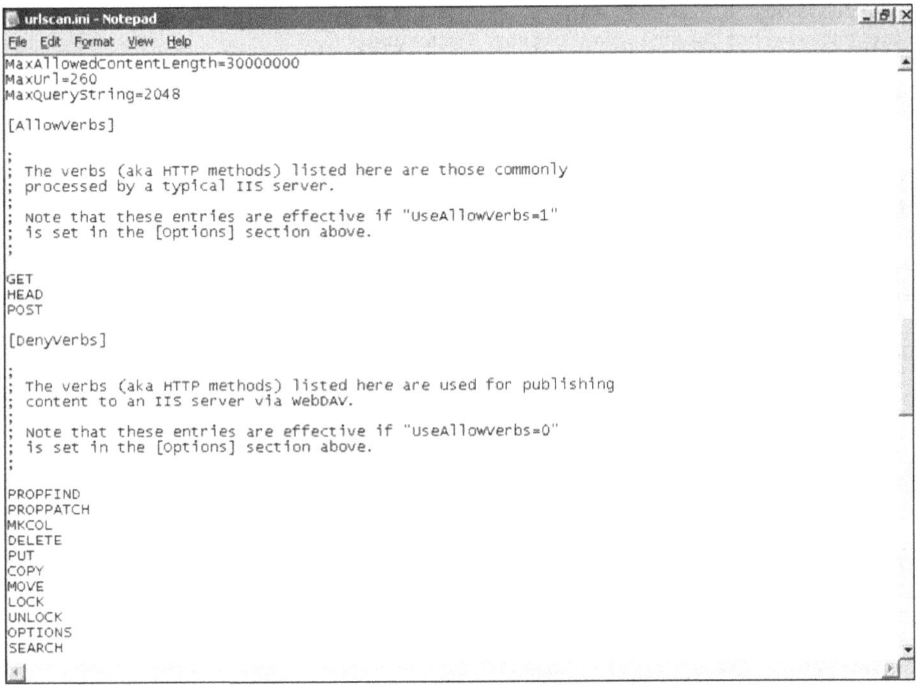

```
urlscan.ini - Notepad                                                    _|8|x
File  Edit  Format  View  Help
MaxAllowedContentLength=30000000
MaxUrl=260
MaxQueryString=2048

[AllowVerbs]

;
; The verbs (aka HTTP methods) listed here are those commonly
; processed by a typical IIS server.
;
; Note that these entries are effective if "UseAllowVerbs=1"
; is set in the [options] section above.
;

GET
HEAD
POST

[DenyVerbs]

;
; The verbs (aka HTTP methods) listed here are used for publishing
; content to an IIS server via WebDAV.
;
; Note that these entries are effective if "UseAllowVerbs=0"
; is set in the [options] section above.
;

PROPFIND
PROPPATCH
MKCOL
DELETE
PUT
COPY
MOVE
LOCK
UNLOCK
OPTIONS
SEARCH
```

Figure 12-11

For more information on URLScan, see http://support.microsoft.com/default.aspx?scid= 307608 or http://msdn.microsoft.com/library/default.asp?url=/library/en-us/secmod/ html/secmod114.asp.

IIS 7 will have more of URLScan's functionality built in.

Secure Web Site(s)

Now that the overall web server is secured, the following settings should be made to each web site.

Harden NTFS Permissions

Do not install any web sites to `\Inetpub\wwwroot`. That's where any hacker will look for web files. Instead, install to almost any other randomly created directory. Consider naming the directory something innocuous, like `D:\Temp`, if you want to fool any local hackers. Most hackers and web server scripts expect web sites to be in the default locations, so use another directory name.

Each web server should have its own web content directories. Each web application pool identity should only have the bare minimum access that it needs to each related content directory. Content directories should be structured to maximize security simplicity. Most administrators structure their web site directories according to the web site's overall linking structure. For example:

```
\Inetpub\wwwroot
\Inetpub\wwwroot\Examplecom
\Inetpub\wwwroot\Examplecom\Main
\Inetpub\wwwroot\Examplecom\Company Structure
\Inetpub\wwwroot\Examplecom\Mission
\Inetpub\wwwroot\Examplecom\Recruiting
```

Most administrators make subdirectory structures that mimic the linking structure and place all content into common parent directories that describe the web site's logical structure. Most of the time, all the files in the same folder share the same permissions. This is completely wrong.

Instead, web site folders should be structured along security lines, so that all content in the same directories truly describes common security permissions. Using the preceding example but improving on it:

```
\Temp\Web
\Temp\Web\Examplecom
\Temp\Web\Examplecom\HTML content
\Temp\Web\Examplecom\HTML content\Main
\Temp\Web\Examplecom\HTML content\Company Structure
\Temp\Web\Examplecom\HTML content\Mission
\Temp\Web\Examplecom\HTML content\Recruiting

\Temp\Web\Examplecom\Scripts
\Temp\Web\Examplecom\Scripts\Main
\Temp\Web\Examplecom\Scripts\Company Structure
\Temp\Web\Examplecom\Scripts\Mission
\Temp\Web\Examplecom\Scripts\Recruiting

\Temp\Web\Examplecom\Executables
\Temp\Web\Examplecom\Executables\Main
\Temp\Web\Examplecom\Executables\Company Structure
\Temp\Web\Examplecom\Executables\Mission
\Temp\Web\Examplecom\Executables\Recruiting

\Temp\Web\Examplecom\Pictures
\Temp\Web\Examplecom\Pictures\Main
```

```
\Temp\Web\Examplecom\Pictures\Company Structure
\Temp\Web\Examplecom\Pictures\Mission
\Temp\Web\Examplecom\Pictures\Recruiting
```

Although this structure may look unnecessarily complicated at first, it's really simple. In the first example, the administrator would have to manually look at each file in each directory and determine what security it should have. In the latter example, the appropriate permissions can be set at the higher parent directories (i.e., HTML content, Scripts, Executables, Pictures), and all the related files automatically inherit the correct permissions. It may take a little bit longer to set up, but it saves in overall administration time and ensures greater security. The former model is bound to break down and cause a security issue. The latter structure makes good security occur naturally.

Then, using Windows Explorer (for NTFS permissions) and IIS Admin (for IIS permissions), set the bare minimum permissions needed for the web site to function appropriately. Remember to tie NTFS permissions to the appropriate application pool identity and the appropriate impersonated user account (e.g., IUSR).

You will have to ensure that identities are in the IIS_WPG group and that identities and impersonated user accounts have the normal User permissions to \System32\Inetsrv. Ensure that any IIS-related user accounts (i.e., IUSR, web pool identity, etc.) do not have access to any files or folders to which they should not have access. There is no reason for IIS-related user accounts to have access to most high-risk files, folders, and registry keys, as detailed in Chapters 5 and 6. For example, unless there is a legitimate reason for the IUSR account to have access to Cmd.exe, Command.com, or Debug.exe, give the IUSR account Deny-Full Control permissions to those files. That way, if the IIS anonymous user account "breaks out" of IIS, then the hacker won't be able to readily access the Windows command prompt, as they often expect. This will defeat many hackers and hacking tools. Appropriately set permissions will help increase the security of any web site.

Web Site IP Settings

Change the IP address of the web site in the IIS Admin console to be a static private address instead of All Unassigned. This will prevent hackers from using unintended IP addresses to gain unauthorized access to the web server. Install the web site to a non-default port, as discussed above, if possible. Moving web servers off ports 80 and 443 will do much to increase the security risk of any affected web site.

Enabled Host Headers

Require a host header to match the appropriate URL name (see Figure 12-12). Host headers are the URLs that are submitted by connecting clients. It's an HTTP standard that allows one web server IP address to host multiple, different web sites. By enabling host headers on all web sites, any request to the web server without a host header will be automatically denied. Most browsers support host headers, but many hacking tools do not. Users almost always connect using fully qualified domain names. Most scanning scripts and worms connect to web servers using IP addresses. The host header requirement would defeat those tools. See www.iisanswers.com/hinders_rant.htm for more details.

Application Pool Changes

Application pools and their identities should be locked down to just the files and folders they need in order to allow the web site to function appropriately. In most cases, every web site should have its own application pool. You can create new application pools in the IIS Manager by right-clicking the Application Pool container object and choosing New ⇨ Application Pool. You can create a custom application pool from scratch or use an existing application pool as a starting template (see Figure 12-13).

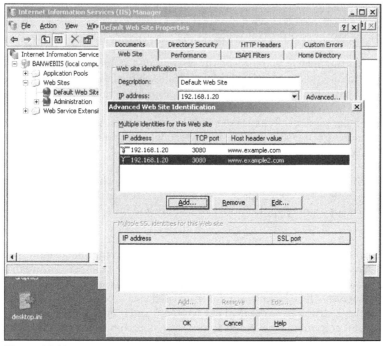

Figure 12-12

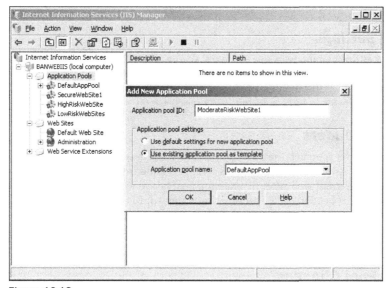

Figure 12-13

If your web site does not need Kerberos authentication, consider creating a new identity account for the web pool. It should not be named anything that might attract the attention of a hacker. It should be named using a similar convention of your regular users. Then give it just the permissions and privileges it needs to load the web site correctly. Don't forget to add new identity accounts to IIS_WPG. Then add the new identity to the web pool (see Figure 12-14).

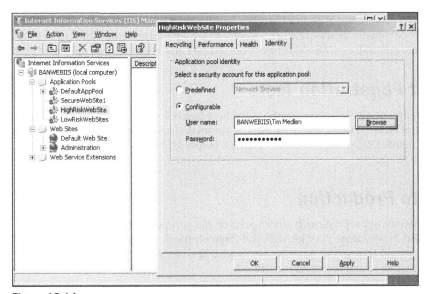

Figure 12-14

After making the appropriate changes, stop and restart IIS to let the new changes take effect. Then rerun the MBSA to check for missing patches.

Configure Logging

Enable Object Access auditing for all files on the web server not authorized to be seen by any IIS accounts. For instance, the IUSR account doesn't access Cmd.exe on most web sites, so enable Object Access auditing for that file and tell it to record success or failure audit events for the user IUSR_<computername>.

Create a new centralized log directory on the server and configure all logs to write there. Enable hourly IIS log files, enable all fields, and configure logs to be saved in the new log folder. Configure URLScan to save its log files to the new central location. Configure the host-based firewall to monitor all successful and dropped packets and to save the log file to the new centralized location.

Clean and Test

When setting up and patching any new computer, there are bound to be temporary files and folders left around. For example, delete the \wutemp folder left over by patching. Look for other temporary files and delete them too. Then empty the Recycle Bin and reboot once more. Check error logs after bootup for any messages to investigate.

Install and Tighten Applications

Now the even harder part. Securing an OS and IIS server are easy compared to installing a secure application. Many penetration experts swear they have never met a secure web application. Coders and the web server administrator should work together to ensure that a secure application is installed on IIS and that the bare minimum permissions have been defined and configured as discussed above.

Conduct Penetration Tests

Open the appropriate web server ports on the host-based firewall to allow for internal penetration testing. Penetration tests, using their own wits or automated tools, should test the OS, IIS, and the application. Any noted deficiencies should be corrected before go-live. Lessons learned should be incorporated into future roll-outs.

Deploy to Production

Finally, open the appropriate web server ports on the perimeter firewall and let the web site be exposed to the world. You've done your job well and there is little to worry about. Every web site can be hacked, but yours should be one that is not easily cracked. You can also open the web site to external penetration testing if another round of testing is required.

Monitor Log Files

Monitor the firewall and log files located in the centralized log directory. Investigate critical or persistent threats.

More Resources

See the following resources for more information on securing IIS:

- ❑ IIS 6 Resource Kit: www.microsoft.com/downloads/details.aspx?FamilyID= 80a1b6e6-829e-49b7-8c02-333d9c148e69&DisplayLang=en

- ❑ Configuring Application Isolation on Windows Server 2003 and Internet Information Services (IIS) 6.0: www.microsoft.com/technet/prodtechnol/windowsserver2003/ plan/appisoa.asp

- ❑ Microsoft IIS 6 Technet Resources: www.microsoft.com/technet/prodtechnol/ windowsserver2003/technologies/featured/iis/default.mspx

- ❑ Brett Hill's IIS Answers.com: www.iisanswers.com

Summary

Chapter 12 covered how to secure one of the most frequently attacked applications on the Internet. It detailed how to harden the network environment, physical location, hardware, operating system, IIS, and applications. Most of the effort is spent hardening the operating system and IIS. If done appropriately and verified, the steps will result in a strongly hardened IIS server that is impervious to easy exploitation.

The author was involved in a hacking contest at www.hackiis6.com (no longer an active domain), where the steps in this chapter were used to harden an IIS 6 static web site. Hackers from around the world were then invited to attempt to exploit the site for a chance to win an Xbox game console. After more than three weeks, the site didn't even come close to being hacked. While the contest may not have proved that IIS is unhackable, it did demonstrate that when appropriately configured, it can be made relatively secure against easy attack. Chapter 13 will cover file and folder encryption using the Encrypting File System.

13

Using Encrypting File System

Microsoft introduced Encrypting File System (EFS) with Windows 2000, and has steadily improved it in its later operating systems. It provides strong, reliable, seamless encryption. When enabled, users can encrypt and decrypt files and folders as desired. EFS-protected files are encapsulated by open, industry-standard encryption ciphers. It's solid security. If the user's EFS decryption key is lost, and no backup or recovery precautions were taken beforehand, it can be difficult to impossible to recover the protected files. This chapter covers how EFS works, how it should be set up, cautionary tales, and best practices.

How EFS Works

EFS requires Windows 2000 or later with NTFS disk volumes and uses both symmetric and asymmetric cipher algorithms. It is globally enabled by default, meaning that any user can encrypt any file or folder at any time simply by choosing to enable it. Files and folders must be individually selected for encryption, although normal inheritance rules apply.

EFS is not supported within XP Home.

Encrypting a File

To disable or enable EFS globally in group policy, choose `Computer Configuration\Windows Settings\Security Settings\Public Key Policies` and right-click the Encrypting File System leaf, select Properties, and enable or remove the *Allow users to encrypt files using EFS* check box. It can also be enabled or disabled using the registry key `HKLM\SOFTWARE\Policies\Microsoft\WindowsNT\CurrentVersion\EFS\EfsConfiguration` or `HKLM\SOFTWARE\Microsoft\WindowsNT\CurrentVersion\EFS\EfsConfiguration`. A `DWord` value of 1 will disable EFS; a value of 0 will enable EFS. EFS is globally enabled by default.

To encrypt a file or folder, a user simply right-clicks the object in Windows Explorer, chooses the Properties option under the General tab, clicks the Advanced button, and enables the *Encrypt contents to secure data* option (see Figure 13-1).

> *Why Microsoft did not put the EFS option under the main Security tab under File Properties along with all the other file security settings is a mystery.*

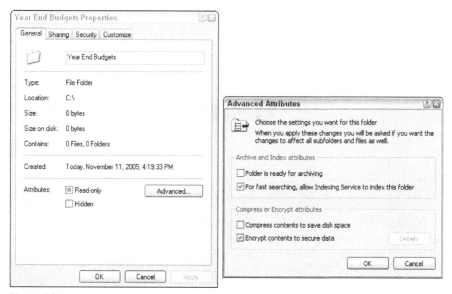

Figure 13-1

If a file in a subfolder is selected for encryption, Windows will prompt the user to decide whether to encrypt only the selected file or to encrypt all files in the current folder. Even when the user decides to encrypt all files (current and future) in the folder, EFS encrypts each file individually and uses separate file encryption keys. If the file contains multiple data streams (i.e., alternate data streams), all data streams will be encrypted, but not the file's attributes.

EFS can be used to encrypt almost any Windows file or folder, but Microsoft made some important exceptions. EFS cannot encrypt the following:

❑ User profiles, because that is where the user's EFS keys are stored

❑ Windows system and root files, because doing so would also encrypt the files needed to use EFS

❑ Any file with the system attribute set, including Hiberfil.sys and the pagefile

❑ Files compressed using Windows NTFS compression

❑ Files stored on FAT volumes

❑ Drive mount or reparse points

> *EFS-protected files are not indexed by the Content Indexing Service to prevent accidental data leakage.*

When files are being encrypted, Windows creates a temporary log file called `Efs0.log` in the System Volume Information folder on the same drive as the encrypted file. The zero in the file name may be incremented (e.g., `Efs1.log`) until the file name is unique. Microsoft uses the log file to keep track of the status of the current or pending EFS transactions. In the event of a crash, EFS will use the log to remove any uncompleted transactions.

Another temporary file called `Efs0.tmp` (or incremented to any unique file name like the log file) is created in the same folder as the file being encrypted. The contents of the original plaintext file are copied into the temporary file, after which the original plaintext file is overwritten with the new encrypted data. When EFS is finished encrypting the file, the log and temporary files are erased. In older versions of EFS, when the EFS temporary file was deleted, the original plaintext from the temporary file was left on disk, which could allow data leakage or discovery. This problem can be minimized by always encrypting entire folders, instead of individual files. You can also use the `Cipher.exe` utility to wipe all free space of any plaintext data left behind by EFS encryption.

Encrypted file names are green when viewed in Windows Explorer. This is a view attribute that can be turned on and off by choosing Tools ➪ Folder Options ➪ View, and enabling or disabling *Show encrypted or compressed NTFS files in color* in Windows Explorer.

Alternative EFS Methods

One or more files can be encrypted at once by using the command-line `Cipher.exe` utility. `Cipher.exe` can participate in over a dozen cryptographic tasks, including many involving EFS. To encrypt multiple files at once, use Cipher's `/E` parameter. To turn off EFS on one or more files, use its `/D` parameter. You can also use Cipher without any command-line parameters to show existing EFS files.

Some organizations may find it easier to enable EFS by placing *Encrypt and Decrypt* on the Windows Explorer context menu when a file is right-clicked with the mouse. To enable this feature, create a DWORD value of 1 for *EncryptionContextMenu* (which you will have to create) under `HKLM\Software\Microsoft\Windows\CurrentVersion\Explorer\Advanced`.

Decrypting Files

One of the most beautiful things about EFS is how transparently the decryption works. If a logged on authorized user opens the file, EFS decrypts the file on the fly into its clear-text representation. If the user copies the file over the network, sends it in an e-mail, or copies it to a non-NTFS partition, the file decrypts transparently. This also means that if intruders can log on as the user or data recovery agent, they can also access the files in their unprotected state. This last point is a big potential weakness.

If the user copies the file to another NTFS partition, or if the file is backed up to an NTFS-aware tape drive, the encryption remains with the file. If an intruder boots around Windows to access the encrypted files without the user's password, they remain encrypted. If the authorized user copies or moves an EFS-protected file from an encrypted folder to an unencrypted folder on the same volume, the file remains encrypted. However, if the user copies or moves an unencrypted file into an encrypted folder, the file will be encrypted.

File Security and EFS

The security mechanisms that determine whether a user can access or modify a particular file are completely separate from EFS mechanisms. This has many repercussions. First, a user must have Read and Modify (or Write, or Change in the Share) permissions to encrypt a file. Second, if multiple users can modify a file prior to EFS being implemented on the file, the first user to encrypt effectively prevents all others from being able to read or modify the file, unless EFS file-sharing is enabled. Third, the file names of encrypted files can still be seen and viewed by other users that have Read or List access to the protected file(s). This is a potential information leakage problem that can only be remedied by removing the unauthorized user's Read and List permissions.

Lastly, even when only one user has the capability to encrypt a file, any user with Modify (or Write) permissions can delete it. While this may be surprising to those new to computer security, EFS is encryption software, not integrity software. Encryption prevents unauthorized users from being able to read, print, extract, copy, or move a file. The confidentiality of the file remains intact at all times. However, the file can be deleted by anyone with the appropriate file permissions, which is an integrity problem. Most encryption programs such as EFS only address confidentiality problems. Integrity concerns must be addressed using normal NTFS file permissions (i.e., remove Modify or Write permissions from unauthorized users).

EFS Certificate

Every time a file is encrypted or decrypted, Windows looks for the user's EFS certificate. If this is the first time the user has encrypted a file on a particular system, Windows will first determine whether a public key infrastructure (PKI) server capable of supporting EFS (like Microsoft's Certificate Services) is active and participating. If so, Windows will request a digital certificate capable of supporting EFS on behalf of the user, and install it to the user's local profile. If a PKI server is not available, Windows will generate a self-signed EFS certificate and install it to the user's profile. Figures 13-2 and 13-3 show an EFS certificate generated by a Microsoft Certificate Services PKI server. EFS certificates are 1,024 bits by default. PKI-supplied EFS digital certificates are good for two years and will automatically renew before they expire, by default. Self-signed EFS certificates are good for 100 years.

> *The expiration period of self-signed EFS digital certifications may seem a month short of the 100-year mark on first examination because the total expiration period does not take into account leap years, so the expiration period is 100×365 days, not exactly 100 years.*

An EFS certificate contains the user's private and public encryption keys. Every user (or sometimes computer, in the case of Offline files) has only one EFS certificate for every stand-alone system or domain computer. Every file the user encrypts will involve the user's single EFS certificate.

As stated above, a user's EFS certificate, with both public and private keys, is stored in the user's local profile. If the user has a roaming profile, the EFS certificate will be stored in the networked roaming profile, and locally wherever the user logs on. If the user encrypts files on a machine that does not have their EFS keys stored locally, they will have to import their EFS certificate locally or make sure the machine is *Trusted for Delegation* (more on this below).

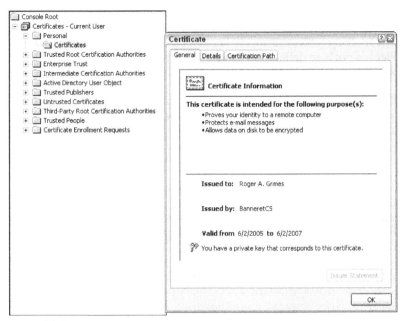

Figure 13-2

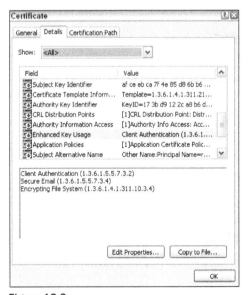

Figure 13-3

The storing of the user's EFS key in their local profile is an extremely important point. If the user loses access to their local profile, either because of corruption or an inadvertent action (e.g., such as reinstalling Windows to fix another problem), their EFS key could become unrecoverable if not backed up. If a data recovery policy has not been defined beforehand (covered below), the protected files could easily be lost forever. This issue is not an uncommon problem.

The user's EFS certificate, which can have up to 16,384 bits of protection (it would be very slow and overkill), is protected by a 512-bit master key. The user's EFS private keys are stored in `C:\Documents and Settings\<userid>\Application Data\Microsoft\Crypto\RSA\<usersid>` and are encrypted by the user's master key, which is stored in `C:\Documents and Settings\<userid>\Application Data\Microsoft\Protect\<userid>` and encrypted based on the user's password.

If an administrator resets the user's password on a stand-alone computer, it causes a new master key to be generated, and the user's EFS certificate can no longer be extracted. Users should always, if possible, change their own password (and not allow an administrator reset). If a user's password is reset, changing the password back to the previous password or using a previously created Password Reset Diskette (if created for the user's old password) should allow the user's EFS keys to be extracted again.

> *Important: Administrators resetting a user's password through the normal methods on a stand-alone computer can cause the user to lose access to their EFS-protected files. Unless impossible, always allow users to change their own password. If an administrator resets a password and the user loses access to their EFS-protected files, the user's original EFS key will have to be restored (if backed up), or the data recovery agent will have to recover the files (if a data recovery agent was in use at the time the files were encrypted).*

File Encryption Key

The actual encryption process behind the scenes is more complicated, of course. When a file is first chosen for encryption, the Windows CryptoAPI will generate a symmetric encryption key, called the *File Encryption Key (FEK)*. Every encrypted file has a unique FEK. No matter how many people can encrypt a single file, only one FEK is used to do the encrypting and decrypting. And just like any symmetric encryption algorithm, the same EFS key that encrypts the file is used to decrypt it.

FEK Ciphers

EFS uses Data Encryption Standard XOR (DESX), Triple-Data Encryption Standard (3DES), or Advanced Encryption Standard (AES) ciphers to create the FEK. By default, EFS uses the 128-bit DESX algorithm in Windows XP (pre-SP1), a slight improvement over the U.S. government's older Data Encryption Standard (DES) algorithm standard, for the FEK symmetric key. See `www.rsasecurity.com/rsalabs/node .asp?id=2232` for more information on the differences between DES and DESX.

> *Non-U.S. versions of EFS may use 56-bit DESX instead of 128-bit.*

Windows XP Pro and later can also be configured to use the stronger 168-bit 3DES cipher algorithm instead of DESX by enabling *System cryptography: Use FIPS compliant algorithms for encryption, hashing, and signing* located in Group Policy or Local Computer Policy under `Computer Configuration\ Windows Settings\Security Settings\Local Policies\Security Options`. The Federal Information Processing Standards (FIPS) are U.S. government recommended or required standards for government agencies, contractors, and solutions. If enabled, all new EFS encryptions in XP pre-SP1 will use 3DES, but any files previously encrypted by DESX will still be able to be decrypted without a problem. A great article on the effective strength of DES, DESX, and 3DES can be found at www .networkcomputing.com/1006/1006colmoskowitz.html.

When FIPS-compliant ciphers are enabled, it affects many other Windows features beyond EFS. If enabled, Windows will use TLS with 3DES, SHA-1, and RSA public keying material instead of the more widely supported standard of SSL for client/server HTTPS transactions, IPSec will use 3DES instead of DESX, and Terminal Services (and RDP services) will only use 3DES for encryption.

Windows XP Pro SP1 and later and Windows Server 2003 use the new and significantly stronger 256-bit AES open, symmetric cipher standard, by default, to create FEKs for EFS. Windows 2000 can use 56-bit DES or 128-bit DESX if installed with SP1 or later and high encryption. Whenever possible, AES should be used to provide the most secure implementation of EFS possible (i.e., AES is more secure than 3DES).

DDF and DRF

When a user encrypts a file, the file's FEK is encrypted by the user's personal EFS public key from the user's EFS digital certificate. The resulting encrypted FEK is stored in one of the file's extended attributes, called $EFS, in the Data Decryption Field (DDF) area. All users who are allowed to encrypt/ decrypt the file will have their own identical copy of the FEK encrypted by their own EFS public key, and stored in the DDF attribute field. Each DDF contains the user's SID, the folder where the EFS key is stored (called the *container name,* based on the computer and user's SIDs), cryptographic provider name (usually Microsoft Base Cryptographic Provider or Enhanced Provider), the user's name, the EFS certificate hash, and, finally, the encrypted FEK.

If a recovery agent is defined (covered in more detail below), a copy of the FEK is encrypted by the EFS recovery agent's public key and stored in a file attribute field called the Data Recovery Field (DRF). There will be a DRF entry for every recovery agent defined at the time the file was encrypted (or re-encrypted). The creation and naming of EFS keys are depicted in Figure 13-4.

New EFS Options in XP and XP SP2

In Windows 2000, EFS was added as a new driver. In Windows XP and later, EFS is integrated as part of NTFS. Microsoft added new EFS features in Windows XP and later (some of the topics have already been covered above):

❏   Data recovery agents are optional, but highly recommended.

❏   The 3DES and AES encryption algorithms can be used instead of DESX.

❏   Additional users can be authorized to access shared encrypted files.

❏   Offline files can be encrypted.

❏   A Password Reset Disk can be used to safely reset a user's password to a previous password.

❏   Encrypted files can be stored in web server (WebDAV) folders.

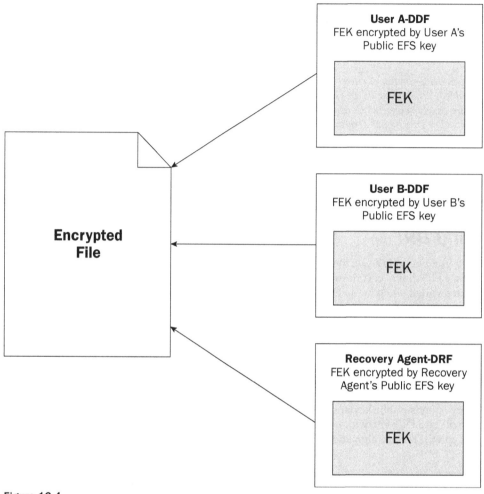

Figure 13-4

EFS File Sharing

Windows XP Pro and later allow multiple users to share EFS-protected files. The first user encrypting the file must add the additional users. All EFS users must have Read and Modify (or Write, or Change on the share) permissions and an already existing EFS certificate installed on the local machine or reachable using Active Directory. To implement the additional users, the original encrypting user chooses the Details button (see Figure 13-5) under the Advanced Attributes dialog box, under File Properties. Then the user clicks the Add button (see Figure 13-6) to add more users. Unfortunately, EFS file-sharing cannot be set on folders and cannot be given to groups. The latter issue is easily understandable because EFS certificates are issued per user and cannot be shared by groups.

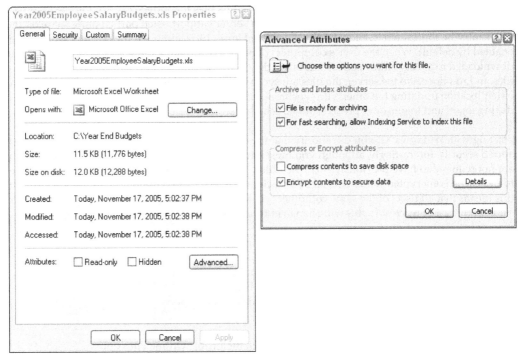

Figure 13-5

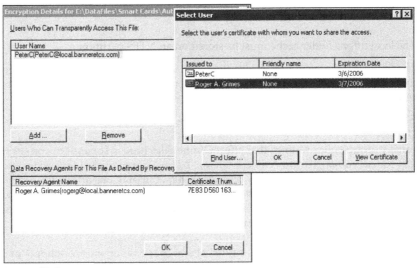

Figure 13-6

Offline File Encryption

Windows' Offline Files feature allows users to store and use remotely accessible files offline when their access to the remote file server is interrupted, intentionally or unintentionally. Starting with Windows

XP Pro, Microsoft allows administrators to encrypt offline files for added security. Offline Files works using shared folders (or web pages) with client and server support. Each participating share on the computer must be configured to allow Offline Files (see Figure 13-7), although the server's settings are often enabled by default. When the user's computer connects to the remote file server share, the files are downloaded to a local offline cache location on the client computer. After the user works with the offline files and reconnects to the server, the files are synchronized with the server, with the latest versions from either location updating the other. File synchronization can occur when the user's computer goes offline, during logoff and logon, or at predetermined schedules.

Starting with Windows XP, you can specify that the offline files that are stored locally be encrypted for added security. Interestingly, although you must have already enabled Offline Files, participating users are not required to have previously encrypted files. When the offline folder cache is encrypted, the folder cache is encrypted with a special EFS machine (i.e., computer) digital certificate. Unfortunately, this means that all users of the same computer will have their personal offline files encrypted with the same EFS key. Per Microsoft, this will change in future Windows versions.

To encrypt the Offline Files database on a local computer:

1. Click the Start button and then click the Control Panel menu option. If Control Panel is in Classic view, double-click Folder Options. If Control Panel is in Category view, click the Appearance and Themes link, and then click Folder Options.

2. Click the Offline Files tab.

3. If Offline Files are not already enabled, click the Enable Offline Files option.

4. Click the *Encrypt offline files to secure data* option (see Figure 13-7). Click OK.

Windows will now automatically encrypt offline files as they are stored in the local Offline Files database. Requirements include the following:

❑ The local offline folder cache must be stored on an NTFS partition.

❑ The first user logging on the local system after offline folder encryption is enabled must be a local administrator. This is because a registry entry must be made and the registry change requires admin rights.

❑ EFS and Offline Folder encryption must not be disabled by the Administrator or group policy.

There are many group policy settings that affect Offline Files (`www.microsoft.com/resources/documentation/Windows/XP/all/reskit/en-us/Default.asp?url=/resources/documentation/Windows/XP/all/reskit/en-us/prde_ffs_phvy.asp`, but only one affects the EFS status of Offline Files, the *Encrypt the Offline Files cache* option. If enabled, the offline files cache will be encrypted if the client is Windows XP or later. When you enable offline folder cache encrypting, the entire database is encrypted, not individual files. You cannot selectively choose which files to encrypt.

A great, short document on Offline EFS is located at `www.microsoft.com/technet/prodtechnol/winxppro/maintain/encryptoffline.mspx`.

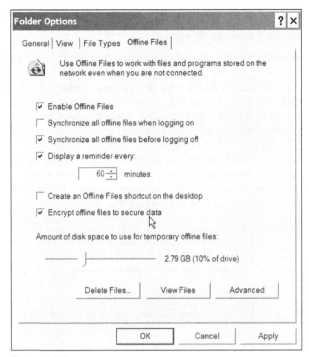

Figure 13-7

Encrypted Web Files

EFS can also be used to encrypt files on WebDAV-enabled directories on IIS 6 web servers. WebDAV stands for Web-based Distributed Authoring and Versioning. It is an open standard from RFC 2518. In order for WebDAV to be used, both the client and the server must support it. Windows 2000 and later have a WebDAV client enabled, called the *Web Client service*. The separate service is not needed if IE 5.x or later is installed or if Microsoft Office 2000 and later is used. The WebDAV service must be enabled in IIS 6 as a web extension. Once enabled, any virtual directory created on IIS becomes automatically WebDAV-enabled. If EFS is also enabled on the server (the default option), any EFS encrypted file stored in a virtual directory remains encrypted when copied to and from a WebDAV-enabled client. Normally, EFS-protected files do not remain encrypted when copied over network connections.

If the file on the web server is not encrypted, it should be encrypted locally on the server is possible. The web server does not have to be trusted for delegation for WebDAV to take advantage of EFS. If the file is unencrypted on the server, and then encrypted by the client, a plaintext version of the file is copied down to the client, encrypted, and then sent back up to IIS. Although WebDAV is a great solution for keeping EFS-protected files encrypted across the wire, IPSec might be a better option because it will work with any protocol, not just HTTP.

Using EFS on Servers

Getting EFS working for local computers is easy, as described above. Getting EFS working on a file server so remote users can use it to encrypt files across a network takes a bit more work. In order for EFS to work on a (remote) server, for a remote user, three things must be true:

❑   The server must be a domain member that uses Kerberos authentication.

❑   The server must be trusted for delegation (covered below).

❑   The user must be logged on with a domain account that can be delegated.

By default, user accounts are usually enabled for delegation, unless in the Account tab under User account object, the following option is enabled: *Account is sensitive and cannot be delegated*. Delegated trust is needed so that the user's EFS private key stored in the user's local profile can be passed to the remote server to encrypt and decrypt the EFS-protected files.

All server computers can be trusted for delegation, but whether delegation is enabled by default depends on the type of server computer. Domain controller computers are trusted for delegation during the domain controller promotion process. Member servers are not trusted by default and must be enabled in Active Directory Users and Computers (see Figure 13-8).

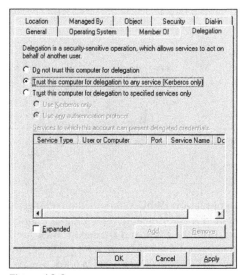

Figure 13-8

In Windows Server 2000 and 2003 domains, there are two or three options to consider in trusting a computer for delegation:

❑   *Do not trust this computer for delegation*. If selected, remote users cannot use EFS on the selected server.

❑   *Trust this computer for delegation to any service (Kerberos only)*. When this option is selected on a computer, all services under the Local System account on the computer will be trusted for delegation. This means an administrator on that computer may install any service, and then that service will have the capability to access any network resource by impersonating a user. This option will work for EFS, but it also makes a system susceptible to some types of malicious attacks (i.e., trojan attacks, etc.).

❏   *Trust this computer for delegation to specified services only.* This is new with Windows Server 2003, and is called *constrained delegation.* With constrained delegation, the administrator can specify which Service Principal Names (SPNs) this account is able to delegate to. This is the safest option to enable, but it takes much more effort to set up for any service, including EFS.

When enabled on a file server for remote users, EFS still does not encrypt files read from the server and sent over the network. If network protection is also desired, use WebDAV, IPSec, or SSL to protect EFS files in transmission.

Setting Up an EFS Recovery Policy

EFS is good encryption. Unfortunately, by storing EFS keys in the user's local profile and using the user's master key to protect the EFS private key, there is a good chance that the user's EFS keys may one day become inaccessible. Administrators must assume this will happen and prepare for recovery. EFS recovery can be accomplished by

❏   Backing up each user's EFS keys individually

❏   Having one or more Default Recovery Agents

❏   Allowing Certificate Services to back up EFS keys automatically

You should choose one of these options and implement an EFS recovery strategy. Users can back up their own EFS keys to a file and then store them in a safe place. If this method is used, users should store their backup EFS keys in a separate physical location away from their primary site, to prevent loss from a single disaster.

Backing Up EFS Keys Individually

Users can back up their EFS keys using many methods, including the following:

❏   Using the Certificates console snap-in

❏   Using `Cipher.exe`

❏   Using EFS GUI

To use the Certificates console snap-in, the user should perform the following steps:

1.   Start the Microsoft Management console by selecting Start ➪ Run, and type **Mmc.exe** in the Open dialog box.

2.   Choose File ➪ Add/Remove Snap-in from the menu bar.

3.   Click the Add button.

4.   Select the Certificates console and click Add, Finish, Close, and then OK.

5.   Expand the Personal and Certificates leaf objects.

6.   Highlight the correct EFS certificate (look for the *Encrypting File System* option under *Enhanced Key Usage* under the Details tab).

7. Under the Details tab, select the *Public Key* field and then click the Copy to File button (see Figure 13-9).

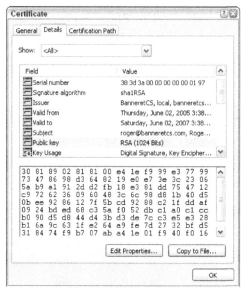

Figure 13-9

8. Click Next in the Certificate Export Wizard dialog box.

9. Select Yes, export the private key, and then click Next.

10. Click Next in the File Format Export dialog box.

11. Type a strong and complex password twice, to protect the private key from compromise, and then click Next.

12. Type in a file name and location in which to save the backed up EFS keys and click Next.

13. Click Finish to create the backup copy.

14. Move to one or more removable media options and store in a secure location.

In Windows XP Pro SP1 and later, you can use the `Cipher.exe` utility to back up user EFS keys. At a command prompt, type in **Cipher.exe /X** and press Enter. The currently logged on user's EFS key will be backed up. Move the resulting backup keys to a secure offsite location.

In Windows 2003 and later, users can back up their EFS keys in the normal EFS GUI. Select File ⇨ Properties ⇨ Advanced, and click the Details button. Then click the Backup Keys button (see Figure 13-10) and follow the Certificate Export Wizard as previously covered above in the first method.

Relying on end users to backup their EFS keys is risky. Many users will find it too complicated and others will simply ignore the good advice. A better option is not to rely on the end user's actions for EFS recovery.

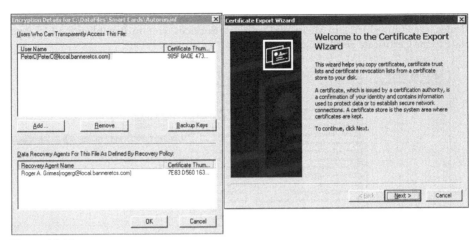

Figure 13-10

Creating a Default Recovery Agent

By default in Windows Server 2000 and Server 2003, the local administrator (on a stand-alone computer) or domain administrator (on a domain member) is the designated Default Recovery Agent (DRA). Windows XP Pro machines in a domain environment also designate the domain administrator as the default DRA, but stand-alone XP Pro machines do not have any DRA installed by default. This latter decision was made by Microsoft to stop local password attacks from compromising the local administrator's or user's accounts and then leveraging the access to recovery EFS files.

You should, unless you have an alternative method, always have one or more DRAs defined. Whenever a file is encrypted, the DRA has a copy of the FEK stored in the DRF file attribute. In the event that a user's EFS key is lost, the DRA agent can log on and recover the files. The DRA should disable the EFS protection during the recovery process, and then copy the files where they are requested. This is because if the DRA does not remove the EFS encryption, anywhere they copy them to (excepting copies off the local NTFS volume) will result in the files remaining encrypted and tied to only the DRA. When unencrypted, the files can be copied to the original user, or to whoever is requesting access, and can be re-encrypted, if desired.

If a DRA is used, two or more DRA accounts should be created and used. This is because every file encrypted makes a backup copy of the FEK and encrypts it with the DRA's private EFS key. If only one DRA is used and something happens to that account (e.g., it is deleted, corrupted, etc.), all the DRF copies could be lost. If a DRA user account is added, only the files newly encrypted, or re-encrypted, will end up with the new DRA's DRF being added to the file. Hence, if an old DRA is deleted before the new DRA's account has had a chance to create DRFs for all encrypted files, files without a valid DRF can be included. If a new DRA is added, consider running the `Cipher.exe /U` command to update all files with the new DRA DRF. The /U option can also be used if the user gets a new EFS digital certificate.

If at all possible, the DRA shouldn't be the administrator, as is the default. This is because the administrator is a high-profile target and if the account is compromised, all encrypted files can be recovered. Instead, it is better to create one or two new DRA accounts, install/import DRA certificates to their accounts, and then run the `Cipher.exe /U` command under both user accounts. Adding a new DRA requires Microsoft Certificate Services or a PKI Certificate Authority that supports *EFS Recovery Agent* certificates (see Figure 13-11). In Microsoft Certificate Services, you must publish the *EFS Recovery Agent* template to the Certificate Services server.

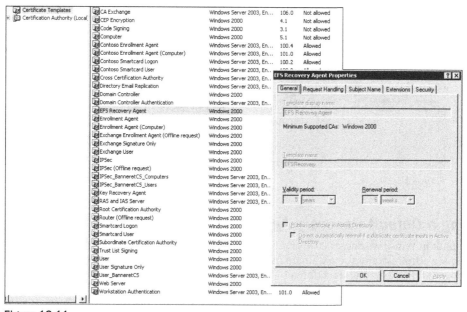

Figure 13-11

The appropriate template permissions must be set so that the correct user accounts can request the certificate. The users then must manually request the certificate (unless auto-enrollment is enabled, which it shouldn't be for EFS Recovery Agent certificates), and a Certificate Authority manager needs to approve the certificate request.

After the certificates are installed in the user's local profiles, the new DRA users can be added as Recovery Agents. To add new DRAs, open the appropriate Group Policy Object and choose `\Computer Configuration\Windows Settings\Security Settings\Public Key Policies`. Right-click the Encrypting File System leaf object, choose Add Data Recovery Agent (see Figure 13-12), and follow the wizard's prompts.

Figure 13-12

For extra security, a DRA's private EFS key should be exported and removed from the system (a selection made possible during the Certificate Export Wizard process), and only added back when needed. Also, the DRA's account should be disabled until needed. That way, if the DRA's account is compromised, the intruder doesn't automatically have access to all encrypted files. Then run the `Cipher.exe` /U command to update the DRF file attributes.

Using Certificate Services

Alternately, you can configure Windows Server 2003 Microsoft Certificate Services to automatically back up (i.e., archive) users' EFS keys if the server is used to issue EFS certificates to users. In order to configure key archival, one or more users must have a *Key Recovery Agent* certificate. The Key Recovery Agent template must have the appropriate permissions and be published to the Certificate Authority server. Then the appropriate users should request KRA certificates and install them.

The appropriate EFS certificate template (its default name is *Basic EFS*) should have the *Archive subject's encryption private key* option selected (see Figure 13-13). Then, whenever an EFS certificate is issued to a user, the user's private key will be archived to a safe location. If the user's private key is ever needed, it can be manually extracted by the Key Recovery Agent and installed back to the user.

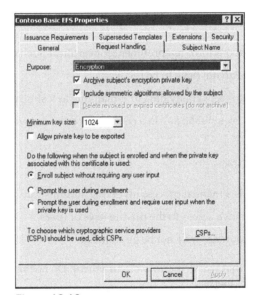

Figure 13-13

DRA versus KRA

EFS recovery can be accomplished automatically using the DRA or KRA. This naturally begs the question of which is a better strategy. Overall, either is fine, but here are the advantages and disadvantages.

Advantages of using a DRA:

❑ It does not require a PKI infrastructure.

❑ Data recovery policies can be managed centrally using the Active Directory.

❏ Users do not have to manage certificates or private keys.

❏ Decryption can be limited to the user only (requires deleting DRA keys while maintaining policy).

Disadvantages of using a DRA:

❏ An administrative process must recover user data. Users cannot recover their own data.

❏ Data recovery occurs on a file-by-file basis as a manual process.

❏ Users must re-enroll for new certificates. This is because only data is recovered, not the original keys of a user.

❏ Administrators must revoke old certificates. This is because it is assumed that when a key is lost it's been compromised.

❏ Stand-alone workstations, or workstations in non-Active Directory environments, cannot be centrally managed.

❏ Data recovery is specific to the EFS application.

Advantages of using a KRA:

❏ Users do not have to perform re-enrollment for certificates, change security settings, etc.

❏ Existing certificates do not have to be revoked.

❏ Users do not have to recover any data or e-mail due to lost private keys.

❏ All data encrypted by a public key in a certificate can be recovered after a private key has been recovered.

Disadvantages of using a KRA:

❏ User key recovery is a manual process involving administrators and users.

❏ It allows administrative access to the private keys of users.

❏ Nonrepudiation assurance may not be guaranteed.

Choose a recovery method that works for your environment. Do not enable EFS without first enabling, and testing, an EFS recovery method.

Setting Up EFS

Here are the basic steps to enable EFS in a stand-alone or domain environment:

1. Turn off until an EFS recovery policy has been enabled.

2. Set up a recovery policy.

3. Educate end users and administrators.

4. Enable EFS (globally, on servers, etc.).

EFS Caveats

Here are a few EFS caveats to remember:

❏ Users cannot encrypt and compress files at the same time using the default Windows tools, but users can use third-party compression utilities and encrypt the results. Just remember that most compression utilities keep the original file along with the compressed copy, and both will need to be encrypted (or the original deleted).

❏ Make sure all used applications support EFS. Many older, legacy applications (e.g., Edit.com) do not understand EFS and can cause corruption problems.

❏ EFS can protect local or remote files, but does not protect any files read from the hard drive and transmitted over the network. Use WebDAV, IPSec, SSL, or some other VPN technology to protect files sent over the network.

❏ You cannot gain access to encrypted files from a Macintosh or other foreign client computers.

❏ You cannot open documents that were stored by others in an encrypted folder that you created.

EFS Best Practices

The following is a list of best practices for utilizing EFS:

❏ Disable EFS until a recovery policy is enabled and tested.

❏ Ensure that a DRA is created on stand-alone XP computers.

❏ Consider implementing Syskey protect (mode 2 or 3) to protect local credentials against password attacks trying to recover EFS keys. Also consider disabling cached logons to prevent the local recovery of passwords in the local LSA cache.

❏ Change the default DRAs from the default administrator accounts to newly created, specialized DRA accounts.

❏ The private keys of DRAs or KRAs should be removed from the environment after creation and only installed when recovery is needed.

❏ Recovery agent certificates must be assigned to special recovery agent accounts that are not used for any other purpose.

❏ Exported private keys should be stored in one or more secure locations, and password-protected with a long and complex password.

❏ Do not destroy recovery certificates or private keys when recovery agents are changed, until after the Cipher.exe /U command is run against all encrypted files.

❏ Help users decide which files and folders should be encrypted (e.g., My Documents, Temp file folders, etc.), and which types should be avoided (e.g., Profile directories, System files, etc.).

❏ Teach users to encrypt folders instead of individual files to prevent unintentional decryption and to prevent leakage from temporary file creation during the encryption process.

❏ Avoid using print spool files, or make sure that print spool files are generated in an encrypted folder.

Other Links

- ❑ Any excellent technical article on EFS by Mark Russinovich is available at www
  .windowsitpro.com/Articles/Index.cfm?ArticleID=5592&Key=Internals

- ❑ Encrypting File System in Windows XP and Windows Server 2003: www.microsoft
  .com/technet/prodtechnol/winxppro/deploy/cryptfs.mspx

- ❑ Windows Data Protection: http://msdn.microsoft.com/library/en-us/dnsecure/
  html/windataprotection-dpapi

- ❑ Certificate Auto-enrollment in Windows XP: www.microsoft.com/technet/prodtechnol/
  winxppro/maintain/certenrl.mspx

- ❑ Key Archival and Management in Windows Server 2003: www.microsoft.com/technet/
  prodtechnol/windowsserver2003/technologies/security/kyacws03.mspx

Summary

Chapter 13 covered Microsoft's Encrypting File System. It described how EFS appears to the end user and how it works behind the scenes. EFS best practices were covered, including ensuring that an EFS recovery policy is enabled before EFS is used. Chapter 14 will begin a two-chapter discussion of group policy by covering each default group policy setting in detail.

Part IV
Automating Security

14

Group Policy Explained

Microsoft's group policy is one of the best management tools ever created for any computer system. No other operating system has anything nearly as sophisticated (although Novell's ZENworks comes the closest). With a few clicks of a mouse, nearly every local computer behavior can be managed. For instance, if a computer worm is found that abuses a particular program or service, the associated program or service can be disabled or turned off with one group policy setting change. Users can be prevented from running a particular program or only allowed to run an approved set of executables. File permissions can be set per user, per organization unit, or per domain. This chapter discusses group policy in detail, including every default OS security setting available in Windows XP SP2 and Windows Server 2003 SP1. Chapter 15 will continue the discussion and detail how group policy should be applied for maximum efficiency and effectiveness.

How Group Policy Works

In one sentence, group policy essentially applies local registry entries and settings that could otherwise be done programmatically or manually, although a few features go beyond that simplified description. Group policy requires Windows 2000 and later computers and Active Directory, although policies can be applied locally using the Local Computer Policy or templates on non-domain computers. XP Home Edition does not support group policy, Local Computer Policy, or the traditional security template tools.

Group policy can be applied by configuring group policy objects (GPOs) in Active Directory. You can configure an unlimited number of GPOs, and each GPO can have a single setting or, literally, hundreds. The GPOs are then attached to Active Directory organization units (OUs) or container objects (e.g., domain, Built-in Users, etc.). If permissions are appropriately set, the settings contained in the GPO apply to the users or computers located in the various OUs and container objects. Multiple GPOs can apply to a single user or computer, and when settings conflict the last one applied wins. Group policy settings can also be applied using the Local Computer Policy object, but any settings that conflict with nonlocal settings will be overwritten. Administrative templates and security templates, which can also contain group policy settings, can be applied locally or imported into GPOs. Chapter 15 will cover the group policy application pathway in detail.

Accessing Group Policy

Group policy settings can be set using GPOs, Local Computer Policy, or locally applied templates. Technically, only settings configured in GPOs are called group policy, but many of the settings that can be set in GPOs can be set in the latter two mechanisms as well.

Group Policy Object Editor

Group policies are often set in Active Directory using an interface that can interact with GPOs. When Active Directory was first released with Windows 2000 Server, GPOs could be created, modified, or deleted using any of the following management console tools:

❑   Active Directory Users and Computers

❑   Active Directory Domains and Trusts (domain-level GPOs only)

❑   Active Sites and Services (site-level GPOs only)

Most GPO work was done using the Active Directory Users and Computers console. In order to create or view GPOs, the user accessing the GPO through the console must have Read and Modify permissions to the GPO (even if they are only viewing the GPO), which is only given to administrators by default. In Active Directory Users and Computers, the administrator would first right-click an OU or container object as the focus, and then choose Properties ➪ Group Policy (see Figure 14-1). There you can create, modify, and delete group policies.

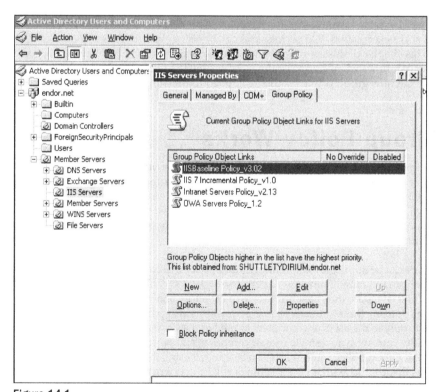

Figure 14-1

Group Policy Management Console

The original Group Policy Editor console (see Figure 14-2) needed a better interface. For one, in order for an administrator to review or modify a policy, they had to find it first. Locating which OU or container the policy was attached to wasn't always easy. The Group Policy Management Console (GPMC) was released around the same time as Windows Server 2003. Once any group policy manager has used it, they never go back to the original editor. It can be downloaded separately from www.microsoft .com/downloads or as part of one of the newer service packs.

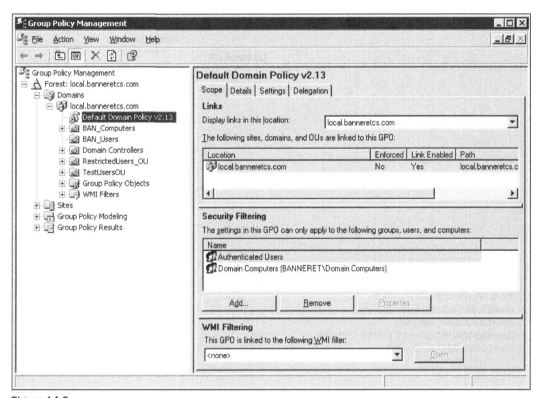

Figure 14-2

The GPMC (see Figure 14-3) allows an administrator to view all group policies in one location, or to see which group policies are attached to which OUs and containers. You can easily see which group policies are directly associated with a particular OU or container, or which GPOs are inherited from parent objects. Even the language used to manage GPOs is improved, substituting more natural language names for the older technical language (e.g., Enforced vs. No Override). The GPMC is the natural way to view and modify GPOs.

Local Computer Policy Editor

Every computer, whether stand-alone or in a domain, also has a Local Computer Policy object. It is applied whenever the computer boots and is applied prior to any user logging on it. It can be configured by choosing Start ⇨ Administrative Tools ⇨ Local Computer Policy. Alternately, it can be started from the command line using Start ⇨ Run, and typing in **Gpedit.msc** in the Open dialog command prompt. Strangely, starting the Local Computer Policy console either way results in a console entitled Group

Policy on workstations or Group Policy Object Editor (see Figure 14-4) on servers. This can be confusing because the consoles configure local policy and not group policy. Local Computer Policy has many, but not all, of the same configuration settings as GPOs (covered in more detail in Chapter 15).

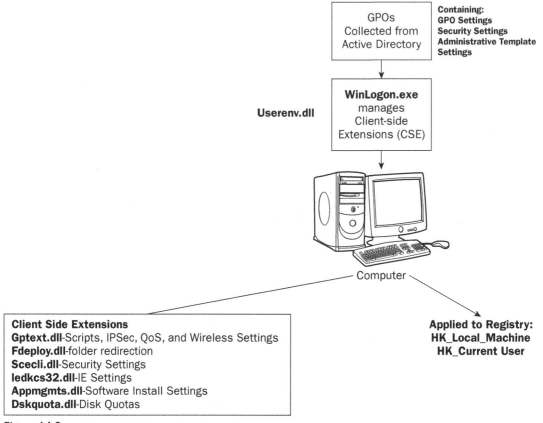

Figure 14-3

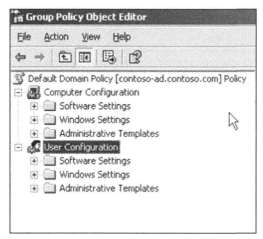

Figure 14-4

Templates

Most GPOs have Administrative Templates settings installed by default, and more can be imported. Administrative Templates often control many default Windows applications, and other applications (e.g., Microsoft Office, Internet Explorer) if vendors provided them. Administrative templates are covered in more detail below. Security templates can also be created and imported.

Security templates contain most, but not all, of the security settings that can be configured in a GPO. Security templates can be imported into GPOs and applied locally against machines (including non-domain machines). Security templates can be created manually (using text editors) or using the Security Templates MMC console. Security templates can be applied locally by importing them using Secedit.exe or the Security Configuration and Analysis MMC console. Templates applied locally tattoo the registry, meaning any changes they make will not automatically be removed if the template is removed.

One of the big differences between Administrative templates and Security templates is that when Security templates are imported, the settings they contain will take effect after importing. Imported Administrative templates enable an administrator to review new application settings and set particular settings, but will not immediately change any settings merely after being imported. Imported Security templates always set configuration choices. Administrative templates reveal choices.

Good computer security requires that administrators effectively and efficiently apply the right combination of settings using GPOs, Local Computer Policy, and templates. Chapter 15 is devoted to this discussion. In defining a security policy plan, it helps to understand how GPOs work under the hood.

GPO Internals

Logically, when a GPO is created, the resulting registry entries and local settings are created in Active Directory (i.e., group policy container) and stored on a domain controller's System Volume (Sysvol) folder. Each GPO gets its own subfolder (named after the GPO's GUID) under the Sysvol parent directory, and various other files and folders are created to hold the GPO settings that will be applied locally. If GPO settings are configured that result in registry entry changes, the following process occurs:

1. When the GPO Editor is started, a temporary registry tree is created for the USER and MACHINE hives. All settings that can affect a user are stored in the USER section. All settings that can affect a computer are stored in the MACHINE hive.

2. When an administrator navigates and configures the various sections of a GPO, the appropriate entries are written to the temporary registry tree.

3. When the GPO Editor is closed, the temporary registry tree is exported to Registry.pol files in GPO's GPT\Machine and GPT\User areas on Sysvol.

4. Whenever a GPO is view or read, Registry.pol settings are read back into a temporary registry tree for viewing and modification.

The GPOs are stored on the Sysvol awaiting computers and users to request group policy application. This is an important point. Computers and users must request group policy to be applied. Microsoft only built the necessary files and processes into Windows 2000 and later (refer to Figure 14-1). The Winlogon.exe and Userenv.dll processes manage the client-side application of GPOs and Local Computer Policy. Various local client files deal with the different parts of the GPO (e.g., security settings, IE settings, etc.). For instance, security settings configured in a GPO are managed by the Scecli.dll file, also known as a local client extension. Microsoft Windows comes with a set of built-in client-side extension files, which do the hard part of collecting and applying group policy settings. The client-side extensions are updated in each newer version of Windows and can be modified and updated by programmers and third-party vendors.

Group Policy Application

Behind the scenes, group policy is applied using the following steps:

1. When a computer starts and accesses Active Directory, it uses the Lightweight Directory Access Protocol (LDAP) to retrieve a list of all the relevant GPOs affecting the OU or container that contains the computer object (each user or computer in Active Directory can only belong as a member of a single OU or container).

2. Active Directory and the client-side extensions work in concert to build the correct resulting `Registry.pol` files for the MACHINE (and eventually, USER) registry hives.

3. The Server Message Block (SMB) protocol is used to download the GPO files to the local host.

4. The client-side extension (CSE) files work to interpret the downloaded GPO settings and apply them to the computer (or user).

Registry settings stored in the `Registry.pol` file in every GPO on the Sysvol are then pulled down to the local client and overwrite or modify the client's existing `Ntuser.pol` file(s). Computer policies are applied whenever a domain computer logs on to a domain (or whenever the computer starts if a Local Computer Policy is defined). Computer settings are stored in the computer's All Users profile. User policies are applied whenever a user first logs on and are saved to the user's personal profile (%Userprofile%). Administrative template policy settings are always applied first. Security policies are applied during the computer and user logons, and reapplied at period intervals, with a maximum default of every 16 hours.

This is a very simplified version of the GPO application process.

Policy versus Preferences

Group policy settings are written to two local registry hives as the primary targets:

```
HKLM\Software\Policies
HKCU\Software\Polices
```

GPO settings are also applied to the following keys as a backup target:

```
HKLM\Software\Microsoft\Windows\CurrentVersion\Policies
HLCU\Software\Microsoft\Windows\CurrentVersion\Policies
```

These are the preferred locations for GPO registry settings to be written and are known as *Fully Managed* or *True* policies. Anything written here will be "undone" if the GPO that applied it no longer applies. GPO settings written to the above registry keys are normally the only ones shown in the Group Policy Editor console when viewing Administrative templates.

GPOs can contain registry keys and settings that target registry entries outside of the fully managed keys. Anything written to registry keys outside the previously listed fully managed "GPO registry keys" will *tattoo* the registry and will not be undone if the related GPO is unlinked or disabled. GPO settings written outside these areas are known as *preferences*. Fully managed policies supersede preferences in conflicts, although if there are existing preferences and the fully managed policies are removed, the Preference settings previously in conflict will again become effective. Preferences can only be seen in the GPO Editor console by selecting Administrative Templates ⇨ View ⇨ Filtering, and then clearing the *Only show policy settings that can be fully managed* setting.

Accessing group policy settings and applying them is the easy part. Figuring out what group policy settings to configure and apply is the harder part. There are several hundred default settings you can review and configure. Most of the settings are moderately documented, but the following section will document all the default GPO settings from Windows XP Pro SP2 and Windows Server 2003 SP1.

Group Policy Settings

This section is divided into two important parts. The first discusses group policy in general, and the second discusses each setting separately.

General Observations

Every GPO has two main sections:

❑   Computer Configuration

❑   User Configuration

Every GPO setting is either set in the Computer Configuration section or the User Configuration section. Settings in the Computer Configuration section can only affect computers. They are applied whenever the computer logs on to the domain (or in the case of some policies, when the computer logs off the domain). User Configuration settings can only affect users. They apply whenever a user logs on to the domain (or with some policies, when the user logs off the domain). At first glance, both sections might appear to be duplicates of each other because they share a lot of the same main category names, but with the exception of Software Installs and a small selection of Administrative Template settings, the settings in one section do not match the settings in the other section. The Computer Configuration section contains more security settings. The User Configuration section contains more desktop/profile settings.

Seeing only these two top-level sections should also remind administrators that, ultimately, group policy can only affect computers or users. Although it may sometimes appear as though a GPO can be applied against a group of computers or users, this is never the case. GPOs must be applied against an OU or container object, and only the computer or user objects contained within are affected.

Main Setting Categories

There are three main setting categories (refer to Figure 14-4):

❑   Software Settings (for automated software installs and updates)

❑   Windows Settings (where most OS security settings are made)

❑   Administrative Templates (for managing applications and components)

Security templates can only be imported into the Computer Configuration Windows Setting\Security Settings object. Administrative templates can be imported into the Administrative Templates category under either Computer Configuration or User Configuration.

Under these three main categories, literally hundreds of choices can be made.

Software Settings

Software can be installed or updated using group policy. Microsoft calls this *software publishing*. Software can be made available for download and install, with the end user choosing when to install. Conversely, software can be forcibly pushed out and mandated when the computer or user logs in. Software publishing works best with programs with MS installer files (.MSI) but can be used to install other types of files. The client PC must be 2000 or later and have Windows Installer and Application Management services either actively running (Automatic startup mode) or in Manual startup mode. Group policy pushes software installs down, but the Windows Installer service installs it. The Application Management service interacts with group policy to download the software and then hands it off to Windows Installer.

Assigned versus Published

Software installs can be:

❑   **Assigned** — to users or computers

❑   **Published** — to users only

If assigned to a computer, the software installs when the PC starts up or reboots. If assigned to the user, it installs when the user logs on. These are mandated modes. The user or computer logs on and the software installs. If the software is published to the user, the user can install the software at their leisure, using the Add/Remove Programs applet (custom categories can be installed), or they can make the application install when the associated file type is double-clicked. For instance, suppose a user wants to send out Microsoft Visio diagrams, but not every user has Microsoft Visio installed. The administrator can download Microsoft's free Visio viewer applet and tell Active Directory to install it when a user without the full version of Microsoft Visio opens a Visio diagram for the first time. Administrators can choose Assign or Publish or choose the Advanced option to further customize their selection (see Figure 14-5).

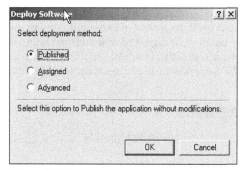

Figure 14-5

Using software publishing you can install the following file types:

- ❏ MSI (Microsoft Installer Files)
- ❏ MST (Transform Files, installed with MSI files only)
- ❏ MSP (Microsoft Patch, becoming less common)
- ❏ ZAP (almost any other type of file — for example, Setup.exe)

MSI files install in the security context of the Windows Installer service, Local System. Thus, when using software publishing, programs can be installed and updated without the user being an administrator or Power User. Microsoft Transform files modify programs installed by MSI files. For instance, you can install Microsoft Office as an MSI file and then customize the security settings and menu bars.

ZAP files allow administrators to install non-MSI files. Administrators must create a special ZAP text file telling the GPO what file to install. They can only be published to users, and because the Windows Installer isn't used, the program will install with the security context of the end user (almost guaranteeing that admin permissions will be needed). ZAP files do not support rollback or install on "first use" features. For more information on Zap files, try http://support.microsoft.com/default.aspx ?scid=kb;en-us;231747.

It usually takes two or three computer reboots before the software publishing GPO takes effect. It takes one reboot to apply the software publishing policy and at least one second to actually push the software install. Software publishing has more options than I can cover in this chapter, but here are the general steps.

Group Policy Software Publishing Steps

Copy the installation package file (MSI, MSP, or ZAP) and related files to a network share distribution point.

Users or computers must have correct permissions to the network share, the install files, and the GPO that will install the package. Ensure that you select all the files that are to be included in the package over a readable accessible network share and not from a local drive (i.e., C:) when creating the software publishing GPO. Network users will probably not be able to access files stored on local drives without a shared folder.

1. Right-click Software Installation and choose New ⇨ Package ⇨ Package.
2. Choose Assigned, Published, or Advanced.
3. Choose appropriate options on the resulting software publishing dialog boxes; for example:
   a. *Auto-install this application by file extension activation* allows an application to be installed when the user clicks on a particular file extension (install on demand).
   b. *Uninstall this application when it falls out of the scope of management* allows *most* applications (not ZAP installed) to be uninstalled when the user or computer is moved out of the OU to which the software install GPO applies. In order for this to work, the package must have been installed with this option selected in the first place.
   c. *Do not display this package in the Add/Remove Programs control panel,* if enabled, will not put the software installation package in Add/Remove Programs as is its normal behavior.
   d. *Install this application at logon* is an option if the package is assigned to a user.

When finished, simply close the software publishing dialog box. Figure 14-6 shows an example install.

Figure 14-6

Group Policy Software Publishing Disadvantages

Unfortunately, software publishing doesn't have a lot of true enterprise management features:

❑   There is no easy way to stagger installs across the enterprise.

❑   Bandwidth throttling is not possible.

❑   There is no reporting available on who did and didn't get the install.

❑   It requires local admin rights for non-MSI files.

❑   Many security patches and service packs can't be rolled back.

❑   It only works with W2K and later.

However, if you don't have another automated software installation tool (such as Microsoft SMS), GPO software publishing is a great way to distribute software quickly. For instance, use software publishing to push out Internet Explorer add-on updates, Sun Java VM updates, and Adobe Acrobat Reader updates. If you can't be assured that end users will consistently update their installed software applications, use GPO software publishing to regain control of your unmanaged software.

GPO Windows Settings

The Windows Settings subcategories include Scripts and Security Settings.

Scripts

Scripts allow an administrator to create shutdown and startup scripts for computers, and logon and logoff scripts for users (see Figure 14-7). It allows scripts, batch files, and command files to be executed when the computer starts up or shuts down, or when the user logs on or off. Any programming and scripting language that the client understands can be used. By default, scripts should be located on the Sysvol share.

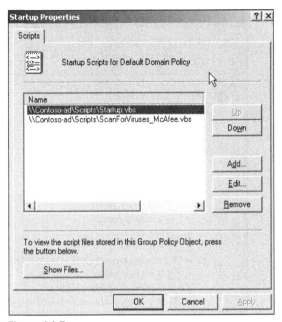

Figure 14-7

Security Settings

Most GPO non-administrative template settings are located under Security Settings (see Figure 14-8). Security Settings include the following:

❑ Account Policies

❑ Local Polices

❑ Event Log Settings

❑ Restricted Groups

❑ System Services

❑ Registry Settings

❑ File System Settings

❑ Wireless Settings

❑ Public Key Policies

❑ Software Restriction Policies

❑ IPSec Policies

Figure 14-8

Importing Security Templates

Security templates can only be imported by right-clicking Security Settings and choosing Import Policy. You can import several templates, one after another, if you want. If any settings conflict between different templates, the last one imported wins.

Security Settings - Account Policies - Password Policy

This setting controls domain or local password settings. As covered in Chapter 4, setting a secure password policy is among the most significant security defenses. Password policy settings can *only* be set at the local and domain level. Well, they can be set elsewhere, but the settings won't take effect. If password policy is set at an OU level, it will only impact the local accounts on the computers within that OU, but not the domain accounts. Rumor has it that Windows versions after W2K3 SP1 will change this requirement.

Enforce password history

Determines how many passwords Windows will remember and not let the user re-use. This should be enabled and set to a reasonable value. Most administrators set the value to 20, which is also the default value if this feature is enabled.

Maximum password age

Indicates how many days users can use a password before they must change it (password expiration period). It can be 0 to 999 days; 0 means there is no password expiration interval. This should be set to a reasonable period of time. Environments requiring strong security should set this value to 90 days or less. Setting it too short (e.g., 15 days) is likely to frustrate users and lead to a more insecure password environment (e.g., users writing their passwords down).

Minimum password age

Specifies how long a password must be used before a user can change it. It is used to prevent users from changing their password a whole bunch of times quickly to defeat the *Enforce password history* setting. It can be 0 to 998 days; 0 means the password can be changed immediately. This value should be set to anything above 0.

Minimum password length

Specifies the minimum password length that will be accepted by Windows or the domain controller. Can be set from 0 to 14. Should be set to 14 in environments requiring strong security, and 8 or above for other environments. Password length is less worrisome if other password defenses have been enabled (e.g., Account Lockout, Auditing, LM password hashes disabled, etc.).

Password must meet complexity requirement

Complexity requirements were covered in Chapter 4. Enabled by default on W2K3 servers. Initial install and a new DCPromo are two times when the password is not forced to be complex even with complexity set.

Store password using reversible encryption for all users in the domain

Can be set on individual accounts in Active Directory Users and Computers. Storing passwords using reversible encryption is essentially the same as storing plaintext versions of the passwords. Disabled by default, this policy should never be enabled unless application requirements outweigh the need to protect password information. This policy is required when using Challenge-Handshake Authentication Protocol (CHAP) authentication through RRAS or Internet Authentication Services (IAS). It is also required when using Digest Authentication in Internet Information Services (IIS).

Security Settings - Account Policies - Account Lockout Policy

Controls account lockout settings. Like password policy, it can only be effectively set at the local and domain level. Recommended settings are covered in Chapter 4.

Account Lockout Duration

Specifies how many minutes an account remains locked out after the Account Lockout Threshold is reached. If set to 0, the account must be unlocked by an administrator. It should be enabled and set to at least 1 minute.

Account Lockout Threshold

Specifies how many invalid logons (without a valid logon) are needed to cause an account to be locked out. Should be set between 3 and 5.

Reset account lockout counter after

Specifies how many minutes invalid logons are tracked in the same threshold counter before resetting the counter to zero. This should be enabled and set to any value.

Security Settings - Account Policies - Kerberos Policy

This controls five Kerberos settings, and can only be set at the domain level. Kerberos Policy does not normally need to be adjusted.

Enforce user logon restrictions

Determines whether the Kerberos server validates every session ticket request only if the user has the *Log on locally* user right (if the requested Kerberos service is running locally) or the *Access this computer from the network* user right (if the requested Kerberos service is running remotely). Although enabled, it may slow network access to services. My recommendation is to leave it enabled.

Maximum lifetime for service ticket

Determines the maximum amount of time (in minutes) that a granted session ticket can be used to access a particular Kerberos service. The setting must be greater than 10 minutes, but less than or equal to the setting for *Maximum lifetime for user ticket*. A decreased time interval will strengthen security. The default is 600 minutes (i.e., 10 hours) and should be left alone unless the administrator has a specific reason to change it.

Maximum lifetime for user ticket

Determines the maximum amount of time (in hours) that a user's ticket-granting ticket (TGT) may be used to request access to Kerberos services without having to re-authenticate and generate another TGT. A decreased time interval will strengthen security. The default setting is 10 hours and should be left as is unless the administrator has a specific reason to change it.

Maximum lifetime for user ticket renewal

Determines the period of time (in days) during which a user's ticket-granting ticket (TGT) may be renewed. A decreased time interval will strengthen security. The default setting is 7 days and should be left as is unless the administrator has a specific reason to change it.

Maximum tolerance for computer clock synchronization

Determines the maximum time difference (in minutes) that Windows Kerberos servers allow between the client's system time and participating Kerberos servers. A decreased time interval will strengthen security. The default setting is 5 minutes and should be left as is unless an administrator has a specific reason to change it.

Security Settings - Local Policies - Audit Policy

These control audit log settings. With few exceptions, they will apply wherever GPO applies.

Audit Account Logon Events

If enabled, all domain logons/authentication events are recorded on the nearest domain controller. This setting has no effect on non-domain controllers.

Audit Account Management

If enabled, this setting tracks creation and manipulation of user and group accounts, including password resets or changes.

Audit Directory Access

If enabled, this setting monitors AD requests on domain controllers only. It can be set per user.

Audit Logon Events

If enabled, logon events are recorded where logon or resource access occurs (i.e., where an object is accessed).

Audit Object Access

If enabled, this will monitor attempted object use (e.g., file, folder, printer, registry entry). It requires that audit permissions be set on the object to be audited. It can be set to monitor particular users or groups.

Audit Policy Change

If enabled, this setting tracks changes to User Rights, Audit policies, or Trust Policies.

Audit Privilege Use

If enabled, this setting tracks usage of User Rights Assignment privileges. It does not track a few privileges (e.g., Backup and Restore privileges) unless the associated User Rights Assignment option is also selected (see below).

Audit Process Tracking

If enabled, this setting audits application processes: starts, stops, and pauses. Turn this on if you are a programmer troubleshooting a program or if you're tracking hackers. Consider enabling on stand-alone domain controllers, which should not be having a lot of process changes.

Audit System Events

If enabled, this setting tracks systemwide events.

The Microsoft Windows Server 2003 Security Guide recommends the audit settings in Table 14-1.

Table 14-1

Computer Environment			
Audit Category	**Legacy**	**Enterprise**	**High Security**
Account logon events	Success, Failure	Success, Failure	Success, Failure
Account management	Success, Failure	Success, Failure	Success, Failure
Directory service access	Success, Failure	Success, Failure	Success, Failure
Logon events	Success, Failure	Success, Failure	Success, Failure
Object access	Success, Failure	Success, Failure	Success, Failure

Table continued on following page

Table 14-1 (continued)

	Computer Environment		
Audit Category	**Legacy**	**Enterprise**	**High Security**
Policy change	Success	Success	Success
Privilege use	No Auditing	Failure	Success, Failure
Process tracking	No Auditing	No Auditing	No Auditing
System events	Success	Success	Success

As stated above, Process tracking should be enabled on stand-alone domain controllers. Also, settings configured under Audit Policy will not affect audit settings configured using Per-User Selective Auditing (new in XP Pro SP2 and Windows Server 2003 SP1).

Security Settings - Local Policies - User Rights Assignment

User Rights Assignments are also known as User Privileges or User Special Privileges. Basically, they allow security principals (users, groups, and computers) to do things they would not otherwise be able to do with NTFS permissions alone. Often, these rights are really meant to be given to service accounts (or less often, computer accounts), and not user accounts.

Every version of Windows comes with default User Rights Assignments given to various users and groups. You can modify membership here. Only security principals defined here can do the particular special privilege. Be careful: If you forget to include existing accounts, System, or Administrator, it is very possible to mess up Windows and/or lock yourself out of functionality of one type or another. This section will discuss the right, give the defaults, and make recommendations. If no recommendation is made, leave the defaults unless you have a specific reason for changing them.

Access this computer from the network

Determines which users and groups are allowed to connect to the computer over the network. This user right is required by a number of network protocols, including server message block (SMB)-based protocols, network basic input/output system (NetBIOS), Common Internet File System (CIFS), Hypertext Transfer Protocol (HTTP), and Component Object Model Plus (COM+). Should be set to Authenticated Users and Administrators, not Everyone, in most environments. Must allow Enterprise Domain Controllers group on Domain Controllers; and add Backup Operators, Everyone, and Pre-Win 2K-compatible groups if they are used. Early versions of OWA required that remote users have this right.

Act as part of the operating system

Allows a process to assume the identity of any user (called *impersonation*) without additional authentication and thus gain access to local resources that the user is authorized to access. The process can therefore gain access to the same local resources as that user. In Windows, a user never accesses a resource directly. A service (e.g., Windows Explorer) does it on behalf of the user by impersonating them. Impersonation is normal. It is also why the LocalSystem account is often the service account for most Windows services — so it can do things on behalf of all authenticated users.

Processes that require this privilege should use the LocalSystem account, which already includes this privilege. It shouldn't be assigned to any additional account, unless needed. If in a W2K or NT domain, you may need to assign this right to processes that need to exchange authentication passwords in clear text. In W2K3, delegation can be constrained by service, but not in W2K. When this right is given to a process, it is given to the process' service account. Only give this right to very trusted accounts.

Add Workstations to the Domain

Allows members to add/join 10 computers (the number is configurable by a registry setting on the domain controller) to the domain. Only valid if set on a domain controller. By default, all Authenticated Users have this right, which you should only consider granting to the Administrators group. If you want a user to be able to add more than 10 computers, you can do a registry edit to increase the number or allow unlimited additions by giving the user the Create Computer Objects right (in the AD Delegation Wizard).

Computers added to the domain using *Add Workstations to the Domain* (vs. the *Create Computer Objects* delegated right) have the Domain Administrators as their owner. W2K has this setting, but by default it does not have any members. NT 4 required that administrators add computer accounts, by default.

Adjust memory quotas for process

Allows a user/programmer to change the memory allocated to a particular program. Normally, you don't need to change this setting unless playing with performance issues. By default, it is granted to Administrators, LocalService, NetworkService, and the IWAM IIS service account. Adjust memory quotas for a process called *Increase quotas* in W2K.

Allow log on locally

User right that determines which users or groups have the right to log on interactively to a particular computer. On a domain controller, only Administrators and various operator accounts have this right. Make sure the Administrators group always has this right. If you modify the *Allow log on locally* right, make sure you add the Administrators group so administrators are not locked out.

By default, the following accounts have the *Allow log on locally* right: On workstations and servers: Administrators, Backup Operators, Power Users, Users, and Guest. On domain controllers: Account Operators, Administrators, Backup Operators, Print Operators, and Server Operators. *Allow log on locally* is known as *Log on locally* in some versions of Windows. W2K Terminal Server users must have this right, but W2K3 users don't (they have a separate group).

Allow log on through Terminal Services

Determines which users or groups have the right to log on from a Terminal Services client. Remote Desktop users and Administrators should have this right. By default the following groups have the *Allow log on through Terminal Services* right: On workstation and servers: Administrators, Remote Desktop Users. On domain controllers: Administrators. Windows 2000 computers must be SP2 or later. If *Deny log on through Terminal Services* is also selected at the same Active Directory level, the deny right will override.

Back up files and directories

This right is needed and used when an application attempts to access a file or directory using the NTFS file system (NTFS) backup application programming interface (API), as most backup software does. The *Back up files and directories* right grants the following permissions: Traverse Folder/Execute File, List

Folder/Read Data, Read Attributes, Read Extended Attributes, and Read Permissions. This right is needed to install Windows updates that use `Update.exe`.

Accounts with this right can circumvent normal file and directory permissions to access unauthorized files. It should only be given to Administrators, Backup Operators, and backup service accounts. Use or attempted use of the *Back up files and directories* right is not automatically tracked if you enable Audit Privileged User under Audit Policy.

Bypass traverse checking

Allows access to files or folders (if the user has correct permissions) regardless of permission restrictions on the parent folder. It's the way Windows works! This privilege does not allow the user to list the contents of a directory, only to traverse the directory tree. *Bypass traverse checking* default memberships on workstations and servers are Administrators, Backup Operators, Power Users, Users , and Everyone. On domain controllers the default members are Administrators and Authenticated Users. If you remove this right, you "break" Windows in most cases.

Change System Time

Allows Windows' system time to be changed. This right is restricted because a user could accidentally mess up the correct time, which is necessary for Kerberos authentication and might allow malicious intruders to hide their tracks (by placing their current activities "in the past." Default users are Administrators and Server Operators (and Power Users on workstations). Does not allow Time Zone to be changed, which is something many mobile users need when traveling. You can allow non-admin users to change the time zone using a registry edit (see `http://support.microsoft.com/default` `.aspx?scid=kb;en-us;300022`).

Create a Pagefile

Allows a security principle to create a virtual memory pagefile or change its size. Normally given to Administrators, it is not normally needed by anyone else.

Create a Token Object

Determines which accounts can be used by processes to create a token that can then be used to get access to any local resources when the process uses an internal API. This user right is used internally by the operating system. Unless it is necessary, do not assign this user right to a user, group, or process other than LocalSystem. You should not assign this to any account that you would not want to take over complete control of the OS.

Create Global Objects

Allows "global objects" (vs. per-user or per-session objects) to be created in Terminal Sessions. Normally given to Administrators and Service. Terminal Services users can still create session-specific objects.

Create permanent shared objects

Allows Active Directory objects to be created. Normally, this right is only needed by programs adding objects or extending the Active Directory schema. LocalSystem has the right be default; it's normally not needed by any other account.

Create Global Objects

Introduced in W2K SP4, a global object can sometimes be something as normal as a graphics file attempting to be inserted into a Word document. This setting should not be modified unless necessary. It is required by some malicious code programs and some remote management programs (e.g., software push programs).

Debug programs

Determines which users can attach a debugger to any process or to the kernel. A very security-sensitive setting to have, it is set to Administrators by default. It's needed for some current and future Microsoft patching (e.g., `Update.exe`) mechanisms. If removed, it may disable forthcoming *hot patching,* a new "in-memory" patching technique used by W2K3 that will require less reboots. For information about why debug programs might be needed for patching, see `http://support.microsoft.com/default .aspx?scid=kb;en-us;888791`.

Deny access to this computer from network

Overrides *Access this computer from the network.* Usually only the default Support account is listed. Modify as required to secure your environment.

Deny log on as a batch job

Overrides the *Log on as batch job* right.

Deny log on as a service

Overrides the *Log on as a service* right.

Deny log on locally

Overrides *Allow Log on locally.* Normally, it contains the Support account and maybe the SQLDebugger account on SQL servers. Normally, non-admin users cannot log on locally to a domain controller.

Deny log on through Terminal Services

Overrides *Allow log on through Terminal Services.*

Enable computer and user accounts to be trusted for delegation

Determines which users can set the *Trusted for Delegation* setting on a user or computer object. A server process running on a computer (or under a user context) that is trusted for delegation can access remote resources on another computer using delegated credentials of a client. Normally, this right is only given to Administrators. This right was created because some trojans and worms (NT Remote Explorer) are programmed to "steal" another user's credentials to access remote resources.

> *More information on the NT Remote Explorer malware program can be found at http://securityresponse .symantec.com/avcenter/venc/data/w32.remoteexplore.html.*

The user or object that is granted this privilege must have write permissions to the user account or the computer object used in the delegation. All computer accounts, except Domain Controllers, have a *Do not trust this computer for delegation* flag that is set by default. Domain Controllers have *Trust this computer for delegation to any service (Kerberos only)* flag that is set by default.

A server process running on a computer (or under a user context) that is trusted for delegation can access remote resources on another computer using delegated credentials of a client, as long as the client account does not have the *Account is sensitive and cannot be delegated* flag set (which can be set in the Account tab in Active Directory Users and Computers).

Force shutdown from a remote system

Allows users to shut down computers running from a remote location on the network. This is set to Administrators and Server Operators by default.

Generate Security Audits

Determines which accounts can be used by a process to add entries to the security log. Normally given to LocalSystem, LocalService, and NetworkService.

Impersonate a client after authentication

Allows programs that run on behalf of the user to impersonate the user. Normally given to Administrator, Administrators, IIS_WPG, and any service. Added with W2K SP4. When you assign the *Impersonate a client after authentication* user right to a user, you permit programs that run on behalf of that user to impersonate a client. This security setting helps to prevent unauthorized servers from impersonating clients that connect to it through methods such as remote procedure calls (RPC) or named pipes.

Increase scheduling priority

Determines which users can change a process' scheduling priority of programs and processes in Task Manager. It contains the Administrators group by default.

Load and unload device drivers

Determines which users can load and unload non-Plug-and-Play device drivers. It contains Administrators and Print Operators by default.

Lock pages in memory

Determines who can force programs to remain in physical memory versus being swapped out to a virtual memory page file. Normally only used by knowledgeable developers. No default members.

Log on as batch job

Determines which accounts can log on as a batch job (versus. interactive). When users create a job in Task Scheduler, Windows will give this right to the user account used when scheduling the task. It normally contains LocalService, IIS accounts, the Support account, and maybe SQLDebuggr. *Deny log on as batch job* will override this right.

Log on as service

Determines which accounts can log on as a service. All "service accounts" must have this right and are assigned it automatically if the account is used on the Service's Logon tab. It allows accounts to be logged on (by the SCM) and be authenticated so the service can start without a user having to log on. It normally contains NetworkService and Administrator. The *Deny log on as service* right will override this right.

Manage auditing and security log

Allows a user to view and clear the security log and enable object access auditing on individual objects. The right is given to Administrators by default. Non-admin users can view the System and Application logs but not the Security log. This is a separate setting under Security Options, which can be enabled to allow the Guest account to view the Security log.

Modify firmware environment values

Allows a user to modify the *Last Known Good* setting. It's normally given to Administrators by default. Needed to install or upgrade Windows OS. On Itanium-based computers, boot information is stored in nonvolatile RAM. Users must be assigned the *Modify firmware environment values* right to run Bootcfg.exe and to change the Default Operating System setting on Startup and Recovery in System Properties. The *Modify firmware environment values* right is needed for Windows updates that use Update.exe.

Perform volume maintenance tasks

Allows user to use applications that access disk volumes, including the Disk Management, volume shadow copies, and defrag. Normally, only Administrators have this right. Users with the *Perform volume maintenance tasks* right can explore disks and extend files into memory that contains other data. When the extended files are opened, the user might be able to read and modify the acquired data.

Profile a single process

Determines which users can use Performance Monitor to profile non-system processes. Given to Administrators, Power Users, and LocalSystem.

Profile system performance

Determines which users can use Performance Monitor to profile system processes. Usually given to Administrators and LocalSystem.

Remove computer from docking station

Determines whether a user can undock a portable computer from its docking station without logging on and still have the laptop automatically go into its undocked profile. Administrators normally have this right. Badly described in help files as a physical security measure.

Replace a process level token

Determines which user (really usually a service) accounts can start another (i.e., call) process. Used by Task Scheduler. Given to LocalService, NetworkService, and IWAM accounts.

Restore files and directories

Determines which users can restore backed up objects to which they would otherwise not have permissions. Given to Administrators, Backup Operators, and Server Operators. Does not automatically allow users to access tape logs stored in user profiles (if needed during a restore). The *Restore files and directories* user right is similar to granting the following permissions to the user or group in question on all files and folders on the system: Traverse Folder/Execute File and Write.

On workstations, the *Restore files and directories* right is given by default to Administrators, Backup Operators, Power Users, and Users. On servers, it is given to Administrators, Backup Operators, and Power Users. On domain controllers, it is given to Account Operators, Administrators, Backup Operators, Server Operators, and Print Operators. *Restore files and directories* and *Shut down the system* rights are needed to install Windows updates that use `Update.exe`.

Shut down the system

Determines which users logged on locally can use the Shutdown menu option to shut down Windows. Normally given to Administrators, Server Operators, and Print Operators.

Synchronize directory service data

Determines which users have the authority to synchronize all directory service data. The default is none.

Take ownership of files or other objects

Allows members to take ownership of an NFTS-secured object. Normally, only Administrators should have this right. It is needed to install Windows patches using `Update.exe`.

Security Settings - Local Policies - Security Options

Security Options contains specific security settings that can be enabled locally. It contains more than 60 settings in Windows XP and later, and more are added with every patch and service pack. In XP and later, Security options are preceded by a category setting (e.g., Accounts, Interactive Logon, etc.). There are some minor changes in setting names between XP and W2K3. There were no category names in W2K. The security options shown below are the most relevant options present in W2K3. Unless otherwise noted, leave them at the defaults. Also, be aware of double-negatives (i.e., disabling the disable of an option).

Administrator account status

Allows the local Administrator account to be disabled in XP Pro and later. This option is disabled by default. If the Administrator account is disabled accidentally, it can be re-enabled by logging on in Safe mode.

Guest account status

This option can be enabled but is disabled by default.

Limit local account user of blank passwords to console logon only

Enabled by default. Disables network users from having or using blank passwords. Local users are still allowed to have blank passwords.

Rename administrator account

Disabled by default. Allows the Administrator account to be renamed. As covered in several previous chapters, this should be enabled and the Administrator account renamed to something inconspicuous.

Rename guest account

Disabled by default. Allows the guest account to be renamed. As covered in several previous chapters, this should be enabled and the guest account renamed to something inconspicuous.

Audit the access of global system objects

If *Audit the access of global system objects* is enabled, it causes system objects, such as mutexes (mutual exclusive), events, semaphores (locking mechanisms used inside resource managers or resource dispensers), and DOS devices to be created with auditing turned on. The access of global system objects is normal, and would generate large security log files if this setting were enabled. It should be disabled or left undefined.

Audit the use of Backup and Restore privilege

Disabled by default. If enabled, it would generate large security log files during a typical backup and restore jobs initiated by normal backup software. This option should be disabled or left undefined.

Shutdown system immediately if unable to log security audit events

Should be left disabled in most environments. If enabled, when the security log reaches its maximum size, it forces the affected system to immediately shut down. No one is allowed to access the system until the administrator logs on locally, clears the security log, and resets a registry entry. This should be enabled in high-security environments where security logs are monitored daily.

Allow undock without having to log on

If enabled, as is its default, it will allow a laptop to go into its Undocked profile without the user having to log on. If *Allow undock without having to log on* is enabled, logon is not required and an external hardware eject button can be used to undock the computer. If disabled, a user must log on and have the *Remove computer from docking station* privilege to undock the computer.

Allowed to format and eject removable media

Defines who can format and eject NTFS removable media, such as tapes and zip disks.

Prevent users from installing printer drivers

If enabled, non-admin users cannot install network print drivers. Enabled by default on servers and disabled on workstations.

Security Options - Devices

Restrict CD-ROM access to locally logged-on user only

Disabled by default. When enabled, it disallows any user from accessing the CD-ROM drive remotely. On the Restrict options, if a local user is accessing the CD-ROM, remote network access is temporarily disabled for the duration of the local access, regardless of settings.

Restrict floppy access to locally logged-on user only

Disabled by default. When enabled, it disallows any user from accessing the floppy drive and its media remotely. On the Restrict options, if a local user is accessing the floppy drive, remote network access is temporarily disabled for the duration of the local access, regardless of settings.

Unsigned driver installation behavior

Determines how drivers not tested and signed by Microsoft as compatible are handled. By default, it's set to *Warn but allow installation prior to Windows Vista*. Can also be set to *Do not allow installation* or *Silently succeed*. Unfortunately, many valid drivers are not signed by Microsoft. However, a very high percentage of system crashes are caused by unsigned drivers. Starting with Windows Vista (and already in Datacenter editions of W2K3), unsigned drivers are not allowed by default.

Allow server operators to schedule tasks

Determines whether server operators can use the legacy At.exe command to schedule batch jobs. Not defined (i.e., doesn't allow) by default.

LDAP server signing requirements

Describes whether the client must have signed LDAP requests to interact with the server (LDAP signing requires W2K servers with SP4 or later). There are two options:

❏   **None** — Not required, but if the client wants to, the server can

❏   **Required** — The LDAP client must use signed LDAP requests

On the face of it, requiring authenticated LDAP to interact with the server is a good thing; unfortunately, unless all participating clients and domain controllers have this setting enabled, proceed with caution.

Refuse machine account password changes

Disabled by default. If enabled, computers trying to change their computer account password (normally done every 30 days without end user involvement) will be prevented by the domain controller from doing so. There are few reasons to enable, but it might be required if a PC has a dual-booting system with NT on one partition and W2K or later on another. See Microsoft KB article #154501 for more details on why you might not want automatic machine password changes to occur.

Domain member: Digitally encrypt or sign secure channel data (always)

Domain member: Digitally encrypt secure channel data (when possible)

Domain member: Digitally sign secure channel data (when possible)

Determines whether all secure channel traffic initiated by the domain member computer must be signed or encrypted. If enabled, computers will not be able to join NT 4 domains. When a computer joins a domain, a computer account and computer account password are created. After that, whenever the system starts, it uses the computer account and password to create a secure channel with a domain controller for its domain. The secure channel is used to perform operations such as service or user logon authentication, NTLM pass-through authentication, LSA SID\Name Lookup, etc. If a system is set to always encrypt or sign secure channel data, it cannot establish a secure channel with a domain controller that is not capable of signing or encrypting all secure channel traffic (i.e., NT), because all secure channel data is signed and encrypted.

Disable machine account password changes

If enabled, prevents computers from even attempting to make computer account password changes. Disabled by default.

Maximum machine account password age

Windows will change the machine account password, which is long and complex already, every 30 days by default.

Require strong (Windows 2000 or later) session key

Disabled by default. If enabled, member computers and domain controllers require strong (128-bit) cryptographic keys to establish a secure channel, versus weaker 64-bit keys used in NT. If enabled, NT and earlier clients will not be able to authenticate to the domain controller.

Do not display last user name

If enabled, the last user account name that logged on to the computer is not displayed in the Windows logon screen. Disabled by default. Should be enabled in high-security or shared computer environments.

Do not require CTRL+ALT+DEL

If enabled, users still have to log on, but they do not have to press the Ctrl+Alt+Del keys to initiate the logon sequence. Disabled by default.

Message text for users attempting to logon

Warning text message for interactive users attempting to log on. Disabled by default. Should be enabled with a legally approved message warning unauthorized users against access, or warning authorized users against unauthorized actions. If enabled, also defeats most automated brute-force password-cracking tools.

Windows XP and the Windows Server 2003 family add support for configuring logon banners that can exceed 512 characters in length and that can contain carriage-return line-feed sequences. However, Windows 2000 clients cannot interpret and display message text that is created by computers running Windows XP or the Windows Server 2003 family. You must use a Windows 2000 computer to create a logon message policy that applies to Windows 2000 computers.

Message title for users attempting to logon

Related to the previous setting. Creates dialog box title bar text surrounding logon message text. Disabled by default, but should be enabled as discussed in the previous setting.

Number of previous logons to cache (in case domain controller is not available)

Determines whether a user using a domain user account can log on to the domain using cached account information when a domain controller is not available. The number value refers to how many separate user profiles can be cached at one time, not how many times an individual user will be allowed to log on. If enabled, allowed users can log on an indefinite number of times without having to contact a domain controller. Often used for roaming laptop users. The default is 10. Set to 0 to disable logon caching.

Users must have made at least one successful logon involving a domain controller in their home domain after the setting was enabled for it to take effect. When enabled, even when a user logs on normally and the domain controller is reachable, the cached credentials are used first to speed up network logons. If enabled, it could cause GPO and security permission problems because cached credentials are used first. There are password-cracking tools that can extract cached credentials from logon caches (if they have local admin access). Recommended setting is 0 for local users and 2–3 for roaming laptop users (i.e., Administrator plus one or two other profiles).

Prompt user to change password before expiration

Determines how far in advance (in days) users are warned that their password is about to expire. The default is 14 days.

Require Domain Controller authentication to unlock workstation

Determines whether or not a domain controller is required to unlock a locked workstation, or whether cached credentials will work. Default is disabled. Should be enabled to prevent timing issues and other types of hacks involving locked screen savers.

Require a smart card

Determines whether or not a smart card is required for an interactive logon. Requires use of a smart card and PKI infrastructure. Can be set per user in Active Directory Users and Computers. Should be enabled on administrator accounts in high-risk environments.

Smart card removal behavior

Determines what happens when the smart card for a logged on user is removed from the smart card reader. Setting this option to *Lock Workstation* locks the workstation when the smart card is removed. Setting this option to *Force Logoff automatically* logs the user off when the smart card is removed. Supported in W2K and later, although this setting cannot be viewed locally on W2K machines.

Security Options - Microsoft Network Client

Windows NT 4.0 SP3 and later (and fully patched Win 9x) computers can digitally sign SMB traffic. Other than the offsetting decrease in performance (up to 15% in some networks), signed SMB traffic is a good thing. It prevents NetBIOS man-in-the-middle attacks. Windows 2000 and 2003 domain controllers require it, dropping all non-signed SMB traffic. However, SMB signing is optional (although often enabled) on all current Windows computers. By default they can participate in SMB signing, but are not required unless connecting to a domain controller.

In most cases, workstations and member servers are configured to digitally sign SMB traffic if the other partner agrees. Because most Windows OSs have this setting enabled, they will communicate with each other using signed traffic by default. Mark Minasi (www.minasi.com) has the best discussion on this topic in his April 2005 Newsletter #46. The default options configured by Microsoft are usually adequate. Essentially, this means older Windows clients will not be able to establish NetBIOS connections to Windows 2000 and 2003 domain controllers.

When reviewing the following settings, "server" does not mean a server-based edition of the operating system. It means the computer acting as a server, hosting shared resources that other remote computers want to access.

Digitally sign communications (always)

Disabled by default on non-domain controllers. If enabled, it requires signed SMB communications to the server.

Digitally sign communications (if server agrees)

Negotiates with the server to see if SMB signing should be enabled. Enabled by default. If the *Digitally sign communications (always)* setting is enabled, the Microsoft network client will not communicate with a Microsoft network server unless that server agrees to perform SMB packet signing. If this policy is disabled, SMB packet signing is negotiated between the client and server.

Digitally sign communications (always)

If enabled, requires signed SMB communications from all clients. Enabled by default for DCs, disabled for member servers. If enabled, participating computers cannot join an NT 4 domain.

Digitally sign communications (if client agrees)

Negotiates with the server to see if SMB signing should be enabled. Enabled by default on DCs.

Because the second option is also selected by default, clients **do not** have to digitally sign SMB communications if they don't want to. The second option overrides the first. NT 4.0 machines will need SP3 and later; Win95 clients needed the Directory Services client. If enabled, copying files and mapping drives between computers takes longer.

Send unencrypted password to third-party SMB servers

Prevents man-in-the-middle (MitM) attacks that modify SMB packets in transit; the SMB protocol supports the digital signing of SMB packets. If this setting is enabled, it instructs Windows to send plaintext passwords to Samba and other third-party SMB services. This policy setting determines whether SMB packet signing must be negotiated before further communication with an SMB server is permitted.

Amount of idle time required before suspending session

Determines how long an idle SMB connection can be idle before being suspended. Set to 15 minutes for servers, not enabled for workstations. When a connection becomes active again, service usually just re-authenticates transparently to the user.

Disconnect clients when logon hours expire

By default, when clients exceed allowed logon hours (as dictated in their User Account tab), they are still allowed to remain connected.

Allow anonymous SID/Name translation

Determines whether or not an anonymous connection can enumerate a user account for its SID. Enabled and required for DCs, disabled for other W2K3 and XP machines. Leave at the defaults.

Do not allow anonymous enumeration of SAM accounts

Determines if an anonymous connection can retrieve the list of local (or domain if stored on an NT domain controller) user and computer accounts. Disabled on servers, enabled on workstations. Leave at the defaults. If the *Do not allow anonymous enumeration of SAM accounts* setting is enabled, it will be impossible to establish down-level trusts to NT 4.0 domains.

Do not allow anonymous enumeration of SAM accounts and Shares

Determines whether anonymous connections can enumerate SAM accounts or shares. Disabled by default. Authenticated users can always do these things. If anonymous SID translation is disabled, many NT 4.0 services will fail. Anonymous enumeration of SAM settings has no effect on DCs.

Security Options - Network Access

Do not allow storage of credentials or .NET Passports for network authentication

Determines whether XP's new Stored User Names and Passwords application will save passwords, credentials, or Microsoft .NET Passports for later use after gaining domain authentication or other participating applications. This setting is disabled by default. Stored User Names and Passwords is not used by many applications. If a hacker has local admin access, they can recover the names and passwords stored in this application. This setting should be enabled in most environments.

Let Everyone permissions apply to anonymous users

Allows anonymous connections to get the same security permissions and rights as the Everyone group (as was allowed prior to W2K3). This was a huge security hole, now closed by default unless you enable this setting. Note: If you disable *Let Everyone permissions apply to anonymous users,* domains with this setting will be unable to establish or maintain trusts with Windows NT 4.0 domains.

Named Pipes that can be accessed anonymously

Remotely accessible registry paths

Remotely accessible registry paths and sub-paths

Restrict anonymous access to Named Pipes and Shares

Shares that can be accessed anonymously

Defines what Named Pipes (an authentication type) and registry paths are accessible to all users (regardless of ACLs) or anonymous connections. Most Windows versions have default entries in these locations.

Leave at the defaults unless you need a highly secured machine. Removing default entries can break some remote management agents (e.g., patch management software, etc.). These settings are named slightly differently in various Windows versions.

Sharing and security model for local accounts

This option has two settings:

❑ Classic — local users authenticate with the logon accounts

❑ Guest only — local users always authenticate as guest

If all users authenticate as guest, their profiles are never saved. Guest only means that all permissions to a resource are either Read only or Modify. XP Home only has Guest model. XP Pro switches from Guest to Classic mode when it is connected to a domain. Should be set to Classic mode. This policy will have no impact on computers running Windows 2000.

Do not store LAN Manager hash value on next password change

LM hashes are very weak and subject to easy attack. By default, all Windows computers store account passwords in LM hash form. The default setting is disabled, but you should enable this setting and make all passwords expire so that users are forced to change their password. You can also instruct users to use passwords longer than 15 characters to manually disable LM hash storage.

Force logoff when logon hours expire

Forces graceful logoff when logon hours expire (versus abrupt disconnection). Disabled by default, but can be enabled when desired.

LAN Manager authentication level

Can be set to allow or reject the following: LM, NTLM, NTLM2 requests or responses. LM and NTLM are legacy authentication protocols, vulnerable to cracking. Whenever possible, you want to refuse to respond to or send LM and NTLM authentication. Test thoroughly first. NT 4.0 must be SP 4 or later. Windows 9x clients must have the Directory Services client installed.

LDAP Signing Requirements

Defines wither the client is required to sign LDAP requests before sending to DC. Settings are None, Negotiate, or Require. The default is Negotiate. W2K3 requires LDAP signing if the client is using Windows Server 2003 Administrative Pack tools.

Network security: Minimum session security for NTLM SSP based (including secure RPC) clients

Network security: Minimum session security for NTLM SSP based (including secure RPC) servers

You can pick and choose requirements, if any. Options include the following:

❑ Require message integrity

❑ Require message confidentiality

❑ Require NTLMv2 session security

❏   Require 128-bit encryption

❏   None

None is set by default.

Security Options - Recovery Console

Allow automatic administrative logon

If enabled, no password is required for use of the Recovery console program. Disabled by default in XP and W2K3; enabled in early versions of W2K.

Allow floppy copy and access to all drivers and folders

Determines whether a Recovery console logon session can access all Windows system drivers and folders. Disabled by default.

Security Options - Shutdown

Allow system to be shut down without having to log on

Enabled on workstations; disabled on servers. Users must have *Shutdown the system* right also to be able to shut down a system without logging on.

Clear virtual memory pagefile

If enabled (default is disabled), Windows will erase the page file when shutting down. Significantly decreases performance during shutdown. Will zero out the Hibernation file (`hyperfil.sys`) when hibernation is disabled, too.

Security Options - System Cryptography

Force strong key protection for user keys stored on the computer

This security setting determines if users' private keys require a password to be used. Can be prompted when using a personal digital certificate. The options are as follows:

❏   User input is not required when new keys are stored and used

❏   User is prompted when the key is first used (user is only allowed to click on OK warning box)

❏   User must enter a password each time they use a key

Use FIPS compliant algorithms for encryption, hashing, and signing

This was discussed in Chapter 13 in more detail. To recap, when enabled, it supports the Transport Layer Security (TLS) protocol as a client and as a server (if applicable) instead of SSL on web servers. Uses only the Triple DES encryption algorithm for the TLS traffic encryption. Uses only the RSA public key algorithm for the TLS key exchange and authentication. Uses only SHA-1 for the TLS hashing requirements. Uses only 3DES for EFS, instead of AES. Uses only 3DES for Terminal Server encryption. FIPS-compliant software is often a requirement of government users.

Security Options - System Objects

Default owner for objects created by members of the Administrators group

By default, when a member of the Administrators group creates an object, ownership is given to the Administrators group, not the individual administrator. This prevents ownership problems if the individual user account is deleted. This option can be enabled and changed to the account that actually created the object, instead.

Require insensitivity for non-Windows subsystems

Determines whether case insensitivity is enforced for all subsystems. Windows supports many different subsystems (e.g., Win32, Posix, etc.). The Win32 subsystem is case insensitive. However, the kernel supports case sensitivity for other subsystems, such as POSIX.

Strengthen default permissions of internal system objects (e.g., Symbolic Links)

If this policy is enabled, as is the default, users who are not administrators can read shared objects but cannot modify shared objects that they did not create.

Security Options - System Settings

Optional subsystems

Windows supports many different subsystems (e.g., Win32, POSIX, OS/2, etc.). You can specify Posix. OS/2 is no longer available as a default option.

Use Certificate Rules on Windows Executables for Software Restriction Policies

Must be enabled for Certificate rules in Software Restriction Policies to work.

Event Log Settings

Configures Event Log settings, such as maximum size and retention method (see Figure 14-9).

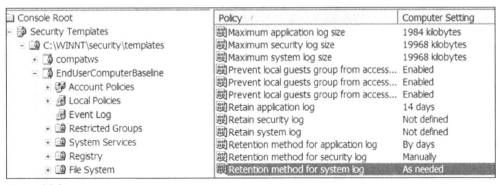

Figure 14-9

Restricted Group Settings

These will enforce group membership, adding and removing users to meet what is set in the Restricted Group setting. This is an excellent GPO setting. You should add any highly privileged administrative group (see Figure 14-10). Then, using the browsing feature (see Figure 14-11), manually select all the users who should belong to a particular group. If anyone adds or deletes a user into those groups outside of the Restricted Group setting, the original members will be restored shortly. This feature is great for preventing "admin creep" whereby various users are accidentally added as administrators during troubleshooting events and then forgotten about. It can also be used to keep highly unprivileged users in restricted permissions groups (as discovered in Chapters 3 and 5).

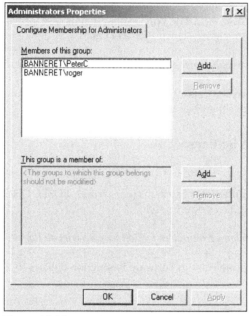

Figure 14-10

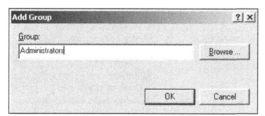

Figure 14-11

You should always browse to select groups or members in the Restricted Groups feature. This causes the SID of the object to be stored, versus the user's name (which could change).

System Services Settings

Another awesome feature of group policy, administrators can define what services are allowed to run on managed machines. The service's Startup mode (i.e., Automatic, Manual, or Disabled) can be defined, along with who has what permissions (see Figure 14-12). This feature was covered in Chapter 7 in more detail. In order to see a particular service to edit in a GPO, the service must be installed and running on the machine on which GPO is being edited. It prevents high-risk services from running on authorized machines. For example, prevent the World Wide Web service from running on computers that don't need IIS. Prevent the Windows Messenger from running on computers not needing its services.

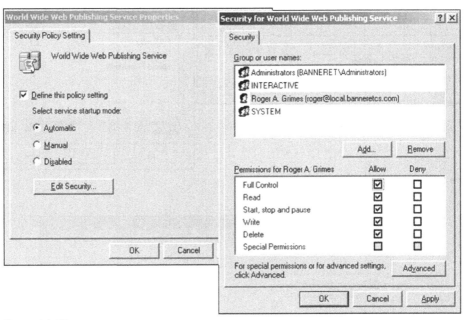

Figure 14-12

Registry Settings

An administrator can define the permissions on existing registry keys (see Figure 14-13). This feature was also covered in Chapter 6. Default GPO settings only allow you to set or change registry permissions, but do not allow registry entries to be modified. A customized Security or Administrative template must be created to modify a custom registry entry value. In order to see a particular registry key permission to edit in a GPO, the registry key must be installed and running on the machine on which the GPO is being edited. Prevent non-admin users from being able to edit or modify high-risk registry keys, as covered in Chapter 6.

File System Settings

An administrator can define the NTFS permissions on existing files and folders (see Figure 14-14). This feature was also covered in Chapter 5. Default GPO settings only allow you to set or change NTFS file or folder permissions, but do not allow files or folders to be created or deleted. A customized Security or Administrative template must be created to modify permissions on a non-existent file or folder. In order to see a particular file or folder permission to edit in a GPO, the file or folder must be on the machine on which the GPO is being edited. Prevent non-admin users from being able to execute high-risk files, as covered in Chapter 5.

513

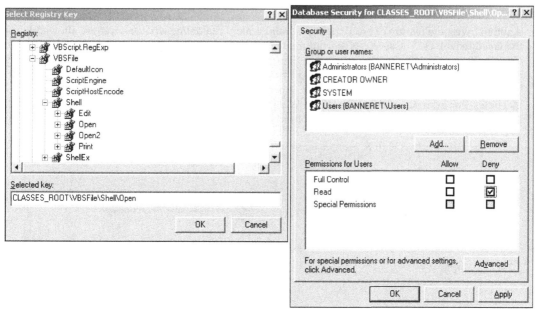

Figure 14-13

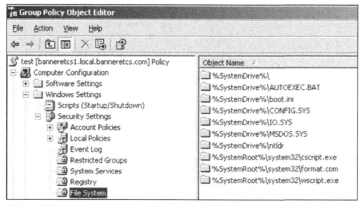

Figure 14-14

Software Restriction Policies

Administrators can set or modify software restriction policies. This feature was covered in detail in Chapter 9.

IP Security Policies

Administrators can set or modify IPSec policies. This feature was covered in detail in Chapter 8.

Administrative Templates

The Administrative Templates area of GPOs allows managed software to be configured and controlled. Administrative templates expose and manipulate registry settings. Each version of Windows comes with hundreds of Administrative template settings, and each service pack adds more. XP SP2 and W2K3 come with over 1,300 template settings. The default adm files shipped with Windows are located in %Windir%\Inf. Most deal with configuring Windows default applications, and many other Microsoft products come with Administrative templates.

Default Windows Administrative Templates

Default Windows Administrative Templates are as follows:

- ❑ System.adm — Configures OS
- ❑ Inetres.adm — Configures IE
- ❑ Wuau.adm — Configures Windows Update
- ❑ Wmplayer.adm — Windows Media Player
- ❑ Conf.adm — Configures NetMeeting

These five default templates are shipped with Windows 2000 SP2 and XP SP1 and later. Wuau (Windows Update) wasn't introduced until those particular versions of 2000 and XP. Wmplayer.adm was called wmp.adm in Windows 2000 and 2000 SP1. System.adm contains the most settings. XP SP2 significantly upgraded the System.adm, Inetres.adm, and Wuau.adm templates.

> *The various Administrative templates, their default settings, and this book's recommendations can be found at www.wrox.com.*

Other Built-in Windows Administrative Templates

Other Built-in Windows Administrative templates (not always installed by default) are as follows:

- ❑ Common.adm — Common settings for Win9x/NT
- ❑ Windows.adm — Settings specific for Win 9x
- ❑ Inetcorp.adm — Configures miscellaneous IE settings
- ❑ Inetset.adm — Configures other miscellaneous IE settings
- ❑ Inetesc.adm — Configures W2K3's IE Enhanced Security Configuration feature. Enabled on W2K3 domain controllers by default.

Common.adm and Windows.adm are policy files meant to be used in NT or 9x systems using System Policy Editor (poledit.exe), because those systems don't understand GPOs.

Loading Administrative Templates into GPOs

New Administrative templates can be imported into both Computer and User-based GPOs, and into Local Computer Policy. Templates must be added to each GPO you want them to be accessible in. When added to a GPO, the template and its settings are uploaded to the GPO on the DC's Sysvol. New Administrative templates can be loaded into a GPO by using the following steps:

1. Open the Group Policy Object Editor or GPMC.

2. Under either Computer Configuration or User Configuration, right-click Administrative Templates, and then click Add/Remove Templates.

3. In the Add/Remove Templates dialog box, click Add.

4. Navigate to the folder containing the `.adm` file that you would like to add. Select the template, and then click Open.

Microsoft Office 2003 Admin Templates

Microsoft releases custom Admin templates with many of its products, including Microsoft Office. Here is a list of the Microsoft Office 2003 Administrative templates:

❑ Access11.adm — Access 2003

❑ Excel11.adm — Excel 2003

❑ Fp11.adm — FrontPage 2003

❑ Gal11.adm — Microsoft Clip Organizer

❑ Inf11.adm — Microsoft InfoPath 2003

❑ Instalr11.adm — Microsoft Windows Installer

❑ Office11.adm — Office 2003 common settings

❑ Outlk11.adm — Outlook 2003

❑ Ppt11.adm — PowerPoint 2003

❑ Pub11.adm — Publisher 2003

❑ Word11.adm — Word 2003

These Office templates contain hundreds of configurable settings that control Microsoft Office settings. You can download these templates from the Office 2003 Resource Kit (`http://office.microsoft .com/en-us/FX011417911033.aspx`).

Custom Administrative Templates

Any third-party vendor or administrator can create custom Administrative templates to manage their product. Although the default Administrative or Security templates have dozens to hundreds of settings, sometimes they don't have exactly what you need. In those cases, you can "roll your own."

Creating a Custom Administrative Template

Custom Administrative templates can be created one of three ways:

❑ Modify an existing template

❑ Use an existing template as a starting point

❑ Create a new template

Administrative templates are Unicode text files, with their own proprietary format, and they require special formatting and syntax. If at all possible, find an existing template that is close to what you want to achieve and modify it to meet your new needs. Don't modify default Administrative templates shipped by Microsoft, as they may be modified or overwritten by future updates. Use these steps:

1. Understand the registry, and the problems you can create for yourself if something goes wrong.

2. Document the registry settings needed for the template.

3. Create the admin template.

4. Save to `%windir%\Inf`.

5. Import into a test GPO.

6. Test, test, test.

7. Release to production.

Here are some links for Administrative template creation and troubleshooting:

❑   http://support.microsoft.com/kb/887303

❑   http://support.microsoft.com/kb/221833

❑   http://support.microsoft.com/kb/216358

❑   http://support.microsoft.com/kb/250842

❑   www.gpanswers.com

❑   www.gpoguy.com/FAQs/troublefaq.htm

GPO Notes/Recommendations

Here are some GPO and Administrative template notes and recommendations:

❑   Start small and test before deploying.

❑   Don't create a policy for *every* setting and application in your environment.

❑   Focus on the most critical settings first.

❑   In the GPO or template name, use a verb that reflects the policy's overall setting (e.g., Allow, Permit, Turn on, Force, Deny, Prohibit, Disable, Turn off, etc.).

❑   In the GPO or template name, use a version number (e.g., Force Corporate Screensaver_1.1) to help keep track of what versions are installed where.

❑   Never modify default templates; copy to a new name, and then modify.

❑   Create smaller, more granular policy settings instead of one larger policy.

❑   Make custom templates on computers with installed software or services.

❑   Create and/or deploy custom templates on the same administrative workstations.

❑   Removing an Admin template does not remove the admin template registry settings!

❑ If you plan to remove an admin template:

    ❑ Modify the settings to be what you want the registry values to be after you remove the template.

    ❑ Let new changes replicate.

    ❑ Remove the admin template.

❑ Remember: admin templates are stored locally on the computer that edits or modifies them; then they are copied up to the DC's Sysvol.

❑ If you modify templates from several different computers, this can potentially cause unwanted "co-mingling" of old and new templates.

❑ Just because you modify an application or setting doesn't mean the related application will prevent users from making changes, or report the current correct setting.

❑ Normally, there is no harm in applying an admin template or GPO setting to a computer that it "doesn't belong on" (i.e., Office templates to a computer without Microsoft Office installed).

Summary

Chapter 14 covered GPO settings and Administrative templates in detail, described the installed defaults, and made recommendations. Chapter 15 will continue the discussion on GPOs, focusing on how to get the most bang for your buck with Active Directory group policy.

Designing a Secure Active Directory Infrastructure

Chapter 15 continues the discussion on Windows security automation by focusing on the mechanisms that exist to apply the group policy settings covered in Chapter 14. Microsoft has incorporated a fair amount of flexibility in Active Directory and group policy objects (GPOs). This flexibility is often described as confusing complexity by administrators beginning their first forays into securing computers with group policy. This chapter covers the different parts of Active Directory, describes the different mechanisms available to apply security policy, and makes best practice recommendations. Readers finishing this chapter will be able to maximize the effectiveness of group policy, keeping Windows computers secure, while minimizing the system performance delays caused by ineffective planning.

Active Directory Introduction

Active Directory is an X.500 directory service introduced by Microsoft with Windows 2000. A *directory service* is simply a namespace distributed database used to name, store, and locate resources. A *namespace* is a collection of objects with a common naming convention and format. Within each namespace, each object or resource must have a unique name and can only exist once. Many different namespaces are used today, both in computer form and non-computer form. An example of a non-computer namespace would be a phonebook. Within each phonebook, each phone entry has its unique address and phone number.

Popular computer namespaces, besides Active Directory, include DNS, WINS, Novell's eDirectory, OpenLDAP, and IBM's SNA. DNS is one of the world's largest namespaces, and no object within DNS shares a name or location. For instance, nobody else in the world is allowed to have my e-mail address of roger@banneretcs.com. By ensuring that all objects have unique names and locations, the directory service can always assist objects and processes in finding other objects.

Active Directory uses the DNS namespace to name and locate many resources.

All X.500 directory services follow a common structure and naming convention. For instance, the collection of all the locations in a single instance of a directory service is called the *tree*. The top of the point, the origination point, is called the *root*. Objects are stored directly off the tree or in subdivisions of the tree called *containers* or *organizational units (OUs)*.

> *Organizational units and containers are essentially the same thing. An OU is an Active Directory container object and there are other types of container objects in Active Directory besides OUs (some other container types are covered below).*

Active Directory comes with a default set of OUs, but administrators can make their own. Table 15-1 discusses the default OUs shown in the Active Directory Users and Computers console.

Table 15-1

Container Name	Description
Saved Queries	Blank container object by default, introduced in W2K3. Can be used to create and store custom LDAP queries. No GPOs can be linked here.
Built-In	Contains many of the built-in security groups present in any domain. All built-in security groups were shown in Table 3-4 in Chapter 3. No GPOs can be linked here.
Computers	Contains all computer object accounts either joined or imported to the domain. No GPOs can be linked here. Computer objects can, and should, be moved out of this container so that custom GPOs can be linked.
Domain Controllers	Contains all domain controller computer accounts for the domain. Should only contain domain controllers, and the domain controller computer accounts should not be removed from this OU. The default domain controller's GPO is linked here and custom GPOs can be linked.
Foreign Security Principals	Contains user, group, and computer objects (actually, their SIDs) from external, trusted domains. In single domain forests, contains no objects. GPOs cannot be linked here.
Users	Contains all new and imported user accounts for the domain, plus many built-in user accounts as shown in Table 3-3 in Chapter 3. No GPOs can be linked here. User account objects can, and should, be moved out of this container so that custom GPOs can be linked.

Table 15-1 shows the built-in OUs in Active Directory displayed by default. More "behind-the-scenes" OUs can be viewed if the View, Advanced Features (under the console menu) setting is enabled in the Active Directory Users and Computer menu. These additional containers are not discussed in Table 15-1, because they are rarely manipulated by administrators to enhance security.

An OU is the smallest container object to which a GPO can be attached. Administrators cannot apply a GPO directly to a user or computer object. In order to affect a computer or user with a GPO, the administrator must link the GPO to the OU in which the user or computer is located.

Although an administrator cannot attach new GPOs to many of the built-in OUs, GPOs linked at the domain or site level can still be inherited by the user or computer objects inside those containers. This is an important point. Either existing users and computers should be moved out of the existing built-in OUs into a custom OU container and GPOs linked directly, or inherited GPOs must be configured correctly to apply the correct policy to objects in the built-in containers.

Custom-made OUs can follow any structure and naming strategy the administrator wants to implement. Later in this chapter, the section "Efficient Active Directory Security Design" covers a structure optimized for security. However, the administrator can shape any structure that best organizes and manages the organization. OUs are essentially created for two reasons only:

- ❑ To organize and manage environment objects in a logical, organized method
- ❑ To apply security settings via group policy in a logical and structured way

If new to Active Directory organizations and group policy, administrators should structure their directory to mimic their entity's physical locations. A location-based tree structure will minimize Active Directory replication issues and allow the administrator to organize security along geographic boundaries.

Top Active Directory Containers

Every Active Directory environment is made up of one or more forests, domains, and sites.

Forests

The top Active Directory container able to be managed by a single security administrator is the *forest*. A forest is one or more domains. The forest is the highest container at which a single group policy or security setting can be applied. Most administrators set the majority of security settings at the domain level to make them more manageable, to improve speed, and because Microsoft didn't make managing security above the domain level easier.

> *The forest name is the same as the name of the first domain in the forest.*

Domains

A forest contains one or more domains, and every forest starts with a single domain. Domains are called by both a NetBIOS and DNS name. All domains in the same forest share the same common parent root name (e.g., south.contoso.com and north.contoso.com are two different child domains under the parent contoso.com domain). Most domains have two or more domain controllers to store the local domain's users, computers, groups, and other resource information. When computers and users log on to the domain, they can connect to any domain controller in the domain to authenticate — usually the one that responds the fastest to their logon request. Every domain controller (DC) in the same domain has a nearly identical copy of the domain Active Directory database, which contains the domain's user, computer, group, and other objects.

Each domain has its own domain administrators group called Administrators. This is an unfortunate name because Administrators is also the name of the local admin group on each Windows computer, and the naming convention doesn't follow the forest example of Enterprise Admins group (one would expect the domain admin group to be called Domain Admins). However, any member of the domain-level Administrators group has full permissions and privileges to all users, computers, and other resources in the domain.

The domain is often incorrectly called the Windows security boundary, even though it is really the forest level that deserves the boundary distinction. The error is common because most security policies are set at the domain level or lower. Some security policies (i.e., Password and Account Lockout policies) must be set at the domain level.

Forest Root Domain

The first domain in a forest (called the *forest root domain*) is the most powerful domain in the forest because it is the only one with the Enterprise admins and Scheme admins forest groups. Only the administrators in this domain can add new members to those two very powerful accounts. Members of the Enterprise admins group are automatically members of each domain's Administrators group, which gives them local Administrator rights to all users, computers, and GPOs in the domain. Of course, any hacker gaining access to the forest root domain has an opportunity to gain control of every resource in the forest.

Trusts

Domains were introduced with Windows NT 4.0. In Windows NT 4.0 networks, trusts had to be set up between every domain that wanted access to another's objects. The *trusting* domain had the resources that the *trusted* (or user) domain wanted to access. Every trust between two domains had to be set up manually. With Windows 2000 and later forests, every domain in the same forest automatically has a two-way, transitive trust. With transitive trusts, if domain A trusts domain B and domain C trusts domain B, domain C will also trust domain A.

Every domain having a two-way transitive trust has huge implications on the forest. Every user in the forest will have the same security permissions as the domain-specific Everyone and Authenticated Users group has in its own domain. This also means that if a hacker breaks into any domain in a forest as an authenticated user, then they have the same access as the Everyone and Authenticated Users group has in any domain in the forest. Of course, the default behavior (of all domains trusting each other) can be modified to limit the damage from a security intrusion.

Windows 2003 forests can also have *forest trusts* with other forests. Cross-forest trusts are always made between a domain in one forest and a single domain in another forest, and cross-forest trusts are not transitive.

Forests trusts can be constrained by a feature called *selective authentication*. If enabled, even though users crossing from their home forest to the remote forest are added to the remote forest's Authenticated Users group, an additional security check is performed that will prevent the home forest user from accessing objects in the remote forest until administrators in the remote forest specifically allow access. If a cross-forest trust is utilized, strongly consider creating the trust with selective authentication to prevent remote users from being added to the local forest's Authenticated Users group automatically.

While GPOs and security policies cannot be inter-forest, a forest trust (one-way, two-way, transitive, or non-transitive) can allow security principals in one forest to access resources in another external forest.

There are other trusts types, such as *external* or *realm trusts*, that can be made from one domain to another type of resource entity (i.e., an NT 4.0 or Kerberos domain), but they don't involve any significant security differences that have not already been discussed. It's important to understand that any trust will allow users from one domain to become an authenticated user in the other domain.

Another security implication to consider is that of the Windows *trust password*. A password must be supplied with every Windows trust created. The password must be identical on both the trusting and trusted domain. After it is initially set and the trust confirmed on both sides, Windows handles changing the trust password thereafter. During the initial setup, the Windows trust password should be long and complex.

For more information on Windows trusts, see `http://support.microsoft.com/default .aspx?scid=kb;EN-US;128489`.

Depending on the version of Windows, the type of trust created, and whether the domain controller involved is in the trusting or trusted domain, the trust password hash is stored in either the LSA secrets cache, Active Directory, or a SAM database. During trust establishment operations, the trust password hash is cached locally on the domain controller. Regardless of the location, each Windows trust password is an additional password that might be recovered and broken. Practically, trust passwords have not been attacked much, but the risk is always there.

Forest Single Master Operations Roles

Even though most of the DCs in a forest only have a copy of the objects in their own domains, some DCs have additional domain- and forest-level roles. Some operations require a single master server to maintain ultimate ownership of the transaction. The five Active Directory Forest Single Master Operations (FSMO) roles and their descriptions are shown in Table 15-2.

Table 15-2

FSMO Role Name	Description
Domain Naming Master	Keeps track of domain names. Needed when creating, deleting, or renaming new domains in a forest. Usually only one per forest.
Relative Identifier Master	In charge of creating and handing out new Relative Identifiers (RIDs), the ending portion of the SID. Hands out new RIDs to DCs. RIDS are given to new users, groups, and computer objects. Usually one per domain.
Infrastructure Master	Keeps track of groups and group memberships. Usually one per domain.
PDC Emulator	PDC Emulator will communicate to NT 4.0 domain DCs. Keeps track of passwords and password changes, and is the time synchronizer for the domain. Usually one per domain. Hackers may want to infiltrate this DC to change the time to hide activities or to download the most current copy of all domain user and computer password hashes.
Schema Master	Keeps track of schema design (i.e., Active Directory database fields). Usually only one per forest. Although not exploited to date, it is essentially the most powerful DC in the forest.

Along with these FSMO roles, usually one or more DCs in each domain contain a *Global Catalog (GC)*. All DCs within a common domain have a nearly identical copy of all the objects, rights, and permissions in the domain (there are always transient differences that they each replicate to each other, such as LastLogonTime field data indicating when a user logs on to a specific DC). Any DC with a GC also has a list of all Active Directory objects in the forest (although not a full list of object attributes). Essentially, a GC is an Active Directory index file. When an object or process looks for an Active Directory object, it often queries the GC for the location. For instance, when a newly booted Windows client attempts to log on, it will query the GC to find DCs with which to authenticate.

Sites

Sites define physical locations for Active Directory replication. Essentially, a site is a logical collection of subnets that contain domain controllers that can talk to each other over relatively fast and constant network connections. In large environments, if all DCs within a domain were to constantly, and immediately, communicate every database change and update to each other the instance it happened (as occurs with all DCs in the same domain within the same site), it could cause traffic congestion problems or cause inefficient economic costs.

By defining some subnets (and thus, some domain controllers) as belonging in the same site, and others as not, replication traffic and costs can be managed by physical location. Domain controllers within the same domain frequently replicate information to each other without any form of encryption. Intersite DCs are configured to replicate at certain times and for certain intervals. When intersite replication occurs, security changes must be transmitted between sites first (bridgehead server to bridgehead server), and then the site's bridgehead DC transmits the changes to the local site's DCs, which then communicate the changes or updates to the users or groups within the domain. In practice, this means that security settings and applied GPOs may not take effect at intersite DCs for a longer period of time than happens intrasite.

By default, Active Directory contains one site, called the *Default-First-Site object*. It contains all DC objects and subnets unless otherwise defined. Sites can be viewed, managed, created, and deleted using the Active Directory Sites and Services console (see Figure 15-1). One or more group policy objects can be applied at the site level (the creator must be an Enterprise admin), using the Active Directory Sites and Services tool or GPMC, but sites are not often the optimum location of GPO security settings because of the potential intrasite replication issues. Enterprises needing security policies applied across a large geographic intrasite location often choose to use domain or OU GPOs instead. However, if the site is smaller in size than the domain, or if the organization has a lot of roaming issues (e.g., IPSec, printers, proxy servers, etc.), it may make sense to set a more granular site-level policy.

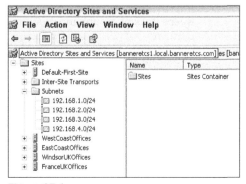

Figure 15-1

Partitions

Starting with Windows Server 2003, Active Directory allows directory (also called *application*) partitions to be defined on one or more DCs. Once a partition is initially created, it can be replicated to one or more other DCs. Only the predefined DCs will replicate partition information to each other and only applications that are specifically written to write information to a partition can. Partitions are not normally used to spread security setting information, but they may be an additional factor in some environments.

LDAP

X.500 directory services are often accessed using a protocol called Lightweight Directory Access Protocol (LDAP). Yes, there was a superset of the protocol called Directory Access Protocol (DAP), but the subset of LDAP has most of the features that administrators, programmers, and users need. Unfortunately, if you've ever done any LDAP programming or queries, the protocol format isn't the friendliest language. Following are two sample LDAP strings:

```
cn=Roger Grimes,o=Contoso.com,c=US

dc=apppartition,dc=contoso,dc=com,dc=server1
```

The former example might identify a user account or e-mail address. The latter represents an object, in this case an application partition, in the Contoso.com domain on a DC called server 1.

Fortunately, most users and administrators never need to interact with Active Directory except through the graphical user interfaces and other types of programs. Most Active Directory manipulations and queries are done using the Active Directory Users and Computers console. Sites are manipulated through the Active Directory Sites and Services console. Forests and trusts are manipulated using the Active Directory Forests and Trusts console. Microsoft also includes dozens of tools to manipulate Active Directory (graphical, command-line, and additional Resource Kit utilities).

LDAP is ripe for hacker exploitation but has so far escaped popular attention. There have been a few attacks specifically coded to exploit Active Directory and its operations, but none that spread beyond a few sites or theoretical discussions. If history proves any guide, when Microsoft releases a next-generation platform security change, like the NT kernel, and now Active Directory, it takes the hackers three to five years to catch up.

Parts of Active Directory Security Policies

The Active Directory security components include forest, site, domain, OUs, computer objects, user objects, group policy objects (GPOs), local computer policy, administrative templates, and security templates.

History of Group Policy

Active Directory group policy was an evolutionary product. Nearly every version of Windows allowed registry edit files to be created manually and applied using various registry tools (such as Reg.exe) or imported using `Regedit.exe`. Prior to group policy, registry edit files were the most common way to modify Windows security settings, but the registry edit mechanism has two big problems:

❏ How to distribute

❏ Registry edits require that the logged on user applying the registry edit file have full administrator permissions to the registry keys being written

The latter issue wasn't a problem in the days before the move to the Windows NT family. In Windows 3.1 and Windows 9x (and Windows ME), every user had full access to all resources. In the Windows NT family, most registry edit files required that the user applying the file have administrator rights. This is the case even today, and entities trying to establish secure environments don't allow their end users to be administrators. This means administrators have to log in locally and apply the registry edit file manually or supply administrator logon credentials using another alternative method. The alternative methods, such as batch or script files, led to their own problems, such as plaintext password use.

Starting with Windows 95, Microsoft provided a way to automate registry-based security using a mechanism called *system policy*. Using a program called the *System Policy Editor* (`Poledit.exe`), administrators could create system policy files and apply them to Windows 9x systems. A similar program was introduced in Windows NT 4.0. System polices could be applied to local users or local machines, but all changes tattooed the registry. Any change made to a user applied globally, affecting all users, although policies could be applied to groups as well. System policy introduced Administrative templates (`*.ADM`) and many of the settings that we still see in group policy today. If you have Windows 9x machines to manage, review the following resources: `http://support.microsoft.com/default .aspx?scid=kb;en-us;Q147381` or `www.zisman.ca/poledit`. Unfortunately, very few administrators took the opportunity to learn about or use system policies.

In Windows NT Service Pack 4, Microsoft introduced security templates, the System Editor (`Secedit.exe`), and the Security Configuration Manager (SCM). Security templates could be created manually with a text editor, or graphically using the SCM. SCM introduced many of the same GPO categories we see today, including Local Policy, Account Policy, Restricted Groups, and System Services.

Security templates and SCM proved wildly popular with many enterprise administrators even though a much larger majority of administrators didn't know they existed or didn't see their potential. But many of Microsoft's largest customers did see the value and asked for even more functionality. Microsoft responded with Active Directory GPOs, Administrative templates, and enhanced security template functionality.

The functionality of GPOs introduced in Windows 2000 Active Directory (known as Active Directory 1.0) was better than anything else that existed for any other platform. In order to do a similar thing for Unix or Windows, vendors or administrators would have to create an enormous amount of batch files or scripts. Even today, only a few similar (although less functional) products are available for non-Windows platforms. Active Directory 1.0 was a great leap forward, but many of the enterprise management tools for better managing group policy didn't arrive until Active Directory 2.0 (released in conjunction with Windows Server 2003). It provided even more GPO functionality, GPO filtering, and the Group Policy Management Console (GPMC). Today, Microsoft continues to expand what GPOs can manage and do, and they are adding improved management tools. Many vendors offer add-on companion tools that extend group policy or offer even easier management.

Security Templates

Prior to the GPMC, security templates were the only way to make Windows security settings transportable. Security templates can be imported into GPOs and Local Computer Policy, even though security templates do not have all the security settings that a GPO does (see Figure 15-2).

Security Template   GPO Security Settings

Figure 15-2

Security templates still allow Windows security settings to be easily portable, and to be applied to non-domain computers. If security templates are applied locally using `Secedit.exe` or the Security Configuration and Analysis console (see Figure 15-3), the security template settings tattoo the registry. Security templates can be created manually or using the Security Templates console (see Figure 15-4).

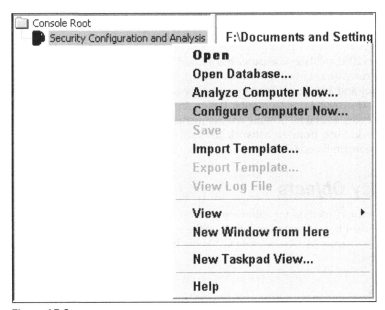

Figure 15-3

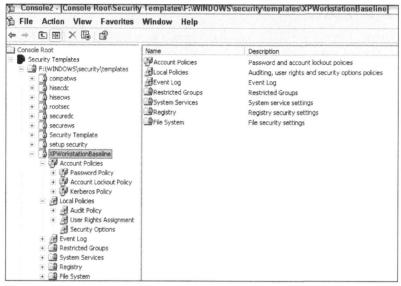

Figure 15-4

Local Computer Policy

Every Windows 2000 and later computer has a Local Computer Policy. It gets applied to the computer every time the computer starts if it contains settings. Security templates can be imported into Local Computer Policy and any Active Directory security settings, if they conflict, override Local Computer Policy settings. However, Local Computer Policy should always be configured, because it applies even when DCs are not contactable. In some environments, legitimate and unauthorized users will sometimes disconnect the computer from the network just long enough during the boot sequence to bypass the application of domain-based GPOs.

Group Policy Objects

GPOs are the primary method for automating computer security settings. GPOs can be created locally (although it's called Local Computer Policy), at the site, domain, or OU level. Common GPO settings were covered in Chapter 14. One or more GPOs can be created and linked at the domain, site, and OU container objects.

Default GPOs

Active Directory includes two GPOs by default:

❑ Default Domain Policy

❑ Default Domain Controllers Policy

These two policies are created when the first domain controller in the domain is created (using Dcpromo.exe). They contain Microsoft's recommended default settings. The *Default Domain Policy* is linked to the domain container (e.g., contoso.com) and is applied to all users and computers in the domain. The *Default Domain Controllers Policy* is linked to the domain controller's OU and applied to all DCs in the domain. All computers, including domain controllers, usually have the Default Domain Policy GPO applied.

Use Chapter 14 to guide you in modifying them to offer more security. In most cases, the original policies should never be modified or implemented. Copy them, rename, and disable the original policies. Make all changes to the new copies so that if something ever goes terrible wrong, the original GPOs can be applied. For W2K3 domain controllers, Microsoft also has a program called Dcgpofix.exe (called *Recreatedefpol* in W2K) installed by default that will restore these two policies to their original default settings.

GPO Application Pathway

GPOs can be applied at the following levels:

- ❏ Locally (using Local Computer Policy)
- ❏ Site
- ❏ Domain
- ❏ OU

Group policy settings are applied when the computer boots up and logs on to the domain, and when the user logs on. The computer settings are applied first, then the user's settings. When a computer boots up, the Local Computer Policy Computer Configuration settings, if any exist, are applied. Then, when the user logs on, the Local Computer Policy User Configuration settings, if any exist, are applied. Then any site-level GPOs are applied. Next, any domain-level GPOs are applied. Lastly, any OU-based GPOs are applied, starting from the top of the directory tree and moving down through the branch containers.

If there are no conflicting settings, all the settings accumulate to create the effective security policy. If any settings conflict between the various GPOs, the last policy applied wins (unless other special settings, as covered below, are involved). The GPO application pathway rule (see Figure 15-5) is known as the *LSDOU rule*.

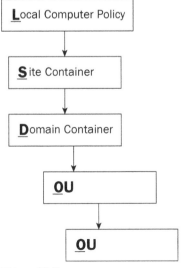

Figure 15-5

If multiple GPOs are linked at the same level and settings conflict, the last applied GPO wins again. In this case, it is the highest GPO in the Group Policy Editor (see Figure 15-6). The Group Policy Editor calls the application order *priority*. The GPMC tool displays a similar listing of GPOs, but calls the precedence order the *link order* (see Figure 15-7). Both tools allow the GPOs to be moved up and down to assist in the correct GPO application order.

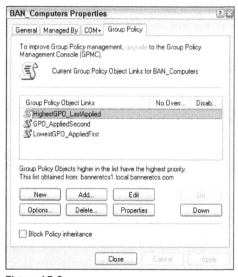

Figure 15-6

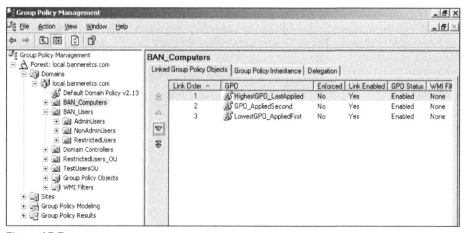

Figure 15-7

Extreme GPO Fighting

The previous GPO application rules can be further controlled using a few other mechanisms:

❑ Disabling

❑ GPO Category Enforcement

- ❏ WMI Filtering
- ❏ Block Inheritance
- ❏ No Override
- ❏ Loopback Policy Processing
- ❏ NTFS Settings

Disabling GPOs

GPOs can be disabled overall, meaning both Computer and User Configuration settings, or just one side of the GPO disabled. Other than domain- or site-level GPOs, each GPO should only be applied to either a computer object or user account, but not both at the same time. Disabling the other side of the GPO (see Figure 15-8) will significantly quicken the application speed of GPOs. For the same reason, completely disable test GPOs not being used by anyone when not in active testing.

Figure 15-8

Category Policy Processing Enforcement

Each GPO category can be disabled or enforced on a per-GPO basis. The following GPO categories can be disabled or enforced under \Computer Configuration\Administrative Templates\System\ GroupPolicy:

- ❏ Registry
- ❏ Internet Explorer
- ❏ Software Installs
- ❏ Folder Redirection
- ❏ Scripts Processing
- ❏ Security
- ❏ IP Security
- ❏ Wireless Policy
- ❏ EFS Recovery Policy
- ❏ Disk Quotas

Figure 15-9 shows the registry category being enforced and reapplied during periodic refreshes even if the GPO hasn't changed. This is another important point. After a GPO is applied, it will not re-apply again until either the GPO changes or the GPO refresh interval is exceeded (usually every 90 minutes with a zero- to 30-minute random offset on non-DCs — to prevent all policies from being re-applied to all PCs at the same time). If the GPO itself has not changed since the last application, the settings are not re-applied until the maximum GPO refresh interval has been met (which is every 17 hours with a random offset).

Figure 15-9

This creates a security issue. Once a GPO is applied, users with appropriate permissions can manually disable or override the setting set by the GPO. The unauthorized change would not be undone until the maximum refresh interval were met. Administrators should require that all GPO settings be re-applied at the regular refresh interval. Of course, this does impose more network and local processing overhead during the GPO application process.

WMI Filtering

Starting with Windows XP, GPOs can be filtered (meaning not applied) to an OU by further selecting additional criteria as queried by the WMI filter. Filters can involve many different fields and criteria, resulting in filters such as the following: only to Windows 2003 machines, only to machines with 100MB free hard drive space, and so on. WMI filters are only understood by XP and later computers, not W2K. W2K will ignore filters and apply GPO.

Blocked Inheritance

GPOs can be blocked on a per-OU basis (see Figure 15-10) using a featured called *block inheritance*. When block inheritance is set on an OU, no GPO set above that level will apply to the current OU or any of its child OU containers. GPOs linked directly at the OU level will still apply. Because blocking inheritance is indiscriminate regarding which policies it will prevent from applying, block inheritance is not used much in the real world.

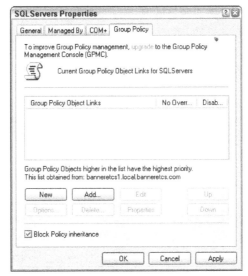

Figure 15-10

No Override

Enabling the *No Override* (it's called *Enforced* in GPMC) attribute will make a GPO apply to objects in an OU even when Blocked Inheritance is enabled also. Any GPO with No Override set will also be applied last, so that if there are any conflicts, its settings will win. If multiple GPOs have No Override set, the rules fall back to the original LSDOU application pathway.

Loopback Policy Processing

A special GPO-specific setting called Loopback Policy Processing can be used to make Computer Configuration settings take precedence over User Configuration settings. Usually, User Configuration settings win in a conflict because they are applied after the Computer Configuration settings. If enabled, the `\Computer Configuration\Administrative Templates\System\GroupPolicy\User Group Policy loopback processing mode` option (see Figure 15-11) will instruct Active Directory to re-apply Computer Configuration settings after the User policies have been applied.

In *Replace* mode, the Computer Configuration settings are the only ones allowed to be applied in the effective settings (even non-conflicting User Configuration settings are removed). In *Merge* mode, only settings in conflict with the Computer Configuration settings are replaced. Loopback policy processing can be set per GPO. It is meant to be used in situations, such as public kiosks, where the User settings should have little to no effect on the settings configured on the computer.

GPO Permissions

The permissions of a GPO determine whether or not a particular GPO will apply to a user or computer, or who can manage, link, and edit it. In order for a GPO to apply to a particular user or computer, two things must be true:

- ❑ The computer or user must be in an OU that the GPO is linked to or inherited into.

- ❑ Computer or user (or a group they belong to) must have the Read and Apply Group Policy permissions enabled.

533

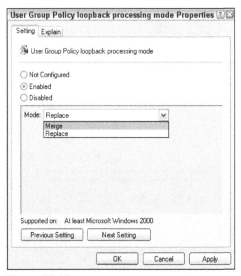

Figure 15-11

If either of those two requirements is not met, the GPO will not apply. Often, administrators deny a user or computer the capability to Apply Group Policy, so that the GPO will not apply. Table 15-3 shows the default GPO permissions, each of which can be allowed or denied.

Table 15-3

GPO Permissions	Description
Full Control	Users with this permission can Read and Apply the GPO, edit the GPO settings, delete the GPO, manage links, and manage GPO permissions.
Read	Users with this permission can read the GPO and its settings. Normal users must have this permission to apply the GPO settings, along with the Apply Group Policy permission.
Write	Users with this permission can read, write, and delete the GPO. Administrators may need this GPO permission to even view the GPO.
Create Child Objects	Allowed to create GPO child objects
Delete Child Objects	Allowed to delete GPO child objects
Apply Group Policy	Users must have this permission to apply GPO settings. Normally given to non-admin users and not given to Administrators. Should be set to Deny to prevent GPO application.
Special Permissions	Any combination of the above permissions

GPO permissions, like regular NTFS settings, are set on a per-user, per-computer, and per-group basis. GPO settings only apply to users and computers, but the security permissions to Read and Apply the group policy can be given to groups (and as long as the group members are in an OU "hit" by the GPO, it will apply). Table 15-4 displays the default GPO permissions assigned to various security groups.

Table 15-4

Group	Default GPO Permissions Assigned
Authenticated Users	Read and Apply Group Policy
Enterprise Admins	Read, Write, Apply Group Policy, Delete and Create Child Objects
Domain Admins	Read, Write, Apply Group Policy, Delete and Create Child Objects
Administrators	Read, Write, Apply Group Policy, and Create Child Objects

By default, Enterprise Admins can create, delete, and manage any OU or GPO in the forest or site. Domain Admins can create, delete, and manage any OU or GPO in their domain (and subdomains). As you can also see, by default, any GPO created that "hits" a user or computer will apply.

Many sources recommend that you use GPO deny permissions to prevent administrators from having GPO settings applied. This is exactly the wrong advice. Administrator accounts are the ones most likely to be sought after by hackers. You should allow GPOs to apply to all accounts by default, and only disable ultra-restrictive GPOs from applying to administrators, and even then only sparingly.

The sheer number of ways in which GPOs can be applied and controlled can make it difficult to determine which setting won and by which GPO.

Determining Effective GPO Policy

With all the possible ways of GPOs to interact, it can sometimes be difficult to determine which GPO caused what security setting. You can use Gpresult.exe (an excellent command-line tool) or the Resultant Set of Policy (RSoP) GUI console to display what domain-based GPO settings and Local Computer Policy settings are affecting a particular user or PC. The RSoP wizard can be initiated in Active Directory Users and Computers (choose All Tasks and Resultant Set of Policy (Logging) after right-clicking a user or computer) or using its own RSoP MMC console tool.

The RSoP tool is a great addition to Windows Server 2003 (it was not available in GUI form in Windows Server 2000), as it leads the administrator through a series of wizard dialog boxes asking whether the user or computer GPOs, or both types, should be reported. It then lists the various GPO settings and what domain-based GPO ended up applying the effective setting (see Figure 15-12). In RSoP *Planning mode,* the administrator can mimic an object move or security group modification (among other options) to see what the impact would be on the effective GPO settings. The only drawback of RSoP is that it does not display the effects of Local Computer Policy settings.

Gpresult.exe is a command-line-based tool. If typed alone at the command prompt without any parameters, it will report what groups the current user and group belong to, other information that might affect GPO application, and then the GPOs applied. If run with the /V parameter, it will report each effective setting (see Figure 15-13) and can display the effects of both domain-based and GPO-based security policies.

Figure 15-12

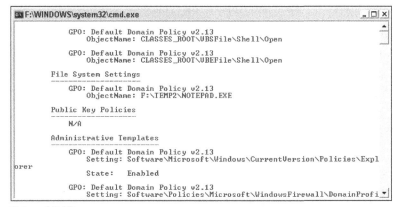

Figure 15-13

Now that we have all the pieces and parts understood, we can begin to apply the knowledge in a thoughtful way.

Efficient Active Directory Security Design

There is an art and a science to effective Active Directory security design. Here are the ideas:

- ❑ Use role-based security.
- ❑ Create a role-based OU structure.
- ❑ Create and use a one-time security template on all computers.
- ❑ Create and use a Local Computer Policy.
- ❑ Create and use a Baseline Security Policy for the domain.
- ❑ Create and use a role-based Incremental Security Policy.
- ❑ Name GPOs with version numbers.

The following sections cover each of these in more detail.

Use Role-Based Security

Using Role-Based Access Control (RBAC) means creating an Active Directory infrastructure that reflects the operational roles of the environment. Ultimately, the most secure security design is one that follows the principle of least privilege. No user or computer should have more rights than is necessary to do the authorized job. In order to accomplish this, the Active Directory OU structure must be role-based.

Most administrators use groups to manage their security permissions. Some readers might think that role-based security and groups are the same. Groups are normally departments (e.g., IT, Admin, HR, Accounting, etc.). Role-based security takes those same groups and breaks them down further into each employee's functional role (i.e., for the IT department, you might have IT Admin, Help Desk, Network Technician, Programmer, etc.). Ideally, you would want a separate OU (and eventually GPO and security template) for each employee role or position. This may sound like overkill at first, but in reality this is what all administrators should have been doing all along. Anything less than this was ineffective security or security managed to the most common denominator (not least privilege).

Create a Role-Based OU Structure

Once role-based groups are created, it's time to create a role-based OU structure to support the role-based security templates and GPOs. Because GPOs are applied to computers and users, the top OU structure must first reflect this branch in the tree. If this step is skipped, it can easily lead to poor GPO performance. The top-level OUs are often named with the word Computers and Users in the name, but they cannot just be Computers and Users, because those are existing containers, which cannot be linked to GPOs. Instead, choose something easy like ContosoUsers and ContosoComputers.

The computer branch should be divided into Domain Controllers (which already exists and should be left alone) and Member Servers (i.e., non-DCs). The Member Servers node should be broken down into all the different roles that a server computer fulfills in the environment. Figure 15-14 shows example roles under the top parent Computer OU, including Web Servers, File Servers, Print Servers, DNS Servers, Exchange Servers, OWA Servers, SQL Servers, Multi-purpose Servers, etc.

Figure 15-14

A more filled-out role-based Active Directory infrastructure would look something like Figure 15-15.

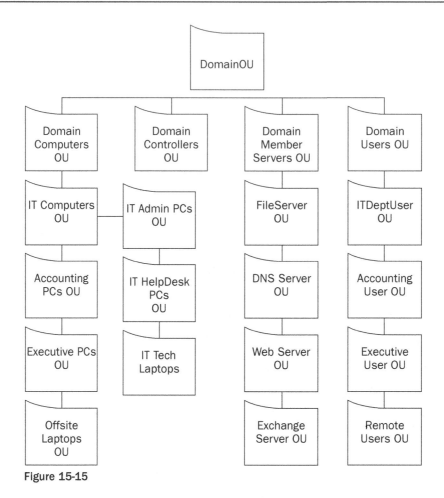

Figure 15-15

Create and Use a One-Time Security Template on All Computers

Think of every possible default security setting, using the previous chapter's recommendations as your guide. For example, from Chapter 5, "Protecting High-Risk Files," create a list of every default installed file that you don't want non-admins to execute. From Chapter 11, "Protecting E-mail," create a list of every file type that should be blocked by default. The idea is to create a detailed list of what is and isn't allowed to run on each PC, develop a security policy from the results, and then implement it using a security template on every PC in your environment.

This is a high bang-for-the-buck proposition. By creating a one-time security template that is applied to all PCs, every Windows workstation, server, and laptop in your environment will be set to the same common default security settings. No need to guess what the baseline is; you've got it documented and applied. Apply it only once, or re-apply once a year or at some other set interval. And because the settings are applied once and tattoo the registry, the hundreds of applied security settings do not slow down the PC, as would a GPO or Local Computer Policy.

Create and Use a Local Computer Policy

Then create and use a Local Computer Policy that reapplies medium to critical computer settings each time the PC starts or the user logs in. If the one-time security template applied hundreds of settings, the local computer policy applies less than a hundred. For example, if the one-time security template blocked 120 different file types, the Local Computer Policy would only block those file types most likely to be seen during the year that you don't want to see executed. The file block list would contain perhaps a dozen or two file types.

A Local Computer Policy is also instrumental in making sure a policy is applied if a domain controller can't be found.

Create and Use a Baseline Security Policy for the Domain

Create two baseline security templates and GPOs: one for the custom top-level Computers OU and one for the custom Users OU. It should contain shared default settings and critical security settings that should be re-applied frequently across a wide swath of users and computers. You want the top-level policies to frequently protect against the biggest threats. For example, the Local Computer Policy re-applied 1-2 dozen file types. The top-level domain policies should block less than a dozen file types— only the ones most likely to affect your users. And if a new file type starts to be used maliciously, add it (for the duration of the biggest threat period) to the domain policy. The other hundred file types have already been blocked by the one-time security template and Local Computer Policy; we're just using a domain-level GPO to make sure the highest-risk stuff is blocked.

Create and Use a Role-Based Incremental Security Policy

Role-based incremental OUs, GPOs, and security templates should be created. The incremental policies should be applied to the role-based OUs and contain settings specific to each computer and user role, plus apply settings to prevent specific threats that might compromise a specific role. For example, don't allow, by default, the IIS or World Wide Web service to be started on normal workstations. Enforce the use of the Enhanced Security Configuration application on W2K3 servers with Internet Explorer. Using Software Restriction Policies, prevent Outlook Express, Outlook, and Microsoft Office from being installed or activated on your servers. Require smart cards for remote admin logons. The idea is to put in a smaller subset of role-based security settings, probably around one to three dozen settings, that will make specific types of users and computers more secure.

Name GPOs with Version Numbers

Lastly, name each of your GPOs with a version number (see Figure 15-16). Every time you modify a GPO, update the version number. This makes troubleshooting GPOs significantly easier. When checking whether a particular computer or user has had the latest GPO applied, run `Gpresult.exe` or RSoP and verify the version number.

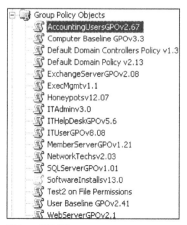
Figure 15-16

Design Summary

Here are the steps for designing and deploying an effective Active Directory security policy:

1. Create and apply locally (using Secedit.exe or the Security Configuration and Analysis console) an extensive one-time security template to all new and existing PCs. Re-apply annually or when needed.

2. Create two top-level OUs, one called XComputers and one called XUsers (e.g., ContosoComputers and ContosoUsers).

3. Create baseline GPO, with critical security settings enabled, for top two GPOs.

4. Create role-based sub-OUs under each parent OU (e.g., File Servers, MemberServers, Web Servers, Exchange Servers, and Remote Laptops, etc., under ContosoComputers; and Executives, IT, HR, and Accounting under ContosoUsers).

5. Create sub-OUs under each parent group (e.g., IT Admin, HelpDesk, Network Techs, etc. under IT).

6. Create role-based incremental GPOs to support role-based OU structure.

7. Create baseline and role-based security templates to support baseline and role-based OU structure.

8. Import the appropriate baseline and role-based security templates into the appropriate baseline and role-based GPOs.

9. Link the appropriate baseline and role-based GPOs with the baseline and role-based OUs (see Figure 15-17).

10. Import baseline and appropriate role-based security templates into the computer's Local Computer Policy.

Figure 15-18 summaries the various parts and criticalities of the Active Directory objects. If done thoughtfully, this method will apply a very effective and efficient security policy with minimal performance delay.

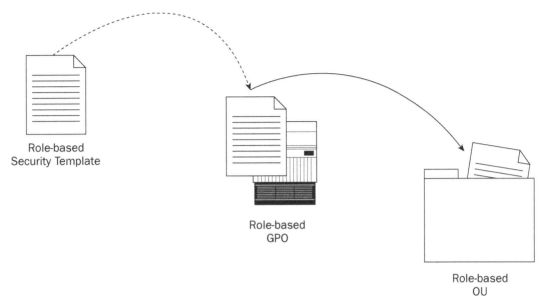

Role-based
Security Template

Role-based
GPO

Role-based
OU

Figure 15-17

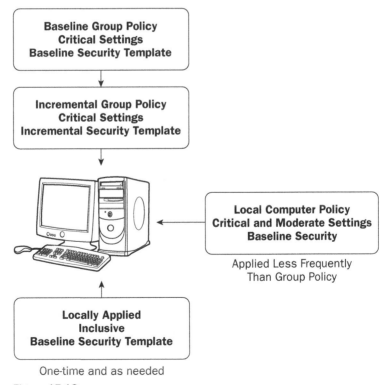

**Baseline Group Policy
Critical Settings
Baseline Security Template**

**Incremental Group Policy
Critical Settings
Incremental Security Template**

**Local Computer Policy
Critical and Moderate Settings
Baseline Security**

Applied Less Frequently
Than Group Policy

**Locally Applied
Inclusive
Baseline Security Template**

One-time and as needed

Figure 15-18

If you already have an existing Active Directory infrastructure that looks nothing like a role-based model, don't panic. A role-based model is the best way to secure a Windows network, but it doesn't have to be implemented in totality immediately. As long as you understand the concept and strengths of role-based security, and how all the various pieces fit together, you can move your organization's existing infrastructure closer to a role-based one with everything that you do. The change can be gradual, but with each move your infrastructure gets stronger and your security better.

Summary

Chapter 15 discussed how to create an efficient and secure Active Directory infrastructure. First, it relies on the administrator to create a role-based OU structure. Then, role-based security templates are imported into role-based GPOs that are then linked to the role-based OUs. A one-time, inclusive security template is applied to all computers. A Local Computer Policy is used to ensure that domain policies aren't bypassed and to apply moderately critical settings again. A domain-level baseline policy is applied to all users and computers. It pushes down critical security settings. Lastly, incremental policies are used to push down policy settings that will help each role-based computer and user. If appropriately planned, Active Directory security can be an efficient asset in the fight against malware and hackers.

Book Summary

If you're reading this, you've made it through all 15 chapters. I hope you agree that this is the best book you've ever read on Windows security. It covered specific problems and made specific recommendations, many of which you'll read nowhere else. Even more important than the massive amount of detail that this book contains are its main points:

❑ Focus on the correct attack threat. The risk coming automated threats is significantly higher than that from the dedicated attacker.

❑ Prevent malware from executing on the desktop in the first place, even if gets by all the other defenses.

❑ Practice defense in depth.

❑ The four single best defenses are as follows: Don't let your non-admin users be logged in as administrators, keep your software updated, prevent unauthorized software execution, and block more things by default.

❑ Security through obscurity works, and works well, but don't rely on it as your only defense.

❑ Don't rely on firewalls, antivirus programs, or end-user education alone to stop malware threats.

❑ Analyze your risks and apply biggest bang-for-the-buck defenses first (i.e., don't let non-admin users be logged in as administrators, disable LM password hash storage, etc.). Prioritize defenses from best to least effective.

❑ Block more stuff (high-risk files, high-risk registry entries) by default.

❑ Lastly, use Active Directory and Group Policy to automate security. If you don't automate your security, it won't be applied efficiently.

If you have any questions, please don't hesitate to e-mail me at roger@banneretcs.com. I always answer my e-mail.

Happy computing!

Index